COHELAN ON CALIFORNIA CLASS ACTIONS

Timothy D. Cohelan

Cohelan & Khoury
San Diego, California

THE EXPERT SERIES

San Francisco, California
WEST GROUP
1997

ISBN 0-314-22196-4

West's Commitment to the Environment

In 1906, West Publishing Company began recycling materials left over from the production of books. This began a tradition of efficient and responsible use of resources. Today, 100% of our legal bound volumes and college texts are printed on acid-free, recycled paper consisting of 50% new paper pulp and 50% paper that has undergone a de-inking process. We also use vegetable-based inks to print many of our books. West recycles nearly 30,000,000 pounds of scrap paper annually—the equivalent of 300,000 trees. Since the 1960s, West has devised ways to capture and recycle waste inks, solvents, oils, and vapors created in the printing process. We also recycle plastics of all kinds, wood, glass, corrugated cardboard, and batteries, and have eliminated the use of styrofoam book packaging. We at West are proud of the longevity and the scope of our commitment to the environment.

WEST GROUP
610 Opperman Drive
P.O. Box 64526
St. Paul, MN 55164-0526
1-800-328-9352

ISBN 0-314-22196-4
Library of Congress Catalog Card No. 97-060489

ABOUT THE AUTHOR

Timothy D. Cohelan is the founding partner of Cohelan & Khoury, a civil litigation firm specializing in class actions and located in its own building in San Diego. Cohelan and the firm have been counsel or co-counsel in civil matters that have recovered for plaintiffs over $225 million in verdicts, judgments, or settlements since September 1993.

Cohelan & Khoury have successfully prosecuted class actions cases on behalf of urban homeless entitled to emergency shelter; victims of a national health insurance fraud scheme; retirees entitled to pension benefits; defrauded investors; victims of discrimination; and workers entitled to back wages. Cohelan & Khoury are AV-rated by Martindale-Hubbell.

Cohelan served as Chairman of San Diego Regional Coastal Commission from 1978 to 1981 and regularly serves as judge pro tem of the municipal court and has co-chaired the San Diego County Bar Association Subcommittee on the Homeless. He is a 1974 graduate of California Western School of Law, where he served as an editor of Law Review. He served as an officer in the U.S. Navy from 1968 to 1971 and received a B.A. from the University of Arizona in 1967. His previous education was received from the public schools of Washington, D.C.; Leeds, England; and Berkeley, California. He is married with one child and resides in San Diego.

WEST GROUP

50 California Street
19th Floor
San Francisco, California 94111

Publisher's Editorial Staff

ROBIN D. KOJIMA, ESQ.
JEFFREY B. SHEA, ESQ.

Page Design and Publishing Services

LABRECQUE PUBLISHING, San Francisco

Preface

The American judicial system draws widespread criticism because the public perceives the typical civil case as too costly, too complex, and too time-consuming. The truth is that few citizens can afford civil litigation, except through contingent-fee representation in a class action. Indeed, the skillfully administered class action is a powerful tool for saving time and expense in civil litigation and resolving significant policy issues.

The public benefits from class actions because of expedited process, reduced cost, and the resolution of issues affecting many individuals. The bench and bar also have a stake in making California class action procedures work effectively. The bench is responsible for learning about class actions and assigning judges interested in both their administrative and legal aspects.

As for the bar, lawyers advancing a class action face the burden of justifying class action treatment. (*City of San Jose* v. *Superior Court of Santa Clara County* (1974) 12 Cal.3d 447 [115 Cal.Rptr. 797, 525 P.2d 701].) This task has become particularly important because of growing skepticism about securities "strike suits" and other perceived abuses of class actions. To prevent both undermining judicial support for class actions and eroding public respect for the administration of justice, lawyers bear the significant responsibility of avoiding spurious, insignificant, or frivolous class actions.

Class actions should be reserved for cases with clear benefits to the litigants on issues of consequence, such as the availability of emergency shelter for homeless persons, loss of life savings or pensions, unpaid health insurance benefits or back wages, and price fixing or other discriminatory anti-competitive activity. In a close case entailing no substantial sum of money or significant public policy questions, the practitioner should determine whether the conduct of the potential defendant or defendants was particularly offensive or involved serious wrongdoing before going ahead with the class action. Is this a wrong that needs a broad class remedy?

Would-be California class action practitioners confront myriad issues: Is it possible to expedite a complex California class case? Can such cases be litigated quickly and efficiently? What responsibilities do lawyers have to process class actions quickly? If complex certification issues derail a class action from the "fast track," is a slower track the only option? Can a civil practitioner with finite resources take on a complex California class action and survive? What are the differences between federal and California class action practice? When should one give notice in a California class action, and why? What evidence, if any, should counsel submit to win class certification? My purpose in writing this book is to answer these and similar questions.

California Class Actions provides the historical perspective necessary for case analysis, including a discussion of the California cases that outline state court procedural divergences from Federal Rules of Civil Procedure rule 23 as amended in 1966 and judicially adopted in California Supreme Court case law in 1967 and 1971. The book also discusses the development of California class action law and procedure, and it summarizes the appellate cases defining California procedure.

Discussion of basic principles of class representation includes the "pitfall" cases cautious practitioners should review in evaluating whether to file a class action. A separate chapter covers the rules of certification developed in case law. The following chapter explains the unique circumstances affecting California class action practice.

Since most certified class actions settle and therefore require judicial approval of dismissal, precertification and pretrial settlement issues are dealt with and secondary authorities provided. Because discovery in a class action usually leads to significant pretrial controversy, the book suggests case management and other methods of organization for the class action moving toward trial. Major substantive class actions in anti-trust, securities, consumer protection, discrimination, and other areas are also reviewed. Finally, the book outlines ways of trying a California case by borrowing from federal authorities such as the *Manual for Complex Litigation, Third*.

Illustrative forms appear at the end of appropriate chapters. The forms are taken from cases filed by my office. My thanks to Gray, Cary, Ware & Friedenrich and Sheppard, Mullin, Richter & Hampton for their permission to use forms.

The appendix includes the text of relevant statutes and rules, including local rules from the courts with the heaviest class action caseloads. Tables of statutes, rules, and cases and an index are also included to expedite your research.

My hope is that *California Class Actions* will increase understanding of the power and importance of the class action in California. Effective and responsible use of class actions will benefit both trial courts and private citizens, enhancing public awareness of, and support for, our system of justice.

You are welcome to fax me comments and suggestions about this book at (619) 595-3000.

Timothy D. Cohelan
Cohelan & Khoury
San Diego, California

COORDINATED RESEARCH IN CALIFORNIA FROM WEST

WEST'S CALIFORNIA LITIGATION FORMS SERIES
West's California Litigation Forms: Civil Procedure Before Trial
Patricia Glaser, Eric Landau, Kirk Pasich, Susan Popik and Laurie Zelon

West's California Litigation Forms: Civil Trials and Evidence
Kathleen V. Fisher, Susan J. Harriman, Karen Randall and James S. Rummonds

West's California Litigation Forms: Civil Appeals and Writs
Justice J. Anthony Kline and Kent Richland

JURY INSTRUCTIONS

[Also available in computer disk and looseleaf formats]

California Jury Instructions—Civil (BAJI)
California Jury Instructions—Criminal (CALJIC)

WEST'S CRIMINAL PRACTICE SERIES
West's California Criminal Law
Douglas Dalton
West's California Criminal Procedure
Laurie L. Levenson
California Criminal Trialbook
Harry M. Caldwell, Sue Steding and Gary Nichols
California Criminal Defense Motions Forms Manual
Albert Menaster

JURY SELECTION PRACTICE BOOKS
Bennett's Guide to Jury Selection and Trial Dynamics: California Criminal Litigation
Bennett's Guide to Jury Selection and Trial Dynamics: California Civil Litigation
Cathy E. Bennett, Robert B. Hirschhorn and Dr. Jo-Ellan Dimitrius

CALIFORNIA HANDBOOK SERIES
California Evidence
Miguel Méndez
California Medical Malpractice
George McDonald

WEST'S CALIFORNIA CODE FORMS
Business and Professions
Joel S. Primes
Civil
Jeanne P. Robinson
Civil Procedure
Gregory L. Ogden and Daryl Fisher-Ogden
Commercial
Stephen N. Hollman and Ray D. Henson
Corporations
Janet E. Kerr
Education
Jay E. Grenig
Elections, Fish & Game, Food & Agricultural, Insurance
Susan J. Orton
Government
Jay E. Grenig and H. Anthony Miller
Probate
Ann E. Stodden and Timothy A. Whitehouse
Public Utilities
Boris H. Lakusta
Revenue and Taxation
Anthony X. McDermott

WEST'S ANNOTATED CALIFORNIA CODES

WEST'S CALIFORNIA DIGEST 2D

WEST'S CALIFORNIA REPORTER

PAMPHLETS

West's California Codes-Compact Edition

Civil Code

Code of Civil Procedure

Commercial Code

Corporations Code

Evidence Code

Penal Code

Probate Code

West's Annotated California Judicial Council Forms

California Education Code

California Environmental Laws

California Family Laws, Rules & Forms

California Insurance Code

California Juvenile Laws, Court Rules & Forms

California Vehicle Code

California Rules of Court-State & Federal

Northern California Local Court Rules–Superior and Municipal Courts

Bay Area Local Court Rules—Superior and Municipal Courts

Central California Local Court Rules—Superior and Municipal Courts

Southern California Local Court Rules—Superior and Municipal Courts

Los Angeles County Court Rules-Superior & Municipal Courts

INTERNET

West's California Catalog

The new California print catalog is on the Internet at http://www.westpub.com/Practice/CA-home.htm

West's Editorial Department

Contact the West Editorial Department directly with your questions and suggestions by e-mail at editor@westpub.com.

West's Home Page

Visit West's home page on the World Wide Web at http://www.westpub.com.

For more information about West California practice tools, please call your West Representative or 1-800-328-9352.

If you have research questions concerning WESTLAW® or West Publications, call West Reference Attorneys at 1-800-733-2889.

WESTLAW ELECTRONIC RESEARCH GUIDE

WESTLAW, Computer Assisted Legal Research

WESTLAW is part of the research system provided by West Publishing Company. With WESTLAW, you find the same quality and integrity that you have come to expect from West books. For the most current and comprehensive legal research, combine the strengths of West books and WESTLAW.

WESTLAW Adds to Your Library

Whether you wish to expand or update your research, WESTLAW can help. For instance, WESTLAW is the most current source for case law, including slip opinions and unreported decisions. In addition to case law, the online availability of statutes, statutory indexes, legislation, court rules and orders, administrative materials, looseleaf publications, texts and periodicals makes WESTLAW an important asset to any library. Check the WESTLAW Directory or the WESTLAW *Database List* for a list of available databases and services. Following is a brief description of some of the capabilities that WESTLAW offers.

You can now search many of the WESTLAW databases using the revolutionary new WIN®, a natural language search method. Instead of formulating a query using terms and connectors, you simply enter a description of your research issue:

> What is the government's obligation to warn military personnel of the danger of past exposure to radiation?

WESTLAW then retrieves the set of documents that has the highest statistical likelihood of matching your description.

Retrieving a Specific Document

When you know the citation to a case, statute, or Constitution section that is not in your library, use FIND to retrieve the document on WESTLAW. The following are sample FIND requests:

```
find 639 p2d 939
find ca elec s 7559
find ca const art 12 s 1
```

Updating Your Research

You can use WESTLAW to update your research in many ways:

- Retrieve cases citing a particular statute or Constitution section.
- Update a state statute or Constitution section by typing UPDATE or by using the appropriate jump marker (> or ➤) from the displayed statute or Constitution section.
- Retrieve newly-enacted legislation by searching in the appropriate legislative service database.
- Retrieve cases not yet reported by searching in case law databases.
- Read the latest U.S. Supreme Court opinions the same day they are released.
- Update West digests by searching topic and key numbers.

Determining Case History

Insta Cite®, a service of West Publishing, is the most current source for the history of a particular case. Insta Cite also provides citation verification and parallel citations. Use Insta Cite when you need to know if the case you are relying on has any subsequent history.

Shepard's® Citations is also available on WESTLAW. Shepard's on WESTLAW offers several advantages, including the following:

- The consolidation of the books, pocket part and update pamphlet into one result
- The ability to view only those references for a specific jurisdiction, treatment code or headnote
- Direct access to citing cases from the West National Reporter System®

Shepard's PreView is a WESTLAW exclusive that offers a preview of citing references from the National Reporter System before they are available in print.

Retrieving Citing Cases

You can supplement existing annotations or create your own set of annotations. Simply use the following approach:

1. Determine the format of the statute or case to which you wish to find references.

2. Select a case database in the desired jurisdiction.
3. Run a search containing key portions of the citation, plus any appropriate terms.*

*Because of the great variety of citations and citing styles, you should refer to the *WESTLAW Reference Manual* or consult with the West Reference Attorneys for more specific examples.

Additional Information

For more detailed information or assistance, contact your WESTLAW Account Representative or call 1-800-WESTLAW (1-800-937-8529).

SUMMARY TABLE OF CONTENTS

Chapter

Foreword: History of California Class Actions
1. Introduction to California Class Actions
2. Prerequisites to Filing a California Class Action
3. Alternatives to Class Actions
4. Preliminary Case Analysis
5. Drafting a California Class Action Complaint
6. The Precertification Stage
7. California Class Certification Procedure
8. Case Management: Controlling the Issues
9. Settlement Issues and Procedure
10. Attorney's Fees
11. Trial Strategies
12. Class Actions Grouped by Substantive Law

Appendix—Relevant Federal and State Statutes and Rules

Tables of Statutes and Cases

Index

DETAILED TABLE OF CONTENTS

Foreword: History of California Class Actions

Chapter 1 Introduction to California Class Actions

1.01 Introduction
- [A] National Importance of California Litigation
- [B] Applicable Law and Rules
- [C] Differences Between California and Federal Practice
- [D] Effect of Local Rules

1.02 Due Process Requirements

1.03 California Class Action Procedure

1.04 The Advantages and Disadvantages of Class Actions
- [A] In General
- [B] Advantages and Disadvantages of Federal Class Actions
- [C] Advantages and Disadvantages of State Class Actions

1.05 California Class Action Authority
- [A] In General
- [B] Code of Civil Procedure Section 382
- [C] Consumer Legal Remedies Act
- [D] Local Rules of Los Angeles, San Diego, San Francisco, and San Mateo Counties

1.06 Federal Authority: Federal Rules Of Civil Procedure, Rule 23

1.07 Differences Between California State and Federal Class Actions

1.08 References

Chapter 2 Prerequisites to Filing a California Class Action

2.01 Introduction

2.02 Ascertainable Class

2.03 Community of Interest

2.04 Adequacy of Representation

2.05 Consumer Legal Remedies Act

2.06 Substantial Benefit

2.07 Class Notice

2.08 Comparison of Federal and State Court Prerequisites

2.09 References

Chapter 3 Alternatives to Class Actions

3.01 Overview

3.02 Injunctive Relief

3.03 Unfair Competition Injunctions

3.04 Taxpayer Lawsuits

3.05 Suit Based on Association Status

3.06 Associations Managing Common-Interest Developments

3.07 Association as Representative Party

3.08 Court-Appointed Receivers

3.09 Mandamus Against Government

3.10 Class Arbitration

3.11 Class Treatment Without Notice

3.12 Consumer Legal Remedies Act

3.13 Mass Torts—Consolidation/Test Cases

3.14 References

Chapter 4 Preliminary Case Analysis

4.01 Deciding Whether to File—An Overview

4.02 Outline the Case
- [A] Class Definition
  - [1] Need for Precision
  - [2] Class Size
- [B] Class Period

[C] Common Questions of Law and Fact
[D] Residual Questions
[E] Relief Sought
[1] Injunctive—Declaratory
[2] Monetary
[F] Class Representation
[1] The Class Representative
[2] Counsel's Conflict with Class
[3] Attorney's Fees
[G] Benefit to Litigants and Court

4.03 Adverse California Case Law
[A] Is There an Obvious Pitfall to Your Case?
[B] Is the Cause Unsympathetic, or Is the Class Deprived of Little?
[C] Are Plaintiff's Recovery Facts Unique, or Is There Insufficient Community of Interest?
[D] Are Multiple Defendants Accused of Wrongdoing?
[E] Are the Class Members the Defendants?
[F] Are Remedial Statutes Superior to Class Treatment?
[G] Is the Case a National Class in a California Court?
[H] Does the Class Have Common Law Negligence Claims or Unique Damage Issues?
[I] Is It a Ticket or Personal Enjoyment Case?
[J] Are Class Members Antagonistic to the Class Action?

4.04 The Effect of Related Litigation
[A] Importance of Early Analysis
[B] Successive Class Actions or Federal Class Actions Precluding State Class Treatment
[C] Successive Class Actions or State Class Actions Precluding Federal Class Treatment
[D] Concurrent Class Actions
[E] Extensive "Group" Litigation
[F] Intervention

4.05 References

Chapter 5 Drafting a California Class Action Complaint

A. Text

5.01 Introduction

5.02 Structuring the Complaint
- [A] The Caption
- [B] Jurisdiction
- [C] Venue and Forum
- [D] The Parties
  - [1] Plaintiffs
  - [2] Subclasses
  - [3] Defendants
- [E] Class Allegations
- [F] Causes of Action

5.03 Key Issues in Class Action Complaints
- [A] Issues Central to Certification
- [B] Focusing and Defining Ascertainable Class
- [C] Class Damages
- [D] Class Representative Issues
  - [1] Primary and Secondary Issues
  - [2] Class Representative
  - [3] Class Counsel's Relationship with Class Representative
- [E] Building the Backbone of the Case
  - [1] Predominance of Common Questions
  - [2] Defendants' Actions
  - [3] Inferences and Presumptions
- [F] Toll the Statute of Limitations for Plaintiff Class
- [G] Multiple Defendants
- [H] Class Claims Against Presently Unknown Defendants

5.04 References

B. Forms

5.10 Class Action Complaint (*Aguilar* v. *Atlantic Richfield*)

5.11 Class Action Complaint (*Marquart* case)

5.12 Notice of Motion and Motion on Special Demurrers and Memorandum of Points and Authorities in Support Thereof (*Dudley* v. *Jones*)

Chapter 6 The Precertification Stage

A. Text

6.01 General Rules for Precertification Activity and Conduct
[A] Fiduciary Responsibility
[B] Precertification Conferences
[C] Demurrers to Class Allegations: The Reasonable-Possibility Standard
[D] No Default
[E] No Dismissal Without Court Approval
[F] Mandatory Dismissal
[G] Communications with Proposed Class Members
[H] Precertification Notices
[I] Limitation on Precertification Merits Rulings

6.02 Precertification Motions
[A] In General
[B] Coordination
[C] Consolidation
[D] Intervention
[E] Complex Designation
[F] Peremptory Challenges to Trial Judge
[G] Challenges for Cause

6.03 Precertification Discovery
[A] In General
[B] Class Discovery
[C] Defendant to Plaintiff Class
[D] Discovery from Plaintiffs to Defendants
[E] Document Depositories
[F] Interrogatories
[1] Judicial Control
[2] Interrogatories to Class Members

[G] Planning for Class Certification—Framing the Issues with the Class
[1] Discovery to Determine Class Composition
[2] Causes of Action
[3] Defendant's Conduct

6.04 References

B. Forms

6.10 Plaintiffs' Memorandum of Points and Authorities in Support of Ex Parte Application for Order Approving Precertification Notice Concerning Class Action

6.11 Declaration of Timothy Cohelan in Support of Ex Parte Application for Order Approving Precertification Notice

Chapter 7 California Class Certification Procedure

A. Text

7.01 Differences in Federal and California Procedure

7.02 Class Certification Hearing
[A] In General
[B] Required Notice of Hearing
[C] Timing: "Earliest Practicable Date"
[D] Nature of the Hearing
[E] Scope of Inquiry
[F] Burden on Plaintiff
[G] Superior Benefit
[H] Findings of Fact and Conclusions of Law
[I] Standard of Review on Appeal

7.03 Class Notice
[A] When Notice Is Required and What It Must Say
[B] Hearing on Class Notice
[C] Costs

7.04 Successive Certification Motions
[A] Difference Between Federal and State Rules
[B] "Intermediate" Class Ruling
[C] Decertification Motion or Procedure

[D] Mandatory Class Certification
[E] Post-Merits Rulings/Notice

7.05 References

B. Forms

7.10 Declaration of Timothy Cohelan and Statement Regarding Time, Manner, and Estimated Cost of Notice and Notice Required by Los Angeles County Rules (*Xiong* case)

7.11 Memorandum of Points and Authorities in Support of Plaintiffs' motion for Class Certification (*Aguilar* v. *Richfield Corp.*)

7.12 Declaration of Timothy Cohelan in Support of Plaintiffs' Motion for Class Certification (*Aguilar* v. *Atlantic Richfield Corp.*)

7.13 Memorandum of Points and Authorities in Opposition to Plaintiffs' Motion for Order Determining Class Issues (*Xiong* case)

7.14 Ruling on Motion for Order Determining Class Issues (First Hearing) (*Xiong* case)

7.15 Ruling on Motion for Order Determining Class Issues (Second Continued Hearing)(*Xiong* case)

7.16 Order Certifying Class (*Aguilar* v. *Atlantic Richfield*)

Chapter 8 Case Management: Controlling the Issues

A. Text

8.01 Proposing a Manageable Trial

8.02 Precertification Case Management
[A] Informal Conferences
[B] Precertification Determinations
[C] Appointing a Discovery Master

8.03 Simplifying Issues Following Certification

8.04 References

B. Forms

8.10 Plaintiffs' Notice of Ex Parte Application for an Order (1) Consolidating Demurrer Hearings, (2) Designating Case as Complex, and (3) Setting Pretrial Conference (*Aguilar* v. *Atlantic Richfield*)

8.11 Memorandum of Points and Authorities in Support of Order (1) Consolidating Demurrer Hearings, (2) Designating Case as Complex, and (3) Setting Pretrial Conference (*Aguilar* v. *Atlantic Richfield*)

8.12 Declaration of Timothy Cohelan in Support of Order (1) Consolidating Demurrer Hearings, (2) Designating Case as Complex, and (3) Setting Pretrial Conference (*Aguilar* v. *Atlantic Richfield*)

8.13 Proposed Order on Ex Parte Application (*Aguilar* v. *Atlantic Richfield*)

8.14 Case Management Order (*Marquart* case)

Chapter 9 Settlement Issues and Procedure

A. Text

9.01 Introduction

9.02 Tactical Considerations
- [A] Realistic Evaluation of Recovery Sources
- [B] Discovery of Insurance Information at the Outset
- [C] Early Appointment of Settlement Master
- [D] Serial Class Settlements
- [E] Defendant Settlement Considerations

9.03 Dismissal
- [A] The Requirement of Court Approval
- [B] Settlement with Class Representative Only
- [C] Settlement Paying Class Attorney's Fees Only

9.04 Class Settlement Procedure
- [A] Ex Parte or Noticed Court Approval of Preliminary Terms of Settlement and Notice
- [B] Notice to Class
- [C] Settlement Hearing
- [D] Standing to Object
- [E] Conditional Classwide and Precertification Settlement
- [F] Postcertification Settlement
- [G] Attorney's Fees Conflicts
- [H] Notice in Declaratory/Injunctive Relief Cases
- [I] Notice in Opt-Out Cases

[J] Scope of Bar Order—State Class Settlements
[K] Scope of Bar Order—Federal Class Settlements
[L] Settlement Effective Date

9.05 References

B. Forms

9.10 Stipulation Regarding Temporary and Conditional Certification of Class for Settlement Purposes Only and Order Thereon

9.11 Stipulation re Settlement

9.12 Memorandum of Points and Authorities in Support of Final Approval of Partial Settlement of Class Action; Award of Attorney's Fees and Costs (*Marquart* case)

9.13 Order of (1) Preliminary Approval of Settlement, and (2) Approval of Notice of Pendency of Class Action, Preliminary Approval of Settlement and Setting Fairness Hearing

9.14 Judgment on Order of Final Approval of Settlement

Chapter 10 Attorney's Fees

A. Text

10.01 Fundamental Principles

10.02 Qualifications of Class Counsel

10.03 Commercial Reality in Compensation

10.04 Common Fund Compensation
[A] Exception to Rule that Party Pay Own Attorney's Fees
[B] Extra Shares and Benchmarks
[C] Enhancing Common Fund Fees with the Private Attorney General Statute
[D] Reasonableness Requirement

10.05 References

B. Forms

10.10 Retainer Agreement and Duties of Class Representative (*Marquart* case)

10.11 Plaintiffs' Memorandum of Points and Authorities in Support of Motion for Order (1) Awarding Attorney's Fees, (2) Allowing Reimbursement of Costs and Expenses, (3) Appointing Settlement Administrator, and (4) Allowing Enhancements for Representatives (Real Property Class)

Chapter 11 Trial Strategies

11.01 Venue and Court for Trial

11.02 Making the Trial Manageable
- [A] In General
- [B] Bifurcation
- [C] Severance
- [D] Pretrial Master or Reference Reports
- [E] Arbitration of Certain Issues
- [F] Contributions of Bar Orders
- [G] Statements of Contested and Uncontested Issues
- [H] Summaries of Voluminous Documents for Exchange with Opposing Parties
- [I] Pretrial Discussion and Disposition of Disruptive Evidentiary Issues

11.03 Additional Considerations
- [A] In General
- [B] Determining Trial Issues Before Certification
- [C] Trial of Remaining Action
- [D] Appropriate Inferences and Presumptions

11.04 References

Chapter 12 Class Actions Grouped By Substantive Law

12.01 Overview

12.02 Antitrust

12.03 Discrimination

12.04 Securities

12.05 Bank and Credit Card Overcharges

12.06 Product Liability

12.07 Partnerships and Investment Schemes

12.08 Brokerage Agreement Charges

12.09 Real Property–Related Class Actions

- [A] Deeds of Trust
- [B] Nuisance and Trespass
- [C] Construction Defect
- [D] Landlord-Tenant
- [E] Mobile Home Rents
- [F] Unlawful Detainers
- [G] Subdivision Land Sales
- [H] Condominiums
- [I] Escrow Practices
- [J] Title Insurance Practices

12.10 Government Benefits and Taxes

12.11 Medical Treatment

12.12 Ticketholders

12.13 Employee-Employer

12.14 Rental Cars

12.15 References

Appendix—Relevant Federal and State Statutes and Rules

Tables of Statutes and Cases

Index

Foreword: History of California Class Actions

From the Nineteenth Century to World War II

During the period when California was shifting from Spanish rule to Mexican, the English political movement that culminated in the Reform Bill of 1832 influenced the development of the representation concept in class-action settings. The political debate of that era refined fundamental ideas such as the role of consent by absent parties. In 1837, Frederick Calver published an influential treatise on the law respecting parties to suits in equity, and he proposed equitable rules concerning representation. J. Story's *Commentaries on Equity Pleading* (1838), a work that strongly influenced American law, articulated a central dilemma of modern class action theory. Is the function of the class action to consolidate suits that would otherwise be brought individually—and thus make the judiciary more efficient? Or is it to make it easier to bring suits that, because the stakes are too small, would not be brought individually—and thus serve substantive goals?

In the United States, the debate in New York over the so-called Field Code for state procedure developed by the brothers and legal reformers David Dudley Field and Stephen Johnson Field coincided with the Mexican War. Both events influenced California's class action law. The New York Field Code Amendment of 1849 created the first state statute on class actions. The law codified two types of representative suits at equity: cases of common or general interest when one sues for the benefit of all, and cases involving parties united by a common interest yet so numerous they cannot practically be brought before the court. That same year gold fever brought waves of Americans—and their legal problems—into California, which had become a United States territory on March 10, 1848 by Senate ratification of the Treaty of Guadalupe Hidalgo ending the Mexican War. The following year, California was admitted into the Union as the 31st free state by the Compromise of 1850. Stephen Johnson Field, who subsequently was a justice of the United States Supreme Court, served as a member of the California Legislature in the 1850s.

Soon after California was admitted to the Union, the state's first class action case, *Von Schmidt* v. *Huntington* (1850) 1 Cal. 55, was decided. The California Supreme Court allowed a bill to be brought by a few shareholders on behalf of themselves and other shareholders for the return of forfeited stock. The court reasoned that an attempt to unite all shareholders in any other fashion would be inconvenient, inefficient, and unjust to those already before the court. The court noted the constant flux of people in and out of the California gold fields created a situation requiring legal adjustment to the facts. Quoting the English jurist Lord Cottenham on defects in parties, the court said that, in order to enforce rights, it needed to fit procedure to social reality, not to strict norms created under quite different circumstances. (*Von Schmidt* v. *Huntington* (1850) 1 Cal. 56, 68.) The court further stated that the 48th Rule of the Supreme Court of the United States adopted in 1842 was the correct rule for the government in cases of this nature. The rule provided that when the parties on either side were very numerous and could not all appear in court, selected representatives of the parties might prosecute the action on behalf of all. (*Von Schmidt* v. *Huntington* (1850) 1 Cal. 55, at 67.)

From 1850 to 1872 California relied on common law equitable principles for class treatment. In 1872 the state adopted Code of Civil Procedure section 382, which allows class action cases, along with other Field Code provisions duplicating the New York reforms of 1849. As adopted in 1872, Code of Civil Procedure section 382 provides that suits may be brought by one on behalf of all when parties are numerous, the question is of general or common interest, and bringing all the parties before the court is impracticable.

In *Carey* v. *Brown* (1881) 58 Cal. 180, defendants claimed an individual interest in an undivided seven-eighths of a 30,000-acre tract held by the plaintiff. Plaintiff stated that he brought the action on behalf of himself and all other persons similarly situated who would in time come to court for relief and contribute to the expense of the litigation. After the plaintiff received judgment in his favor, the would-be class members presented themselves. The court, however, held that no class existed because the plaintiff's interest in the land was not united as one entity with the interests of the others. The court construed Code of Civil Procedure section 382 as permitting one to sue or defend for the benefit of many persons only in cases where they are so united in interest as to make them necessary parties. The court also pointed out that if the other would-be plaintiffs wished to intervened, they should have done so before the final judgment, which determined only the plaintiff's rights against the defendants and not the rights of any other persons. Would the result have been different if the court was forced to rule on a common question of law other than adverse possession to all of those who took title? The court stated that the only issue before the court was the plaintiff's effort to quiet title to his land and that no one else had any interest.

In *Noroian* v. *Bennett* (1919) 179 Cal. 806, a group of farmer plaintiffs alleged that they were fraudulently induced to execute a series of promissory notes on a variety of occasions. The court denied class treatment because the transactions were legally separate and distinct. There was no single fact or act whose determination would fix the rights of all of the plaintiffs. This result stands in fascinating contrast to the *Vasquez* decision rendered 52 years later, which will be discussed below.

Federal Equity Rule 48 incorporated a res judicata effect on nonparty class members and operated in the federal courts from 1842 to 1912. Equity Rule 38 replaced rule 48 between 1912 and 1938, when the original Federal Rules of Civil Procedure rule 23 was adopted. Commentators have stated that rule 23 was a "bold and well-intentioned attempt to encourage the more frequent use of class actions." (*Wright, Miller & Kane*, Vol. 7, ¶ 1752.) This important change in federal class action procedural practice made class relief acceptable and justifiable, but a quarter-century of experience clarified the rule's serious defects and showed it to be in need of revision.

Postwar Cases in the Shadow of Federal Rule 23

The United States Supreme Court's 1938 adoption of the Federal Rules of Civil Procedure codified all common law and equity procedural aspects. It included a formalized provision for class actions in federal courts that clarified the general American concepts of class action law. The 1938 codification organized class actions according to the substantive character of the right asserted. The "true" class action concerned joint, common, derivative, or secondary rights. The "hybrid" class action consisted of an adjudication of specific property claims. The "spurious" class action was really a permissive joinder device.

Seven states now have class action statutes modeled on what is called the original federal rule 23 model. That provision states that, if a class is so numerous that bringing its members before the court is impracticable, one or more adequate representatives may prosecute the matter provided that the right to be enforced is one of three types: (1) joint, common, or secondary, in that the owner of a primary right refuses to enforce it and the class becomes entitled to enforcement; (2) several, and the action concerns specific property; and (3) several, and the questions of law or fact are common.

Within 10 years of the adoption of original federal rule 23, the California Supreme Court defined the limits of a community of interest in an important and oft-cited case. *Weaver* v. *Pasadena Tournament of Roses* (1948) 32 Cal.2d 833 [198 P.2d 514] centered on the public sale of tickets to the 1947 Rose Bowl. Advertising for the heavily publicized sale said 7,500 tickets would be available, and a large crowd appeared. Would-be ticketholders were given numbered identification stubs, but only 1,500 were allowed to buy tickets. The class action suit was brought on behalf of those denied tickets. The ruling denied class certification. The court established that a defined community of interest in questions of law and fact must exist between those bringing the suit and those to be represented, and that the suit should be brought on behalf of a definite ascertained or ascertainable group. Reviewing and summarizing California cases in which a class suit had been held proper, the court noted that they involved a trust fund, a common fund of some sort, or a common property interest uniting all the parties in interest. In the *Weaver* case, however, the alleged wrongful conduct required judicial inquiry into the myriad reasons why individuals were refused Rose Bowl admittance. The court noted that the case involved no one simultaneous set of acts or series of acts that created or conferred rights or interests and thereby established a common interest in all members of the group. The *Weaver* case assisted subsequent California courts in determining when to allow class certification.

Hefferman v. *Bennett & Armour* (1952) 110 Cal.App.2d 564 [243 P.2d 846] involved the successful prosecution of a fraudulent conveyance or a transfer action with the intent to defraud creditors. The court found it was a valid representative class brought both for the benefit of the plaintiff and all the rest of the defendant's creditors. The common issue was whether the questionable transfers were made with the intent to defraud. Since the issue was determined in favor of plaintiff and the other creditors, the court found that he represented other creditors.

Two years later, in *Barber* v. *California Employment Stabilization Commission* (1954) 130 Cal.App.2d 7 [278 P.2d 762], a California appellate court refused class certification to a group of unemployed sailors seeking unemployment benefits. Since the sailors were not on strike, and since they were unemployed for a variety of specific reasons, determining eligibility required individual threshold eligibility criteria that diluted the community of interest. Each class member's facts applied only to the individual, and no class existed.

Three years later, *Fanucchi* v. *Coberly-West Co.* (1957) 151 Cal.App.2d 72 [311 P.2d 33] involved a defendant cotton-ginning company that over a period of years wrongfully retained overcharges belonging to the plaintiff growers. The trial court sustained the defendant's demurrer to the class allegations because they alleged misconduct as the product of numerous transactions. The growers, who said that individual lawsuits were too costly to be justified, prevailed on appeal. They argued that proof of a common set of facts was required only on the real issue—the overage the growers had been denied. This proof established the existence of a fund and set each grower's pro rata share. Although created by separate commercial transactions, the misconduct still supported a community of interest and class certification. (*Fanucchi* v. *Coberly-West Co.* (1957)151 Cal.App.2d 72, 83 [311 P.2d 33].)

Chance v. *Superior Court* (1962) 58 Cal.2d 275 [23 Cal.Rptr. 761, 373 P.2d 849] went further. The court stated that a class action could be certified without a common fund or common property. Separate parcels of property with separate deeds of trust were sold in the same overall transaction, with the same paperwork, provisions, and conditions. The only difference was the face amounts of the notes. Accordingly, a class action was appropriate.

The Contemporary Period: 1966 to 1997

Federal Rules of Civil Procedure rule 23 was refined in 1966 to its present form, setting the procedural path for certification issues in federal court followed to this day. The courts have since defined most of the practical and important cases dealing with procedural class action issues according to the 1966 Federal Rule of Civil Procedure amendments and the California Supreme Court's ruling in *Daar* v. *Yellow Cab Co.* (1967) 67 Cal.2d 695 [63 Cal.Rptr. 724, 433 P.2d 732]. These cases can be misleading on procedural issues, however, since a number of them have subsequently been overruled or modified. Factual settings of cases prior to 1966 may compare to a present controversy and all judges, of course, like to see a previous case on "all fours."

Although the amended form of rule 23 did not greatly affect California's statutory law, with the minor exception of the Consumer Legal Remedies Act, it extensively influenced the development of case law. The California Supreme Court followed the revision with a series of benchmark cases encouraging class actions.

The seminal modern California case is *Daar* v. *Yellow Cab Co.* (1967) 67 Cal.2d 695, 698 [63 Cal.Rptr. 724, 433 P.2d 732]. This case represented a major departure from the postwar rules regarding common funds and property and extended existing California law. The proposed class comprised people who had used Yellow Cab within the past four years and paid cash. Although class members were unidentified, the lack of identification did not preclude a complete determination of the issues affecting the class. Yellow Cab had agreed in writing with the City of Los Angeles that rates would be set by a commission, yet the actual rates charged to the class were higher by a uniform percentage known to the defendant. The community of interest in the case required neither common fund nor common recovery to support certification of the class. In its opinion, the California Supreme Court cited the noteworthy changes to rule 23 applicable to state class actions and substantially consistent with Code of Civil Procedure section 382 (*Daar* v. *Yellow Cab Co.* (1967) 67 Cal.2d 695, 709 [63 Cal.Rptr. 724, 433 P.2d 732].)

Vasquez v. *Superior Court* (1971) 4 Cal.3d 800 [94 Cal.Rptr. 796, 484 P.2d 964] is often taken together with *Daar* as constituting judicial adoption of rule 23 in California. In *Vasquez*, the court stated, among other things, that where California law is silent, rule 23 prescribes procedural devices trial courts might find useful. (*Vasquez* v. *Superior Court* (1971) 4 Cal.3d 800 [94 Cal.Rptr. 796, 484 P.2d 964].) The court also held to *Daar*'s notion of community of interest. The case concerned retail installment sales contracts sold to residents of San Joaquin and Stanislaus counties. Alleged misrepresentations were made in the contracts themselves and the prepared sales pitch. As in *Daar*, the transactions were separate, yet this fact was not controlling. Instead, the memorized statement delivered by salespeople and the standardized terms of the written contracts created the community of interest. The court also extended an inference of reliance and encouraged trial courts to use pragmatic procedural devices, taking the courts one step closer to rule 23 yet not limiting them to those procedures. By 1973, the Los Angeles Superior Court, for instance, had adopted a series of *Vasquez*-motivated trial court procedures that, after review by the appellate courts in a series of cases, began to set pretrial standards for class actions.

A case that came between *Daar* and *Vasquez*, *Gerhard* v. *Stephen* (1968) 68 Cal.2d 864 [69 Cal.Rptr. 612, 442 P.2d 692], somewhat limited the community of interest notion. The facts of the case involved an alleged ownership of undivided mineral interests, but each claim presented important individual issues of title requiring individual litigation to determine the right to recovery. The interested parties were numerous, but they could bring individual actions.

It also appeared to the court that a large number had actual knowledge of the case. A class action in the situation was ruled inappropriate.

La Sala v. *American Sav. & Loan Ass'n* (1971) 5 Cal.3d 864 [97 Cal.Rptr. 849, 489 P.2d 1113] defined the class representative's responsibilities. Defendants sought to stop the action through the procedural ploy of mooting the representative plaintiff's claim. At the same time, some plaintiffs tried to benefit at the expense of absent class members by settling and dropping class allegations. The attempt was deterred by requiring judicial review of class allegation dismissal to ensure that settlement supports the fiduciary responsibility to the class.

Collins v. *Rocha* (1972) 7 Cal.3d 232 [102 Cal.Rptr. 1, 497 P.2d 225] further expanded the rules regarding certification and served to expand the factual setting for community of interest beyond *Vasquez*. The case turned on oral misrepresentations of available work the defendant made knowingly to farm workers. As a result of the misrepresentations, the workers were brought into a setting where they defrauded and abused. Although there was no common fund and communications were oral, not written, the court held a community of interest did exist and the class was certified.

The opinion in *City of San Jose* v. *Superior Court of Santa Clara County* (1974) 12 Cal.3d 447 [115 Cal.Rptr. 797, 525 P.2d 701], which was written by Justice Clark for the California Supreme Court's majority, clearly circumscribed the bounds of earlier expansive class action cases. This case has become a mandatory and prominent citation in all opposition briefs by defendants in California class actions. The matter arose from real property condemnation and nuisance cases. The unique characteristics of each piece of real estate created individual questions, and the nuisance allegations likewise involved individual reactions to smoke and noise, thereby preventing a class action.

Home Sav. and Loan Ass'n v. *Superior Court, Los Angeles County* (1974) 42 Cal.App.3d 1006 [117 Cal.Rptr. 485] concerned a class action in which Home Savings and Loan was sued for damages and declaratory relief arising from late charges on loans. Before the class was certified or notice given to the class, the trial court allowed bifurcation under Code of Civil Procedure section 1048, subdivision (b), ordering a separate trial of liability issues. The appellate court ruled this error. It stated that the primary question in a class action is certification of the class. Until the class is certified, no binding judgment may be rendered. The court noted the pragmatic devices mentioned in *Vasquez* for postponing certification and dispensing with notice to members of the class fail to protect the defendant's right to a fair trial and due process of law. They fail equally in protecting the rights of absent class members.

In *Eisen* v. *Carlisle and Jacquelin* (1974) 417 U.S. 156 [40 L.Ed.2d 732, 94 S.Ct. 2140], the court restated the requirement for class determination as soon as practicable and before any other action.

Cartt v. *Superior Court of Los Angeles County* (1975) 50 Cal.App.3d 960 [124 Cal.Rptr. 376] further circumscribed and defined procedure for notice. The court had certified the matter as a class action and ordered the named plaintiff to mail notice to the 700,000 persons who owned credit cards issued by the defendant. The cost was nearly $70,000, well out of reach for the plaintiff, a school teacher who earned less than $15,000 a year. The trial court apparently felt its hands were tied by *Eisen* v. *Carlisle and Jacquelin* (1974) 417 U.S. 156 [40 L.Ed.2d 732, 94 S.Ct. 2140]. The appellate court reversed. In doing so, it allowed the trial court the flexibility to balance the economic feasibility of notice against the desire for res judicata and decide what notice is realistic and required. The court stated that notice protects the integrity of the class action process and prevents burdening the courts with multiple claims where one will do. (*La Sala* v. *American Sav. & Loan Ass'n* (1971) 5 Cal.3d 864 [97 Cal.Rptr. 849, 489 P.2d 1113].)

In 1976 two notable cases were decided. In the first, *Occidental Land, Inc.* v. *Superior Court of Orange County* (1976) 18 Cal.3d 355 [134 Cal.Rptr. 388, 556 P.2d 750], the Supreme Court reviewed and approved a class certification order for 155 homeowners suffering partial oral and written misrepresentation. The court reconfirmed the subsequently discredited trial court procedure of successively applying for class certification as Federal Rule of Civil Procedure 23 contemplates. It also found that moving to decertify a class within eighteen months was not a delay. The opinion in the second case, *Blue Chip Stamps* v. *Superior Court of Los Angeles* (1976) 18 Cal.3d 381 [134 Cal.Rptr. 393, 556 P.2d 755], was rendered by the court on the same day as *Occidental Land*. It provides a clue to the judicial view of smaller and apparently less worthy claims.

Richmond v. *Dart Industries, Inc.* (1981) 29 Cal.3d 462 [174 Cal.Rptr. 515, 629 P.2d 23] strengthened the concept of community of interest created by written misrepresentations. It also set out rules tolerating some conflicts within the class, and described the legal criteria for both ascertainable class and community of interest.

Green v. *Obledo* (1981) 29 Cal.3d 126 [172 Cal.Rptr. 206, 624 P.2d 256] held that circumstances must have changed to decertify a class. Absent such changes, it was error to decertify.

McConnell v. *Merrill Lynch, Pierce, Fenner & Smith, Inc.* (1983) 33 Cal.3d 816 [191 Cal.Rptr. 458, 662 P.2d 916] held that the procedural failure to request findings of fact and conclusions of law when the trial court denied class certification made significant review of any error on the court's part impossible. Now counsel must request findings and conclusions to protect the record and provide for a meaningful analysis on appeal.

California clarified rules on the tolling of the statute of limitations for absent class members in *Jolly* v. *Eli Lilly & Co.* (1988) 44 Cal.3d 1103 [245 Cal.Rptr. 658, 751 P.2d 923]. This significant ruling sets forth the policy criteria that determine tolling in cases where defendants are on notice as to the approximate identity of the proposed class and as to either the nature and substance of the claims for relief or the causes of action.

California courts have used the tripartite analysis of Federal Rules of Civil Procedure rule 23, subdivision (b), to determine whether notice to class members about the pending action is required. The courts have taken this language to heart and acknowledged that the notice requirements of rule 23 do not bind California courts. (*Cartt* v. *Superior Court of Los Angeles County* (1975) 50 Cal.App.3d 960 [124 Cal.Rptr. 376].) *Bell* v. *American Title Ins. Co.* (1991) 226 Cal.App.3d 1589 [277 Cal.Rptr. 583] was the first discussion by a California appellate court on opt-outs. The Federal Rules of Civil Procedure determine no right to opt out in classes certified under rule 23, subdivisions (b)(1) or (b)(2). Rule 23, subdivision (b)(1), weighs the risk of separate actions or cases that would otherwise impair a uniform remedial pattern of conduct by a defendant. Rule 23, subdivision (b)(2), deals with declaratory relief or final injunctive relief on grounds that are generally appealable to the class. By contrast, Code of Civil Procedure section 382 does not say when the trial court should afford a right to opt out. The trial court ruling had precluded opt-outs in *Bell* v. *American Title Ins. Co.*, a decision the appellate court agreed with. The court confirmed that California courts have the discretion to determine whether the requirements of Federal Rule of Civil Procedure rule 23, subdivision (b)(1) or (b)(2), apply. This case also allows the court to determine whether the primary or predominant relief is injunctive and any corresponding monetary relief subordinate.

In *Stephen* v. *Enterprise Rent-A-Car* (1991) 235 Cal.App.3d 806 [1 Cal.Rptr.2d 130], California settled its different approach from that of the federal courts on appeal of a denial of class certification. California does not allow successive motions to attempt certification, but only successive motions to attempt decertification. If a plaintiff fails to certify the class unsuccessfully and there is no partial certification, plaintiff must appeal since the denial is a final order terminating the action for absent class members.

1 INTRODUCTION TO CALIFORNIA CLASS ACTIONS

Sec.

1.01 Introduction

[A] National Importance of California Litigation

[B] Applicable Law and Rules

[C] Differences Between California and Federal Practice

[D] Effect of Local Rules

1.02 Due Process Requirements

1.03 California Class Action Procedure

1.04 The Advantages and Disadvantages of Class Actions

[A] In General

[B] Advantages and Disadvantages of Federal Class Actions

[C] Advantages and Disadvantages of State Class Actions

1.05 California Class Action Authority

[A] In General

[B] Code of Civil Procedure Section 382

[C] Consumer Legal Remedies Act

[D] Local Rules of Los Angeles, San Diego, San Francisco, and San Mateo Counties

1.06 Federal Authority: Federal Rules of Civil Procedure, Rule 23

1.07 Differences Between California State and Federal Class Actions

1.08 References

§ 1.01 Introduction

[A] National Importance of California Litigation

The bulk of civil litigation in the United States passes through the state courts. By any such measure as population, gross domestic product, or number of lawyers and general caseload, California plays a significant role in the state court system of civil litigation. California already handles more than its share of complex litigation. With recent Supreme Court rulings giving greater deference to state class action settlements, California class actions will only become more important.

[B] Applicable Law and Rules

California superior courts have original jurisdiction in all cases not assigned by statute to other courts. (Cal. Const., art. VI, § 10.) The California Supreme Court directed California trial courts to use federal rules for class action procedures whenever state authority proves inadequate. (*Richmond* v. *Dart Industries, Inc.* (1981) 29 Cal.3d 462, 469 [174 Cal.Rptr. 515, 629 P.2d 23].) This mandate, however, has not produced a predictable, clear, and understandable set of procedural rules.

California's class action procedures evolved after the state adopted the Field Code in 1872. The Field Code reforms were an attempt to simplify legal principles extracted from centuries of case law. Included in California's code was Code of Civil Procedure section 382, which dealt in part with class actions. California case law expanded the application of this statute to new circumstances. In 1971 the California Supreme Court "judicially adopted" Federal Rules of Civil Procedure, rule 23, which establishes current federal class action procedure, but the state kept the final say on certification. Subsequent case law required that the benefit of class action to the court and the litigants be substantial. (See *Daar* v. *Yellow Cab Co.* (1967) 67 Cal.2d 695, 698 [63 Cal.Rptr. 792, 433 P.2d 732]; *Vasquez* v. *Superior Court* (1971) 4 Cal.3d 800 [94 Cal.Rptr. 796, 484 P.2d 964].)

[C] Differences Between California and Federal Practice

California case law often diverges from federal practice. Instances include procedures for class certification, such as:

- The scope and type of evidentiary hearing. (*Carabini* v. *Superior Court* (1994) 26 Cal.App.4th 239 [31 Cal.Rptr.2d 520].)

- The form of objections to class certification. (*Hamwi* v. *Citinational-Buckeye Investment Co.* (1977) 72 Cal.App.3d 462 [140 Cal.Rptr. 215].)
- Method and timing of appeal. (*Stephen* v. *Enterprise Rent-A-Car* (1991) 235 Cal.App.3d 806 [1 Cal.Rptr.2d 130].)
- The question of whether precertification must be determined. (*Home Savings & Loan Ass'n* v. *Superior Court (Home I)* (1974) 42 Cal.App.3d 1006 [117 Cal.Rptr. 485]; *Home Savings & Loan Ass'n* v. *Superior Court (Home II)* (1976) 54 Cal.App.3d 208 [126 Cal.Rptr. 511].)
- Partial class settlement issues, such as bar orders under Code of Civil Procedure section 877.6.
- The scope and method of required notice to the class. (*Cartt* v. *Superior Court of Los Angeles County* (1975) 50 Cal.App.3d 960 [124 Cal.Rptr. 376].)

Only when there is no relevant state precedent do California courts turn to federal law and rule 23 for guidance. (*Bell* v. *American Title Ins. Co.* (1991) 226 Cal.App.3d 1589, 1603 [277 Cal.Rptr. 583].) Indeed, unless a constitutional right is impaired, federal cases interpreting federal rule 23 do not bind state courts. (*Rosack* v. *Volvo of America Corp.* (1982) 131 Cal.App.3d 741, 806 [182 Cal.Rptr. 800].) As a result, class action practitioners must be familiar with California case law to determine where California and federal law part company.

Since California Code of Civil Procedure section 382, the primary statutory authority for class actions in the state, provides no formal procedures, California lawyers must wend their way through a tangled thicket of complex statutes and rules ranging from statutory yardsticks like the Consumer Legal Remedies Act (Civ. Code, § 1750 et seq.) to local superior court rules (see, e.g., Super. Ct. L.A. County Rules, Ch. 15, Class Actions; Super. Ct. San Diego County Rules, div. II, sec. three; Super. Ct., S.F. County Manual for Conduct of Pretrial Proc. in Class Actions; Super. Ct. San Mateo County Rules, div. VII, Pretrial Proc. in Class Actions; and Appendix.)

Efforts to standardize state class actions have yet to reach California. The National Conference of Commissioners on Uniform State Laws argues that states strongly need to adopt a uniform class action act, in part because federal restrictions on the availability of class actions send more and more claimants to state court (Uniform Law Commissioners Model Class [Act] [Rule] Prefatory Note). California briefly attempted to adopt a statute similar to federal rule 23 in enacting the Consumer Legal Remedies Act (hereafter CLRA).

However, most California appellate courts ignore CLRA in favor of Code of Civil Procedure section 382 except when a case falls within CLRA's strict definition of unfair consumer transactions. (See, e.g., *Clemons* v. *Western Photo Camera Hut* (1981) 117 Cal.App.3d 392 [172 Cal.Rptr. 782]; *Hogya* v. *Superior Court* (1977) 75 Cal.App.3d 122 [142 Cal.Rptr. 325].) Unless faced squarely with CLRA, recent California class action procedural cases rarely discuss it. (See, e.g., *Carabini* v. *Superior Court* (1994) 26 Cal.App.4th 239 [31 Cal.Rptr.2d 520]; *Daniels* v. *Centennial Group, Inc.* (1993) 16 Cal.App.4th 467 [21 Cal.Rptr.2d 1]; *National Solar Equipment Owners' Ass'n, Inc.* v. *Grumman Corp.* (1991) 235 Cal.App.3d 1273 [1 Cal.Rptr.2d 325].)

[D] Effect of Local Rules

Local rules may further render CLRA and its foundation in federal rule 23 moot. Many local jurisdictions provide detailed procedural guidelines for class certification that appellate courts have held applicable at the trial court level. Generally, however, local rules bind only the court that promulgated them. (*Hypolite* v. *Carleson* (1975) 52 Cal.App.3d 566, 578 [125 Cal.Rptr. 221].) Indeed, some appellate districts have sought to expand the use of local rules in class actions. (See, e.g., *Union Mutual Life Ins. Co.* v. *Superior Court* (*Bobby Ray Scott, Real Party in Interest*) (1978) 80 Cal.App.3d 1, 13 [145 Cal.Rptr. 316].)

§ 1.02 Due Process Requirements

Rendering a judgment for or against a nonparty to a lawsuit may constitute a denial of due process under the United States and California Constitutions. (*Lambert* v. *California* (1957) 355 U.S. 225 [2 L.Ed.2d 228, 78 S.Ct. 240].) California has recognized for the past 50 years that a judgment may not be entered either for or against someone who is not party to an action. (*Bronco Wine Co.* v. *Frank A. Logoluso Farms* (1989) 214 Cal.App.3d 699, 703 [214 Cal.Rptr. 899].)

Class action practice, however, does allow a court to constitutionally extend jurisdiction over a nonparty. In a typical class action lawsuit, a resident of Los Angeles County may represent the interests of, for example, Tulare County residents who never appear before the Superior Court of Los Angeles. In sharp contrast to individual litigation, in which plaintiffs present themselves to the court and are highly attentive, motivated, and aware of their claims, a class action may bind people who never appear and pay little or no attention to the proceeding and its outcome.

In a class action trial, the evidence offered and the advocacy advanced by the class representative and class counsel affect the entire class, for better or worse. In a settlement, the class representative and class counsel may negotiate on behalf of the interests of the class. Either way, a few affect the rights of many. Thus, notice of the action and a chance to be heard are essential components of the trial court's jurisdiction and due process in class actions. (*Environmental Coalition of Orange County Inc.* v. *Local Agency Formation Com.* (1980) 110 Cal.App.3d 164, 173 [167 Cal.Rptr. 735].)

The "leveraged" effect of a class action makes it substantially different from basic litigation. When individual litigants appear in the courtroom to contest issues, they are bound by normal due process concepts only if they have been designated as parties and duly served with process in a manner consistent with in personam jurisdiction. In a class action, by contrast, the persons litigating in court represent interests beyond the courtroom.

Class action treatment is an equitable concept in that it allows a suit to proceed when the number of interested parties is so large that joining them is impractical under usual rules of procedure and might actually obstruct justice. (*Uniform Law Commissioners Model Class Actions* [Act] [Rule] prefatory note; *Hansberry* v. *Lee* (1941) 311 U.S. 32 [85 L.Ed. 22, 61 S.Ct. 115].) The class action device modifies the legal process to maximize expediency and necessity yet still satisfy due process.

Class actions serve the important function of resolving the claims of many individuals at once, saving time and reducing cost. (*Kaye* v. *Mt. La Jolla Homeowners Ass'n* (1988) 204 Cal.App.3d 1476 [252 Cal.Rptr. 67].) This benefits the judicial system by eliminating repetitious litigation and providing a method of obtaining redress for claims too small to warrant litigation on their own. (*Richmond* v. *Dart Industries, Inc.* (1981) 29 Cal.3d 462 [174 Cal.Rptr. 515].)

§ 1.03 California Class Action Procedure

Generally, state class action procedures in the United States fall into four basic categories. First, some states have implemented statutes that follow the express terms of Federal Rules of Civil Procedure, rule 23, as adopted and revised in 1966. Second, some states still follow the pre1966 rule 23, which dates to 1938. Third are states with Field Code statutes, of which California is one. Fourth and finally, some states have no class action statutes whatsoever. (Uniform Law Commissioners Model Class [Act] [Rule] Prefatory Note.)

Obviously, class action procedures differ substantially from state to state, and California has its own unique set of class action procedures.

When can an active California litigant represent other, passive persons in a lawsuit? Class action procedure and practice answer this question. The relevant statutes and case law apply in this order:

1. Code of Civil Procedure section 382.
2. Civil Code section 1781(b)(1)(4).
3. California case law, if specifically applicable.
4. Federal Rules of Civil Procedure, rule 23 (supplementing Civ. Code, § 1781; see *McGhee* v. *Bank of America* (1976) 60 Cal.App.3d 442 [131 Cal.Rptr. 482]).
5. Local rules of the county in which the matter is filed.
6. Federal case law interpreting rule 23 (unless a constitutionally protected right is involved, in which case it is binding on the California court).

Certain provisions (Civ. Code, § 1781(b)(1)(4)) of the CLRA (Civ. Code, § 1750 et seq.) closely track federal rule 23. Their importance to standard (nonconsumer) class action practice over the past 20 years of California case law is open to question.

Class action procedure cannot alter substantive law. (*City of San Jose* v. *Superior Court* (1974) 12 Cal.3d 447 [115 Cal.Rptr. 797, 525 P.2d 701].) However, because of its expanded effect, class certification powerfully affects the total substantive rights of class members. As a result, policy issues underlying the substantive area of law work to the advantage or disadvantage of the class device. For example, because of the policy preference accorded antitrust issues, an antitrust consumer class action will likely fare better than a minor consumer claim against the representations of an advertiser.

Since a class action lawsuit affects the rights of persons not before the court, the individual representative, or litigant, represents the interests of those absent persons. The success or failure of the individual litigant binds the absent class members. The person bringing a class action must adequately represent and protect the interests of the other members of the class who will be bound by the judgment. (*La Sala* v. *American Sav. & Loan Ass'n* (1971) 5 Cal.3d 864, 871, 872 [97 Cal.Rptr. 849, 489 P.2d 1113]). Thereafter, res judicata bars members of the class from relitigating claims related to the primary right already decided. (*Johnson* v. *American Airlines, Inc.* (1984) 157 Cal.App.3d 427 [203 Cal.Rptr. 638].)

This critical difference in the scope and extent of the undertaking of litigant and counsel in class actions results in special procedural complexities and additional fiduciary obligations that will be discussed later.

§ 1.04 The Advantages and Disadvantages of Class Actions

[A] In General

The primary advantage of a class action is that it effectively and efficiently brings together small claims unlikely or impractical to litigate individually. By aggregating small claims, class actions lower the cost of litigation and bring superior resources and legal talent to bear.

Additionally, a certified class action strengthens the plaintiff's negotiating position. A certified class action levels the playing field when individuals of little power find themselves up against strong economic entities.

The leading disadvantage is the procedural complexity of class actions. From the plaintiff's perspective, class actions can be expensive to prosecute and defend. Additionally, class actions need to be resolved in a common manner that precludes attention to the idiosyncratic nature of individual claims. Class actions usually become a liability in certain types of emotional distress, negligence, or other issues. Absent certification, the practitioner is left with the need and duty to prosecute the case on a far narrower scope than originally anticipated.

In extensive class actions, consolidation of cases and assignment of lead counsel to different individuals eliminates direct litigation control. Also, large consolidated cases necessarily proceed slowly and sharply restrict settlement.

Class actions are generally, but not necessarily, more timeconsuming and expensive for practitioners. Unlike individual litigation, class actions must undergo a series of precertification steps that increases counsel's burden of time and expense.

[B] Advantages and Disadvantages of Federal Class Actions

Federal class actions offer the considerable advantage of remedying wrongs on behalf of litigants located in any number of states. If two or more cases involving a similar defendant or common liability questions are pending in different districts, defendant or plaintiff may ask to have them transferred under the auspices of the Multidistrict Litigation Panel in federal law. (28 U.S.C., § 1407.) This jurisdictional benefit can greatly streamline consolidation of similar cases. It should be noted that California has a similar capability; the Judicial Council can coordinate similar cases pending in different superior courts. (See Code Civ. Proc., § 404 et seq.; Cal. Rules of Court, rule 1501 et seq.)

The well-defined federal procedural rules in effect since July 1, 1966 also work to counsel's benefit. Additionally, certain substantive causes of action can be heard only in federal courts, such as federal antitrust claims or certain environmental matters.

The federal court system works to the benefit of a class action because one judge handles the entire proceeding. Assignment to an individual judge allows the same jurist to rule on class certification after dealing with extensive pretrial motions and other activity that has "educated" him or her to the benefit or merits of the case.

Local venue is less likely in large class actions because of the use of the Multidistrict Litigation Panel. Federal forums are also subject to jurisdictional restrictions. The U.S. Supreme Court has held, for instance, that each of the class members in a diversity case under federal rule 23 must have a monetary claim of more than $10,000 and or be dismissed from the case. (*Zahn* v. *International Paper* (1973) 414 U.S. 291 [38 L.Ed.2d 511, 94 S.Ct. 505].) This issue does not, however, apply in most securities class actions, which are usually brought under the jurisdictional provisions of federal securities law.

Also, most authorities believe that federal rules require stricter adherence to notice provisions than California state practice does. The federal rules are set forth in *Eisen* v. *Carlisle and Jacquelin* (1974) 417 U.S. 156 [40 L.Ed.2d 732, 94 S.Ct. 2140]. The state rules appear in *Cartt* v. *Superior Court of Los Angeles County* (1975) 50 Cal.App.3d 960 [124 Cal.Rptr. 376].

[C] Advantages and Disadvantages of State Class Actions

Once counsel understands the rules of class action, the California courts provide a more direct and expeditious venue than the federal. While this primarily benefits cases whose class members are mostly California residents, national class actions can be venued in a California court in some instances. California substantive law can be applied in areas where federal law is less favorable, such as securities violations or indirect purchaser requirements in antitrust law. Additionally, recent United States Supreme Court rulings boost respect for state class action settlements and make them more attractive (*Matsushita Electric Industrial Co., Ltd* v. *Epstein* (1996) _U.S_ [134 L.Ed.2d 64, 116 S.Ct. 873]; see discussion in Chapter 4.)

The leading disadvantage to state class actions is the inability to venue larger national claims without raising serious dueprocess issues. In addition, a number of superior courts, including smaller courts, face serious pressures because of criminal calendars swollen by "three strikes" criminal laws. Judges who are busy and overburdened are likely to find it difficult to handle the extensive factual investigation class action demands and to constantly monitor the conduct of plaintiff and defense counsel for potential harm to absent class members. Class actions require a great deal more work than the average civil case, and they fare best with judges who are seriously interested in them and willing to bear the extra workload.

§ 1.05 California Class Action Authority

[A] In General

Getting a case certified as a class action in California requires adherence to this state's unique rules. (See discussion under [B]–[D], below.)

[B] Code of Civil Procedure Section 382

California Code of Civil Procedure section 382 provides that in issues of widespread interest or with a substantial effect upon a number of people too large to practically bring to court, one or more claimants may litigate on behalf of all. This is the basis for class actions in California.

[C] Consumer Legal Remedies Act

The Consumer Legal Remedies Act (Civ. Code, § 1750 et seq., hereafter CLRA), passed by the California Legislature in 1970, provides that any consumer entitled to bring an action under section 1780 of the Civil Code may do so on behalf of others besides himself or herself if an unlawful method, act, or practice has done damage to a number of individuals in similar situations. (Civ. Code, § 1781.) These provisions on when a class action may be filed are very similar to rule 23(a)(1)(4) of the Federal Rules of Civil Procedure. In certain cases, CLRA offers an effective alternative or additional way for proceeding with class actions. This approach is discussed in detail in Chapter 3.

[D] Local Rules of Los Angeles, San Diego, San Francisco, and San Mateo Counties

Because certain jurisdictions impose requirements more detailed than the state's, practitioners must become familiar with the local rules of Los Angeles, San Diego, San Francisco, and San Mateo counties, as well as any other counties that defer to their pretrial procedures. The local rules of various superior courts govern the procedural process and, because of their specificity, have some substantive effect. For a complete discussion of the substantive effects of procedural rules, see Chapter 4. The class action rules for Los Angeles, San Diego, San Francisco, and San Mateo counties are set forth in the Appendix to this book.

§ 1.06 Federal Authority: Federal Rules of Civil Procedure, Rule 23

The Federal Rules of Civil Procedure, rule 23, revised and substantially adopted in 1966, has had broad effect. Because it is a relatively straightforward description of the types of situations in which class actions can be certified, it is a touchstone for analysis of California cases. However, in the event of a difference between federal and state law on a given practice, California decisional law controls.

Federal Rule of Civil Procedure, rule 23(a) sets forth four prerequisites to asserting a class action:

1. Numerous parties making joinder impracticable.
2. Common questions of law and fact.
3. Typical claims and defenses by the representative parties.
4. Adequacy of representation.

Once these "threshold criteria" are met, and only then, the court must move on to the analysis required by federal rule 23(b), which requires the court to decide whether the action is a "mandatory" class action requiring no notice. (See Fed. Rules Civ.Proc., rule 23(b)(1) & (2).) The mandatory classification covers class actions in which there is a risk of inconsistent or incompatible standards of conduct, the potential for adjudications that would be dispositive of the interests of the class, or a suggestion of injunctive relief or declaratory. The more common notice and opt-out requirements satisfying due process in claims for monetary damages are governed by federal rule 23(b)(3) and require courts, on the other hand, apply the criteria of federal rule 23(a) and (b) in a more structured way, with at least the appearance of a tighter framework of analysis.

As this book is going to press, there have been hearings held before the Committee on Proposed Reforms of Rule 23 of the Federal Rules of Civil Procedure which would have an impact on the federal handling of class actions. These changes include expressly a settlement class provision, a provision similar to that of a "substantial benefit" requirement, and other changes. Practitioners are advised to monitor these recommendations.

§ 1.07 Differences Between California State and Federal Class Actions

California has judicially evolved a unique set of procedural rules for certifying class actions. The rather cryptic terms of Code of Civil Procedure section 382 required an evolutionary development of the rules. As a result, the broad principles applicable to federal class actions do not automatically hold for state class actions. Differences between federal and state practice include the scope and extent of notice, procedural rules surrounding certification of a class, precertification conduct, and the procedure for appealing from an unfavorable class ruling and its finality. (For further discussion of these limits, see Chapter 6.)

California's rules allow a far smaller number of individuals to form a class. As long as the number is large enough to make bringing them before the court "impracticable," a class action is permitted. The federal rule requires numerosity, or a large number.

The California standard allows for dominant common action or in actions in which the opposing party has acted on terms applicable to a larger group as it may not be required to bind affected parties.

These are minor differences, however, compared with the gap between state and federal class action practice on California final rules on the superiority of the class process and the ability to provide substantial benefits to the public and the court. California courts may step back and ask if the proposed remedy of a state class action is "superior" to other methods of resolving the controversy.

§ 1.08 References

NEWBERG For a discussion of the advantages and disadvantages of class actions, see 2 Newberg on Class Actions (3d ed. 1992), Chapter 5.

WITKIN For discussion of class actions generally, see 4 Witkin, Cal. Procedure (4th ed. 1997) Pleading, § 246 et seq.

THE RUTTER GROUP See California Practice Guide: Civil Procedure Before Trial (CPBT), Chapter 14, regarding California class actions generally. See also California Practice Guide: Federal Civil Procedure Before Trial (FCPBT), §§ 10:225–10:626, regarding federal class actions generally.

WEST'S KEY NUMBER SYSTEM See the following Key Numbers in West's California Digest 2d, Federal Civil Procedure (Topic 170A):

- Factors and grounds in general (Federal Civil Procedure 🔑 161–166).
- Certification proceedings (Federal Civil Procedure 🔑 171–180).
- Particular class represented (Federal Civil Procedure 🔑 181–189).

See also Parties (Topic 287):

- Representative and class actions in general (Parties 🔑 35.1–35.21).
- Certification proceedings (Parties 🔑 35.31–35.53).
- Particular class represented (Parties 🔑 35.61–35.89).

WESTLAW® See the WESTLAW Electronic Research Guide at the beginning of this volume.

2 PREREQUISITES TO FILING A CALIFORNIA CLASS ACTION

Sec.

2.01 Introduction
2.02 Ascertainable Class
2.03 Community of Interest
2.04 Adequacy of Representation
2.05 Consumer Legal Remedies Act
2.06 Substantial Benefit
2.07 Class Notice
2.08 Comparison of Federal and State Court Prerequisites
2.09 References

§ 2.01 Introduction

As we have seen in Chapter 1, California approaches class actions differently from other states or the federal courts. Since California Code of Civil Procedure section 382 has never been replaced by an updated class action statute, procedural prerequisites in California class actions are largely defined by case law. Case law has interpreted section 382 to mean that a class action requires the demonstration of an ascertainable class and a well-defined community of interest among the members of that class in questions of law and fact (*Richmond* v. *Dart Industries, Inc.* (1981) 29 Cal.3d 462, 470 [174 Cal.Rptr. 515, 629 P.2d 23]). Other prerequisites include substantial benefit, the terms of the Consumer Legal Remedies Act, the adequacy of representation by class representative and representative, and the class notice requirement.

§ 2.02 Ascertainable Class

California law requires that class be defined in a manner that is "precise, objective and presently ascertainable." (*Manual For Complex Litigation, Third*, § 30.14.) The definition of an ascertainable class starts with a review of whether the class members can be located with reasonable efficiency. This differs substantially from the federal perspective, which approaches class analysis with the more structured framework discussed later in this chapter.

For a class action to occur in California, the persons to be bound by the litigation must be located and, when appropriate, advised that a lawsuit is pending on their behalf. The ability to identify, locate, and bind a class depends upon "ascertainability." Ascertainability requires an objective definition of the persons in the class—that is, who they are, and how, if notice is required, they can be told about the case and their interest in it. Ascertainability is further determined by examining the size of the class and the means available for identifying class members. (*Reyes* v. *Board of Supervisors* (1987) 196 Cal.App.3d 1263 [242 Cal.Rptr. 339] quoting *Vasquez* v. *Superior Court* (1971) 4 Cal.3d 800 [94 Cal.Rptr. 796, 484 P.2d 964].)

A classic early example of an ascertainability issue arose in *Weaver* v. *Pasadena Tournament of Roses* (1948) 32 Cal.2d 833, 835 [198 P.2d 514]. The plaintiff alleged that 7,500 tickets to the 1948 Rose Bowl were advertised, but only 1,500 were actually sold. The remaining 6,000 purported "class members" were refused admittance even though they were willing to pay for the tickets. The court found no ascertainable class, such as stock holders, bond holders, or creditors of an organization, but only a large number of individuals, each one of whom may or may not have cared to assert a claim for wrongful refusal of admission. A class action could not be pursued because no class could be ascertained.

§ 2.03 Community of Interest

Community of interest refers to an interest—usually, but not always, economic—that one person shares with other persons. Class actions require a community of interest. Simply, everyone in the class must be in the same boat. Only if there is a community of interest can the interests of one be litigated for the benefit of others in a fair and efficient way.

The community of interest requirement consists of three factors (*Reyes* v. *Board of Supervisors* (1987) 196 Cal.App.3d 1263, 1271 [242 Cal.Rptr. 339]):

1. The common questions of law or fact in the case predominate over individual questions.
2. Class representatives offer claims or defenses that typify the class.
3. Class representatives can adequately represent the class.

§ 2.04 Adequacy of Representation

California requires that a proposed class representative be a member of an ascertainable class united by a common interest. (*City of San Jose* v. *Superior Court* (1974) 12 Cal.3d 447 [115 Cal.Rptr. 797, 525 P.2d 701].) The interests of the class representative, however, need not be identical with those of the class. (*B.W.I. Custom Kitchen* v. *Owens-Illinois, Inc.* (1987) 191 Cal.App.3d 1341 [235 Cal.Rptr. 228].) Rather, the requirement is that the class representative be situated similarly to the class's other members. (*Classen* v. *Weller* (1983) 145 Cal.App.3d 27, 46 [192 Cal.Rptr. 914].)

A key element in determining the class representative's adequacy is that person's ability and willingness to pursue the class members' claims vigorously. This issue is repeatedly raised in a settlement wherein a conflict develops between compensation of counsel and the interests of the class. When the proportional benefit to counsel outweighs that to the class, the criticism is heightened. Clearly, to prevent prejudice against the interests of absent parties, a class action requires the same vigorous advocacy by plaintiff and counsel as individual litigation.

§ 2.05 Consumer Legal Remedies Act

The Consumer Legal Remedies Act (Civ. Code, § 1750 et seq., hereafter CLRA) and its provisions directly apply to the sale of either "goods" or "services" within the meanings defined by California Civil Code section 1761, subdivisions (a) and (b). CLRA requires California courts to permit a suit on behalf of all members of the representative class when the class is too large to bring to court, the common questions of law or fact are similar for all individuals in the class, the plaintiff's claims represent the class, and the plaintiff protects the class's interest. (Civ. Code, § 1781, subd. (b); see Chapter 1.)

The California Supreme Court has prescribed that CLRA's class action procedures can and should be used by trial courts in all class actions. (*Civil Service Emp. Ins. Co.* v. *Superior Court of City and County of San Francisco* (1978) 22 Cal.3d 362 [149 Cal.Rptr. 360, 584 P.2d 497].) For further discussion of CLRA rules and procedures, see Chapter 3.

§ 2.06 Substantial Benefit

The requirement to permit a class action under CLRA when its criteria are met contrasts with the balancing test trial courts may apply in class actions brought under Code of Civil Procedure section 382. The balancing test allows the court to decide against class action on the basis that the benefit to litigants and the court is too small to justify class action. A proposed California class action must present a superior method of resolving the controversy with substantial benefits to the court and litigants. The party seeking class certification bears the burden of proving substantial benefit.

Ultimately, the court can simply state that the benefits of a class action do not exceed its costs in specific circumstances. (*Kaye* v. *Mt. La Jolla Homeowners Ass'n* (1988) 204 Cal.App.3d 1476 [252 Cal.Rptr. 67] citing *Blue Chip Stamps* v. *Superior Court* (1976) 18 Cal.3d 381, 389 [134 Cal.Rptr. 393, 556 P.2d 755].)

§ 2.07 Class Notice

Federal Rules of Civil Procedure, rule 23(b) breaks class actions into two categories: "mandatory" class actions, where no notice to class members is required (see Fed. Rules Civ. Proc., rule 23(b)(1)–(2)); and "opt-out" class actions, where notice is required and members of the class of plaintiffs must be afforded an opportunity to opt out of the action (see Fed. Rules Civ.Proc., rule 23(b)(3)). To prevent confusing the court, you should explain early on in the proceeding which of these two "roads" you are taking.

When class notice is required (see Chapter 7 for further explanation of the rules on notice requirements), it should be the "best practicable under the circumstances" to all persons who can be identified through "reasonable effort." These requirements of rule 23 demand that members of the proposed class be advised that the court will exclude them from the class if they request exclusion by a specified date. Judgment will cover everyone in the class who does not request exclusion. Any included class member may appear in court through counsel.

If notice is clearly required, counsel must consider the cost and the reasonableness of notice early in the process. California notice cases provide direction. (See, e.g., *Cartt* v. *Superior Court* (1975) 50 Cal.App.3d 960 [124 Cal.Rptr. 326].) The trial judge, assigned research staff, and the client benefit from your command of these principles, which will be discussed in detail in Chapter 7. For instance, since notice may not be required in order to bind the affected parties in declaratory or injunctive relief actions or in actions where the opposing party acted on terms applicable to a larger group, there in no reason to belabor the adequacy and reasonableness of notice in such cases. (See. e.g., *Bingham* v. *Obledo* (1983) 147 Cal.App.3d 401, 406 [195 Cal.Rptr. 142]; *Reyes* v. *Board of Supervisors* (1987) 196 Cal.App.3d 1263 [242 Cal.Rptr. 339].)

§ 2.08 Comparison of Federal and State Court Prerequisites

Federal courts apply the criteria of Federal Rules of Civil Procedure, rule 23(a) and (b) in a more structured way than do California courts, creating at least the appearance of a tighter framework of analysis.

Federal rule 23(a) demands four prerequisites to a class action: (1) parties so numerous that joining them is impracticable; (2) common questions of law and fact; (3) typical claims and defenses by the representative parties; and (4) adequacy of representation. (See Fed. Rules Civ.Proc., rule 23; see also Chapter 1. For text of rule 23, see Appendix A.)

When—and only when—these threshold criteria are met, the court moves on to the analysis required by federal rule 23(b). This entails deciding whether the action is a "mandatory" class action or an "opt-out" class action. A mandatory class action requires no notice. (See Fed. Rules Civ. Proc., rule 23(b)(1) and (2).) An opt-out class action requires full notice to members of the plaintiff class offering them the opportunity to exclude themselves from the action. (See Fed. Rules Civ. Proc., rule 23(b)(3).) Class action treatment under federal rule 23(b)(1) and (2) involves actions with a risk of inconsistent or incompatible standards of conduct, adjudications that will be dispositive of the interests of the class, or injunctive or declaratory relief. Claims for monetary damages fall under the more common notice and opt-out requirements of federal rule 23(b)(3).

The California standard allows for dominant common action or actions in which the opposing party has acted on terms applicable to a larger group as it may not be required to bind affected parties.

Additional differences in the standards focus on the issue of class size. California allows a far smaller number of individuals to form a class, provided that it is "impracticable" to bring them before the court. The federal rule, in contrast, requires numerosity, or a large number.

These are minor differences, however, between state and federal class action practice compared to the final California rules concerning the superiority of the class process and the ability to show substantial benefit to the public and the court. Above all else, California rules require a demonstration that class action treatment is the best and most beneficial way to proceed.

§ 2.09 References

📖 **NEWBERG** For a discussion of whether an action is a "mandatory" or "opt-out" class action, see 1 Newberg on Class Actions (3d ed. 1992), Chapter 3.

📖 **WITKIN** For discussion of prerequisites to filing a California class action, see the following:

- Questions of common interest (4 Witkin, Cal. Procedure (4th ed. 1997) Pleading, §§ 256–258).
- The class (4 Witkin, Cal. Procedure (4th ed. 1997) Pleading, §§ 259–263).
- Adequacy of representation (4 Witkin, Cal. Procedure (4th ed. 1997) Pleading, §§ 264–266).

- Notice of action (4 Witkin, Cal. Procedure (4th ed. 1997) Pleading, §§ 282–286).

TRG **THE RUTTER GROUP** See the following sections in California Practice Guide: Civil Procedure Before Trial (CPBT) regarding prerequisites to filing a California class action:

- Prerequisite conditions (CPBT, § 14:11).
- Grounds for class action (CPBT, §§ 14:12–14:20).
- Application of requirements (CPBT, §§ 14:21–14:61).
- Governmental claim as prerequisite to suit (CPBT, §§ 14:65–14:67).

See also the following sections in California Practice Guide: Federal Civil Procedure Before Trial (FCPBT) regarding prerequisites to federal class actions:

- Class action requirements in general (FCPBT, §§ 10:235–10:253).
- Size of class (“numerosity”) (FCPBT, §§ 10:255–10:260).
- Common questions of law or fact (“commonality”) (FCPBT, §§ 10:261–10:267).
- Representative's claim typical ("typicality") (FCPBT, §§ 10:268–10:285).
- Adequate representation requirement (FCPBT, §§ 10:286–10:326).
- Grounds—risk of prejudice from separate suits (FCPBT, §§ 10:328–10:338).
- Grounds—injunctive or declaratory relief benefitting class (FCPBT, §§ 10:339–10:344.2).
- Grounds—common questions “predominate” and class action “superior” (FCPBT, §§ 10:345–10:386.1).

WEST'S KEY NUMBER SYSTEM See the following Key Numbers in West's California Digest 2d, Federal Civil Procedure (Topic 170A):

- Factors and grounds (Federal Civil Procedure ⚷ 161.1).

- Superiority and manageability (Federal Civil Procedure ⚷ 161.2).
- Representation of class (Federal Civil Procedure ⚷ 164).
- Common interest in subject matter (Federal Civil Procedure ⚷ 165).

See also Parties (Topic 287):

- Factors and grounds (Parties ⚷ 35.5).
- Superiority and manageability (Parties ⚷ 35.7).
- Impracticability of joining all members; numerosity (Parties ⚷ 35.11).
- Representation of class; typicality (Parties ⚷ 35.13).
- Community of interest; commonality (Parties ⚷ 35.17).

WESTLAW® See the WESTLAW Electronic Research Guide at the beginning of this volume.

3 ALTERNATIVES TO CLASS ACTIONS

Sec.

3.01 Overview

3.02 Injunctive Relief

3.03 Unfair Competition Injunctions

3.04 Taxpayer Lawsuits

3.05 Suit Based on Association Status

3.06 Associations Managing Common-Interest Developments

3.07 Association as Representative Party

3.08 Court-Appointed Receivers

3.09 Mandamus Against Government

3.10 Class Arbitration

3.11 Class Treatment Without Notice

3.12 Consumer Legal Remedies Act

3.13 Mass Torts—Consolidation/Test Cases

3.14 References

§ 3.01 Overview

There are ways other than a class action to secure relief, resolve issues, or clarify rights for an active litigant in a manner that also affects passive litigants. Each of these alternatives to class action allows one or more persons to pursue claims on behalf of themselves and thereby affect the rights of similarly situated persons. If financial recovery in the form of damages for past wrongs is not an immediate or primary goal, one of these alternatives may offer a mode of relief that avoids the pretrial procedural complexity of a typical class action. These alternatives include injunctive relief, including unfair competition injunctions; taxpayer lawsuits; lawsuits based upon association status; court-appointed receiver actions; writs of mandamus; "hybrid" class actions involving declaratory or injunctive relief; injunctions under the Consumer Legal Remedies Act; and consolidated mass torts with test cases.

§ 3.02 Injunctive Relief

When a party seeks equitable or preventive relief, the requested injunction may affect the rights of similarly situated persons. If one individual is seeking to invalidate a statute, enjoin a practice, or challenge a governmental statute with broad application, injunctive relief affords a less cumbersome alternative to a class action. (See Code Civ. Proc., § 527, subd. (a).)

Courts normally abbreviate procedures in hearing requests for temporary restraining orders and preliminary injunctions, typically attending to them well before trial on the merits. This makes injunctive relief substantially more expeditious than class action. Code of Civil Procedure section 527, subdivision (b), authorizes courts to grant a temporary restraining order, a preliminary injunction, or both in an action involving one or more parties suing or defending for the benefit of numerous parties on the same grounds as in other actions. This authorization holds true whether a class action has been certified or not.

Gardner v. *County of Los Angeles* (1995) 34 Cal.App.4th 200 [40 Cal.Rptr.2d 271] shows the practical effect of injunctive relief prior to class certification. In *Gardner*, the trial court was directed to enter an order granting a preliminary injunction on behalf of a class of indigent Los Angeles County residents who had received aid from the county's general assistance program. Although the trial did not formally certify a class action, it produced three temporary restraining orders for the benefit of persons other than the named plaintiffs.

Recently, in a case handled by the author, a complete and final writ of mandamus judgment was issued against the defendant city for failure to update its general plan and to site transitional housing and homeless shelters. The class was never formally certified nor was any motion made. Obviously, the entry of this relief performed the function sought.

For additional discussion on seeking injunctions generally, see The Rutter Group's Cal. Prac. Guide: Civ. Pro. Before Trial, Chapter 9, Part III.

§ 3.03 Unfair Competition Injunctions

Under the California Unfair Competition Act, one person can bring an action on behalf of the general public. (See Bus. & Prof. Code, § 17204.) Business and Professions Code section 17200 provides broad equitable and injunctive remedies for unfair competition. In California unfair competition is defined as unlawful, unfair, or fraudulent business practices and unfair, deceptive, untrue, or misleading advertising. In addition to giving standing to the attorney general, district attorney, or city attorney to assert an action for relief, section 17200 allows suits by any board, officer, person, corporation, or association acting for the benefit of itself, its members, or the general public. (See Bus. & Prof. Code, § 17204; *Saunders* v. *Superior Court (California Reporting Alliance)* (1994) 27 Cal.App.4th 832, 839 [33 Cal.Rptr.2d 438].)

Business & Professions Code section 17082, which authorizes plaintiffs to seek injunctive relief, allows certain unfair trade practices to be enjoined. Though these two injunctive relief provisions (Bus. & Prof. Code, §§ 17082 and 17204) are somewhat specialized, Code of Civil Procedure section 527 apparently authorizes their use early in a proceeding.

Injunctive relief brought in the name of a private party on behalf of itself or its members would seem to provide a res judicata effect as well the other benefits of class treatment. However, in *Bronco Wine Co.* v. *Frank A. Logoluso Farms*, the trial court's judgment in favor of nonparty growers was reversed on due process grounds. The reversal held that the *Bronco* court did not deal with the issue of whether an individual representative action asserting unfair competition can be properly maintained outside the confines of a class action. (*Bronco Wine Co.* v. *Frank A. Logoluso Farms* (1989) 214 Cal.App.3d 699 [214 Cal.Rptr. 899].)

The provisions of the Unfair Competition Act often accompany other competitive cases. The author has used it in cases alleging below cost sales, price fixing, and related anti-competitive conduct. It provides an appropriate complement to class cases of this kind, and in an appropriate setting can resolve preliminary issues in a class action case under the guise of an unfair competition injunction.

§ 3.04 Taxpayer Lawsuits

California Code of Civil Procedure section 526a authorizes actions by an individual citizen against a town, city, or county officer to obtain a judgment restraining and preventing illegal expenditures of, waste of, or injury to state funds or county, town, or city property. Such actions may take precedence over other civil matters on court dockets. (See Code Civ. Proc., § 526a.) Section 526a gives city or county taxpayers a way to seek relief outside the cumbersome class certification process.

However, statutes and case law substantially modify taxpayer class action lawsuits. To begin with, efforts on behalf of taxpayers to secure immediate pecuniary relief—as opposed to broader-based taxpayer challenges to governmental action—are handled procedurally in a restricted "opt in" fashion instead of the normal class action opt-out provisions. This means simply that each party needs to agree in advance to participate and file appropriate papers. It reverses the normal class action opt-out situation, in which a party must act affirmatively to be excluded. (*Farrar* v. *Franchise Tax Bd.* (1993) 15 Cal.App.4th 10 [18 Cal.Rptr.2d 611].)

Revenue and Tax Code section 19055 provides for a refund of income taxes to a class of taxpayers if each taxpayer provides written authorization that includes him or her in the class, carries the signature of the taxpayer or the taxpayer's representative, and states the specific grounds for the claim. By statute, tax refund cases are handled differently than broad-based taxpayer lawsuits authorized under Code of Civil Procedure section 526a.

Recent decisions, however, preclude class actions in tax refund cases unless specifically allowed by statute. (*Woosley* v. *State of California* (1992) 3 Cal.4th 758 [13 Cal.Rptr.2d 30, 838 P.2d 758] (reaffirmed in *Neecke* v. *City of Mill Valley* (1995) 39 Cal.App.4th 946 [46 Cal.Rptr.2d 266]).) As a result of these decisions, a taxpayer lawsuit undertaken as an alternative to a class action should not seek class eligibility for any refund.

§ 3.05 Suit Based on Association Status

California Code of Civil Procedure section 369.5 provides that an unincorporated association, either for-profit or not-for-profit, may sue and be sued under its assumed or known name. This statute gives an unincorporated association rights to sue in order to challenge a governmental action. In one such case, the complaint argued that the association's membership lived in an area affected by the project it challenged and alleged that the membership would suffer injury if the project was allowed to proceed. The court looked to the public nature of the question and noted that the right to sue is greatly relaxed where the question is of public interest. (*Residents of Beverly Glen, Inc.* v. *City of Los Angeles* (1973) 34 Cal.App.3d 117 [109 Cal.Rptr. 724].)

Labor unions, as unincorporated associations, have the right to sue in a representative capacity. (*Daniels* v. *Sanitarium Ass'n, Inc.* (1963) 59 Cal.2d 602 [30 Cal.Rptr. 828, 381 P.2d 652] (libel action by labor union).) Similarly, an unincorporated association of "taxpayers, residents, land owners, and/or registered voters" may challenge governmental action. (*Citizens Against Forced Annexation* v. *County of Santa Clara*, (1984) 153 Cal.App.3d 89 [200 Cal.Rptr. 166].)

§ 3.06 Associations Managing Common-Interest Developments

Code of Civil Procedure section 383 grants associations established to manage common-interest developments the standing to institute, defend, settle, or intervene in litigation, arbitration, mediation, or administrative proceedings. Associations may engage in such activity in their own names as the real party in interest, without joining together the individual owners of the common-interest development. This statute specifically grants such associations the ability to assert claims for damages to common areas and other separate interests the association must maintain or repair. (Code Civ.Proc., § 383, subd. (a)(4).) Any practitioner who has handled construction defect litigation will be familiar with this particular section because it facilitates resolution of construction defect cases involving a common-interest management association.

§ 3.07 Association as Representative Party

An unincorporated association with standing to sue in a representative capacity may bring claims for individual damages on behalf of a class. Likewise, an unincorporated association can sue in a representative capacity when it has been injured itself. It can also bring an action for prospective relief, such as an injunction or a declaration of rights. (*Tenants Association of Park Santa Anita* v. *Southers* (1990) 222 Cal.App.3d 1293 [272 Cal.Rptr. 361] citing *Del Mar Beach Club Owners Ass'n.* v. *Imperial Contracting Co.* (1981) 123 Cal.App.3d 898, 907 [176 Cal.Rptr. 886].) An association advancing this type of case needs to delete from the case specific causes of action that would not otherwise be permitted in a class action, such as emotional distress and highly idiosyncratic damages. Such injuries are too intangible and inherently individual to reasonably form a community of interest. (*Tenants Ass'n of Park Santa Anita* v. *Southers* (1990) 222 Cal.App.3d 1293, 1304 [272 Cal.Rptr. 361].)

The court in *Tenants Ass'n of Park Santa Anita* found that considerations of necessity, convenience, and justice supported the use of the representative procedural device. There was an ascertainable class—namely, members of the association, who were tenants or former tenants of the park—and a community of interest regarding the questions of law and fact. Furthermore, association members were victims of the park owners' and managers' allegedly fraudulent actions. (*Tenants Ass'n of Park Santa Anita* v. *Southers* (1990) 222 Cal.App.3d 1293, 1303 [272 Cal.Rptr. 361]; see also *National Solar Equipment Owners' Ass'n, Inc.* v. *Grumman Corporation* (1991) 235 Cal.App.3d 1273 [1 Cal.Rptr.2d 325].)

Another complaint involving an association asked for damages or rescission and restitution of land sales contracts. The plaintiffs alleged that the defendants had used a "canned sales pitch" to induce the purchase of the defendants' property. The court permitted a representative action by the unincorporated property owners association after analyzing the essential nature of the action and finding it to be a class action on behalf of a "self-defined class." (*Salton City, etc., Owners Ass'n* v. *M. Penn Philips Co.* (1977) 75 Cal.App.3d 184, 188 [141 Cal.Rptr. 895].)

§ 3.08 Court-Appointed Receivers

A superior court in which an action or proceeding is pending or a judge of that court may appoint a receiver. If the receiver is appointed before judgment, the receiver essentially represents all creditors of the entity being liquidated or supervised. (See Code Civ. Proc., § 564, subd. (b)(8).) As a result, a receiver can assert the claims of or obligations to a large group of individuals. For example, when a receiver is appointed to liquidate an insolvent insurance company, the receiver becomes a trustee for the benefit of all the company's creditors. (See, e.g., *Title U.S.A. Ins. Corp.* v. *Armato, Gaims, Weil, West, and Epstein* (1995) 36 Cal.App.4th 363 [42 Cal.Rptr.2d 498].)

§ 3.09 Mandamus Against Government

If a governmental agency or a governmental body fails to perform a clearly ministerial duty, and if this failure affects a significant group of individuals, such as welfare beneficiaries or homeless persons entitled to emergency shelter, a writ of ordinary mandamus may be an appropriate remedy. (See Code Civ. Proc., § 1085.) Mandamus actions offer the advantage of calendar priority, and they can be filed either directly in the superior court of original jurisdiction or in the court of appeal. Hearings conducted in the superior court also may be subject to a "briefing schedule" with supplementary oral testimony at various hearings, such as an order to show cause or other earlier application.

§ 3.10 Class Arbitration

In several cases, California courts have discussed classwide arbitration as an alternative to judicial class certification. In *Southland Corp.* v. *Keating*, the court considered classwide arbitration as a method of resolving a controversy over widely used contracts of adhesion. The court stated that a judicially ordered classwide arbitration would clearly entail more judicial involvement than is normal with arbitration, but ideally it would still require no use of court facilities. The court would have to make initial determinations regarding certification and notice to the class. The court would also have to supervise the arbitration to ensure safeguarding of the rights of absent class members in the event of dismissal and settlement. *(Southland Corp.* v. *Keating* (1984) 465 U.S. 1 [79 L.Ed.2d 1, 104 S.Ct. 852]; see *Keating* v. *Superior Court of Alameda County* (1982) 31 Cal.3d 584 [183 Cal.Rptr. 360, 645 P.2d 1192] rev'd. on other grounds *sub nom).*)

In *Izzi* v. *Mesquite Country Club*, the appellate court instructed the trial court to determine whether classwide arbitration could proceed. The case was brought by condominium purchasers against the condominiums' sellers because the sellers failed to disclose that the buyers were subject to assessments for certain improvements. The appeals court made a point of underscoring repeatedly the strong public policy favoring class actions and arbitrations. *(Izzi* v. *Mesquite Country Club* (1986) 186 Cal.App.3d 1309 [231 Cal.Rptr. 315].) The court also noted that since the *Keating* decision, classwide arbitration has been ordered in securities margin account disputes involving classes numbering in the hundreds of thousands. (*Lewis* v. *Prudential-Bache Securities* (1986) 179 Cal.App.3d 935, 945–946 [225 Cal.Rptr. 69].) In the *Lewis* case, the court held that without class arbitration each Prudential customer would have to arbitrate his or her claim individually, an overly costly and time-consuming way of proceeding. (*Lewis* v. *Prudential-Bache Securities* (1986) 179 Cal.App.3d 935, 946 [225 Cal.Rptr. 69].)

Arbitration clauses are usually asserted at the demurrer stage when a defendant seeks to stay the proceeding pending arbitration. This action affects the merits and the court's ability to handle the matter with normal class action judicial procedures.

In response to motions to compel arbitration in a class setting, the author's firm has sought class-wide arbitration as opposed to individual arbitration. As a general rule, however, the existence of arbitration clauses can raise significant individual questions precluding certification.

§ 3.11 Class Treatment Without Notice

One way to streamline the class certification process and save substantial amounts of time is to style the case as one that requires no prejudgment notice. (See Chapter 7 for rule on notice.) The court may hear the merits of the case earlier than otherwise, possibly along with other dispositive motions, such as those for summary judgment. (See, e.g., *Bingham* v. *Obledo* (1983) 147 Cal.App.3d 401 [195 Cal.Rptr. 142] (court ordered postjudgment notice).) These actions require no notice because they are procedurally related to a federal rule 23(b)(1) or (b)(2) action as declaratory or injunctive relief. These sections apply when any of the following circumstances hold true:

1. Separate actions by or against individual members of the class would create a "risk of inconsistent or varying adjudications that would establish incompatible standards of conduct for the party opposing the class."

2. Separate actions by or against individual members of the class would create the risk of adjudications dispositive of the interests of members of the class not party to the adjudications. (Fed. Rules Civ.Proc., rule 23(b)(1).)

3. "The party opposing the class has acted or refused to act on grounds generally applicable to the class, making appropriate final injunctive

relief or corresponding declaratory relief with respect to the class as a whole." (Fed. Rules Civ.Proc., rule 23(b)(2).)

Certain types of class actions require no notice because members of the class lack the right to opt out. In *Bell* v. *American Title Ins. Co.*, the court noted that, since Code of Civil Procedure section 382 does not address when the trial court should afford the right to opt out of class actions, California courts are urged to follow the procedures prescribed in federal rule 23 for conducting class actions. (*Bell* v. *American Title Ins. Co.* (1991) 226 Cal.App.3d 1589, 1603 [277 Cal.Rptr. 583].) A class member's ability to exclude himself or herself from judgment by opting out of the class generally depends upon which of the subdivisions apply. The federal courts have determined that class actions certified under rule 23b(1) or b(2) involve no right to opt out. California follows the same rule. (See Chapters 7 and 9 for more complete discussions of the three types of class actions under rule 23.)

Likewise, prejudgment notice is not required in welfare class actions where declaratory and injunctive relief are the primary objectives. (*Reyes* v. *Board of Supervisors* (1987) 196 Cal.App.3d 1263, 1274 [242 Cal.Rptr. 339].)

One of the author's earliest class actions provides an example of class treatment without notice. The case alleged entitlement to retroactive pay by county probation officers. The assigned law and motion judge at the demurrer hearing certified the class but shortly thereafter granted the county's demurrer for failure of the probation officers to make "claims against the county." The net effect was to provide an adverse class-wide determination.

§ 3.12 Consumer Legal Remedies Act

The Consumer Legal Remedies Act (Civ. Code, § 1750 et seq.; hereafter CLRA) is a hybrid of Federal Rules of Civil Procedure rule 23 enacted five years after the 1966 revisions to rule 23. (Compare, e.g., Civ. Code, § 1781(b)(1)–(4) with Fed. Rules Civ.Proc., rule 23(a)–(d).) Under CLRA, a consumer may, in certain circumstances, bring an action on behalf of other consumers situated similarly to himself or herself to recover damages or attain other relief for unfair competition or unfair or deceptive acts or practices. (See Civ. Code, §§ 1781, subd. (a), 1780, 1770.) Even though CLRA allows defendants to correct any wrongdoing and avoid damages after a demand (see Civ. Code, § 1782, subd. (b) (agreement to remedy within thirty days)), it can still be considered as an alternative to true class action relief.

At least 30 days before beginning an action for damages under the CLRA, consumers must provide notice to the potential defendant of the alleged wrongdoing and demand that the defendant correct, repair, replace, or rectify the alleged violation. The notice must be written and it must be sent by certified or registered mail, return receipt requested. No action for damages can be brought until after the notice and demand is sent. (See Civ. Code, § 1782, subd. (a).) Additionally, no damages may be awarded if the defendant can prove that the violation was unintentional and resulted from a "bona fide error." (See Civ. Code, § 1784.)

California courts must permit suit to be maintained on behalf of all members of the representative class under the CLRA if all of the following conditions exist (Civ. Code, § 1781, subd. (b)):

1. It is impractical to bring every member of the class before the court.
2. The questions of law or fact common to the class are substantially similar, and they predominate over questions affecting individual members.
3. The claims or defenses of the representative plaintiffs typify the claims or defenses of the class.
4. The representative plaintiffs will fairly and adequately protect the interests of the class.

These four conditions are the exclusive criteria for class certification in suits brought under CLRA. (See *Hogya* v. *Superior Court (National Meat Packers, Inc., Real Party In Interest)* (1977) 75 Cal.App.3d 122, 138 [142 Cal.Rptr. 325].) If these criteria are met, the court has no choice but to certify the class. The court lacks discretion to deny certification based on other considerations. (*Hogya* v. *Superior Court (National Meat Packers, Inc., Real Party In Interest)* (1977) 75 Cal.App.3d 122, 138 [142 Cal.Rptr. 325].) This contrasts with the balancing test trial courts may apply in class actions brought under Code of Civil Procedure section 382, in which the court may consider, for example, whether class action will deliver greater benefit to litigants and court than another form of action.

Often a class action under CLRA accompanies a full-blown (Code Civ. Proc., § 382) class action. CLRA specifically provides that it is not an exclusive remedy. If any act or practice proscribed by CLRA also constitutes a cause of action in common law, or if that act or practice violates another statute, a consumer may assert that common law or statutory cause of action under the procedures and obtain the remedies provided in that law in addition to the remedies provided by CRLA. (See Civ. Code, § 1752.) Remedies under CLRA include actual damages, an order enjoining the practices, punitive damages, and other relief the court deems proper. (Civ. Code, § 1770.)

§ 3.13 Mass Torts-Consolidation/Test Cases

Recently, "mass tort" and group litigation cases have placed tremendous pressure on California trial courts. Efficient trial practices have compelled test cases and bifurcation or consolidation of certain issues to keep already crowded court calendars from being even further impacted. Although new to our courts, certain broadly initiated types of tort actions have benefited from aggregation and other procedures that provide for de facto class treatment yet obviate formal class certification. Courts have used a number of procedures to expedite these matters, including the incorporation and filing of "model complaints" that summarize the salient and common features of various actions.

§ 3.14 References

NEWBERG For additional discussion of the availability of class actions for mass torts, see 3 Newberg on Class Actions (3d ed. 1992), Chapter 17.

WITKIN See the following sections regarding alternatives to class actions:

- Association's capacity to sue or be sued (4 Witkin, Cal. Procedure (4th ed. 1997) Pleading, §§ 82, 84, 85).
- Common interest development as real party in interest (4 Witkin, Cal. Procedure (4th ed. 1997) Pleading, § 133).
- Taxpayers' actions (4 Witkin, Cal. Procedure (4th ed. 1997) Pleading, §§ 144–151).
- Consumers' actions (4 Witkin, Cal. Procedure (4th ed. 1997) Pleading, §§ 268–270).
- Consolidation of actions (4 Witkin, Cal. Procedure (4th ed. 1997) Pleading, §§ 305–311).
- Unfair competition injunctions (5 Witkin, Cal. Procedure (4th ed. 1997) Pleading, §§ 735, 786).

- Injunctions (6 Witkin, Cal. Procedure (4th ed. 1997) Provisional Remedies, § 276 et seq.).
- Receivers (6 Witkin, Cal. Procedure (4th ed. 1997) Provisional Remedies, § 416 et seq.).
- Mandamus against acts of administrative agencies (8 Witkin, Cal. Procedure (4th ed. 1997) Extraordinary Writs, § 30).

TRG **THE RUTTER GROUP** See the following sections in California Practice Guide: Civil Procedure Before Trial (CPBT) regarding alternatives to class actions:

- Injunctions (CPBT, § 9:500 et seq.).
- Unfair competition injunctions (CPBT, § 9:684 et seq.).
- Receivers (CPBT, § 9:733 et seq.).
- Consolidation of separate lawsuits (CPBT, § 12:340 et seq.).

WEST'S KEY NUMBER SYSTEM

See the following Topics and Key Numbers in West's California Digest 2d regarding alternatives to class actions:

- Consolidation of actions (Actions 🔑 54–59).
- Injunctions (Topic 212).
- Mandamus against government (Mandamus 🔑 63 et seq.).
- Receivers (Topic 323).

WESTLAW® See the WESTLAW Electronic Research Guide at the beginning of this volume.

4 PRELIMINARY CASE ANALYSIS

Sec.

4.01 Deciding Whether to File—An Overview

4.02 Outline the Case

[A] Class Definition

[1] Need for Precision

[2] Class Size

[B] Class Period

[C] Common Questions of Law and Fact

[D] Residual Questions

[E] Relief Sought

[1] Injunctive—Declaratory

[2] Monetary

[F] Class Representation

[1] The Class Representative

[2] Counsel's Conflict with Class

[3] Attorney's Fees

[G] Benefit to Litigants and Court

4.03 Adverse California Case Law

[A] Is There an Obvious Pitfall to Your Case?

[B] Is the Cause Unsympathetic, or Is the Class Deprived of Little?

[C] Are Plaintiff's Recovery Facts Unique, or Is There Insufficient Community of Interest?

[D] Are Multiple Defendants Accused of Wrongdoing?

[E] Are the Class Members the Defendants?

[F] Are Remedial Statutes Superior to Class Treatment?

[G] Is the Case a National Class in a California Court?

[H] Does the Class Have Common Law Negligence Claims or Unique Damage Issues?

[I] Is It a Ticket or Personal Enjoyment Case?

[J] Are Class Members Antagonistic to the Class Action?

4.04 The Effect of Related Litigation

[A] Importance of Early Analysis

[B] Successive Class Actions or Federal Class Actions Precluding State Class Treatment

[C] Successive Class Actions or State Class Actions Precluding Federal Class Treatment

[D] Concurrent Class Actions

[E] Extensive "Group" Litigation

[F] Intervention

4.05 References

§ 4.01 Deciding Whether to File—An Overview

The first task for a practitioner considering a class action in California is to review the basics of the case and determine if a class action truly is the best choice for litigation. As discussed in Chapter 3, a number of alternative solutions are available for particular types of cases. Review the proposed case with these alternatives in mind to decide whether any of them offers an effective yet procedurally simpler choice than a class action.

- Once the practitioner determines that a class action offers the best route, the next step is to outline the case step by step. This involves the following steps.
- Define the class as precisely as possible, stating the causes of action and potential damages.
- Compare and contrast the position of the class representative with the identity and location of defendants.
- Review adverse California case law for similar cases in which certification was denied (so-called "pitfall" cases).
- Search for prior class actions involving the same "primary right."
- Determine whether pending class actions could affect your ability to certify the class or otherwise control the case's progress.
- Assess the likelihood of extensive group actions or intervention.

§ 4.02 Outline the Case

[A] Class Definition

[1] Need for Precision

Early on in a proposed class action, it is important to work through the key elements of the action to determine how each one contributes to or detracts from the case. First, the class needs to be defined clearly and objectively since the definition determines who will be bound by the judgment or entitled to notice of its pendency. In California, class definition starts with ascertainability: How difficult is it to locate the class members?

The question to be answered is whether class members can be easily identified at the remedial stage. (*Reyes* v. *Board of Supervisors* (1987) 196 Cal.App.3d 1263, 1275 [242 Cal.Rptr. 339].) For example, you should determine whether the defendant's records allow identification of the class members. If no such records exist, will the expense of locating and identifying the class be so undue as to prevent certification of the class?

Since the group may be the basis for a legally enforceable judgment under the doctrine of res judicata, it must be defined in a manner consistent with the legal and factual basis of class claims. Make sure the class definition is extremely precise so that when, and if, the court certifies your class, it is quite clear who will be entitled to the effect of a judgment.

Problems occur when the class definition is less than precise. An ambiguous class definition will expose you to post-certification motions to "clarify class rulings," a tactic that offers yet another source of unanticipated delay and attack and creates additional grounds for appeal. Recently, unnecessary post-certification hearings were required in a discrimination case handled by the author's firm because of an ambiguity in the precise class definition, including the policy holder periods who might benefit from a judgment. Several class definition clarification hearings were conducted that obviously taxed the trial judge's patience. Avoid this whenever possible by utilization of a precise definition.

[2] Class Size

As part of the class definition, estimate the size of the class. California courts have construed Code of Civil Procedure section 382 to mean only that a class action requires many parties. (*Rose* v. *City of Hayward* (1981) 126 Cal.App.3d 926 [179 Cal.Rptr. 287], citing *Renken* v. *Compton City School District* (1962) 207 Cal.App.2d 106 [24 Cal.Rptr. 347].) There is no set "magic" number in California, but the state minimum class membership appears to be lower than federal requirements, where 100 or more persons are typically needed. Class certification has been won with far smaller numbers, however. In *Rose* v. *City of Hayward*, 42 retirees were held to be "quantitatively" sufficient for class action. *(Rose* v. *City of Hayward* (1981) 126 Cal.App.3d 926 [179 Cal.Rptr. 287].) In *Hebbard* v. *Colgrove*, 28 beneficiaries of a trust alleging improper conduct by the trustees were also sufficient for a class. *(Hebbard* v. *Colgrove* (1972) 28 Cal.App.3d 1017 [105 Cal.Rptr. 172].) *Collins* v. *Rocha*, declared nine named representatives enough to bring suit on behalf of 35 others. *(Collins* v. *Rocha* (1972) 7 Cal.3d 232 [102 Cal.Rptr. 1, 497 P.2d 225].) By contrast, another court ruled that 22 members were too few for a class action. (*Slakey Brothers Sacramento, Inc.* v. *Parker* (1968) 265 Cal.App.2d 204 [71 Cal.Rptr. 269].) The apparent rule is that questions of equity prevail over objective considerations of number. (*Rose* v. *City of Hayward* (1981) 126 Cal.App.3d 926 [179 Cal.Rptr. 287].)

At the other end of the scale, extremely large classes can become highly problematic, particularly when claims are insignificant. Large classes pose difficulties with notice, its cost, and general manageability of the case. An example is *Cartt* v. *Superior Court*, in which the plaintiff, a teacher, was ordered by the trial court to give notice to approximately 700,000 persons on the defendant's mailing list at a cost of nearly $70,000. (*Cartt* v. *Superior Court* (1975) 50 Cal.App.3d 960 [124 Cal.Rptr. 376].) The author's firm has secured certification of a class composed of over 20 million members, demonstrating that a large size is not necessarily a bar.

[B] Class Period

In some cases, the class definition includes a time period, such as all persons who signed a certain kind of sales contract with the defendant between two dates. Statutes of limitation applicable to the substantive cause of the class action typically affect class periods. Efforts to extend class periods to extremely early dates run up against this problem. The further dates and times are pushed into the past, the more vulnerable your case is to criticism about its manageability and class ascertainability.

[C] Common Questions of Law and Fact

The definition of the class should so narrow the focus of the wrongdoing that it is easy to prove classwide damage or impact. If the defendants have engaged in unfair competition or deceptive consumer sales practices, the Consumer Legal Remedies Act (CLRA) may apply. CLRA offers distinct advantages, including mandatory class certification when its prerequisites are met (see Chapter 2).

Examine the elements of a prima facie case for each cause of action in light of the class definition. For example, the court has held that, in cases alleging price fixing, common questions predominate over those affecting only individual class members. Proving the existence of the conspiracy itself determines liability to class members. (*B.W.I. Custom Kitchen* v. *Owens-Illinois, Inc.* (1987) 191 Cal.App.3d 1341, 1348 [235 Cal.Rptr. 228].)

Similarly, employment discrimination is often class discrimination by its very nature and therefore appropriate for class action treatment. In a case in which the plaintiff alleged a pattern and practice of excluding women from management positions in certain departments of a major retailer, statistics presented in court showed women to be significantly underrepresented. Over a seven-year period women made up two-thirds of all sales employees and managers in some departments yet represented only 13% of managers in the departments where discrimination was alleged. (*Stephens* v. *Montgomery Ward & Company* (1987) 193 Cal.App.3d 411, 419 [238 Cal.Rptr. 602].)

[D] Residual Questions

The California test for a class action is whether common questions of fact predominate over individual. Although the courts allow subsequent determination of individual class damages, questions that factually intertwine on both damages and liability will generally prevent class certification.

Every case contains corollary questions of law and fact. Look carefully to determine whether these questions are in fact residual, such as those involving damage calculations. If these residual claims are also involved in the liability analysis, they are likely to prevent certification.

[E] Relief Sought

[1] Injunctive—Declaratory

You should review case law requirements associated with classwide injunctive and declaratory relief (see Chapter 3). For declaratory relief, prejudgment class notice may not be required, which simplifies the proceeding and cuts costs. Injunctive relief may be given entirely prior to class certification. Examples include welfare actions seeking declaratory and injunctive relief. California decisions have followed the lead of federal courts in holding that prejudgment notice serves no apparent purpose in welfare class actions lacking factual disputes and offering adequate class representation by counsel. (*Miller* v. *Woods* (1983) 148 Cal.App.3d 862, 875 [196 Cal.Rptr. 69]; *Reyes* v. *Board of Supervisors* (1987) 196 Cal.App.3d 1263, 1274 [242 Cal.Rptr. 339].)

[2] Monetary

If class damages are extremely small in relation to the size of the class, certification will be a problem. An example is *Stilson* v. *Reader's Digest Ass'n, Inc.*, (1972) 28 Cal.App.3d 270 [104 Cal.Rptr 581], in which damages amounted to only $1.00 per class member. (For other ascertainability of damage questions, see, e.g., *Collins* v. *Safeway Stores*, Inc. (1986) 187 Cal.App.3d 62 [231 Cal.Rptr. 638].)

Methods of damage distribution such as that of cy pres or fluid recovery can also be employed. The doctrine of cy pres, or fluid recovery, allows the court to utilize class action damages, where appropriate, to direct relief toward fulfilling the underlying causes of the action. (*State* v. *Levi Strauss & Co.* (1986) 41 Cal.3d 460, 472 [224 Cal.Rptr. 605, 715 P.2d 564].) A review of applicable statutes can help in determining whether damages may be aggregated for calculation. Under Business and Professions Code section 16760, subdivision (d), antitrust damages can be proven by statistical or sampling methods, with overcharges allocated on a pro rata basis.

Code of Civil Procedure section 384, subdivision (b), provides "that prior to the entry of any judgment in a class action established pursuant to Section 382, the court shall determine the total amount that would be payable to all class members if all class members are paid the amount to which they are entitled pursuant to the judgment." This provision applies to the residue of a common fund created for the benefit of the class. Absent settlement, this provision substantially guides the disposition of any residue. A number of cases deal with the interpretation of this statute, such as *Granberry* v. *Islay Investments* (1995) 9 Cal.4th 738 [38 Cal.Rptr.2d 650, 889 P.2d 970].

[F] Class Representation

[1] The Class Representative

For a class to be considered ascertainable, its members must have a plausible cause of action against the defendant. If multiple plaintiffs fail to meet this elementary standard, no ascertainable class exists and the class action will not be maintained. (*American Suzuki Motor Corp.* v. *Superior Court* (1995) 37 Cal.App.4th 1291 [44 Cal.Rptr.2d 526].)

The class representative must be a class member and must make claims typical of the class. However, the case does not hinge on any one representative if replacements are available. (*La Sala* v. *American Sav. & Loan Ass'n* (1971) 5 Cal.3d 864 [97 Cal.Rptr. 849, 489 P.2d 1113].)

In the initial planning of the case, concerns arise about the individual relief the class representative wants. Counsel is responsible for explaining carefully the limited ability of a class representative to benefit apart from the class. (*La Sala* v. *American Sav. & Loan Ass'n* (1971) 5 Cal.3d 864 [97 Cal.Rptr. 849, 489 P.2d 1113]; Super. Ct. L.A. County Rules, rule 15.41.) A plaintiff suing on behalf of a class assumes a fiduciary obligation to the members of that class and surrenders any right to compromise the group action in return for individual gain. Even if the named plaintiff receives all the benefits sought in the complaint, he or she still has a duty to continue the action for the benefit of others in the class (*La Sala* v. *American Savings & Loan Ass'n* (1971) 5 Cal.3d 864, 871 [97 Cal.Rptr. 849, 489 P.2d 1113]). Although compensation enhancements are appropriate when supported by documented efforts on behalf of the representative, they are to a large extent subject to judicial review and approval. Some local rules generally call for disapproval of benefits to the class representative not also made to other members of the class. (See., e.g., Super Ct. L.A. County Rules, rule 15.41.) Similar local rules require the class representative to inform the court of conflicts with the class's position, including the share of damages awarded in the case of a plaintiff or damages suffered in the case of defendant. (See, e.g., Super. Ct. L.A. County Rules, rule 15.18(e).)

Since most class representation is contingent, the written retainer agreement between class counsel and class representative should identify and discuss this "conflict" between individual and class.

[2] Counsel's Conflict with Class

Class counsel may not be a percipient witness to the important events in the case. If counsel is a percipient witness, he or she will be disqualified to act as an attorney for the class. (See *Reich* v. *Club Universe* (1981) 125 Cal.App.3d 965 [178 Cal.Rptr. 473].)

[3] Attorney's Fees

The question of counsel's compensation is addressed in Chapter 10.

[G] Benefit to Litigants and Court

An important aspect of convincing the judge that class treatment benefits both the court and the parties is to make every attempt to expedite the case. Effective representation depends on explaining to the judge how you propose to turn a complex factual pattern into something relatively simple, manageable, and capable of resolution within a reasonable time and expense. Like a bar examination, case planning is best mastered by dealing with the issues logically and in order of importance. Charting the path of the case before the class certification hearing demonstrates to the court that you have given careful thought to how this potentially complex undertaking can be broken down into manageable parts.

§ 4.03 Adverse California Case Law

[A] Is There an Obvious Pitfall to Your Case?

Often lawyers and clients wonder if their case is suitable as a California class action. One quick way to answer the question is to skim "pitfall" cases in which certification was denied for reasons that reflect critical judicial attitudes. Case review prevents a practitioner from filing an action that could waste court time and resources, undermine respect for the bar, and prevent counsel from doing something better with his or her time.

[B] Is the Cause Unsympathetic, or Is the Class Deprived of Little?

In his dissent in *Blue Chip Stamps* v. *Superior Court*, Justice Mosk accused his brethren of manifest antipathy to a class action whose cause prompted little sympathy. The facts of the case, however, hardly resounded with unfairness, undercutting Mosk's point. The proposed class plaintiffs, who collected Blue Chip stamps, were represented by their attorney-husbands. The trial court had certified the case in a very half-hearted manner, stating that since only small sums were involved, the class was deprived of little. Sensing something other than a strong signal from the trial court, the appellate court reversed. (*Blue Chip Stamps* v. *Superior Court* (1976) 18 Cal.3d 381 [134 Cal.Rptr. 393, 556 P.2d 755].)

A similar case, *Stilson* v. *Readers Digest Ass'n Inc.*, involved a sweepstakes mailing sent to 20 million people. The cause of action concerned unauthorized use of contestants' names. The court refused to certify class action because nominal damages totaled at best only $1 per person. The court was following the basic concept of failing to certify a class action in which benefits do not exceed costs. (*Stilson* v. *Readers Digest Ass'n Inc.* (1972) 28 Cal.App.3d 270 [104 Cal.Rptr 581]; see *Kaye* v. *Mount La Jolla Homeowners Ass'n* (1988) 204 Cal.App.3d 1476 [252 Cal.Rptr. 67].)

[C] Are Plaintiff's Recovery Facts Unique, or Is There Insufficient Community of Interest?

In 1974, the California Supreme Court established a major limitation on class actions in *City of San Jose* v. *Superior Court*. The court held that a court cannot certify a class action for liability and damages that are highly individual in nature, such as real property condemnation and nuisance cases. (*City of San Jose* v. *Superior Court* (1974) 12 Cal.3d 447 [115 Cal.Rptr. 797, 525 P.2d 701].)

Since this case is frequently cited for principles well beyond its actual holding, the practitioner should become very familiar with it.

[D] Are Multiple Defendants Accused of Wrongdoing?

Multiple defendants generally so compound the number of individual questions that the case becomes unmanageable. (*Diamond* v. *General Motors Corp.* (1971) 20 Cal.App.3d 374 [97 Cal.Rptr. 639]; see also *Devidian* v. *Automotive Service Dealers Ass'n* (1973) 35 Cal.App.3d 978 [111 Cal.Rptr. 228] (1,000 service stations) and *Kennedy* v. *Baxter Healthcare* (1996) 43 Cal.App.4th 799 [50 Cal.Rptr.2d 736].) Exceptions arise if your complaint alleges facts that make one defendant vicariously liable for the acts of others or that indicate a conspiracy.

[E] Are the Class Members the Defendants?

Both Federal Rules of Civil Procedure, rule 23, and Code of Civil Procedure section 382 authorize class actions on behalf of defendants. However, unless your proposed defendants are unincorporated associations or partnerships, you face a series of adverse California cases that work against certification. These include *Simons* v. *Horowitz* (1984) 151 Cal.App.3d 834 [199 Cal.Rptr. 134]; *Pinnacle Holdings, Inc.* v. *Simon* (1995) 31 Cal.App.4th 1430 [37 Cal.Rptr.2d 778]; and *Kaye* v. *Mount La Jolla Homeowners Ass'n* (1988) 204 Cal.App.3d 1476 [252 Cal.Rptr. 67]. This issue is discussed further in Chapter 5.

[F] Are Remedial Statutes Superior to Class Treatment?

In *Caro* v. *Procter & Gamble Co.*, a consumer moved for class certification in a lawsuit against an orange juice processor for falsely representing reconstituted orange juice as "fresh." The trial court denied certification, indicating that the plaintiff did not demonstrate how class treatment would benefit both litigants and court, particularly in light of alternative remedies. (*Caro* v. *Procter & Gamble Co.* (1993) 18 Cal.App.4th 644 [22 Cal.Rptr.2d 419].)

The trial court permitted *Dean Witter Reynolds, Inc.* v. *Superior Court of Alameda County* to proceed as a class action, but the court of appeal issued a writ of mandamus instead. The court of appeal had not been shown to be demonstrably superior to individual actions, suggesting choices that mitigated or eliminated the unfairness of the situation. Also, competing IRAs with alternative fee structures were available, as one would expect in a free market system. The reversal in this case has further defined the standard for benefit to litigants and court. (See *Dean Witter Reynolds, Inc.* v. *Superior Court of Alameda County* (1989) 211 Cal.App.3d 758 [259 Cal.Rptr. 789].)

[G] Is the Case a National Class in a California Court?

The prosecution of national class actions in California courts depends on the application of California law and jurisdiction over non-California class members. Since jurisdictional issues predominate in such cases, you need to establish California jurisdiction as part and parcel of the certification hearing. (*Union Mutual Life Insurance Co.* v. *Superior Court* (1978) 80 Cal.App.3d 1 [145 Cal.Rptr. 316].) Local rules now require a statement of the jurisdictional issues at the class certification stage. (See, e.g., Super. Ct. L.A. County Rules, rule 15.18.)

In *Osborne* v. *Subaru of America, Inc.*, plaintiffs sought to certify a nationwide class of current or former owners of allegedly defective automobiles. Denial was based on the complex, numerous, and substantial questions needing to be resolved, including the application of other states' laws. (*Osborne* v. *Subaru of America, Inc.* (1988) 198 Cal.App.3d 646 [243 Cal.Rptr. 815].) Similar reasoning occurred in *Baltimore Football Club* v. *Superior Court* (1985) 171 Cal.App.3d 352 [215 Cal.Rptr. 323]. In *Anthony* v. *Superior Court*, a national class was requested, but a state class certified. (*Anthony* v. *Superior Court* (1976) 59 Cal.App.3d 760 [130 Cal.Rptr. 758]; see also *General Motors Corp.* v. *Superior Court* (1988) 199 Cal.App.3d 247 [244 Cal.Rptr. 776].)

[H] Does the Class Have Common Law Negligence Claims or Unique Damage Issues?

The court in *Rose* v. *Medtronics, Inc.* dismissed class action allegations on behalf of an individual who had a second pacemaker implanted after the first device proved defective. The court held that even after the common questions had been determined in this action—which entailed negligent conduct, product liability, strict liability, and implied warranty—each member of the class would still have to litigate numerous substantial issues affecting his or her individual right to recover. (*Rose* v. *Medtronics, Inc.* (1980) 107 Cal.App.3d 150 [166 Cal.Rptr. 16].)

Bifurcation of liability issues may allow for certification when liability issues are common to the class and predominant over individual questions. However, certain types of damages, such as emotional distress or mental anguish, require determination so individual and unique that no community of interest can exist. (*Altman* v. *Manhattan Savings Bank* (1978) 83 Cal.App.3d 761 [148 Cal.Rptr. 100].) In *Fuhrman* v. *California Satellite Systems*, the trial court sustained a demurrer without leave to amend on the issue of certifying class in a case of emotional distress. Plaintiff maintained that 8,700 persons receiving a letter from the defendant had experienced distress, alarm, frustration, dismay, and shock as a result. The court found that common questions were lacking and a class action inappropriate. While receipt of the letter placed the class members in a similar situation, each class member needed to establish the right to recover on the basis of facts peculiar and personal to his or her own case. (*Fuhrman* v. *California Satellite Systems* (1986) 179 Cal.App.3d 408 [231 Cal.Rptr. 113] citing *Daar* v. *Yellow Cab Co.* (1967) 67 Cal.2d 695 [63 Cal.Rptr. 724, 433 P.2d 732].) *Brown* v. *Regents of the University of California*, which concerned the ability of class members to recover damages resulting from treatment at a university hospital, likewise depended on facts known only to each individual. The case was dismissed at the pleading stage. (*Brown* v. *Regents of the University of California*, (1984) 151 Cal.App.3d 982 [198 Cal.Rptr. 916]; see also *Silva* v. *Block* (1996) 49 Cal.App.4th 345 [56 Cal.Rptr.2d 613].)

[I] Is It a Ticket or Personal Enjoyment Case?

Class certification in actions concerning ticket sales or personal enjoyment is at best problematical. In *Weaver* v. *Pasadena Tournament of Roses*, the court denied class certification because the 6,000 people denied Rose Bowl tickets were not an ascertainable class but a large number of individuals, each of whom may or may not have been entitled to relief. (*Weaver* v. *Pasadena Tournament of Roses* (1948) 32 Cal.2d 833 [198 P.2d 514].) *D'Amico* v. *Sitmar Cruises, Inc.*, another personal enjoyment case, raised many critical questions as to the individual types of proof, such as what it would take to prove a plaintiff's personal enjoyment of a pleasure cruise. (*D'Amico* v. *Sitmar Cruises, Inc.* (1980) 109 Cal.App.3d 323 [167 Cal.Rptr. 254].) *Bartlett* v. *Hawaiian Village, Inc.* required an evaluation of personal characteristics including subjective standards for admission to a gay bathhouse. (*Bartlett* v. *Hawaiian Village, Inc.* (1978) 87 Cal.App.3d 435 [151 Cal.Rptr. 392].) *Baltimore Football Club* v. *Superior Court* also reasoned that too many multiple individual questions of fact and law, including application of the laws of eighteen states, had to be resolved to provide relief. (*Baltimore Football Club* v. *Superior Court* (1985) 171 Cal.App.3d 352 [215 Cal.Rptr. 323].)

[J] Are Class Members Antagonistic to the Class Action?

Individual plaintiffs who feel threatened by a proposed class action or sympathetic to the defendant often criticize and attack it. Antagonism or hostility, however, does not rule out a class action. (*Richmond* v. *Dart Industries, Inc.*, (1981) 29 Cal.3d 462 [174 Cal.Rptr. 515, 629 P.2d 23]; see *Fanucchi* v. *Coberly-West Co.* (1957) 151 Cal.App.2d 72 [311 P.2d 33] (over one-third of the class was allegedly antagonistic).) If a proposed class action satisfies the other criteria for class certification, antagonism from some members of the class will not derail certification.

In the *Fanucchi* case, one-third of the class members did not appear to support litigation. A more common problem, however, involves circumstances when individual litigants have filed numerous individual cases. These situations also include those where there are "mass filings" and the potential class may be viewed as a threat to their viability or to client control. On numerous occasions the author's office has had to deal with initial class status conferences and certification hearings that are conducted under a climate of a hostility due to competing plaintiffs' cases. Trial judges need to identify these competing forces and attempt to encourage a negotiated "truce" or, in fact, impose one of some type.

§ 4.04 The Effect of Related Litigation

[A] Importance of Early Analysis

As part of the early analysis of the case, it is highly advisable to find out about pending or prior federal or state class actions. Such litigation may affect control of your case and even the existence of your claim.

[B] Successive Class Actions or Federal Class Actions Precluding State Class Treatment

In some circumstances, a federal class action litigated to a final order may preclude a subsequent state court class action under the doctrine of res judicata.

In *Johnson* v. *American Airlines, Inc.*, the court found that, under both California and federal law, res judicata bars a subsequent suit if the same cause of action has been previously adjudicated in a suit between the same parties. The plaintiff asserted that res judicata did not apply to her because she was not a named party in the federal lawsuit settled without notice to the class. The court found that as long as she was a member of the class, even though unnamed, and as long as she was adequately represented, the settlement in the federal class action bound her. The court asserted that review of the two actions should focus on the "primary right" the litigation seeks to protect. The state class action can proceed only if the causes of action are distinct and different from those in the federal lawsuit. If a final judgment through settlement and/or trial has already determined the primary right, any subsequent California state action is precluded. (*Johnson* v. *American Airlines, Inc.* (1984) 157 Cal.App.3d 427 [203 Cal.Rptr. 638].) *Frazier* v. *City of Richmond* involved a similar interpretation of an ordinance regarding salaries. The final judgment in the first class action prevented a member of that class from relitigating the issue in a second class action. (*Frazier* v. *City of Richmond* (1986) 184 Cal.App.3d 1491 [228 Cal.Rptr. 376].)

Distinguish your case from any known prior matter and refer to it in your class certification papers and in the proposed notice. Describe why your class is different and why its primary rights have not been previously compromised or affected.

[C] Successive Class Actions or State Class Actions Precluding Federal Class Treatment

Recently the United States Supreme Court ruled that a state court settlement judgment (Delaware) releasing otherwise exclusive federal claims is entitled to full faith and credit. (*Matsushita Electric Industrial Co., Ltd.* v. *Epstein* (1996) __U.S.__ [134 L.Ed.2d 6, 116 S. Ct. 873].) A state court settlement judgment may now have a broader preclusive effect and be of greater value to settling parties.

[D] Concurrent Class Actions

Class actions pending at the same time as your case can cause problems. *Trotsky* v. *Los Angeles Fed. Sav. & Loan Ass'n* involved settlement of a class action while a similar case was pending (*Trotsky* v. *Los Angeles Fed. Sav. & Loan Ass'n* (1975) 48 Cal.App.3d 134, 141 [121 Cal.Rptr. 637]; see *Barwig* v. *Los Angeles Federal Savings & Loan Ass'n.*, Los Angeles Superior Court case no. C14608). The *Trotsky* settling parties failed to inform the court of the pendency of *Barwig* and the nature of that case's claims, which concerned related but slightly different theories. Since the *Trotsky* settlement notice did not refer to the pendency of the *Barwig* case, the entire judgment was reversed. Class members need to be advised whenever a similar case is pending, particularly if they are releasing their rights in a settlement. (See *Trotsky* v. *Los Angeles Fed. Sav. & Loan Ass'n* (1975) 48 Cal.App.3d 134, 141 [121 Cal.Rptr. 637].)

Schneider v. *Vennard* dealt with an unsuccessful attempt to file and certify both federal and state class actions. The California state securities class action failed certification largely because a federal class action on essentially the same grounds was pending. The increasingly strict statute of limitations and other recent reforms in federal securities law make this a difficult dilemma for practitioners. Which is the better approach: certifying a national class in a California court, or facing the ever-tougher requirements of federal securities law in federal court? (*Schneider* v. *Vennard* (1986) 183 Cal.App.3d 1340 [228 Cal.Rptr. 800].)

Bell v. *American Title Ins. Co.* presented an extreme example of a successive class action in state court and some of the remedies available to the trial judge. The plaintiff lawyer and the class representative in the second action attempted to undermine the settlement in the first case by sending mailers to the class urging them to "opt out"—an apparent test of the boundaries of ethical and appropriate conduct. The court imposed a sanction of $77,000 on plaintiff's counsel, staying all but $7,000. The case discusses the powers of the court to cite counsel for interfering with a settlement. (*Bell* v. *American Title Ins. Co.* (1991) 226 Cal.App.3d 1589 [277 Cal.Rptr. 583].)

In *Reich* v. *Club Universe*, the class representative's lawyer attempted to file a successor lawsuit to an identical action already filed on behalf of his wife. The trial court ruled that the attorney was disqualified from acting as the attorney for the class in the first action since he was a percipient witness. The disqualification order was final and appealable. Since it had not been appealed, however, the lawyer was barred from attempting to have it set aside in the case. (*Reich* v. *Club Universe* (1981) 125 Cal.App.3d 965 [178 Cal.Rptr. 473].)

[D] Extensive "Group" Litigation

Much class action law and procedure developed before substantial changes in the Rules of Professional Conduct allowed lawyers to advertise by mail. Often these communications to potential clients contain detailed information regarding potential claims as well as terms and conditions of representation. Numerous individual filings often result.

Superior courts can, and usually do, consolidate such extensive group lawsuits with proposed class actions. Numerous individual filings substantially affect class certification by giving the defendant an opportunity to argue that, since all parties are coming forward to participate in the extensive group, the class action is unneeded. For their part, plaintiffs can argue that the multiplicity of proceedings compel certification to prevent unfairness to absent class members. Numerous individual filings usually lead to "test cases" something like an action on behalf of a class representative, except that test cases involve collateral estoppel effects rather than the res judicata of class actions.

[F] Intervention

A related case can actually merge or join with a pending class action. Rule 23 of the Federal Rules of Civil Procedure requires that in cases requiring notice "any member who does not request exclusion, if he desires, may enter an appearance through his counsel." (Fed. Rules Civ.Proc., rule 23(e)(2)(c).) In California state courts this rule suggests that intervention is permitted but not required. Intervention is a procedural method of allowing participation in an action pending between other parties. Code of Civil Procedure section 387 allows anyone who has an interest in the litigation to intervene. In a class action, caution should be exercised before alignment with either plaintiff or defendant in intervention inasmuch as the intervening party takes the filed complaint as it stands.

Intervention also requires a showing of adequate interest in the litigation outcome and inadequate representation of the intervenor's interest by either party. (*Estate of Davis* (1990) 219 Cal.App.3d 663 [268 Cal.Rptr. 384].) Alternatively, a class member may opt out of the matter or enter an "appearance" in the matter. Undue delay or prejudice are key considerations when intervention is proposed well into litigation. Intervention motions, if granted, may impact control of a class matter more than would be the case with consolidation.

Recently individual plaintiffs' attorneys moved to intervene in a class action filed by the author's law firm. The class action complaint did not allege fraud. The statute of limitations for the class was governed by the class complaint, so we asked the court to defer a decision. If the motion was granted, the intervenor's clients may have adversely impacted the statute of limitations as to their cases since intervenors would take the complaint of the class as they found it. (See Code Civ. Proc., § 387.) A better result would be for the court to consolidate the class and individual cases.

§ 4.05 References

NEWBERG For a discussion of prefiling considerations under federal law, see 2 Newberg on Class Actions (3d ed. 1992), Chapter 6.

WITKIN See the following sections regarding general requirements for class actions:

- Questions of common interest (4 Witkin, Cal. Procedure (4th ed. 1997) Pleading, §§ 256–258).
- The class (4 Witkin, Cal. Procedure (4th ed. 1997) Pleading, §§ 259–263).
- Adequacy of representation (4 Witkin, Cal. Procedure (4th ed. 1997) Pleading, §§ 264–266).

TRG **THE RUTTER GROUP** The following sections in California Practice Guide: Civil Procedure Before Trial (CPBT) regarding general requirements for class actions:

- Prerequisite conditions (CPBT, § 14:11).
- Grounds for class action (CPBT, §§ 14:12–14:20).
- Application of requirements (CPBT, §§ 14:21–14:61).

See also the following sections in California Practice Guide: Federal Civil Procedure Before Trial (FCPBT) regarding general requirements for federal class actions:

- Class action requirements in general (FCPBT, §§ 10:235–10:253).
- Size of class ("numerosity") (FCPBT, §§ 10:255–10:260).
- Common questions of law or fact ("commonality") (FCPBT, §§ 10:261–10:267).
- Representative's claim typical ("typicality") (FCPBT, §§ 10:268–10:285).
- Adequate representation requirement (FCPBT, §§ 10:286-10:326).

⚷ **WEST'S KEY NUMBER SYSTEM** See the following Key Numbers in West's California Digest 2d, Federal Civil Procedure (Topic 170A):

- Factors and grounds (Federal Civil Procedure ⚷ 161.1).
- Superiority and manageability (Federal Civil Procedure ⚷ 161.2).
- Representation of class (Federal Civil Procedure ⚷ 164).
- Common interest in subject matter (Federal Civil Procedure ⚷ 165).

See also Parties (Topic 287):

- Factors and grounds (Parties ⚷ 35.5).
- Superiority and manageability (Parties ⚷ 35.7).
- Impracticability of joining all members; numerosity (Parties ⚷ 35.11).
- Representation of class; typicality (Parties ⚷ 35.13).
- Community of interest; commonality (Parties ⚷ 35.17).

WESTLAW® See the WESTLAW Electronic Research Guide at the beginning of this volume.

5 DRAFTING A CALIFORNIA CLASS ACTION COMPLAINT

A. TEXT

Sec.

5.01 Introduction

5.02 Structuring the Complaint

[A] The Caption

[B] Jurisdiction

[C] Venue and Forum

[D] The Parties

[1] Plaintiffs

[2] Subclasses

[3] Defendants

[E] Class Allegations

[F] Causes of Action

5.03 Key Issues in Class Action Complaints

[A] Issues Central to Certification

[B] Focusing and Defining Ascertainable Class

[C] Class Damages

[D] Class Representative Issues

[1] Primary and Secondary Issues

[2] Class Representative

[3] Class Counsel's Relationship with Class Representative

[E] Building the Backbone of the Case

[1] Predominance of Common Questions

[2] Defendants' Actions

[3] Inferences and Presumptions

[F] Toll the Statute of Limitations for Plaintiff Class

[G] Multiple Defendants

[H] Class Claims Against Presently Unknown Defendants

5.04 References

B. FORMS

5.10 Class Action Complaint (*Aguilar* v. *Atlantic Richfield*)

5.11 Class Action Complaint (*Marquart* case)

5.12 Notice of Motion and Motion on Special Demurrers and Memorandum of Points and Authorities in Support Thereof (*Dudley* v. *Jones*)

§ 5.01 Introduction

A California class action complaint differs structurally from a normal litigation filing in important ways. This chapter details the various elements that go into a successful class action complaint and reviews issues practitioners should consider as they draft the document. For illustrative allegations in class action complaints, see the sample forms in Chapter 13.

§ 5.02 Structuring the Complaint

[A] The Caption

The complaint should be clearly captioned with the words "Class Action." The caption should also refer to the applicable class action statue—Code of Civil Procedure section 382; Consumer Legal Remedies Act, section 1781; or one of the specialized areas under Corporations Code section 17501, such as limited partnerships.

[B] Jurisdiction

If the case is likely to be removed to federal court, perhaps a state case is not advisable. The section addressing jurisdiction and venue should tell the court why the case is being brought in state court. This provision assumes particular importance when the complaint describes a national class. If the action may possibly be removed to federal court, questions such as federal preemption should be analyzed to determine their effect on the cause of action in state court. (See, e.g., *Mark J. Fenning* v. *Glenfed. Inc.* (1995) 40 Cal.App.4th 1285 [47 Cal.Rptr.2d 715].)

For additional discussion of removing a state court action to federal court, see The Rutter Group's Cal. Prac. Guide: Fed. Civ. Pro. Before Trial, Chapter 2D.

[C] Venue and Forum

The class representative's cause of action should support venue in the county of choice. (*General Motors Corp.* v. *Superior Court of Alameda County* (1983) 141 Cal.App.3d 966 [190 Cal.Rptr. 742].) In a class action, the question of appropriate venue depends on wider considerations than usual, such as convenience to witnesses and attention to the underlying claims of the class representatives. Since class action trials are often complex, you should take into account the ability of the chosen court to calendar such demanding litigation. It pays to consider early on the likelihood of whether the action may subsequently be transferred to another jurisdiction.

Code of Civil Procedure section 410.30 provides that the court, on either its own motion or the motion of a party in the interest of substantial justice, can stay or dismiss an action in whole or part that should apparently be heard in a forum in another state. California class actions brought by a represented party on behalf of other California residents should not face dismissal on this ground because of the state's unquestioned interest in providing a forum adequate to resolution of the controversy. (*Archibald* v. *Cinerama Hotels* (1976) 15 Cal.3d 853 [126 Cal.Rptr. 811, 544 P.2d 947].)

For additional discussion of venue requirements in state courts, see The Rutter Group's Cal. Prac. Guide: Civ. Pro. Before Trial, Chapter 3.

[D] The Parties

[1] Plaintiffs

Representative plaintiffs should be organized around the claims for the action. The complaint should show that common questions of law and fact predominate and that class representatives are situated similarly to other members of the class. (*Classen* v. *Weller* (1983) 145 Cal.App.3d 27 [192 Cal.Rptr. 914].)

[2] Subclasses

Rule 23 of the Federal Rules of Civil Procedure allows subclasses, and no California cases have yet proscribed their use. Subclasses can be an effective device when it is possible to divide a defined set of legal standards or factual issues into logical, manageable increments. One example might be defenses available under the law to some class members but not others. Another example would be factual issues relating only to certain subclasses and not to others.

Subclasses may be appropriate in a multiple-defendant situation where conduct affects class members' damages separately, but liability issues unite them collectively. Other examples might include various security issues of different preferences and priorities. Additional examples might include persons who intervene in a larger class action and who present a minority or differing opinion on issues that affect only their interests. As a general concept, members of a subclass should have a broad unifying interest with minor differences in their individual situations.

[3] Defendants

The complaint needs to connect the specific defendants to the claims of the class. If any of the defendants are subsidiaries or wholly owned entities, this relationship needs to be made known. The complaint should also mention any defendant's claims grounded solely in the rights of a subclass.

[E] Class Allegations

The important class allegations section clearly distinguishes a class action complaint from typical litigation. This section needs to list the parties clearly, state their representative nature, and say why they are situated similarly to others in the class.

Additionally, the complaint should state the common questions of law and fact for the whole class or each subclass as needed. Typical language for this section reads as follows:

> Among the questions of law and fact common to the class are:
>
> (a) Whether California law, including but not limited to principles of ________ of securities law have been violated by the defendants, and each of them, as hereinafter alleged.

[F] Causes of Action

In general the complaint should give two or three primary causes of action suitable for class action certification. The complaint may also name other causes of action that are not the basis of class certification, although these causes of action should be subordinate or neutral, as with injunctive relief (see Chapter 3).

§ 5.03 Key Issues in Class Action Complaints

[A] Issues Central to Certification

A well-structured class action complaint deals with a number of issues central to successful certification. As you are drafting the complaint, pay particular attention to these concerns.

[B] Focusing and Defining Ascertainable Class

It is important to understand the difference between establishing the existence of an ascertainable class and identifying the individual members of that class. A class may be ascertainable even if the specific identities of class members are unknown on the date of the filing. For example, a successful complaint defined the plaintiffs as "all persons whose arrest record contains or will contain an entry relating to an arrest or detention not resulting in conviction and whose arrest record has been or will be disseminated by respondents to public employers. . . ." (*Central Valley Chapter 7th Step Foundation, Inc.* v. *Younger* (1979) 95 Cal.App.3d 212 [157 Cal.Rptr. 117].)

It is important that class members can be identified without unreasonable expense or delay. (*Hypolite* v. *Carleson* (1975) 52 Cal.App.3d 566 [125 Cal.Rptr. 221].) One way of limiting expense and delay and ensuring ascertainability is basing class identification on the defendant's records rather than information from individual plaintiffs. In *Daar* v. *Yellow Cab Co.* (1967) 67 Cal.2d 695 [63 Cal.Rptr. 724, 433 P.2d 732], although the class members were defined as those who purchased the taxicab script, the court actually found that the defendant's records determined who the class members were by showing their purchase of the script. As a contrasting example, *Weaver* v. *Pasadena Tournament of Roses* (1948) 32 Cal.2d 833 [198 P.2d 514] failed certification because the class of would-be ticket buyers could be identified only by each individual coming forth and presenting proof of the facts authorizing recovery. Since no records stated who received tickets and who did not, the class could not be ascertained.

Some local rules require that the complaint contain information regarding the approximate number of class members, their geographic location, status, methods of identification, and, where appropriate, any jurisdictional class questions. (See, e.g., Super. Ct. L.A. County Rules, rule 15.18.)

[C] Class Damages

What untoward events happened to the people you seek to represent? When and how did damages occur, and who is primarily responsible for them? These questions lie at the heart of your class definition.

For instance, how and when your class was damaged is important in defining it. Case law has allowed class actions where there is a common fund, common property, or a "mass of fungible goods" even though assembled separately. (*Fanucchi* v. *Coberly-West Co.* (1957) 151 Cal.App.2d 72 [311 P.2d 33].) A series of transactions and events can also result in certification. (*Daar* v. *Yellow Cab Co.* (1967) 67 Cal.2d 695 [63 Cal.Rptr. 724, 433 P.2d 732].) Antitrust damages can be proven by statistical or sampling methods with a pro rata allocation of overcharges. (Bus. & Prof. Code, § 16760, subd. (d).)

Misrepresentations, even on separate occasions and involving assignees of contracts, can also be certified. (*Vasquez* v. *Superior Court* (1971) 4 Cal.3d 800 [94 Cal.Rptr. 796, 484 P.2d 964].) Written misrepresentations or communications may likewise support class certification. (*Richmond* v. *Dart Industries, Inc.* (1981) 29 Cal.3d 462 [174 Cal.Rptr. 515, 629 P.2d 23].) Another form of misrepresentation is, of course, an omission. (See Civ. Code, § 1710.) The author's firm obtained class certification in a case involving 4,000 thrift and loan depositors uninformed of a looming FDIC deadline. When the institution was taken over by state regulatory authorities, the funds were unavailable during liquidation.

Do common statutory interpretations, welfare benefits, pension benefits, or other relief affect your class? If so, you may be able to avoid prejudgment notice and simplify the proceeding. (*Rose* v. *City of Hayward* (1981) 126 Cal.App.3d 926 [179 Cal.Rptr. 287].)

Fluid recovery should be proposed if the defendants' ill-gotten gains came from conduct that took a little each from large numbers of individuals instead of great deal from only a few. (*State v. Levi Strauss* (1986) 41 Cal.3d 460 [224 Cal.Rptr. 605, 715 P.2d 564].)

[D] Class Representative Issues

[1] Primary and Secondary Issues

Primary issues relate to whether adequacy of the individual representative is adequately representative of the class, willing to undertake a representation on behalf of the class, and connected to the matter in a way that allows him or her to represent others similarly situated. Secondary issues concern the adequacy of class counsel, conflicts of interest on the part of counsel, and the class attorney's willingness and ability to prosecute the claims of the class vigorously.

[2] Class Representative

The class representative must have claims typical of, but not necessarily identical to, the class. The most important test is whether the class representative is situated similarly to other class members on the common questions of law and fact. (*B.W.I. Custom Kitchen* v. *Owens-Illinois, Inc.* (1987) 191 Cal.App.3d 1341 [235 Cal.Rptr. 228]; *La Sala* v. *American Sav. & Loan Ass'n* (1971) 5 Cal.3d 864 [97 Cal.Rptr. 849, 489 P.2d 1113]; *Vasquez* v. *Superior Court* (1971) 4 Cal.3d 800 [94 Cal.Rptr. 796, 484 P.2d 964]; *Classen* v. *Weller* (1983) 145 Cal.App.3d 27 [192 Cal.Rptr. 914].) The class representative must also be prepared to vigorously prosecute the claims of the class. This requirement and the case law suggest that the class representative needs to have more than a passing approach to the case. At a minimum, a class representative should be prepared for deposition testimony and possibly even participation in the trial of the matter on behalf of the class.

[3] Class Counsel's Relationship with Class Representative

If the relationship between class counsel and class representative blurs the merits of the case, as happens when attorney and plaintiff are husband and wife, the filing of a class action may run into difficulty. (See, e.g., *Blue Chip Stamps* v. *Superior Court* (1976) 18 Cal.3d 381 [134 Cal.Rptr. 393, 556 P.2d 755].) Class certification will be denied if the plaintiff's attorney serves as a class representative, as in *Dean Witter Reynolds, Inc.* v. *Superior Court of Alameda County* (1989) 211 Cal.App.3d 758 [259 Cal.Rptr. 789]. Denial will also result if the attorney is deeply involved as a percipient witness. (See *Reich* v. *Club Universe* (1981) 125 Cal.App.3d 965 [178 Cal.Rptr. 473].)

[E] Building the Backbone of the Case

[1] Predominance of Common Questions

A key element in creating a successful class action complaint is demonstrating that common questions predominate over individual ones. Look for inferences and presumptions that expedite proof of the predominance of common questions. For example, most courts hold that in cases alleging a conspiracy to fix prices, common questions predominate over issues affecting class members only individually. (*B.W.I. Custom Kitchen* v. *Owens-Illinois, Inc.* (1987) 191 Cal.App.3d 1341 [235 Cal.Rptr. 228].) It is critical that the complaint avoid causes of action requiring individual proof, except in the calculation of damages. If each member of the class can recover only on the basis of facts unique to that individual, the class action will certainly be dismissed at the pleading stage as inappropriate. (*Brown* v. *Regents of the University of California* (1984) 151 Cal.App.3d 982 [198 Cal.Rptr. 916].)

For instance, damages for recovery of the market value of property lost because of aircraft noise, vapor, dust, and vibration led to detailed factual inquiries on liability and damages that precluded class certification in *City of San Jose* v. *Superior Court of Santa Clara County* (1974) 12 Cal.3d 447 [115 Cal.Rptr. 797, 525 P.2d 701].

[2] Defendants' Actions

How many defendants are there? Were they acting in concert? What are they alleged to have done? California courts may look to a continuous series of acts as the cause of the alleged wrong provided that the class is otherwise ascertainable. (*Daar* v. *Yellow Cab Co.* (1967) 67 Cal.2d 695 [63 Cal.Rptr. 724, 433 P.2d 732].)

[3] Inferences and Presumptions

Inferences and presumptions ease proof in cases involving multiple defendants, and they can persuade the court to certify a class action. Some types of proof offered by a representative class plaintiff provide inferences sufficient to shift the burden of persuasion to the defendant. (*La Sala* v. *American Savings & Loan Ass'n* (1971) 5 Cal.3d 864 [97 Cal.Rptr. 849, 489 P.2d 1113].) For instance, in *B.W.I. Custom Kitchen* v. *Owens-Illinois, Inc.* (1987) 191 Cal.App.3d 1341 [235 Cal.Rptr. 228], the court presumed classwide injury through antitrust violations once certain facts were proved.

[F] Toll the Statute of Limitations for Plaintiff Class

At the federal level, filing a class action tolls the statute of limitations for all members of the purported class until the class action is certified or dismissed. (*American Pipe & Construction Co.* v. *Utah* (1974) 414 U.S. 538 [38 L.Ed.2d 713, 94 S.Ct. 756].) The exact application of this principle to California law has been discussed in three important cases: *Bangert* v. *Narmco Materials Inc.* (1984) 163 Cal.App.3d 207 [209 Cal.Rptr. 438]; *Jolly* v. *Eli Lilly & Co.* (1988) 44 Cal.3d 1103 [245 Cal.Rptr. 658, 751 P.2d 923]; and *Becker* v. *McMillin Construction Co.* (1991) 226 Cal.App.3d 1493 [277 Cal.Rptr. 491]. A practitioner should be aware of the effect and holdings of these cases in drafting a California class action complaint. Filing the complaint has the tolling effect if it is drafted and handled correctly, but may not do so may not if the tolling issue is overlooked. Tolling becomes critical should the class complaint later amended be to add defendants or its structure otherwise be changed.

The most recent case, *San Francisco Unified School Dist.* v. *W.R. Grace & Company—Connecticut* (1995) 37 Cal.App.4th 1318 [44 Cal.Rptr.2d 305], confirms the present rule in California concerning equitable tolling of the statute of limitations in a pending class action. The court argued that this ruling stood at the intersection of two lines of California Supreme Court cases, namely *Jolly* v. *Eli Lilly & Co.*, (1988) 44 Cal.3d 1103 [245 Cal.Rptr. 658, 751 P.2d 923], and *Seely* v. *White Motor Co.*, (1965) 63 Cal.2d 9 [45 Cal.Rptr. 17, 403 P.2d 145].

Although the court stated that the federal ruling in *American Pipe & Construction Co.* v. *Utah* (1974) 414 U.S. 538 [38 L.Ed.2d 713, 94 S.Ct. 756] did not bind California courts, they should consider its applicability. As an example, the court cited *Becker* v. *McMillan Construction Co.* (1991) 226 Cal.App.3d 1493 [277 Cal.Rptr. 461] and agreed with the federal rule that the statute of limitations is tolled for a plaintiff who opts out of the class during the period he or she remained a member of the class.

Whether tolling affects absent class members depends on the scope and quality of notice given defendants. To the extent possible, defendants should be made aware of the requested class relief and the identity of class members. (See *Jolly* v. *Eli Lily & Co.* (1988) 44 Cal.3d 1103, [245 Cal.Rptr. 658, 751 P.2d 923].) Plaintiff's counsel should invite defendants and defense counsel to inquire as to the nature, scope, and type of claims in the complaint. Notice may affect the ability of additional parties to intervene in the case or file an individual action later. Generally, final denial of a class certification motion runs the statute of limitations against unnamed plaintiffs.

Use the statute of limitations tolling argument to support a precertification notice. We often seek to advise the proposed class members that the statute of limitations is tolled as to their claims against the then named defendants, avoiding the need to file an individual action to "protect their rights."

[G] Multiple Defendants

The more defendants named in the action, the more difficult it is to certify the class. Without either conspiracy allegations or action in concert, the case easily becomes unmanageable. (See *Diamond* v. *General Motors Corp.* (1970) 20 Cal.App.3d 374 [97 Cal.Rptr. 639]; *Devidian* v. *Automotive Service Dealers Ass'n* (1973) 35 Cal.App.3d 978 [111 Cal.Rptr. 228].) For example, an individual plaintiff with a claim against one of thirty-five defendant savings and loan associations was held an inadequate class representative because he lacked a legal nexus with all of the defendants. (*Petherbridge* v. *Altadena Federal Sav. and Loan Ass'n* (1974) 37 Cal.App.3d 193 [112 Cal.Rptr. 144].) However, such a legal nexus did exist in *Daniels* v. *Centennial Group, Inc.*, which arose from the consolidation of six limited partnerships into a single corporate entity. Class representatives did not need to be limited partners in each of the partnerships because the single corporation had linked them into one entity acting in concert. (*Daniels* v. *Centennial Group, Inc.* (1993) 16 Cal.App.4th 467 [21 Cal.Rptr.2d 1].)

[H] Class Claims Against Presently Unknown Defendants

Plaintiff's counsel may not know the exact identity of a defendant yet wish to prevent the running of the statute of limitations while attempting to discover who that defendant is. There are three ways to achieve this effect: filing a complaint designating fictitious persons as defendants (so-called Doe defendants; see Code Civ. Proc., § 474), and then amending upon learning their identity; proposing a defendant class (Code Civ. Proc., § 382); or combining the two. Notice must be given to the prospective defendants upon learning their identity, or must be given constructively if a defendant class is employed.

A plaintiff ignorant of a defendant's identity may amend the complaint to substitute the true names of the defendants once they are learned. Filing a proper complaint against a Doe defendant tolls the statute of limitations. (See Code Civ. Proc., § 474; *Balon* v. *Drost* (1993) 20 Cal.App.4th 483 [25 Cal.Rptr.2d 12] (laying out requirements for use of Doe defendants under Code Civ. Proc., § 474).) This approach can be extremely valuable in complicated state class actions.

A more arguable method for tolling the statute of limitations against a large group of defendants is to propose a defendant class. *Simons* v. *Horowitz* is one of the few cases in California that deals with defendant class actions. The reasoning behind the tolling of the statute of limitations on behalf of a plaintiff class would also seem to apply to a defendant class receiving proper notice. There is, however, a dearth of authority on defendant class suits. (See *Simons* v. *Horowitz* (1984) 151 Cal.App.3d 834 [199 Cal.Rptr. 134].) No California cases have construed tolling of the statute of limitations for a defendant class. Still, tolling would appear to apply as long as the representative defendant is not collusive—that is, not unfairly associated with the plaintiff or inadequately representative of the defendant class. Defendant class certification applies best to unincorporated associations or partnerships, which can sue and be sued as entities on their own, quite apart from their class status. Most successful uses of defendant classes involve clearly defined groups, such as owners of a common property.

§ 5.04 References

📖 **NEWBERG** For additional discussion of prefiling considerations, see 2 Newberg on Class Actions (3d ed. 1992), Chapter 6.

📖 **WITKIN** See the following sections regarding key issues in filing a California class action:

- Questions of common interest (4 Witkin, Cal. Procedure (4th ed. 1997) Pleading, §§ 256–258).
- The class (4 Witkin, Cal. Procedure (4th ed. 1997) Pleading, §§ 259–263).
- Adequacy of representation (4 Witkin, Cal. Procedure (4th ed. 1997) Pleading, §§ 264–266).

TRG **THE RUTTER GROUP** See the following sections in California Practice Guide: Civil Procedure Before Trial (CPBT) regarding key issues in filing a California class action:

- Prerequisite conditions (CPBT, § 14:11).
- Grounds for class action (CPBT, §§ 14:12–14:20).
- Application of requirements (CPBT, §§ 14:21–14:61).
- Jurisdiction (CPBT, §§ 14:69–14:79).
- Venue (CPBT, § 14:80).
- Pleadings (CPBT, §§ 14:81–14:83).

See also the following sections in California Practice Guide: Federal Civil Procedure Before Trial (FCBPT) regarding prerequisites to federal class actions:

- Class action requirements in general (FCPBT, §§ 10:235–10:253).
- Size of class ("numerosity") (FCPBT, §§ 10:255–10:260).
- Common questions of law or fact ("commonality") (FCPBT, §§ 10:261–10:267).
- Representative's claim typical ("typicality") (FCPBT, §§ 10:268–10:285).
- Adequate representation requirement (FCPBT, §§ 10:286–10:326).
- Jurisdiction and venue (FCPBT, §§ 10:392–10:426).
- The complaint (FCPBT, §§ 10:427–10:434).

WEST'S KEY NUMBER SYSTEM See the following Key Numbers in West's California Digest 2d, Federal Civil Procedure (Topic 170A):

- Factors and grounds (Federal Civil Procedure ⚷ 161.1).
- Superiority and manageability (Federal Civil Procedure ⚷ 161.2).
- Impracticability of joining all members (Federal Civil Procedure ⚷ 163).
- Representation of class (Federal Civil Procedure ⚷ 164).
- Common interest in subject matter (Federal Civil Procedure ⚷ 165).

See also Parties (Topic 287):

- Factors and grounds (Parties ⚷ 35.5).
- Superiority and manageability (Parties ⚷ 35.7).
- Impracticability of joining all members; numerosity (Parties ⚷ 35.11).
- Representation of class; typicality (Parties ⚷ 35.13).
- Community of interest; commonality (Parties ⚷ 35.17).

WESTLAW® See the WESTLAW Electronic Research Guide at the beginning of this volume.

B. FORMS

§ 5.10 Class Action Complaint (*Aguilar* v. *Atlantic Richfield*)

Timothy D. Cohelan (60827)
Isam C. Khoury (58759)
COHELAN & KHOURY
701 C Street
San Diego, California 92101-5305
Telephone: (619) 595-3001

Daniel J. Mogin (95624)
Angela Milea Mogin (153920)
THE MOGIN LAW FIRM
401 West A Street, Suite 2200
San Diego, California 92101-7909
Telephone: (619) 687-6700

Attorneys for Plaintiffs

COPY
KENNETH E. MARTONE
Clerk of the Superior Court
JUN 12 1996
By: L. MARTIN, Deputy
BUSINESS

SUPERIOR COURT OF THE STATE OF CALIFORNIA
FOR THE COUNTY OF SAN DIEGO

THERESA AGUILAR, individuals, on behalf of themselves and all others similarly situated, Plaintiffs, vs. ATLANTIC RICHFIELD CORPORATION, CHEVRON CORPORATION, EXXON CORPORATION, MOBIL OIL CORPORATION, SHELL OIL COMPANY, TEXACO, INC., TOSCO CORPORATION, ULTRAMAR CORPORATION, UNOCAL CORPORATION, and DOES 1 Through 40, inclusive, Defendants.	Case No. 00700810 CLASS ACTION FIRST AMENDED COMPLAINT FOR DAMAGES AND EQUITABLE RELIEF FOR: 1) VIOLATIONS OF CARTWRIGHT ACT 2) VIOLATIONS OF UNFAIR COMPETITION ACT JURY TRIAL DEMANDED

Plaintiffs, Theresa Aguilar, on behalf of themselves and all others similarly situated, and demanding trial by jury, complain and allege upon information and belief as follows:

JURISDICTION

1. This is a civil antitrust action seeking treble damages, injunctive relief and attorneys' fees pursuant to California Business and Professions Code §§16750(a) due to violations by the defendants and their co-conspirators, as alleged herein, of Bus. & Prof. Code §16720(a), et. seq., commonly known as the Cartwright Act. Plaintiffs' claims also arise and are brought pursuant to Bus. & Prof. Code §§17203 and 17204 for equitable relief including full restitution and/or disgorgement of all revenues, earnings, profits, compensation and benefits obtained by defendants as a result of their unlawful, unfair or fraudulent business acts or practices alleged herein as prohibited by Bus. & Prof. Code §§17200, et. seq., commonly known as the Unfair Competition Act.

VENUE

2. Venue as to each defendant is proper in this judicial district, pursuant to Bus. & Prof. Code §§16750(a) and 17203 and California Code of Civil Procedure §§395(a) and 395.5. Each defendant either maintains an office, transacts business, has an agent, or is found in the County of San Diego and each defendant is within the jurisdiction of this Court for purposes of service of process. The unlawful acts alleged herein had a direct effect on consumers within the State of California and, more particularly, within the County of San Diego. Additionally, the trade and commerce described herein is carried on, in part, in the State of California and, more particularly, within the County of San Diego.

DEFINITIONS

3. As used herein, the terms "CARB GAS" or "gasoline" mean all grades and types of reformulated or California Air Resources Board ("CARB") Phase 2 gasoline refined for retail sale in the State of California, including, without limitation, regular, premium and super premium, excluding diesel. Without limiting the foregoing, "CARB GAS" or "gasoline" includes all grades of CARB Phase 2 gasoline sold by defendants in California.

2

CARB GAS is a cleaner burning fuel than conventional gasoline and is expected to improve air quality in California by reducing polluting emissions.

4. As used herein, the terms "rack" or "rack price" refer to the wholesale price of CARB GAS.

5. As used herein, the terms "person" or "persons" shall have the same meaning as set forth in Bus. & Prof. Code §§16702 and 17021.

6. Plaintiffs allege that each of paragraphs 31-56 are likely to have evidentiary support after reasonable opportunity for further investigation and discovery.

PLAINTIFFS

7. a. Plaintiff Theresa Aguilar is a resident of the State of California and the County of San Diego. During the Class Period, Plaintiff Aguilar purchased CARB GAS within this state for her own use and not for resale and has paid supra-competitive prices.

b. Plaintiff is a resident of the State of California and the County of San Diego. During the Class Period, Plaintiff purchased CARB GAS within this state for her own use and not for resale and has paid supra-competitive prices.

c. Plaintiff is a resident of the State of California and the County of San Diego. During the Class Period, Plaintiff purchased CARB GAS within this state for his own use and not for resale and has paid supra-competitive prices.

d. Plaintiff is a resident of the State of California and the County of San Diego. During the Class Period, Plaintiff purchased CARB GAS within this state for his own use and not for resale and has paid supra-competitive prices.

DEFENDANTS

8. Defendant Atlantic Richfield Company ("Arco") is a corporation, either directly or through its subsidiaries, engaged in the business of refining, distributing and retailing gasoline in California. During the Class Period, Arco refined CARB GAS at its

3

refinery in Carson, California that it sold and distributed within the State of California and the County of San Diego.

9. Defendant Chevron Corporation ("Chevron") is a corporation, either directly or through its subsidiaries, engaged in the business of refining, distributing and retailing gasoline in California. During the Class Period, Chevron refined CARB GAS at its refineries in El Segundo and Richmond, California that it sold and distributed within the State of California and the County of San Diego.

10. Defendant Exxon Corporation ("Exxon") is a corporation, either directly or through its subsidiaries, engaged in the business of refining, distributing and retailing gasoline in California. During the Class Period, Exxon refined CARB GAS at its refinery in Benicia, California that it sold and distributed within the State of California and the County of San Diego.

11. Defendant Mobil Oil Corporation ("Mobil") is a corporation, either directly or through its subsidiaries, engaged in the business of refining, distributing and retailing gasoline in California. During the Class Period, Mobil refined CARB GAS at its refinery in Torrance, California that it sold and distributed within the State of California and the County of San Diego.

12. Defendant Shell Oil Company ("Shell") is a corporation, either directly or through its subsidiaries, engaged in the business of refining, distributing and retailing gasoline in California. During the Class Period, Shell refined CARB GAS at its refinery in Martinez, California that it sold and distributed within the State of California and the County of San Diego.

13. Defendant Texaco, Inc. ("Texaco") is a corporation, either directly or through its subsidiaries, engaged in the business of refining, distributing and retailing gasoline in California. During the Class Period, Texaco refined CARB GAS at its refineries in Bakersfield and Wilmington, California that it sold and distributed within the State of California and the County of San Diego.

4

14. Defendant Tosco Corporation ("Tosco") is a corporation, either directly or through its subsidiaries, engaged in the business of refining, distributing and retailing gasoline in California. Tosco retails gasoline through a number of arrangements including as a licensee, lessee or operator of BP ("British Petroleum") brand stations in California. During the Class Period, Tosco refined CARB GAS at its refinery in Avon, California that it sold and distributed within the State of California.

15. Defendant Ultramar Corporation ("Ultramar") is a corporation, either directly or through its subsidiaries, engaged in the business of refining, distributing and retailing gasoline in California. During the Class Period, Ultramar refined CARB GAS at its refineries in Wilmington, California that it sold and distributed within the State of California and the County of San Diego.

16. Defendant Unocal Corporation ("Unocal") is a corporation, either directly or through its subsidiaries, engaged in the business of refining, distributing and retailing gasoline in California. During the Class Period, Unocal refined CARB GAS at its refineries in San Francisco and Los Angeles, California that it sold and distributed within the State of California and the County of San Diego.

CO-CONSPIRATORS

17. Various individuals, partnerships, corporations and associations, including other refiners and retailers of gasoline, not named as defendants in this Complaint, have participated as co-conspirators in the violations alleged herein and have performed acts and made statements in furtherance thereof.

DOE DEFENDANTS

18. DOES 1-10 are residents of the State of California and officers, employees or agents of the defendants and/or entities owned or controlled by the defendants. DOES 1-10 participated in the course of conduct that is the subject of this action as alleged herein.

5

19. DOES 11-20 are institutes, central agencies, private individuals, associations, partnerships, corporations, institutions or other entities which participated in the course of conduct that is the subject matter of this action, as alleged herein. Certain of DOES 11-20 are corporations, partnerships or other entities and are organized under the laws of the State of California with their principal place of business in the State of California. Certain DOES 11-20 are private individuals who are residents of the State of California.

20. DOES 21-30 are central agencies, private individuals, associations, partnerships, corporations, institutions or other entities which participated in the course of conduct that is the subject matter of this action, as alleged herein. Certain of DOES 21-30 are corporations, partnerships or other entities and are organized under the laws of the several states with their principal place of business in one of the states of the United States other than California.

21. DOES 31-40 participated in the concerted activity alleged herein in ways that are unknown to plaintiffs at this time. DOES 31-40 may be residents of the State of California.

22. Except as described herein, plaintiffs are, as yet, ignorant of the true names, capacities and nature and extent of participation in the course of conduct alleged herein of the persons sued as DOES 1 through 40 inclusive, and therefore sue these defendants by such fictitious names. Plaintiffs will amend this complaint to allege the true names and capacities of the DOE defendants when ascertained.

CLASS ACTION ALLEGATIONS

23. Plaintiffs bring this action, on behalf of themselves and all others similarl situated, as a class action pursuant to Section 382 of the California Code of Civil Procedure an Section 1781 of the California Civil Code. The class which plaintiffs seek to represent i composed of and defined as follows:

6

All persons (as defined above) residing in California who, during the time period March 1, 1996 through the present (the "Class Period"), purchased, in California, for their own use and not for resale, CARB GAS sold by any of the defendants ("Plaintiff Class"). Specifically excluded from the Plaintiff Class are the defendants herein; officers, directors or employees of any defendants; any entity in which any defendant has a controlling interest; the affiliates, legal representatives, attorneys, heirs, or assigns of any defendant; and any federal, state or local governmental entity.

24. This action has been brought and may properly be maintained as a class actio pursuant to the provisions of CCP §382 because there is a well-defined community of interest i the litigation and the proposed class is easily ascertainable:

a. Numerosity: The Plaintiff Class is so numerous that the individu joinder of all members is impracticable under the circumstances of this cas While the exact number of class members is unknown to plaintiffs at this tim plaintiffs are informed and believe that approximately 13.5 billion gallons c gasoline are sold in California annually and that sales during the Class Peric were approximately $50 to $60 million per day, involving hundreds c thousands of class members located throughout California. Joinder of a members of the Plaintiff Class is not practicable.

b. Common Questions Predominate: Common questions of law an fact exist as to all members of the Plaintiff Class and predominate over ar questions which affect only individual members of the class. These commo questions of law and fact include, without limitation:

(i) Whether defendants violated the Cartwright Act;

7

(ii) The existence, duration, and illegality of the restrictions, limitations, obligations, combinations, agreements, trusts and conspiracies alleged herein;

(iii) Whether defendants and each of them was a participant in the restrictions, limitations, obligations, combinations, agreements, trusts and conspiracies alleged herein;

(iv) The effect upon and the extent of injuries sustained by plaintiffs and members of the Plaintiff Class and the appropriate type and/or measure of damages;

(v) Whether defendants violated the Unfair Competition Act;

(vi) The amount of additional revenues and profits obtained by defendants attributable to their violations of the Unfair Competition Act; and,

(vii) The appropriate nature of class wide equitable relief.

c. Typicality: Plaintiffs' claims are typical of the claims of the members of the Plaintiff Class. Plaintiffs and all members of the Plaintiff Class sustained injuries and damages arising out of defendants' common course of conduct in violation of law as complained of herein. The injuries and damages of each member of the Plaintiff Class were caused directly by the defendants' wrongful conduct in violation of law as alleged herein.

d. Adequacy: Plaintiffs will fairly and adequately protect the interest of the members of the Plaintiff Class. Plaintiffs reside in California, purchased, in California, gasoline manufactured by defendants during the Class Period for their own use and not for resale, and are adequate representatives of the Plaintiff Class as they have no interests which are adverse to the interests of absent class members. Plaintiffs have retained counsel who have substantial experience and success in the prosecution of complex class action and antitrust litigation.

8

e. Superiority: A class action is superior to other available means for the fair and efficient adjudication of this controversy since individual joinder of all members of the class is impracticable. Class action treatment will permit a large number of similarly situated persons to prosecute their common claims in a single forum simultaneously, efficiently, and without the unnecessary duplication of effort and expense that numerous individual actions would engender. Furthermore, as the damages suffered by each individual member of the class may be relatively small, the expenses and burden of individual litigation would make it difficult or impossible for individual members of the class to redress the wrongs done to them while an important public interest will be served by addressing the matter as a class action. The cost to the court system of adjudication of such individualized litigation would be substantial. Individualized litigation would also present the potential for inconsistent or contradictory judgments.

25. Plaintiffs are unaware of any difficulties that are likely to be encountered in the management of this action that would preclude its maintenance as a class action.

TRADE AND COMMERCE

26. CARB GAS is a cleaner burning fuel than conventional gasoline and is expected to improve air quality in California by reducing polluting emissions. As of March 1, 1996 CARB GAS is required to be sold in California pursuant to the federal Clean Air Act Amendments and the regulations of the California Air Resources Board ("CARB"). CARB GAS has had the effect of transforming California's gasoline market and setting California apart from other fuel markets.

27. The defendants named herein were and are the major refiners, distributors and retailers of all types of gasoline, including CARB GAS, in the State of California. During the Class Period defendants and their co-conspirators were engaged in the business of

9

refining, distributing and selling CARB GAS in the State of California, collectively controlling almost 100% of the wholesale market for CARB GAS and approximately 92% of the retail market.

28. The defendants and their co-conspirators sell and distribute CARB GAS in California to wholesalers, distributors and retailers (commonly referred to as "dealers") including dealers owned by, operated or affiliated with defendants, who, in turn, re-sell CARB GAS to plaintiffs and the other members of the Class. Plaintiffs and the other members of the Class are end-users and do not resell CARB GAS; accordingly none of the supra-competitive prices paid by plaintiffs and the class members are passed on by them, as they use the CARB GAS directly.

29. CARB GAS is a fungible product; consumer demand for CARB GAS is relatively inelastic. The California Energy Commission estimates an ongoing and constant retail demand for gasoline of approximately 864,000 barrels per day, rising to more than 910,000 barrels per day during the summer driving season.

30. Defendants began refining CARB GAS in late December, 1995. Beginning on March 1, 1996 only CARB GAS was refined for sale in California. Commencing June 15, 1996 only CARB GAS may be sold in California. As a result of defendants' acts and practices, the market for CARB GAS is a closed market, economically inaccessible by other, potentially competitive producers. For these reasons, *inter alia*, the California gasoline market has been transformed and is unique.

31. Defendants have acted to restrict the supply of CARB GAS. In 1982 there were 44 operating refineries in California. At present there are only 12 refineries in California producing CARB GAS, each of which is operated by the defendants. Since 1982, the California refinery utilization rate has reportedly increased from 71% to over 95% at present. This restricted number of refineries operating at virtually full capacity allows the defendants to control the supply of CARB GAS and to use their control to

10

restrict the supply of CARB GAS, artificially inflating the price of CARB GAS and causing prices to rise rapidly and dramatically.

32. Defendants have also acted to restrict and reduce the number of independent and non-affiliated dealers. Defendants' reduction of the number of operating refineries and increase in refinery utilization rate in conjunction with a practice known in the industry as "KILL" (Keep Inventories Low and Lean), have resulted in the virtual elimination of independent dealers as supplies of unbranded rack, surplus rack or spot market rack gasoline. The existence and operation of the competitive surplus or spot markets acted as a check on defendants' ability to control prices. In 1982, there was a substantial market presence of independent dealers; whereas today less than 8% of all gas stations in California are independently owned or unaffiliated with the major refiners and distributors of gasoline, including, primarily the defendants. As a result, retail gas stations must purchase at dealer tank wagon prices set at the refinery. In fact, at least 2 years prior to the implementation of the CARB Phase 2 program, refiners brazenly warned independents that there would be a shortfall of CARB GAS supply and that independent dealers had better "brand-up" (affiliate with a defendant) or risk being unable to obtain supplies of CARB GAS.

33. The California Energy Commission issues a "Weekly Fuels Watch Report" which details refinery production and stock levels. Several of these reports, commencing in January of 1996, reveal restricted production of CARB GAS and diminishing stocks of CARB GAS, despite the impending deadlines for the production and sale of CARB GAS. For example, for the week ending January 12, 1996, refinery production of CARB GAS decreased 7.4% from the previous week, while refinery stock of CARB GAS plummeted 11.7% from the previous week. In the weeks immediately preceding the March 1, 1996 deadline, at a time when defendants knew that they needed to build up refinery inventories or stocks in order to meet demand and make an orderly transition to CARB GAS, defendants' production of CARB GAS was hundreds of thousands of barrels per day less

11

than estimated demand. In fact, beginning the week ended February 16, 1996 until the week ended June 6, 1996, defendants' production of CARB GAS has been significantly less than estimated demand, except for a brief period of intense media and governmental scrutiny. Thereafter, as the pubic has adjusted to supra-competitive prices and media and governmental scrutiny has diminished, defendants' production of CARB GAS has again declined to levels significantly below estimated demand and retail prices have thus been maintained at supra-competitive prices.

34. As alleged above, as of March 1, 1996, CARB GAS is the only type of gasoline refined for sale in California. Prior to March 1, 1996, defendants issued repeated assurances that the transition to production of CARB GAS would be accomplished without major disruptions. From the end of December, 1995 to approximately March 1, 1996, the increases in the price of gasoline in general and CARB GAS in particular were relatively small or were closely tied to the cost of crude oil. According to the reports of the California Energy Commission – which has declared a state of energy emergency and implemented certain emergency measures– however, beginning about March 1, 1996, defendants, and each of them, caused rapid price increases to occur. For the week ending March 22, reported CARB GAS production increased only 0.9% from the previous week. The following week saw a restriction or decline in CARB GAS production by 1.9% from the previous week. The April 5 report reveals further supply restriction, as CARB GAS production plummeted by 3.2% from the previous week. CARB GAS production reportedly fell again in the weeks ending May 10 (-2.9%), May 24 (-6.8%) and May 31(-6.7%) compared to the prior weeks. These reports indicate that notwithstanding the emergency and repeated public assurances that supplies would be adequate and prices would decline production has continued to be restricted, particularly compared to demand and production capacity estimates prepared by the California Energy Commission based upon data supplied, in large part, by defendants. As a result, prices of CARB GAS have risen or stabilized at supra-competitive levels. The following chart illustrates defendants'

12

reported production of CARB GAS compared to estimated demand and estimated production capacity:

Week Ending	Reported Production (000s of barrels)	Estimated Demand (000s of barrels)	% of Est. Demand
2-16-96	3735	6048	61.76
2-23-96	4175	6048	69.03
3-01-96	4023	6048	66.51
3-08-96	4759	6048	78.69
3-15-96	5681	6048	93.93
3-22-96	5730	6048	94.74
3-29-96	5621	6048	92.94
4-05-96	5440	6048	89.95
4-12-96	5508	6048	91.07
4-19-96	6033	6048	99.75
4-26-96	5992	6048	99.07
5-03-96	6375	6230	102.33
5-10-96	6190	6230	99.36
5-17-96	6470	6230	103.85
5-24-96	6029	6230	96.77
5-31-96	5628	6230	90.34
6-06-96	6041 (est.)	6342	95.25

Week Ending	Est. Prod. Cap. (000s of barrels)	Rep. Production as % of Est. Prod. Capacity
2-16-96	6475	57.68
2-23-96	6475	64.48
3-01-96	6475	62.13
3-08-96	6475	73.49
3-15-96	6475	87.73
3-22-96	6475	88.49
3-29-96	6475	86.81
4-05-96	6475	84.05
4-12-96	6475	85.07
4-19-96	6475	93.17
4-26-96	6475	92.54
5-03-96	6475	98.46
5-10-96	6475	95.60
5-17-96	6475	99.92
5-24-96	6475	93.11
5-31-96	6475	86.92
6-06-96	6475	93.30(est.)

(See Exhibit 1)

35. Since March 1, 1996, the defendants have each engaged in massive price increases, raising their prices by nearly identical increments at almost precisely the same time throughout California. (See Exhibit 2.) Such price increases have increased the average refiner's margin from approximately $ 0.213 per gallon in December of 1995, to

13

$0.464 per gallon as of April 23, 1996, an increase of $0.251 or 135%. In contrast, during the same period, the dealers' average margin shrank from $0.083 to $ (-0.012), a decrease of 1.2%. (See Exhibit 3.)

36. As a result of these massive price increases, on April 17, 1996 the California Energy Commission declared an energy emergency and implemented the verification phase of the legislatively mandated Energy Emergency Contingency Plan which required defendants to report their actual production of CARB GAS. These reports reveal a continued attempt to maintain high prices by restricting production and supplies. Comparison of the intermittent daily reports issued by the Energy Commission pursuant to the Energy Emergency Contingency Plan reveals that the weekly reports of defendants' reported production as detailed in the Energy Commission's "Weekly Fuels Watch Report" has been overstated as defendants have continued to produce less CARB GAS than estimated demand and production capacity.

37. These price increases have been led in Southern California by defendant Texaco. Texaco, however, is a relatively small market participant, with only about a 5% share of the Southern California gasoline market, and only about 10% of California's CARB GAS refinery capacity. Yet, Texaco led the "steady drumbeat of price increases" during the relevant period. These price increases were closely followed by the other defendants, notwithstanding the fact that Texaco had insufficient market power to lead and sustain such price increases without risking substantial loss of volume and market share, but for the other defendants' lockstep price increases. Normally, anytime any one of the defendants takes the lead in a price "restoration," they do so risking the loss of a portion of their market share. While such a loss can be absorbed by defendants with more robust market shares, Texaco, with its limited share of the market, could not logically engage in such actions under normal economic conditions. Despite this reality, Texaco was the most aggressive leader in the recent round of price increases.

14

38. Texaco's actions, coupled with the subsequent moves of other defendant refiners, were the principal factors in the rise of retail gasoline prices by more than $0.38 per gallon between January 1, 1996 and April 19, 1996 and thereafter. The defendants each raised prices and maintained their existing market shares by means of dramatic increases in their refiner's margins.

39. As a result of the collective conduct of defendants, California's price increases have led the nation by a significant margin.

40. The defendants have offered conflicting and false explanations of their conduct, and the resulting dramatic increases in California prices to supra-competitive levels:

a. <u>Increased Price of Crude Oil Due to Cold Winter and the Continued Production of Heating Oil Rather than Gasoline</u>:

The defendants have cited an increased cost of crude oil due to the cold winter and the need to continue to refine heating oils to meet sustained demand restricting their ability to produce gasoline. This explanation is false. Very little, if any, heating oil is refined in California. Moreover, to the extent that the cost of crude oil has increased at times during the Class Period by approximately $5 per barrel, this translates to an increase of only approximately $0.12 per gallon of gasoline at the pump or retail level. In contrast, to the extent that the cost of crude oil has decreased during the Class Period, such decreases have not been fully reflected in the price of CARB GAS at the pump.

b. <u>Increased Cost Of Crude Oil Due To Uncertainty In World Oil Markets Caused By U.N. Negotiations With Iraq</u>:

Defendants have also blamed the increased cost of crude oil on the possibility of Iraq producing crude oil exports, in other words the uncertainty caused by a potential increase in world crude oils supply has caused the price of crude oil to increase. This explanation is, at best, a red

15

bearing. In fact, California's crude oil supply for CARB GAS comes from non-OPEC sources, primarily from Alaska and California.

c. Operational Disruptions at West Coast Refineries:

Operational disruptions and maintenance at West Coast refineries, such as the Shell and Arco refinery fires, have also been incorrectly blamed for the enormous price increases. This explanation is also misleading. Historically, mechanical difficulties and operational disruptions have not resulted in substantial price hikes. In fact, operational disruptions, such as refinery fires and maintenance shut-downs are routine and common place. Defendants and their co-conspirators have reduced refinery production in order to decrease supply, allowing defendants to implement price hikes upon the occurrence of any operational disruptions.

d. Increased Costs Associated With the Transition to CARB GAS:

Defendants have also blamed increased costs associated with the transition to refining California's cleaner-burning CARB GAS for the huge price jumps. This excuse is also false and misleading. Defendants previously indicated that costs associated with retooling the refineries to produce California's cleaner burning gasoline are between $3 and $5 billion dollars. Increasing the cost of gas $0.05 per gallon would allow defendants to recoup $5 billion in just 5 years, excluding any possible tax advantages the companies might receive. Moreover, California allows certain tax credits to defendants to allow them to partially recoup the cost of conversion to CARB GAS. Based upon the tax credits claimed by defendants, the aggregate cost of conversion to CARB GAS production appears to have been materially overstated and substantially less than the publicly stated amounts which have, in fact, been incurred.

16

41. The $0.05 per gallon increase due to the retooling costs, coupled with the approximately $0.12 increase per gallon as a result of increased crude oil costs, provides the defendants with at least a $0.17 per gallon increase in the refinery margin. Yet refiners' margins have increased by approximately $0.38 or 135%. In fact, the defendants have reported large increases in their profits during the first quarter of 1996 and industry analysts have forecast that defendants will continued to enjoy record profits as a result of increased refinery margins.

VIOLATIONS ALLEGED

FIRST CAUSE OF ACTION
VIOLATIONS OF THE CARTWRIGHT ACT
(Against all Defendants)

42. Plaintiffs incorporates by reference and reallege paragraphs 1-41, above, as though fully set forth herein.

43. The defendants' conduct with respect to the supply and pricing of CARB GAS reveals that they do not compete and have agreed not to compete in California, particularly with respect to the refiner's margin set before dealer delivery.

44. Beginning at a time presently unknown to plaintiffs, and continuing thereafter to the present, defendants and co-conspirators entered into and engaged in a continuing unlawful trust in restraint of the trade and commerce described above in violation of Bus. & Prof. Code §16720. Within the last four years the defendants, and each of them, have acted in violation of §16720 to increase their refinery margins and, correspondingly, the retail price through their dealers by wrongfully restricting supplies of CARB GAS and thereby fix, raise, stabilize and maintain prices at supra-competitive levels.

45. Each of the defendants knew all of the information relative to the dealer margin, crude oil cost, and federal and state taxes.

17

46. Defendants have exchanged, communicated and signaled, through themselves and through third-parties and devices unknown to plaintiffs, confidential information regarding production plans, supplies and prices and have agreed to wrongfully restrict supplies of CARB GAS, sustain an artificially high level of refiner "margin" and thereby fix, raise, stabilize and maintain prices at supra-competitive levels.

47. The aforesaid violations of Bus. & Prof. Code §16720 consisted, without limitation, of a continuing combination, agreement, understanding and concert of action among the defendants and co-conspirators, the substantial terms of which were to limit the production and to fix, raise, maintain and stabilize the prices of CARB GAS sold in the State of California to plaintiffs and the members of the Plaintiff Class at supra-competitive levels.

48. For the purpose of forming and effectuating the aforesaid combination and conspiracy, the defendants and co-conspirators have done those things which they combined and conspired to do, including among other things:

(a) agreed to and did exchange current and future price information;

(b) agreed to and did communicate other confidential competitive information;

(c) agreed to and did coordinate output and inventory levels;

(d) agreed to and did coordinate pricing levels and movements;

(e) agreed on prices and price levels;

(f) agreed to and did fix, raise, stabilize, inflate and maintain and increase prices and price levels in relation to each other;

(g) agreed to and did restrict manufacture and supply of CARB GAS, and;

(h) agreed to and did refrain from competing among themselves on the basis of price.

18

EFFECTS

49. The aforesaid combination and conspiracy has had the following effects, among others:

(a) price competition in the sale of CARB GAS has been suppressed, restrained and eliminated;

(b) prices of CARB GAS purchased by plaintiffs and other members of the Class have been raised, fixed, maintained and stabilized at artificial and non-competitive levels;

(c) supplies of CARB GAS have been restricted;

(d) buyers of CARB GAS were deprived of free and open competition in the purchase of CARB GAS.

INJURY TO PLAINTIFFS AND MEMBERS OF THE PLAINTIFF CLASS

50. During the period covered by this Complaint, plaintiffs and the other members of the Plaintiffs Class purchased CARB GAS directly or indirectly from defendants. By reason of the alleged violations of the antitrust laws, plaintiffs and the members of the Plaintiff Class paid more for CARB GAS than they would have paid in the absence of the illegal combination and conspiracy and, as a result, have been injured in their business and property and have suffered damages in an amount according to proof at trial.

SECOND CAUSE OF ACTION
UNFAIR COMPETITION ACT
(Against all Defendants)

51. Plaintiffs incorporate by reference and reallege paragraphs 1-41, above, as though fully set forth herein.

52. This Complaint is filed and these proceedings are instituted pursuant to §§17203 and 17204 of the California Business and Professions Code, to obtain restitution

19

from these defendants for acts, as alleged herein, that violated §17200 of the California Business and Professions Code, commonly known as the Unfair Competition Act.

53. The defendants' conduct as alleged herein violates §17200. The acts, omissions, misrepresentations, practices, and non-disclosures of defendants, as alleged herein, constituted and constitute a common continuous and continuing course of conduct of unfair competition by means of unfair, unlawful and/or fraudulent business acts or practices within the meaning of California Business and Professions Code Section 17200, et seq., including, but in no way limited to, the following:

a. the violations of Bus. & Prof. Code §16720, et seq. set forth in paragraphs 1-50, above;

b. defendants' acts, omissions, misrepresentations, practices, and non-disclosures as described in paragraphs 1-41 above, whether or not in violation of Bus. & Prof. Code §16720, et seq. are otherwise unfair, unconscionable, unlawful and fraudulent;

c. violation of Section 5 of the Federal Trade Commission Act [15 U.S.C. §45(a)];

d. defendants' acts and practices are unfair to consumers in the State of California within the meaning of Bus. & Prof. Code §17200; and

e. defendants' acts and practices are fraudulent within the meaning of Bus. & Prof. Code §17200.

54. Plaintiffs and the Plaintiff Class are entitled to equitable and injunctive relief, including full restitution and/or disgorgement of all revenues, earnings, profits, compensation and benefits which may have been obtained by defendants as a result of such business acts or practices and enjoining defendants to cease and desist from engaging in the practices described herein.

55. The illegal conduct alleged herein is continuing and there is no indication that defendants will not continue such activity into the future.

20

FRAUDULENT CONCEALMENT

56. The running of any statute of limitations has been suspended with respect to any claims which the plaintiffs and the other members of the class have sustained as a result of the unlawful course of conduct alleged herein and with respect to their rights to injunctive relief by virtue of the doctrine of fraudulent concealment in that:

(a) defendants and co-conspirators through various devices and techniques of secrecy affirmatively and fraudulently concealed the existence of the unlawful combination and conspiracy alleged herein; and

(b) plaintiffs and the other members of the Plaintiff Class had no knowledge of such unlawful conduct or of fact which might have led to the discovery thereof with the exercise of due diligence until some time shortly before filing this Complaint.

PRAYER FOR RELIEF

WHEREFORE, plaintiffs pray:

(a) That the Court determine that this action may be maintained as a class action;

(b) That the unlawful combination and conspiracy alleged herein be adjudged and decreed to be a violation of Section 16720 of the California Business and Professions Code, and that plaintiffs and the members of the Plaintiff Class have been injured and damaged as a result of said violation of the Cartwright Act;

(c) That plaintiffs and each and every member of the Plaintiff Class recover threefold the damages determined to have been sustained by them, and that joint and several judgment in favor of plaintiffs and each and every member of the Plaintiff Class, respectively, be entered against the defendants, and each of them;

(d) That plaintiffs and the other members of the Plaintiff Class recover their costs of suit, including reasonable attorneys' fees, as provided by §16750(a) of the California Business and Professions Code;

21

(e) That defendants be found to have engaged in unfair competition in violation of §17200 of the California Business and Professions Code;

(f) That defendants be ordered and enjoined to make restitution to plaintiffs and the members of the Plaintiff Class due to their unfair competition, including disgorgement of their wrongfully obtained revenues, earnings, profits, compensation and benefits, pursuant to California Business and Professions Code §§17203 and 17204;

(g) That defendants further be enjoined to cease and desist from unfair competition in violation of §17200 of the California Business and Professions Code;

(h) That plaintiffs be awarded costs of suit and attorneys' fees pursuant to §1021.5 of the California Code of Civil Procedure;

(i) That defendants be enjoined from further acts in restraint of trade or unfair competition; and

(j) That plaintiffs and the other members of the Plaintiff Class be granted such other and, further relief as the nature of the case may require or as my seem just and proper to this Court.

Dated: June 11, 1996

Timothy D. Cohelan (60827)
Isam C. Khoury (58759)
COHELAN & KHOURY

by: ____________________
Timothy D. Cohelan
701 C Street
San Diego, California 92101-5305
(619) 595-3001

Daniel J. Mogin (95624)
Angela Milea Mogin (153920)
THE MOGIN LAW FIRM

by: ____________________
Daniel J. Mogin
401 West A Street, Suite 2200
San Diego, California 92101-7909
(619) 687-6700

Attorneys for Plaintiffs

22

JURY DEMAND

Plaintiffs individually and on behalf of all others similarly situated, hereby demand a trial by jury on all issues so triable.

Dated: June 11, 1996

Timothy D. Cohelan (60827)
Isam C. Khoury (58759)
COHELAN & KHOURY

by ______________________
Timothy D. Cohelan
701 C Street
San Diego, California 92101-5305
(619) 595-3001

Daniel J. Mogin (95624)
Angela Milea Mogin (153920)
THE MOGIN LAW FIRM

by: ______________________
Daniel J. Mogin
401 West A Street, Suite 2200
San Diego, California 92101-7909
(619) 687-6700

Attorneys for Plaintiffs

calgas.1stamcmpt
June 11, 1996

23

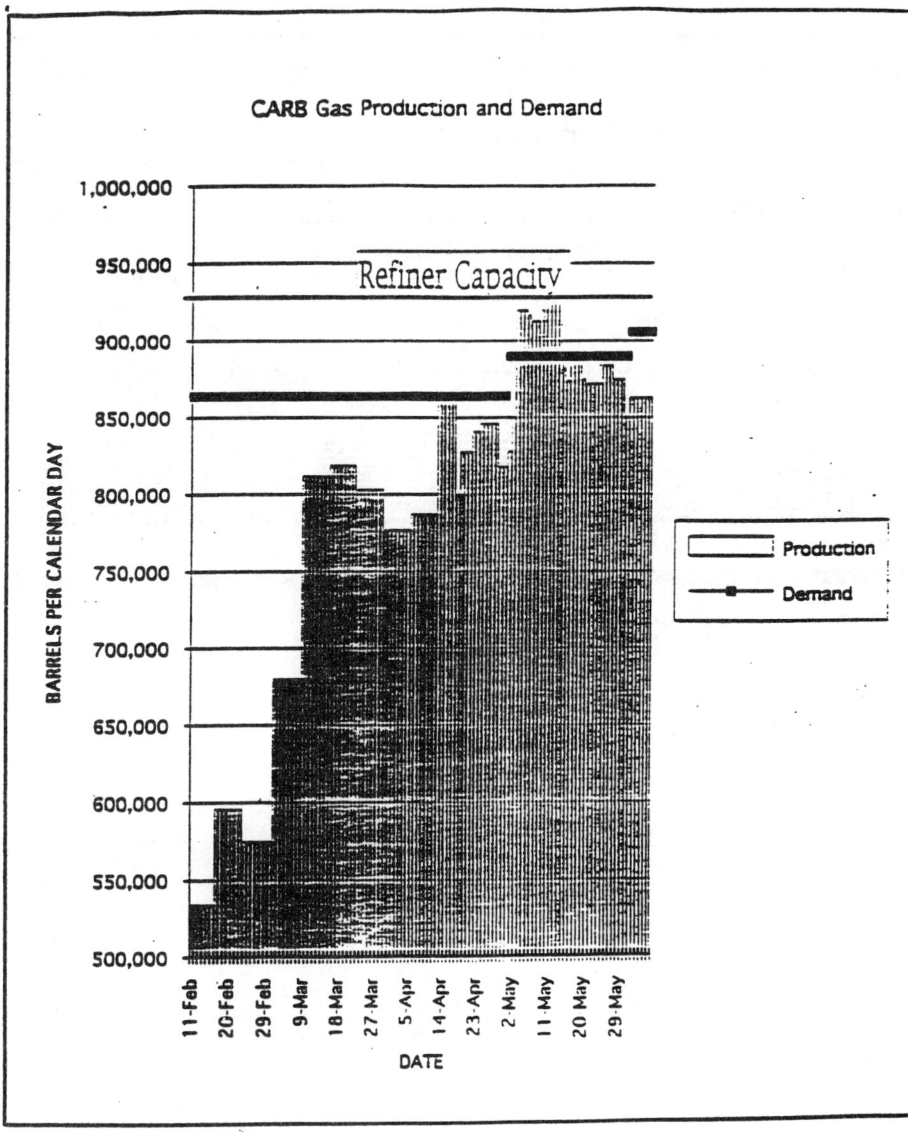
CARB Gas Production and Demand
Refiner Capacity
BARRELS PER CALENDAR DAY
1,000,000
950,000
900,000
850,000
800,000
750,000
700,000
650,000
600,000
550,000
500,000
11-Feb
20-Feb
29-Feb
9-Mar
18-Mar
27-Mar
5-Apr
14-Apr
23-Apr
2-May
11-May
20-May
29-May
DATE
Production
Demand

EXHIBIT

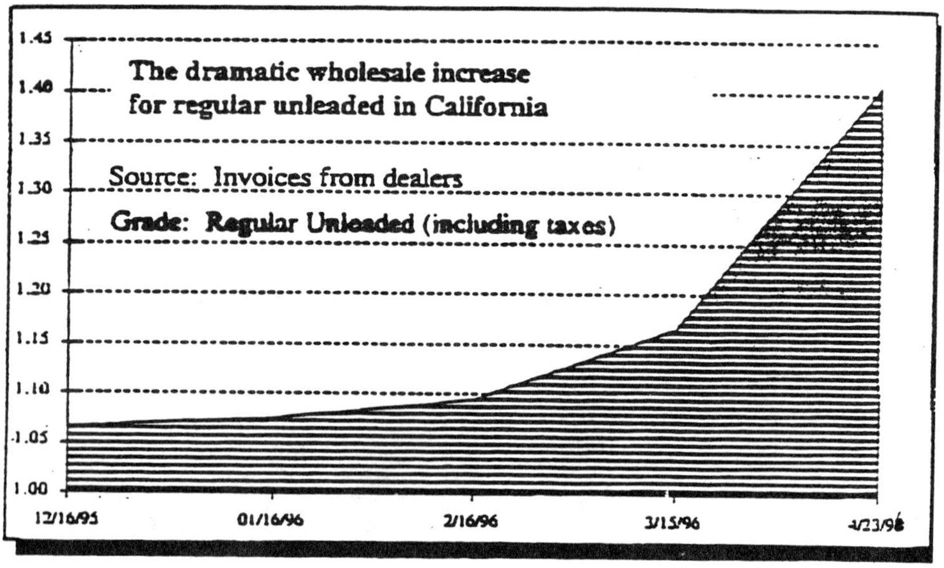
The dramatic wholesale increase
for regular unleaded in California
Source: Invoices from dealers
Grade: Regular Unleaded (including taxes)
1.45
1.40
1.35
1.30
1.25
1.20
1.15
1.10
1.05
1.00
12/16/95
01/16/96
2/16/96
3/15/96
4/23/96

EXHIBIT 2

Figure 6

MOTOR GASOLINE
APRIL 23, 1996 • $1.473 PER GALLON

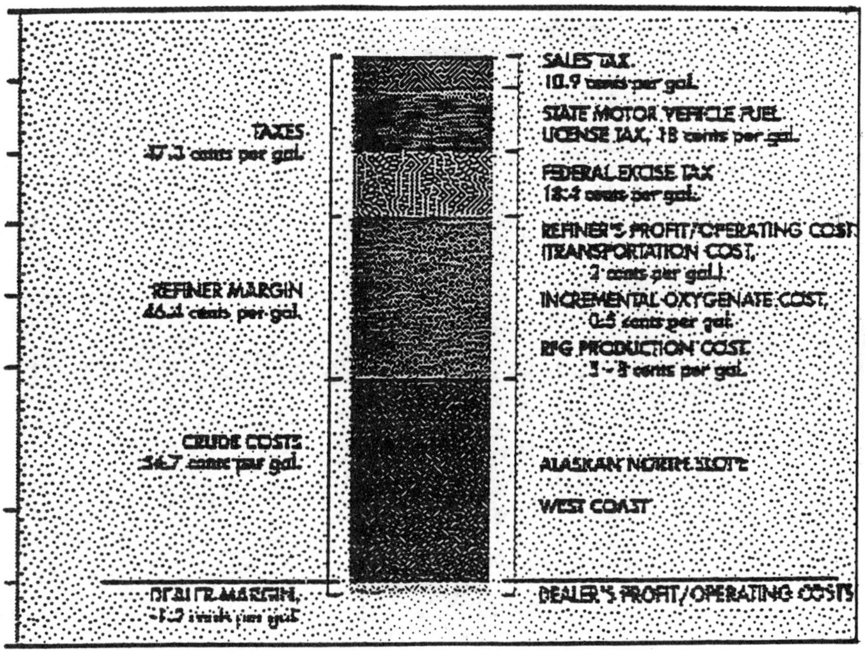

EXHIBIT 3

figure 5

MOTOR GASOLINE
DECEMBER, 1995 • $1.15 PER GALLON

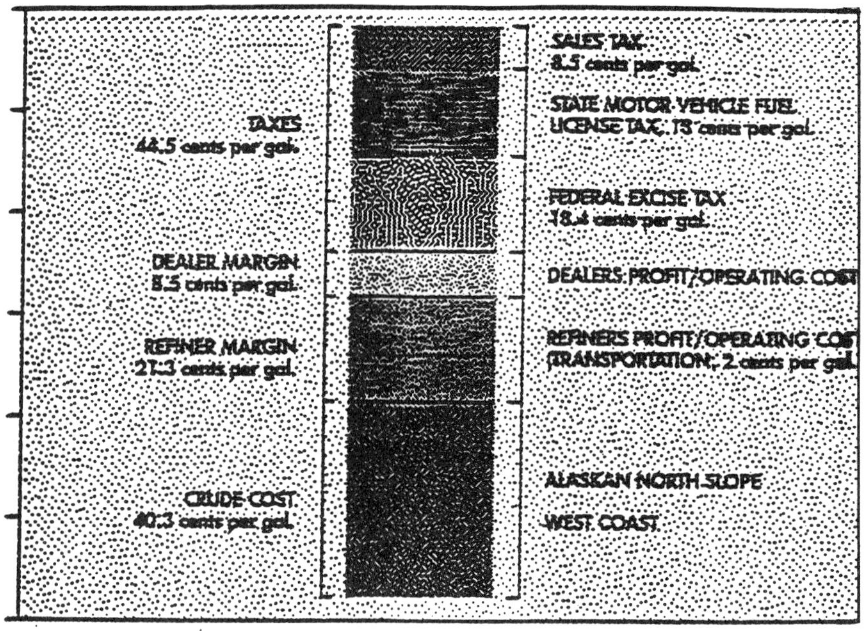

§ 5.11 Class Action Complaint (*Marquart* Case)

Timothy D. Cohelan, Esq. (CA State Bar #60827)
Isam C. Khoury, Esq. (CA State Bar #58759)
William C. Herring, Esq. (CA State Bar #144899)
J. Mark McNeill, Esq. (CA State Bar #153531)
COHELAN & KHOURY
701 "C" Street
San Diego, California 92101-5307
Telephone: (619) 595-3001

Attorneys for Plaintiffs

SUPERIOR COURT OF CALIFORNIA

COUNTY OF ORANGE

WESLEY MARQUART; on behalf of themselves and all others similarly situated, Plaintiffs, v. CHARTWELL FINANCIAL, a California corporation; an individual; CORPORATION, a Delaware corporation; a law firm; an individual; an individual; DOES 1-1000, inclusive, Defendants.	Case No. COMPLAINT FOR: 1. Intentional Misrepresentation and Fraudulent Concealment; Aiding and Abetting 2. Breach of Fiduciary Duties; Aiding and Abetting 3. Negligent Misrepresentations and Omissions 4. Violation of Corporations Code §§25110, 25120 5. Violation of Corporations Code §§25400(d), 25401, 25501 and 25504.1 6. Negligence CLASS ACTION (Plaintiff Class) (Cal. Code Civ. Proc. §382)

I.

INTRODUCTION

1. This case arises out of the financial collapse of a group of related trusts and business entities organized, assembled and financed through a California corporation – Chartwell Financial, Inc. Beginning in 1989, a variety of limited partnerships, trusts and other securities offerings (sometimes hereinafter referred to as the "trusts") were organized and sold by Chartwell and its predecessors. Over $10 million was raised through sales primarily to California investors. These securities were purportedly exempt from federal and state securities laws. Chartwell personnel and various brokers and investment advisors told the Chartwell investors that all of Chartwell's investments were fully secured and that audits of the "asset-based lenders" would be conducted by "Big Six" accounting firms. Chartwell touted itself as managing "loans" in excess of $170 million on an annual basis.

2. Chartwell investors purchased participation interests in commercial and medical "accounts receivable." Chartwell described "asset-based lending" as a banking function in which loans were made against "accounts receivable" for the services of various health care providers and other commercial accounts. This is commonly known as "factoring." Short-term loans with a maximum term of ninety days were supposedly underlying the investors' notes. The medical trust investors were told that the loans were secured by accounts receivable obligations of the government and solid insurance carriers – Medicare, Medicaid and Blue Cross or Blue Shield. Although investors were told by the selling brokers and others, and by the offering materials, that Chartwell had never experienced losses, Chartwell ultimately collapsed when a series of bankruptcies involving its asset-based lenders completely undermined its financial viability.

3. By 1992 Chartwell had, through its own negligence and inadvertence, loaned the lion's share of its funds, after payment of fees and commissions, to two primary "asset-based lenders" – Park Helena Corporation ("PHC") and Health Care Finance Company ("HCFC"). Both organizations subsequently collapsed under circumstances in which the principals were accused of misusing all funds entrusted to them.

4. The Chartwell securities were marketed through a web of NASD-registered

1

broker/dealers, or "participating dealers." The "private placement memoranda," or offering circulares, were circulated by financial planners, most if not all of whom acted as registered representatives of these broker/dealers.

5. Chartwell and its principal then undertook a common practice and pattern of repeatedly lulling investors, who by this time had become concerned about their investments, by use of mailed "monthly status reports" and other correspondence, which sometimes included interest payments. These tactics only served to falsely reassure investors and plaintiffs herein that their investments were completely safe and that Chartwell would recover from its financial troubles. Copies of these documents were also provided to the original selling broker/dealers and investment advisors. Plaintiffs could not have known of the true scope and extent of the fraud or the unregistered nature of the securities until July of 1994, when Chartwell informed them of the futility of implementing the "Recovery Plan," which had previously been approved by investor vote.

6. These Chartwell investment products were and are unqualified, unregistered and nonexempt securities, and are presently valueless. As a result of the fraudulent and negligent conduct of the Defendants herein, the class damages are in excess of $10 million plus interest.

II.

JURISDICTION AND VENUE

7. The Orange County Superior Court has jurisdiction in this matter due to alleged violations of the California Corporate Securities Laws of 1968, as amended, and to related common law principles applicable to California residents.

8. The sales of the unregistered securities and the misleading statements and omissions and other violations of California securities laws generally occurred in Orange County and Southern California and therefore venue is appropriate.

9. Defendants and other out-of-state participants can be brought before this Court pursuant to the provisions of California Corporations Code § 25501 in that they participated in violations of California law.

2

III.

THE PARTIES

A. **The Plaintiffs:**

10. Plaintiff Wesley Marquart is now, and at all relevant times was, a resident of Orange County, State of California. Plaintiff Wesley Marquart invested $ in Medical Trust II and $ in Medical Trust VII.

11. Plaintiff is now, and at all relevant times was, a resident of Orange County, State of California. Plaintiff invested $ in Medical Trust VII.

12. Plaintiff is now, and at all relevant times was, a resident of Clark County, State of Nevada. Plaintiff invested $ in Medical Trust VII.

13. Plaintiff is now, and at all relevant times was, a resident of Orange County, State of California. Plaintiff invested approximately $ in Medical Trust II.

14. Plaintiff is now, and at all relevant times was, a resident of Orange County, State of California. Plaintiff invested $ in Medical Trust II.

15. Plaintiffs are now, and at all relevant times were, residents of Orange County, State of California. Plaintiffs invested a total of $ in TR4 Trust.

B. **The Chartwell Financial Defendants:**

16. Chartwell Financial, a California corporation, was founded in 1988 by Mr. served, and presently serves, as Chartwell Financial's president and sole shareholder and is a general securities representative registered with the National Association of Securities Dealers, Inc. ("NASD"). Chartwell was organized for the purpose of acting as the trustee of private offerings.

17. DOES 1 through 20 are affiliates, subsidiaries and related entities and the alter-

3

egos of Chartwell Financial, corporate or otherwise, who participated in and are liable for the actions herein alleged. Plaintiffs will seek to amend this complaint to allege the true names and capacities of these DOE Defendants when they are ascertained.

18. DOES 21 through 100 are other individuals or entities whose identities are presently unknown to plaintiffs who were officers, directors, or employees of Chartwell Financial. Plaintiffs will seek to amend this complaint to allege the true names and capacities of these DOE Defendants when they are ascertained.

C. <u>Defendant</u>

19. Defendant is the remaining officer (president) of Chartwell Financial and sole shareholder during the time of the violations. Chartwell Financial and were and are the alter-egos of each other.

D. <u>The Underwriting Defendants</u>:

20. DOES 101 through 500 were marketing entities which conducted and underwrote the unregistered securities on a "best-efforts" basis. Plaintiffs will seek to amend this complaint to allege the true names and capacities of these DOE Defendants when they are ascertained.

21. DOES 501 through 600 are officers, directors and persons otherwise subject to liability pursuant to California Corporations Code § 25503 for the underwriting violations (DOE Underwriters). Plaintiffs will seek to amend this complaint to allege the true names and capacities of these DOE Underwriting Defendants when they are ascertained.

E. <u>The Broker/Dealer Defendants</u>:

22. Defendant Corporation ( ) is a registered broker/dealer and a member of the NASD and the Securities Investors Protective Corporation, through which a variety of registered professional investment advisers offered securities, including the various Chartwell trusts.

23. DOES 601 through 620 are directors and officers of Corporation who are

4

otherwise liable for the violations of the Corporations Code. Plaintiffs will seek leave to amend this complaint to allege the true names and capacities of these DOE Defendants when they are ascertained.

24. DOES 621 through 800 are additional Broker/Dealer Defendants and their respective directors and officers, whose identities are unknown to plaintiffs at this time and who participated in the marketing of the registered securities and the transmittal of misleading statements as hereinafter set forth. Plaintiffs will seek leave to amend this complaint to allege the true names and capacities of these DOE Defendants when they are ascertained.

F. <u>Defendant Registered Investment Advisors/Agents</u>:

25. Defendant   is a registered investment advisor who sold the Chartwell Financial investment vehicles to one or more Plaintiffs herein.

26. Defendant   is a registered investment advisor who sold the Chartwell Financial investment vehicles one or more Plaintiffs herein.

27. DOES 801 through 950 are other registered investment advisors who sold the Chartwell Financial investment vehicles to members of the Plaintiff Class. Plaintiffs will seek leave to amend this complaint to allege the true names and capacities of these DOE Defendants when they are ascertained.

G. <u>Attorney Defendants</u>

28. The law firm of   acted as counsel to the trust and trustee and subsequently became involved in advising the trustee as to what step to take in connection with its modifications, as hereinafter set forth.

29. DOES 951 through 975 are other law firms or attorneys that acted as counsel for any of the Chartwell Financial-related trusts. Plaintiffs will seek leave to amend this complaint to allege the true names and capacities of these DOE Defendants when they are ascertained.

///

///

5

H. Other Defendant Professionals

30. DOES 976 through 1000 are other professionals or professional firms that participated directly or indirectly in the preparation for sale, marketing or sales of the Chartwell Financial-related trusts. Plaintiffs will seek leave to amend this complaint to allege the true names and capacities of these DOE Defendants when they are ascertained.

IV.

ACTS OF CHARTWELL FINANCIAL AND THE CHARTWELL DEFENDANTS

A. The Trusts: Unregistered and Nonexempt Securities in the Form of "Promissory Notes"

31. Beginning in 1989, a variety of private placement memorandums were circulated through the investment community in California. San Francisco-based Chartwell Financial circulated the private offering memoranda for "promissory notes" to investors, broker/dealers and financial advisors.

32. These investment vehicles sponsored by Chartwell and its predecessor, King & Company, included the following:

1) TR Income Fund ("TRIF"), a California limited partnership, organized on December 26, 1989 to acquire participation interests in commercial accounts receivable financing transactions generated by Concord Growth Corporation ("CGC");

(2) TR2 Trust ("TR2"), a California grantor trust, organized on May 18, 1990 for the purpose of investing as a limited partner in Concord Growth Corporation Credit;

(3) TR3 Trust ("TR3"), a California grantor trust, formed on September 26, 1990 to acquire participation interests in commercial accounts receivable financing transactions generated by PHC;

(4) TR4 Trust ("TR4"), a California grantor trust, formed on September 26, 1990 to acquire participation interests in commercial accounts receivable financing transactions generated by PHC;

(5) Medical Financial Trust I ("MFTI") was formed on November 15, 1990 to acquire participation interests in health care accounts generated by Maximum Finance Associates ("MFA");

(6) Medical Financial Trust II (MFTII") was formed on January 2, 1991 to acquire participation interests in health care accounts receivable generated by

6

MFA; and,

(7) Chartwell Medical VII-Short Term Trust ("CMSTT") was formed on May 15, 1992 to acquire participation interests in medical accounts receivable acquired from, or collateralizing loans made by, independent finance companies who originate such participation interests;

33. The trusts were characterized as California grantor trusts and organized with Chartwell Financial as trustee.

34. The trusts' stated intentions were, among other things, to reinvest the proceeds derived from the participation interests originated by the "independent finance companies" known as "asset-based lenders" or "ABLs" into new participation interests during the term of the trust and to liquidate the participation interests at the maturity of the promissory notes. The notes themselves were to have an initial term of ninety days and were to bear interest at ten or twelve percent.

35. Chartwell represented that the medical insurance trusts would make loans secured by the accounts receivable obligations of insurance carriers such as Blue Cross/Blue Shield or the federal government, i.e., Medicare and Medicaid. Chartwell stated that the distribution of "loans" would be represented as follows: forty percent (40%) private insurance carriers; twenty percent (20%) Blue Cross/Blue Shield, and forty percent (40%) the federal government. The medical financial trusts were to have all of their interests ultimately secured by medical accounts receivable.

36. These Trusts, or "secured" promissory notes, were marketed as an investment alternative for investors seeking a high rate of interest and capital preservation.

37. The Trusts were also marketed with an emphasis on certain "Safety Features" as stated in the respective offering material. These features included "[p]ersonal guarantees of Customers' principals," a "Full faith and credit guarantee" and "full audit to prevent fraud."

38. For all of the originated investments of Chartwell, Chartwell informed investors, broker/dealers, investment advisors and others by mail and facsimile that it had "experienced no losses" and that "Big Six accounting firms, including Ernst & Young, Deloitte & Touche and Arthur Anderson, conducted audits of all asset-based lenders who received funding from

7

Chartwell Financial."

39. Chartwell Financial declared it was organized for the purpose of acting directly or through other entities as the trustee of these private offerings and further held itself out as "engaging in investment banking activities." Plaintiffs are informed and believe that at no time was it formally authorized by state authorities to conduct investment banking activities, although it substantially undertook that function.

B. <u>The "Asset-Based Lenders" - PHC, HCFC and GCC</u>:

1. **The Park Helena Corporation ("PHC"):**

40. PHC was given an inordinate amount of the funds raised through Chartwell. PHC was subsequently revealed to have little, if anything, to do with the alleged purposes for which the Chartwell money was raised, as hereinafter set forth.

41. By June 17, 1992 PHC had filed a voluntary petition for protection from its creditors under Chapter 11 of the Bankruptcy Act. The recovery of the trust assets that were listed by PHC in its bankruptcy filing was uncertain. Shortly after the bankruptcy, the bankruptcy trustee further discovered that at least $1.3 million had been misappropriated by the officers of PHC.

2. **Health Care Finance Corporation ("HCFC"):**

42. HCFC was located in Richmond, Virginia, and received almost $2 million of funds from the trusts. In late March, 1993, a Petition of Involuntary Bankruptcy was filed by a judgment creditor of HCFC. By this time, PHC, the other primary "asset-based lender", had denigrated to a financial debacle.

3. **Growth Capital Corporation ("GCC"):**

43. GCC was located in Richmond, Virginia and together with HCFC managed over $4.2 million of Chartwell trust funds. was President of both HCFC and GCC.

8

C. Chartwell's "Loans" to the ABLs:

44. On August 13, 1992, after PHC's problems became known, Chartwell considered and in fact agreed to transfer all of the assets of PHC to GCC, owned and controlled by who proved to have misappropriated the funds of another entity he controlled - HCFC.

45. GCC was to be the beneficiary of a transfer of the PHC assets on or about September 1, 1992. This transaction was not consummated by Chartwell at the time solely because Chartwell felt that the cooperation of the principals of PHC was not "forthcoming."

46. Partly because Chartwell Financial's trusts were essentially the sole creditors of PHC, GCC entered into an agreement with Chartwell Financial, announced to investors on November 23, 1992, whereby GCC would assume the obligations of PHC. The agreement was described as designed to resume payments to investors and to recover losses from all of the Chartwell trusts. at the time already was managing a substantial portion of the Chartwell Financial trust funds' assets.

47. Notwithstanding the representation to the various investors as to the security of the accounts receivable, Chartwell Financial loaned funds to the "asset-based lenders" in sharp contrast to the careful audited process represented to investors.

48. PHC received over half of the funds from the Chartwell trusts, but in July of 1992 filed bankruptcy and collapsed in a "complicated morass of entities which had no legal relationship with each other." The trustee for PHC on the first year anniversary of its bankruptcy filing found accounting records incomplete, inaccurate and misleading, and evidence of a conscious scheme to defraud and mislead investors. Numerous corporate subsidiaries were shams calculated to deceive investors and others. Plaintiffs are informed and believe that none of the alleged subsidiaries of PHC were ever audited by a Big Six accounting firm, or anyone else.

49. The assets of these "subsidiaries" had little, if anything, to do with medical or health care receivables. Investors subsequently learned that the funds were used by the "ABLs" and their "subsidiaries" for personal purposes and a variety of other illicit ends.

9

50. HCFC, the underlying asset-based lender for many of the medical trusts, was likewise insolvent under circumstances suggesting fraud. misappropriated over $4,500,000 in class investors' funds.

D. <u>The "Recovery - Workout Plan" - October 1992 Through May 1993</u>:

51. Commencing on or about the date of the bankruptcies of PHC and HCFC, Chartwell Financial and began to transmit to security holders of all the grantor trusts copies of a "Workout Proposal for your review - TR Trusts" and a "Recovery Plan" for the medical trusts.

52. Proxy statements and note modifications were transmitted to each of the unit holders in or about May of 1993 requesting and soliciting the active involvement of the noteholders, in part, by representing to the noteholders that no funds would be recovered without approval by a special noteholder vote.

53. The representations made to the noteholders included that over $5 million would be recovered from the Workout and Recovery Plans and that a failure to execute and approve said plan would result in the loss of investment.

54. All of the broker/dealer defendants and the underwriting defendants were actively involved in structuring the noteholders modification forms, including, but not limited to, a purported arbitration clause and other active efforts to impede, complicate and discourage civil redress on the part of the investors, plaintiffs herein.

55. A summary of communications to investors and the broker/dealers clearly reveals the information selectively leaked to investors prior to requesting an important modification of their rights in May of 1993. The summary below makes it clear that the true state of affairs known to Chartwell Financial and ascertainable by the broker/dealer and other defendants was withheld from investors at the time they were asked to vote on the approval for the "Recovery Plan" as well as the modified promissory notes. In fact, the true state of affairs was only made known to investors on September 23, 1993, when a letter previously sent by facsimile to on June 30, 1993 by the trustee of PHC, was finally transmitted to investors -

10

almost ninety days after had originally received it. Plaintiffs are informed and believe that the reason for this delay from June 30, 1993 to September 23, 1993 was to allow and others to receive back the executed modified promissory notes in accordance with the modification solicited through the proxy statements.

E. <u>Summary of Communications to Investors and Broker/Dealers By Trustee Chartwell Financial and the Chartwell Defendants</u>:

<u>1992 Representations</u>:

Statement	Source and Date
Chartwell Financial experienced no losses - Big Six accounting firms conduct audits of all asset-based lenders who receive funding from Chartwell Financial.	Chartwell Financial handout - February 20, 1992.
Investor purchases of fully secured promissory note through an escrow account at an FDIC bank.	Chartwell Financial handout - February 20, 1992.
Participatory interest in the loans to the asset-based lender are secured with Uniform Commercial Code (UCC) filings, corporate and personal guarantees and further require the asset-based lender to deposit twenty percent of the financing advance.	Chartwell Financial handout - February 20, 1992.
Chartwell is ceasing its business relationship with Park Helena Corporation - Chartwell will transfer the Park Helena assets to Growth Capital Corporation.... Chartwell anticipates upon consummation the trust's historical need for liquidity will be unaffected.	Status report letter dated August 13, 1992.
The principals of Park Helena may have engaged in unethical conduct....Chartwell believes that ultimately losses to the trust, if any, will be made up by the trust's continuation of its participation business and thus will not ultimately affect the trust's obligations to its noteholders....	Status report letter dated September 10, 1992.
The U.S. Trustee and Chartwell Financial ...are in the process of preparing a joint restructuring plan...Chartwell's trusts are the sole creditors...Chartwell has filed suit	October 15, 1992 letter to investors.

11

against the principals of Park Helena to enforce their guarantees....	
The bankruptcy court did not release any funds to the trusts for the month of October. This resulted in the mispayment with the October 15th mailing...Chartwell anticipates the resumption of payments in November to the extent possible... approximately forty-five percent of the medical trust funds raised were placed with asset-based lenders other than Park Helena and are performing unaffected by the Park Helena situation....	November 6, 1992 letter to investors.
Chartwell Financial is pleased to announce the signing of an agreement with Growth Capital Corporation (GCC) of Richmond, Virginia. The agreement is designed to resume payments to the investors and to eventually recover any losses realized with Park Helena Corporation (PHC) in TR3, TR4, Medical Financial Trust I, Medical Financial Trust II and Chartwell Medical Trust VII.... is president of GCC and Healthcare Finance Corporation. They currently manage over $4.2 million of Chartwell Financial Trust Funds....	November 23, 1992 Park Helena Corporation (PHC) update.
Chartwell's...Growth Capital Corporation management of the trust is "on track".	Status Report - December 15, 1992.
<u>1993 Representations</u>:	
The proposal of the Workout Plan Chartwell has been engaged in with Capital Growth has been finalized and the final memorandum should be in the office in mid-week....	January 18, 1993 letter from Chartwell Financial.
Due to the bankruptcy of Park Helena Corporation (PHC) and the effect on the trust, Chartwell Financial, the trustee, has determined that it is necessary to modify the terms of the notes originally offered. This step is necessary in order to provide the trust with the needed time and capital resources to recoup losses that are likely to be incurred as a result of PHC's bankruptcy....	February 18, 1993 letter.
A recovery plan was developed in mid-October 1992 and has evolved since then.	February 18, 1993 letter.

12

On February 5, 1993, an exposure draft was sent to your financial advisor...Chartwell held meetings with... financial advisors and...broker/dealers.	
Things continue to move along favorably and quickly at Park Helena...we feel confident that we are in the final two weeks of getting the recovery plan and voting ballot to you and your financial planners. We are currently awaiting the final contracts and are in the process of changing Chartwell's procedure of loan management....	March 19, 1993 letter to investors.
Enclosed is a copy of our long-awaited Workout Proposal for your review and with it is your ballot...Chartwell has recently made some operational changes in order to better provide security for the investors.	April 7, 1993 Notice.
The Pallet Company is operating profitably. As of August 1993, the recovered assets will be managed by Chartwell Financial Group - CFG will be continually reinvesting all of the reclaimed assets until all investor funds have been made whole. The time period for this plan is three years to be extended to five, if necessary. The recovered assets will be deployed proportionally across the five trusts involved in the bankruptcy....	Park Helena Workout - Recover of Assets mailed to investors April 7, 1993.
We are happy to inform you that we received majority votes for approval of the Recovery Plan for the trust.	June 15, 1993 Chartwell Financial documentation.
The following is a letter from Chartwell and exhibits from involved parties that will bring you up-to-date on the status of your investment.	September 23, 1993 letter.
The Park Helena Corporation...a complicated morass of entities, many of whom had no "legal" relationship with... Park Helena...accounting records incomplete, inaccurate, misleading... appears to be a conscious scheme to defraud and mislead investors...value of subsidiaries and accounts receivable of (Park Helena) grossly overstated...ongoing fraud...factual dollar amount of accounts receivable a fraction of the number touted by the principals of PHC...PHC engaged	September 23, 1993 letter to investors with Exhibit "B" (a June 30, 1993 letter sent to Court-Appointed Trustee of PHC).

13

in the artificial inflation of the value of its accounts receivable as a part of what appears to have been a fraudulent scheme to generate investment funds....	
"Approximately half of the medical trust assets were invested by HCFC in Richmond, Virginia. HCFC was placed in involuntary bankruptcy by Healthline, a subsidiary of Blue Cross/Blue Shield of Maryland....We have served the president of HCFC in a civil capacity in order to make good on his personal guarantees."	September 23, 1993 letter.
<u>**1994 Representations**</u>:	
We are happy to report the continued progress we are making in implementing the "Workout Plan"....	January 15, 1994 letter to investors.
Healthcare Finance Corporation/ - In the case of HCFC we are waiting for the sister judgment in the state of Virginia...this will enable us to seize his assets. The trustee has also brought legal action against wife, who received money from HCFC....Park Helena Corporation - originally we expected to receive over $5 million in the liquidation of the estate. This was the assumption that prompted the Recovery Plan....Our recover plan relies heavily on the outcome of the Healthcare Finance Corporation...we are happy to report we have signed Settlement/Workout Agreement which will be filed with the court....	January 15, 1994 letter to investors.
Chartwell has a judgment against excess of $4,500,000. In addition, the court ordered that and his wife not spend more than $8,000 per month.	April 15, 1994
In the past fourteen months since the approval of the Workout Plan for the Trust we have continued to have one setback after another with the estate assets under the control of the bankruptcy trustees. This turn of events has made a tremendous impact on our Workout Plan. As a result, Chartwell Financial Trustee, has concluded that the Workout Plan is no longer viable.	July 15, 1994 report to investors.

14

F. **Collapse of the "Workout Plan":**

56. By July 15, 1994, each investor in the medical trusts and the TR Trusts was advised that, "Chartwell Financial has concluded that the Workout Plan is no longer viable."

57. The transmittal of the July 15th letter was the first opportunity that investors had to realize that the communications from Chartwell Financial and others were significantly deficient in imparting information concerning their investments.

58. On or about May 22, 1994, approximately two months before the transmittal to investors, Chartwell Financial and transmitted to the U.S. Trustee's Office a communication indicating a detailed understanding of the nature of the problems associated with the underlying investment.

V.

ACTS OF THE BROKER/DEALER DEFENDANTS

59. At all relevant times, each of the Defendant broker/dealers and the respective registered representatives or investment advisors (together sometimes referred to as "brokers" or "broker/dealers"), including Defendants represented and held themselves out to plaintiffs and to the public as possessed of a special expertise in the analysis and handling of securities investments and as willing and able of adhering to the customary and required standards of integrity, fidelity, knowledge and experience in advising their clients with respect to their investments. Defendants were registered representatives of and acted at all times pursuant to that authority.

60. A confidential business relationship was established between the broker/dealers and their clients, the investors, including a reliance upon the broker/dealer's or advisor's business judgment, and their exercising ordinary reasonable care in that degree of circumspection and diligence possessed of other financial planners and broker/dealers in the community in which the securities were sold.

61. Plaintiffs, and each of them, were inexperienced and unknowledgeable regarding investments in securities markets and particularly those of the type in which

15

Chartwell was involved, i.e., nonexempt private placements. Plaintiffs entrusted substantial sums of money to Defendant Chartwell on the advice, analysis and judgment of the broker/dealer defendants, and each of them.

62. The broker/dealer defendants agreed to act as brokers, dealers and advisors in connection with the sale of Chartwell trusts. The sale of the Chartwell trusts was accomplished by the Defendant broker/dealers for and in consideration of their receipt of commissions from Chartwell and its organizations. At all times herein, the financial advisors, broker/dealers were acting as fiduciaries for their clients and receiving compensation from the Chartwell organization for the sale of the securities hereinafter.

63. The broker/dealer defendants, and each of them, from time to time communicated directly with the plaintiffs advising clients to execute revised promissory notes. A reasonable inquiry would have revealed several things including, but not limited to, that the alleged audits were not being performed, that the Chartwell trusts were not a viable or reasonable investment due to, among other things, the financial woes and impending bankruptcy of the ABLs, and that the investments' safety features were misrepresented, such as the stated intention to provide for principal safety by diversifying the investors' funds among several ABLs.

VI.

CONDUCT GIVING RISE TO VIOLATIONS OF THE LAW

A. Violations of California Securities Laws:

64. Each of the initial medical trusts was not a qualified security or subject to any valid exemption and the sale in California to the broker/dealer network accordingly violated California Corporations Code §§ 25110 and 25120.

65. The note modifications and the accompanying solicitation and proxy material sent between April and June of 1993 further were violative of California securities law, since they were, in fact, subject to California securities law. These proposed transactions as consummated with investors in 1993 were, in fact, sales, offers or offers to sell and

16

otherwise affected transactions within the meaning of California Corporations Code § 25017, which provides in pertinent part as follows:

Sale; Offer or Offer to Sell:

(a) Sale or Sell includes every contract of, contract to sell, or disposition of, a security or interest in a security for value. Sale or sell includes any exchange of securities and any change in the rights, preferences, privileges or restrictions of or on outstanding securities.

66. Persons associated with the modification, including, but not limited to, the broker/dealers and financial advisors who materially participated in this important change in the rights, preferences, privileges or restrictions of outstanding securities are likewise liable as hereinafter set forth.

B. <u>Breaches of Fiduciary Duties – Misinforming Class Members</u>:

67. Defendants Chartwell Financial, and their predecessors owed a fiduciary duty to the beneficiaries of the trust and the investors who relied upon the superior knowledge and skill of Chartwell and its broker/dealers and investment advisors who represented to them that the underlying security for the participation interests was appropriate for persons interested in capital preservation.

68. Misleading communications from Chartwell and the advice from the broker/dealers, and each of them, was given in circumstances in which they knew, or should have known, that information necessary to make an informed decision on the part of the investors was not being communicated.

69. Defendants, and each of them, attempted to consciously structure a pattern of communications which was calculated to lull, deceive and delay informed and intelligent analysis of legal responsibilities. These communications provided on a quarterly basis by Chartwell through the broker community consciously and continually misrepresented the underlying state of affairs.

70. The information transmitted to investors by the trustee, including, but not

17

limited to, the monthly status reports materially understated the known facts at the time they were each solicited. For example, the true state of affairs regarding HCFC was only revealed to investors in the spring of 1994, when, in fact, the active attempts to secure a judgment against the principal of HCFC, and his wife, was well known to the trustee, or could easily have been discovered by others, including the broker/dealers, with reasonable effort.

71. The PHC debacle, first mentioned to investors in the fall of 1992, was likewise known to Chartwell and others well prior to the denouement. had an ongoing series of disputes with the principals of PHC who had previously threatened to place PHC in bankruptcy. Accordingly, this contentious series of negotiations with PHC's principal was well known to the trustee well before the actual filing of the Involuntary Bankruptcy Petition.

72. Additionally, at no time did make it clear to investors that PHC was not directly involved in the medical accounts receivable business.

73. Another example of the attempt to lull investors and to mislead them was the failure to acknowledge the trustee's letter of Ronald Durkin, received by on June 30, 1993 by facsimile. This important and critical revelation as to the true state of affairs with regard to PHC was only mailed to investors on September 23, 1993 ostensibly so that could secure executed copies of the previously transmitted amendments to the promissory notes.

VII.

CLASS ALLEGATIONS

74. Plaintiff Wesley Marquart is a purchaser and holder of a secured promissory note issued by the Chartwell Medical Trusts II and VII, and, as such, is entitled to bring, pursuant to California Corporations Code § 15701, and as a purchaser of a secured promissory note issued by a trust, a class action, on behalf of all or a class of such purchasers, to enforce any claim of those purchasers.

75. Plaintiff is a purchaser and holder of a secured promissory

18

note issued by the Chartwell Medical Trust VII, and, as such, is entitled to bring, pursuant to California Corporations Code § 15701, and as a purchaser of a secured promissory note issued by a trust, a class action, on behalf of all or a class of such purchasers, to enforce any claim of those purchasers.

76. Plaintiff is a purchaser and holder of a secured promissory note issued by Chartwell Medical Trust VII, and, as such, is entitled to bring, pursuant to California Corporations Code § 15701, and as a purchaser of a secured promissory note issued by a trust, a class action, on behalf of all or a class of such purchasers, to enforce any claim of those purchasers.

77. Plaintiff is a purchaser and holder of a secured promissory note issued by Chartwell Medical Trust II, and, as such, is entitled to bring, pursuant to California Corporations Code § 15701, and as a purchaser of a secured promissory note issued by a trust, a class action, on behalf of all or a class of such purchasers, to enforce any claim of those purchasers.

78. Plaintiff is a purchaser and holder of a secured promissory note issued by Chartwell Medical Trust II, and, as such, is entitled to bring, pursuant to California Corporations Code § 15701, and as a purchaser of a secured promissory note issued by a trust, a class action, on behalf of all or a class of such purchasers, to enforce any claim of those purchasers.

79. Plaintiffs are purchasers and holders of a secured promissory note issued by Chartwell TR4 Trust, and, as such, are entitled to bring, pursuant to California Corporations Code § 15701, and as purchasers of a secured promissory note issued by a trust, a class action, on behalf of all or a class of such purchasers, to enforce any claim of those purchasers.

///

///

///

///

19

80. The Plaintiff Class is defined as:

> all persons or entities which purchased interests in notes issued by Chartwell Medical Trusts I, II, or VII, or TR3 or TR4 Trusts, or any combination thereof, and were damaged thereby, excluding the DEFENDANTS named in this Complaint, their officers, directors, agents, trustees, parents, children, corporations, trusts or entities controlled by the Defendants and their heirs, successors or assigns, or other persons or entities related to or affiliated with the Defendants, or any of them, or the general partner.

81. Upon application by plaintiffs' counsel for certification of the class, the Court may be requested to also incorporate subclasses in the interests of justice and judicial economy.

82. The investors in the earlier trusts received substantial distributions from the investors in the later trusts, and were the primary recipients of the "Ponzi" arrangement, as hereinafter set forth. Many of the investors in (earlier trusts) were voluntary or involuntary "rollovers" into (later trusts) and, therefore, there is a substantial identity among the noteholders. Finally, the substantial commingling of partnership funds and distribution funds makes it inequitable and otherwise difficult or impossible to accurately trace the proceeds of capital contributions and income distributions without the presence of the (earlier trusts) participants and, therefore, investors in all five trusts (I, II, VII and TR3 and TR4) are proposed to be members of the class.

83. Substantial evidence of the unity of interest and the significant commingling of assets and business functions among the Trusts was provided to the bankruptcy court in a filing in connection with the Park-Helena bankruptcy proceedings. Accordingly, all class members are equal victims of the ongoing fraud and share common questions of fact and law, as between them.

84. The total Plaintiff Class consists of approximately 400 investors and is so numerous that the joinder of all members is impractical. This sum is the aggregate of the total number of known investors in each of the Trusts.

85. The Representative Plaintiffs' claims are typical of the claims of the Plaintiff Class because the WESLEY MARQUART and

20

and all Class members have sustained or will sustain damages which arose out of the Defendants' wrongful conduct in violation of California securities law and common law as complained of herein.

86. Plaintiffs are representative parties who will fully and adequately protect the interests of the Class members and have retained class counsel who are experienced and competent both in class action and securities litigation. Plaintiffs have no interests which are contrary to or conflict with those of the Class they seek to represent. The number and identity of the members of the Class are determinable from the records of the five trusts, and Class members may be easily and quickly notified of the pendency of this class action by mail.

87. Plaintiffs know of no difficulty to be encountered in the management of this action which would preclude its maintenance as a class action. Relief concerning Plaintiffs' rights under the laws alleged herein and with respect to the Class as a whole would be appropriate.

88. The likelihood of individual Class members prosecuting separate claims is remote and individual members of the Class do not have a significant interest in individually controlling the prosecution of separate actions. Additionally, the prosecution of separate actions by individual Class members would create a risk of inconsistent and varying adjudications concerning the subject of this action, which adjudications could establish incompatible standards of conduct for Defendants under the laws alleged herein.

89. There is a well-defined community of interest in the questions of law and fact involved affecting the parties to be represented. Questions of law and fact common to the members of the aforesaid Class predominate over any questions which may affect only individual members, in that by use of various newsletters and literature and other means of disseminating [misleading] information, the DEFENDANTS have communicated through means generally available to the entire Class. Among the questions of law and fact common to the Class are:

///

21

(a) whether California law, including but not limited to Corporations Code §§ 25401 and 25400(d), have been violated by the DEFENDANTS, and each of them, as alleged herein;

(b) whether DEFENDANTS participated in, and/or pursued the course of conduct complained of herein;

(c) whether the documents and statements disseminated to the investors, including but not limited to the private placement memoranda by which the trust investments were offered to Plaintiffs and the financial reports prepared by the internal accountants, omitted to state and/or misrepresented material facts about the business of the trusts and, in particular, about the trustees' conduct with respect to the assets of the trusts;

(d) whether DEFENDANTS materially misrepresented or omitted material facts necessary in order to make the statements made, in the light of circumstances under which they were made, not misleading;

(e) whether the DEFENDANTS, and each of them, acted wilfully, recklessly and/or with gross or ordinary negligence in omitting to state and/or in misrepresenting material facts or in aiding and abetting the making of such misstatements or in conspiring with others to make such misstatements;

(f) whether the DEFENDANTS breached their fiduciary duties owed to the members of the Plaintiff Class;

(g) whether the members of the Class have sustained damages and, if so, the proper measure of damages;

(h) whether DEFENDANTS' solicitations were targeted to appeal to potential investors who were interested in predictable and stable monthly income;

(i) whether investors were told that the underlying asset-based lenders would be audited in accordance with representations of Chartwell;

(j) whether investors received misleading and erroneous attempts to modify their rights in 1993, in contravention of California securities law;

(k) whether the securities as originally sold and modified were unregistered

22

and nonexempt and whether plaintiffs, and each of them, are entitled to rescission;

(l) whether the underwriters share corresponding joint and several liability therefor; and,

(m) whether the communications transmitted to all investors by Chartwell and its agencies were misleading or failed to transmit material facts and omitted to transmit facts and circumstances in which they might be misleading.

VIII.

CAUSES OF ACTION

FIRST CAUSE OF ACTION

<u>Intentional Misrepresentation and Fraudulent Concealment; Aiding and Abetting</u>
(Against All Defendants Except the Attorney Defendants)

90. Plaintiffs hereby incorporate by reference paragraphs 1 through 89 above as though fully set forth herein.

91. As plaintiffs in this matter and other investors became increasingly concerned about their investment and the roles and relationships to the subsidiaries and the "asset-based lenders", the investors were reassured repeatedly in the letters and communications outlined above. Such conduct took the form of written and oral reports to plaintiffs provided on at least a monthly basis and which were materially misleading.

92. These defendants had a continuing duty to disclose and to correct statements that they later learned to be false. For instance, the Chartwell Defendants failed to mention that no certified audits had ever been conducted and that the representations made as to the value, type, scope, collateral and security underlying the promissory notes were inaccurate and nonexistent.

93. It was further part of a conspiracy to conceal from the plaintiffs and other investors the true facts in order to lull said investors into a false sense of security and to

23

effectively defer any prompt and efficient redress of their legal rights.

94. The conduct of the Chartwell Defendants, Defendant the Underwriting Defendants and the Broker/Dealer and Advisor Defendants and DOES 1 through 950, and each of them, and their affiliated business entities constituted a fraud against plaintiffs, both by misrepresenting and concealing material facts as alleged above, which injured plaintiffs by causing losses as aforesaid.

95. At the time said misrepresentations and concealments were undertaken by said defendants, they had a fiduciary duty to the investors, including plaintiffs, to disclose the material facts misrepresented and suppressed as they had an ongoing duty to disclose any materially adverse facts about the investment.

96. When these Defendants, and each of them, made these representations, they knew them to be false; and these representations were made by said defendants, and each of them, with the intent to defraud and deceive plaintiffs, or were made recklessly, in that defendants had no belief in the truth of these statements, and were made with the intent to induce plaintiffs to act in the manner herein alleged. In addition, said defendants owed the plaintiffs a fiduciary duty to prevent the perpetration of a fraud on investors, and that said defendants' actual or constructive notice of the fraud and the intentional reckless and/or negligent failure to disclose the existence of the same to investors constitutes constructive as well as actual fraud on their part.

97. When said defendants, and each of them, failed to disclose information and suppressed information they had a duty to divulge to plaintiffs, defendants knew of the misleading nature of such omissions, and by these omissions, defendants, and each of them, intended to defraud and deceive plaintiffs, and intended to induce plaintiffs to act in the manner alleged.

98. Plaintiffs, at all times these misrepresentations and concealments were made by said defendants and at the time plaintiffs took actions herein alleged, were ignorant of the facts suppressed by defendants, and believed defendants' statements to be true.

99. Plaintiffs reasonably relied upon the material misrepresentations of defendants,

24

and were induced to and did invest with defendants as a direct result thereof. Had plaintiffs known the actual facts, plaintiffs would not have taken such actions. Plaintiffs' reliance upon the representations of said defendants was justified, and plaintiffs' investment decisions were substantially influenced thereby.

100. and DOES 1 through 950, and each of them, knew that Defendants Chartwell and were engaged in the fraudulent conduct as aforesaid, and that said conduct constituted a breach of duty and a fraud. Notwithstanding this, said defendants, and each of them, engaged in conduct as hereinbefore described which rendered substantial assistance to and aided and abetted the fraud.

101. With knowledge of the unlawful purpose of Defendants Chartwell and said defendants, and each of them, entered into an agreement to accomplish the aforesaid scheme, and by their actions assisted that scheme and result.

102. As a proximate result of defendants' and each of their conduct as aforesaid, plaintiffs were damaged, including, but not limited to, injury to their property and business, loss of principal investment, lost profits, loss of future income, injury to their economic credit, and other general and specific damages, all in an amount to be determined according to proof.

103. As a further proximate result of the aforementioned fraudulent conduct of the defendants, and each of them, plaintiffs have suffered, and will suffer in the future, pain, discomfort, fears, anxiety, worries and mental, physical and emotional distress, all to the plaintiffs' general damages in an amount to be determined according to proof.

104. Pursuant to California Civil Code § 3287(a), plaintiffs are further entitled to pre-judgment interest as a direct and proximate result of said defendants' wrongful conduct as hereinabove alleged. The amount of damages suffered by plaintiffs as a result of said acts was a sum certain, capable of calculation under the terms of the subject investments, and plaintiffs are entitled to interest in an amount to be set forth according to proof based on the terms thereof.

105. The aforementioned acts of defendants, and each of them, were done

25

maliciously, oppressively and with intent to defraud, and plaintiffs are entitled to punitive and exemplary damages in an amount to be ascertained according to proof.

SECOND CAUSE OF ACTION

<u>Breach of Fiduciary Duties; Aiding and Abetting</u>
<u>Breach of Fiduciary Duties</u>
(Against the Chartwell Defendants, the Broker/Dealers, Their Registered Representatives and Investment Advisors)

106. Plaintiffs hereby incorporate by reference paragraphs 1 through 105, inclusive, of this complaint as though fully set forth herein.

107. The Chartwell Defendants, the broker/dealers, investment advisors and registered representatives, acting in the scope and course of their employment, instituted a relationship of trust and confidence with the plaintiffs. The defendant investment advisors, broker/dealers and others had superior knowledge of the transactions which were to be funded by investment of capital from plaintiffs and had reason to believe that the plaintiffs would rely upon them. Defendant Broker/Dealers received compensation for their investment advice in the form of commissions and other consideration. Defendants therefore had a duty to investigate and to disclose all material facts related to these transactions.

108. Defendants failed to investigate, inquire or otherwise attempt to determine whether any of the promised audits were performed, or whether the asset valuations were reasonable or if the security/collateral even existed.

109. Because of their business, social and personal relationships, as well as superior skill and knowledge in the mortgage business possessed of these Defendants and DOES 1 through 950, and each of them, plaintiffs reposed the utmost trust and confidence in said defendants at the time plaintiffs decided to first invest in Chartwell Financial. At that time, and thereafter, by virtue of plaintiffs' investment and plaintiffs' transfer of funds to Defendants, these defendants owed to plaintiffs a fiduciary duty of the highest good faith, integrity and fair dealing. Said fiduciary duty extended to any rollovers as well as the continued obligation to monitor and protect plaintiffs' investments under the offering materials.

26

110. On account of their position as title insurers, and the position of public trust so held, Defendants owed plaintiffs a fiduciary duty to act with the highest degree of care and not to withhold any information that would materially affect investors' decisions to invest, to undertake any conveyance that impaired the security of that investment, or transferred/reconveyed it without express authority.

111. In doing the things heretofore alleged, Defendants breached the fiduciary duties they owed to plaintiffs.

112. Defendants and the DOE Broker/Dealer, Investment Advisor and Underwriter Defendants, and each of them, knew that Defendants Chartwell and and DOES 1 through 100, and each of them, owed fiduciary duties to plaintiffs as aforesaid, and that said conduct constituted a breach of those duties. Notwithstanding this, said defendants, and each of them, engaged in conduct as hereinbefore described which rendered substantial assistance to and aided and abetted said breach of fiduciary duty of Defendants Chartwell and and DOES 1 through 100 and each of them.

113. With full knowledge and awareness the above-described fiduciary relationships and duties and of the wrongful conduct of Defendants Chartwell and and DOES 1 through 100 and each of them, said Defendants, and each of them, entered into an agreement to accomplish the aforesaid breaches of duty, and by their actions materially aided and abetted in breaching the fiduciary duties of others.

114. As a direct and proximate result of Defendants' breach of fiduciary duty and aiding and abetting of said breach of duty, plaintiffs and members of the class have suffered the injuries and damages alleged above, together with interest thereon as provided by law, all in an amount to be determined according to proof at trial.

115. As a further proximate result of the aforementioned breach of fiduciary duty by defendants, and each of them, plaintiffs have suffered, and will suffer in the future, pain, discomfort, fears, anxiety, worries, and mental, physical and emotional distress, all to the plaintiffs' general damage in an amount to be determined according to proof.

27

116. Pursuant to California Civil Code § 3287(a), plaintiffs are further entitled to pre-judgment interest as a direct and proximate result of said defendants' wrongful conduct as hereinabove alleged. The amount of damages suffered by plaintiffs as a result of said acts was a sum certain, capable of calculation under the terms of the subject investments, and plaintiffs are entitled to interest in an amount to be set forth according to proof based on the terms thereof.

THIRD CAUSE OF ACTION

Negligent Misrepresentations and Omissions

(Against All Defendants)

117. Plaintiffs hereby incorporate by reference paragraphs 1 through 116, inclusive, of this complaint as though fully set forth herein.

118. Defendants, and each of them, owed Plaintiffs an affirmative duty to act with reasonable diligence to ascertain the true state of affairs and to disclose all necessary and relevant facts to Plaintiffs.

119. The misrepresentations and omissions alleged above at Section IV. E. above were made by Defendants negligently and carelessly and without any reasonable grounds for asserting them. Defendants, and each of them, knew of or should have known the true facts and that the representations made top Plaintiffs were false and or misleading.

120. Defendant   and DOES 951 through 975, and each of them, (the Attorney Defendants) played critical roles in the operation of all the business fraud of Chartwell Financial from their arrival on the scene in 1989. In addition to the activities and conduct outlined herein, the Attorney Defendants assisted in the "transmittal" of the investment funds from the Medical Trusts I, II and VII directly into TR Trusts 3 and 4. They prepared, reviewed, and transmitted the corrections to the prospectuses which were to be mailed to investors and relied upon by the investors in connection with all the Chartwell Financial offerings. For the reasons set forth herein, each of the prospectuses, as well as the various other materials prepared for investor review, were misleading because

they omitted the material facts relating to the underlying operation of Chartwell Financial entities, including the scope and extent of the fraud. The Attorney Defendants also assisted in the preparation, review and approval of various other communications sent to investors, such as the newsletters. The attorneys knew and expected that the work that they were performing and for which they were compensated would be relied upon by the investors and that their misleading work product would be transmitted to investors.

121. As such, the Attorney Defendants owed to the members of the Plaintiff Class, as investors in the Chartwell Trusts, a duty to prevent the promulgation of false or misleading statements concerning their investments. The Attorney Defendants, because they held themselves out as specializing in the field of corporate securities, must meet the standard of knowledge and skill of such specialists.

122. In this case, the surrounding circumstances included an offering circular in which the Attorney Defendants participated in the drafting that described Chartwell Financial projects as safe and that "there has been no prior performance."

123. The Attorney Defendants prepared false and/or misleading documents, including but not limited to the prospectuses, the purpose of which were to influence the Plaintiffs' conduct, i.e., to induce Plaintiffs to purchase interests in notes issued by one or more of the Chartwell trusts. These Defendants' knowledge regarding the purpose of these documents establish a duty to those whose conduct has been influenced (Plaintiffs herein). The Attorney Defendants breached that duty, as described herein, by, among other things, failing to disclose material information of which they had knowledge.

124. Had the Attorney Defendants performed a reasonable, independent investigation into the facts, Plaintiffs allege upon information and belief that it would have revealed, *inter alia*, that, since at least early 1992, Chartwell Financial had insufficient income from sources other than investors' funds to pay the 10-12% interest on the notes, and consequently, to make the monthly distributions to the Plaintiff Class. An independent investigation would have also revealed that neither the Park-Helena bankruptcy plan which commenced with the July 1992 filing, nor the now-abandoned 5-year "Recovery Plan"

29

espoused by the Chartwell principals, would be of any real benefit to investors and Plaintiffs herein.

125. From early 1992, the date of the organization of more than one of the trusts and just prior to the PHC bankruptcy filing, the Attorney Defendants, and each of them, knew or should have known of the existence of the fraud. A reasonable attorney processing private offerings would have known that the Chartwell organization was, in essence, a Ponzi arrangement which could only fail. Notwithstanding this awareness and likelihood, the Attorney Defendants assisted in the preparation, approval and marketing of the private placement memoranda for Medical Trusts I, II, VII and TR 3 and TR4 and, as a result, the class damages are in excess of $10 million.

126. As a proximate result of the Attorney Defendants' negligence, the members of the Plaintiff Class have been damaged in an amount to be determined according to proof at trial.

127. The Chartwell Defendants, the Underwriter, Broker/Dealer and Advisor Defendants, and all DOES, and each of them, likewise owed to the members of the Plaintiff Class, as investors in the Chartwell Trusts, a duty to prevent the promulgation of false or misleading statements concerning their investments.

128. The Chartwell Defendants, the Underwriter, Broker/Dealer and Advisor Defendants, and all DOES, and each of them, breached that duty of care by doing the things alleged herein.

129. In doing the things alleged herein, Defendants, and each of them, were also acting to aid and abet each other and Chartwell Financial. Defendants, and each of them, did so knowing that their conduct was assisting in carrying out the primary wrong and or in furtherance of a conspiracy.

130. As a proximate result of defendants' negligence, Plaintiffs have been damaged in an amount to be determined according to proof at trial, together with interest thereon as provided by law. These damages include injury to property and business, loss of principal investment, lost profits, loss of future income, injury to economic credit, and other general

30

and specific damages.

131. As a further proximate result of the aforementioned negligent misrepresentations of the defendants, and each of them, plaintiffs have suffered, and will continue to suffer in the future, pain, discomfort, fears, anxiety, worries, and mental, physical and emotional distress, all to the plaintiffs' general damage in an amount to be determined according to proof.

132. Pursuant to California Civil Code § 3287(a), plaintiffs are further entitled to pre-judgment interest as a direct and proximate result of said defendants' wrongful conduct as hereinabove alleged. The amount of damages suffered by plaintiffs as a result of said acts was a sum certain, capable of calculation under the terms of the subject investments, and plaintiffs are entitled to interest in an amount to be set forth according to proof based on the terms thereof.

FOURTH CAUSE OF ACTION

Violations of California Corporations Code §§ 25110, 25120 and 25504.1
(Against All Defendants Except the Attorney Defendants)

133. Plaintiffs hereby incorporate by reference paragraphs 1 through 132, inclusive, of this complaint as though fully set forth in this action.

134. The securities in the instant matter, and each of them, were sold in reliance on Federal Regulation D (17 C.F.R. 230.501 - 230.508) promulgated under the Securities Act of 1933 (15 U.S.C. § 77a - 77aa, the '33 Act). Limited offerings, however, are not without regulatory limitations in the states in which they were sold.

135. The basic qualification requirement of the California Corporate Securities Law of 1968 is Corporations Code § 25110. Pursuant to Corporations Code § 25102(f) and the associated administrative regulations, the sale or modification of these securities in California would need to conform to this exemption to be legal.

136. Violations and the otherwise inapplicability of § 25102(f) occurred when the

31

broker/dealers were compensated for their advice, and when sales of the security were made to more than thirty-five persons, including persons not in California, and no preexisting personal or business relationship existed between the offeror and the investors and the selling agents, and additionally the selling agents, the issuer and the broker/dealers and the broker/dealers were in fact compensated by the issuer and its affiliates for selling the product.

137. In doing the acts alleged herein, Defendants Chartwell, the Broker/Dealer, Advisor and Underwriter Defendants and DOES 1 through 950, and each of them, offered and sold securities in the State of California without qualification or exemption and in doing so violated California Corporations Code §§ 25110 and 25120.

138. Defendants, and DOES 1 through 950, and each of them, materially assisted said violations as hereinabove alleged and facilitated the sale of unqualified and non-exempted securities in violation of California Corporations Code § 25504.1. Said defendants intended by their conduct, or were reckless in not knowing that the proximate result of their conduct would be, to deceive and defraud plaintiffs and other investors.

139. As a proximate result of defendants' violations, and the conduct of each of them as aforesaid, plaintiffs were damaged, including, but not limited to, injury to their property and business, loss of principal investment, lost profits, loss of future income, injury to their economic credit, and other general and specific damages, all in an amount to be determined according to proof.

FIFTH CAUSE OF ACTION

Violations of California Corporations Code §§ 25401, 25501 and 25504.1
(Against All Defendants Except the Attorney Defendants)

140. Plaintiffs hereby incorporate by reference paragraphs 1 through 139, inclusive, of this complaint as though fully set forth herein.

32

141. The conduct of the Chartwell and Broker/Dealer Defendants extended through to a continuous and integrated series of acts, occurring from at least 1990 through to 1994, and said acts and communications were conducted over that period of time in connection with the transmittal of interest to the investors with communications that included misrepresentations, and with concealed information and omissions of material facts, and said conduct occurred on a continual basis through to the time of the solicitation for the amended promissory notes and the subsequent attempted securing of the release of important rights on the part of plaintiffs.

142. But for the continual communications from the Chartwell Defendants as hereinbefore set forth, the plaintiffs would have promptly attempted to seek civil redress and were without sufficient information upon which to understand that a claim had arisen. In addition, the wrongful conduct pursuant to § 25401 continued up to and including that time of the July 15, 1994 communication in that all of the communications were in connection with the sale of these securities.

143. The acts of Defendants Chartwell and   and the Broker/Dealer Defendants violate California Corporations Code § 25401 in that defendants sold securities by means of misrepresentations, fraudulent concealment and omissions of material facts as hereinabove alleged.

144. Defendants, and each of them, materially assisted said violations as hereinabove alleged and facilitated the sale of unqualified and non-exempted securities in violation of California Corporations Code § 25504.1. Said defendants intended by their conduct, or were reckless in not knowing that the proximate result of their conduct would be, to deceive and defraud plaintiffs and the other investors.

145. As a direct and proximate result of defendants' violations, and the conduct of each of them as aforesaid, plaintiffs were damaged, including, but not limited to, injury to their property and business, loss of principal investment, lost profits, loss of future income, injury to their economic credit, and other general and specific damages, and plaintiffs are therefore entitled to rescission or damages under California Corporations Code § 25501, all

33

in an amount to be determined according to proof.

SIXTH CAUSE OF ACTION

Negligence
(Against All Defendants)

146. Plaintiffs hereby incorporate by reference paragraphs 1 through 145, inclusive, of this complaint as though fully set forth herein.

147. Defendants Chartwell, the Broker/Dealer, Advisor, Attorney and Underwriter Defendants, and DOES 1-1000, and each of them, owed plaintiffs a duty of due care in the solicitation, offering, sale and management of plaintiffs' investments as hereinabove alleged.

148. In doing the hereinabove-alleged acts, said defendant violated that duty of care and was negligent in committing those acts.

149. As a proximate result of defendants' negligence, and each of their conduct as aforesaid, plaintiffs were damaged, including, but not limited to, injury to their property and business, loss of principal investment, lost profits, loss of future income, injury to their economic credit, and other general and specific damages, all in an amount to be determined according to proof.

150. Pursuant to California Civil Code § 3287(a), plaintiffs are further entitled to pre-judgment interest as a direct and proximate result of said defendants' wrongful conduct as hereinabove alleged. The amount of damages suffered by plaintiffs as a result of said acts was a sum certain, capable of calculation under the terms of the subject investments, and plaintiffs are entitled to interest in an amount to be set forth according to proof based on the terms thereof.

///

///

///

///

34

IX.

PRAYER FOR RELIEF

WHEREFORE, Plaintiffs pray as follows:

1. for compensatory and general damages according to proof;
2. for punitive damages according to proof;
3. for costs of the proceedings herein and prejudgment interest according to law; and,
4. for such other and further relief as the Court deems appropriate.

COHELAN & KHOURY
Attorneys for Plaintiffs

DATED: 9/21, 1994

By: J. Mark McNeill

JURY TRIAL DEMANDED

Plaintiffs demand a trial by jury of all issues so triable.

COHELAN & KHOURY
Attorneys for Plaintiffs

DATED: 9/21, 1994

By: J. Mark McNeill

35

§ 5.12 Notice of Motion and Motion on Special Demurrers and Memorandum of Points and Authorities in Support Thereof (*Dudley* v. *Jones*)

L.B. CHIP EDLESON
LAURA G. SCHAEFER
GRAY, CARY, AMES & FRYE
401 B Street, Suite 1700
San Diego, CA 92101-4219
(619) 699-2740/2820

Attorneys for Defendants

SUPERIOR COURT OF THE STATE OF CALIFORNIA

FOR THE COUNTY OF SAN DIEGO

SEAN A. DUDLEY, LESLEE DUDLEY, individually and on behalf of all others similarly situated,, Plaintiffs, vs. an individual, an individual, an individual, an individual, an individual, an individual, and DOES 1 through 20, inclusive,, Defendants.	Case No. NOTICE OF MOTION AND MOTION ON SPECIAL DEMURRERS Date: October 5, 1990 Time: 8:30 a.m. Dept: 32 - Honorable Jeffrey T. Miller ICJ [Telephonic Ruling] Trial Date: None

TO: PLAINTIFFS AND THEIR ATTORNEYS OF RECORD:

NOTICE IS HEREBY GIVEN that on October 5, 1990 at 8:30 a.m., or as soon thereafter as the matter can be heard in Department 32 of the above-entitled Court, located at 220 West Broadway, San Diego, California, defendants

-1-

08/16/90:LGS
20036732

will demurrer generally and specially to plaintiffs' complaint on the grounds that the alleged second, third and fourth causes of action fail to state facts sufficient to constitute a cause of action. Defendants also specially demurrer on the grounds that the complaint fails to state facts sufficient to constitute a class action.

These general and special demurrers will be based upon this Notice, the Memorandum of Points and Authorities attached to this Notice and served and filed herewith, the complete pleadings, papers and records of this action and such oral testimony and documentary evidence as may be presented at the time of the hearing.

DATED: August 17, 1990

GRAY, CARY, AMES & FRYE

By: [signature]
L.B. Chip Edleson
Laura G. Schaefer
Attorneys for Defendants

-2-

08/16/90:LGS
20036732

L.B. CHIP EDLESON
LAURA G. SCHAEFER
GRAY, CARY, AMES & FRYE
401 B Street, Suite 1700
San Diego, CA 92101-4219
(619) 699-2740

Attorneys for Defendants

SUPERIOR COURT OF THE STATE OF CALIFORNIA

FOR THE COUNTY OF SAN DIEGO

SEAN A. DUDLEY, LESLEE DUDLEY, individually and on behalf of all others similarly situated, Plaintiffs, vs. an individual, an individual, an individual, an individual, an individual, an individual, and DOES 1 through 20, inclusive, Defendants.	Case No. MEMORANDUM OF POINTS AND AUTHORITIES IN SUPPORT OF DEFENDANTS' GENERAL AND SPECIAL DEMURRERS Date: October 5, 1990 Time: 8:30 a.m. Dept: 32 - Honorable Jeffrey T. Miller (ICJ) Trial Date: None [Telephonic Ruling]

TABLE OF CONTENTS

		Page
PRELIMINARY STATEMENT		1
SUMMARY OF ARGUMENT		2
I	THE COMPLAINT IS DEMURRABLE BECAUSE IT FAILS TO ALLEGE FACTS SUFFICIENT TO SUSTAIN A CLASS ACTION	3
II	PLAINTIFFS DO NOT STATE CAUSES OF ACTION FOR FRAUD, CONCEALMENT, OR MISREPRESENTATION BECAUSE THEY FAIL TO ALLEGE THE FACTS UNDERLYING THOSE CLAIMS WITH PARTICULARITY	10

-i-

TABLE OF AUTHORITIES

Page

CASES

Altman v. Manhattan Savings Bank (1978) 83 Cal.App.3d 761 . . . . 5, 6

Bartlett v. Hawaiian Village, Inc. (1978) 87 Cal.App.3d 435 3

Bozaich v. State of California (1973) 32 Cal.App.3d 688 3

City of San Jose v. Superior Court (1974) 12 Cal.3d 447 5

Collins v. Rocha (1972) 7 Cal.3d 232 8

Committee on Children's Television, Inc. v. General Foods Corp. (1983) 35 Cal.3d 197 10

D'Amico v. Sitmar Cruises, Inc. (1980) 109 Cal.App.3d 323 . . . . 5, 6

Darr v. Yellow Cab Co., 67 Cal.2d 695 4

Fuhrman v. California Satellite Systems (1986) 179 Cal.App.3d 408 . . . . 5, 6

Hills Trans. Co. v. Southwest Forest Industries, Inc. (1968) 266 Cal.App.2d 702 11

Leeper v. Beltrami (1959) 53 Cal.2d 195 12

Occidental Land, Inc. v. Superior Court (1976) 18 Cal.3d 355 8

Richmond v. Dart Industries, Inc. (1981) 29 Cal.3d 462 . . . . 4, 8

Rose v. Medtronics, Inc. (1980) 107 Cal.App.3d 150 . . . . 5, 6

Slakey Brothers Sacramento, Inc. v. Parker (1968) 265 Cal.App.2d 204 9

Vasquez v. Superior Court (1971) 4 Cal.3d 800 . . . . 4, 8

-ii-

Yandl v. PPG Industries, Inc. (E.D. Tex. 1974) 65 F.R.D. 566 7

MISCELLANEOUS

5 Witkin, California Procedure (3d ed. 1985), § 661, p. 109 10

-iii-

Defendants .

respectfully submit the following points and authorities in support of their general and special demurrers.

PRELIMINARY STATEMENT

The plaintiffs purport to sue on behalf of 1,782 individuals who maintained deposits at American Thrift & Loan, a California industrial loan corporation, as of June 6, 1990. (First Amended Complaint, ¶ 5.) On that date, American Thrift filed bankruptcy. The deposits of American Thrift are insured by the Thrift Guaranty Association. Nevertheless, the plaintiffs seek to impose personal tort liability on various officers, directors, and employees of American Thrift. They allege fraud, misrepresentation, concealment, negligence, and intentional infliction of emotional distress. American Thrift is not a named defendant in this action.

This demurrer challenges two aspects of the plaintiffs' tort allegations. First, from the face of the complaint, the plaintiffs' effort to state a class action are inadequate and misplaced.[1] Second, the plaintiffs' fraud and related claims are too general and nonspecific to state a cause of action for

---

1 This demurrer challenges the plaintiffs' class action allegations based solely upon facts stated in the complaint. The defendants will present additional facts and legal arguments, beyond those appearing from the face of the complaint, in their opposition to the plaintiffs' motion for an order certifying this matter as a class action. For example, the existence of deposit insurance, and its effect on the class, will be established in papers filed opposing the plaintiffs' motion.

-1-

personal liability against individual officers, directors, and employees, rather than against American Thrift itself.

SUMMARY OF ARGUMENT

California law is well established that class actions are improper where plaintiffs allege negligence or seek emotional distress damages. Every plaintiff would have to establish damages and liability on an individual basis. Also, the plaintiffs in this case even individualize their claims for fraud, misrepresentation, and concealment. Although ambiguous, the complaint appears to state that each individual was told something different, most likely at different times and places and by different individuals. Because class actions are not intended to present an opportunity for hundreds or thousands of plaintiffs to come forward and testify concerning their emotional distress, or their reliance on specific and varied representations, the court should sustain the defendants' demurrer to the class action allegations.

The plaintiffs' causes of action for fraud, misrepresentation, and concealment allege that directors, officers, and employees failed to disclose a state law which required American Thrift to either obtain federal deposit insurance or close its doors. In addition, the plaintiffs allege factual misrepresentations concerning the financial stability of American Thrift. However, throughout their complaint the plaintiffs are vague and general concerning what misrepresentations were made and who made them. The following is typical:

-2-

> Plaintiffs [sic] DUDLEY were repeatedly given verbal assurances as to the adequacy and safety of their investment in said deposit account by the agents and employees of American Thrift & Loan, acting at the direction of the officers and directors.

Accordingly, even if these allegations were sufficiently specific to state a proper claim against American Thrift, they are far too general to state a claim for personal tort liability against individuals. As framed, the pleadings do not provide the court or the defendants with a proper framework for testing or measuring the adequacy of the facts and claims presented against each separate and distinct individual named as a defendant. No single defendant has anyway of knowing, or challenging, what, if anything, he allegedly did or said. The court should not allow individual officers, directors, or employees to be personally sued on account of corporate conduct absent claims stated with particularity.

I

THE COMPLAINT IS DEMURRABLE BECAUSE IT FAILS TO ALLEGE FACTS SUFFICIENT TO SUSTAIN A CLASS ACTION.

A class action complaint must contain allegations showing the existence of the requirements for maintaining a class action. Bartlett v. Hawaiian Village, Inc. (1978) 87 Cal.App.3d 435, 437-438. When the complaint on its face does not allege facts sufficient to establish a class interest, the class issue may be properly disposed of by demurrer. Id. If the court sustains the demurrer on these grounds, it must order the class

/////

-3-

allegations stricken from the complaint. Bozaich v. State of California (1973) 32 Cal.App.3d 688.

Authority for maintaining a class action is found in section 382 of the Code of Civil Procedure which provides, in relevant part:

> . . . when the question is one of common or general interest, of many persons, or when the parties are numerous, and it is impracticable to bring them all before the court, one or more may sue or defend for the benefit of all.

Under this section, there must be not only an ascertainable class but a well-defined "community of interest." Darr v. Yellow Cab Co., supra, 67 Cal.2d 695; Vasquez v. Superior Court (1971) 4 Cal.3d 800. Three separate requirements exist for there to be a "community of interest." They are: (1) common questions of law or fact which predominate; (2) class representatives with claims typical of the class; and (3) class representatives who can adequately represent the class. Richmond v. Dart Industries, Inc. (1981) 29 Cal.3d 462, 470.

In this case, the plaintiffs' complaint on its face establishes that the first requirement cannot be met. Apart from whether the class representatives have claims typical of the entire class, or can adequately represent the class, the complaint establishes that the predominant questions of law and fact in this case vary with the particular circumstances of each plaintiff.

/////

/////

/////

/////

-4-

For this reason alone, the court should sustain this demurrer and strike the class action allegations.[2]

Where each member of a class would be required to litigate numerous and substantial issues affecting each individual's right to recover damages, the requirement of a community of interest is not satisfied. City of San Jose v. Superior Court (1974) 12 Cal.3d 447, 459-460. For this reason, courts have uniformly held that a class action is inappropriate where plaintiffs either allege negligence or seek emotional distress damages. Fuhrman v. California Satellite Systems (1986) 179 Cal.App.3d 408, 425, overruled on other grounds, Silberg v. Anderson (1990) 50 Cal.3d 205, 213; D'Amico v. Sitmar Cruises, Inc. (1980) 109 Cal.App.3d 323, 326; Rose v. Medtronics, Inc. (1980) 107 Cal.App.3d 150, 155; Altman v. Manhattan Savings Bank (1978) 83 Cal.App.3d 761.

In Fuhrman, the court sustained a demurrer without leave to amend as to class action allegations where the plaintiffs sought emotional distress damages claiming that the defendant sent letters accusing them of illegally acquiring cable TV signal without payment. The court held the plaintiffs' claims were ill-suited for prosecution as a class action because each would have to testify to their emotional distress. Fuhrman, supra, 179 Cal.App.3d at 425. The court explained at page 425:

---

2 As previously indicated, this demurrer can and does challenge only matters appearing in the face of the complaint. The defendants believe the other two requirements for a "community of interest" are also missing. However, those arguments are based upon facts extraneous to the complaint. Therefore, those arguments will be presented by the defendants in their opposition to the plaintiffs' motion to certify this matter as a class action.

-5-

> The injury alleged in each of the first six causes of action is "severe intimidation, shock, distress, humiliation, alarm, frustration, harassment, embarrassment, defamation and disruption . . ." Perhaps no cause of action is less susceptible to a class action than one for infliction of emotional distress. Recovery in each case necessarily depends on the particular characteristics of each plaintiff. Every plaintiff will have a different degree of susceptibility and emotional reaction to the conduct in question. If the legal issues were common to all class members, the individual right of each member to damages and the extent of those damages would have to be separately litigated. While each class member is similarly situated in that each received the letters in question, each member must establish his or her right to recover on the basis of facts peculiar to his or her own case. The class action is inappropriate in such a case. (Citations.) [Emphasis added.]

For similar reasons, the courts disallow class actions for negligence claims. See D'Amico v. Sitmar Cruises, Inc. (1980) 109 Cal.App.3d 323, 326; Fuhrman v. California Satellite Systems, supra, 179 Cal.App.3d at 424; Rose v. Medtronics, Inc. (1980) 107 Cal.App.3d 150, 155; Altman v. Manhattan Savings Bank (1978) 83 Cal.App.3d 761. The courts have recognized that negligence actions give rise to damages dependent upon the testimony of individual plaintiffs. As the court in Rose explained at page 155:

> In general, mass tort actions for personal injuries are not appropriate for class action treatment, (citations), in that the major elements in tort actions for personal injuries - liability, causation, and damages - may vary widely from claim to claim. Reluctance to extend class action treatment to mass torts governs even those types of claims which necessarily contain common questions of law and fact. . . . Consolidation of actions is the preferred procedure for disposition of such causes. The reasons behind the reluctance to process mass torts as class

-6-

> actions are twofold: first, the great importance of tort claims for personal injuries to the claimants themselves and the consequent desire of claimants to be represented by counsel of their own choosing rather than by strangers, and second, the wide disparity in damages that ordinarily arises from such claims.

Moreover, the court in Rose distinguished between "single mass accident cases" and those cases, such as this one, which allege multiple breaches of duty over a period of time and involve multiple defendants. As the Rose court explained at page 156:

> [Mass accident cases] have normally involved a single tragic happening which caused physical harm or property damage to a group of people, and affirmative defenses are absent. Usually, one set of operative facts will establish liability. Here the nine defendants acted differently at different times. The court is in agreement with the defendant that there is not a single act of negligence or proximate cause which would apply to each potential class member and each defendant in this case. (Quoting Yandl v. PPG Industries, Inc. (E.D. Tex. 1974) 65 F.R.D. 566, 571.)

In this case, as in Fuhrman, plaintiffs seek emotional distress damages and even allege a separate cause of action for emotional distress. (First Amended Complaint, ¶¶ 49 and 50.) Paragraph 49 of the seventh cause of action alleges that plaintiffs "have been subjected to embarrassment, humiliation, and mental anguish" due to the alleged conduct of the defendants. Each of the 1,782 plaintiffs would have to come forward to testify regarding the extent of his or her emotional distress damages, if any. It is for this very same reason that the Fuhrman court refused to permit plaintiffs to entertain their class action.

/////

-7-

Not only would damages vary, but the facts needed to establish liability would also be diverse and dependent upon a different set of facts. The plaintiffs allege different factual scenarios with multiple defendants. This action involves the conduct of six different defendants who necessarily acted differently at different times. Some defendants are outside directors who will be held to a different standard of care. This case does not involve a single act of alleged negligence but multiple acts involving multiple players over an indefinite time period. Moreover, the plaintiffs did not all become depositors the same day. The representations made to depositors, the truth of the representations, and any justified reliance will greatly depend upon when deposits were made.

A similar argument applies to plaintiffs' claims for misrepresentation, concealment, and fraud. Although California courts permit class actions for fraud, they do so only under limited and specific factual circumstances, where the alleged fraud arose from a single set of operative facts. Several California Supreme Court cases are instructive on this point.

For example, in <u>Richmond</u> v. <u>Dart Industries, Inc.</u>, <u>supra</u>, 29 Cal.3d 462, the alleged misrepresentations were contained in a written "Final Subdivision Public Report" distributed to each class member. In <u>Occidental Land, Inc.</u> v. <u>Superior Court</u> (1976) 18 Cal.3d 355, 361, the plaintiffs again alleged misrepresentations contained in a "Final Subdivision Public Report." In <u>Collins</u> v. <u>Rocha</u> (1972) 7 Cal.3d 232, 237, the court permitted a class of farmworkers to pursue a class action

/////

-8-

only because false representations were allegedly made at one time and one place by a farm labor contractor.

In Vasquez v. Superior Court, 4 Cal.3d 800, consumer plaintiffs alleged that the defendant made fraudulent misrepresentations to them when they purchased frozen food and freezers. The court held that the plaintiffs could establish their right to recover on a class basis because the defendant utilized a uniform or standard sales approach which made use of a memorized statement. The Vasquez court distinguished a case almost identical to that alleged by the plaintiffs here, Slakey Brothers Sacramento, Inc. v. Parker (1968) 265 Cal.App.2d 204, stating at page 819:

> Slakey Brothers Sacramento, Inc. v. Parker . . . was a class action for fraud by some of the creditors of an insolvent subdivider suing on behalf of themselves and other creditors. It was alleged that defendants concealed the subdivider's financial peril, causing plaintiffs to refrain from attempts to collect their debts. The alleged misrepresentations were in form and motive communications so varied as to "exhaust the legal possibilities"; some of them were made to the purported class as a group, others only to some, and still others to public officers. It was held that proof that misrepresentations reached each creditor was required and that the reliance of each creditor upon the misrepresentations which reached him would have to be shown individually.

Plaintiffs here do not allege representations made only in a single written document. Nor do they rely on a "common sales recitation." It cannot be seriously maintained, nor do plaintiffs allege, that all six defendants, in unison, orally made misrepresentations to all 1,782 plaintiffs as a group. Instead, it is apparent from a reading of the complaint that each

-9-

individual plaintiff was told something different, at a different time, at a different place, in a different manner, by different individuals.

The plaintiffs have alleged claims which require that each of them testify individually to establish when they made deposits with American Thrift, when they received information (misrepresentations) concerning the financial condition of American Thrift, who made misrepresentations to them and what were the misrepresentations, and finally the nature and extent of any emotional distress or other consequential loss which they suffered beyond the amount of their deposits (which are insured and should be paid prior to any trial of this action). In reality, the plaintiffs' claims have nothing in common other than the legal issue of whether the various officers, directors, and employees of American Thrift owed them a duty of disclosure. That simple legal question does not override the diverse factual and legal issues presented by the plaintiffs' allegations. In short, the plaintiffs' claims are extremely ill-suited for prosecution as a class action, yet each plaintiff could bring an individual action which would provide a sufficient legal remedy for any uncompensated damages suffered.

II

PLAINTIFFS DO NOT STATE CAUSES OF ACTION FOR FRAUD, CONCEALMENT, OR MISREPRESENTATION BECAUSE THEY FAIL TO ALLEGE THE FACTS UNDERLYING THOSE CLAIMS WITH PARTICULARITY.

The elements of fraud are: (1) representations; (2) falsity; (3) intent to deceive; and (4) reliance resulting in

-10-

damage. 5 Witkin, California Procedure (3d ed. 1985), § 661, p. 109.

Fraud actions are subject to strict requirements of particularity in pleading. Committee on Children's Television, Inc. v. General Foods Corp. (1983) 35 Cal.3d 197, 216. This specificity requirement serves two purposes. It furnishes a defendant with certain definite charges which can be intelligently met, and it enables the court to determine whether, on the facts pled, there is any foundation for the charge of fraud. Id.

In Hills Trans. Co. v. Southwest Forest Industries, Inc. (1968) 266 Cal.App.2d 702, 707-708, the court sustained both general and special demurrers because:

> No specific facts were pleaded to show how, when, where, to whom, and by what means the representations were tendered, from what data the falsity of [defendants'] intentions could be inferred, or how, when, where, through whom, and in what circumstances [plaintiff] became justified in relying upon these representations.

In this case, as in Hills Trans. Co., plaintiff's allegations of fraud are devoid of the required specific statement of facts as to when, to whom, by whom, and by what means the alleged representations were transmitted to the plaintiffs. Paragraphs 9 through 15 constitute the representations allegedly made in their entirety. These paragraphs do not identify which defendants, if any, made the alleged representations. The most the plaintiffs allege is in paragraph 9, as to plaintiff DUDLEY, and in paragraph 15, as to plaintiff where the plaintiffs merely state that the representations were made by "agents and employees of American Thrift & Loan, acting at the

-11-

direction of the officers and directors." (First Amended Complaint, ¶ 9.) The mere statement that representations were made by employees of American Thrift is not the specificity contemplated by Hills Trans. Co., nor is it fair to force an individual to defend himself against personal liability for corporate debts based upon such vague and general conclusions of fact.

Plaintiff's second, third, and fourth causes of action for misrepresentation, negligent misrepresentation, and concealment are based on, and incorporate by reference, the allegations from the first cause of action for fraud. (First Amended Complaint, ¶¶ 22, 28 and 32.) Each of these causes of action merely lump together the defendants. For example, paragraph 23 states that "defendant directors, officers, agents and employees of American Thrift" engaged in a course of misrepresentation. Paragraph 29 states that "defendants, and each of them" concealed facts. Similarly, the fourth cause of action for negligent misrepresentation alleges that "defendants, and each of them, their agents and employees" misrepresented facts. Again, as with the first cause of action, neither the court nor the defendants can ascertain which of the defendants, if any, engaged in the alleged wrongdoing. Thus, the court should sustain the demurrer as to these causes of action as well. The rule that fraud must be pleaded with particularity applies to these causes of action because, like fraud, they are claims based on alleged misrepresentations. Leeper v. Beltrami (1959) 53 Cal.2d 195, 216 ("Where the cause of action depends upon the proof of the fraud, the facts constituting the fraud must be averred.").

-12-

CONCLUSION

For the reasons stated, the court should sustain the defendants' demurrer as to the class allegations and dismiss all unnamed class plaintiffs without leave to amend. In addition, as a separate and distinct matter, the court should sustain the defendants' demurrer to the first through fourth causes of action and require that the plaintiffs provide greater specificity.

DATED: August 17, 1990

Respectfully submitted,

GRAY, CARY, AMES & FRYE

By: [signature]
L.B. Chip Edleson
Laura G. Schaefer
Attorneys for Defendants

-13-

6 THE PRECERTIFICATION STAGE

A. TEXT

Sec.

6.01 General Rules for Precertification Activity and Conduct
- [A] Fiduciary Responsibility
- [B] Precertification Conferences
- [C] Demurrers to Class Allegations: The Reasonable-Possibility Standard
- [D] No Default
- [E] No Dismissal Without Court Approval
- [F] Mandatory Dismissal
- [G] Communications with Proposed Class Members
- [H] Precertification Notices
- [I] Limitation on Precertification Merits Rulings

6.02 Precertification Motions
- [A] In General
- [B] Coordination
- [C] Consolidation
- [D] Intervention
- [E] Complex Designation
- [F] Peremptory Challenges to Trial Judge
- [G] Challenges for Cause

6.03 Precertification Discovery
- [A] In General
- [B] Class Discovery
- [C] Defendant to Plaintiff Class

[D] Discovery from Plaintiffs to Defendants

[E] Document Depositories

[F] Interrogatories

[1] Judicial Control

[2] Interrogatories to Class Members

[G] Planning for Class Certification—Framing the Issues with the Class

[1] Discovery to Determine Class Composition

[2] Causes of Action

[3] Defendant's Conduct

6.04 References

B. FORMS

6.10 Plaintiffs' Memorandum of Points and Authorities in Support of Ex Parte Application for Order Approving Precertification Notice Concerning Class Action

6.11 Declaration of Timothy Cohelan in Support of Ex Parte Application for Order Approving Precertification Notice

A. TEXT

§ 6.01 General Rules for Precertification Activity and Conduct

[A] Fiduciary Responsibility

Filing a class action creates a fiduciary responsibility in favor of the class owed by class attorneys and representatives to absent members. (*City of San Jose* v. *Superior Court of Santa Clara County* (1974) 12 Cal.3d 447 [115 Cal.Rptr. 797, 525 P.2d 701].) As part of this fiduciary responsibility, counsel must pay careful attention to the precertification steps defined by judicial practice for the conduct of the action, its parties, counsel, and the court.

[B] Precertification Conferences

Local rules for class actions suggest early informal conferences upon written notice from any named party or the court (see, e.g., Super. Ct. San Mateo County Rules, rule 7.4.). Informal conference in chambers or open court can discuss and determine class issues, priority in case management, discovery hearings, and other pre– and post–class-certification questions. Most local rules provide that no evidence be presented at the informal conference, but they do require all parties to have sufficient knowledge of class issues to discuss proposed stipulations. (See Super. Ct. L. A. County Rules, rule 15.4.)

[C] Demurrers to Class Allegations: The Reasonable-Possibility Standard

The court should not sustain demurrers to class allegations as long as class treatment is a reasonable possibility. The court needs to schedule an evidentiary hearing and make a finding consistent with the recognized legal criteria. If it does not, it faces the prospect of error requiring reversal.

Successful demurrers should now be rarer than ever since case law has clearly informed the bar of the allegations that will not pass muster at the class certification stage. (See, e.g., *Brown* v. *Regents of the University of California* (1984) 151 Cal.App.3d 982 [198 Cal.Rptr. 916]—medical malpractice; *Fuhrman* v. *California Satellite Systems* (1986) 179 Cal.App.3d 408 [231 Cal.Rptr. 113]—emotional distress; *Collins* v. *Safeway Stores, Inc.* (1986) 187 Cal.App.3d 62 [231 Cal.Rptr. 638]—highly problematic damages; *Silva* v. *Block* (1996) 49 Cal.App.4th 34 [56 Cal.Rptr.2d 613]—police dog bites; *Kennedy* v. *Baxter*

Healthcare (1996) 43 Cal.App.4th 799 [50 Cal.Rptr.2d 736]—medical problems from latex gloves. See also Chapter 4 on adverse California case law.)

[D] No Default

Because class issues still need to be resolved, a defendant who defaults by failing to answer makes no admission in regard to the merits of class certification. The default taken when a rock performer failed to answer a purported class action against him was appropriately vacated. Since the class had not been certified and no provision made for notice, there was a jurisdictional deficiency. (*Kass* v. *Young* (1977) 67 Cal.App.3d 100 [136 Cal.Rptr. 469]).

[E] No Dismissal Without Court Approval

Pursuant to California Rules of Court, rule 365, a class action can be dismissed only with court review and approval, usually in a noticed hearing. Likewise, settlement must serve the interests of the class. (*La Sala v. American Sav. & Loan Ass'n* (1971) 5 Cal.3d 864 [97 Cal.Rptr. 849, 489 P.2d 1113].) The case law behind these rules is discussed in Chapter 9 on settlement and dismissal.

[F] Mandatory Dismissal

A class action is subject to dismissal under Code of Civil Procedure section 583, subdivision (b), if class issues are not determined within sufficient time for class members to exercise their options. (*Massey* v. *Bank of America Nat. Trust and Sav. Ass'n* (1976) 56 Cal.App.3d 29 [128 Cal.Rptr. 144].) This time period, which includes notice to the class, is five years from the complaint filing date. The five-year period may not include appeal. (*Kaye* v. *Mount La Jolla Homeowners Ass'n* (1988) 204 Cal.App.3d 1476 [252 Cal.Rptr. 67].)

[G] Communications with Proposed Class Members

Since time often elapses between the filing of a class action complaint and the formal certification hearing, the court needs to maintain the status quo by objectively reviewing communications with the class. The court's involvement preserves its ability to certify the matter as a class and helps prevent the action from splintering unnecessarily into many individual cases or becoming unmanageable.

Miscommunication to the class in a number of cases highlights the damage that can be done. In *Richmond* v. *Dart Industries, Inc.*, the defendant tried to discourage class membership. (*Richmond* v. *Dart Industries, Inc.*, (1981) 29 Cal.3d 462 [174 Cal.Rptr. 515, 629 P.2d 23].) An even more egregious example arose in *Bell* v. *American Title Insurance Co.*, which was settled by a court-approved "non–opt-out" arrangement for the class. Counsel for a competing class action filed at a later date sent numerous misrepresentations to class members of the first matter, saying that they could opt out of the settlement if they chose. The court fined the offending attorney $77,000. (*Bell* v. *American Title Insurance Co.* (1991) 226 Cal.App.3d 1589 [277 Cal.Rptr. 583].)

Judicial review of communications, however, runs up against individuals' constitutional right to communicate with class members. Since ethical constraints on contact with potential clients have eased, attorneys enjoy first amendment rights to communicate directly with members of an uncertified class. This right may extend as far as expressing opinions on the case and even, under certain circumstances, seeking formal retainer to prosecute an individual matter. Defendants may also communicate with an uncertified class, seeking to undermine class representatives in their claims.

[H] Precertification Notices

California expressly authorizes court-approved precertification communication. (*Atari* v. *Superior Court* (1985) 166 Cal.App.3d 867 [212 Cal.Rptr. 773].) A notice sends a neutral, court-approved message to class members, who are commonly confused about what to do. Often they need to know about the class action so they can make an informed decision on individual litigation. The notice should state the tolling of the statute of limitations for absent class members. It should also explain that they can wait without penalty to see whether the class is certified before filing individual litigation that may well prove needless.

[I] Limitation on Precertification Merits Rulings

A trial court order requiring the defendant to go to trial on major substantive issues before class issues, including notice, have been determined is an error requiring reversal. (*Home Savings and Loan Ass'n* v. *Superior Court, Los Angeles County* (1974) 42 Cal.App.3d 1006 [117 Cal.Rptr. 485]; but see Post-Merits Class Rulings and Code Civ. Proc., § 527.) *Green* v. *Obledo* restated the proposition that procedural class-action issues, including the composition of the class, must ordinarily be resolved before the merits can be decided. (*Green* v. *Obledo* (1981) 29 Cal.3d 126, 146 [172 Cal.Rptr. 206, 624 P.2d 256] citing *Home Savings & Loan Ass'n* v. *Superior Court* (1976) 54 Cal.App.3d 208, 211–214 [126 Cal.Rptr. 511].)

A quiescent defendant who allows adjudication of issues on the merits before class certification can imply a waiver of this limitation. (*Civil Service Emp. Ins. Co.* v. *Superior Court of City and County of San Francisco* (1978) 22 Cal.3d 362 [149 Cal.Rptr. 360, 584 P.2d 497].) The merits can be heard if the parties stipulate to bifurcation, separating trial of class issues from trial on the merits. (*Colwell Company* v. *Superior Court of County of Los Angeles* (1975) 50 Cal.App.3d 32 [123 Cal.Rptr. 228].)

§ 6.02 Precertification Motions

[A] In General

Certain precertification motions can set the stage for resolving the matter by identifying related litigation and reviewing its effect on the pending class action. Counsel should also consider assigning a single judge to all matters related to the class action.

[B] Coordination

If similar or related cases filed in different counties involve common questions of law or fact, the court usually considers a coordination motion before it spends much time on the matter. When all involved courts are aware of the extent of related litigation, the benefits to the class and the litigants can be more meaningfully analyzed during the class certification hearing. (Code Civ. Proc., § 404.)

[C] Consolidation

If individual cases pending in the same court allege one or more similar causes of action between the same parties, and if the court does not move to consolidate, counsel should bring a consolidation motion of its own. Consolidation saves time, focuses issues, enhances settlement possibilities, and cuts fees and costs. (Code Civ. Proc., §§ 378, 379.)

[D] Intervention

Before or after certification, plaintiffs may intervene under the circumstances authorized by Code of Civil Procedure section 387. (See the discussion of intervention in Chapter 4.)

[E] Complex Designation

A motion to designate a case complex may help in having one judge assigned to hear all matters. The Judicial Council has called for early and continuous judicial management to determine complexity and assign matters to one judge. (Cal. Standards Jud. Admin., § 19; see also, *Manual For Complex Litigation, Third*, § 21.213 (the court should consider the appropriate procedure for dealing with the certification issues).) The litigants, however, should be prepared before filing to anticipate problem areas and point out possible solutions to court.

[F] Peremptory Challenges to Trial Judge

When numerous parties will appear at various stages in the case, counsel must give thought to the potential application of challenges under Code of Civil Procedure section 170.6. For example, if one judge commences pretrial motion activity and subsequent Doe defendants appear and challenge that judge, do you need to start over? At the first case management conference, the court should establish a procedure that defines and limits which "sides" are "parties" for purposes of Code of Civil Procedure section 170.6 challenges.

[G] Challenges for Cause

Code of Civil Procedure section 170.1 governs the circumstances under which a jurist may hear certain matters, such as those involving relatives, defined as "persons within the third degree." The same section outlines additional bases for challenges, including representation by a law firm that previously employed the judge. Case law has not yet developed in the wake of the 1984 amendments to this statute, which added much specificity to the grounds and procedure for challenges of the trial judge for cause. Confusion can also arise when parties intervene in matters that were formerly consolidated under, or handled by, the same judge

§ 6.03 Precertification Discovery

[A] In General

California's precertification procedures countenance pretrial discovery sufficient to establish the community of interest as a "matter of fact" at the class certification hearing. The judge then applies the legal criteria to this "factual predicate." Denial of class treatment is an appealable order, stopping the absent parties in their tracks. The federal rule, by contrast, allows successive motions for class certification because of the court's inherent ability to alter, amend, or modify class rulings. (See *Stephen* v. *Enterprise Rent-A-Car Co.* (1991) 235 Cal.App.3d 806 [1 Cal.Rptr.2d 130].)

Discovery at the earliest stages of a class action typically focuses on the existence of the class and the suitability of the matter for class action. Substantial arguments arise over what is class discovery as opposed to merits discovery. The line is often unclear and difficult to define. For example, necessary class discovery against a defendant must include questions that in other contexts would constitute merits discovery.

Initial discovery in most class actions aims at class issues rather the merits of the case, although the differences are typically difficult to ascertain. Often plaintiffs lack information on the scope and extent of their class and seek discovery to that point. An example is *Union Mut. Life Ins. Co.* v. *Superior Court* (1978) 80 Cal.App.3d 1 [145 Cal.Rptr. 316]. Plaintiff's cause of action stated an informed belief in the existence of other similarly situated plaintiffs. Certain interrogatories from the plaintiffs sought information not to support the class action, but to enable plaintiffs to amend the complaint to state a class action on behalf of yet another potential group including members outside California. The court held this discovery to be appropriate, saying plaintiffs should not be denied opportunity to obtain further information simply because it was uncertain whether the discovery would support a national class action. A discovery referee can devote the focused attention necessary to produce solid precertification discovery recommendations, which are usually adopted by the trial court.

[B] Class Discovery

The key questions guiding discovery in the early stages of a class action are:

1. How is the class defined? Who are the class representatives, and what is their unifying interest or injury?
2. What are the common or similar causes of action? Classwide discovery should be conducted only on those causes of action alleging classwide conduct.
3. What are the elements of a prima facie case for the classwide causes of action?
4. What issues are critical to establishing of liability? Defer damages until later.

Once the class is certified, discovery can be organized around the remaining issues and dealt with in a simplified case-management order.

Imprecise or broad allegations may cloud the issues between the parties. Plaintiffs, defendants, or both may oppose efforts to clarify and narrow the causes of action. Plaintiffs assert that clarification can occur only after substantial discovery, and defendants contend that discovery is impracticable until the claims are refined.

[C] Defendant to Plaintiff Class

Discovery based upon the preliminary definition of issues may lead to a revision of those issues, which in turn may alter the conduct of discovery. Notwithstanding this fact, "discovery from class members is susceptible to being used by parties opposing class certification as a device to harass and embarrass and should be necessary only in unusual circumstances." (*Manual for Complex Litigation, Third,* § 30.12.)

The defendant's right to conduct discovery of absent class members is extremely circumscribed. Typically, the defendant may not conduct depositions or other burdensome discovery on absent class members, at least not before certification. After certification such discovery is permitted only under judicially controlled conditions.

In *National Solar Equipment Owners' Ass'n, Inc.* v. *Grumman Corp.*, the appeals court reversed the trial judge for refusing to certify the matter as a class unless the proposed class counsel agreed to full discovery, including depositions of the more than two thousand class members. The appeals court agreed that unnamed class members are parties for purposes of discovery, but the right to such discovery is not absolute. The trial court erred in making certification contingent on granting defendants full discovery rights. (*National Solar Equipment Owners' Ass'n, Inc.* v. *Grumman Corp.* (1991) 235 Cal.App.3d 1273 [1 Cal.Rptr.2d 325].)

Precedent for this holding included *Southern California Edison Co.* v. *Superior Court of Los Angeles County* in which the defendant had proposed excluding from the class persons who refused to appear for their deposition. The court held against this, stating that named plaintiffs often have little or no control over unnamed class members. The California Supreme Court stated that the trial court did not abuse its discretion in requiring Southern California Edison Company to subpoena unnamed plaintiffs to take their depositions. It said further that defendants should not be allowed to effectively stifle a class action at the discovery stage, either by imposing impossibly expensive burdens on the named plaintiffs or by chipping away at the size of the class by excluding unnamed plaintiffs. (*Southern California Edison Co.* v. *Superior Court of Los Angeles County* (1972) 7 Cal.3d 832 [103 Cal.Rptr. 709, 500 P.2d 621].)

Carlson v. *Superior Court for Los Angeles County* was the follow-up case to *Edison*. The trial judge included a cover letter that essentially required unnamed plaintiffs to submit to a deposition or opt out of the case. A writ of mandate vacated this order, because of the objectionable nature of the either/or notice. (*Carlson* v. *Superior Court for Los Angeles County* (1973) 33 Cal.App.3d 640 [109 Cal.Rptr. 240].)

Although defendants have no unfettered right to depose unnamed plaintiffs, selected depositions could very well be authorized under certain circumstances. Examples are damage information defendants need for their case and the size of the class. In *Spoon* v. *Superior Court*, (1982) 130 Cal.App.3d 735 [182 Cal.Rptr. 44], the trial court appropriately required unnamed class members to answer interrogatories about the identity and amount of their claims and their reliance on certain documents. This case, however, involved only 146 purchasers of condominium units, a considerably small number than the thousands of unnamed class members in the *Carlson* and *Southern California Edison* cases.

[D] Discovery from Plaintiffs to Defendants

At least before class certification, discovery from plaintiffs to defendants will focus on common questions of fact, composition of the class, and possibly the location of absent class members. See the discussion under [H], below.

[E] Document Depositories

Class actions, like most complex litigation, benefit from a joint agreement to place documents in one standard depository and have copies of the documents made available with shared costs. This arrangement cuts expenses for both plaintiffs and defendants. (See § 8.14 (illustrative form of Case Management Order).)

[F] Interrogatories

[1] Judicial Control

The court should attempt to control interrogatories. Discovery, when appropriate, should be modified by the trial court to reflect the circumstances and be based upon good cause. Except for contention interrogatories before trial, interrogatories should focus narrowly on important issues.

[2] Interrogatories to Class Members

In *Danzig* v. *Superior Court for Alameda County*, the court commented on the California law governing whether all members of a plaintiff class must answer interrogatories from the defendant. Surveying the relevant case law, the court concluded that unnamed class members were on different footing than named parties to whom interrogatories have been propounded. (*Danzig* v. *Superior Court for Alameda County* (1978) 87 Cal.App.3d 604 [151 Cal.Rptr. 185].) *National Solar Equipment Owners' Ass'n, Inc.* v. *Grumman Corp* is again important for stating the principle that allowing full discovery of every unnamed member of a class would probably eliminate class actions altogether. (*National Solar Equipment Owners' Ass'n, Inc.* v. *Grumman Corp.* (1991) 235 Cal.App.3d 1273 [1 Cal.Rptr.2d 325].)

[H] Planning for Class Certification—Framing the Issues with the Class

[1] Discovery to Determine Class Composition

California law permits discovery to get information necessary to plead a cause of action. A key case in this regard is *Union Mutual Life Insurance Co.* v. *Superior Court* in which the plaintiffs propounded discovery requiring the defendant insurance company to provide names and addresses of persons who might be class members. Plaintiffs also served interrogatories requesting information on disability benefits, including the amount paid each employee and additional information concerning the location of the class. The court ruled the plaintiffs were entitled to the information. (*Union Mut. Life Ins. Co.* v. *Superior Court* (1978) 80 Cal.App.3d 1 [145 Cal.Rptr. 316].) This case shows that plaintiffs should not be denied the opportunity to obtain full information simply because it is uncertain whether such information will allow a class action. In fact, this is precisely why the discovery should be permitted. (*Union Mut. Life Ins. Co.* v. *Superior Court* (1978) 80 Cal.App.3d 1 [145 Cal.Rptr. 316].)

In *Colonial Life & Acc. Ins. Co.* v. *Superior Court of Los Angeles County*, the Supreme Court held that the discovery of the names, addresses, or files of absent claimants with whom individual claims adjusters had attempted settlements was relevant to the subject matter of the class action. The defendant insurer was not entitled to a writ of mandate requiring the trial court to specifically prohibit counsel from seeking employment from other prospective class members as a result of certain information being tendered in discovery. Presumably, defendant feared additional individual actions in the event class certification failed. (*Colonial Life & Acc. Ins. Co.* v. *Superior Court of Los Angeles County* (1982) 31 Cal.3d 785 [183 Cal.Rptr. 810, 647 P.2d 86].)

The right to discover other similarly situated persons from defendant's records was also the subject of *Budget Finance Plan* v. *Superior Court In and For Santa Cruz County* in which this discovery was available to the plaintiff even after a demurrer had been sustained. (*Budget Finance Plan* v. *Superior Court In and For Santa Cruz County* (1973) 34 Cal.App.3d 794 [110 Cal.Rptr. 302].)

[2] Causes of Action

Because plaintiffs bear the burden of meeting the requirements for class certification, initial discovery should focus carefully on these requirements. Subjects include the constitution of the class, class members' geographic location, and the nature and extent of information on class composition.

[3] Defendant's Conduct

The uniformity of defendant's conduct is relevant to discovery during precertification. For instance, in cases involving printed contracts of adhesion that result in uniform commercial transactions, certification may succeed. (*McGhee* v. *Bank of America* (1976) 60 Cal.App.3d 442 [131 Cal.Rptr. 482].) If the action alleges a conspiracy, discovery must focus on multiple defendants to uncover some "juridical glue" binding them together. Otherwise, significant certification and manageability problems will arise. The defendant's conduct and underlying motivation are also important in terms of the policy issues raised by the wrongdoing.

§ 6.04 References

NEWBERG For additional discussion of absent class members, see 3 Newberg on Class Actions (3d ed. 1992), Chapter 16.

WITKIN See the following sections regarding precertification procedures:

- Interrogatories to unnamed members (4 Witkin, Cal. Procedure (4th ed. 1997) Pleading, § 288).
- Prior trial of liability issue (4 Witkin, Cal. Procedure (4th ed. 1997)Pleading, §§ 289–292).
- Default or dismissal (4 Witkin, Cal. Procedure (4th ed. 1997) Pleading, §§ 293, 294).

TRG **THE RUTTER GROUP** See the following sections in California Practice Guide: Civil Procedure Before Trial (CPBT) regarding precertification procedures:

- Intervention in general (CPBT, § 2:400 et seq.).
- Discovery in general (CPBT, Ch. 8).
- Dismissal in general (CPBT, Ch. 11).
- Consolidation in general (CPBT, § 12:340 et seq.).
- Coordination in general (CPBT, § 12:370 et seq.).
- Governmental claim as prerequisite to suit (CPBT, §§ 14:65–14:67).
- Communication with class members before certification hearing (CPBT, §§ 14:84–14:93).
- Rulings prior to certification hearing (CPBT, §§ 14:94–14:97).
- Discovery before certification (CPBT, § 14:135).
- Limited right to discovery from unnamed class members (CPBT, § 14:137).

See also the following sections in California Practice Guide: Civil Trials and Evidence (CTE) regarding precertification procedures:

- Challenges to trial judge in general (CTE, Ch. 3).

See also the following sections in California Practice Guide: Federal Civil Procedure Before Trial (FCBPT) regarding precertification procedures in federal class actions:

- Motion to dismiss (FCPBT, §§ 10:435, 10:436).
- Injunctive relief (FCPBT, §§ 10:437, 10:438).
- Summary judgment (FCPBT, §§ 10:439–10:444).
- Limited discovery before certification (FCPBT, §§ 10:518–10:524).
- Right to discovery from unnamed members (FCPBT, §§ 10:525–10:536).
- Limitations on communications with unnamed class members (FCPBT, §§ 10:537–10:550).

WESTLAW® See the WESTLAW Electronic Research Guide at the beginning of this volume.

B. FORMS

§ 6.10 Plaintiffs' Memorandum of Points and Authorities in Support of Ex Parte Application for Order Approving Precertification Notice Concerning Class Action

Timothy D. Cohelan, Esq. (CA State Bar #60827)
Isam C. Khoury, Esq. (CA State Bar #58759)
Diana M. Khoury, Esq. (CA State Bar #128643)
J. Mark McNeill, Esq. (CA State Bar #153531)
COHELAN & KHOURY
701 "C" Street
San Diego, California 92101-5307
Telephone: (619) 595-3001

Attorneys for Plaintiffs

SUPERIOR COURT OF CALIFORNIA

COUNTY OF

on behalf of themselves and all others similarly situated,

Plaintiffs,

v.

XYZ CORPORATION, et al.

Defendants.

Case No. 00000

PLAINTIFFS' MEMORANDUM OF POINTS AND AUTHORITIES IN SUPPORT OF EX PARTE APPLICATION FOR ORDER APPROVING PRECERTIFICATION NOTICE CONCERNING CLASS ACTION

Date: February 2, 1995
Time: 1:15 p.m.
Dept: 3, Hon.

CLASS ACTION (Plaintiff Class)
(Cal. Code Civ. Proc. §382)

I.

INTRODUCTION

This procedure, a request for approval to mail a precertification notice to the proposed class, is being employed at this point in the litigation in order that over two thousand County homeowners will become informed of the pendency of this action which could affect their rights, and in order that the potential for massive misunderstanding of classwide interests be eliminated. (See, Declaration of Timothy Cohelan, submitted herewith.)

The original complaint in this matter was originally filed on October 7, 1994, as a class action pursuant to California Code of Civil Procedure §382 on behalf of all persons who purchased a home built by XYZ Corporation in a well-defined area County, California, including the cities of This proposed class is defined in both the complaint and the attached Notice.

The purpose of the instant application is to seek approval of a precertification notice (attached hereto as Exhibit "A") to the over 2,000 homeowners, some of whom have been vigorously solicited by individual plaintiff law firms. (A certified equivalent Spanish version will accompany the Notice.)

If the present precertification notice is not allowed, present counsel believes that a **substantial number of individual filings will occur, which will tremendously inconvenience the Court and otherwise cause the matter to be unduly burdensome upon the court system.** The interests of justice likewise require that each and every prospective class member make an informed decision as to how they elect to seek compensation for damages sustained in connection with their purchase of an XYZ home.

II.

THE PURCHASERS OF XYZ HOMES LOCATED IN COUNTY ARE ENTITLED TO MAINTAIN A CLASS ACTION PURSUANT TO CALIFORNIA CODE OF CIVIL PROCEDURE § 382 AND THE LAWS OF STRICT LIABILITY.

California Code of Civil Procedure § 382 provides in pertinent part as follows:

> ...[W]hen the question is one of a common or general interest, of many persons, or when the parties are numerous, and it is impracticable to bring them all before the court, one or more may sue or defend for the benefit of all.

California Code Civ. Proc. § 382. Accordingly, this provision sanctions the use of this mechanism to redress grievances in accordance with class policy.

The requirement of an ascertainable class are met. Certain issues, such as those involving strict liability for construction defects and classwide expansive soil conditions, support a community of interest finding with damage questions capable of being determined by formula approaches. Vasquez v. Superior Court, 4 Cal. 3d 800, 94 Cal. Rptr. 796 (1971); Daar v. Yellow Cab, 67 Cal.2d 698 (1967).

2

III.

THE COURT CAN AND SHOULD AUTHORIZE A PRECERTIFICATION NOTICE OF THE PENDENCY OF CLASS ACTION IN THIS MATTER TO PRESERVE THE STATUS QUO AND ALLOW THE COURT TO LATER ANALYZE THE BENEFIT TO THE LITIGANTS AND THE COURT.

Unlike the lawyers who direct those gratuitous legal solicitation letters which currently seem to permeate our society today, the firm of Cohelan & Khoury, must seek court authorization for communication with proposed class members.

The complexity of class matters, and the Court's ability to analyze carefully certification questions, often lead to substantial delays in hearing complete and total certification issues in due course. In the instant case, however, since the California Code of Civil Procedure specifically sanctions the use of the class action device, early class certification will, and should, focus primarily on whether certain issues are common to class representatives.

If a substantial number of what would otherwise be passive class members (approximately 2,000+) file individual actions in the Superior Court of County, it will unduly burden this particular Court.

Present class counsel has heard homeowner comments such as, "We didn't know your case was pending", "I thought I had to sign up with another attorney" and other comments which indicate a general misunderstanding of available rights and which strongly suggest that at the very least a precertification notice should go out advising individual homeowners of the existence of this action.

The Court has authority to take this action pursuant to *Atari, Inc. v. Superior Court*, 166 Cal. App. 3d 867 (6th Dist. 1985). The Atari Court found a broadly worded notice permissible where the trial court had the advance opportunity of making sure there was no specific impropriety. Counsel here assures the Court that this Notice serves the beneficial interests of both the Court and the litigants. (See, Cohelan Declaration, paras. 5, 10, 13.)

///

///

///

3

IV.

GOOD CAUSE APPEARS FOR THE APPROVAL OF THE ATTACHED PRECERTIFICATION NOTICE.

It has been the practice of this firm to respond only to requests from potential class members for information. This practice is based in part upon *Colonial Life and Accident Ins. Co. v. Superior Court*, (1982) 31 Cal.3d 785. This, however, places class counsel in a situation of needing to respond to persons who are willing to place a phone call, but are unaware of this pending class action and the rights pertaining thereto. Absent a notice such as the one proposed herein, the present situation does not allow for an effective communication of the legal alternatives available to individual members.

V.

CONCLUSION.

The interests of class members and judicial economy will be served by allowing the attached nonargumentative Precertification Notice Concerning Class Action to be mailed in a timely fashion to the [proposed] members of the class. For the foregoing reasons, Plaintiffs request that the Precertification Notice be so approved and an Order be issued.

Respectfully submitted,

COHELAN & KHOURY

DATED: January 30, 1995 By:____________________
J. Mark McNeill
Attorneys for Plaintiffs

4

EXHIBIT A

SUPERIOR COURT OF CALIFORNIA

COUNTY OF

on behalf of themselves and all others similarly situated,	**Case No. 00000**
Plaintiffs,	**COURT-APPROVED PRECERTIFICATION NOTICE CONCERNING CLASS ACTION**
v.	
XYZ CORPORATION, et al.,	
Defendants.	

THIS NOTICE MAY AFFECT YOUR RIGHTS. PLEASE READ IT CAREFULLY.

TO THE PURCHASERS OF HOMES BUILT OR MARKETED BY XYA CORPORATION BEFORE JANUARY 1, 1994 IN THE FOLLOWING CITIES AND SUB-DIVISIONS:

[1] City of ______

[2] City of ______

[3] City of ______

[4] City of ______

[5]

Your rights may be affected by this lawsuit, v. *XYZ Corporation, et al.*, which has been filed and is presently pending in the County Superior Court, Civil Action No. 00000.

1

DESCRIPTION OF THE ACTION

XYA Corporation has built approximately 2100 homes in the subdivisions listed above, which are located in the cities of California. Representative Plaintiffs through their attorneys, the offices of COHELAN & KHOURY, have filed this lawsuit as a class action on behalf of all persons or entities who purchased homes (either as original purchasers or as subsequent purchasers) in those subdivisions built or marketed by XYZ Corporation before January 1, 1994, and who were damaged or may be damaged thereby. The First Amended Complaint in this case alleges that certain expansive soil conditions have caused or may cause foundation and structural problems to these homes, including progressive property damage, and that additionally certain homes in these subdivisions have other related defects (hereinafter "the defects"). Defendant XYZ Corporation denies each and every allegation and additionally asserts certain affirmative defenses.

This Notice has been directed to you as a member of the Class described below. This Notice is not to be understood as an expression of any opinion of this Court as to the merits of any of the claims or defenses asserted by either side in the subject action, but is sent for the sole purpose of informing you of the pendency of this action and the rights which you may have with respect to it.

On ____________________, 1995, the Court approved this Precertification Notice Concerning Class Action so that you might more fully understand that a class action lawsuit has been filed in this case which, if ultimately certified by the Court, may affect your rights. The proposed Plaintiff Class is defined as follows:

> All persons or entities which purchased, either as original purchasers or subsequent purchasers, homes in the below-listed CLASS PROPERTIES in County, California, in the cities listed below, and which were built or marketed by XYZ Corporation, and which were damaged thereby, excluding the DEFENDANTS named in this First Amended Complaint, their officers, directors, agents, trustees, parents, children, corporations, trusts or entities controlled by the DEFENDANTS and their heirs, successors or assigns, or other persons (except non-officer/director employees of DEFENDANTS) or entities related to or affiliated with the DEFENDANTS, or any of them.

The CLASS PROPERTIES are further divided into subclasses as follows:

(a) City of ________

(b) City of ________

(c) City of ________
Park;

2

(d) City of ______

(e)

The Court has not ruled on class certification. If the Court ultimately approves an order certifying this matter as a class action, you will receive additional notice. It is possible that such a notice may include a settlement proposal by defendants. Pursuant to that notice, unless you elect to be excluded from the class, your interests will be represented by the law offices of Cohelan & Khoury, the attorneys who filed this class action. If the action is not certified as a class, you will also be so advised so that you may protect your rights to pursue litigation in this matter. No action on your part is necessary at this time.

TOLLING OF THE STATUTE OF LIMITATIONS

Plaintiffs' counsel in this matter, the law offices of Cohelan & Khoury, believe that the statute of limitations on the claims of the individual class members has been tolled (suspended) by the filing of this matter as a class action. Class Counsel rely upon the case of *American Pipe and Construction Co. v. Utah*, 414 U.S. 538 (1974), wherein the United States Supreme Court held that, "The commencement of a class action suspends the applicable statute of limitations as to all asserted members of the class who would have been parties had the suit been permitted to continue as a class action."

This notice is provided to you for informational purposes only. You will not be bound by any class judgment or prospective class settlements, if any, without further notice.

RIGHTS AND OBLIGATIONS OF CLASS MEMBERS IF A CLASS IS CERTIFIED

If the class described above is certified and you remain a member of the class:

(a) and any other plaintiffs named in the lawsuit, and their attorneys, the law offices of Cohelan & Khoury, will act as your representatives and counsel for the presentation of the charges against the defendants. If you desire, you may appear by your own attorney. You may also seek to intervene individually and may advise the Court if at any time you consider that you are not being fairly and adequately represented by the Representative Plaintiffs and/or their attorneys.

(b) Your participation in any recovery which may be obtained from the defendants through trial or settlement will depend upon the results of this lawsuit. If no recovery is obtained for the class, you will be bound by that result also.

3

(c) You may be required, as a condition to participating in any recovery through settlement or trial, to present evidence respecting the purchase of your home or information relating to any alleged damages thereto. You should, however, preserve information and evidence relating to the condition of your home and problems related thereto.

(d) You will be entitled to notice of any ruling reducing the size of the class, reducing and allowing subclasses by subdivision with an opportunity to be heard respecting any proposed settlement or dismissal of any class claims. (For this reason, as well as to participate in any recovery, you are requested to notify the Class Counsel of any corrections or changes in your name or address.)

ATTORNEYS' FEES AND COSTS

As Class Counsel, COHELAN & KHOURY may be eligible to receive attorneys' fees of 25% of any class recovery. However, class counsel has agreed to modify any fee application to request fees of 17 1/2 % of any class recovery if settlement is effectively accomplished during calendar year 1995. This agreement is set forth in writing between the parties and is available for review in the court file. In addition, the Court may be requested to approve the reimbursement of costs and expenses incurred by COHELAN & KHOURY on behalf of the class in the conduct of the lawsuit. In any circumstance, attorneys' fees, costs and expenses sought by Class Counsel must be approved by the Court.

FURTHER PROCEEDINGS/SETTLEMENT NEGOTIATIONS

Settlement discussions may be held between plaintiffs' counsel and defendants. If any settlements are reached, you will receive additional notice with a full and complete explanation of the terms and conditions of same. As noted, the essential allegations of the charges against the defendants are denied by them. You may communicate with Class Counsel if you have evidence you believe would be helpful to the establishment of class claims. Further, you will be entitled to fill out and complete a full questionnaire in the future identifying all the background information concerning your home. Your cooperation with Class Counsel may be required to allow for testing and other site inspection of your residence.

ADDITIONAL INFORMATION

Any questions you have concerning the matters contained in this notice and any corrections or changes of name or address should not be made to the Court. If you wish to communicate with Class Counsel as your attorneys in this litigation, you may contact them by writing or calling:

4

Timothy D. Cohelan, Esq.
COHELAN & KHOURY
701 "C" Street
San Diego, California 92101-5307
Telephone: (619) 595-3001

You may, of course, seek the advice and guidance of your own attorney if you desire. **If you are currently represented by an attorney in a similar matter against XYZ Corporation, you may discuss this class action with your attorney. Nothing in this notice is intended to interfere in any way with any relationship you may presently have with any attorney.** The pleadings and other records in this litigation may be examined and copied at any time during regular business hours at the Office of the Clerk of the Superior Court, County of

§ 6.11 Declaration of Timothy Cohelan in Support of Ex Parte Application for Order Approving Precertification Notice

Timothy D. Cohelan, Esq. (CA State Bar #60827)
Isam C. Khoury, Esq. (CA State Bar #58759)
J. Mark McNeill, Esq. (CA State Bar #153531)
COHELAN & KHOURY
701 "C" Street
San Diego, California 92101-5307
Telephone: (619) 595-3001

Attorneys for Plaintiffs

SUPERIOR COURT OF CALIFORNIA

COUNTY OF

on behalf of themselves and all others similarly situated, Plaintiffs, v. XYZ CORPORATION, et al., Defendants.	**Case No. 00000** **DECLARATION OF TIMOTHY COHELAN IN SUPPORT OF EX PARTE APPLICATION FOR ORDER APPROVING PRECERTIFICATION NOTICE CONCERNING CLASS ACTION** **DATE:** **TIME:** **DEPT: 3** **Hon.**

///

///

///

///

///

///

///

I, TIMOTHY D. COHELAN, declare that I am licensed to practice law in the State of California and if called as a witness would testify of my own personal knowledge as follows:

1. I was admitted to practice law in California on December 18, 1974. I am also admitted to practice in the United States District Court, Central and Southern Districts of California. I have also litigated in the Federal Courts of Texas and New York, and am presently class counsel in a case set for trial in April 1995 in the Southern District of New York pursuant to the Multidistrict Litigation Panel. I am a founding partner of Cohelan & Khoury, which has been in existence since 1981. Our attorneys, including the undersigned, regularly try to a conclusion jury and non-jury matters. Our firm, and the undersigned, are "AV"-rated by Martindale-Hubbell.

2. Our firm specializes in civil litigation, with an emphasis on cases involving group relief. Class actions we have litigated have involved emergency shelter for the homeless, pension benefits, health insurance fraud, securities fraud, back pay and wages, unfair business practices, and other matters. We have prosecuted class action and other civil cases to settlement or conclusion which, together with our co-counsel, has generated over $54 million in class-wide recoveries since September of 1993.

3. Our firm has either been counsel or co-counsel in the following cases which were certified as class actions by state or federal courts:

(a) Bailey, et al., v. National Association of Professionals and Executives, Inc., et al., Case No. 92-260(IEG)LSP in the U.S. District Court for the Southern District of California, certified November 9, 1992 in the Southern District of California, re-certified July 1994 in the Southern District of New York;

(b) Alberts, et al., v. Service Technicians, Inc., et al., Case No. 92-526(H)P in the U.S. District Court for the Southern District of California, certified July 20, 1992;

(c) Goldman, et al., v. Pioneer Mortgage, et al., Case No. 91-0005 King(BTM) in the U.S. District Court for the Southern District of California, certified October 7, 1991;

(d) Beatty, et al., v. National Steel and Shipbuilding Company, Case No. 87-1602 JLI(M) in the U.S. District Court for the Southern District of California, conditional class certification/settlement;

2

(e) Dudley, et al., v. ______________, Case No. 625336 in the Superior Court for the County of San Diego, certified June 28, 1991; and

(f) Arthur, et al., v. City of San Diego, et al., Civil Case No. 639789 in the Superior Court for the County of San Diego, certified May 1991;

(g) Alpha Group Consultants, Ltd. v. ______________. Case No. 91-0143 IEG(HRM) in the U.S. District Court for the Southern District of California, certified 1993;

(h) Soriano, et al., v. ______________, Case No. 92-0953 AWT(Tx) in the U.S. District Court for the Central District of California;

(i) Evans, et al. v. ______________, No. BC 052392 in the Superior Court for the County of Los Angeles, conditionally certified September 1993; and

(j) Marcus, et al. v. ______________, Case No. 92-1198-H(M) in the United States District Court for the Southern District of California, conditionally certified September 1993.

4. This application is filed in accordance with California state class action procedure after extensive review of the governing law and the underlying facts of this action, originally filed on October 7, 1994, as a class action pursuant to California Code of Civil Procedure §382 and California Corporations Code §15701. The Court has authority to take this action pursuant to *Atari, Inc. v. Superior Court*, 166 Cal. App. 3d 867 (6th Dist. 1985).

5. A key problem for the bench and bar involved in a proposed class action is the maintenance of the status quo during the precertification stages. Based upon my work on this case thus far and my years of both California and federal class action work, I firmly believe that approval of a precertification notice (attached as Exhibit "A" to the Memorandum of Points and Authorities, submitted herewith) to the [proposed] class of the pendency of this class action will (1) protect absent class members; (2) enhance settlement with numerous defendants; (3) minimize unnecessary and duplicative discovery; (4) shorten the proposed trial time; (5) provide ease of judicial administration; and (6) save costs, attorneys' fees and avoid confusion and delay.

6. We are currently engaged in an analysis of the pervasive problems confronting the proposed class and possible solutions therefor, and the need to preserve the ability to globally resolve this matter. Since there is clearly an ascertainable class and the requisite community of interest, the ability to determine the appropriate degree of compensation in a settlement context is enhanced.

3

7. I have reviewed the background of the civil litigation which has been initiated in County and have become familiar with the various allegations in connection with soil subsidence and other problems associated with alleged construction defects. I have made a good faith effort to understand and appreciate the technical aspects of each of these and have come to the conclusion that the overriding and extensive nature of the defects require that the interests of the class be preserved on an ongoing basis in a fashion which can only be accomplished through a class action and associated settlement activity, if at all possible.

8. I have interacted and discussed with representatives and a variety of other non-party insurance carriers the progress of the above class action and methods of proceeding in that regard. Without committing or in any way advising or communicating any position whatsoever with regard to the proposed class in this matter, we have predetermined that the ability to process a class action will be affected by the initiation of significant individual lawsuits.

9. In recent years I have noticed a substantial increase in the direct contacting of class members by lawyers. Usually, but not always, this occurs in directed mailings that encourage individual case filings.

10. The benefit to the Court and the litigants of a proposed class action can be undermined if class members are unaware of such an action and the potential benefits that may inure to them, if any, including the protection of their rights to "sit on the fence" as absent class members, rather than file a multiplicity of individual actions. Based upon my experience, the instant situation requires an objective, court-approved communication, such as that agreed to by the Plaintiffs and Defendants.

11. The confusion and miscommunication will place the class in a position whereby the time a formal certification or settlement were announced to the community, enough individual cases could have been initiated that it would be burdensome and expensive and would not substantially benefit the court or the litigants.

12. The proposed Precertification Notice (a certified equivalent Spanish version will accompany it), modeled upon other precertification notices, is calculated to advise the recipient

4

of the pendency of this action and the substance of the underlying case without committing the defendants to any admissions of liability.

13. I respectfully suggest, based upon my years of experience in class actions which have involved thousands of individuals, that this communication, or notice, would serve the best interests of the litigants and the Court.

I declare under penalty of perjury under the laws of the State of California that the foregoing is true and correct. Executed this 30 day of January, 1995, at San Diego, California.

Timothy D. Cohelan

5

7 CALIFORNIA CLASS CERTIFICATION PROCEDURE

A. TEXT

Sec.

7.01 Differences in Federal and California Procedure

7.02 Class Certification Hearing

[A] In General

[B] Required Notice of Hearing

[C] Timing: "Earliest Practicable Date"

[D] Nature of the Hearing

[E] Scope of Inquiry

[F] Burden on Plaintiff

[G] Superior Benefit

[H] Findings of Fact and Conclusions of Law

[I] Standard of Review on Appeal

7.03 Class Notice

[A] When Notice Is Required and What It Must Say

[B] Hearing on Class Notice

[C] Costs

7.04 Successive Certification Motions

[A] Difference Between Federal and State Rules

[B] "Intermediate" Class Ruling

[C] Decertification Motion or Procedure

[D] Mandatory Class Certification

[E] Post-Merits Rulings/Notice

7.05 References

B. FORMS

7.10 Declaration of Timothy Cohelan and Statement Regarding Time, Manner, and Estimated Cost of Notice and Notice Required by Los Angeles County Rules (*Xiong* case)

7.11 Memorandum of Points and Authorities in Support of Plaintiffs' Motion for Class Certification (*Aguilar* v. *Atlantic Richfield*)

7.12 Declaration of Timothy Cohelan in Support of Plaintiffs' Motion for Class Certification (*Aguilar* v. *Atlantic Richfield Corp.*)

7.13 Memorandum of Points and Authorities in Opposition to Plaintiffs' Motion for Order Determining Class Issues (*Xiong* case)

7.14 Ruling on Motion for Order Determining Class Issues (First Hearing) (*Xiong* case)

7.15 Ruling on Motion for Order Determining Class Issues (Second Continued Hearing) (*Xiong* case)

7.16 Order Certifying Class (*Aguilar* v. *Atlantic Richfield*)

A. TEXT

§ 7.01 Differences in Federal and California Procedure

Where California case law has something to say, it controls class action procedure up to and including the class certification hearing. Where case law is silent, Federal Rules of Civil Procedure rule 23 and California Civil Code section 1781 guide the trial court. The California Supreme Court has consistently followed this general standard, requiring the prudent practitioner to scrutinize state precedent to determine if and how California case law differs from rule 23.

The outcome of the case often hinges on the class certification hearing. In California, unlike federal court, counsel for the proposed class may not make successive class certification motions. Rather, an evidentiary hearing that often extends beyond the declarations of the parties and pleadings provides the basis for certifying or denying the class. A final ruling that denies certification is then subject to appeal as a final order. Findings of fact and conclusions of law are generally mandated in federal practice, but California counsel must request them to allow for appellate review.

The California class action statute (Code Civ. Proc., § 382) is silent on the question of when the court may order a class certified or denied. Federal rule 23, however, explicitly provides in subdivision (c)(1) that the court shall determine by order whether a class action is to be maintained as soon as practicable after the action commences. In federal procedure, the certification order may be conditional, and it may be altered or amended before decision on the merits. (*Green* v. *Obledo* (1981) 29 Cal.3d 126 [172 Cal.Rptr. 206, 624 P.2d 256].

§ 7.02 Class Certification Hearing

[A] In General

Classwide settlements often call for conditional class certification or certification consensual with the defendant, subject to the terms of a settlement agreement. Conditional settlement generally includes a negotiated opt-out position so that defendants understand full well the scope and extent of the final settlement they have agreed to. The following rules apply to opposed class certification hearings.

[B] Required Notice of Hearing

Federal practice has not formally defined the degree of notice required before class certification, nor do the flexible procedures of Federal Rules of Civil Procedure rule 23 specifically require a noticed motion. Indeed, there is no absolute requirement of a hearing for maintaining a class. (*Wright, Miller & Kane*, Vol. 7, 1785; *Jones* v. *Hutto* (1985) 763 F.2d 979.) Federal courts hold hearings only if necessary. Indeed, the author has made successful oral motions for class certification in federal court without notice in a class action where the class had been certified, decertified, redefined, and conditionally certified by certain settling defendants. Also, in an important California case, the trial court certified the class although the plaintiffs had not yet moved for certification or put out a notice. (*City of San Jose* v. *Superior Court of Santa Clara County* (1974) 12 Cal.3d 447 [115 Cal.Rptr. 797, 525 P.2d 701].) Such is no longer the practice.

Current California procedure requires notice to all parties and an opportunity to brief before class certification. (*Carabini* v. *Superior Court* (1994) 26 Cal.App.4th 239 [31 Cal.Rptr.2d 520].) The court may act on the plaintiffs' motion to certify, the opposition's motion to dismiss, or the court's own motion.

[C] Timing: "Earliest Practicable Date"

California decisions uniformly hold that the propriety of class actions must be decided at the earliest possible stage. (*Danzig* v. *Jack Grynberg & Associates* (1984) 161 Cal.App.3d 1128 [208 Cal.Rptr. 336].) Delaying this decision can result in dismissal. (*Massey* v. *Bank of America Nat. Trust and Sav. Ass'n* (1976) 56 Cal.App.3d 29 [128 Cal.Rptr. 144].) However, counsel should not move for class certification until the issues raised by the complaint are "settled" and the complaint states a cause of action against the appropriate defendants. (*Los Angeles County Democratic Central Committee* v. *County of Los Angeles* (1976) 61 Cal.App.3d 335, 343 [132 Cal.Rptr. 43].)

Some local rules state that defendant or plaintiff may submit a motion for class certification 60 days after defendant has filed an answer. California state policy favors prompt and early class determination. (*Massey* v. *Bank of America* (1976) 56 Cal.App.3d 29 [128 Cal.Rptr. 144].) However, considerations of equity predominate. Trial courts should avoid ruling on the merits until they are satisfied that the plaintiffs have had a fair opportunity to present the case for certification. (*Stephen* v. *Enterprise Rent-A-Car* (1991) 235

Cal.App.3d 806 [1 Cal.Rptr.2d 130].) The proceeding may be delayed with continuances requested by plaintiffs if denial of the class certification request will stop the case and result in an appeal. Since pending discovery may define the scope of the class and prevent a premature ruling based on insufficient evidence, plaintiffs should avoid allowing a class certification motion to be thrust on them. (*Union Mutual Life Insurance Co.* v. *Superior Court* (1978) 80 Cal.App.3d 1 [145 Cal.Rptr. 316]; see discussion in Chapter 6 regarding pretrial discovery and litigation on the composition of the class.)

Some local rules call for briefing schedules. The hearing must be noticed not less than 60 days nor more than seventy-five days after service of the motion for class certification. Each responding party may submit documents within 45 days after service. (Super. Ct. L.A. County Rules, rule 15.10.)

[D] Nature of the Hearing

The class certification stage requires an evidentiary hearing. (*Hamwi* v. *Citinational Buckeye Insurance Co.* (1977) 72 Cal.App.3d 462 [140 Cal.Rptr. 215].) Declarations, discovered evidence, and matters judicially noticed determine the evidence submitted at the hearing. Typically, the hearing should address the constitution of the class, including the approximate number, geographic location, status of members, description of subclasses, and method of identifying class members. Counsel for the class needs to frame common as well as similar questions of law together with those unique to class members. The hearing must also deal expressly with the superiority of class action for fairly and efficiently adjudicating the controversy, the status of class representatives as members of the class, and the representatives' ability to protect the interests of the class. (See, e.g., Super. Ct. L.A. County Rules, rule 15.18; Super. Ct. San Mateo County Rules, rule 7.2.)

[E] Scope of Inquiry

The trial court has great discretion in certifying class actions. (*Bell* v. *American Title Ins.* (1991) 226 Cal.App.3d 1589 [277 Cal.Rptr. 583].) The court's inquiry focuses not on the merits of the lawsuit itself, but on the validity of the community of interest as a matter of fact. (*Caro* v. *Procter & Gamble* (1993) 18 Cal.App.4th 644 [22 Cal.Rptr.2d 419].) A class determination generally involves considerations enmeshed in the factual and legal issues raised by the plaintiffs' cause of action. It is up to the court to balance the benefits to the prospective class against the burden on the judicial system. This process continues well into the trial, if necessary, as the issues become more precise. (*Beckstead* v. *Superior Court* (1971) 21 Cal.App.3d 780 [98 Cal.Rptr. 779.) The court can also answer legitimate questions about the action's lack of merit. (*Collins* v. *Safeway Stores* (1986) 187 Cal.App.3d 62 [231 Cal.Rptr. 638].)

[F] Burden on Plaintiff

Plaintiff bears the burden of establishing that the requisites for continuing the litigation as a class action exist. The hearing stage requires more than the reasonable possibility standard of the demurrer stage. Community of interest must be proven as a matter of fact. (*Hamwi* v. *Citinational-Buckeye Investment Co.* (1977) 72 Cal.App.3d 462 [140 Cal.Rptr.215].)

In evaluating the evidence presented to render a decision on class certification, the court uses these legal criteria (*Daniels* v. *Centennial Group, Inc.* (1993) 16 Cal.App.4th 467 [21 Cal. Rptr.2d 1]):

1. The existence of an ascertainable class.
2. A well-defined community of interest among class members, including:
   a. Predominant questions of fact and law.
   b. Class representatives with typical claims or defenses who adequately represent the class interest.

A commonly cited case detailing extensive and specific requirements for findings is *Abella* v. *Riverside Unified School District.* The court concluded that, in addition to ascertainable class and common questions of law and fact, the record needed to cover the impracticability of bringing all members of the class before the court, the predominance of common questions of fact over unique questions affecting only individual class members, the form of notice to absent members of the class, and adequate representation. (*Abella* v. *Riverside Unified School District* (1976) 65 Cal.App.3d 153 [135 Cal.Rptr. 177].) Although this decision does not refer specifically to the Consumer Legal Remedies Act (Civ. Code, § 1750 et seq.; hereafter, CLRA), it gives the appearance of CLRA grafted onto Code of Civil Procedure section 382. Many of these requirements appear in the local rules of Los Angeles County Superior Court as amended January 1, 1995.

An additional caveat on legal criteria arises from the holding of *Hogya* v. *Superior Court, County of San Diego* (1977) 75 Cal.App.3d 122 [142 Cal.Rptr. 325]. Limited strictly to an interpretation of CLRA, this case suggests that, once the court makes the appropriate findings under the statute, certification is mandatory. Standard class actions based on very minor infractions fail to gain certification because benefit to litigants and court cannot be shown. With CLRA, however, certification is mandatory whether the cause of action is large or small.

[G] Superior Benefit

Certifying a class action requires demonstrated substantial benefit to litigants and court. (*Caro* v. *Procter & Gamble* (1993) 18 Cal.App.4th 644, 657 [22 Cal.Rptr.2d 419].) The burden of this demonstration rests with the plaintiff. (*Collins* v. *Safeway Stores, Inc.* (1986) 187 Cal.App.3d 62 [231 Cal.Rptr. 638].)

[H] Findings of Fact and Conclusions of Law

Although a request for findings of fact and conclusions of law is not technically required in the certification hearing, failure to request will prevent the court from meaningfully reviewing the legal reasoning of the trial court in the event of an appealed denial. (*Stephens* v. *Montgomery Ward & Company* (1987) 193 Cal.App.3d 411 [238 Cal.Rptr. 602].) The application of improper criteria and erroneous legal standards presents grounds for reversal. Without findings, however, the review needed for reversal is impossible.

[I] Standard of Review on Appeal

The right result is an inadequate substitute for an incorrect process. (*Clothesrigger, Inc.* v. *GTE Corporation* (1987) 191 Cal.App.3d 605 [236 Cal.Rptr. 605].) The appellate courts may agree with the trial court's result, but it will reverse if the trial court's reasoning is incorrect.

§ 7.03 Class Notice

[A] When Notice Is Required and What It Must Say

Since the holding in *Home Savings and Loan Ass'n* v. *Superior Court*, notice to the class in certain opt-out class actions is required to bind absent class members. (*Home Savings and Loan Ass'n* v. *Superior Court* (1974) 42 Cal.App.3d 1006 [117 Cal.Rptr. 485].) Still, there are clear limitations on the court's ability to order notice. In some situations, notice imposes such a burden on class representatives that it effectively defeats class claims. *Cartt* v. *Superior Court* applied a sliding scale to determine whether the interests of the absent class members required full notice. (*Cartt* v. *Superior Court* (1975) 50 Cal.App.3d 960 [124 Cal.Rptr. 376].)

This decision fits with accepted California notice considerations, which appear more discretionary than federal requirements. Typically, the court may make its own decisions about reasonable notice under the circumstances of the case, including the location of the plaintiffs and the nature of the causes of action. Many times mailing is presumed to be the appropriate means of giving notice when the names of class members are known. With less focused, more diffused causes of action, publication may be required, and sometimes mailing combined with publication.

At a minimum the court notice should provide the following information:

1. A brief nonargumentative explanation of the case, including basic contentions or denials of the parties.
2. The right of any member of the class to exclude himself or herself from the class by making a request before a specified date (opting out).
3. Information concerning how class members may give notice to opt out.
4. A statement that, under the rule of res judicata, judgment in the action will terminate the claim of any member who does not request exclusion.
5. Identity of proposed counsel for the class and other information concerning the methods of communicating with the class.

Local rules for Los Angeles and San Francisco counties require that notice also include the estimated recovery, anticipated fees, costs and expenses, and the net amount if the case is successful. (Super. Ct. L.A. County Rules, rule 15.18(4)(f); Super. Ct. S.F. County Rules, rule 427(6)(c)(vi).)

[B] Hearing on Class Notice

In one case, after the court approved plaintiffs' draft of a notice describing the litigation and giving an opt-out date, defendant sent out a separate notice emphasizing the disadvantages of the class action and enclosing an opt-out form. The court said that notice is far too important to leave to the litigants' whim. (*Gainey* v. *Occidental Land Research* (1986) 186 Cal.App.3d 1051 [231 Cal.Rptr. 249].)

To avoid similar situations, local rules often provide for a separate hearing to approve the class notice. After the court rules in favor of class certification, a status conference is scheduled for the court to review the proposed notice to class members. (Super. Ct. L.A. County Rules, rule 15.18(f).) Alternatively, the notice approval hearing is not scheduled until the court has ruled in favor of other class action issues (Super. Ct. S.F. County Rules, rule 427). This local rule, however, allows the court to "generally shorten" the time for the notice hearing. Both San Francisco and Los Angeles require that a copy of the proposed notice to the class regarding the pending class action be attached to the motion.

It is important that opposing counsel work together to mediate disputes about content or the obviously argumentative language that somehow creeps into the notice following spirited or contentious pretrial activity. A simple rule to remember is that, since the notice is a court document sent to the litigants, it should be totally neutral and express no opinion on the merits.

Under the notice provisions for consumer class actions under CLRA, the court may require either party to notify every class member of the action. The notice must say that the class will include anyone who does not request exclusion by a specified date, that the judgment will include all who do not request exclusion, and that any included member may enter an appearance through counsel. (Civ. Code, § 1781, subds. (d) & (e).)

[C] Costs

California's rules on who pays the costs of class action notice are similar to federal provisions. Before the class is certified, the court is prohibited from inquiring into the merits of a suit to decide which party should bear the cost. (*People* v. *Pacific Land Research Co.* (1977) 20 Cal.3d 10 [141 Cal.Rptr. 20, 569 P.2d 125].) Civil Code section 1781, subdivision (d), authorizes imposition of notice costs on either party to a class action. This approach has been held to be an appropriate procedure that does not violate defendant's due process rights. (See *Vasquez* v. *Superior Court* (1971) 4 Cal.3d 800, 802 [94 Cal.Rptr. 796]; *Civil Service Emp. Ins. Co.* v. *Superior Court of City and County of San Francisco* (1978) 22 Cal.3d 362 [149 Cal.Rptr. 360, 584 P.2d 497].) Local rules require that costs for obtaining addresses, preparing the notice, and delivering it be detailed in a statement with factual support for the estimate. The party advancing the notice may propose how costs are to be divided between the parties. (Super. Ct. L.A. County Rules, rule 15.18(f)(3)(b), (c).)

§ 7.04 Successive Certification Motions

[A] Difference Between Federal and State Rules

Rule 23 of the Federal Rules of Civil Procedure suggests that counsel may make successive motions of class action certification without appealing denials. The reasoning is that initial orders can be conditional and may be altered or amended before judgment on the merits. California rules are quite different, and they can be a trap for the unwary practitioner used to federal procedure.

California does not permit successive motions, a point made clear by the ruling in *Stephen* v. *Enterprise Rent-A-Car Co.*, which the Supreme Court refused to review. Arguing that federal procedure was impractical, the court significantly limited plaintiff's ability to bring renewal motions in so-called death knell rulings. *(Stephen* v. *Enterprise Rent-A-Car Co.* (1991) 235 Cal.App.3d 806 [1 Cal.Rptr.2d 130].) The death knell doctrine, defined by the United States Supreme Court and incorporated into California procedure, holds that without the incentive of group recovery, the individual plaintiff may find a particular ruling makes it economically imprudent to pursue the lawsuit to final judgment and seek appellate review of an adverse determination. (*Coopers & Lybrand* v. *Livesay* (1978) 437 U.S. 463 [57 L.Ed.2d 351, 98 S.Ct. 2454].) An example is *Daar* v. *Yellow Cab*, which held that an order dismissing class allegations and transferring the matter from superior to municipal court was legally tantamount to dismissing the action for all members of the class other than the plaintiff and virtually demolishing it as a class action. *(Daar* v. *Yellow Cab* (1967) 67 Cal.2d 695 [63 Cal.Rptr.724, 433 P.2d 732].)

California case law mandates that an order denying certification sounds the death knell for the matter and that the order must be appealed immediately. Plaintiffs who fail to appeal from such an order lose forever their right to attack it. California law does not allow relitigation of class certification once the denying order class becomes final. As long as the denial was based on the merits, it makes no difference whether the trial court rules "without prejudice" or otherwise enters an order contemplating additional class certification.

On several occasions the author's firm has experienced a California trial court denying a motion for class certification "without prejudice." Be alert to the potential peril of allowing 60 days to pass after entry of such an order. An alert defendant will resist any subsequent effort to certify the class, citing the rules on finality and the failure to appeal the order. In such an event we ask the court to "continue the hearing," which keeps the hearing open and allows counsel to supplement the record as requested by the court. The court can explain in detail what evidentiary or legal deficiencies exist and, if possible, can be cured by plaintiffs.

[B] "Intermediate" Class Ruling

Immediate appeal lies only when the court's action disposes of the entire action. (*Rosack* v. *Volvo of America* (1982) 131 Cal.App.3d 741, 749 [182 Cal.Rptr. 800] cert. denied (1983) 460 U.S. 1012.) If the order allows further proceedings—certifying, for instance, a class smaller than originally proposed—the order is not appealable. Likewise, a writ does not lie. (*General Motors* v. *Superior Court* (1988) 199 Cal.App.3d 247 [244 Cal.Rptr. 776.) Certification of a state class rather than a national is not a death knell and, therefore, not appealable. Practitioners who achieve a partial class certification or anything else short of a death knell may not bring an appeal as a matter of right. Allowing appeal as a matter of right from each detail of class certification order would delay trials and multiply proceedings needlessly. (*General Motors Corp.* v. *Superior Court* (1988) 199 Cal.App.3d 247 [244 Cal.Rptr. 776].)

[C] Decertification Motion or Procedure

The rule against successive motions does not, however, apply to defendants, who may make any number of motions to decertify. When it becomes clear to the trial court that common issues no longer predominate over individual questions requiring separate adjudication, the court may decertify the case, as long as it employs correct criteria. (*Grogan-Beall* v. *Ferdinand Roten Galleries, Inc.* (1982) 133 Cal.App.3d 969 [184 Cal.Rptr. 411].) Absent findings of fact and conclusions of law, the appellate court is responsible for affirming the trial court if it used proper standards in decertification.

[D] Mandatory Class Certification

So-called mandatory state class action results from the application of rule 23, subdivision(b)(1) and (2), of the Federal Rules of Civil Procedure. (See Chapter 1 and Rule 23 in Appendix A.) In matters governed by these rules, the court focuses on common questions as a key to determining class certification. California's adoption of the common question or community of interest requirement as set forth in Code of Civil Procedure section 382 has been determined to be jurisdictional.

[E] Post-Merits Rulings/Notice

Some post-merits rulings have been upheld because it was clear that class issues were resolved as readily after trial as before. Generally these are creditor types of cases. An example was an AFDC welfare benefits class action seeking declaratory and injunctive relief case with a writ of mandamus. The court held it was no error to enter a class certification order to those entitled to benefits after the matter had been remanded to the trial court following a finding in validity of the statute. (*Hypolite* v. *Carleson* (1975) 52 Cal.App.3d 566 [125 Cal.Rptr. 221].) In *Bingham* v. *Obledo*, a clear explanation of the court's actions on a postjudgment basis was deemed adequate. (*Bingham* v. *Obledo* (1983) 147 Cal.App.3d 401 [195 Cal.Rptr. 142].)

§ 7.05 References

NEWBERG For a discussion of the federal rules and case law on notice to class members, see 2 Newberg on Class Actions (3d ed. 1992), Chapter 8.

WITKIN See the following sections regarding certification procedures:

- Certification as class action (4 Witkin, Cal. Procedure (4th ed. 1997) Pleading, §§ 279–281).
- Notice of action (4 Witkin, Cal. Procedure (4th ed. 1997) Pleading, §§ 282–286).

TRG **THE RUTTER GROUP** See the following sections in California Practice Guide: Civil Procedure Before Trial (CPBT) regarding certification procedures:

- Certification hearing (CPBT, §§ 14:98–14:116).
- Notice to class members (CPBT, §§ 14:117–14:132).
- Right of class members to stay in or "opt out" (CPBT, §§ 14:133, 14:134).

See also the following sections in California Practice Guide: Federal Civil Procedure Before Trial (FCPBT) regarding certification procedures in federal class actions:

- Certification proceedings (FCPBT, §§ 10:445–10:491.1).
- Notice to class (FCPBT, §§ 10:492–10:508).

- Right to "opt out" (FCPBT, §§ 10:509–10:517).

WEST'S KEY NUMBER SYSTEM See the following Key Numbers in West's California Digest 2d, Federal Civil Procedure (Topic 170A):

- Certification proceedings (Federal Civil Procedure ⚷ 171–180).

See also Parties (Topic 287):

- Certification proceedings (Parties ⚷ 35.31–35.51).

WESTLAW® See the WESTLAW Electronic Research Guide at the beginning of this volume.

B. FORMS

§ 7.10 Declaration of Timothy Cohelan and Statement Regarding Time, Manner, and Estimated Cost of Notice and Notice Required by Los Angeles County Rules (*Xiong* case)

Daniel J. Callahan, Esq. (CA State Bar #91490)
Andrew A. Smits, Esq. (CA State Bar #146659)
CALLAHAN, BLAINE & WILLIAMS
18500 Von Karman, Suite 800
Irvine, California 92715
(714) 553-1155

Timothy D. Cohelan, Esq. (CA State Bar #60827)
Isam C. Khoury, Esq. (CA State Bar #58759)
COHELAN & KHOURY
701 "C" Street
San Diego, California 92101-5307
Telephone: (619) 595-3001

Attorneys for Plaintiffs

SUPERIOR COURT OF CALIFORNIA

COUNTY OF FRESNO

YIA XIONG on behalf of themselves and all others similarly situated, Plaintiffs, v. an unincorporated inter-insurance exchange; a California corporation; INSURANCE COMPANY; and DOES 1 through 500, inclusive, Defendants.	CASE NO. DECLARATION OF TIMOTHY COHELAN AND STATEMENT REGARDING TIME, MANNER, AND ESTIMATED COST OF NOTICE [Super. Ct. L.A. County Rules 15.18(f)] DATE: January 12, 1996 TIME: 8:30 a.m. DEPT: 51 TRIAL: NONE SET

I, TIMOTHY D. COHELAN, declare:

1. I am one of the attorneys for the Plaintiffs in the above-captioned lawsuit certified as a class action on November 9, 1995.

2. I am licensed to practice law before all the courts of California and if called as a witness would testify of my own personal knowledge as follows:

3. This declaration is offered in direct response to the Court's November 9, 1995 Order requiring Plaintiffs to submit a proposed recommendation and proposed Order regarding notice to Class Members.

Summary of Proposed Notices

4. Plaintiffs propose that the Court approve three complementary methods of notice.

5. Since Defendants have raised certain privacy concerns, the Plaintiffs recommend that notice by mail be achieved by the transmittal of a "Notice to Policyholders" by Defendants to those existing policyholders in the form of a normal business correspondence. Plaintiffs agree to reimburse reasonable costs of such mailing. The proposed "Notice to Policyholders" attached hereto as Exhibit "A" conforms to the basic requirements of class action notice and the Local Rules of the Superior Court of Los Angeles County.

6. Exhibit "B" is a proposed second supplementary Notice. It is a more comprehensive and traditional notice of class certification that would be mailed by Plaintiffs to persons who request a more definitive explanation after receiving the Notice to Policyholders, or after receiving notice through publication, and additionally to persons who have been identified as no longer maintaining a relationship with Plaintiffs propose to have this Notice directly mailed as a supplement at the conclusion of the Class Identification Period to those Class Members who will not be receiving for one reason or another the Notice to Policyholders.

Notice by Publication:

7. Finally, Plaintiffs have included as Exhibit "C" a draft of a Summary Notice of Class Certification, which Plaintiffs propose to have published in summary form in the Fresno Bee, The Merced Sun-Star Daily, The Sacramento Bee, California Hmong Times and The Stockton Record, newspapers covering large portions of the Merced Regional Office operating area, and additionally in selected ethnic newspapers after translation into appropriate Class dialects where applicable.

2

Class Identification Period:

8. Upon approval by the Court of this methodology, Plaintiffs, through a review of the master policy list and declination letters provided by will assemble a list of those persons identified by the experts as Members of the Class of Southeast Asian motorists as approved by the Court in the Class Definition in the companion documentation. The Class Identification Period will be utilized to compile a list which will then result in the transmittal by of the Notice to Policyholders with a supplementary mailing by Plaintiffs to those who for one reason or another do not receive same. At present, the Class Identification Period is estimated to take approximately ten weeks from the date of Court approval.

Actual Notice Period:

9. The Actual Notice Period will commence on or about the halfway point of the Class Identification Period as the names of Class Members become available and as Southeast Asian policyholder names are transmitted to for a direct mailing, a process believed to require three to six months. Additionally, during the actual Class Notice Period the other Notice modality, which includes the publication on at least four separate occasions of the small Summary Notice, will be achieved in the general newspapers, as well as those newspapers which serve the larger ethnic concentrations.

Cost of Notice:

10. The Plaintiffs estimate the cost based upon their past experiences in mailing notices to classes, including printing, for a group of approximately 10,000 individuals to be $5,015.33 for printing and mailing of the full notice. The one page notice would cost less to print, but the same to mail.

11. Since the Notice to Policyholders is proposed to be transmitted directly through a mailing by the postage cost is unknown. However, Plaintiffs are prepared to bear all of the printing costs of any such Notice and will transmit same to the Defendants for mailing, as previously stated, during the Class Identification Period.

12. The cost for legal publication of the Summary Class Notice in newspapers of

3

general circulation is estimated to be approximately $1500 for four separate publication dates. The cost for the ethnic publications is unknown as of this date, but will be made available at the hearing on this matter.

I declare under penalty of perjury under the laws of the State of California that the foregoing is true and correct.

Executed on the 28th day of December, 1995, in San Diego, California.

____
Timothy D. Cohelan

4

NOTICE TO POLICYHOLDERS OF

The Superior Court of the County of Fresno has certified the matter entitled *Yia Xiong, et al. v. et al.* as a class action and has ordered the enclosed Notice to be transmitted to you as a policyholder of one of the above-referenced companies. A class action lawsuit is a lawsuit which is filed by certain individuals to protect the interests or to represent the interests of a large group of absent parties. Since this Notice may affect your rights, you should read it carefully. Although the Court has expressed no opinion as to the merits of the lawsuit, the Court has approved this method of advising you of the pendency of this lawsuit and your rights, including your right to exclude yourself from the action.

This Notice is directed to persons of Southeast Asian origin as defined in the Ruling On Motion For Order Determining Class Issues approving Class certification dated November 9, 1995 and as clarified by the Court on January 12, 1996. The Class Description includes Hmong, Cambodian, Laotian, Vietnamese, Thai, Mien and Lahu currently residing in counties within the operating area of Regional Office.

Background and Description of the Action

The lawsuit alleges that systematically discriminated against persons of Southeast Asian ethnicity. denies the Plaintiffs' allegations and transmits this information to you pursuant to a Court Order entered on January 12, 1996.

Class Action Ruling and Class Action Counsel

On November 9, 1995, the Court ruled that the Second and Fourth Causes of Action of the Second Amended Complaint should be entitled to class treatment and that representative parties be allowed to proceed representing the interests of all absent Class Members through proposed Class Counsel identified as Timothy D. Cohelan of COHELAN & KHOURY, 701 "C" Street, San Diego, California 92101-5307, telephone: (619) 595-3001; and Daniel J. Callahan of CALLAHAN, BLAINE & WILLIAMS, 18500 Von Karman, Suite 800, Irvine, California 92715, telephone: (714) 553-1155. These attorneys will be paid only if they recover for the Class and the Court approves their request for fees and costs reimbursement.

Consequences of Class Membership and Election to Opt Out

If you come within the definition of the Class as described above, you will automatically become a Member of the Class unless you elect to be excluded from the Class within forty-five (45) days of the receipt of this Notice. A Class Member may exclude himself or herself from the Class by filing a valid election to be excluded from the Class discussed below. In no event will any Class Member be allowed to exclude themselves after July 31, 1996. If you do not request exclusion, you may additionally move the Court for permission to appear as a named Class co-representative if you so desire. As a Class Member you will be represented by existing Class Representatives acting on behalf of the Class and will receive notice of any ruling affecting the size of the Class and notice of any proposed settlement or dismissal of Class claims or any judgment rendered. You will be bound by any judgment or other final disposition of the Class lawsuit, whether that disposition is favorable or unfavorable. You will participate upon proof of membership in the Class and the filing of a proper claim form in a distribution of any damages recovered in the litigation.

If you elect to be excluded from the Class, you will not be bound by any disposition of the class action and you will retain any claims you may have against However, you will likewise not share in any recovery which might be paid to Class Members upon any settlement of this case or if the Class Representatives are successful at trial. In determining whether you want to be excluded from the Class, you are advised to consult your own attorney.

Importance of this Notice

Additionally, you have a right to receive free of charge from Class Counsel an updated and more definitive notice of your rights pursuant to this matter upon mailing to them at the above-listed address any inquiry concerning the status of this case. Class Counsel will promptly provide to you background information, including a more detailed notice of the pendency of the claim, upon receipt of such request. Additionally, you may examine any of the papers in this case in the Court file of the Office of the County Clerk, Superior Court of Fresno County, 1100 Van Ness, Room 402, Fresno, California 93721-2012. Please direct any inquiries to Class Counsel, not to the Court.

Dated:____________________ ______________________________

James L. Quaschnick
Judge of the Fresno County Superior Court

SUMMARY NOTICE OF PENDENCY OF CLASS ACTION

TO: PERSONS OF SOUTHEAST ASIAN ORIGIN, INCLUDING HMONG, CAMBODIAN, LAOTIAN, VIETNAMESE, THAI, MIEN, AND LAHU, CURRENTLY RESIDING IN COUNTIES WITHIN THE OPERATING AREA OF MERCED REGIONAL OFFICE WHO MAY HAVE BEEN DISCRIMINATED AGAINST BY ITS AFFILIATES OR OPERATING ENTITIES IN THE PURCHASE OF OR APPLICATION FOR AUTOMOBILE INSURANCE.

On November 9, 1995, the Superior Court of the County of Fresno certified the matter entitled *Yia Xiong, et al. v.* as a class action involving race discrimination against Southeast Asians. The discrimination includes the overcharging for auto insurance coverage or the denial of auto insurance coverage. It is alleged that and its primary operating entities, Insurance Company engaged in such discriminatory practices.

This summary is to advise you that you will automatically become a Member of the Class unless you elect to be excluded from the Class by filing the appropriate exclusion request with the Court or with Class Counsel. As a Class Member you will be represented by existing representatives acting on behalf of the Class and will receive notice of any ruling affecting the Class, including settlement, dismissal or judgment in favor of or against the Class. You will be bound, however, by any judgment or other final disposition.

You have a right to receive information from Class Counsel and should request it if you have questions concerning your rights in this matter. Class Counsel are listed below.

Timothy D. Cohelan
COHELAN & KHOURY
701 "C" Street
San Diego, California 92101-5307
Telephone: (619) 595-3001

Daniel J. Callahan
CALLAHAN, BLAINE & WILLIAMS
18500 Von Karman, Suite 800
Irvine, California 92715
(714) 553-1155

Although this Notice is being sent to you by Order of the Superior Court, the Court has not expressed any opinion on the merits of the case.

Dated:____________________

____
James L. Quaschnick
Judge of the Fresno County Superior Court

§ 7.11 Memorandum of Points and Authorities in Support of Plaintiffs' Motion for Class Certification (*Aguilar* v. *Atlantic Richfield*)

Timothy D. Cohelan, Esq. (SBN60827)
Isam C. Khoury, Esq. (SBN58759)
COHELAN & KHOURY
701 C Street
San Diego, California 92101-5307
Telephone: (619) 595-3001

Daniel J. Mogin (SBN95624)
Angela Milea Mogin (SBN153920)
THE MOGIN LAW FIRM
701 C Street, Suite 200
San Diego, California 92101-5307
Telephone: (619) 687-6611

Attorneys for Plaintiffs

SUPERIOR COURT OF THE STATE OF CALIFORNIA

FOR THE COUNTY OF SAN DIEGO

THERESA AGUILAR, individuals, on behalf of themselves and all others similarly situated, Plaintiffs, v. ATLANTIC RICHFIELD CORPORATION, CHEVRON CORPORATION, EXXON CORPORATION, MOBIL OIL CORPORATION, SHELL OIL COMPANY, TEXACO, INC., TOSCO CORPORATION, ULTRAMAR CORPORATION, UNOCAL CORPORATION, and DOES 1 through 40, inclusive, Defendants.	Case No. 00700810 MEMORANDUM OF POINTS AND AUTHORITIES IN SUPPORT OF PLAINTIFFS' MOTION FOR CLASS CERTIFICATION DATE: TIME: DEPT: 49 I/C JUDGE: Hon. Jeffrey T. Miller TRIAL DATE: N/A

///

///

///

///

///

TABLE OF CONTENTS

Page

I. INTRODUCTION 1

II. SUMMARY OF FACTS 2

III. PLAINTIFFS MEET ALL APPLICABLE REQUIREMENTS FOR CERTIFICATION OF THE CLASS 4

A. Legal Standards for Determining Motion 4

B. Plaintiffs Case Satisfies The Legal Standards For Class Certification 7

1. The Proposed Class is Ascertainable 7

2. Commonality and Community of Interest 7

a. Common Issues of Fact and Law Predominate 7

b. Proof Of The Conspiracy/Combination Of Defendants Unites The Class 8

c. The Evidence Adduced In Discovery To Date Provides A Factual Predicate In The Form Of An Inference That A Combination Or Conspiracy To Raise And Stabilize CARB 2 Prices Exists 9

d. The Classwide Impact Can Be Presumed By The Application Of Statistical Analyses Of Damages To The Class 1

e. Common Issues of Fact and Law Also Predominate in Plaintiffs' Second Cause of Action for Unfair Competition 1

3. Numerosity 1

4. Typicality 1

5. Adequacy of Representation by the Named Plaintiffs and Class Counsel 1

6. Superiority 1

CONCLUSION 1

ii

TABLE OF AUTHORITIES

FEDERAL CASES

Alton Box Bd. Co. v. Esprit de Corp. (9th Cir. 1982) 682 F.2d 1267 8

Blackie v. Barrack (9th Cir. 1975) 524 F.2d 891 6

Continental Ore Company v. Union Carbide & Carbon Corp. (1962) 370 U.S. 690 8

Edward J. Sweeney & Sons v. Texaco (3d Cir. 1980) 637 F.2d 103 8

Eisen v. Carlisle & Jacquelin (1974) 417 U.S. 156, 94 S.Ct. 2140 5

Guarantee Ins. Agency Co. v. Mid-Continental Rlty Co. (N.D. Ill. 1972) 57 F.R.D. 555 14

Illinois Brick Co. v. Illinois (1977) 431 U.S. 720, 97 S.Ct. 2061 8

In re Consolidated Pretrial Proceedings in Petroleum Products Antitrust Litigation (9th Cir. 1990) 906 F.2d 432 . . . . 4, 10

U.S. v. Container Corp. of America (1968) 393 U.S. 333 . . . . 4, 9

STATE CASES

Anthony v. General Motors (1973) 33 Cal.App.3d 699 5

B.W.I. Custom Kitchen v. Owens-Illinois, Inc. (1987) 191 Cal.App.3d 1341 . . . . 2, 5-8, 11

Bank of the West v. Superior Court (1992) 2 Cal.4th 1254 12

Bruno v. Superior Court (1981) 127 Cal.App.3d 120 . . . . 6, 11

Carabini v. Superior Court (1994) 26 Cal.App.4th 239 5

Carey v. Brown (1881) 58 Cal. 180 5

Cellular Plus v. Superior Court (1993) 14 Cal.App.4th 1224 . . . . 2, 3, 8

Classen v. Weller (1983) 145 Cal.App.3d 27 . . . . 6, 8, 13

Committee on Children's Television, Inc. v. General Food Corp. (1983) 35 Cal.3d 197 12

Daar v. Yellow Cab Company (1967) 67 Cal.2d 695 . . . . 5, 15

Diesel Electric Sales & Service, Inc. v. Marco Marine San Diego, Inc. (1993) 16 Cal.App.4th 202 11

Fanucchi v. Coberly-West Co. (1957) 151 Cal.App.2d 73 6

Gleske v. Anderson (1888) 77 Cal. 247 5

Green v. Obledo (1981) 29 Cal.3d 126 5

Jellen v. O'Brien (1928) 89 Cal.App. 505 5

Keating v. Superior Court (1982) 31 Cal.3d 584, appeal dismissed in part, rev'd in part on other grounds sub nom., *Southland Corp. v. Keating* (1984) 465 U.S. 1. 14

La Sala v. American Savings & Loan Assn. (1971) 5 Cal.3d 864 . . . . 5, 6, 14, 15

Lazar v. Hertz Corp. (1983) 143 Cal.App.3d 128 12

McGhee v. Bank of America (1976) 60 Cal.App.3d 442 . . . . 13, 14

Miller v. Woods (1983) 148 Cal.App.3d 862 . . . . 7, 13

Motors, Inc. v. Times-Mirror Co. (1980) 102 Cal.App.3d 735 12

People v. National Association of Realtors (1981) 120 Cal.App.3d 459 . . . . 4, 9

Reyes v. Board of Supervisors of San Diego County (1987) 196 Cal.App.3d 1263 . . . . 5, 7, 11, 12, 14

Richmond v. Dart Industries, Inc. (1981) 29 Cal.3d 462 . . . . 4-6, 12-15

Rosack v. Volvo of America Corporation (1982) 131 Cal.App.3d 741; cert. denied (1983) 460 U.S. 1012 . . . . 2, 4, 11, 13

San Jose v. Superior Court (1974) 12 Cal.3d 447 6

Saxer v. Phillip Morris, Inc. (1975) 54 Cal.App.3d 7 7

State ex. rel Van de Kamp v. Texaco (1988) 46 Cal.3d 1147 3

State of California v. Levi Strauss & Co. (1986) 41 Cal.3d 460 . . . . 4, 15

Stephens v. Montgomery Ward (1987) 193 Cal.App.3d 411 5

Union Carbide Corp. v. Superior Court (1984) 36 Cal.3d 15 . . . . 3, 5, 15

Vasquez v. Superior Court (1971) 4 Cal.3d 800 . . . . 5-7, 11, 15

STATUTES AND RULES

Federal Rules of Civil Procedure
rule 23(b)(1)(A) 15

California Business and Professions Code
§ 16702 1
§ 16720, *et seq.* 1
§ 16720(b) 8
§ 16750 8
§ 16760(d) 11
§ 17021 1
§ 17200 . . . . 11, 12
§ 17200, *et seq.* 1

California Civil Code
1781(b) 5

California Code of Civil Procedure
§ 382 . . . . 1, 6
§ 384 11

OTHER AUTHORITIES

Weil & Brown, Cal. Practice Guide: Civil Procedure Before Trial (The Rutter Group 1993) ¶14:100, p.14-20.3 5

iv

I.

INTRODUCTION

This is an antitrust and unfair competition class action brought by representative Plaintiffs Theresa Aguilar,

on behalf of a class of California motorists who purchased "CARB GAS"[1] for their own use and not for resale since March 1, 1996. The Defendants are the nine major refiners, distributors and retailers of all types of CARB GAS in California. Defendants collectively control almost 100% of the wholesale market for CARB GAS and approximately 92% of the retail market. The State Board of Equalization reports that over 13.5 billion gallons of gasoline are sold in California annually. Thus, the case is a matter of significant public interest and importance to the State's economy.

Plaintiffs' First Amended Complaint ("Complaint") alleges two causes of action arising from Defendants' common course of conduct: the first for violations of the Cartwright Act (Cal. Bus. & Prof. Code, § 16720, *et seq.*); the second for violations of the Unfair Competition Act (Cal. Bus. & Prof. Code, § 17200, *et seq.*).[2]

Pursuant to Code of Civil Procedure section 382, Plaintiffs seek certification of a plaintiff class defined as:

> All persons (as defined by Bus. & Prof. Code §§ 16702 and 17021) residing in California who, during the time period March 1, 1996 through the present (the "Class Period"), purchased, in California, for their own use and not for resale, CARB GAS sold by any of the defendants ("Plaintiff Class"). Specifically excluded from the Plaintiff Class are the defendants herein; officers, directors or employees of any defendants; any entity in which any defendant has a controlling interest; the affiliates, legal representatives, attorneys, heirs, or assigns of any defendant; and any federal, state or local governmental entity.

---

1 As defined in the Complaint, "CARB GAS" means all grades and types of reformulated o California Air Resources Board ("CARB") Phase 2 gasoline refined for retail sale in the State of California As of March 1, 1996 CARB GAS was required to be refined for sale in California pursuant to the federa Clean Air Act Amendments and the regulations of the California Air Resources Board ("CARB"). As c June 15, 1996, only CARB GAS could be sold in California.

2 Plaintiffs filed an Amendment to the First Amended Complaint correcting the caption by deletin several early class representatives and adding several new ones. References to the Complaint are cite hereafter as "¶__."

1

This is precisely the type of case that courts have repeatedly found should be certified for class treatment. The class is united with respect to proof of the conspiracy and proof of injury. (*B.W.I. Custom Kitchens v. Owens-Illinois, Inc.* (1987) 191 Cal.App.3d 1341, 1350-55; *Rosack v. Volvo of America Corporation* (1982) 131 Cal.App.3d 741, 753.) Injury and damages are inferred upon a showing that the conspiracy exists. (*Id.*) This class is ascertainable, a well-defined community of interest exists and common issues of fact and law predominate. Further, the proposed Class Representatives meet each of the applicable criteria for certification. For these reasons, Plaintiffs' motion should be granted.

II.

SUMMARY OF FACTS

The Complaint alleges a prototypical class action case for horizontal price-fixing, a per se violation of the Cartwright Act, brought by ordinary consumers victimized by a conspiracy. (*B.W.I. Custom Kitchen v. Owens-Illinois, Inc., supra,* 191 Cal.App.3d at 1348; *Rosack v. Volvo of America Corporation, supra,* 131 Cal.App.3d at 751-52; <u>cert. denied</u> (1983) 460 U.S. 1012; *Cellular Plus v. Superior Court* (1993) 14 Cal.App.4th 1224.)[3] It alleges that "[b]eginning at a date unknown to plaintiffs, and continuing thereafter to the present, the ... defendants ... engaged in a continuing unlawful trust in restraint of trade and commerce" (¶44), "the substantial terms of which were to limit the production and to fix, raise, maintain and stabilize the prices of CARB GAS sold in the State of California to Plaintiffs and the members of the Plaintiff Class at supra-competitive levels." (¶47) The effects of the conspiracy were to fix and maintain the cost of CARB GAS at artificially high and supra-competitive levels and to unreasonably restrain competition in the sale of CARB GAS. (¶33)

Defendants have acted to restrict the supply of CARB GAS (¶31), in that only 12 refineries in California produce CARB GAS, each of which is operated by the Defendants.

[3] Certain practices in violation of the antitrust laws are deemed per se violations. Price fixing i such a practice and is unlawful per se under both Section 1 of the [federal] Sherman Act as well as th Cartwright Act. (*Rosack v. Volvo of America Corp. supra,* 131 Cal.App.3d at 751.)

(¶31) Defendants use their control of these refineries to restrict the supply of CARB GAS, artificially inflating the price of CARB GAS and causing prices to rise rapidly and dramatically. (¶31)

California's antitrust laws are more far reaching than federal antitrust laws (*State ex. rel Van de Kamp v. Texaco* (1988) 46 Cal.3d 1147, 1164-65; *Cellular Plus v. Superior Court, supra*, 14 Cal.App.4th at 1240-43 ["the Cartwright Act is broader in range and deeper in reach than the Sherman Act"]) and its class action procedures must be liberally applied in favor of certification in consumer antitrust actions. (*Union Carbide Corp. v. Superior Court* (1984) 36 Cal.3d 15, 21-22.) Proof of a violation requires only evidence of a conspiracy among defendants to fix prices; the offenses charged are per se violations; no defense or justification is recognized. "Whatever economic justification particular price-fixing agreements may be thought to have, the law does not permit an inquiry into their actual reasonableness. They are all banned because of their actual or potential threat to the central nervous system of the economy ...." It is no defense that the price fixed was a "reasonable price," nor is it necessary to show an actual effect on prices. (*Id.*)

Since the March 1, 1996 deadline for refining CARB GAS, the Defendants have each engaged in massive price increases, raising their prices by nearly identical increments at almost precisely the same time throughout California. (¶35) Those price increases increased the average <u>refiner's</u> margin from approximately $0.213 per gallon in December of 1995, to $0.464 per gallon as of April 23, 1996, an increase of $0.251 or 135%! Refiners margins have remained high since that period. Moreover, since the introduction of CARB GAS, retail prices have hit historic and breathtaking levels.[4] The resulting injury is readily apparent and class wide in its effects. As Plaintiffs allege, "these outrageous price hikes"

[4] According to CARB Chairman John Dunlop, after hearing testimony from defendants' executives:

> Californians currently are paying an extra five to eight cents a gallon for cleaner, healthier air. The rest of these outrageous price hikes reflect events within the state, national and global oil markets that are unrelated to California regulations. After listening to the oil industry's testimony, I still have not heard anything that fully explains these price increases.

California Air Resources Board, Release 96-11, April 26, 1996, p.1.

3

were the result of understandings among the Defendants: agreements to exchange [competitive information] in order to facilitate price stabilization and restrictions on production capacity and supply. (See, *In re Coordinated Pretrial Proceedings in Petroleum Products Antitrust Litigation* ("*Petroleum Products*") (9th Cir. 1990) 906 F.2d 432, 463.)

Furthermore, a jury can infer the fact of injury when a conspiracy to fix prices has been established and Plaintiffs have established that they purchased the affected goods or services. Based upon the limited discovery conducted to date, such an inference is justified. The Defendants are, by their own admission, exchanging price information through third party facilitators such as Oil Price Information Services ("OPIS"),

in a fashion that causes anti-competitive effects. Such practices have long been sufficient to establish the combination or conspiracy required by the antitrust laws. (*U.S. v. Container Corp. of America* (1968) 393 U.S. 333; *People v. National Association of Realtors* (1981) 120 Cal.App.3d 459, 481-482; *Petroleum Products, supra,* 906 F.2d 432.)

III.

PLAINTIFFS MEET ALL APPLICABLE REQUIREMENTS FOR CERTIFICATION OF THE CLASS

A. Legal Standards for Determining Motion

Plaintiffs have stated claims of illegality and injury which can be proved predominantly with facts applicable to the class as a whole, rather than by a series of facts relevant only to individual or small groups of plaintiffs. As such, prosecution as a class action is appropriate and desirable. (*Rosack v. Volvo of America Corp., supra,* 131 Cal.App.3d at 752-754.) The existence of the price-fixing conspiracy is the predominant common issue determinative of liability to all class members. (*Id.*)

Indeed, the express judicial policy of California is to favor the maintenance of appropriate class actions. (*Richmond v. Dart Industries, Inc.* (1981) 29 Cal.3d 462 "[T]his state has a public policy which encourages the use of the class action device...") California also has a long standing commitment to using the class action device to further consumer protection. (*State of California v. Levi Strauss & Co.* (1986) 41 Cal.3d 460, 471 ["the

4

consumer class action is an essential tool for the protection of consumers against exploitative business practices"]; *Union Carbide Corp. v. Superior Court* (1984) 36 Cal.3d 15, 21-22, [courts are bound by legislative "mandate to avoid unnecessary procedural barriers to [consumers'] prosecution of California antitrust suits"]; *La Sala v. American Savings & Loan Assn.* (1971) 5 Cal.3d 864, 875-6; *Vasquez v. Superior Court* (1971) 4 Cal.3d 800, 820-21.)

In applying these principles, the merits of a plaintiff's claims are not examined at the class certification stage. (*Green v. Obledo* (1981) 29 Cal.3d 126, 146; *Stephens v. Montgomery Ward* (1987) 193 Cal.App.3d 411, 418 (citing *Eisen v. Carlisle & Jacquelin* (1974) 417 U.S. 156, 177-78, 94 S.Ct. 2140); *Reyes v. Board of Supervisors of San Diego County* (1987) 196 Cal.App.3d 1263, 1271.) "A motion to certify a class action is not a trial on the merits, nor does it function as a motion for summary judgment. The court may consider the merits of a claim only to determine whether there is a realistic chance for recovery." (*Carabini v. Superior Court* (1994) 26 Cal.App.4th 239, 245 (citing Weil & Brown, Cal. Practice Guide: Civil Procedure Before Trial (The Rutter Group 1993) ¶14:100, p.14-20.3); *Anthony v. General Motors* (1973) 33 Cal.App.3d 699.) Any doubts as to the appropriateness of class treatment must be resolved in favor of certification, subject to later modification. (*Richmond v. Dart Industries, Inc., supra*, 29 Cal.3d at 473-475.)

For over 110 years, California courts have expressed only two primary requirements in order to maintain a California class action:

1. An ascertainable class; and
2. A well-defined community of interest in the questions of law and fact involved affecting the parties to be represented.

(*Carey v. Brown* (1881) 58 Cal. 180; *Gleske v. Anderson* (1888) 77 Cal. 247; *Jellen v. O'Brien* (1928) 89 Cal.App. 505; *Daar v. Yellow Cab Company* (1967) 67 Cal.2d 695, 704; *B.W.I. Custom Kitchen v. Owens-Illinois, Inc.* (1987) 191 Cal.App.3d 1341, 1347.) The elements of numerosity, typicality, adequacy, superiority and the predominance of common questions of law and fact are considered under the Consumer Legal Remedies Act, Civil Code section 1781(b), which has also been expressly adopted by the California Supreme

5

Court for use by trial courts in determining whether the requirements of certification under Code of Civil Procedure section 382 have been met. (*Vasquez v. Superior Court, supra,* 4 Cal.3d at 821;[5] *Richmond v. Dart Industries, Inc., supra,* 29 Cal.3d. at 473.)

Class certification does not require any preexisting relationship among class members, simultaneous or identical injuries, a single episode or transaction, or any absolute identity among the numerous transactions or representations that are the particular indicators of an underlying "systemic course of dealing." (*Fanucchi v. Coberly-West Co.* (1957) 151 Cal.App.2d 73, 80-82.) "Courts take a common sense approach that the class is united by a common interest in determining whether a defendant's course of conduct is in its broad outlines actionable, which is not defeated by slight differences in class members' positions." (*Blackie v. Barrack* (9th Cir. 1975) 524 F.2d 891, 902-903.) "The only requirements are that common questions of law and fact *predominate* and that the class representatives be *similarly* situated [citations omitted]." (*B.W.I. Custom Kitchens v. Owens-Illinois, Inc., supra,* 191 Cal.App.3d at 1347, citing *Classen v. Weller* (1983) 145 Cal.App.3d 27, 46 [emphasis original].) Class actions are utilized and encouraged to preclude a defendant from avoiding exposure for wrongdoing because individual victims may lack the sophistication, financial motivation or resources to sue on their own. (*Vasquez v. Superior Court, supra,* 4 Cal.3d at 808.)[6]

Using these criteria, antitrust class actions of this type have frequently been certified. (See e.g., *Bruno v. Superior Court* (1981) 127 Cal.App.3d 120 [certified class of purchasers

---

[5] In the absence of California authority, California courts are instructed to refer to Federal Rules of Civil Procedure, rule 23 on class action issues. (*Vasquez v. Superior Court* (1971) 4 Cal.3d 800, 821; *La Sala v. American Savings & Loan Assn.* (1971) 5 Cal.3d 864, 872; *San Jose v. Superior Court* (1974) 12 Cal.3d 447, 453.)

[6] "Frequently numerous consumers are exposed to the same dubious practice by the same seller so that proof of the prevalence of the practice as to one consumer would provide proof for all. Individual actions by each of the defrauded consumers is often impracticable because the amount of individual recovery would be insufficient to justify bringing a separate action; thus an unscrupulous seller retains the benefit of its wrongful conduct. A class action by consumers produces several salutary byproducts including a therapeutic effect upon those sellers who indulge in fraudulent practices, aid to legitimate business enterprises by curtailing illegitimate competition, and avoidance to the judicial process of the burden of multiple litigation involving identical claims. The benefit to the parties and the courts would in many circumstances, be substantial." (*Vasquez*, 4 Cal.3d at 808.)

6

of milk]; *B.W.I. Custom Kitchen v. Owens-Illinois, Inc., supra,* 191 Cal.App.3d 1341 [certified class of purchasers of glass containers]; *Saxer v. Phillip Morris, Inc.* (1975) 54 Cal.App.3d 7 [home purchasers class action certified against developer-sales company].)

B. Plaintiffs' Case Satisfies The Legal Standards For Class Certification.

1. The Proposed Class is Ascertainable.

Whether a class is ascertainable is determined by examining (1) the class definition, (2) the size of the class, and (3) the means available for identifying class members. (*Reyes v. Board of Supervisors of San Diego County, supra,* 196 Cal.App.3d at 1271; *Vasquez v. Superior Court, supra,* 4 Cal.3d at 821-22; *Miller v. Woods* (1983) 148 Cal.App.3d 862, 873.) Here the class definition is objective and merits-neutral: all persons who purchased CARB GAS in California for their own use and not for resale during the Class Period. As described below, the proposed Class numbers in the millions. The Class is identifiable from public records, such as those at the Department of Motor Vehicles.

2. Commonality and Community of Interest.

a. Common Issues of Fact and Law Predominate.

Plaintiffs have alleged that each Member of the proposed Class is a victim of a common course of conduct. The Complaint (¶24b) details the common nucleus of facts and resulting common questions of law and fact including:

(i) Whether defendants violated the Cartwright Act;

(ii) The existence, duration, and illegality of the restrictions, limitations, obligations, combinations, agreements, trusts and conspiracies alleged herein;

(iii) Whether defendants and each of them was a participant in the restrictions, limitations, obligations, combinations, agreements, trusts and conspiracies alleged herein;

(iv) The effect upon and the extent of injuries sustained by plaintiffs and members of the Plaintiff Class and the appropriate type and/or measure of damages;

7

(v) **Whether defendants violated the Unfair Competition Act;**

(vi) **The amount of additional revenues and profits obtained by defendants attributable to their violations of the Unfair Competition Act; and,**

(vii) **The appropriate nature of class wide equitable relief.**

Each of these issues is best suited to proof and adjudication on a classwide basis.

In this case the class members are both direct and indirect purchasers, purchasing CARB GAS from company operated stations and/or from franchisees or lessees. In contrast to federal law, California expressly provides for actions by indirect purchasers. (Bus. & Prof. Code, §16750; *Cellular Plus, supra,* 14 Cal.App.4th at 1233; c.f. *Illinois Brick Co. v. Illinois* (1977) 431 U.S. 720, 731, 97 S.Ct. 2061.) These actions are not preempted by federal law and must be pursued in the California courts. (*Id.*; *Alton Box Bd. Co. v. Esprit de Corp.* (9th Cir. 1982) 682 F.2d 1267, 1269-70.)

b. Proof Of The Conspiracy/Combination Of Defendants Unites The Class.

Restrictive and coordinated inventory practices that limit production output of a commodity violate the Cartwright Act. (Bus. & Prof. Code § 16720(b) [restricting trusts created to "limit or reduce the production, or increase the price of merchandise or of any commodity"].) "[W]hen a conspiracy to fix prices has been alleged, common questions of fact predominate over any questions affecting only individual class members." (*B.W.I. Custom Kitchen v. Owens-Illinois, Inc., supra,* 191 Cal.App.3d at 1350-55.) "[T]he existence of the conspiracy is the predominant issue determinative of liability to all class members. . . . violation as to each class plaintiff will be proved by facts of the same conspiracy." (*Classen v. Weller* (1983) 145 Cal.App.3d 27, 47.)

The law applicable to proving price fixing or stabilization is well established. Plaintiffs may rely on an inference of a common understanding drawn from basic evidence . . . . (*Edward J. Sweeney & Sons v. Texaco* (3d Cir. 1980) 637 F.2d 103.) (*Continental Ore Company v. Union Carbide & Carbon Corp.* (1962) 370 U.S. 690.) An illegal conspiracy

8

can also involve restrictions of the supply or production of refined petroleum products; in fact, agreements regarding capacity/production restrictions or mutual decelerations have been found sufficient to impose antitrust liability.

c. The Evidence Adduced In Discovery To Date Provides A Factual Predicate In The Form Of An Inference That A Combination Or Conspiracy To Raise And Stabilize CARB 2 Prices Exists.

Although the Court should not consider the merits of the claim in the context of a class certification motion, the Defendants have recently indicated an intention to submit expert declarations regarding the merits of the case in opposition to this motion. Accordingly, Plaintiffs have included herein a brief discussion of the facts supporting their allegations. Discovery to date clearly indicates the predominance of class issues regarding the alleged conspiracy. The reciprocal exchange of price information can be concerted action sufficient to establish a combination or conspiracy violative of antitrust law. (*People v. National Association of Realtors, supra,* 120 Cal.App.3d at 481-482; *United States v. Container Corp., supra,* 393 U.S. at 335.) In this case, competitive price information is exchanged between the Defendants at every critical point in the distribution chain from refinery to pipeline to terminal to dealer. The Defendants admit that they receive and rely upon up-to-the-minute pricing information of each others prices at all levels of trade from the refinery, at the terminal gate, the dealer tank wagon and at the pumps; provided with their participation or authorization through certain third party providers.[7] The CARB GAS spot pipeline price is provided by Oil Price Information Service ("OPIS") to the Defendants. Moreover, each of the Defendants had a representative at an OPIS seminar held in Santa Monica, California on December 4, 1995. The ostensible purpose for the seminar was to advise each of the participants of how the CARB GAS spot, pipeline, and terminal or rack prices would be reported.

[7] The prices for gasoline vary depending upon where in the line of distribution the product is being purchased. Defendants set a price for CARB GAS as it leaves the refinery, again when it leaves the terminals, once again when it is picked up to be transported to the dealers and at the pumps. The "spot" price refers to the ostensible price that would be paid by purchasers of the product in an open market. The lack of sufficient supply and small number of transactions and actors in the spot market makes the "spot" market merely an artifice.

9

The terminal prices and dealer tank wagon ("DTW") prices, which track the prices of refined CARB gas to franchise dealers, are also exchanged through several sources, including the . The deposition of revealed that each Defendant subscribes in one form or another to the wholesale price report of which provides each company with dealer tank wagon ("DTW") surveys and other wholesale price and volume information. (See Declaration of Timothy Cohelan and Daniel J. Mogin filed concurrently herewith, citing relevant portions of Defendants' deposition transcripts.)

The Defendants in this case have admitted that they provide pricing information in one manner or another to third party services knowing that these third parties would provide specific pricing information back to each company. The dealer tank wagon information is given to purportedly by franchise dealers, yet no defendant prohibits its dealers from providing this proprietary information. No one deposed to date has indicated that they charge for any information. Interestingly, Ms. acknowledged that "posting of prices" and direct transfer of such pricing information was curtailed in March of 1991, coinciding with the denial of cert. in the *Petroleum Products* case. The transfer of information, however, continues in an enhanced and improved fashion through the artifice of "third party" conduits. In addition certain of this information is also transmitted by each company's product traders or others who are in a position to know what those prices are.

Plaintiffs will demonstrate there is no rational competitive economic basis for this activity. This behavior serves only to establish agreed upon pricing levels and to coordinate the supplies of CARB GAS that each company is putting on the market. (*Petroleum Products, supra,* 906 F.2d at 445-560.) Accordingly, an inference of collusion is justified and the class is united in its proof of common issues of fact and law regarding the understanding alleged.

///

///

///

10

d. The Classwide Impact Can Be Presumed By The Application Of Statistical Analyses Of Damages To The Class.

The Cartwright Act specifically allows the utilization of aggregate or statistical or sampling methods with a pro rata allocation of illegal overcharges or excess profits. (Bus. & Prof. Code, § 16760(d).) The Cartwright Act also expressly sanctions the proof of price fixing damages by statistical proof. (Bus. & Prof. Code, § 16760(d).) There is no need to separately prove the individual claim of, or the amount of damage to, persons on whose behalf the suit was brought. Code of Civil Procedure section 384 allows the Court to identify classwide damages and to retain jurisdiction over such funds, serving where possible, the public interests involved.

The only issue of fact not common among all class members is the precise amount of damages or restitution each may be entitled to receive. Such individual variations, however, are not a bar to class certification. (*Vasquez v. Superior Court, supra,* 4 Cal.3d at 815; *Rosack v. Volvo of America Corp., supra,* 131 Cal.App.3d at 761-64; *B.W.I. Custom Kitchens, supra,* 191 Cal.App.3d at 1354; *Reyes v. Board of Supervisors of San Diego, supra,* 196 Cal.App.3d at 1278 "the necessity for class members to individually establish eligibility and damages does not mean that individual fact issues prevail." It is unnecessary to show injury and damages on an individual basis in price fixing class actions. (*Bruno v. Superior Court* (1981) 127 Cal.App.3d 120.) An aggregation of overcharges passed on to an individual driver can be calculated statistically or according to some other pattern. (*B.W.I. Custom Kitchen, supra,* 191 Cal.App.3d at 1354; *Rosack v. Volvo of America Corporation, supra* 31 Cal.App.3d at 762-63; *Diesel Electric Sales & Service, Inc. v. Marco Marine San Diego, Inc.* (1993) 16 Cal.App.4th 202, 219-20.)

e. Common Issues of Fact and Law Also Predominate in Plaintiffs' Second Cause of Action for Unfair Competition.

This common nucleus of facts and law is also present in Plaintiffs' Unfair Competition Act claim, which requires only the showing of an unfair, unlawful or fraudulent practice by the Defendants. The "purpose [of Bus. & Prof. Code, § 17200] is to deter futur

cs-mot

11

violations of the unfair trade practice statute and to foreclose retention by the violator of its ill gotten gains [internal citations omitted]. The Legislature considered this purpose so important that it authorized courts to order restitution without individualized proof of deception, reliance and injury if necessary to prevent the use or employment of an unfair practice." (*Bank of the West v. Superior Court* (1992) 2 Cal.4th 1254, 1267; *Committee on Children's Television, Inc. v. General Food Corp.* (1983) 35 Cal.3d 197, 211.) Even a showing of conspiracy is not required in an antitrust related claim brought under section 17200 of the Business and Professions Code. (*Motors, Inc. v. Times-Mirror Co.* (1980) 102 Cal.App.3d 735, 741-42.) Thus Plaintiffs' Unfair Competition Act claims are also well suited to certification because they present predominant common issues of law and fact.

Accordingly, the proposed class presents a well defined community of interest and common issues of law and fact prevail over individual issues. Class certification is therefore appropriate.

3. Numerosity.

The proposed Plaintiff Class must be sufficiently numerous so that joinder of its members is impracticable. (*Richmond v. Dart Industries, supra,* 29 Cal.3d at 470.) Plaintiffs need not allege the exact number and identity of class members, but must only establish that joinder is impracticable through some reasonable estimate of the number of potential class members. (*Reyes v. Board of Supervisors of San Diego County, supra,* 196 Cal.App.3d at 1274-75.) That requirement is easily met here since the members of the proposed class number in the millions. (*Richmond v. Dart Industries, supra,* 29 Cal.3d at 478, [size of proposed class that numbers in the thousands makes joinder impractical]; *Lazar v. Hertz Corp.* (1983) 143 Cal.App.3d 128, 138, [certifying class of over 5 million members].)

There are 20,390,000 licensed drivers in California (10.7 million men and 9.6 million women) and there are an estimated 14,629,000 automobiles registered.[8] The Board of

[8] Source: The Federal Highway Administration, Selected Highway Statistics and Charts, Tabl SS94-6, January 1996 lodged herewith.

12

Equalization records indicate that in 1995 Californians consumed 13,258,139,000 gallons of gasoline (taxable sales). This is more than sufficient to satisfy the numerosity requirement for class treatment.

4. **Typicality.**

In order to meet the requirement of typicality, the named Plaintiffs' interest in the action must be similar to that of the other members of the proposed class. (*Richmond v. Dart Industries, supra,* 29 Cal.3d at 47-75.) The claims of each class member need not be identical. (*Classen v. Weller* (1983) 145 Cal.App.3d 27, 46-47.)

Here, the class representatives have demonstrated that they are similarly situated to the conspiracy or course of conduct that gives rise to the claims of the other class members, and their claims are based on the same legal theory. (*Id.; Rosack v. Volvo of America Corporation, supra,* 131 Cal.App.3d at 741, 763.) Each proposed class representative and each class member purchased CARB GAS for their own use and not for resale within the Class Period. (See Class Representatives' Declarations filed concurrently herewith.) No further showing is required to satisfy the requirement of typicality.

5. **Adequacy of Representation by the Named Plaintiffs and Class Counsel.**

The representative Plaintiffs will fairly and adequately represent the interests of the class. The adequacy requirement is met here by fulfilling two conditions. First, the named Plaintiffs must be represented by counsel qualified to conduct the litigation. Second, the named Plaintiffs' interest in the litigation must not be antagonistic to the class; in other words, they must have no disabling conflict of interest that might hinder the prosecution of the action on behalf of the class. (*McGhee v. Bank of America* (1976) 60 Cal.App.3d 442, 451.)

All of the Class representatives meet both of these criteria. Class Counsel are qualified to handle this litigation. (See Declarations of Daniel Mogin and Timothy Cohelan.) They are experienced in prosecuting complex antitrust, consumer and public interest class actions, and are thus "qualified, experienced and generally able to conduct the proposed litigation." (*Miller v. Woods* (1983) 148 Cal.App.3d 862, 875; Mogin and Cohelan

13

Declarations filed concurrently herewith.) Further, absent a showing to the contrary, adequacy may be assumed. (*Guarantee Ins. Agency Co. v. Mid-Continental Rlty. Co.* (N.D. Ill. 1972) 57 F.R.D. 555, 565-66, [absent any conflicts between the interests of the representative plaintiff and other purchasers and absent any indication that the representative will not aggressively conduct the litigation, fair and adequate protection of the class may be assumed].)

The representative Plaintiffs' interests in the litigation are co-extensive with the interests of the class. Each of them has been injured in the same manner by the same practices or course of conduct as the other class members and each seeks the same relief. They have further agreed to serve as class representatives and have retained experienced counsel. This demonstrates their commitment to bringing about the best possible results for the benefit of the class, and thus meets the adequacy requirement. (*McGhee v. Bank of America, supra,* 60 Cal.App.3d at 451.) (See Class Representative Declarations.)

6. Superiority.

As previously demonstrated, the express judicial policy of California is to favor the maintenance of appropriate class actions. (*Richmond v. Dart Industries, Inc. supra,* 29 Cal.3d. at 462; *La Sala v. American Savings & Loan Assn., supra,* 5 Cal.3d at 883.) A class action is plainly superior to the other methods available for the fair and efficient adjudication of this controversy. (*Richmond v. Dart Industries, Inc., supra,* 29 Cal.3d at 469.) The California Supreme Court has repeatedly emphasized the importance of the class action device for vindicating the rights asserted by large groups of persons. (*Keating v. Superior Court* (1982) 31 Cal.3d 584, 610, appeal dismissed in part, rev'd in part on other grounds sub nom., *Southland Corp. v. Keating* (1984) 465 U.S. 1.) "Class actions serve an important role by establishing a judicial process within which the claims of many individuals can be resolved simultaneously, eliminating repetitive litigation and proving a practical method of securing redress for claims which because of their size do not warrant individual litigation." (*Reyes v. Board of Supervisors of San Diego County, supra,* 196 Cal.App.3d at 1270.)

14

Class actions by and for consumers, in particular, are recognized as "an essential tool for the protection of consumers against exploitative business practices." (*State of California v. Levi Strauss & Co., supra,* 41 Cal.3d at 471; *La Sala v. American Savings & Loan Assn., supra,*5 Cal.3d at 875-6, *Vasquez v. Superior Court, supra,*4 Cal.3d at 820-21.) For these reasons, the courts of this state have consistently strived to remove unnecessary barriers to the effective utilization of class action procedures. (*Union Carbide Corp. v. Superior Court, supra,*36 Cal.3d at 21-22; *Richmond v. Dart Industries, Inc., supra,* 29 Cal.3d at 462; *La Sala v. American Savings & Loan Assn., supra,* 5 Cal.3d at 864; *Vasquez v. Superior Court, supra,* 4 Cal.3d at 800; *Daar v. Yellow Cab, supra,* 67 Cal. 2d at 695.) Meaningful access to the court system and the deterrence of unfair and illegal conduct underlie the superiority of class litigation. (*Vasquez v. Superior Court, supra,*4 Cal.3d at 807-8; *Daar v. Yellow Cab, supra,* 67 Cal.2d at 715.)

This class action provides the best method to resolve this controversy due to the likelihood of repetitious litigation, the fact that individual litigation would simply be too expensive to pursue, and the need for deterrence. Further, a multitude of individual actions presents a risk of inconsistent or varying adjudications which could establish incompatible standards of conduct for the Defendants and the other members of the refining industry. (See Federal Rules of Civil Procedure, Rule 23 (b)(1)(A).) A class action in this matter is therefore superior to alternative methods for adjudicating this controversy.

The deterrence of illegal conduct and the courts' commitment to the use of class actions to resolve controversies involving large numbers of potential claimants clearly are the primary factors that underlie the superiority element. This element is easily met in this public interest litigation.

///

///

///

///

///

15

CONCLUSION

This case meets all of the requirements for class certification: There is an ascertainable class and a well-defined community of interest in the litigation. Plaintiffs have demonstrated the predominance of common issues of fact and law, numerosity, typicality, adequacy and superiority. For these reasons, Plaintiffs respectfully submit the proposed class should be certified.

Dated: December 18, 1996

Respectfully submitted,

COHELAN & KHOURY

By: Timothy Cohelan

Dated: December 18, 1996

THE MOGIN LAW FIRM

By: Daniel J. Mogin

16

§ 7.12 Declaration of Timothy Cohelan in Support of Plaintiffs' Motion for Class Certification (*Aguilar* v. *Atlantic Richfield Corp.*)

Timothy D. Cohelan, Esq. (SBN60827)
Isam C. Khoury, Esq. (SBN58759)
COHELAN & KHOURY
701 C Street
San Diego, California 92101-5307
Telephone: (619) 595-3001

Daniel J. Mogin (SBN95624)
Angela Milea Mogin (SBN153920)
THE MOGIN LAW FIRM
701 C Street, Suite 200
San Diego, California 92101-5307
Telephone: (619) 687-6611

Attorneys for Plaintiffs

SUPERIOR COURT OF THE STATE OF CALIFORNIA

FOR THE COUNTY OF SAN DIEGO

THERESA AGUILAR, individuals, on behalf of themselves and all others similarly situated, Plaintiffs, v. ATLANTIC RICHFIELD CORPORATION, CHEVRON CORPORATION, EXXON CORPORATION, MOBIL OIL CORPORATION, SHELL OIL COMPANY, TEXACO, INC., TOSCO CORPORATION, ULTRAMAR CORPORATION, UNOCAL CORPORATION, and DOES 1 through 40, inclusive, Defendants.	**Case No. 00700810** **DECLARATION OF TIMOTHY COHELAN IN SUPPORT OF PLAINTIFFS' MOTION FOR CLASS CERTIFICATION** **DATE:** **TIME:** **DEPT: 49** **I/C JUDGE: Hon. Jeffrey T. Miller** **TRIAL DATE: N/A**

I, TIMOTHY COHELAN, declare:

1. I am one of the attorneys for the Plaintiffs in the above-captioned lawsuit and I submit this Declaration in support of Plaintiffs' Motion for Class Certification.

2. I am licensed to practice law before all the courts of California and if called as a witness would testify of my own personal knowledge as follows:

ccertdec.sc

3. Since my admission to the bar I have represented numerous parties in civil actions of various types and degrees of complexity. To date, I have been either counsel or co-counsel in the following cases which were certified as class actions:

A. Goldman, et al. v. Pioneer Mortgage, et al., USDC for the Southern District of California, Case No. 91-005 King (BTM). Co-counsel for certified plaintiff class in federal case filed on behalf of investors in failed mortgage-backed securities issuer;

B. Marcus v. ________ Inc., USDC for the Southern District of California, Case No. 921198 H(M);

C. Evans v. ________ Inc., Los Angeles County Superior Court Case No. BC 0529392;

D. Soriano v. ________ Inc., USDC for the Central District of California, Case No. 92-0953 AWT(TX). Co-counsel in class action filed on behalf of purchasers of units in master limited partnership controlled by Cal Fed Bank;

E. Dudley, et al. v. ________ American Thrift, San Diego Superior Court Case No. 625336;

F. Bailey, et al. v. Empire Blue Cross/Blue Shield, et al., USDC for the Southern District of New York, MDL Docket No. 902, 93 Civ. 6179 (MP). Co-counsel for nation-wide certified class action filed on behalf of 8,000 victims of phony health insurance scam against RICO Defendants who engineered scam and approximately 800 insurance brokers who sold the faulty insurance. Judgments of approximately $150 million per company were entered against 84 offshore insurance companies on October 3, 1996.

G. Yia Xiong v. ________ Insurance Company, Fresno County Superior Court. Co-counsel for approximately 6,600 Hmong residents who were allegedly discriminated against by defendants in the purchase of automobile insurance.

H. Wesley Marquart v. Chartwell Financial, Orange County Superior Court. Counsel for approximately 400 investors who invested in promissory notes sold in violation of the securities code.

I. ________ v. ________ County Superior Court Case No. Certified class, for settlement purposes, of 1,391 homeowners who purchased allegedly defective homes built by in California. This matter recently settled for $22 million on behalf of the class (approved December 9, 1996).

J. Janice D. Loyd, as Trustee and Liquidator of First Assurance and Casualty Co., Ltd. v. ________. USDC for the Southern District of California, Case No. 951194T(BTM). Co-counsel - conditional settlement purposes - failed offshore insurance company with class of policyholders brought together with the bankruptcy trustee for the estate of the company.

K. Hoffmaster, et al. v. City of San Diego, San Diego County Superior Court Case No. 682920. Pro bono class action brought on behalf of homeless persons against City based on failure to provide winter shelter and failure to comply with state and federal law concerning Housing Element. (Certification not filed because mandamus issued to benefit class.)

coendec.sc

2

L. Arthur, et al. v. City of San Diego, San Diego County Superior Court Case No. 639789. This lawsuit was filed on behalf of retired police officers and firemen for unpaid health benefits.

M. Alberts v. Service Technicians, Inc., USDC for the Southern District of California, Case No. 92-526H (P).

4. I have researched and written *California Class Actions*, a treatise on handling California class action lawsuits, scheduled for publication by West Publishing in 1997.

5. The Plaintiff Class is defined as: All persons (as defined by Bus. & Prof. Code §§ 16702 and 17021) residing in California who, during the time period March 1, 1996 through the present (the "Class Period"), purchased, in California, for their own use and not for resale, CARB GAS sold by any of the Defendantts.

6. The size of the Class is approximately 20,390,000 licensed drivers based upon records of the Federal Highway Administration.[1]

7. Any factual differences in the status of the named Plaintiffs are *de minimis* and irrelevant. Neither differences in age, sex, marital status, employment, nor the number of gallons purchased by the Plaintiffs are determinative factors for class representation. The factors common to the named Plaintiffs who submit their Declarations herewith are: (1) The Plaintiffs are all licensed California drivers; (2) Each purchased CARB gasoline from one of the Defendantts during the applicable period; and (3) Each purchased that gasoline for their own use and not for resale.

8. I am unaware of any legal differences in the representatives' status as Class Members, nor of any unique factual issues pertaining to any representative which much be litigated.

9. In my opinion, the Plaintiffs' Declarations submitted herewith clearly indicate that the Plaintiffs are properly before this Court as representatives of the proposed Class.

10. Our office, together with The Mogin Law Firm, is prepared to zealously pursue this case on behalf of the Class if the Class is certified. We seek to have an early trial date and, as of the date of this application for certification and according to our

[1] See Exhibit "A" to Notice of Lodgment.

ccertdec.tc

3

discovery plan, expect to be in a position to disclose the identity and opinion of experts in early spring. As Plaintiffs' counsel we will vigorously pursue the matter through to a trial.

I declare under penalty of perjury under the laws of the State of California that the foregoing is true and correct. Executed this 10th day of December, 1996, at San Diego, California.

TIMOTHY COHELAN

coordec.tc

4

§ 7.13 Memorandum of Points and Authorities in Opposition to Plaintiffs' Motion for Order Determining Class Issues (*Xiong* case)

THEODORE R. FORREST, JR., CAL. BAR NO. 76429
WILLIAM T. McLAUGHLIN II, CAL. BAR NO. 116348
FORREST & MCLAUGHLIN
6790 North West Avenue, Suite 104
Fresno, California 93711-1393

Telephone: (209) 261-9100

PIERCE T. SELWOOD, CAL. BAR NO. 36174
DANI JO MERRYMAN, CAL. BAR NO. 130346
ELENA MURAVINA, CAL BAR NO. 160037
SHEPPARD, MULLIN, RICHTER & HAMPTON
333 South Hope Street, 48th Floor
Los Angeles, California 90071-1448

Telephone: (213) 620-1780

Attorneys for Defendant

AND RELATED ENTITIES

SUPERIOR COURT OF CALIFORNIA

COUNTY OF FRESNO

YIA XIONG, on behalf of themselves and all others similarly situated, Plaintiffs, v. an unincorporated inter-insurance exchange; a California corporation; and DOES 1 through 500, inclusive, Defendants.	Case No. 1. MEMORANDUM OF POINTS AND AUTHORITIES IN OPPOSITION TO PLAINTIFFS' MOTION FOR ORDER DETERMINING CLASS ISSUES; 2. DECLARATION OF IN SUPPORT THEREOF; 3. DECLARATION OF IN SUPPORT THEREOF; and 4. DECLARATION OF IN SUPPORT THEREOF. [Declarations Filed Concurrently Herewith.] DATE: May 31, 1995 TIME: 8:30 a.m. DEPT: 70 TRIAL: NONE SET

2\M\P076638X.LEO -i-

Defendants

erroneously sued as

(hereinafter occasionally

collectively referred to as) respectfully submit the following memorandum of points and authorities in opposition to plaintiffs Yia Xiong,

(hereinafter occasionally collectively referred to as "Plaintiffs"), Motion for order determining class issues ("Certification Motion").

2\M\P076638X.LEO -ii-

TABLE OF CONTENTS

	Page
MEMORANDUM OF POINTS AND AUTHORITIES	1
I. INTRODUCTION	1
II. PLAINTIFFS HAVE THE BURDEN OF PROOF TO SHOW THAT THE CLAIMED CLASS SHOULD BE CERTIFIED	5
III. PLAINTIFFS FAILED TO MEET THEIR BURDEN OF SHOWING THAT CLASS TREATMENT IS APPROPRIATE IN THIS ACTION.	7
A. No Class Can Be Ascertained	8
1. The proposed class cannot be ascertained under the Plaintiffs' own definition	8
2. Plaintiffs' method of ascertaining the class does not withstand scrutiny	9
3. Plaintiffs failed to provide any means of ascertaining who among the minority policyholders was inappropriately rated . . .	12
4. Legal authority does not support Plaintiffs' position that the class can be ascertained here	13
B. Individual Issues Of Law And Fact Predominate Over Common Questions	15
1. No common question of law exists as to the alleged violation of the Cartwright Act . . .	16
2. Individual questions of fact predominate as to alleged violations of the Cartwright Act and the Unruh Civil Rights Act	17
(1) Statistical analysis cannot be used to prove discriminatory conduct of the type alleged in Plaintiffs' Complaint	18
(2) Named class representatives fail to substantiate Complaint allegations . . .	19
3. Individual issues of fact clearly predominate	22
4. Plaintiffs misapprehend the caselaw applicable to class certification in this lawsuit	25
5. Plaintiffs failed to demonstrate the causal connection between the alleged wrongful acts and the injury sustained by the members of the putative class	26

2\M\P076638X.LEO

-i-

C. Plaintiffs Have Failed To Meet The Superiority Requirement 29

D. Named Class Representatives Are Not The Members of The Class 32

E. Ability Of Class Representatives To Fairly And Adequately Protect The Interests Of The Class . . . 33

1. Named representatives' claims are not typical 33

2. Named class representatives cannot properly discharge their fiduciary obligations 34

IV. CONCLUSION 37

2\M\P076638X.LEO

-ii-

TABLE OF AUTHORITIES

Page(s)

Cases

Brown v. Regents of University of California,
151 Cal. App. 3d 982 (1984) 15

Burhalter Travel Agency v. MacFarms Intern., Inc.,
141 F.R.D. 144 (N.D.Cal. 1991) 34, 35

Caro v. Procter & Gamble Co.,
18 Cal. App. 4th 644, n.13, 667, n.20 (1993) . 6, 15, 17, 27, 33, 37

City of San Jose v. Superior Court,
12 Cal. 3d 447 (1974) 6, 15, 27, 37

Collins v. Safeway Stores, Inc.,
187 Cal. App. 3d 62 (1986) 27

Crogan-Beall v. Ferdinand Roten Galleries, Inc.,
133 Cal. App. 3d 969 (1982) 15

Daar v. Yellow Cab Co.,
67 Cal. 2d 695 (1967) 12-14, 25

Dean Witter Reynolds, Inc. v. Superior Court,
211 Cal. App. 3d 758 (1989) 6, 20, 37

Fanucchi v. Coberly-West Co.,
151 Cal.App.2d 72 (1957) 26

General Telephone Co. of Southwest v. Falcon,
457 U.S. 148, 102 S.Ct. 2364 (1982) 17

Hamwi v. Citinational-Buckeye Investment Co.,
72 Cal. App. 3d 462 (1977) 6, 29

Mechigian v. Art Capital Corp.,
612 F. Supp. 1421 (D.C.N.Y. 1985) 36

National Auto Brokers Corp. v. General Motors Corp.,
376 F. Supp. 620 (S.D.N.Y. 1974),
aff'd, 572 F.2d 953 (2d Cir. 1978),
cert. den'd, 439 U.S. 1072, 99 S. Ct. 844 (1979) 36

Osborne v. Subaru of America, Inc.,
198 Cal. App. 3d 646 (1988)
reh'g den'd and rev. den'd 7, 37

Ralston v. Volkswagenwerk, A.G.,
61 F.R.D. 427 (W.D.Mo. 1973) 36

2\M\P076638X.LEO -iii-

Spoon v. Superior Court,
130 Cal. App. 3d 735 (1982) 28

State of Alabama v. Blue Bird Body Co., Inc.,
573 F.2d 309 (5th Cir. 1978) 31

Stephens v. Montgomery Ward, Inc.,
193 Cal. App.3d 411 (1987) 9, 18

Teamsters v. United States,
431 U.S. 324 (1977) 18

Union Mutual Life Ins. Co., v. Superior Court,
80 Cal. App.3d 1 (5th Dist. 1978) 7

Vasquez v. Superior Court of San Joaquin County,
4 Cal. 3d 800 (1971) 13, 14

Weaver v. Pasadena Tournament of Roses,
32 Cal. 2d 833 (1948) 15

Welling v. Alexy,
155 F.R.D. 654 (N.D.Cal. 1994) 34

Yia Xiong, Tou Vue Moua and Theng Moua v. Farmers, et al.,
Case No. BC 089365, Los Angeles Superior Court 2

Statutes

Cal. Civ. Code §§ 1750 *et seq*. 5

Cal. Code Civ. Proc. § 382 5

Cal. Ins. Code § 1861.025 9

Other Authorities

Barclays Official California Code of Regulations,
Title 10, Section 2646.6 10

Los Angeles County Superior Court Rules,
Chapter 15 7

2\M\P076638X.LEO -iv-

MEMORANDUM OF POINTS AND AUTHORITIES

I.

INTRODUCTION

Based upon the Second Amended Complaint in the present lawsuit, plaintiffs' counsel have filed a Motion for an Order Determining Class Issues ("Certification Motion") on the second cause of action for alleged violations of one provision of the Cartwright Act, Business and Professions Code § 16721, and the fourth cause of action for alleged violations of the anti-discrimination Unruh Act, Civil Code Sections 51 and 52. Plaintiffs' counsel ask the Court to certify a class with the following definition:

> "Persons of Southeast Asian origin, defined as Hmong, Cambodians, Laotians, and Vietnamese, who reside within the Fresno and Merced County areas and who purchased automobile insurance through including the subsidiaries operating between March 29, 1990 and March 29, 1994, inclusive, and who were discriminated against economically by being placed into a higher-risk category at greater expense than that allowed by the law of California, including the "Good Driver Discount" of Insurance Code § 1861.025, and who were damaged thereby by said overcharges."

The plaintiff class representatives in this action are a group of twelve Fresno area Southeast Asian immigrants, some of whom do not want to be part of the lawsuit, and all of whom show little interest or concern about the issues raised by it. The defendants are several affiliated entities from the

Z\M\P076638X.LED -1-

which are headquartered in is a California reciprocal interinsurance Exchange owned by its policyholders. Historically, has insured only those drivers who presented low risk based on numerous different rating criteria.

a California Corporation, has historically insured those drivers who are typically considered "standard" i.e., those drivers who present a greater risk of loss.

Defendants contend that this action is a lawyers' creation. Plaintiffs' counsel represent unwilling and unsophisticated individuals, many of whom do not speak any English, are indigent and on government assistance. The action now pending in the Fresno Superior Court is a result of obvious forum shopping. Plaintiffs' counsel were clearly dissatisfied with the progress of their case as originally filed in the Los Angeles Superior Court in September of 1993.[1] Following removal of that action to the U.S. District Court, and a massive sanctions motion being filed against plaintiffs' counsel, plaintiffs attempted to voluntarily dismiss their federal action. After a lengthy hearing, Judge Keller granted plaintiffs' motion, on the condition that the plaintiffs' and their counsel reimburse $15,500 for its reasonable fees and costs incurred in defending the action. This court can take judicial notice of the "Notice of Entry of Order" (in Los Angeles U.S.D.C. Case No.) filed in this action in the Fresno Superior Court on

[1] See Yia Xiong, v. et al., Case No. Los Angeles Superior Court.

2\M\P076638X.LEO -2-

July 21, 1994.[2] Plaintiffs' counsel had already started forum shopping by filing this case in Fresno on March 29, 1994, two weeks after filed its Opposition to Plaintiffs' Rule 11 Certification, which Opposition demonstrated the lack of merit of plaintiffs' claims.

Plaintiffs' counsel have constantly revised and narrowed the class definition they seek to have certified. In the original Los Angeles Superior Court case the class was defined as "all California residents of Southeast Asian race and heritage, who were denied coverage or overcharged for insurance coverage or had existing policies unjustly cancelled by ." By the time of the Second Amended Complaint filed in this action on August 9, 1994, counsels' constantly changing "class" had greatly contracted. The class no longer consisted of "all Southeast Asians in California," but only of ethnically Hmong, Laotian, Mien and Lahu residents of Fresno or Merced Counties "who purchased a automobile policy, or who attempted to purchase such a policy or obtain an insurance quotation for such a policy" during the relevant time period. Second Amended Complaint, ¶ 60.

Finally, as can be seen from plaintiffs' instant motion, the class has once again been narrowed to include only those "who were discriminated against economically by being placed into a higher risk category at greater expense than that allowed by the law of California, including the 'Good Driver Discount' . . . ,

[2] The Court is respectfully requested to take judicial notice of all pleadings and papers on file with this Court.

2\M\P076638X.LEO -3-

and who were damaged thereby by said overcharges." Obviously, counsel for plaintiffs are making a desperate effort, long after filing the lawsuit, to come up with a class definition which will "stick to the wall."

vigorously and unconditionally denies plaintiffs' allegations of discrimination against the plaintiffs or anyone else. has always strictly enforced a written company-wide policy of non-discrimination. is absolutely confident that a trial on the merits would demonstrate that plaintiffs' allegations have no basis whatsoever in fact. However, the merits of plaintiffs' case may not be assessed at the present time, and must await resolution following the Certification Motion. The scope of the Class Certification phase of this lawsuit is narrow: Plaintiffs' must prove that class treatment is appropriate and superior to individual actions. As this opposition demonstrates, plaintiffs failed to sustain their burden. The defendants are confident that the Court, in weighing whether plaintiffs have met their burden of proof on each of the required elements in a Class Certification Motion, will find that plaintiffs have totally failed to meet their burden on a number of the class issues, thereby requiring the Court to deny plaintiffs' Certification Motion.

Plaintiffs failed to demonstrate how the class as defined can be ascertained in the instant case. No showing that the class is ascertainable is made in the Certification Motion. In addition, plaintiffs failed to sustain their burden in

2\M\P076638X.LEO -4-

demonstrating that a common issue of law exists with respect to their Cartwright Act cause of action. On both causes of action, alleged violation of the Cartwright Act and alleged violation of the Unruh Act, individual issues of fact clearly predominate, yet plaintiffs here failed to present a method by which these issues can be resolved on a class-wide basis. Given the extremely detailed and time-consuming analysis of each class member's individual factual situation that Plaintiffs will have to develop in order to demonstrate the alleged discrimination, this class action is not superior as it will inevitably disintegrate into a series of mini-trials. Finally, the named class representatives cannot adequately represent the class as they have not suffered the injury alleged in the Second Amended Complaint and are unable to vigorously prosecute this action on behalf of the absent class members.

For these reasons, as more fully set forth below, plaintiffs' motion requesting that the class be certified should be denied.

II.

PLAINTIFFS HAVE THE BURDEN OF PROOF TO SHOW THAT THE CLAIMED CLASS SHOULD BE CERTIFIED

This Court has the authority, under California Code of Civil Procedure, Section 382, and California Civil Code, Sections 1750 *et seq*., to determine whether class treatment is appropriate. Under California Code of Civil Procedure,

2\M\P076638X.LEO -5-

Section 382, there are two basic prerequisites to certification of a class action: (1) the existence of an ascertainable class, and (2) a well-defined community of interest in the questions of law and fact which affect the parties to be represented. See also Certification Motion, at 3. The courts have made it clear that any class action plaintiff bears the burden of establishing that the action meets these requirements:

> "A plaintiff moving for class treatment bears the burden of establishing that the requisites for such treatment are present. . . In ordinary class actions, this requires the plaintiff to show that there is 'an ascertainable class and a well-defined community of interest among the class members.'"

Dean Witter Reynolds, Inc. v. Superior Court, 211 Cal. App. 3d 758, 764 (1989); Hamwi v. Citinational-Buckeye Investment Co., 72 Cal. App. 3d 462, 471 (1977).

Moreover, as the court held in Hamwi, "satisfaction of that burden requires that the plaintiff establish more than 'a reasonable probability' that class treatment is appropriate." Hamwi, supra, at 471-72. The community of interest issue must be determined "on the merits" and the plaintiff "must establish the community as a matter of fact." Id., Caro v. Procter & Gamble Co., 18 Cal. App. 4th 644, 665, n.13, 667, n.20 (1993).

Additionally, plaintiffs have the burden of meeting a "superiority requirement." As the Supreme Court explained:

> "Before the imposition of a judgment binding on absent parties can be justified, it must be shown that substantial benefits both to the litigants and to the court will result . . . . The burden of such a showing falls on plaintiff. . ."

2\M\P076638X.LEO -6-

City of San Jose v. Superior Court, 12 Cal. 3d 447, 460 (1974) (citations omitted); Osborne v. Subaru of America, Inc., 198 Cal. App. 3d 646, 653 (1988), reh'g den'd and rev. den'd.

Accordingly, Los Angeles County Superior Court Rules, Chapter Fifteen governing class actions ("Class Action Rules"), recommended to this Court by the Fifth District Court of Appeal[3/], provide in Rule 15.17(f):

> "The burden of proof on all class issues is on the party alleging the existence of a class. All issues of fact will be proved by a preponderance of the evidence presented in the hearing."

Plaintiffs' moving papers do not carry the burden of establishing that the class action prerequisites are met, and for a simple reason: this action is not suitable for class treatment. Failure to meet the burden of proof requires denial of Plaintiffs' motion.

III.

PLAINTIFFS FAILED TO MEET THEIR BURDEN OF SHOWING THAT CLASS TREATMENT IS APPROPRIATE IN THIS ACTION.

[3/] Los Angeles County Superior Court Rules, Chapter 15, formerly, the Manual for the Conduct of Pretrial Procedures in Class Actions, govern all class actions pending in the Los Angeles Superior Court; however, they are persuasive authority for other courts that are urged to follow the same guidelines, See Union Mutual Life Ins. Co., v. Superior Court, 80 Cal. App.3d 1, 13 n.2. (5th Dist. 1978). In fact, Plaintiffs have previously referred this Court to these rules for guidance in their Motion for Order Compelling Production of Documents, at 10, n.4, on file with this Court.

2\M\P076638X.LEO -7-

A. No Class Can Be Ascertained.

1. The proposed class cannot be ascertained under the Plaintiffs' own definition.

The way Plaintiffs define the class has changed throughout the history of this action. In their first Complaint filed in 1993 in Los Angeles Superior Court (the predecessor lawsuit), Plaintiffs defined it as "all California residents of Southeast Asian race and heritage, who were denied coverage or overcharged for insurance coverage or had existing policies unjustly cancelled by ." (See footnote 1, supra.) However, the class, as defined in the operative Second Amended Complaint filed on August 9, 1994 in this case, no longer consists of all Southeast Asians in California, but only of ethnically Hmong, Laotian, Mien and Lahu residents of Fresno or Merced Counties who purchased a automobile insurance policy, or attempted to purchase such a policy or obtain an insurance quotation for such a policy during the relevant time period. Second Amended Complaint, ¶ 60.

This definition has further evolved in the present Certification Motion which now defines the class as ethnically Hmong, Cambodians, Laotians and Vietnamese residing within Fresno and Merced County who purchased automobile insurance from and "were discriminated against economically by being placed into a higher-risk category at greater expense than that allowed by the law of California, including the "Good Driver Discount" of

2\M\P076638X.LEO -8-

Insurance Code § 1861.025, and who were damaged thereby by said overcharges." Certification Motion, at p. 1.

Yet, even under this more narrow definition, the class cannot be ascertained. While Plaintiffs are correct in asserting that ascertaining the precise identity of each absent class member is not required at this time, Plaintiffs may not merely speculate as to the existence of class members: it remains their burden to demonstrate that some reasonable means of ascertaining absent class members' identities exist. Stephens v. Montgomery Ward, Inc., 193 Cal. App.3d 411, 417 (1987). Plaintiffs have failed to meet this burden.

2. Plaintiffs' method of ascertaining the class does not withstand scrutiny.

Plaintiffs propose to ascertain the class by using a California Department of Insurance Statistical Analysis which provides some statistics as to the number of automobile insurance policies issued by in 1991 for the Fresno area, not including Merced. Certification Motion, at p. 4. Obviously, taken by itself, this "slice of life" statistical sample which covers neither the entire relevant geographic area nor time period, even if accurate,[6] proves nothing. To bolster their claim that the class can be ascertained, Plaintiffs requested that produce certain evidence at the hearing. See Plaintiffs' Request for Testimony at Hearing on Class Issues

[6] See Objections to Plaintiffs' Evidence filed concurrently herewith.

2\M\P076638X.LEO -9-

and Request for Production of Documents at Hearing ("Request for Testimony and Documents"). Setting the propriety of such a demand aside[5/], the statistical data Plaintiffs seek simply does not exist at the present time. See Declaration of (" Decl."), ¶ 2. Moreover, Section 2646.6 of the Barclays Official California Code of Regulations, Title 10, cited by Plaintiffs does not require to have such data for the time period relevant to this litigation and consequently, no such data has been gathered or maintained. Declaration of (" Decl."), ¶ 3; Decl., ¶ 2.

Plaintiffs' intent is to compare the statistical data in the California Department of Insurance Statistical Analysis to the data in the Department of Insurance Community Service statement, to be prepared by .[6/] Such Community Service Statement, when filed, will contain certain information regarding the national origin or race of the applicants or policyholders, to be voluntarily provided by the applicants. However, is required to provide the first such Community Service statement only on March 1, 1996, not March 1, 1995 as Plaintiffs erroneously state. See Decl. Moreover, when assembled, this Community Statement will contain only information for the year of 1995, which is outside the relevant time period defined by

---

5/ have filed an Opposition to Plaintiffs' Request for Testimony and Documents, filed concurrently herewith.

6/ As Plaintiffs' do not expressly explain how they are going to demonstrate ascertainability of the class through the use of the Community Service Statement, their methodology has to be deduced from their motion.

2\M\P076638X.LEO -10-

Plaintiffs as the period between March 29, 1990 and March 29, 1994. Plaintiffs' Motion, at 1.

At this time, has no data concerning the race and/or national origin of its insureds. Decl., ¶ 2. In fact, requesting such information is specifically prohibited by the non-discrimination policy, and consequently, there is no question addressing this issue on initial policy application form, or any other forms. Declaration of , (" Decl."), ¶ 15. Thus, Plaintiffs' method of ascertaining the identities of putative class members fails because the information Plaintiffs need to identify the class does not in fact exist, contrary to Plaintiffs' assumption.

In the alternative, Plaintiffs propose to identify putative class members by their last names, through the expertise of Dr. . As Objections to Plaintiffs' Evidence demonstrate, Dr. 's proposed method of identifying minority class members by their names lacks any scientific foundation.[7] Moreover, his expertise in identifying individuals' national origin by their names apparently applies only to some of the minority class members, namely, Hmong and Laotian. Plaintiffs have yet to find an expert capable of divining the national origin of Cambodians, Vietnamese, Mien and Lahu policyholders.

---

[7] Objections to Plaintiffs' Evidence, at pp. 11-13.

Z\M\P076638X.LEC -11-

3. <u>Plaintiffs failed to provide any means of ascertaining who among the minority policyholders was inappropriately rated</u>.

Even if it is assumed that the policyholders of certain defined Southeast Asian origin can somehow be identified with some degree of precision, it does not automatically make them members of the Plaintiffs' class. <u>In order to fall within Plaintiffs' own class definition, those minority policyholders must also sustain damages from being economically discriminated against by by being placed into a higher-risk category, specifically Insurance Company, and by depriving them of the Good Driver Discount benefit.</u> Thus, in addition to showing how they will identify the minority policyholders, Plaintiffs also must demonstrate the method by which they can identify on a class-wide basis among those minority policyholders the ones who (a) were inappropriately put in a higher-risk insurance category; (b) were not given the benefit of a deserved Good Driver Discount; and (c) suffered damages as a result. As more fully explained below, such analysis requires a close scrutiny of a great number of individual facts affecting the assignment of risk and is not capable of being performed on a class-wide basis.

Plaintiffs' attempts to analogize the instant case to <u>Daar v. Yellow Cab Co.</u>, 67 Cal. 2d 695 (1967) are unavailing. Every single passenger who entered a Yellow Cab in <u>Daar</u> was subjected to the same uniform overcharge. The only task left for plaintiffs in that case was to identify the passengers who used Yellow Cab during the relevant time period. Yet, the instant

2\M\P076638X.LEC -12-

situation is strikingly dissimilar. The assignment of risk, insurance rating and application of the Good Driver Discount do not apply uniformly and automatically to all policyholders, minority or not, but turn on the specific individual facts, unique to each policyholder. In fact, the analysis of the factual circumstances and rating decisions for just the named class representatives in this action refutes any notion of uniformity, see Decl. ¶ 14. As demonstrated below, none of the named representatives was in fact overcharged by or in a discriminatory manner placed in a higher-premium insurance category, or denied a Good Driver Discount. However, while the outcome -- absence of discrimination -- is the same for all the named plaintiffs, in each case this determination was reached based on a variety of different factors. See Plaintiffs Information Table, supra, at 21.

4. Legal authority does not support Plaintiffs' position that the class can be ascertained here.

Plaintiffs cite no authority in support of their contention that the "ascertainable class" requirement can be met in these circumstances, and there is none. To the contrary, the California Supreme Court made it clear in both Daar, supra, and Vasquez v. Superior Court of San Joaquin County, 4 Cal. 3d 800 (1971), that the "ascertainable class" requirement cannot be met in such circumstances. The Court stated in Daar:

> [I]n observing the ascertainable class requirement . . ., [courts] are at the same time giving recognition to the principle that a group of individuals' rights to recover,

2\H\P076638X.LEC -13-

> each of which is based on a separate set of facts, cannot be determined by a judgment in a class action."

Daar, supra, at 704. Similarly, in Vasquez, the Court noted that: "As to the necessity for an ascertainable class, the right of each individual to recover may not be based on a separate set of facts applicable to him." Vasquez, supra, at 809.

Yet, it is precisely a separate set of facts that each putative class member would have to prove in this case. Each would have to prove, among other things, that he or she answered approximately sixty questions on the application form in such a way as to qualify for placement with and for obtaining a Good Driver discount during the relevant time period, yet was denied proper placement. Moreover, each would have to prove that he or she sustained ascertainable harm as a result thereof.[8] This cannot be done by generalized proof on a class-wide basis. Plaintiffs failed to make any showing whatsoever that even the named plaintiffs, let alone anyone else, were purportedly harmed by the alleged discriminatory conduct. Accordingly, the "ascertainable class" requirement cannot be met here. Plaintiffs failed to sustain their burden of proof on the critical issue of ascertainability of the class.

---

[8] Given the fact that during the majority of the relevant period, the rates of were identical, proving damages becomes a daunting task. See infra at 24, 25.

2\M\P076638X.LEO -14-

B. Individual Issues Of Law And Fact Predominate Over Common Questions.

To meet the "community of interest" requirement, plaintiffs must demonstrate that common questions of law and fact predominate over individual issues, and therefore, the right of each putative class member to recover would not require individual proof. As the Supreme Court stated in City of San Jose:

> "Holding that a class action cannot be maintained where each member's right to recover depends on facts peculiar to his case. . . remains viable in this state. The rule exists because the community of interest requirement is not satisfied if every member of the alleged class would be required to litigate numerous and substantial questions determining his individual right to recover following the "class judgment" determining issues common to the purported class."

City of San Jose, supra, at 459; Caro, supra, at 668; Weaver v. Pasadena Tournament of Roses, 32 Cal. 2d 833, (1948); Crogan-Beall v. Ferdinand Roten Galleries, Inc., 133 Cal. App.3d 969, 976 (1982).

Thus, the right to bring a class action is not unlimited. Class actions will not be permitted where there are diverse factual issues to be resolved, even though there may be many common questions of law. Brown v. Regents of University of California, 151 Cal. App. 3d 982, 988 (1984). The Certification Motion is flawed at its very heart because, as more fully set below, the alleged discriminatory placement into a higher-premium risk category is not susceptible to proof on a class-wide basis.

2\M\P076638X.LEO -15-

1. <u>No common question of law exists as to the alleged violation of the Cartwright Act</u>.

Business and Professions Code Section 16721 of the Cartwright Act provides that no person can be excluded from a business transaction on the basis of a policy expressed in any <u>document</u> or <u>writing</u>. . . where such policy requires discrimination against that person on the basis of the person's race, sex or national origin. The Certification Motion offers no evidence of any such document or writing expressing discriminatory policy toward people of Southeast Asian origin or any other minority. All the named class representatives have uniformly denied any knowledge of such a written document. <u>See</u> Decl., ¶ 4. This is for a good reason: no such document exists. In fact, exactly the opposite is true: a fully articulated non-discriminatory policy is enforced by management and explained to all agents. Decl., ¶¶ 15-16.

The antitrust cases cited by Plaintiffs are inapposite: none of them deals with Section 16721. The statutory requirement is clear -- in the absence of a written document, no violation of Section 16721 can be found. As Plaintiffs have failed to demonstrate the existence of such a written document, no community of interest can be found among the individual class members with respect to the alleged violation of Section 16721 of the Cartwright Act. Hence, it is clear that no class could be certified as to the cause of action alleged under the Cartwright Act.

2\M\P076638X.LEC -16-

2. Individual questions of fact predominate as to alleged violations of the Cartwright Act and the Unruh Civil Rights Act.

While discrimination cases may indeed often be found susceptible to class treatment, as the United States Supreme Court explained in the context of an alleged employment discrimination case:

> "Conceptually, there is a wide gap between (a) an individual's claim that he has been denied a promotion on discriminatory grounds, and his otherwise unsupported allegation that the company has a policy of discrimination, and (b) the existence of a class of persons who have suffered the same injury as that individual, such that the individual's claim and the class claims will share common questions of law and fact and that the individual's claim will be typical of the class claims."

General Telephone Co. of Southwest v. Falcon, 457 U.S. 148, 157, 102 S.Ct. 2364 (1982).[9]

The gap that the U.S. Supreme Court has described is particularly wide here as the alleged discriminatory conduct is simply not susceptible to class-wide proof. The fallacy of the Plaintiffs' case is that the injury alleged here, unlike a uniform denial of coverage or uniform overcharging of all Southeast Asian applicants, is so individual in character and requires such an extensive, facts-driven analysis, that any national origin commonality is completely undermined and refuted by many varying individual issues of fact. Thus, it is not surprising that Plaintiffs

[9] California courts may look to federal authority for guidance on matters involving class action procedures. Caro, supra, at 656, n. 7 (1993).

2\M\P076638X.LEC -17-

failed to demonstrate how they intend to deal with the great number of individual issues of fact that must be addressed. Calling this complex inquiry "simply a California-overcharging case" (Certification' Motion, at 11) is, of course, begging the issue.

(1) Statistical analysis cannot be used to prove discriminatory conduct of the type alleged in Plaintiffs' Complaint.

The proof of discriminatory conduct of the type alleged in Plaintiffs' Second Amended Complaint is not susceptible to class treatment. The most common method of proving discriminatory conduct is by utilizing statistical analysis to create a broad inference of discrimination which is illustrated by the named plaintiff's individual case. Thus, a statistical data analysis of a disproportionate number of women as compared to men who were promoted to supervisorial positions was introduced to support an inference of discrimination in Stephens, supra, at 416. A low number of Blacks or Hispanics in desirable positions, when compared to the percentage of the workers of the same race or national origin in the company labor force was held to raise an inference of discrimination in Teamsters v. United States, 431 U.S. 324 (1977).

However, no statistical data is, or could be available to demonstrate the disparity in premiums paid by different ethnic groups insured by   to support the inference of discrimi-

2\M\P076638X.LEC -18-

nation alleged by Plaintiffs.[10] The amount of premium is determined by a great number of individual facts pertaining to each insured, such as his or her age, driving experience, mileage driven, number of cars, number of drivers in the household, age and experience of those drivers and a multitude of other factors. See Decl., ¶ 42. Even if had information regarding the national origin of its insureds, any statistical analysis under these circumstances would have been meaningless. However, as does not have any information regarding its insureds' national origin, such statistical analysis is simply impossible. Plaintiffs have made no showing of how an inference of discrimination by against the Southeast Asians can be raised under the facts of this case.

(2) Named class representatives fail to substantiate Complaint allegations.

Moreover, Plaintiffs similarly failed to substantiate the allegations in the Second Amended Complaint with any evidence that discriminated against the named representatives of

[10] Plaintiffs have included a portion of their argument in the Declaration of Timothy D. Cohelan ("Cohelan Decl."). Thus, additional documents introduced there are apparently relied on by Plaintiffs to demonstrate the ascertainability of the class and are intended to serve as "representative information upon which informed analysis can be conducted on a statistical basis." Cohelan Decl., at 9. The evidentiary value of these documents is addressed elsewhere, see Objections to Plaintiffs' Evidence, at pp. 10-11. However, the time for the informed statistical analysis is now, when Plaintiffs must meet their burden of showing that the class is ascertainable. Again, Plaintiffs failed to sustain that burden.

2\M\P076638X.LEO -19-

the class. When the claim of a named class representative patently lacks merit, it precludes an action by the class he purports to represent. Dean Witter Reynolds, Inc., supra, at 772. This is precisely the case here: as demonstrated by the table below, none of the named representatives has a meritorious claim.

The analysis of the insurance history of each named representative is involved and lengthy. It has been performed by the underwriting specialist, , and is set forth in her declaration. See Decl., ¶¶ 82-207. For the purposes of illustration, has organized in the table below the information pertinent to the initial application for insurance during the relevant time period by each named class representative. The table is illustrative of the fact that out of twelve named class representatives none was discriminated against by being inappropriately placed in a higher-premium category[11/] and/or denied a Good Driver Discount. Decl., ¶¶ 93-99, 115-118, 124-134, 166-190, 193-198, 203 and 207.

11/ As discussed, infra, the very notion of a "higher-premium" insurance is, at best, misleading, as during most of the relevant time period, both offered identical rates for identical coverage, and identical good driver discounts. See, infra at 24.

2\M\P076638X.LEO -20-

Table Omitted

-21-

In reviewing the table, it is apparent that all named representatives who qualified for the Good Driver Discount were granted such a discount in 1991 when the good driver discount provisions of the Proposition 103 were first implemented by . Equally apparent is the fact that those named representatives who were not insured with did not qualify for such a placement, typically, because of the lack of prior insurance. However, those who qualified for placement with the were so placed. In fact, if information undisclosed by the named representatives and revealed through discovery in this action were revealed by them at the time of their application, such individuals as would not have been placed with the . Thus, in fact, some of the named representatives were not only not overcharged, but rather undercharged by . *See* Decl., ¶ 83.

3. Individual issues of fact clearly predominate.

Even more significantly, the table above illustrates the extent of a factual inquiry necessary to determine whether each individual class member has sustained the injury alleged. Those disparate questions of fact include:

- Territory of operations (where car principally garaged);
- Age of drivers;
- Smoking habits of drivers;
- Occupation of drivers;

2\H\P076638X.LEO

-22-

- Prior insurance coverage;
- Sex of drivers;
- Marital status of drivers;
- Type of automobile(s);
- Number of automobile(s);
- Use of automobile(s) (work, pleasure, etc.);
- Expected yearly mileage;
- Amount of coverage requested;
- Accident record of all drivers;
- Driving violations of all drivers.

Plaintiffs state that "Defendants' records will allow Plaintiffs' counsel to examine objective criteria to determine whether overcharged the class." Certification Motion, at 10. Yet, as time-consuming as such an examination of records would be, it will not be sufficient. As the named Plaintiffs' deposition testimony amply demonstrates, the information provided by Plaintiffs in their insurance applications cannot be relied on in making such a determination.[12] Actual discovery of pertinent facts and separate adjudication of each individual claim for each putative class member will be required. A great number

[12] Some of the discrepancies between information found in plaintiffs' applications and what they testified to in their depositions involve not disclosing information regarding additional youthful drivers. For example, did not indicate any additional youthful drivers residing in his household, however, three of his children of driving age were residing with him at the time. One of them, Tiffany, in 1991, while driving a car insured by was involved in an accident resulting in a complete loss of the car. Other plaintiffs did not disclose their smoking habits on their applications and received a non-smoking discount, while smoking a pack per day. See Decl., ¶ 11.

2\M\P076638X.LEC -23-

of mini-trials will absolutely be required if this litigation is permitted to proceed on a class basis.

Similarly, Plaintiffs' reliance on the "now-codified rules regarding acceptable insurance rates" is misplaced. Different rules, including those governing the Good Driver Discount, applied at different times throughout the applicable period. Therefore, an applicant who arguably qualified for placement with and/or a good driver discount at one time, would not have necessarily qualified for it at another time. No less than three separate rating plans were applicable during the relevant time period. Thus, class members who applied for new insurance coverage between March 29, 1990 and February 1, 1991, were offered rates based on the pre-Proposition 103 rating plan. From February 1, 1991 through March 1, 1994, implemented a post-Proposition 103 rating plan. Effective March 1, 1994 and pursuant to the Stipulation and Order entered into by and the Department of Insurance, implemented further modifications to its rating plan. Decl., ¶¶ 82-84.

During most of the relevant period, between February 1, 1991 and March 1, 1994, applicants were placed either in based on their prior insurance history and other factors. However, during that time, both companies offered identical rates. Moreover, both companies offered identical good driver discount. The only difference between the two companies was that also offered a preferred 30/60 plan and a non-smoking discount. Thus, Plaintiffs' allegations that they were over-

2\M\P076638X.LEO -24-

charged as a result of being placed in Company have no basis in reality. Decl., ¶¶ 82-84.

Therefore, in addition to analyzing differing individual circumstances of each putative class member, this Court will also have to verify which of the three above-described rating plans applied to each class member at the time he or she applied for insurance. Plaintiffs did not and could not propose any method by which they will provide a uniform analysis of all of these diverging separate issues of fact. Consequently, they failed to sustain their burden of proof that individual issues of fact do not predominate here.

4. Plaintiffs misapprehend the caselaw applicable to class certification in this lawsuit.

Plaintiffs attempt to skirt the issue of disparate individual facts predominating here by trying to squeeze their case into the legal precedent of Daar, supra. The Cinderella shoe simply does not fit: the fact pattern of Daar bears no resemblance to the issues in this case. There were no individual issues of fact, other than the amount of damages, that separated Yellow Cab passenger plaintiffs in Daar. The fact of injury for all Daar plaintiffs was established when it was proved that the Yellow Cab meters were rigged. Here, on the other hand, the fact of injury cannot be established without an extensive analysis of all relevant individual questions of fact for each putative class member.

Z\M\P076638X.LEO -25-

Similarly, Plaintiffs have misapprehended the issues in Fanucchi v. Coberly-West Co., 151 Cal.App.2d 72 (1957), where the cotton growers sued a ginning company for underpaying them for their cottonseed (not overcharging, as erroneously stated in the Certification Motion, at 10). Growers alleged that the defendant commingled all the cottonseed delivered by the plaintiffs before weighing it, and then paid them for less than true weight of the cottonseed delivered. Thus, each of them was entitled to an additional payment. The price of the cottonseed was the same for all the class members, thus the only individual issue of fact pertained to the amount of underpayment which could have been established based on the records of cotton actually delivered by each grower. One fails to see the relevance of Fanucchi to the instant situation.

Plaintiffs' assertion that the alleged discrimination by improperly rating the insurance risk of putative class members is an issue "squarely presenting questions of fact and law suitable for class treatment" (Certification Motion, at 9) misapprehends the law and the reality of this case. Plaintiffs failed to sustain their burden in demonstrating that individual issues of fact do not predominate.

5. Plaintiffs failed to demonstrate the causal connection between the alleged wrongful acts and the injury sustained by the members of the putative class.

The absence of any proof that even the named class representatives, let alone the absent class members, have

2\M\P076638X.LEO -26-

sustained the injury alleged in the Second Amended Complaint demonstrates that there is no causal connection between the

alleged misconduct and Plaintiffs' alleged injury. Yet, proof of causation is central to the Plaintiffs' ability to certify the class. "[T]here can be no class certification unless it is determined by the trial court that similarly situated persons have sustained damage. There can be no cognizable class unless it is first determined that members who make up the class have sustained the same or similar damage." Caro, supra, 664. The fact of damage must be distinguished from the amount of damage. While the courts have generally allowed a class action to proceed despite the individual character of proof of the amount of damage, plaintiffs still have the burden of proof on the fact of damage on a class-wide basis. Id. As the courts noted on many an occasion, "[o]nly in an extraordinary situation would a class action be justified where, subsequent to the class judgment, the members would be required to individually prove not only damages but also liability." City of San Jose, supra, at 463; Caro, supra, at 668.

Two cases are particularly instructive. In Collins v. Safeway Stores, Inc., 187 Cal. App. 3d 62 (1986), plaintiffs brought a class action on behalf of all state residents who purchased eggs that may have been contaminated. The contaminated and non-contaminated eggs were commingled before sale, and there was no way to show whether any individual customer purchased the contaminated eggs. Thus, it was possible that some members of the class sustained harm, but the fact of damage was not susceptible to proof. The court explained that "California law has long

2\M\P076638X.LEO

-27-

required that a person must suffer detriment in order to have a claim for recovery of damages . . . . If multiple plaintiffs fail to meet these elementary standards, no ascertainable class exists." Id., at 72.

In Spoon v. Superior Court, 130 Cal. App. 3d 735 (1982), condominium owners filed a class action against a developer. Noting the distinction between the amount and the fact of damage, the Spoon court explained: "The amount of damage is an incidental and unavoidably necessary part of the other legitimate part of inquiry, i.e. whether damage has in fact been truly suffered and if so, from what cause." Id. at 741.

In the present case, Plaintiffs have failed to meet their burden of proving the fact of damage on a class-wide basis. Plaintiffs failed to come up with any evidence, let alone any credible evidence, that named class representatives or anyone else was overcharged for insurance services by . They simply assume that if class members were placed with the , they must have been wronged. Yet, this assumption is negated by the fact that during the majority of the relevant period, charged rates identical to . Decl., ¶¶ 31-34. Thus, the fact of damage cannot be deduced from the mere placement with . An individual analysis of each insured's situation is required to prove that the damage, if any, was indeed sustained. Plaintiffs failed to demonstrate how the proof of causation can be demonstrated on a class-wide basis under the facts of this case.

2\M\P076638X.LEO -28-

C. <u>Plaintiffs Have Failed To Meet The Superiority Requirement</u>.

Like the "ascertainable class" and "community of interest" requirements, this requirement demands that Plaintiffs demonstrate that members of the putative class can establish their right to recover without the need for individualized proof:

> "A class action is appropriate only where there exists a 'sufficient community of interest' in 'common questions of law and fact' so that proceeding in the class action would result in 'substantial benefits' both to the litigants and the court."

<u>Hamwi</u>, <u>supra</u>, at 471.

The Class Action Rules, Rule 15.18(c) breaks this requirement into seven separate issues. Plaintiffs did not significantly address any of these issues, but simply stated that this "case would serve the public policies of judicial economy and manageability." Cohelan Decl., ¶ 11.d. Yet, Plaintiffs' conclusory assertions notwithstanding, four of the issues outlined by the Rules that are applicable here demonstrate that a class action is not a superior vehicle under the present facts.

1. Alternative procedures are available here since the Department of Insurance, which regulates the insurance industry, has the powers to investigate and address the alleged violation; (<u>See</u> Ins. Code, Section 12921.3) such proceedings would be more economical than the lengthy and expensive adjudication of each putative class member's claim.

2. The remedies available under the alternative proceedings through the Department of Insurance can effectively grant relief to minorities if any alleged discrimination is indeed found; such relief would be broader than relief that can be obtained in the

Z\M\P076638X.LEO -29-

instant action; alternatively, individual Plaintiffs may seek damages.

3. The Department of Insurance has the administrative powers to conduct such an investigation and manage the proceedings. On the other hand, the manageability of a trial where the individual claims of allegedly numerous class members must be adjudicated is highly questionable. Plaintiffs assert that "an abbreviated and expedited trial" is possible through selective use of expert and summarized testimony. Cohelan's Decl., ¶ 11.a[13] Yet, they fail to explain how such summarized testimony will address all the numerous individual issues of facts and what kind of expert testimony may be available at trial. The reality of this case is that it inevitably will deteriorate into separate individual cases and mini-trials.

4. The benefit to the public from curing discriminatory conduct, if such conduct can be proven, is, of course, unquestionable. However, manageability of this action, if the class is certified, would become a serious issue for this Court, when forced to separately litigate numerous issues as they affect individual members of the putative class. Little efficiency is to be gained from adjudicating issues of liability, causation and damages for each putative class member separately in one monster trial. Confusion and delays are more likely to result if the class is certified. The inefficiency of proceeding as a class action is amply demonstrated here by the fact that on April 14, 1995, two plaintiffs have served on all three defendants a total

---

[13] See footnote 10, supra.

2\M\P076638X.LEO -30-

of approximately 25,000 Special Interrogatories.[14] Answering thousands of Special Interrogatories is not likely to promote efficiency or manageability of this action.

Plaintiffs assert that the instant action can be manageable and superior because "much proof will depend upon statistical information and evidence." Certification Motion, at 15. However, as this Memorandum has demonstrated, Plaintiffs not only failed to come up with any such statistical evidence, but also failed to explain how such statistical evidence can be obtained. In State of Alabama v. Blue Bird Body Co., Inc., 573 F.2d 309 (5th Cir. 1978), the circuit court noted that "if the effect of class certification is to bring in thousands of possible claimants whose presence will in actuality require a multitude of mini-trials (a procedure which will be tremendously time-consuming and costly), then the justification for class certification is absent." Id., at 328. The "multitude of mini-trials" addressing the issues of alleged injury, causation and damages would be the inevitable result should this action be certified. Plaintiffs failed to demonstrate why a proceeding by the Department of Insurance is not superior to a class action under the present facts. They have not sustained their burden of proof in meeting the "superiority" requirement.

[14] This Court is requested to take a judicial notice of the Special Interrogatories propounded by the plaintiffs, lodged with this Court.

2\M\P076638X.LEC -31-

D. Named Class Representatives Are Not The Members of The Class.

Under the Class Action Rules, Rule 15.18(d), the class representatives must submit declarations containing legally admissible evidence supporting their membership in the class. No such declarations have been submitted by Plaintiffs, and for a good reason: none of the named class representatives is a member of the class!!

In order to be a member of the class in this action, an individual must (1) be of the defined Southeast Asian origin; (2) have purchased automobile insurance through between March 29, 1990 and March 29, 1994; (3) have been discriminated against by being improperly placed into a higher-premium risk-category, including being denied a Good Driver Discount; and (4) have sustained damages therefore.

There are twelve named class representatives in this action.[15] Out of twelve, one, , is not a member of the class because he did not purchase any automobile insurance through during the applicable time period. Decl., ¶ 5. The other eleven are not the members of the class because they were neither improperly placed into a higher-premium risk-category, nor improperly denied a Good Driver

[15] Plaintiffs have "dropped" two of the named class representatives, from their Motion. Yet, these two individuals have not dismissed their claims, have not filed a substitution of attorney, and thus, continue to remain parties to this action and named class representatives.

2\M\P076638X.LEC -32-

Discount. Decl., ¶¶ 82-207. Thus, out of all named class representatives, none is a member of the class.[16]

E. Ability Of Class Representatives To Fairly And Adequately Protect The Interests Of The Class.

1. Named representatives' claims are not typical.

To adequately represent a class, the class representative's claim must be typical of those of the other class members. Caro, supra, at 669. As this Memorandum has demonstrated, none of the named representatives has suffered the alleged injury being claimed by the class members and thus, can provide adequate representation. In fact, Plaintiffs themselves acknowledged that "[a]dequacy of representation means that damages of the representative party are representative of those of the class members." Certification Motion at 11. None of the named representatives suffered any damages due to the alleged injury, and consequently, Plaintiffs failed to meet their own test.

---

[16] In apparent anticipation of this argument, Plaintiffs remind the Court that it has the power to substitute named plaintiffs, if necessary. While this is true, the cases cited by Plaintiffs involve either a single pro per plaintiff, Scott v. Indian Wells, 6 Cal.3d 541 (1972), or newly discovered facts which necessitated a substitution, Tenants' Assn. of Park Santa Anita v. Southern, 222 Cal.App.3d 1292 (1990). The instant situation is clearly distinguishable: Plaintiffs' counsel had an ample to discover the basic facts pertaining to the named representatives, including whether they have ever suffered the alleged injury. In fact, Plaintiffs' counsel state unequivocally that they have reviewed DMV records, records, and other background information on the representatives. Cohelan Decl., ¶ 11b.

2\M\P076638X.LEO -33-

Plaintiffs' showing of typicality of class representatives' claims is not only insufficient, but in fact, is designed to mislead the Court. To demonstrate that the named representatives have qualified for a Good Driver Discount, Plaintiffs attached as exhibits current DMV records of the representative plaintiffs. Of course, the December 1994 DMV driving records, which go only three years back, have no bearing whatsoever on whether Plaintiffs so qualified when they applied for insurance coverage; it is the three years prior to application that would be relevant here. See Objections to Evidence, at 8-9.

2. Named class representatives cannot properly discharge their fiduciary obligations.

Named class representatives' credibility and familiarity with the issues involved in the lawsuit must also be considered by the Court in assessing their ability to adequately represent the class. "The Court must feel certain that the class representative will discharge his fiduciary obligations by fairly and adequately protecting the interests of the class." Burhalter Travel Agency v. MacFarms Intern., Inc., 141 F.R.D. 144, 154 (N.D.Cal. 1991) (citations omitted). The courts have developed a standard of "striking unfamiliarity" to assess a representative's adequacy in policing the prosecution of his or her lawsuit, and have observed that a class representative who is unfamiliar with the case will not serve the necessary role of "checking the otherwise unfettered discretion of counsel in prosecuting the suit." Welling v. Alexy, 155 F.R.D. 654, 659 (N.D.Cal. 1994) (citations

2\M\P076638X.LEO -34-

omitted). Or, in the words of the Burhalter court, supra, there has to be a "sense that there is an actual party behind counsel's prosecution of the action." Burhalter, supra, at 153.

The named representatives in this lawsuit demonstrate "striking unfamiliarity" with the issues of this case. In fact, two of them refused to even participate in the discovery process. See, fn. 15, supra. While the essence of the Plaintiffs' allegations is that they were discriminated against by by being inappropriately placed into while they qualified for , the majority of the named representatives are unaware of even the existence of the two separate insurance companies and do not know with which of the two companies they had been insured. Decl., ¶ 6. They are unaware of any other putative class members. Decl., ¶ 7. They are "strikingly unfamiliar" with the allegations of the Second Amended Complaint. Decl., ¶ 8. They show "striking unfamiliarity" with many essential terms relevant to the issues of insurance coverage, such as "full coverage", "deductible", "comprehensive insurance", "policy limits" and others. Decl., ¶ 9. In fact, in a case where the details and particulars of each individual class member's driving history and personal and family background are of extreme relevance in order to ascertain whether discriminatory placement has occurred, many named representatives are unable to answer very basic questions such as what is the make of their car, the year they were born, the age or spelling of the names of their children. Decl., ¶ 10.

2\M\P076638X.LEO -35-

Moreover, the information elicited during deposition testimony by the named representatives is often in direct conflict with the answers they have given to written discovery, and even more so, with the information contained in their insurance applications. Decl., ¶ 11. In fact, the discrepancies are of such magnitude that they call into question Plaintiffs' credibility and the means through which Plaintiffs' counsel accomplish their representation of the case.[17]

Additionally, financial status of a class representative is relevant to the Plaintiffs' ability to adequately protect interests of the class. Class representatives must have funds available to "effectively prosecute" a lawsuit of such magnitude as at issue here. See Mechigian v. Art Capital Corp., 612 F. Supp. 1421, 1433 (D.C.N.Y. 1985); National Auto Brokers Corp. v. General Motors Corp., 376 F. Supp. 620, 637 (S.D.N.Y. 1974), aff'd, 572 F.2d 953 (2d Cir. 1978), cert. den'd, 439 U.S. 1072, 99 S. Ct. 844 (1979); Ralston v. Volkswagenwerk, A.G., 61 F.R.D. 427 (W.D.Mo. 1973). Plaintiffs here have not demonstrated the financial stability required to serve as class representatives in a lawsuit of this magnitude. In fact, all but one of them are

[17] Perhaps, most disturbing of all is the evidence of apparent perjury. Mr. Yia Xiong whose name leads the list of named plaintiffs has never read nor had translated for him either the Second Amended Complaint, or the interrogatories propounded to him. It appears that his daughter-in-law has answered the interrogatories instead of him, often falsely, and simply asked him to affix his signature. Decl. , ¶ 12. Mr. Yia Xiong, as some of the other named plaintiffs, appeared confused and baffled throughout his deposition. Decl., ¶ 12. The requirement of adequacy of representation is designed, inter alia, to protect individuals from becoming pawns in the games not of their own design. The instant case cries out for these rules to be invoked.

2\M\P076638X.LEO

-36-

indigent and receive governmental assistance. Decl., ¶ 13. Although that fact alone should not stay in the way of a legitimate class action, when coupled with the disturbing facts of the representatives' lack of comprehension and interest in prosecution of this action, discussed supra, it raises serious concerns as to whether there actually is a party behind the counsel prosecuting this action.

IV.

CONCLUSION

In order for a class action to be certified each and every requirement for class certification must be met. Plaintiffs have failed to sustain their burden of proof on each and every requirement for class certification. Their Motion for Order Determining Class Issues is meritless, and should be denied. Although class actions can serve an important function in our judicial system, not every case is susceptible of class treatment. In City of San Jose v. Superior Court, the Supreme Court cautioned:

> "[D]espite this court's general support of class actions, it has not been unmindful of the accompanying dangers of injustice or of the limited scope within which these suits serve beneficial purposes. Instead, it has consistently admonished trial courts to carefully weigh respective benefits and burdens and to allow maintenance of the class action only where substantial benefits occur to both the litigants and the court."

12 Cal. 3d 447, 459 (1974); accord Caro, supra, at 658; Dean Witter Reynolds, Inc., supra, at 772-73; Osborne, supra, at 653.

2\M\P076638X.LEO -37-

This Memorandum demonstrates that no substantial benefits will incur to either litigants or the court if this action is certified for class treatment. Therefore, respectfully requests that the Court issue an order denying Plaintiffs' Motion for Order Determining Class Issues and that Plaintiffs' class not be certified.

Dated: April 18, 1995

SHEPPARD, MULLIN, RICHTER & HAMPTON

By Pierce T. Selwood
PIERCE T. SELWOOD
Professional Corporation

Attorneys for Defendant

AND RELATED ENTITIES

2\M\P076638X.LEO -38-

§ 7.14 Ruling on Motion for Order Determining Class Issues (First Hearing) (*Xiong* case)

FILED
AUG 26 1995
FRESNO COUNTY CLERK
By K.C. - DEPUTY

SUPERIOR COURT OF CALIFORNIA, COUNTY OF FRESNO

YIA XIONG, , on behalf of themselves and all others similarly situated, Plaintiffs, v. an unincorporated inter-insurance exchange; a California corporation; and DOES 1 through 500, inclusive, Defendants.	No. Dept. 51 RULING ON MOTION FOR ORDER DETERMINING CLASS ISSUES

The Motion for Order Determining Class Issues came on regularly for hearing in Department 51 on July 6, 1995. Timothy Cohelan and Andrew Smits appeared on behalf of the plaintiffs. Pierce Selwood, Ted Forrest, and Royal Oakes appeared on behalf of defendant and related entities.

Plaintiffs seek an order determining that certain issues

COUNTY OF FRESNO
FRESNO, CALIFORNIA

be given class treatment: (a) The Second Cause of Action of the Second Amended Complaint for Unlawful Restraints of Trade-Cartwright Act section 16721 for discrimination against plaintiffs as a group based on ethnic criteria; and (b) The Fourth Cause of Action of the Second Amended Complaint for violation of the Unruh Civil Rights Act, Civil Code sections 51.5 and 52.

The Court having considered the papers submitted and the arguments presented continues this motion to September 13, 1995 in Department 51 at 8:30 a.m., and will delay its ruling on the evidentiary objections until that time.

To obtain class certification, plaintiffs will be required to demonstrate, to the court's satisfaction, the following issues:

1. Ascertainability of the Class

Plaintiffs argue that the means of identifying the class of overcharged purchasers in the Merced/Fresno area is possible because: (1) lists of insureds by Fresno/Merced zip codes are available from defendants and the State Department of Insurance; and (2) the ethnicity of each name on the lists of insureds can be ascertained to be Hmong, Laotian, Cambodian, and Vietnamese by those familiar with these language groups.

Plaintiffs also maintain that the Declaration, submitted by the opposition, sets forth the ascertainability of the class by virtue of the computer records. Specifically, the Declaration states that the Declaration Sheet (a computer-generated form) contains information which reflects:

-2-

OUNTY OF FRESNO
FRESNO CALIFORNIA

"the company issuing the policy, name and address of the insured, agent of record, policy number, vehicle, effective date of coverage, renewal date, coverages, premium due and/or paid, discounts, territory, filing requirements...." (Declaration, paragraph 18)

The class must be ascertainable; however, there is no need to identify its individual members to bind them by the judgment. Thus, a class action was permitted on behalf of several thousand unidentified customers of a taxicab company to recover fare overcharges over a four-year period. Daar v. Yellow Cab Co. (1967) 67 Cal.2d 695, 63 Cal.Rptr.724.

In this case, plaintiffs' plan to use zip codes, computer records, and the Southeast Asian names of policyholders is one method of determining the ascertainability of the class.

However, plaintiffs have not provided the court with any competent evidence that one may discern these specific Asian nationalities based on the surnames of the policyholders. Plaintiffs have submitted the declaration of Dr. however, this declaration does not establish Dr. as an expert in such matters (Dr. teaches courses in theater arts and the humanities at Fresno State). A true expert, such as a linguist trained in Southeast Asian culture and language, may be able to competently ascertain the membership of this class based on the policyholders' surnames.

In addition to providing competent evidence that it is possible to discern specific Asian nationalities based on names, plaintiffs should submit declarations providing additional facts

-3-

COUNTY OF FRESNO
FRESNO, CALIFORNIA

regarding the constitution of the class as set forth in the Los Angeles County Superior Court Rules section 15.18(a)(1)-(7). The Fifth District urged other superior courts to follow these guidelines in Union Mutual Life Ins. Co. v. Superior Court (5th Dist. 1978) 80 Cal.App.3d 1, at 13, n. 2.

For example, the declaration should provide information as to the approximate number of persons in the class. If there are subclasses, the declaration should describe each and set out the approximate number of persons in each subclass. The declaration should also set forth the time when the individual class members will be identified if such identification is contemplated. See Los Angeles County Superior Court Rules section 15.18(a)(1)-(7).

2. Membership of the Class Representatives in the Class

Plaintiffs have named twelve class representatives in this action. The general rule is that a purported class representative must be a member of the class he seeks to represent, and his claims must be typical of those asserted by the other members. See Payne v. United Calif. Bank (1972) 23 Cal.App.3d 850, 858, 100 Cal.Rptr. 672; Petherbridge v. Altadena Fed. Savings & Loan Assn. (1974) 37 Cal.App.3d 193, 200, 112 Cal.Rptr. 144. The purpose is to assure adequacy of representation. Parker v. Bowron (1953) 40 Cal.2d 344, 352.

Plaintiffs, however, have failed to demonstrate that each named class representative is actually a member of the purported class. For example, plaintiff does not appear to be a member of the class because he did not buy any auto insurance through defendant during the applicable

-4-

COUNTY OF FRESNO
FRESNO CALIFORNIA

time period (March 29, 1990 and March 29, 1994); rather, his auto insurance during this period was purchased through State Farm. (Declaration, paragraph 5; Deposition, 36:14-23; Ex J of Declr.)

Plaintiffs also do not appear to be members of the alleged class.

Plaintiff applied for insurance on August 25, 1993, and he was bound for auto insurance with MCA. was issued a policy in MCA without a GDD due to the fact that at the time of his application, he had not been a licensed driver for three years. His policy was cancelled on January 31, 1994 due to nonpayment. (Declaration, paragraph 114-118.) Thus, it would appear does not fit the requirements of a class member.

Plaintiff was issued a companion policy on October 2, 1990. received the 30/60 "Ultra Preferred" program offered by . Upon 's April 2, 1991 renewal of the policy, he received the GDD. was not qualified to maintain his policy due to a reckless driving citation effective April 14, 1994. (Declaration, paragraph 194-198.) Thus, it would appear does not fit the requirements of a class member (i.e, he was properly denied coverage under).

To prove the purported class representatives are members of the class, plaintiff should submit one or more declarations providing the following evidence: (1) when and in what manner the representative became a class member; (2) factual differences in the representative's status as a class

-5-

COUNTY OF FRESNO
FRESNO, CALIFORNIA

member and those of any other persons within the class; (3) legal differences (if any) in the representative's status as a class member; and (4) any unique legal/factual issues pertaining to the representative which must be litigated. See Los Angeles Los Angeles County Superior Court Rules section 15.18(d)(1)-(5).

3. <u>Adequacy of Representation</u>

Adequate representation of interests of all members of a class by its representatives is a prerequisite to a class action, and it must be achieved so as to satisfy the requirements of due process. Whether a plaintiff can fairly protect the rights of the group he purports to represent is one of fact for the court. The court must use any procedures available to insure that all legally relevant interests are before it in administering a class action, . 4 Witkin, California Procedure (3rd ed.) Pleading, paragraph 207, page 245.

To demonstrate that the class members can fairly and adequately protect the interests of the class, plaintiffs should submit one or more declarations showing: (1) the amount of damages the representative estimates will be awarded to the class and his or her share; (2) other class actions that the representative or his/her spouse has been named a party. See Los Angeles Los Angeles County Superior Court Rules section 15.18(e)(1)-(2).

DATED this 26 day of July, 1995.

JAMES L. QUASCHNICK
Judge of the Superior Court

-6-

COUNTY OF FRESNO
FRESNO, CALIFORNIA

SUPERIOR COURT OF CALIFORNIA, COUNTY OF FRESNO
1100 Van Ness, P.O. Box 1628
Fresno, California 93717–1628

TITLE OF ACTION: XIONG, et al. v.	CASE NUMBER:

rtify that I am not a party to this cause and that a copy of the attached was mailed first class, postage prepaid, in a sealed envelope ddressed as shown below, and that the mailing of the foregoing and execution of this certificate occurred at Fresno, California:

Date): . . July 26, 1995 . . . . Clerk of Court, By Nancy L. Wallace
Nancy L. Wallace, Deputy Sr.Crt.Clerk

Theodore R. Forrest Jr.
Attorney at Law
P.O. Box 3317
Pinedale, CA 93650-3317

Timothy D. Cohelan
Attorney at Law
701 "C" St.
San Diego, CA 92101-5307

Pierce T. Selwood
Attorney at Law
333 S. Hope St., 48th Fl.
Los Angeles, CA 90071-1448

Royal Oakes
Attorney at Law
515 S. Flower St., 34th Fl.
Los Angeles, CA 90071

Daniel J. Callahan
Attorney at Law
18500 Von Karman, Ste. 800
Irvine, CA 92715

☐ Name and address continued on reverse side.

The singular includes the plural. This certificate must be attached to the original or a true copy of the document served by mail and filed in the action. If the copy of the document served by mail does not bear a notation of the date and place of mailing, an unsigned copy of this certificate must accompany the document served by mail.

CLERK'S CERTIFICATE OF MAILING

SC CLK 0004 86 CCP 1013; 1013a

§ 7.15 Ruling on Motion for Order Determining Class Issues (Second Continued Hearing) (*Xiong* case)

FILED
NOV 9 1995
FRESNO COUNTY CLERK
By G.R. - DEPUTY

SUPERIOR COURT OF CALIFORNIA, COUNTY OF FRESNO

YIA XIONG. on behalf of themselves and all others similarly situated, Plaintiffs, v. an unincorporated inter-insurance exchange; a California corporation; and DOES 1 through 500, inclusive, Defendants.	No. Dept. 51 RULING ON MOTION FOR ORDER DETERMINING CLASS ISSUES

The Motion for Order Determining Class Issues came on regularly for hearing in Department 51 on October 27, 1995. Timothy Cohelan and Andrew Smits appeared on behalf of the plaintiffs. Pierce Selwood, Ted Forrest, and Royal Oakes appeared on behalf of defendant and related entities.

Plaintiffs seek an order determining that certain issues be given class treatment: (a) The Second Cause of Action of the Second Amended Complaint for Unlawful Restraints of

COUNTY OF FRESNO
Fresno, CA

Trade-Cartwright Act section 16721 for discrimination against plaintiffs as a group based on ethnic criteria; and (b) The Fourth Cause of Action of the Second Amended Complaint for violation of the Unruh Civil Rights Act, Civil Code sections 51.5 and 52.

The Court having considered the papers submitted and the arguments presented grants plaintiffs' motion to certify the class.

Plaintiffs charge that defendants (one of its subsidiaries, and its related insurance exchange group) have, since at least 1990, intentionally and systematically discriminated against Southeast Asians both directly and through coercion and control over its "independent agents."

This discrimination is alleged to have taken the form of discouraging the solicitation, sale and renewal of car insurance to plaintiffs' class, pressuring agents to insure them only through their higher-priced subsidiary (defendant costing 80-100% more) rather than under the less expensive policies available through other subsidiaries without making any determination of eligibility, encouraging the independent agents to cancel policies or increase premiums on renewal without good cause or changed circumstances, and penalizing agents who write too many "undesirable" policies to this group. allegedly failed to implement and honor the regulations of Proposition 103 and California Insurance Code sections 1861.02, 1861.025, and 1861.03 by using unapproved criterion for insurance rating purposes, which constitutes "unfair discrimination" under California Insurance Code section

COUNTY OF FRESNO
Fresno, CA

-2-

1861.02(a)(4).

I. Class Certification-Generally

Code of Civil Procedure section 382 provides:

> ...when the question is of a common or general inter
> of many persons, or when the parties are numerous, a:
> it is impracticable to bring them all before the cou:
> one or more may sue or defend for the benefit of all

The California Supreme Court has directed local cour: to follow the procedures set forth in Federal Rules of Civil Procedure, rule 23 wherever California authority is lacking. (*of San Jose v. Sup. Ct.* (1974) 12 Cal.3d 447, 453 [115 Cal.Rpt: 797, 801].

(a) Class Action requirements

To maintain a class action, certain prerequisite conditions must exist, and the action must be based on one or m recognized grounds.

(I) Prerequisite Conditions: all of the follow conditions must be established:

Numerous parties: the class must be so numerous that joinder of all members individually would be impractical.

Common question: the action must involve questi of law and fact common to the class;

Representative's claim typical: the claims of t person representing the class must be typical of the class generally; and

Adequacy of representation: the person representing the class must be able to fairly and adequately to protect the interests of all members of the class. (Fed. Rules

COUNTY OF FRESNO
Fresno, CA

-3-

Civ.Proc., rule 23(a).)

(ii) Code of Civil Procedure section 382

There are two basic prerequisites to certification of a class action under Code of Civil Procedure section 382: (1) the existence of an ascertainable class; and (2) a well-defined community of interest in the questions of law and fact which affect the parties to be represented. *Daar v. Yellow Cab Co.* (1967) 695, 704.

The "community of interest" embodies three factors:

(1) Predominant common questions of law or fact;

(2) Class representatives with claims or defenses typical of the class; and

(3) Class representatives who can adequately represent the class. Weil and Brown, CPBT (1995) 14.11.1

The court will now turn to examining whether plaintiffs have sustained their burden of proof of the five prerequisites for class certification.

A. Is the Class Ascertainable?

On July 6, 1995, this court heard plaintiff's Motion for Order Determining Class Issues. In its July 26, 1995 Ruling, this court denied plaintiffs' motion without prejudice and requested plaintiffs provide the court with certain information as set forth in Chapter 15 of the Los Angeles Superior Court Rules on Class Actions.

This court specifically requested that plaintiffs submit the following evidence regarding ascertain ability of the class: (1) a declaration from an expert such as a linguist trained in

COUNTY OF FRESNO
Fresno, CA

-4-

Southeast Asian culture and language who may be able to competently ascertain the membership of the class based on defendants' policyholders' surnames; (2) declarations providing additional facts re the constitution of the class such as the approximate number of persons in the class; and (3) with respect to any subclasses, declarations describing the same and setting forth the approximate number of persons in each subclass, as well as when the individuals will be identified.

Plaintiffs have submitted declarations from who are experts in linguistics and cultural anthropology. These experts are familiar with Southeast Asian cultures and language including Hmong and Lao. and are also conversant in Lao, Thai and other Southeast Asian Languages.

Plaintiffs argue that the declarations of establish that they are competent to ascertain the membership of the class based on the surnames of defendants' policyholders. can review master list of the names of all of its policyholders (about 250,000) in the Fresno/Merced regions, and they can create as list of Southeast Asian policyholders.

Plaintiffs estimate the class size to be at least 8,747 people. This estimate is based on data provided in the 1990 United States Census and California Department of Insurance, Statistical Analysis Bureau's Reports.

(I) Potential Subclasses

Plaintiffs state the sub-classes might be practical as follows:

COUNTY OF FRESNO
Fresno, CA

-5-

1. **Those persons denied the Good Driver Discount Completely;**

2. **Those persons never rewritten to a policy but qualified for such;**

3. **Those persons who were given Good Driver Discounts and/or rewritten to but not in a timely fashion; and**

4. **Those persons who applied for insurance with but were denied, not for legitimate underwriting reasons, but because they were of Southeast Asian heritage, or other unlawful reasons.** (Cohelan Declaration, paragraph 10.)

Defendants concede that plaintiffs can probably use experts to identify the individuals of Hmong and Laotian ancestry by their last names from the client master list.

Defendants, however, argue that in order to fall within plaintiffs' own class definition, including the three subclasses identified by the Cohelan Declaration, those minority policyholders must also sustain damages from being economically discriminated against by by: (1) being placed into a higher-risk category, specifically the (2) by depriving them of the Good Driver Discount benefit; or (3) by being denied any coverage.

As noted above, the class must be ascertainable; however, there is no need to identify its individual members in order to bind them by the judgment. Thus, a class action was permitted on behalf of several thousand unidentified customers of a taxicab company to recover fare overcharges over a four-year

COUNTY OF FRESNO
Fresno, CA

-6-

period. *Daar v. Yellow Cab Co.* (1967) 67 Cal.2d 695 [63 Cal.Rptr.724].

> **If the rights of each member of the class are dependent upon facts applicable only to him, there is not the requisite ascertainable class required for a representative suit.**

Barber v. California Emp. Stab. Com., 130 Cal.App.2d 7, 14.

In this case, the court finds that plaintiffs have demonstrated they can ascertain their class. Plaintiffs assert that they can identify the class of overcharged purchasers in the Merced/Fresno area because: (1) lists of insureds by Fresno/Merced zip codes are available from defendants and the state Department of Insurance; and (2) the ethnicity of each name on the lists of insureds can be ascertained to be Hmong or Laotian by those familiar with these language groups.

Plaintiffs will also utilize the defendants' computer records to ascertain the class. Specifically, the Declaration states that the Declaration Sheet (a computer-generated form) contains information which reflects:

> the company issuing the policy, name and address of the insured, agent of record, policy number, vehicle, effective date of coverage, renewal date, coverages, premium due and/or paid, discounts, territory, filing requirements.... (Declaration, paragraph 18.)

The court thus finds that plaintiffs have established the ascertain ability of the class.

B. <u>Do common questions of law/fact predominate over individual issues</u>?

Plaintiffs argue that questions of law and fact

COUNTY OF FRESNO
Fresno, CA

-7-

predominate in this case. Specifically, plaintiffs maintain that common questions surrounding the Cartwright Act section 16721 (overcharging on the basis of ethnicity and national origin) exist. Plaintiffs note they are simply victims of discrimination, and that no individualized analysis such as knowledge is necessary because, in an action where violation of a statute is alleged, knowledge of individual class members is no obstacle to certification.

Plaintiffs note that common questions of law also exist as to overcharging on the basis of national origin in violation of the Unruh Civil Rights Act (Civ. Code, section 51). Plaintiffs allege that the conduct alleged in the Second Amended Complaint raises substantial public policy concerns which require adjudication as a matter of public policy.

Plaintiffs further argue that common questions of fact predominate as well. Plaintiffs note that the exact amount of overcharge would be known to defendants and can be ascertained by their records.

Defendants argue, *inter alia*, that no common question of law exists as to the alleged violation of the Cartwright Act. Business and Professions Code section 16721 of the Cartwright Act provides that no person can be excluded from a business transaction on the basis of a policy expressed in any document or writing, where such policy requires discrimination against that person on the basis of the person's race, sex or national origin. Because plaintiffs have failed to demonstrate the existence of such written document, defendants note that no community of interest can be found among the individual class members with respect to section 16721 of the Cartwright Act.

Defendants also argue that individual questions of fact predominate as to the alleged Cartwright Act and Unruh Civil Rights Act violations. Defendant maintains that the injury to each minority is so individual in character and requires such an extensive, fact-driven analysis, that any national origin commonality is undermined by individual issues of fact.

The following statement appears to be a rough approximation of the test re the question of common interest settled by California decisions: There must be a question of common or general interest, to a group of persons similarly situated. 4 Witkin, California Procedure (3rd ed.) Pleading, section 202, page 238.

Many decisions have held the showing of a question of common interest sufficient. See *Reyes v. Board of Supervisors* (1987) 196 Cal.App.3d 1263 [242 Cal.Rptr.339] (action by welfare claimants seeking retroactive relief from alleged impermissible denial of benefits); *Rosack v. Volvo of America Corp.* (1982) 131 Cal.App.3d 741, 760 [182 Cal.Rptr. 800] (auto price fixing action; certification proper despite ability of individual purchasers to negotiate price and possibility of variable injury among class members).

To meet the "common questions" requirement of class certification, the moving party must demonstrate "that the questions which they will be required to litigate separately are not numerous or substantial...." *Vasquez v. Superior Court* (1971) 4 Cal.3d 800, 820 [94 Cal.Rptr. 796]. Certification is properly denied where "the individual questions to be decided may prove too

COUNTY OF FRESNO
Fresno, CA

-9-

complex, numerous or substantial to allow the class action...or the benefits to be gained may not be significant enough to justify imposition of a judgment binding on absent parties." *Harrison v. Board of Supervisors* (1975) 44 Cal.App.3d 852, 861-2 [118 Cal.Rptr. 828].

The most common ground for class actions is simply that the questions of law or fact common to the class predominate over questions affecting the individual class members ... and, on balance, a class action is superior to other methods available for adjudicating the controversy. Federal Rules of Civil Procedure, rule 23(b)(3); Weil and Brown, *supra*, section 14:15.

A class action is not "superior" where there are substantial questions affecting each class member's right to recover, following determination of liability to a class as a whole. *City of San Jose v. Sup. Ct.* (1974) 12 Cal.3d 447 [115 Cal.Rptr.797].

Plaintiffs seeking class certification need not show they will necessarily prevail at trial. "It is enough that it appears that evidence in support of plaintiffs' theory may be available when the case goes to trial." *Osborne v. Subaru of America. Inc.* (1988) 198 Cal.App.3d 646, 652 [243 Cal.Rptr. 815, 818], citing *Anthony v. General Motors Corp.* (1973) 33 Cal.App.3d 699, 707 [109 Cal.Rptr. 254].

In this case, while it is likely that plaintiffs may vary as to amount of damages suffered, the common question of law (whether race-based discrimination in issuance of insurance policies is permitted) and the common questions of fact (whether defendants did promulgate a discriminatory policy and violate its

COUNTY OF FRESNO
Fresno, CA

-10-

own rate schedule or otherwise refuse to insure Southeast Asians on the same basis as non Asians) appear to predominate. If a plaintiff was put into when he was entitled to the "Good Driver" rate, he is owed the difference. The Cartwright Act and Unruh Act provide statutory remedies, including damages. The court thus finds that common questions of law and fact predominate over individual issues.

C. <u>Have plaintiffs met the Superiority Requirement</u>?

Plaintiffs argue that certification of the class would provide substantial benefits to the court and the litigants. Specifically, plaintiffs argue the class would benefit as important anti-discrimination rights would be litigated. Plaintiffs assert that defendants would have the opportunity to prove to the court that they did not discriminate, and the court would benefit in that it would deal with a simplified trial since much proof will depend upon statistical information and evidence in one proceeding.

Plaintiffs also argue that this class is sufficiently numerous to make joinder impracticable, due to the size of the class (thousands of individuals) and geographic dispersion (counties of Merced and Fresno).

Defendants, on the other hand, argue that a class action is not a superior vehicle under these circumstances. Defendants note that alternative procedures are available since the Department of Insurance has power to investigate and address the alleged violations. Defendants maintain the remedies available through the Department can grant relief to the minorities.

COUNTY OF FRESNO
Fresno, CA

-11-

In determining whether a class action would be "superior" to individual lawsuits, the court will usually consider:

The interest of each member in controlling his own case personally;

The difficulties, if any, that are likely to be encountered in managing a class action;

The nature and extent of any litigation by individual class members already in progress involving the same controversy;

The desirability of consolidating all claims in a single action before a single court. (Fed. Rules Civ.Proc., rule 23(b)(3); Weil and Brown, *supra*, section 14:16)

California courts have identified other factors that are "germane" to class certification, including:

Whether substantial benefits will accrue to the litigants, the class, the public and to the court; and

Whether it is likely that a high percentage of class members would ultimately come forward to prove separate claims to a portion of the total class recovery. *Caro v. Proctor & Gamble Co.* (1993) 18 Cal.App.4th 644 [22 Cal.Rptr. 2d 419, 423]; Weil and Brown, *supra*, section 14:17.

In this case, the court finds that a class action would be superior to individual lawsuits. Class members would probably be unable to institute actions on an individual basis due to the prohibitive costs of litigation and the small size of the individual losses. Thus, it is unlikely that a high percentage of class members would ultimately come forward to prove separate claims to a portion of the total class recovery. Plaintiffs

COUNTY OF FRESNO
Fresno, CA

-12-

assert that a manageable trial is possible with selective use of expert and summarized testimony. Much of the data necessary to try this case will be available at trial from defendants since the insurance industry is highly regulated and defendant is required to maintain records as to the rates charged and type of insurance program (such as) on an annual basis.

D. Are the named Class Representatives members of the Class?

In the court's July 26, 1995 Ruling, the court requested plaintiffs provide additional evidence concerning membership of the class representatives in the class.

The court specifically requested that plaintiffs submit declarations providing: (1) when and in what manner the representative became a class member; (2) factual differences in the representative status as a class member and those of any other persons within the class; (3) legal differences (if any) in the representative's status as a class member; and (4) any unique legal/factual issues pertaining to the representative which must be litigated.

In response to the court's July 26, 1995 Ruling, plaintiffs submit declarations of the following four plaintiffs: Yia Xiong, . There are a total of 10 plaintiffs.

Plaintiffs note that the declarations establish the factors common to the plaintiffs: (1) plaintiffs are Hmong or Lao; (2) plaintiffs purchased coverage during the period in question (March 29, 1990 through March 29, 1994); (3) did not give applicable discounts at the time of

COUNTY OF FRESNO
Fresno, CA

-13-

purchase; and (4) placed the plaintiffs in the more expensive coverage and did not place plaintiffs in the less expensive coverage.

Plaintiffs assert there are no legal differences in the representatives' status as class members, and there are no unique factual issues pertaining to any representative which must be litigated.

Defendants, on the other hand, argue that of the ten representative plaintiffs, only four have submitted declarations in support of plaintiffs' supplemental filing. Defendants maintain that these declarations contain incompetent information and do not negate the results of analysis; that is, that has not discriminated against any of the named representatives.

The general rule is that a purported class representative must be a member of the class he seeks to represent, and his claims must be typical of those asserted by the other members. See *Payne v. United Calif. Bank* (1972) 23 Cal.App.3d 850, 858 [100 Cal.Rptr. 672]; *Petherbridge v. Altadena Fed. Savings & Loan Assn.* (1974) 37 Cal.App.3d 193, 200 [112 Cal.Rptr. 144]. The purpose is to assure adequacy of representation. *Parker v. Bowron* (1953) 40 Cal.2d 344, 352.

Here, in order to be a member of the instant class, an individual must: (1) be of a defined Southeast Asian origin; (2) have a valid California driver's license; (3) have purchased auto insurance through between March 29, 1990 and March 29, 1994; (4) have been discriminated against by being improperly placed into a higher-premium

COUNTY OF FRESNO
Fresno, CA

-14-

risk-category, including being denied a Good Driver Discount (section 1861.025); and (5) have suffered damages.

To qualify for the "Good Driver Discount", a person must meet the following criteria under section 1861.025:

(a) be a licensed driver for the previous 3 years;

(b) has not done the following during the 3 previous years:

1. had more than 1 point as defined in subds. a-e, g, h of Vehicle Code section 12810.

2. had more than 1, Vehicle Code section 1803.5 during those 3 years.

3. been guilty of Vehicle Code section 23140.

4. been principally at-fault in an accident resulting in fatality or substantial bodily injury.

Insurance Code section 1861.02(c) provides:

> The absence of prior automobile insurance coverage, in and of itself, shall not be a criterion for determining eligibility for a good driver discount policy, or generally for automobile rates, premiums or insurability.

The court will examine each declaration in turn.

(I) ______________________

Defendants object to portions of this declaration:

1. <u>Paragraph 4</u>: states that he applied for auto insurance with Mr. , a Insurance Agent, on July 5, 1989 to obtain coverage for his 1984 Toyota Celica. filled out an application for insurance and signed it that date.

Defendants object to this paragraph on the grounds of lack of relevance (as to time - Evid. Code, §§ 210, 350) and

COUNTY OF FRESNO
Fresno, CA

-15-

estoppel by contradiction, Evidence Code section 623, *D'Amico v. Board of Medical Examiniers* (1974) 11 Cal.3d 1, 21.

Specifically Evidence Code 623 states:

> Whenever a party has, by his own statement or conduct, intentionally and deliberately led another to believe a particular thing true and to act upon such belief, he is not, in any litigation arising out of such statement or conduct, permitted to contradict it.

In *D'Amico v. Board of Medical Examiners* (1974) 11 Cal.3d 1, 21, the court did not allow a party in a summary judgment motion to artificially create a "triable issue of material fact" in order to defeat a motion for summary judgment by filing a declaration which was contradictory to deposition testimony previously given by that party.

Defendants argue that instant declaration directly contradicts his January 9, 1995 deposition testimony, where he testified that: (1) he did not know a insurance agent named (Ex. A to Forrest Declaration, p. 8:22); (2) he forgot the name of the agent to whom he spoke re his application for insurance with defendants (Forrest Declaration, Ex. A, pg. 20:17); and (3) the application was filled out by the agent to whom the application was being submitted. (Forrest Declaration, Ex. A, p. 28:10.) See Forrest Declaration, in Support of Defendants' Objections to Evidence, p. 6.

In this case, a witness is entitled to refresh his memory in order to provide accurate testimony re such matters under Evidence Code section 771. In addition, as noted by plaintiffs, some of the information contained in

COUNTY OF FRESNO
Fresno, CA

-16-

declaration is supported by the exhibits attached to the April 17, 1995 Declaration of For example, Exhibit 22A of the declaration provides a copy of application with the agent's signature, could have used this document to refresh his memory before completing his declaration.

The court thus overrules this objection.

2. Paragraph 6: states that during the application process, the agent asked him questions to which he responded truthfully and fully.

Defendants object to this paragraph on the grounds of lack of relevance (as to time - Evid. Code, §§ 210, 350) and estoppel by contradiction, Evidence Code section 623, *D'Amico v. Board of Medical Examiners* (1974) 11 Cal.3d 1, 21.

Here, prior deposition testimony contradicts with this more recent declaration (see, e.g., discussion on paragraph 9, *infra*), and the objections to this paragraph are sustained.

3. Paragraph 9: states that he was placed with policy and was quoted a premium of $500 for a 15/30 liability plus $100/$500 deductible policy. asserts he was not offered any good driver discounts despite not having any accidents or tickets in the three previous years. He states he was not offered insurance with .

Defendants object to this paragraph on the grounds of lack of relevance (as to time - Evid. Code, §§ 210, 350) and estoppel by contradiction, Evidence Code section 623, *D'Amico v.*

COUNTY OF FRESNO
Fresno, CA

-17-

Board of Medical Examiners (1974) 11 Cal.3d 1, 21.

Defendants note that at deposition, he testified that he had never heard of but that he had only heard of . (Ex. A of Declaration, p. 9:2.) also testified at his deposition that he had received <u>one ticket prior</u> to the time he initially met with the insurance agent. (Ex. A of Forrest Declaration, p. 50:24) and that he had never owned a policy of insurance through . (Ex. A of Declaration, p. 80: 25.) See Declaration, in Support of Defendants' Objections to Evidence, p. 7

Here, prior deposition testimony re the fact that he <u>had indeed received a ticket</u> contradicts with his more recent declaration, and the objection as to his declaration statement that he never received a ticket is sustained.

states in his declaration that he did not receive the Good Driver Discount during his renewal notice in December, 1990 through June 12, 1991, despite the fact that he had no accidents or tickets. Defendants have offered evidence to contradict assertion that he had no ticket.

To qualify for the "Good Driver Discount", a person must meet the following criteria under section 1861.025:

(a) be a licensed driver for the previous 3 years;

(b) has not done the following during the 3 previous years:

1. had more than 1 point as defined in subds. a-e, g, h of Veh. Code, § 12810.

2. had more than 1 Vehicle Code section 1803.5

COUNTY OF FRESNO
Fresno, CA

-18-

during those 3 years.

3. been guilty of Vehicle Code section 23140.

4. been principally at-fault in an accident resulting in fatality or substantial bodily injury.

Since there is no information as to what type of ticket received, it is unclear that discriminated against by denying him the Good Drivers Discount (i.e., may have properly denied the Discount based on this ticket- it is unclear). It is the plaintiffs' burden to prove that their named class representatives are members of the class. Plaintiffs have thus not demonstrated that is a proper representative of the class.

(ii) <u>Declaration of</u>

1. <u>Paragraphs 4-10</u>: states that on November 23, 1987 he applied for auto insurance, that the application agent asked him questions to which he responded truthfully, that he told the agent he had insurance during the last 12 months, and that he was placed with and quoted a certain premium. He was not offered the Good Driver Discount.

Defendants object to this evidence on the ground of lack of relevance. (Evid. Code, §§ 210, 350.)

The court overrules this objection as plaintiff is simply supplying information re his eligibility into the class that the court requested in its June 26, 1995 ruling.

2. <u>Paragraph 15</u>: states that rewrote his policy to a policy in November, 1993. (Paragraph 14.) then asserts that on July 16, 1994, he

COUNTY OF FRESNO
Fresno, CA

-19-

allowed that policy to lapse.

Defendants object to this paragraph on the ground of estoppel by contradiction. Evidence Code section 623.

Specifically, defendants conducted an investigation which revealed that was not the registered owner of the vehicle he was insuring with defendants. Defendants requested provide information re the owner of the vehicle, and failed to submit the information. Defendants canceled the policy for missing information effective July 16, 1994. (See paragraph 114 of the Declaration.)

The court thus sustains this objection as to the issue of his policy "lapsing".

Despite defendants' evidentiary objections, the declaration establishes that is a member of this class. Specifically, declaration demonstrates that Moua: (1) is of Hmong ancestry; (2) purchased auto insurance from between March 29, 1990 and March 29, 1994; (3) was discriminated against by being improperly placed into a higher premium risk category; and (4) sustained damages.

(iii) Declaration of

1. Paragraph 4: states that on May 4, 1990, he applied for auto insurance with a agent, Mr. . states that he filled out an application for insurance and signed the application on that date.

Defendants object to this evidence on the ground of estoppel by contradiction. Specifically, defendants note that at 's deposition, he testified that he did not recall the name of his insurance agent. (Ex. B of

COUNTY OF FRESNO
Fresno, CA

-20-

Declaration, pp. 41:6, 41:15.) In addition, the application for insurance shows that 's wife signed as the policyholder with identified only as a rated driver on the policy. (Declaration in Support of Defendants' Objection, p. 10.).

In this case, a witness is entitled to refresh his memory in order to provide accurate testimony re such matters under Evidence Code section 771. In addition, as noted by plaintiffs, some of the information contained in 's declaration is supported by the exhibits attached to the April 17, 1995 Declaration of . For example, Exhibit 23A of the declaration provides a copy of 's application with the agent's signature, . could have used this document to refresh his memory before completing his declaration.

The court thus overrules this objection.

2. <u>Paragraph 6</u>: states that during the application process the agent asked him questions to which he responded truthfully and fully.

Defendants object to this paragraph on the ground of estoppel by contradiction. Evidence Code section 623. Specifically, defendants note that pursuant to 's deposition testimony, his son and daughter were allowed to drive the vehicle even though failed to identify the presence of youthful drivers residing in the household. (Declaration, Ex. B-1, p. 31:22, 33:2.) Moreover, defendants note that the application shows that Mr. and Mrs. signed a non-smoker statement when in fact admitted during his

COUNTY OF FRESNO
Fresno, CA

-21-

deposition that both he and his wife smoke cigarettes. (Ex. B-1 of Declaration, pp. 47:7, 47:25.) Defendants maintain that none of this information was contained in 's application, in direct contradiction to the statements contained in the declaration which profess that he answered "fully and truthfully."

Here, 's application contradicts with his recent declaration, and the objections to this paragraph are sustained.

3. Paragraph 9: states that he was placed with policy #12622 87 10 and was quoted a premium of $374 for a 15/30 with $5,000 medical. states he had received a ticket in 1988 and had been in an accident not his fault in 1989. He was not offered insurance with .

Defendants object to this paragraph on the ground of estoppel by contradiction. Evidence Code section 623. Specifically, defendants note that during 's deposition he was questioned re his driving record. at that time admitted that he had been stopped for speeding and had received a second ticket for turning on a yellow light. (Ex. B-1, p. 54:11, 54:24 of Forrest Declaration.) Defendants argue that this is incorrect information based on 's deposition testimony as well as Sayasane's response to Special Interrogatory No. 33 which admits that he had two tickets during the three years immediately preceding the date which he became insured with defendants. (Ex. B-2 of Forrest Declaration.)

Plaintiffs argue that defendants' attorney Forrest has taken this testimony out of context by omitting page 57 of

COUNTY OF FRESNO
Fresno, CA

-22-

's deposition testimony. Pages 55-57 of 's deposition reveal that believed that the insurance agent who had his driver's license number, would investigate 's driving/citation record. (See Ex. A of Plaintiff's Evidentiary Objection to Forrest Declaration.)

While may have believed the insurance agent would investigate his record and discovery the second citation, the fact still remains that the Declaration incorrectly states that he only received one citation in 1988. The court thu sustains this portion of the paragraph on the basis of estoppel b contradiction.

4. Paragraphs 11 and 12: states that he renewed his policy on April of 1991 for $487.35 but was still not offered a policy. alleges that canceled the policy in August of 1991.

Defendants object to this paragraph on the ground of estoppel by contradiction. Evidence Code section 623. Specifically, defendants note that in 's answer to Specia: Interrogatory No. 4, he answered that "[ ] did not cancel m: insurance; I had decidea to obtain insurance elsewhere." (Declaration, Ex. B-2.)

The court sustains the objection to paragraph 12. 's declaration that he received only one ticket in 1988 is contradicted by prior deposition testimony as well as his interrogatory answers, where he admitted that he had two tickets during the three years immediately preceding the date which he became insured with defendants. (Ex. B-2 of Forrest Declaration.)

COUNTY OF FRESNO
Fresno, CA

-23-

To qualify for the "Good Driver Discount", a person must meet the following criteria under section 1861.025:

(a) be a licensed driver for the previous 3 years;

(b) has not done the following during the 3 previous years:

1. had more than 1 point as defined in subds. a-e, g, h of Veh. Code, § 12810.

2. had more than 1 Vehicle Code section 1803.5 during those 3 years.

3. been guilty of Vehicle Code section 23140.

4. been principally at-fault in an accident resulting in fatality or substantial bodily injury.

Since received two tickets before being insured with defendants, it is unclear that discriminated against by denying him the Good Drivers Discount (i.e., may have properly denied the Discount based on this ticket- it is unclear). However, it is the plaintiffs' burden to prove that their named class representatives are members of the class. The court thus finds that plaintiffs have not demonstrated that is a proper representative of the class.

5. Declaration of Yia Xiong

1. Paragraph 4: Xiong states that on September 4, 1990, he applied for auto insurance with a agent, Mr. Xiong. He filled out an application for insurance and signed the application on that date.

Defendants object to this paragraph on the ground of estoppel by contradiction. Evidence Code section 623. However, defendants provide no contradictory evidence to Xiong's

COUNTY OF FRESNO
Fresno, CA

-24-

assertion. (See Forrest Declaration in Support of Defendants' Objections to Evidence, p. 12.) The court overrules this objection.

2. <u>Paragraphs 6-9</u>: Xiong states that during the application process, his agent asked him questions to which he responded fully and truthfully. (Paragraph 6.) Xiong told his agent he wished full coverage for his 1978 Chevy van. (Paragraph 7.) Xiong told his agent he did <u>not</u> have insurance during the 12 months prior to the application and that he had an accident in 1988. (Paragraph 8.) Xiong was placed with Company, Policy # 95 12881 63 28, and was quoted a premium of $300 for 15/30 liability only policy. (Paragraph 9.)

Defendants object to these paragraphs on the ground of estoppel by contradiction. Evidence Code section 623. Specifically, defendants argue that during Xiong's deposition on January 24, 1995, he stated that he told his Agent that he <u>did</u> have prior auto insurance with Mutual of Omaha (Ex. C-1 of Forrest Declaration, p. 89:15-18), and that he had been insured by AAA for one and one-half years. (Ex. C-1 of Forrest Declaration, p. 90:14.) Xiong's response to Special Interrogatory No. 13 (Ex. C-2 of Forrest Decl.) stated that he had owned a policy of insurance from during the three years immediately preceding the date which he purchased his auto insurance from . (Ex. C-2 of Forrest Declaration.) Xiong's response to Special Interrogatory #16 stated that he had "no citations, no accidents." (Ex. C-2 of Forrest Declaration.)

Xiong's current declaration is in direct contradiction

COUNTY OF FRESNO
Fresno, CA

-25-

with his previous deposition and interrogatory responses. Thus, the court sustains the objections to paragraphs 6 and 8. Paragraph 7 is uncontradicted and the objection is overruled.

Defendants then object to paragraph 9. Defendants note that at his deposition, Xiong failed to produce any documents demonstrating that he was quoted a premium of $300 for a 15/30 liability policy and Xiong testified that he threw away all copies of checks and insurance policies he had received or which were related to his auto insurance policy with defendants.. (Ex. C-1 of Forrest Declaration, p. 80:25.) See Forrest Declaration in Support of Defendants' Objections to Evidence, page 12-13.

As to paragraph 9; Xiong's current declaration does not significantly contradict his prior testimony. Xiong actually states that he threw away copies of any checks (and not insurance policies) that he had sent to . (See Ex. C-1, p. 80:25 of Forrest Declaration.) The court thus overrules the objection to paragraph 9.

3. Paragraph 12: Xiong states that on March 4, 1993, the company canceled his policy allegedly because his license had expired.

Defendants object to this paragraphs on the ground of estoppel by contradiction. Evidence Code section 623. Specifically, defendants note that in Xiong's deposition testimony, two of Xiong's children informed him that his California Driver's License had expired. (Forrest Declaration, Ex. C-1, p. 28:9.) This is not truly a contradiction, and the court overrules the objection to paragraph 12.

Xiong's declaration that he told his agent he did not

COUNTY OF FRESNO
Fresno, CA

-26-

have insurance during the 12 months prior to the applicatio contradicted by prior Xiong's deposition on January 24, 199 that time, he stated that he told his he did have prior auto insurance with Mutual of Omaha (Ex. (Forrest Declaration, p. 89:15-18), and that he had been insı AAA for one and one-half years. (Ex. C-1 of Forrest Declarã p. 90:14.)

While Xiong may have contradicted himself re his p insurance, he has established himself as a representative of class. Specifically, his declaration establishes that Xionç is of Hmong ancestry; (2) purchased auto insurance from between March 29, 1990 and March 29, 1994; (3) was discrir against by being improperly placed into a higher premium ris category, including being denied the Good Driver Discount; (4) sustained damages.

The court thus finds that of the ten individuals plaintiffs assert are representatives of the class, plaintif have demonstrated only that Xiong and are proper representatives of the class.

E. Can Class Representatives fairly and adequately protect interest?

The court requested in its July 26, 1995 Ruling th plaintiffs submit evidence demonstrating that the class memb can fairly and adequately protect the interests of the class.

Specifically, the court requested that plaintiffs declarations showing: (1) the amount of damages the representative estimates will be awarded to the class and his

COUNTY OF FRESNO
Fresno, CA

-27-

share; and (2) other class actions that the representative or his/her spouse has been named a party.

Plaintiffs estimate that their damages are at least $10 million dollars and that under the Unruh Civil Rights Act, plaintiffs' damages are trebled and would amount to $30 million dollars. (Cohelan Declaration, par. 20-21.)

The declarations of plaintiffs Xiong and establish that they are willing and able to assume their duties as class representatives. These declarations also establish that neither of these two plaintiffs or their spouses have participated in class actions or as class representatives.

Defendants argue that there are serious doubts re the named class representatives' ability to discharge their fiduciary duties. Defendants note that the named representative repeatedly exhibited a pattern of "striking unfamiliarity" with the issues central to this suit. In addition, defendants maintain that much of the information submitted by plaintiffs in their declarations in support of the plaintiffs' supplemental filing directly contradicts their prior testimony.

Fair and adequate representation of interests of all members of a class by its representatives is a prerequisite to a class action, and it must be achieved in such a way as to satisfy the requirements of due process. Whether a particular plaintiff can fairly protect the rights of the group he purports to represent is one of fact for the court. The court, in administering a class action, must use any procedures available to insure that all legally relevant interests are before it. 4 Witkin, California Procedure (3rd ed.) Pleading, paragraph 207,

COUNTY OF FRESNO
Fresno, CA

-28-

page 245.

Adequacy of representation depends on whether the plaintiff's attorney is qualified to conduct the proposed litigation and the plaintiff's interests are not antagonistic to the interests of the class. *McGhee v. Bank of America* (1976) 60 Cal.App.3d 443, 450 [131 Cal.Rptr.482, 487]. The primary criterion in determining adequacy of representation is whether the class representative, through qualified counsel, has "vigorously and tenaciously protected the interests of the class". *Simons v. Horowitz* (1984) 151 Cal.App.3d 834, 846, 199 Cal.Rptr.134, 142.

Other decisions suggest that adequacy of representation is simply another aspect of the requirement that plaintiff's claims be "typical" of the class. See *Caro v. Procter & Gamble Co.* (1993) 18 Cal.App.4th 644 [22 Cal.Rptr.2d 419, 43-] (claims of plaintiff purchaser of defendant's orange juice were not typical of class members' claims, since he thought the juice was "premium" instead of "fresh", and he had read only the top portion of the alleged false label).

In this case, the court finds that there is no indication that plaintiffs' counsel are not qualified to act as attorneys for the class. There is also no evidence that plaintiffs have any interests that would be antagonistic to those of the class. Plaintiffs' counsel states his law firm has advanced the costs in this matter and will continue to do so if the class is certified. (Cohelan Declaration, par. 4.) While it is true that eight of the ten named plaintiffs may not be representative members of the class, at least two are. The court finds that these two plaintiffs, Xiong and   , could adequately

COUNTY OF FRESNO
Fresno, CA

-29-

represent the class.

The court thus certifies this action as a class action. Plaintiffs shall submit a proposed recommendation and proposed order regarding notice to the class members.

DATED this 9 day of November, 1995.

James L. Quaschnick
JAMES L. QUASCHNICK
Judge of the Superior Court

COUNTY OF FRESNO
Fresno, CA

-30-

SUPERIOR COURT OF CALIFORNIA, COUNTY OF FRESNO
1100 Van Ness, P. O. Box 1628
Fresno, California 93717-1628

TITLE OF ACTION: XIONG, et al. VS.
CASE NO.

-o0o-

I certify that I am not a party to this cause and that a copy of the attac Ruling on Motion for Order Determining Class Issues was mailed first cla postage prepaid, in a sealed envelope as addressed as shown below, and tl the mailing of the foregoing and execution on this certificate occurred Fresno, California:

on November 9, 1995

Superior Court Clerk

Timothy Cohelan, Esq.
Cohelan & Khoury
701 "C" Street
San Diego, CA 92101-5307

Theodore Forrest, Jr., Esq.
Forrest & McLaughlin
6790 N. West Avenue, Ste. 104
Fresno, CA 93711-1393

Daniel Callahan, Esq.
Callahan & Gauntlett
18500 Von Karman, Ste. 800
Irvine, CA 92715

Pierce Selwood, Esq.
Sheppard, Mullin, Richter & Hampton
333 S. Hope Street, 48th Floor
Los Angeles, CA 90071-1448

Todd R. Howell, Esq.
Tharpe & Howell
25 East Anapamu
Third Floor
Santa Barbara, CA 93101

Royal Oakes, Esq.
BARGER & WOLEN
515 South Flower Street
Thirty-Fourth Floor
Los Angeles, CA 90071

RECEIVED
NOV 13 1995

§ 7.16 Order Certifying Class (*Aguilar* v. *Atlantic Richfield*)

SUPERIOR COURT OF THE STATE OF CALIFORNIA

COUNTY OF SAN DIEGO

THERESA AGUILAR, individuals, on behalf of themselves and all others similarly situated, Plaintiffs, v. ATLANTIC RICHFIELD CORPORATION, CHEVRON CORPORATION, EXXON CORPORATION, MOBIL OIL CORPORATION, SHELL OIL COMPANY, TEXACO, INC., TOSCO CORPORATION, ULTRAMAR CORPORATION, UNOCAL CORPORATION, and DOES 1 through 40, inclusive, Defendants.	CASE NO. 700810 **ORDER GRANTING MOTION FOR CLASS CERTIFICATION**

On March 25, 1997, the motion of plaintiffs for class certification was heard in Department 49 of this court, The Honorable Jeffrey T. Miller presiding. After carefully considering the file in this action, all pleadings concerning the motion, and the oral argument of counsel, the Court rules as follows:

Initially, the Court advises it has neither read nor considered the declarations of originally submitted with plaintiffs' rebuttal papers, pursuant to the voluntary withdrawal of these declarations by plaintiffs' counsel. (Tr. of Oral Argument, pp. 6-8.)

This is an action brought by plaintiffs Theresa Aguilar, etc.. Plaintiffs purport to be representatives of a class consisting of all California motorists who purchased any grade or type of reformulated or California Air Resources Board ("CARB") Phase 2 gasoline (hereafter "Carb Gas") from March 1, 1996. Defendants are nine major refiners, distributors and retailers of Carb Gas.

Plaintiffs' First Amended Complaint sets forth causes of action for violations of the California Cartwright Act (Bus. & Prof. Code § 16720, et seq.) and the California Unfair Competition Act (Bus. & Prof. Code § 17200, et seq.). Plaintiffs, in this motion, submit this is a case well suited for class treatment as "[t]his class is ascertainable, a well-defined community of interest exists and common issues of fact and law predominate." Defendants, on the other hand, contend common questions of law and fact do not predominate over individual issues. Specifically, defendants assert neither impact nor damages can be proven on a classwide basis as each class member would have to prove individual damage. Further, defendants contend, the inherent pricing complexities of the gasoline industry from the refinery to the retail station, create a maze of conditions which renders individual retail purchaser impact impossible.

Defendants also assert in their pleadings and at oral argument (Tr. of Oral Argument, pp. 18-22) plaintiffs must bear a threshold evidentiary burden of establishing a realistic chance of ultimate success on the merits. In that regard, defendants cite to the existence of three federal governmental agency studies into the price spike of 1996 which have been concluded without civil

-2-

or criminal prosecution. (Tr. Oral Argument, pp. 22-23.) Defendants suggest this Court should not "take on [the] burden . . ." of this purported class action in light of the extensive governmental analysis into the issue. (Tr. Oral Argument, pp. 25-26.)

For the reasons stated below, the Court finds this case is appropriate for class treatment and grants the motion for class certification.

DISCUSSION

The beginning of the inquiry into class certification in this case must focus on the nature of the claims brought by plaintiffs. Basically, plaintiffs claim defendant oil companies got together and unlawfully conspired to artificially raise prices of Carb Gas to be sold in California. This is precisely the type of claim to be litigated within the context of class treatment. The class, although huge, is ascertainable. Common issues of fact and law on the question of conspiracy or unfair business practices will predominate. The interests and claims of the named plaintiffs are similar to those of class members. There exist economic disincentives for California motorists to bring individual actions for themselves. Further, the prospect of a myriad of subclaims being filed would do violence to judicial economy. Moreover, any practical subgroup of motorists, whether defined by region, county, municipality, individual oil company, or minimum purchase level, would result in a massive class action. Judicial economy and uniformity would dictate these similar claims be litigated in one massive class action rather than many.

Defendants argue there is some threshold evidentiary standard the law imposes on plaintiffs by which a reasonable chance of prevailing on the merits must be established before a class certification motion may be granted. They cite Vasquez v. Superior Court (1971) 4 Cal.3d 800; Carabini v. Superior Court (1994) 26 Cal.App.4th 239; and Caro v. Procter & Gamble Co. (1993) 18 Cal.App.4th 644. The state of the law, however, is to the contrary.

-3-

Indeed, the Court may consider the merits of a claim to determine whether there is a realistic chance for recovery. Carabini, at 245. However, a motion for class certification is not a trial on the merits or tantamount to a motion for summary judgment. Id. Indeed, allegations of a conspiracy to fix prices in a context similar to this case has been observed to establish common questions of law and fact which predominate over individual issues. B.W.I. Custom Kitchens v. Owens-Illinois, Inc. (1987) 191 Cal.App.3d 1341, 1347-9. Given the allegations of the First Amended Complaint, the proof necessary to establish the alleged conspiracy will require a "common thread of evidence" applicable to all class members. Id. Further, doubts as to the suitability of a class treatment should be resolved in favor of certification, consistent with California's public policy encouraging use of the class action. Richmond v. Dart Industries Inc. (1981) 29 Cal.3d 462, 473.

Defendants, while recognizing this Court may not consider the contents of three governmental studies into the Carb Gas price hike, urge the Court to take notice of the existence of the studies. Defendants, however, do not cite any authority for the proposition such studies should preempt the right of consumers to press private claims of the type brought here. These studies should not deprive California consumers of their day in court.

Defendants forcefully argue that pricing complexities at the various levels from the oil refinery to the retail pump pose mammoth practical impediments to certifying this matter as a class action. They argue the reasoning of Illinois Brick Co. v. Illinois (1977) 431 U.S. 720, while conceding the case is not controlling precedent here. (Tr. Oral Argument pp. 32-35.) Illinois Brick held that generally indirect purchasers of an alleged price-fixed product may not sue under federal antitrust law on the theory the price-fixers' overcharge has been passed on to the indirect purchaser. It cannot be disputed the majority opinion of Justice White in Illinois Brick recognized the

-4-

uncertainties and difficulties in analyzing whether a price overcharge to the direct purchaser of an alleged price-fixed product has been passed on to the indirect purchaser who brings a federal antitrust action. The true holding, however, of Illinois Brick is that fundamental fairness and reciprocity principles bar such an action based upon an offensive use of a pass-on theory where the Court has already determined a pass-on theory may not be used defensively by an antitrust violator against a direct purchaser plaintiff.

In 1978, the California legislature rejected the reasoning of Illinois Brick when it amended the Cartwright Act [Bus. & Prof. Code § 16750, subdivision (a)] to allow any person to bring an action under the act, "regardless of whether such injured person dealt directly or indirectly with the defendant". (Italics added.) See B.W.I., supra, at 1346. Of course, this Court is bound by the controlling California precedent. Although defendants greatly argue their position on impact and damage complexities, at this juncture these arguments simply point out the potential need for fashioning creative remedial devices in the event liability is established on either of the theories advanced by plaintiffs.

The case of Devidian v. Automotive Service Dealers Assn. (1973) 35 Cal.App.3d 978, provides neither aid nor comfort to defendants. The purported class in Devidian consisted of all retail purchasers of gasoline in Fresno County, and the defendants were identified as over one thousand price-fixing gasoline distributors supplying gasoline to retailers with a two-cent per gallon overcharge. The Court recognized that where it is alleged a myriad of defendants have allegedly conspired to impose a de minimis price increase in an industry with great marketing complexities, the case is not appropriate for class treatment. The Devidian case, of course, was decided prior to the 1978 amendment to the Cartwright Act. More importantly, however, this action can easily be distinguished from Devidian. Here, there are only nine defendants who, it is alleged, entered into a straightforward conspiracy to

-5-

artificially hike the price of Carb Gas a significant sum. This action is directed at an initial and fundamental price level. Liability, if any, of this limited group of defendants is not greatly impacted by the retail pricing complexities which existed at the retail pump in the Devidian case.

In summary, this Court finds this case involves an ascertainable class and a well-defined community of interest as shown by typicality, adequacy, and the predominance of common issues of law and fact. This is the type of consumer state antitrust case the courts and legislature have mandated is suitable for class action treatment. The motion of plaintiffs for class certification is granted.

DATED: May 1, 1997

JEFFREY T. MILLER
Judge of the Superior Court

-6-

8 CASE MANAGEMENT: CONTROLLING THE ISSUES

A. TEXT

Sec.

8.01 Proposing a Manageable Trial

8.02 Precertification Case Management

[A] Informal Conferences

[B] Precertification Determinations

[C] Appointing a Discovery Master

8.03 Simplifying Issues Following Certification

8.04 References

B. FORMS

8.10 Plaintiffs' Notice of Ex Parte Application for an Order (1) Consolidating Demurrer Hearings, (2) Designating Case as Complex, and (3) Setting Pretrial Conference (*Aguilar* v. *Atlantic Richfield*)

8.11 Memorandum of Points and Authorities in Support of Order (1) Consolidating Demurrer Hearings, (2) Designating Case as Complex, and (3) Setting Pretrial Conference (*Aguilar* v. *Atlantic Richfield*)

8.12 Declaration of Timothy Cohelan in Support of Order (1) Consolidating Demurrer Hearings, (2) Designating Case as Complex, and (3) Setting Pretrial Conference (*Aguilar* v. *Atlantic Richfield*)

8.13 Proposed Order on Ex Parte Application (*Aguilar* v. *Atlantic Richfield*)

8.14 Case Management Order (*Marquart* case)

A. TEXT

§ 8.01 Proposing a Manageable Trial

Too often failure by plaintiff's counsel to control a class action moving through the judicial system makes the matter look procedurally more difficult than it needs to. Since class certification is meant to save time, minimize cost, and simplify complex litigation, unwittingly casting it as a time-consuming and costly web of complication works against your interests. (*Kaye* v. *Mt. La Jolla Homeowners' Ass'n* (1988) 204 Cal.App.3d 1476 [252 Cal.Rptr. 67].) Prosecution of a class action is more likely to succeed if you give sufficient thought to advancing the case towards trial or settlement by slicing the elephant into bite-sized pieces.

For instance, when numerous aggressive and talented defense attorneys launch simultaneous criticisms of a class action, it is easy for plaintiffs' counsel to succumb to intimidation. Certain initial mass motions are unavoidable, such as group demurrers. You can make an early clear proposal of selective omnibus or consolidated responses to the assigned judge, helping the court simplify the proceeding and reduce your fear factor. The successful plaintiffs' counsel will divide and conquer, determining which issues to resolve when.

§ 8.02 Precertification Case Management

[A] Informal Conferences

Los Angeles Superior Court allows for one or more informal conferences scheduled by notice from any named party. (Super. Ct. L.A. County Rules, rules 15.4 & 15.6.) The parties can discuss class issues, establish the precedence of discovery, schedule hearings, or determine any other matters concerning pretrial determination of class issues. Once the plaintiff has thought through these preliminary questions and dealt with them in informal conference, the proceeding moves more efficiently for everyone involved, including the court.

Typically, discovery centering on defendants' attempts to defeat the class certification motion and plaintiffs' attempts to prove certifiability occupies the early stages of class action. Depositions of plaintiffs concerning their representatives' adequacy and other related issues should give the defendants ample opportunity to understand the nature of common claims. Defendants focus on what they deem the eccentricities or idiosyncracies of the proposed class representative. Plaintiffs by and large attempt to simplify the characteristics of class members to the lowest common denominator.

From plaintiff's perspective, a case management order limiting defendant's discovery is a matter of life and death. The successful plaintiff's practitioner will move to advance only important issues and refuse to be lured into a Russian winter of defense depositions and prolonged, expensive pretrial discovery. It is better to advance dispositive issues early, even if this timing seems unfavorable to the plaintiff's position, than to be dragged through an endless, expensive, and ultimately unsuccessful discovery process. Be prepared to advance a case management plan that protects your right either to conduct aggressive discovery, if you represent the plaintiff, or places sensible limitations on discovery, if you are counsel for the defendant.

[B] Precertification Determinations

Although the court may not hear issues on the merits before class certification, there are two ways of achieving early hearing on merits issues. Both of them need to be addressed in any case management order. (See *Home Savings & Loan Assn.* v. *Superior Court* (1974) 42 Cal.App.3d 1006 [117 Cal.Rptr. 485].)

The first way is injunctive relief. As discussed in chapters 3 and 4, injunctive relief may be brought prior to class certification in accordance with Code of Civil Procedure section 527, subdivision (a). The second method is agreement by the parties to a stipulation allowing resolution of issues before class certification. (*Colwell Co.* v. *Superior Court of County of Los Angeles* (1975) 50 Cal.App.3d 32 [123 Cal.Rptr. 228].)

[C] Appointing a Discovery Master

Since certification of the class hinges on proving the community of interest as a predicate of fact, discovery issues occupy much of the trial court's time before the certification hearing. Typically, the issue of which facts are relevant is a battleground between the parties. A discovery master can be very helpful at this stage of the proceeding. Prompt and well-reasoned rulings are well worth the cost.

§ 8.03 Simplifying Issues Following Certification

Simplifying issues speeds a class action proceeding. It also works to the practitioner's benefit to simplify issue resolution. Substantive and procedural issues, defined as application of law to facts developed and proved at the time of trial, determine the resolution of the case.

After the class is certified, arrange the classwide issues in an order of resolution that recognizes the need to expedite, economize, and simplify. Liability issues and special defenses, for example, can and should be resolved early. (Code Civ. Proc., §§ 597 & 598.) Local rules encourage this by allowing early class issues to be bifurcated where appropriate. (See, e.g., Super. Ct. L.A. County Rules, rule 15.36; Super. Ct. S.F. County Rules, rule 441; Super. Ct. San Mateo County Rules, rule 7.7.)

Where complicated facts or voluminous records make simplification more difficult, consider a reference under the Code of Civil Procedure (Code Civ. Proc., §§ 638, 639). The court can order the reference on agreement of the parties (Code Civ. Proc., § 638) or, if the parties do not consent (Code Civ. Proc., § 639), on its own authority, provided that the evidentiary record supports the order. Evidentiary support for a reference arises when a long account from either side needs to be taken and/or examined, or when a question of fact other than upon the pleadings arises upon motion or otherwise and/or requires account information necessary for the court before it may enter judgment pursuant to Code of Civil Procedure section 639. By agreement of the parties, the reference can try any or all issues of fact or law and report a statement of decision The reference may also ascertain a fact necessary for the court in its determination of action or proceeding. The reference procedure can allow the parties to determine underlying factual predicates before or after formal certification and before trial. This kind of dual-track procedure saves the parties from expensive, wasteful, and unfocused discovery.

In cases involving detailed financial records, such as in a Ponzi fraud scheme, a special master appointed to conduct an accounting can expedite a determination of liability and damages. In partnership cases (including limited partnerships) there is a statutory right to such an accounting.

A practitioner needs to be aware of when issues might appear that call for a dual-track proceeding. For instance, an independent master or the court in a separate simplified proceeding can determine equitable issues surrounding an accounting in a complicated case. There is no reason to decide against dual-track hearings before class certification, particularly since much of the factual information developed in the proceeding will bear significantly on the certification issue. If evidentiary hearings can provide the factual predicate to class certification, the court should be willing to allow them as a way of helping it determine objectively whether class treatment serves class interests.

One worthwhile concept is an order scheduling and consolidating all pretrial motion activity 60, 90, or 120 days into the response. A proposed checklist of issues and a timetable for their resolution are very helpful to the trial court. After providing the framework for the court to decide the methods of resolving the matter, determine the level of discovery appropriate to buttressing the theory of the case.

§ 8.04 References

NEWBERG For a discussion of the federal approach to managing class actions for damages, see 2 Newberg on Class Actions (3d ed. 1992), Chapter 9.

§ 8.10 Plaintiffs' Notice of Ex Parte Application for an Order (1) Consolidating Demurrer Hearings, (2) Designating Case as Complex, and (3) Setting Pretrial Conference (*Aguilar v. Atlantic Richfield*)

Timothy D. Cohelan, Esq. (60827)
Isam C. Khoury, Esq. (58759)
COHELAN & KHOURY
701 C Street
San Diego, California 92101-5307
Telephone: (619) 595-3001

Daniel J. Mogin (95624)
Angela Milea Mogin (153920)
THE MOGIN LAW FIRM
701 C Street, Suite 200
San Diego, California 92101-5307
Telephone: (619) 687-6611

Attorneys for Plaintiffs

SUPERIOR COURT OF THE STATE OF CALIFORNIA

FOR THE COUNTY OF SAN DIEGO

THERESA AGUILAR, et al., individuals, on behalf of themselves and all others similarly situated, Plaintiffs, v. ATLANTIC RICHFIELD CORPORATION, CHEVRON CORPORATION, EXXON CORPORATION, MOBIL OIL CORPORATION, SHELL OIL COMPANY, TEXACO, INC., TOSCO CORPORATION, ULTRAMAR CORPORATION, UNOCAL CORPORATION, and DOES 1 through 40, inclusive, Defendants.	**Case No. 00700810** **<u>CLASS ACTION</u>** **NOTICE OF *EX PARTE* APPLICATION FOR AN ORDER:** **1) CONSOLIDATING DEMURRER HEARINGS;** **2) DESIGNATING CASE AS COMPLEX; AND,** **3) SETTING PRETRIAL CONFERENCE;** **MEMORANDUM OF POINTS & AUTHORITIES; DECLARATION OF TIMOTHY D. COHELAN; [PROPOSED] ORDER THEREON** **Date: July 31, 1996** **Time: 8:30 a.m.** **Dept: 49** **I/C Judge: Honorable Jeffrey T. Miller**

TO ALL PARTIES AND THEIR ATTORNEYS OF RECORD:

PLEASE TAKE NOTICE that on July 31, 1996, at 8:30 a.m., in Department 49 of this Court, located at 330 West Broadway, San Diego, California, Class Plaintiffs, through their attorneys of record herein, will request *ex parte* that the Court:

1) Consolidate all demurrers for one hearing;

2) Designate this case as complex; and,

3) Set an early preliminary pretrial conference and order that all counsel meet and confer and attempt to stipulate to a pretrial order in advance thereof.

This *ex parte* motion is made pursuant to § 19 of the California Rules of Court, Judicial Administration Standards and is based upon this Notice, the accompanying Memorandum of Points and Authorities and the Declaration of Timothy D. Cohelan and such other and further matters as the Court may consider at the time of hearing.

Respectfully submitted,

Dated: July 30, 1996

Timothy D. Cohelan (60827)
Isam C. Khoury (58759)
COHELAN & KHOURY

By______________________
Timothy D. Cohelan

Daniel J. Mogin (95624)
Angela Milea Mogin (153920)
THE MOGIN LAW FIRM

Attorneys for Plaintiffs

motions\exparte1.not

2

§ 8.11 Memorandum of Points and Authorities in Support of Order (1) Consolidating Demurrer Hearings, (2) Designating Case as Complex, and (3) Setting Pretrial Conference (*Aguilar* v. *Atlantic Richfield*)

Timothy D. Cohelan, Esq. (60827)
Isam C. Khoury, Esq. (58759)
COHELAN & KHOURY
701 C Street
San Diego, California 92101-5307
Telephone: (619) 595-3001

Daniel J. Mogin (95624)
Angela Milea Mogin (153920)
THE MOGIN LAW FIRM
701 C Street, Suite 200
San Diego, California 92101-5307
Telephone: (619) 687-6611

Attorneys for Plaintiffs

SUPERIOR COURT OF THE STATE OF CALIFORNIA

FOR THE COUNTY OF SAN DIEGO

THERESA AGUILAR, et al., on behalf of themselves and all others similarly situated, Plaintiffs, v. ATLANTIC RICHFIELD CORPORATION, CHEVRON CORPORATION, EXXON CORPORATION, MOBIL OIL CORPORATION, SHELL OIL COMPANY, TEXACO, INC., TOSCO CORPORATION, ULTRAMAR CORPORATION, UNOCAL CORPORATION, and DOES 1 through 40, inclusive, Defendants.	**Case No. 00700810** **<u>CLASS ACTION</u>** **CLASS PLAINTIFFS' MEMORANDUM OF POINTS AND AUTHORITIES IN SUPPORT OF *EX PARTE* APPLICATION FOR AN ORDER:** **1) CONSOLIDATING DEMURRER HEARINGS;** **2) DESIGNATING CASE AS COMPLEX; AND,** **3) SETTING PRETRIAL CONFERENCE** **Date: July 31, 1996** **Time: 8:30 a.m.** **Dept: 49** **I/C Judge: Honorable Jeffrey T. Miller**

I.

INTRODUCTION

This is a complex antitrust and unfair competition class action brought by plaintiffs on behalf of a class of California motorists who purchased "CARB GAS" in California for their

motions\exparte1.pka

own use and not for resale since March 1, 1996. As defined in the Complaint[1], "CARB GAS" means all grades and types of reformulated or California Air Resources Board ("CARB") Phase 2 gasoline refined for retail sale in the State of California. CARB GAS is a cleaner burning fuel than conventional gasoline and is expected to improve air quality in California by reducing polluting emissions. As of March 1, 1996 CARB GAS is required to be sold in California pursuant to the federal Clean Air Act Amendments and the regulations of the California Air Resources Board ("CARB"). The defendants are the nine major refiners, distributors and retailers of all types of CARB GAS in California. Defendants collectively control almost 100% of the wholesale market for CARB GAS and approximately 92% of the retail market. Plaintiffs allege that over $13.5 billion gallons of gasoline are sold in California annually. Thus, the case is a matter of significant public interest and importance to the State's economy.

The Complaint demands treble damages, injunctive relief and attorneys' fees pursuant to California Business and Professions Code §§16750(a) due to violations of Bus. & Prof. Code §16720(a), et. seq., commonly known as the Cartwright Act. Plaintiffs' also seek equitable relief including injunctions, full restitution and/or disgorgement of all revenues, earnings, profits, compensation and benefits obtained by defendants as a result of their alleged unlawful, unfair or fraudulent business acts or practices as prohibited by Bus. & Prof. Code §§17200, et. seq., commonly known as the Unfair Competition Act, pursuant to Bus. & Prof. Code §§17203 and 17204.

Plaintiffs have alleged that the major refiners, distributors and retailers of all types of CARB GAS in California, including some of the world's largest corporations, have acted to restrict supplies of CARB GAS in California and drive prices to astronomical, supra-competitive levels, injuring millions of California motorists and the State's fragile economy. For several years prior to the March 1, 1996 deadline, defendants publicly stated that the transition to CARB GAS would be handled without major disruptions in supplies or prices. Since the March 1, 1996 deadline mandating production of CARB GAS, however, the defendants have each engaged in

[1] The Complaint refers to plaintiffs' First Amended Complaint filed on June 12, 1996.

motions\exparte1.p&a

2

massive price increases, raising their prices by nearly identical increments at almost precisely the same time throughout California. Such price increases have increased the average refiner's margin from approximately $ 0.213 per gallon in December of 1995, to $0.464 per gallon (as of April 23, 1996) an increase of $0.251 or 135%. In contrast, during the same period, the retail dealers' average margin shrank from $0.083 to $ (-0.012), a decrease of 1.2%. Defendants' have failed to produce at levels sufficient to meet estimated demand or production capacity, creating a shortage of supply. As a result of these massive price increases and supply shortages, on April 17, 1996 the California Energy Commission declared an energy emergency. This official state of emergency restricted production, and inflated prices are continuing.

Even as the world price of crude oil has declined, the price of CARB GAS has remained at historic highs. For a short time of intense media and governmental scrutiny, production of CARB GAS rose. As the pubic has "adjusted" to supra-competitive prices and media and governmental, scrutiny has diminished, however, production of CARB GAS has again declined to levels significantly below estimated demand and capacity and retail prices have thus been maintained at supra-competitive prices.

In an effort to serve the interests of judicial economy and coordinate all the various proceedings that this complex matter will necessarily engender, Plaintiffs herein are requesting this Court issue an Order with respect to at least three pretrial issues. In particular, this Court is requested to:

1) Consolidate all demurrers for one hearing;

2) Designate this case as complex; and,

3) Set an early preliminary pretrial conference and order that all counsel meet and confer and attempt to stipulate to a pretrial order, including the establishment of certain time limits, in advance thereof.

II.

ARGUMENT

A. One Hearing For All Demurrers Will Help Make This Case More Manageable.

The instant action involves a lawsuit against nine corporate defendants. Eight of the nine

motions\experte1.pda

3

defendants have jointly executed a Notice of General Appearance and Stipulation Regarding Extension of Time to respond to the First Amended Complaint (to **August 14, 1996**) and to certain discovery.

However, one of the defendants, Tosco Corporation ("Tosco"), has filed a demurrer, scheduled to be heard by this Court telephonically on **August 16, 1996**, at 2:00 p.m. Plaintiffs' counsel has suggested to Tosco on more than one occasion that all parties and the Court would be better served by means of consolidated proceedings. But attempts to secure Tosco's agreement to have their demurrer heard on the same date as the demurrers of the other eight defendants have been unsuccessful. See, Declaration of Timothy Cohelan, submitted herewith.

Given the fact that almost all of these defendants may wish to file appropriate pretrial proceedings, in the interest of judicial economy, and for reasons stated herein, the Court is respectfully requested to either request all parties to join the presently scheduled demurrer hearing on August 16, 1996, by filing a joinder in the current (Tosco) demurrer or by Answer, or to consolidate, to a later convenient time, the hearings on these pretrial matters.

B. This Case Is Complex And Should Be So Designated.

Additionally, for the reasons set forth, the Court should at this time designate this matter as complex litigation and address the related pretrial issues discussed in this memorandum from a complex perspective.

California Rules of Court, Standards for Judicial Administration §19 ("§19") applies to complex litigation and instructs that in such cases, "judicial management should begin early and be applied continuously and actively, based upon knowledge and circumstances of the case." §19(a). The court may examine the issue of whether litigation is complex on its own motion or may do so upon either the ex parte motion or noticed motion of any party. §19(b).

Section 19 defines "complex litigation" as "those cases that require specialized management to avoid placing unnecessary burdens upon the court or litigants." §19(c). Although "not capable of precise definition," complex litigation may involve:

> multiple related cases, extensive pretrial activity, extended trial times, difficult or novel issues and post-judgment judicial supervision, or may concern special categories such as class

motions\exparte1.p&a

4

> actions; however no particular criterion is controlling and each situation must be examined separately.

California Rules of Court, Standards for Judicial Administration §19(c).

As detailed below and in the accompanying Declaration of Timothy D. Cohelan, this case meets the definition of "complex litigation" within the meaning of §19(c) and would benefit from such treatment, for the following reasons:

a. Class Action: This case is a class action brought on behalf of a class defined as follows:

> All persons residing in California who, during the time period March 1, 1996 through the present (the "Class Period"), purchased, in California, for their own use and not for resale, CARB GAS sold by any of the defendants ("Plaintiff Class"). Specifically excluded from the Plaintiff Class are the defendants herein; officers, directors or employees of any defendants; any entity in which any defendant has a controlling interest; the affiliates, legal representatives, attorneys, heirs, or assigns of any defendant; and any federal, state or local governmental entity.

b. Extensive Pretrial Issues: At the appropriate time, plaintiffs must seek certification of the class. Thereafter, assuming certification is granted, class notice must be given to potentially millions of class members.

c. Difficult And Novel Issues Of Law Concerning Complex Subject Matters: The case presents difficult and novel issues of law concerning complex subject matters. The case challenges, inter alia, certain of defendants' business practices and may require highly technical discovery and expert testimony.

d. Protective Order Issues: Defendants will, undoubtedly, request entry of a protective or confidentiality order before engaging in substantive discovery. Due to the public interest and importance of the subject matter, plaintiffs will insist on a very narrow protective order consistent with Local Rule 6.9.

e. Injunctive Relief Hearing: This would include a Cal. Bus. & Prof. Code §17200 injunction request. The Court would need to anticipate a hearing

motions\exparte1.p&a

5

date and briefing schedule, e.g., a November 15, 1996 hearing, with opening briefs due October 15, 1996.

f. Post-judgment Judicial Supervision: Because this is a class action, post-judgment judicial supervision may be required in connection with such issues as compliance with equitable relief, administration of the distribution of any settlement or judgment funds, claims processing and post-judgment notice.

g. Avoid Conflicting Discovery: The parties are already engaged in serving conflicting and proliferating discovery. It is likely the Court will be asked to rule on injunction issues early in the case, in particular, discovery issues relating to the production of non-proprietary documents.

C. The Court And The Litigants Would Benefit From the Establishment of a Preliminary Pretrial Conference and Order.

In complex cases the court should conduct a preliminary conference "at the earliest practical date." §19(g). California courts interpret Section 19(g) as a mandate to "assume an aggressive role at the earliest possible time to efficiently move the case to settlement or trial." See, Asbestos Claims Facility v. Berry & Berry, 219 Cal. App. 3d 9, 19, (Cal. App. 1990) (quoting, Advisory Committee Comment to Section 10 of the California Standards of Judicial Conduct.). [To date, the parties have not agreed upon a proposed pretrial schedule.] Section 19 advises that time limits should be used throughout the litigation and that they should be established early. §19(f).

Here, the Court and parties would clearly benefit from an early preliminary pretrial conference which would, among other things, establish timetables and a schedule for settling the pleadings, setting a hearing on plaintiffs' motion for preliminary injunction, class certification, merits and expert discovery and reduce litigation over such issues. The following subjects, among others, may be discussed at the pretrial conference:

(1) Settle the pleadings . . .

(3) Schedule discovery proceedings

motions\exparte1.pda

6

(4) Issue protective orders

(5) Arrange settlement conferences ...

(7) Provide for the exchange of documents ...

(11) Schedule further conferences as necessary.

§19(g).

Principal objects of the preliminary pretrial conference are to expose at an early date the essential issues in the litigation and to suppress unnecessary and burdensome discovery procedures. §19(h).

Plaintiffs believe that this matter is complex litigation and accordingly request that the court set an early pretrial conference, pursuant to §19, and order that all counsel meet and confer and attempt to stipulate to a pretrial order in advance thereof.

III.

CONCLUSION

For the foregoing reasons, and in the interest of judicial economy, class plaintiffs respectfully request that the Court issue an Order to:

1) Consolidate all demurrers for one hearing, and require defendants (other than Tosco) to demur only by joinder;

2) Designate this case as complex; and,

3) Set an early pretrial conference, pursuant to §19, and require counsel for plaintiffs and defendants meet and confer and attempt to stipulate to a pretrial order in advance thereof.

Respectfully submitted,

Dated: July 30, 1996

Timothy D. Cohelan (60827)
Isam C. Khoury (58759)
COHELAN & KHOURY

By____________________
Timothy D. Cohelan

Daniel J. Mogin (95624)
Angela Milea Mogin (153920)
THE MOGIN LAW FIRM

Attorneys for Plaintiffs

motions\exparte1.pda

7

§ 8.12 Declaration of Timothy Cohelan in Support of Order (1) Consolidating Demurrer Hearings, (2) Designating Case as Complex, and (3) Setting Pretrial Conference (*Aguilar v. Atlantic Richfield*)

Timothy D. Cohelan, Esq. (60827)
Isam C. Khoury, Esq. (58759)
COHELAN & KHOURY
701 C Street
San Diego, California 92101-5307
Telephone: (619) 595-3001

Daniel J. Mogin (95624)
Angela Milea Mogin (153920)
THE MOGIN LAW FIRM
701 C Street, Suite 200
San Diego, California 92101-5307
Telephone: (619) 687-6611

Attorneys for Plaintiffs

SUPERIOR COURT OF THE STATE OF CALIFORNIA

FOR THE COUNTY OF SAN DIEGO

THERESA AGUILAR, et al., individuals, on behalf of themselves and all others similarly situated, Plaintiffs, v. ATLANTIC RICHFIELD CORPORATION, CHEVRON CORPORATION, EXXON CORPORATION, MOBIL OIL CORPORATION, SHELL OIL COMPANY, TEXACO, INC., TOSCO CORPORATION, ULTRAMAR CORPORATION, UNOCAL CORPORATION, and DOES 1 through 40, inclusive, Defendants.	**Case No. 00700810** **<u>CLASS ACTION</u>** **DECLARATION OF TIMOTHY D. COHELAN IN SUPPORT OF CLASS PLAINTIFFS' EX PARTE APPLICATION FOR AN ORDER: 1) CONSOLIDATING DEMURRER HEARINGS; 2) DESIGNATING CASE AS COMPLEX; AND, 3) SETTING PRETRIAL CONFERENCE** **Date: July 31, 1996** **Time: 8:30 a.m.** **Dept: 49** **I/C Judge: Honorable Jeffrey T. Miller**

1. I am an attorney at law duly admitted to practice in the State of California. I am one of plaintiffs' counsel in the above-entitled matter. This declaration is submitted in support of Class Plaintiffs' Ex Parte Application, Pursuant to California Rules of Court ("CRC"), Judicial Administration Standards, §19. I have personal knowledge of the matters set forth herein and, if called as a witness, I could and would competently testify thereto.

2. On or about July 29, 1996, my office gave notice to defendants that plaintiffs would present this ex parte application pursuant to California Rules of Court, Judicial Administration Standards, §19. This notification provided to defendant counsel complies with CRC, Rule 379. (See, "Exhibit A" attached hereto.)

3. The First Amended Complaint was filed on June 12, 1996, and all defendants were served shortly thereafter. (Immediately after filing, a courtesy copy was delivered to counsel for Tosco Corporation, at his telephonic request.) To date, all but one defendant have executed a Notice of General Appearance and Stipulation Regarding Extension of Time, and plaintiffs' counsel have entered into certain agreements regarding the time in which these defendants must file responsive pleadings. (See, "Exhibit B" attached hereto.)

Consolidated Demurrer Hearing:

4. One defendant however, Tosco Corporation, has filed a demurrer and set it for hearing with this Court on August 16,1996, and has resisted efforts to allow for consolidation of this demurrer with others.

5. On or about July 16, 1996, I communicated with Mr. Tosco's counsel, expressing my desire that we coordinate the pretrial activities. Again, on July 25, 1996, I communicated with Mr. asking if they were unwilling to consolidate or coordinate pretrial activity with the other defendants in the action in the interest of judicial economy and ease of administration of the matter. Mr. has not so agreed. (See, "Exhibits C, D & E" attached hereto.)

6. To date I have received no indication of a change in TOSCO's position and, therefore, plaintiffs seek relief from this Court in doing one of the following with regard to the presently scheduled demurrer:

a. Require all defendants to file, by joinder, demurrers to be heard on August 16, 1996, or, in the alternative,

b. Schedule a date convenient to all parties in which the Court may hear all such joinders, demurring to the First Amended Complaint, in a coordinated fashion.

motions\exparte1.dec 2

Complex designation:

7. Additionally, plaintiffs seek to have the Court consider designating this matter as a complex case.

8. CRC, Judicial Admin. Standards, §19 applies to complex litigation and expressly allows that the court may consider the issues raised by complex litigation on either its own motion or "the ex parte notice or noticed motion of any party." §19(b).

9. It is plaintiffs' counsels' position that this case is complex within the meaning of §19(c) and would benefit from such treatment, including the establishment of certain time limits (§19(f)) and a preliminary conference (§19(g-h)), for the following reasons:

a. This case is a [proposed] class action brought on behalf of a class defined as follows:

> All persons residing in California who, during the time period March 1, 1996 through the present (the "Class Period"), purchased, in California, for their own use and not for resale, CARB GAS sold by any of the defendants ("Plaintiff Class"). Specifically excluded from the Plaintiff Class are the defendants herein; officers, directors or employees of any defendants; any entity in which any defendant has a controlling interest; the affiliates, legal representatives, attorneys, heirs, or assigns of any defendant; and any federal, state or local governmental entity.

b. At the appropriate time, plaintiffs must seek certification of the class. Thereafter, assuming certification is granted, class notice must be given to potentially millions of class members.

c. The case presents difficult and novel issues of law concerning complex subject matters. The case challenges, inter alia, certain of defendants' business practices and may require highly technical discovery and expert testimony.

d. Defendants will, undoubtedly, request entry of a protective or confidentiality order before engaging in substantive discovery. Due to the public interest and importance of the subject matter, plaintiffs will insist on a very narrow protective order consistent with Local Rule 6.9.

motions\exparte1.doc 3

e. Because this is a class action, postjudgment judicial supervision may be required in connection with such issues as administration of the distribution of any settlement or judgment funds, claims processing and postjudgment notice.

f. The parties are already engaged in serving conflicting and proliferating discovery.

<u>Preliminary Pretrial Conference:</u>

10. As alluded to above, Plaintiffs furthermore request that the court set a pretrial or case management conference as soon as practicable and require that the parties meet and confer in advance of the conference in an attempt to stipulate to a pretrial scheduling order.

I declare under penalty of perjury under the laws of the State of California that the foregoing is true and correct.

Executed this 30th day of July, 1996, at San Diego, California.

____
Timothy D. Cohelan

motions\exparte1.dec 4

§ 8.13 Proposed Order on Ex Parte Application (*Aguilar* v. *Atlantic Richfield*)

SUPERIOR COURT OF THE STATE OF CALIFORNIA

FOR THE COUNTY OF SAN DIEGO

THERESA AGUILAR, et al., individuals, on behalf of themselves and all others similarly situated, Plaintiffs, v. ATLANTIC RICHFIELD CORPORATION, CHEVRON CORPORATION, EXXON CORPORATION, MOBIL OIL CORPORATION, SHELL OIL COMPANY, TEXACO, INC., TOSCO CORPORATION, ULTRAMAR CORPORATION, UNOCAL CORPORATION, and DOES 1 through 40, inclusive, Defendants.	**Case No. 00700810** **<u>CLASS ACTION</u>** **[PROPOSED] ORDER RE CLASS PLAINTIFFS' *EX PARTE* APPLICATION** **Date: July 31, 1996** **Time: 8:30 a.m.** **Dept: 49** **I/C Judge: Honorable Jeffrey T. Miller**

Class Plaintiffs' *ex parte* application pursuant to California Rules of Court, Standards of Judicial Administration §19, came on for hearing on July 31, 1996, the Honorable Jeffrey T. Miller, presiding. The Plaintiffs, on behalf of themselves and all those similarly situated, i.e., a proposed class, requested that the Court issue an Order 1) consolidating all demurrers for one hearing; 2) designating this case a complex case; and, 3) establishing a date for a preliminary pretrial conference and requiring all counsel meet and confer beforehand for the purpose of stipulating to a pretrial order.

After hearing the arguments of counsel and considering §19 of the California Rules of

Court, Judicial Administration Standards, Class Plaintiffs' Memorandum of Points and Authorities in support of their application and the Declaration of Timothy D. Cohelan, and good cause appearing therefor,

IT IS HEREBY ORDERED:

1. Any party wishing to demur to the operative complaint shall join in Tosco's demurrer, the points & authorities for which shall not exceed two (2) pages in length, and which demurrer shall be heard in one consolidated hearing on August 16, 1996, or on __________, 1996, or on such other date as the Court may elect. Any party choosing to so demur by joinder should file and serve its moving papers timely so as to be heard on that date. Any party not wishing to so demur shall file its answer to the operative complaint by the same date as the demurrer would be due.

2. This matter is hereby deemed complex and is so designated for all purposes.

3. A preliminary pretrial conference is hereby set for ______________, 1996, at ____.m., in Department 49 of the above-entitled court. The parties shall be prepared to discuss the issues specified in Cal. Rules of Court, Standards of Judicial Administration §19(g) at that time, including the scheduling of discovery, briefing and hearing on Plaintiffs' motion for preliminary injunction.

4. The parties shall meet and confer and attempt to stipulate to a pretrial order in advance of the preliminary pretrial conference.

Dated:____________________

____
HON. JEFFREY T. MILLER
Judge of the Superior Court

motions\exparte1.ord

2

§ 8.14 Case Management Order (*Marquart* case)

FILED
ORANGE COUNTY SUPERIOR COURT

JUL 06 1995

ALAN SLATER, Executive Officer/Clerk
By MV DEPUTY

SUPERIOR COURT OF THE STATE OF CALIFORNIA

FOR THE COUNTY OF ORANGE

WESLEY MARQUART et al., Plaintiffs, v. CHARTWELL FINANCIAL, et al., Defendants.	Case No.
	CASE MANAGEMENT ORDE
	Date: May 16, 1995 Time: 2:00 p.m. Dept: 30
	Assigned For All Purposes To:
AND RELATED CROSS-ACTIONS.	The Honorable Tully H. Seymour

It appearing that a Case Management Order is appropriate to assist in the efficient management of this litigation,

IT IS ORDERED:

A. Purposes of Discovery.

The parties mutually agree that discovery is a fact-finding process and has as its purpose the ascertainment of truth. As such, the parties have an obligation to share and disclose all facts and information requested by opposing parties within their custody or control which pertain or relate to the subject matter of this lawsuit. To that end, the parties agree not to withhold information or documents pursuant to unreasonable objections or legalistic interpretations of requests for documents or information.

B. <u>Discovery Schedule</u>.

The parties shall use all reasonable efforts to complete discovery in this action as quickly and as efficiently as possible. The parties shall use best efforts to complete all non-expert discovery no later than June 31, 1996, and all expert discovery no later than August 15, 1996. The parties reserve the right to expand the discovery cut-off if necessary.

C. <u>Depositions</u>.

No deposition shall take place in this case except pursuant to the procedures set forth herein, unless otherwise ordered by this Court.

1. <u>Scheduling of Depositions</u>.

Depositions will commence on June 15, 1995. A party shall provide at least twenty (20) days notice of any oral deposition. Prior to noticing the oral deposition of any witness (party or otherwise), counsel wishing to depose the witness shall contact opposing counsel to discuss mutually convenient dates for the conduct of the deposition, and shall take all reasonable steps to arrange for such depositions to proceed on dates and at locations convenient to all counsel and witnesses.

this matter along with the designation of the stage in which they will be deposed. This listing is an estimate based on information known at this time and is subject to change based on further information discovered as well as the course of the depositions themselves:

Stage 1

Plaintiff's depositions (as to class certification only).

Stage 2

Chartwell affiliated parties and witnesses.

Stage 3

All remaining Defendants and witnesses.

Stage 4

Plaintiffs.

D. Court Reporters.

Counsel shall strive to use the same court reporter for all depositions so that the reporter will be familiar with the names and terminology unique to this litigation. Counsel have negotiated a discount rate with Barkley Court Reporters to use said service for this action. Accordingly, all depositions shall be reported by Barkley Court Reporters.

E. Expert Discovery.

Whether or not any party serves a demand for exchange of expert witness information, all parties shall designate any experts they intend to have testify at trial on or before July 5, 1996. Such expert designations shall in all other respects comply with Ca..ifornia Civil Procedure Cc . section 2034.

The scheduling and conduct of any expert witness depositions shall in all respects comply with the procedures set forth in Section C above.

F. <u>Production of Documents</u>.

Counsel may seek documents throughout the discovery phase of this action as deemed appropriate. All documents will be stamped (Bates or otherwise) to identify the producing party. Such indentification will be by producing intity if represented by counsel in this matter, otherwise, identification will be by the document reposting. Callahan, Blaine & Williams will act as the Document Repository. Documents need only be produced, whether by parties or witnesses, to the Document Repository who shall maintain all documents on behalf of all parties. All documents produced prior to the execution of this order shall be deposited with the Document Repository within fifteen (15) days of execution of this order. All documents will be scanned, organized, and indexed by the Document Repository upon receipt and immediately upon completion of same the Document Repository shall send to all parties computer disk and/or hard copies of the produced documents (according to preference) together with an index of same. Documents may be reviewed and additional copies will be produced, upon reasonable notice.

G. <u>Protection of Confidential Documents</u>.

All information contained in documents produced in thi. action which are marked as "confidential" shall be maintained as confidential by counsel the named parties and the Document Repository and shall not be disclosed to third parties for any purpose outside of this litigation unless ordered by a court of competent jurisdiction.

Counsel may provide copies of any of the confidential documents produced in this action to consultants or experts as counsel deems necessary in this case. Such consultants or experts must agree, however, to maintain such information as confidential and not to divulge it to anyone or use it for any purpose other than in this litigation.

H. Status Conferences.

The Court shall hold status conferences as it deems appropriate. No less than ten (10) days prior to each status conference, the parties shall meet and confer for the purpose of negotiating a joint agenda for such status conference. An agenda for the status conference shall be submitted to the Court no less than three (3) court days prior to the scheduled conference. In the event an agreement regarding a joint agenda cannot be reached, each side shall submit a separate agenda to the Court within the time prescribed above.

I. Amendment of Case Management Order.

This Order may be amended by the Court or supplemented by additional order upon motion of any party or by stipulation.

J. Dea. ines Are Based On Parties ood Faith.

The deadlines set forth herein are good faith estimates. The parties acknowledge that the deadlines set forth herein may, in spite of the parties' best efforts, require modification or extension in light of the circumstances.

SO STIPULATED.

Dated: 5-16-95

CALLAHAN, BLAINE & WILLIAMS

By: ______________________
Michael J. Sachs
Attorneys for Defendants

Dated:

COHELAN & KHOURY

By: ______________________
Timothy Cohelan
William C. Herring
Attorneys for Plaintiffs

Dated:

By: ______________________

Attorneys for Defendant
CHARTWELL FINANCIAL

Dated:

By: ______________________

Defendant in Pro Per

J. Deadlines Are Based On Parties' Good Faith.

The deadlines set forth herein are good faith estimates. The parties acknowledge that the deadlines set forth herein may, in spite of the parties' best efforts, require modification or extension in light of the circumstances.

SO STIPULATED.

Dated: CALLAHAN, BLAINE & WILLIAMS

By: ______________________
Michael J. Sachs
Attorneys for Defendants

Dated: 5/15/95 COHELAN & KHOURY

By: William C. Herring
Timothy Cohelan
William C. Herring
Attorneys for Plaintiffs

Dated:

By: ______________________

Attorneys for Defendant
CHARTWELL FINANCIAL

Dated:

By: ______________________

Defendant in Pro Per

Dated:

By: ______________________

Attorneys for Defendant

Dated:

By: ______________________

Attorneys for Defendant

Dated:

By: ______________________

Attorneys for Defendant

Dated:

By: ______________________

Attorneys for Defendant

Dated:

By: ______________________

Attorneys for Defendant

Dated:

By: ______________________

Attorneys for Defendant

Dated:

By: ______________________

Attorneys for Defendant

Dated: 5-15-95

By: ______________________

Attorneys for Defendant

Dated: 5/16/95

By: ______________________

Attorneys for Defendant

IT IS SO ORDERED.

Dated this 6th of ~~May~~ July 1995.

TULLY H. SEYMOUR

Honorable Tully H. Seymour
Judge of the Superior Court

SERVICE LIST

Marquart, et al., v. Chartwell Financial, et al.
OCSC Case No.

Timothy Cohelan, Esq. William C. Herring, Esq. Cohelan & Khoury 701 "C" Street San Diego, CA 921201-5307 Phone: 619/595-3001 Fax #: 595-3000	Plaintiffs WESLEY MARQUART; and on behalf of themselves and all others similarly situated.
c/o Phone:	Defendant CHARTWELL FINANCIAL
Phone:	Defendant IN PRO PER
San Francisco, CA 94105 Phone: Fax:	Defendants

9 SETTLEMENT ISSUES AND PROCEDURE

A. TEXT

Sec.

9.01 Introduction

9.02 Tactical Considerations

[A] Realistic Evaluation of Recovery Sources

[B] Discovery of Insurance Information at the Outset

[C] Early Appointment of Settlement Master

[D] Serial Class Settlements

[E] Defendant Settlement Considerations

9.03 Dismissal

[A] The Requirement of Court Approval

[B] Settlement with Class Representative Only

[C] Settlement Paying Class Attorney's Fees Only

9.04 Class Settlement Procedure

[A] Ex Parte or Noticed Court Approval of Preliminary Terms of Settlement and Notice

[B] Notice to Class

[C] Settlement Hearing

[D] Standing to Object

[E] Conditional Classwide and Precertification Settlement

[F] Postcertification Settlement

[G] Attorney's Fees Conflicts

[H] Notice in Declaratory/Injunctive Relief Cases

[I] Notice in Opt-Out Cases

[J] Scope of Bar Order—State Class Settlements

[K] Scope of Bar Order—Federal Class Settlements

[L] Settlement Effective Date

9.05 References

B. FORMS

9.10 Stipulation Regarding Temporary and Conditional Certification of Class for Settlement Purposes Only and Order Thereon

9.11 Stipulation re Settlement

9.12 Memorandum of Points and Authorities in Support of Final Approval of Partial Settlement of Class Action; Award of Attorney's Fees and Costs (*Marquart* case)

9.13 Order of (1) Preliminary Approval of Settlement, and (2) Approval of Notice of Pendency of Class Action, Preliminary Approval of Settlement and Setting Fairness Hearing

9.14 Judgment on Order of Final Approval of Settlement

A. TEXT

§ 9.01 Introduction

Like most civil litigation, class actions that are adequately prepared for trial tend to settle. Well-conceived and well-executed cases that receive class certification usually settle with some or all defendants. Counsel needs to begin considering tactical issues and procedural rules for settlement even in the early stages of the proceeding.

§ 9.02 Tactical Considerations

[A] Realistic Evaluation of Recovery Sources

Particularly in a multiparty case, plaintiffs should realistically analyze defendants' financial position and the prospects of recovery. With multiple defendants, their individual ability to respond may range from a cost-of-defense perspective to a substantial recovery source. Defense counsel should not be shy about discussing these commercial realities with plaintiffs' counsel early in a case. Most experienced defense attorneys understand the benefits of providing enough information to a settlement master to better the chances of early resolution for their clients.

If you seek to remedy a significant wrong, and if the defendants appear obviously incapable of responding to damage claims, you should analyze the likelihood of a financial result. This is a particular concern when ongoing, overt patterns of wrongdoing, such as fraud, leave a trail of bankruptcy estates and disappearing defendants. If there are no realistic sources of relief, settlement will be unlikely.

[B] Discovery of Insurance Information at the Outset

Many class actions benefit from early analysis of insurance questions, including the type of coverage involved. Defendants are often influenced in settlement analysis by their insurance carriers, deductible amounts, and coverage restrictions.

Other relevant insurance information reveals whether policies are errors and omissions, crime bonds, surety bonds, or possibly even comprehensive general liability policies. Comprehensive general liability policies typically are occurrence-based, while many other types of coverage are claims-made, with important provisions governing the date of the claim, not the underlying events giving rise to coverage.

Early analysis of insurance information should also cover primary, excess, and umbrella policies. Check to see whether the policies have burning limits or are self-consuming—that is, whether the cost of defending the action is subtracted from the reserves available to indemnify the insured for loss. If the policy is self-consuming, and if the underlying insured cannot respond to damages, policy limits demands and other actions must be taken to preserve class interests against depletion of the insurance reserve. Even when defendants have the resources to grant the relief on their own, coverage still plays a role in decisions to settle.

[C] Early Appointment of Settlement Master

When the settlement fund is limited and various parties are competing for it, defendant and plaintiff should consider the appointment of a settlement master by a court reference. Appointed by a case management or other court order, the settlement master can be given authority to receive, control, administer, and distribute settlement proceeds as well as render findings in connection with settlement.

Common practice suggests the settlement master should not be the trial judge. An outside settlement master allows the parties to begin discussing their differences in the context of prospective conditional classwide resolution. A retired judge or experienced attorney serving as settlement master should be familiar with the procedures and processes of conditional class certification, including required notice to the class and the tremendous benefit of settlement to the defendant. A settlement master who senses the momentum of the case can make a critical difference by encouraging early notification of partial class settlement, which often helps the court reach conclusions on class certification. Simply put, a good settlement master illuminates the exit sign.

[D] Serial Class Settlements

In a case with substantial merit and numerous parties, a prudent plaintiff's counsel sees the value of a continuous, ongoing settlement process entailing a series of notices to class members updating them on the status of the case. The court tends to view counsel more sympathetically when the practitioner appears to be resolving claims for the class. All parties benefit when the process hedges or lessens risks.

[E] Defendant Settlement Considerations

Defendants who settle early achieve a degree of certainty in terms of exposure and legal costs, and they can close their files to get on to other business. Unless the defendant is convinced that the claim is wholly without merit, unjustified, malicious, or undertaken in complete bad faith, he or she should begin the settlement analysis with a realistic estimate of the cost of defense. Defendant's counsel should try to determine objectively what damages could be proven under the defendant's worst case (i.e., plaintiffs' best case) and discount for the risk of loss. For example, let us assume defendant's counsel estimates that the case will cost $250,000 to defend, joint and several liability with other defendants may exceed $5 million, and plaintiffs have a 30 percent chance of success. Now defendant and counsel can complete a series of calculations that guide them in making a settlement offer.

§ 9.03 Dismissal

[A] The Requirement of Court Approval

With or without class certification, the court must approve dismissal before the clerk may process it. Counsel should provide background information explaining the purposes and reasons for the dismissal and its effect on absent class members. This is particularly important if the settlement involves the class representatives or delivers unusual benefit to class counsel. A pure dismissal may not have a res judicata effect on absent class members, but it can have other consequences, such as allowing the statute of limitations to run, that require class notice.

[B] Settlement with Class Representative Only

California Rules of Court, rule 365, expressly requiring court approval of class action dismissal is grounded in *Marcarelli* v. *Cabell* (1976) 58 Cal.App.3d 51 [129 Cal.Rptr. 509]. The case involved an attempt to settle benefiting class representatives only. Plaintiffs filed an amended class action complaint against the defendant alleging a massive real estate fraud and asking for restitution, compensatory and exemplary damages, and other relief. Plaintiffs claimed further to represent several thousand persons. Within three months of the original filing, the plaintiffs and defendants filed a joint request for dismissal of the action with prejudice under Code of Civil Procedure section 581, subdivision (2). They also submitted a "consent to dismissal" stating that the parties to the action wished to adjust and settle fully all claims and controversies. When the clerk orally refused to enter the dismissal, the plaintiffs and the defendants filed a writ of mandate seeking to compel the clerk to perform what they called the "nondiscretionary duty to dismiss the case." (*Marcarelli* v. *Cabell* (1976) 58 Cal.App.3d 51 [129 Cal.Rptr. 509].)

The court found without merit the plaintiffs' contention that they had an absolute right to dismiss the class action under Code of Civil Procedure section 581. Citing *La Sala* v. *American Savings & Loan Ass'n*, the court reaffirmed that when a class action is to be dismissed because defendants are granting benefits to class representatives but not to other members of the class, the dismissal may not proceed without notice to the class. The court pointed to a simple reason for the rule. A plaintiff suing on behalf of a class assumes a fiduciary obligation and surrenders any right to compromise the group action in return for individual gain. Even if the named plaintiff receives all the benefits sought in the complaint, he or she still must continue the action for the benefit of others similarly situated. (*Marcarelli* v. *Cabell* (1976) 58 Cal.App.3d 51 [129 Cal.Rptr. 509] quoting *La Sala* v. *American Savings & Loan Ass'n* (1971) 5 Cal.3d 864, 871 [97 Cal.Rptr. 849, 489 P.2d 1113], and also referring to *City of San Jose* v. *Superior Court of Santa Clara County* (1974) 12 Cal.3d 447 [115 Cal.Rptr. 797 525 P.2d 701].)

In addition to the representative party's fiduciary duty, the court itself has a duty to protect the class. (*Bingham* v. *Obledo* (1983) 147 Cal.App.3d 401 [195 Cal.Rptr. 142].) Declarations in support of the facts and circumstances surrounding the dismissal will allow the court to complete the record required for dismissal. Local rules such as Los Angeles Superior Court revised rule 15.47 expressly direct the clerk of the superior court to process requests for dismissal of a class action only with prior court approval.

[C] Settlement Paying Class Attorney's Fees Only

Settlements that appear to primarily benefit class attorneys run up against the same questions of individual gain at the expense of fiduciary responsibility. Although there are a number of well-known examples of courts refusing to approve sweetheart class settlements, a 1976 California case set the standard for judicial review of settlements and required supporting information.

That case is *Anthony* v. *Superior Court of Los Angeles County* in which a settlement agreement largely called attention to defendant's actions in satisfying class claims and awarded plaintiff's counsel over $300,000 in fees. The court affirmed the lower court's decision not to issue a writ of mandate compelling dismissal of the matter despite the supposed settlement. Plaintiffs had filed a class action against General Motors alleging defects in certain disc wheels made by a separate corporation but sold by General Motors as optional equipment on 1960 to 1965 model trucks. Plaintiffs originally requested that the defendants recall and pay for the replacement of the wheels. Defendants subsequently mailed out a notice that they would replace the wheels on all the affected trucks at their expense. The plaintiffs then filed a supplemental complaint alleging that the settlement would mislead three-fourths of the truck-owner class. Later, the Federal Highway Administration notified General Motors that the defect in the wheels resulted in an unreasonable risk of harm. General Motors filed suit against the Department of Transportation to invalidate the finding. The original class complaint alleged claims beyond the scope of the recall and regulatory issues involving the federal Highway Administration. (*Anthony* v. *Superior Court* (1976) 59 Cal.App.3d 760, 771 [130 Cal.Rptr. 758].)

Six years after the original filing, class lawyers and representatives requested dismissal. The attorneys' declaration stated that plaintiffs' primary concern was replacement of the defective wheels, a fact seemingly controverted by, among other things, the original complaint. The settlement agreement called for General Motors to pay plaintiff's law firm $300,000 for fees over and above the regulatory action. The appellate court found the settlement agreement deficient in several particulars. There had been no showing that $300,000 adequately compensated the class for surrendering its damage claims, nor that the attorneys should take the entire settlement, nor that the attorney's work had been worth $300,000, nor even that the attorney's efforts had produced the regulatory settlement. (*Anthony* v. *Superior Court* (1976) 59 Cal.App.3d 760, 771 [130 Cal.Rptr. 758]. *Anthony* was finalized when the Supreme Court denied petitioners' application for a hearing on September 29, 1976.)

The court found that notice should be given so that class members have the opportunity to express their opinion about a proposed settlement that benefits class attorneys monetarily. This problem obviously does not arise when counsel is compensated pursuant to the common fund theory, since the fund is established for the benefit of the class and attorneys are paid a percentage of the recovery. (*Anthony* v. *Superior Court* (1976) 59 Cal.App.3d 760, 771 [130 Cal.Rptr. 758].)

§ 9.04 Class Settlement Procedure

[A] Ex Parte or Noticed Court Approval of Preliminary Terms of Settlement and Notice

The first step in settling a class action is to prepare the settlement documentation and a summary notice for approval by the court. Since most monetary claims are resolved as opt-out actions under rule 23, subdivision(b)(3), of Federal Rules of Civil Procedure, the court must approve the contents of the notice to class members. In most cases, the need for, and contents of, class settlement notices are subject to local rules as well.

At the preliminary stage, the court considers general settlement terms. It reviews information on the arms-length nature of the negotiation, any obvious signs of collusion, presence or absence of conflicts within the class, and possible preferential treatment within the class. The court also determines whether the settlement is likely to be approved at the hearing to be scheduled after notice.

The court-approved preliminary notice includes the opt-out dates and other provisions of the settlement, and it states that the court has given preliminary approval to the terms of the settlement. The notice is sent to absent class members after the court approves a preliminary order of approval reciting the settlement terms and dates of the settlement hearing. This essentially follows federal practice. District courts are not required to conduct hearings to evaluate the adequacy of a settlement before ordering settlement notice. (*In re "Agent Orange" Products Liability Litigation* (2d Cir. 1987) 818 F.2d 11.) A preliminary notice of approval is included in the Appendix.

[B] Notice to Class

Notice of a class settlement must tell class members everything they need to know in order to make an informed decision about being bound by the settlement or opting out or to object to its terms if the class is certified. Much as in federal procedure, parties to settlement agreements submit a written notice of the motion for the court's preliminary approval. This is accompanied by the original executed settlement agreement and a copy of the proposed order with notice to the class. (See Super. Ct. San Mateo County Rules, rule 7.9, Settlement of Class Actions.)

Class settlement documentation must include information on a number of topics. These include a brief explanation of the case, the exclusion date for persons not wishing to be bound by the settlement, specific exclusion criteria, attorney's fees to be paid by the class as part of the settlement, and total recovery and anticipated benefit to the class with expenses and costs specified. Documentation should state that class members who do not exclude themselves will be subject to a binding judgment in favor of the settling defendant under res judicata and that the attorneys for the proposed class in the settlement will continue to represent all class members who do not opt out. (See, e.g., Super. Ct. L.A. County Rules, Class Actions Man., § 15.18(f), "Necessity for Class Actions.") Information on pending but unresolved class cases as of the date of the proposed settlement is also important. (*Trotsky* v. *Los Angeles Fed. Sav. & Loan Ass'n* (1975) 48 Cal.App.3d 134 [121 Cal.Rptr. 637].)

[C] Settlement Hearing

All class settlements are subject to a settlement hearing and court approval before entry of judgment or final order. The trial court has broad powers to determine whether a proposed settlement is fair. (*Mallick* v. *Superior Court* (1979) 89 Cal.App.3d 434 [152 Cal.Rptr. 503].) The California standard for approval of class settlements is similar to the federal requirement that the settlement be fair, reasonable, and adequate for class members overall. (*Piambino* v. *Bailey* (1980) 610 F.2d 1306 (5th Cir.) cert. denied, 449 U.S. 1011.) Federal courts do not decide the merits of the case or resolve unsettled legal questions at settlement. (*Carson* v. *American Brands, Inc.* (1981) 450 U.S. 79, 88 [67 L.Ed.2d 59, 101 S.Ct. 993].)

The initial presumption of fairness in a class settlement may be established by showing arm's length bargaining, sufficient discovery or investigation, experience of counsel in similar cases, and the quantity and scope of any objections to the settlement. The trial court should closely scrutinize settlement terms outside the scope of the operative complaint to determine whether the plaintiff genuinely contests those issues and adequately represents the class. (*Mallick* v. *Superior Court* (1979) 89 Cal.App.3d 434 [152 Cal.Rptr. 503].)

The considerations relevant to approval of a class settlement are (*Armstrong* v. *Board of School Directors* (7th Cir. 1980) 616 F.2d 305, 314):

1. The strength of the plaintiffs' case on the merits balanced against what is offered.

2. The defendant's ability to pay.

3. The complexity, length, and expense of further litigation.

4. The degree of opposition within the class.

5. The presence of collusion.

6. The reaction of class members to the settlement.

7. The opinions of counsel

8. The stage of proceedings and amount of discovery conducted.

In support of the proposed class settlement, counsel should discuss the strength of the case and analyze its legal or factual underpinnings. Juxtaposing the facts known on the date of settlement against the applicable law allows the judge to draw reasonable inferences about the risk of loss.

The court has broad discretion to approve a settlement and the trial court's action in that regard is "limited to review of the trial court's approval for a clear abuse of discretion." (*Dunk* v. *Ford Motor Company* (1996) 48 Cal.App.4th 1794, 1802 [56 Cal.Rptr.2d 483].)

Local rules now give courts considerable discretion in determining the fairness, reasonableness, and adequacy of a proposed settlement (Super. Ct. L.A. County Rules, rule 15.45). They encourage procedures that may involve the taking of evidence by declaration, points, and authorities and offer an opportunity for class members to be heard. Under San Francisco Local Rules, the court conducts an independent inquiry on fairness, and it may refuse to approve any settlement it determines is unfair. The court may also modify the terms of settlement to achieve fairness. If the parties agree to be bound by the changes, the court may then approve. (Super. Ct. S.F. County Rules, rule 461.)

In California, plaintiff may settle with one of several joint tortfeasors or co-obligors on a contract without releasing the others. Provided that the settlement is in good faith, it also discharges the settling defendant from liability to other defendants for equitable contribution or comparative indemnity pursuant to Code of Civil Procedure section 877, subdivisions (a) and (b). This protects a settling defendant against future claims of class members and codefendant cross-complaints other than those based upon written express indemnity agreements. The settlement should roughly approximate the settling defendant's proportion of total responsibility. Obviously, collusion, fraud, or tortious conduct must be absent. (*Tech-Bilt, Inc.* v. *Woodward, Clyde & Associates* (1985) 38 Cal.3d 488, 499 [213 Cal.Rptr. 256, 698 P.2d 159].)

[D] Standing to Object

Only a party aggrieved by deficiencies in the settlement may object to it. Generally class members can object to a class settlement even if they could have opted out.

[E] Conditional Classwide and Precertification Settlement

In certain circumstances the parties may wish to negotiate and seek court approval of a settlement stipulating to certification before the court has actually ruled on the issue. In conditional settlements, the class agrees to be bound if the conditions are met. The defendant usually agrees to settle with the class by paying or performing, subject to conditions that usually include a limit on the number of class members opting out and some sort of bar order against cross-complaints from other defendants.

Conditional settlements can arise from a defendant's desire to avoid further legal expense and settle early for less. Such settlements often occur after adverse results in pending individual litigation, test cases, or other relevant matters. Regulatory pressures and the problems raised by large, multiparty cases often lead to proposed classwide settlements. Plaintiff benefits from precertification settlements by the value of an early ruling and notice to the as-yet-uncertified class, which increases the prospects of certification over remaining opposition. Damage and liability responses from the settling defendant often enhance plaintiff's position in the eyes of the remaining defendants as well.

Procedural steps begin with an agreement of conditional class certification, for settlement purposes only. Preliminary court approval of the general terms and authorization of notice follow. The final step is an open noticed hearing on all aspects of the proposed settlement.

Conditional class settlements before formal certification are sometimes controversial if significant pending individual cases are not included or simultaneously settled. While differences in settlement may only be in the minds of counsel, a court must understand the merits of criticisms in the context of the overall facts, including the potential merits, of all the cases. In a substantial conditional class settlement the author's firm negotiated, the court initially refused to formally calendar the settlement, in effect sending all back to mediation of a "global resolution" that subsequently occurred.

[F] Postcertification Settlement

Most certified class actions settle. In the postcertification stage of the proceeding, the size and scope of the class is known and therefore not conditional, fundamentally changing the relative status of the negotiating parties. The period after certification and before notice offers plaintiff's counsel a unique opportunity to involve defendants in developing the class notice. Often this interaction leads to some discussion of settlement.

Assuming that the settlement is based upon noncollusive factors and a commensurate comparison of ability to pay against degree of exposure to liability, the parties face far fewer unknowns after certification than before. Postcertification settlements normally win court approval.

If the court has also approved notice before settlement is agreed, the class has been defined, and class representatives and counsel represent their interests. Since the non–class member opt-outs have already been identified, remaining class members may not opt out of additional settlements, although they may object to the fairness, reasonableness, and adequacy of the settlement and to attorneys' fees and costs. If objections from a party in this situation are overcome, the objecting party may not initiate individual litigation and is confined to the subsequent class proceedings. Generally the threshold for final court approval is lower and the burden for the objecting party higher than in opt-out situations, where an objecting party can simply walk away from the settlement and pursue individual litigation.

[G] Attorney's Fees Conflicts

Settlement entails significant potential conflicts of interest between counsel, both plaintiff's and defendant's, and the real parties in a class action. Plaintiff's counsel, particularly in common fund situations, faces the tension of a contingent fee crystallizing into a set amount in settlement discussions. Defense counsel may be anticipating the conclusion of a substantial portion of his or her workload. Therefore, a well-structured settlement explicitly subordinates the interests of the lawyers to the interests of the clients.

[H] Notice in Declaratory/Injunctive Relief Cases

A case that attacks a statute or rule is easily settled by changing the rule to conform to the alleged deficiency. In other situations, too, considerations of judicial economy allow a California court to render a settlement mandatory or non–opt-out.

In *Bell* v. *American Title Ins. Co.*, the court spelled out the relationship of federal and state rules on mandatory judgments. (*Bell* v. *American Title Ins. Co.* (1991) 226 Cal.App.3d 1589 [277 Cal.Rptr. 583].) California, like Federal Rules of Civil Procedure rule 23, distinguishes different types of class actions and establishes different requirements of notice. Federal cases certified under Federal Rules of Civil Procedure, rule 23, subdivison(b)(1) or (b)(2), involve no opt-out right and may be called mandatory. (See the Appendix A for the complete text of federal rule 23.)

Rule 23, subdivison (b)(1), applies to class actions in which individual adjudication would either establish incompatible standards of conduct for the opposing party or would be dispositive of the interests of other class members and substantially impair their ability to protect their own interests. (*Bell* v. *American Title Ins. Co.* (1991) 226 Cal.App.3d 1589 [277 Cal.Rptr. 583].) In matters seeking injunctive relief, the trial court has the discretion to classify the action as a mandatory judgment requiring no notice. By its nature, injunctive relief easily could create potentially incompatible standards of conduct for the opposing party if it were awarded in some cases and denied in others.

Rule 23, subdivision (b)(2), applies to situations in which the party opposing the class has acted or refused to act on grounds generally applicable to the class. Final injunctive or declaratory relief for the class as a whole is appropriate. Class members have no right to "opt out." Accordingly, in actions requesting final injunctive or declaratory relief against the party opposing the class, notice is not required before adjudication on the merits.

If doubts arise how an action should be classified under rule 23, California courts favor resolution in favor of subdivision (b)(2) status. (*Frazier* v. *City of Richmond* (1986) 184 Cal.App.3d 1491, 1501 [228 Cal.Rptr. 376].)

[I] Notice in Opt-Out Cases

See Chapter 6 for the required contents of class notice in opt-out class actions under rule 23, subdivision (b)(3).

[J] Scope of Bar Order—State Class Settlements

When a class action is settled with fewer than all the defendants, two issues arise. First, the settling defendant wants a bar order preventing indemnity or contribution claims from nonsettling parties. The bar order is generally granted after the court conducts the appropriate hearing pursuant to a motion seeking confirmation for good faith settlements under Code of Civil Procedure sections 877 and 877.6. The settling defendant asks the court to determine that any pending cross-complaints for equitable indemnity or contribution against the settling parties be dismissed and all future actions barred.

The second issue, the degree of offset or credit to be afforded the nonsettling party at trial, comes into play after the settling defendant has an award confirmed. Statute and case law govern the degree of this credit or setoff at the trial after the trier of fact apportions liability. Setoffs for settlement payments cover only economic damages against the jury's verdicts. Settlement payments attributable to noneconomic damages are not subject to the setoff. (*Espinoza* v. *Machonga* (1992) 9 Cal.App.4th 268 [11 Cal.Rptr.2d 498].)

A trial court's certification of a nationwide settlement class was recently approved. Prior to the settlement, the trial court had originally certified only a class of California residents. The reasoning of the appeal court was that the normal arguments against a nationwide class, such as the application of different laws, do not apply in a settlement situation. There was no requirement of a "protracted determination of other states' laws inasmuch as it was a settlement." (*Dunk* v. *Ford Motor Company* (1996) 48 Cal.App.4th 1794 [56 Cal.Rptr.2d 483].)

[K] Scope of Bar Order—Federal Class Settlements

When notice in a state class action includes without limitation claims asserted in a federal action, the settlement is entitled to full faith and credit under 28 U.S.C. section 1738. Such was the recent holding of *Matsushita Electric Industrial Co., Ltd.* v. *Epstein*, which allows state court class action settlements that meet the criteria for extinguishing federal claims. (*Matsushita Electric Industrial Co., Ltd.* v. *Epstein* (1996) __ U.S.__ [134 L.Ed. 2d 64, 116 S.Ct. 873].)

[L] Settlement Effective Date

Most settlement documentation defines the settlement effective date as 60 days after a final judgment or order is entered and mailed to all parties in accordance with California Rules of Court, rule 2, subdivision (a)(2). This simply means that approximately sixty days after the court approves a settlement, it becomes final and operative. If codefendants or other parties make objections that result in either a request for a writ or the filing of a formal appeal, the settlement does not become final until the court rules on the writ or appeal.

§ 9.05 References

NEWBERG For a discussion of the federal procedure for submitting class settlement for approval and settlement effective dates, see 2 Newberg on Class Actions (3d ed. 1992), Chapter 11.

TRG **THE RUTTER GROUP** See the following sections in California Practice Guide: Civil Procedure Before Trial (CPBT) regarding settlement:

- Settlement and notice (CPBT, §§ 14:138, 14:139).

See also the following sections in California Practice Guide: Federal Civil Procedure Before Trial (FCPBT) regarding settlement in federal class actions:

- Settlement procedures (FCPBT, §§ 10:551–10:595).

WESTLAW® See the WESTLAW Electronic Research Guide at the beginning of this volume.

B. FORMS

§ 9.10 Stipulation Regarding Temporary and Conditional Certification of Class for Settlement Purposes Only and Order Thereon

TIMOTHY D. COHELAN, ESQ.
ISAM C. KHOURY, ESQ.
COHELAN & KHOURY
701 "C" Street
San Diego, CA 92101-5307
(619) 239-8148
Attorneys for Plaintiffs

MERRILL F. STORMS, JR. (078333)
TERRY D. ROSS (042660)
CINDY M. CIPRIANI (144402)
GRAY CARY WARE & FREIDENRICH
A Professional Corporation
401 B Street, Suite 1700
San Diego, CA 92101-4297
(619) 699-3526
Attorneys for Defendants

SUPERIOR COURT OF THE STATE OF CALIFORNIA

FOR THE COUNTY OF

on behalf of themselves and all others similarly situated, Plaintiffs, vs. a California general partnership; a California Corporation; and DOES 1-100, inclusive, Defendants.	CASE NO. STIPULATION REGARDING TEMPORARY AND CONDITIONAL CERTIFICATION OF CLASS FOR SETTLEMENT PURPOSES ONLY AND ORDER THEREON Date: October 17, 1996 Time: 4:00 p.m. Dept 3 Judge:

IT IS HEREBY STIPULATED by and between and on behalf of themselves and all others similarly situated, as defined more precisely in the Stipulation re Settlement filed concurrently herewith, and a California general partnership, and a California Corporation ( ) as follows:

1. Conditional on the execution and filing by this Court of the Order of Final Approval of Settlement in accordance with the Stipulation re Settlement submitted concurrently herewith, agrees that the Court shall simultaneously order that the Class referred to in the Stipulation re Settlement and defined immediately below shall be temporarily and conditionally certified for settlement purposes only:

> "Class" means all persons subject to this Class Action and specifically all persons who are shown in the records of the County Recorder of the County of to have owned a home at any time between April 1, 1994 and October 15, 1996 located in the County of constructed by with respect to which the Notice of Completion was recorded on or after January 1, 1983 and before April 1, 1994, except (a) such persons who have previously reached settlements, released or dismissed claims against (b) named plaintiffs in lawsuits pending in County against for construction defects and specifically in County Superior Court Case Nos.
>
> and (c) any owners, officers or directors of in the following cities and subdivisions:
>
> City of ______
> City of ______
> City of ______
>
> City of ______

2. This Stipulation is made for the sole purpose of attempting to consummate Settlement of the Class Action in accordance with the Stipulation re Settlement submitted concurrently herewith. enters into this Stipulation in compromise of disputed claims. In the event that the Court does not execute and file the Order of Final Approval and Order Determining Good Faith of the Settlement, or in the event that either such Order of Final Approval or Order Determining Good Faith does not become final for any reason whatsoever, or is

-2-

modified in any material respect, or in the event that the Effective Settlement Date, as defined in the Stipulation re Settlement, does not occur, this Stipulation shall be deemed void *ab initio* and shall be of no force or effect whatsoever, and shall not be referred to or utilized for any purpose whatsoever, specifically including, without limitation, any later attempt by or on behalf of plaintiffs to seek class certification in this or any other matter. denies all of plaintiffs' claims as to liability and damages as well as plaintiffs' class allegations, and does not waive, but rather expressly reserves, all rights to challenge all such claims and allegations on all procedural and factual grounds including the assertion of any and all defenses.

IT IS SO STIPULATED.

DATED:________________

____

DATED:________________

____

DATED: 10.14.96

Approved:

COHELAN & KHOURY

By: ____________________
TIMOTHY D. COHELAN
Attorneys for Plaintiffs

DATED: ________________

A California general partnership

By:____________________

-3-

DATED: ____________________

A California Corporation

By:______________________________

DATED: 10/14/96

GRAY CARY WARE & FREIDENRICH
A Professional Corporation

By: MERRILL F. STORMS
Attorneys for Defendants

ORDER

THE COURT, having considered and accepted the above Stipulation, and Good Cause Appearing,

IT IS SO ORDERED.

DATED:________ ______________________________
JUDGE OF THE SUPERIOR COURT

-4-

§ 9.11 Stipulation re Settlement

TIMOTHY D. COHELAN, ESQ.
ISAM C. KHOURY, ESQ.
COHELAN & KHOURY
701 "C" Street
San Diego, CA 92101-5307
(619) 239-8148
Attorneys for Plaintiffs

MERRILL F. STORMS, JR. (078333)
TERRY D. ROSS (042660)
CINDY M. CIPRIANI (144402)
GRAY CARY WARE & FREIDENRICH
A Professional Corporation
401 B Street, Suite 1700
San Diego, CA 92101-4297
(619) 699-3526
Attorneys for Defendants

SUPERIOR COURT OF THE STATE OF CALIFORNIA

FOR THE COUNTY OF

on behalf of themselves and all others similarly situated, Plaintiffs, vs. a California general partnership; a California Corporation; and DOES 1-100, inclusive, Defendants.	CASE NO. STIPULATION RE SETTLEMENT

IT IS HEREBY STIPULATED by and between and on behalf of themselves and all others similarly situated, as defined more precisely below, and a California general partnership, and a California corporation ( ) as set forth below.

1. CONDITIONAL NATURE OF STIPULATION. This Stipulation re Settlement is made for the sole purpose of attempting to consummate Settlement of the case on a class wide basis. This Stipulation re Settlement and the Settlement it evidences is made in compromise of disputed claims. Because this is a Class Action, this Settlement must receive preliminary and final approval by the Court. Accordingly, enters into this Stipulation on a conditional basis. In the event that the Court does not execute and file the Order of Final Approval or Order Determining Good Faith of the Settlement, or in the event that any such Order of Final Approval or Order Determining Good Faith does not become final for any reason, or is modified in any material respect, or in the event that the Effective Settlement Date, as defined herein, does not occur, this Stipulation re Settlement shall be deemed null and void *ab initio* and shall be of no force or effect whatsoever, and shall not be referred to or utilized for any purpose whatsoever. denies all of plaintiffs' claims as to liability and damages as well as plaintiffs' class allegations, and does not waive, but rather expressly reserves, all rights to challenge all such claims and allegations upon all procedural and factual grounds including the assertion of any and all defenses.

2. DEFINITIONS. The following definitions apply with respect to this Stipulation re Settlement and all related documents:

a. "Agreement & Release" means a document entitled "Agreement & Release Affecting Real Property & Covenant Running With the Land," in a recordable form to be signed by Participating Class Members and notarized, with respect to each Participating Class Home, releasing all Released Claims, to be promptly recorded by Class Counsel as a condition of payment of any of the Settlement Amount to such Participating Class Members.

b. "Class" means all persons subject to this Class Action and specifically all persons who are shown in the records for the County Recorder of the County of to have owned a home at any time between April 1, 1994 and

SD\1019338-1

-2-

October 15, 1996 located in the County of constructed by with respect to which the Notice of Completion was recorded on or after January 1, 1983 and before April 1, 1994, except (a) such persons who have previously reached settlements, released or dismissed claims against (b) named plaintiffs in lawsuits pending in County against for construction defects and specifically in County Superior Court Case Nos. and (c) any owners, officers or directors of in the following cities and subdivisions:

i. City of ______

ii. City of ______

iii. City of ______

iv. City of ______

v. ______

c. "Class Action" means the Class Action lawsuit herein, generally known as " v. ," County Superior Court Case Number .

d. "Class Action Settlement Claim Form" means a document bearing that title to be completed by Participating Class Members as specified therein in order to claim and recover any amounts pursuant to this Settlement.

e. "Class Counsel" means the Cohelan & Khoury law firm.

f. "Class Counsel Fees and Expenses" means the reasonable attorneys' fees and litigation expenses incurred by Class Counsel in prosecuting the Class Action, in an amount to be approved by the Court.

g. "Class Home" means any home constructed by in the County with respect to which the Notice of Completion was recorded on

SD\1019358-1

-3-

or after January 1, 1983 and before April 1, 1994.

h. "Class Member(s)" means any person who is a member of the Class defined in paragraph 2.b. above.

i. "Court" means the Superior Court of the State of California for the County of

j. "Effective Settlement Date" as defined below is a condition to performance of obligations under this Settlement. obligations are conditioned on (1) the execution and filing by the Court of the Order of Preliminary Approval of the Settlement, (2) the execution and filing by the Court of the Order of the Final Approval and Order Determining Good Faith of the Settlement and Entry of Judgment accordingly, and (3) said Orders and Judgment becoming final through the first to occur of the following, the date of which shall constitute the Effective Settlement Date: (a) the failure of any person with standing to file objections to the Settlement or otherwise object to the Settlement at or before the Fairness and Good Faith Determination Hearing; (b) expiration of all potential appeal and writ periods without an appeal or other request for writ review having been filed; (c) final affirmance of any and all orders issuing out of any timely appeal or writ review proceeding, or final dismissal or denial of all such appeals or writ proceedings (including petitions for review, rehearing, certiorari, etc.); or (d) final disposition of any supplemental or subsequent proceedings resulting from any appeal or writ proceeding. Until and unless the Effective Settlement Date occurs, shall have no obligation to perform under this Stipulation re Settlement.

k. "Fairness and Good Faith Determination Hearing" means a hearing set by the Court to take place on or about December 9, 1996 for the purpose of determining (1) the fairness, adequacy and reasonableness of the Settlement pursuant to class action procedures and requirements, (2) the good faith of the Settlement pursuant to Code of Civil Procedure section 877.6, and (3) Class Counsel Fees and Expenses.

SD\1019338-1

-4-

l. "Judgment" means a Judgment on Order of Final Approval of Settlement to be executed by the Court and entered in the Court records in the form attached hereto as Exhibit 1.

m. " " means a California general partnership, a California Corporation, their insurance carriers, successors, and all related entities and individuals.

n. "Notice of Final Approval" means a notice entitled "Notice of Final Approval of Settlement," to be approved by the Court and to be mailed and published to Class Members as directed by the Court. Said Notice of Final Approval shall be in the form attached hereto as Exhibit 2.

o. "Notice of Pendency of Class Action" means a notice entitled "Notice of Pendency of Class Action, Preliminary Approval of Settlement and Hearing for Final Approval" to be approved by the Court and to be mailed to Class Members as directed by the Court; and a short form thereof to be approved by the Court that shall be published as directed by the Court; said Notice of Pendency of Class Action shall be in the form attached hereto as Exhibit 3A and the short form thereof shall be in the form attached hereto as Exhibit 3B.

p. "Opt-Out" means a written, signed request by a Class Member to be excluded from the Class, filed within the time and as directed by the Court in the Notice of Pendency of Class Action.

q. "Order Determining Good Faith" means an order executed and filed by the Court finding the Stipulation re Settlement and Settlement to be in good faith pursuant to Code of Civil Procedure section 877.6. Said Order Determining Good Faith shall be in the form attached hereto as Exhibit 4.

r. "Order of Final Approval" means an order executed and filed by the Court entitled "Order of Final Approval of Settlement" granting final approval to the Stipulation re Settlement and Settlement. Said Order of Final Approval shall be in

SD\1019338-1

-5-

the form attached hereto as Exhibit 5.

s. "Order of Preliminary Approval" means an order executed and filed by the Court entitled "Order of Preliminary Approval of Settlement, Approval of Notice of Pendency of Class Action, Preliminary Approval of Settlement and Setting Fairness Hearing" granting preliminary approval of the Stipulation re Settlement and Settlement, approving the Notice of Pendency of Class Action and setting the Fairness and Good Faith Hearing. Said Order of Preliminary Approval shall be in the form attached hereto as Exhibit 6.

t. "Participating Class Home(s)" means a Class Home as to which no Class Member effectively files an Opt-Out (except as otherwise provided in paragraph 6.d. below).

u. "Participating Class Members" means any Class Member who does not effectively Opt-Out of the Class. Every Participating Class Member will be bound by the Settlement of the Class Action and permanently enjoined and forever barred from seeking further relief arising out of the subject matter of the Class Action.

v. "Released Claim(s)" means all claims of Class Members and their successors in interest against in any way related to the subject matter of the Class Action, including without limitation, any and all claims asserted therein or which could have been asserted therein on any theory whatsoever, any and all claims for construction defects of any nature whatsoever, and any and all claims for breach of or pursuant to any express or implied warranty including the Ten-Year Limited Warranty (House Foundation – Foundation-related problems) issued by with respect to certain Class Homes.

w. "Settlement Amount" means the amount to be paid by or on behalf of for the benefit of Class Members to be deposited by Class Counsel into a Settlement Trust Account, upon terms and conditions set forth herein.

x. "Settlement Trust Account" means a client trust account to be set up by Class Counsel in which the Settlement Amount is to be deposited by Class

SD\1019338-1

-6-

Counsel for the benefit of Class Members, to be administered in a manner to be recommended by Class Counsel and approved by the Court consistent with the terms of this Stipulation Re Settlement.

y. "Stipulation re Settlement" and "Settlement" mean this document, which the parties acknowledge sets forth all material terms and conditions of the Settlement between them, and which is subject to Court approval. Performance of obligations under the Stipulation re Settlement is expressly conditioned on the occurrence of the Effective Settlement Date.

z. "Stipulation Regarding Temporary and Conditional Certification of Class for Settlement Purposes Only" means a document so entitled submitted to the Court simultaneously with this Stipulation, to be executed and filed by the Court as part of the Settlement.

3. CONDITIONS OF SETTLEMENT. Performance by of the obligations set forth in this Stipulation re Settlement is subject to all of the following material conditions:

a. Execution and filing by the Court of the Order of Preliminary Approval.

b. Execution as an Order and filing by the Court of the Stipulation Regarding Temporary and Conditional Certification of Class for Settlement Purposes Only.

c. Mailing and publication of the Notice of Pendency of Class Action to Class Members in accordance with the Court's Order of Preliminary Approval.

d. Participation in the Settlement of no less than one thousand two hundred (1,200) Participating Class Homes, (subject to waiver by as provided in paragraph 4.b. below).

e. The Court conducting a Fairness and Good Faith Determination Hearing on or about December 9, 1996.

/////

SD\1019338-1

-7-

f. Execution and filing by the Court of the Order Determining Good Faith of Settlement.

g. Execution and filing by the Court of the Order of Final Approval of the Settlement.

h. Execution and entry of Judgment by the Court.

i. Mailing and publication of the Notice of Final Approval in accordance with the Court's Order of Final Approval.

j. Occurrence of the Effective Settlement Date.

k. Funding of the Settlement by insurance carriers, suppliers and subcontractors and their carriers in accordance with the mediated global settlement.

The parties hereby covenant and agree to cooperate reasonably and in good faith for the purpose of achieving occurrence of the conditions set forth above, including, without limitation, timely filing of all motions, papers and evidence necessary to do so, and refraining from causing or encouraging directly or indirectly any appeal or petition for writ proceedings seeking review of any Order or the Judgment contemplated by this Stipulation re Settlement. Class Counsel represent and warrant that they have authority to enter into this Stipulation re Settlement and that by doing so they are not in breach or violation of any agreement with any third parties. The parties further agree that the Class Action shall be stayed in all respects pending the occurrence or failure of the Effective Settlement Date.

4. <u>CLASS/CLASS MEMBER RECOVERY</u>. Payment of the Settlement Amount shall be as set forth below:

a. The total Settlement Amount to be paid by or on behalf of shall be the sum of approximately Dollars ($ .00) predicated on

SD\1019338-1

-8-

participation of all 1,391[1] Class Homes covered by this Class Action. Said Settlement Amount includes all amounts to be paid to participating Class Members and to be paid to Class Counsel as reasonable attorneys' fees and for reimbursement of litigation expenses. Said Settlement Amount shall be reduced by (a) the amount allocated to any Class Home that chooses to be excluded from the Settlement by Participating Class Members as to such Class Home effectively filing an Opt-Out with the Court and (b) the amount allocated to any Class Home as to which no claim is timely submitted as provided herein or as to which no Agreement and Release is properly signed, notarized and submitted as provided herein and as ordered by the Court. Said Settlement Amount shall also be reduced by any amount less than ($) approved by the Court to be paid to Class Counsel as reasonable attorneys' fees and reimbursement for litigation costs.

b. Payment of any Settlement Amount is conditioned on the occurrence of all conditions set forth in paragraph 3 above; provided, however, that in its sole and unfettered discretion, may waive the condition set forth in paragraph 3d above requiring participation of no less than 1,200 participating Class Homes.

c. Payment of the Settlement Amount as provided herein shall be made by or on behalf of within 30 days of the occurrence of the Effective Settlement Date and may be made by one or more drafts payable to the Cohelan & Khoury Settlement Trust Account for the Class Action. Such payment shall fully satisfy the obligation of under this paragraph 4.

d. Procedures for Participating Class Members to make claims shall be as set forth in the Notice of Final Approval of Settlement attached hereto as Exhibit 2 including the completion and execution of the Class Action Settlement Claim

---

[1]The exact amount will be finally calculated after the expiration of the Opt-Out period. Class Counsel shall file a declaration in advance of the hearing documenting the exact number of Participating Class Homes and the exact Settlement Amount.

SD\1019338-1

-9-

Form and execution before a notary public of the Agreement and Release form attached as exhibits to the Notice of Final Approval of Settlement. The completion, execution and submittal of the Claim Form and Release and Agreement (including acknowledgment by a notary) by each Participating Class Member as provided in the Notice of Final Approval shall be a condition precedent to the payment of any settlement money to such Participating Class Member.

e. The Settlement Amount, after deduction of Class Counsel's reasonable attorneys' fees and reimbursement of litigation expenses as approved by the Court, will be paid to Participating Class Members based on subclasses consisting of the various subdivisions. Participating Class Members shown in the records of the County Recorder's Office as owners of record of a Participating Class Home at close of business on October 15, 1996 presumptively will be entitled to payment of the amount specified herein as to their respective Participating Class Homes; provided, however, in the event one or more former owners of record of a Participating Class Home who qualifies as a Participating Class Member makes application for payment within a time frame to be set by the Court, entitlement to said payment will be decided by the Court or other person designated by the Court and subject to Court approval.

f. The amount to be paid to Participating Class Members in the various subdivisions has been based on a balancing by Class Counsel of a number of objective considerations, including the square footage of the home, the model of the home, the original selling price, the date of construction, actual or potential damage to the home, and the presence or absence of a concrete apron and cut-off wall (moisture barrier) and related work paid for by

g. Amounts to be paid to Participating Class Members in each subdivision are set forth by Participating Class Home address on the attached Exhibit 7.

/////

SD\1019338-1

-10-

h. All amounts paid to the Cohelan & Khoury Settlement Trust Account in accordance with this Stipulation re Settlement shall be held in trust and shall be paid in strict accordance with the terms of this Settlement and only upon Court approval. To the extent any amount is paid to the Settlement Trust Account over and above the amount actually required to pay Class Counsel's reasonable attorneys' fees and reimbursement of litigation expenses as approved by the Court, and actually paid to Participating Class Members in accordance with Exhibit 7 and in strict accordance with the claim filing procedures and deadlines and other requirements as set forth in the Notice of Final Approval of Settlement, said amounts shall be held in trust for the benefit of . Any amounts allocated to Participating Class Homes for which no Claim Form is received by Class Counsel on or before February 10, 1997 shall within ten days thereafter be refunded to . If for any reason, including without limitation: (1) the effective filing of one or more Opt-Outs, (2) the failure of one or more Participating Class Members entitled to recovery under this Settlement to submit timely and complete Claim Forms, or deficiencies in such claims; (3) the failure of one or more Participating Class Members entitled to recovery under this Settlement to submit timely and complete Agreement and Release forms, or deficiencies in any such Agreement and Release, etc., any amounts remain in the Settlement Trust Account on April 14, 1997 in excess of the amounts actually required for distribution to Participating Class Members in strict accordance with this Stipulation re Settlement, said excess amounts shall be returned to no later than April 21, 1997.

5. <u>NOTICES TO CLASS MEMBERS</u>. There shall be two notices mailed to Class Members and published as directed by the Court as follows:

a. Notice of Pendency of Class Action shall be mailed (long form) to Class Members and published (short form) in the County of as directed by the Court in the Order of Preliminary Approval; and

b. Notice of Final Approval shall be mailed to Class Members and

SD\1019338-1

-11-

published in the County of as directed by the Court in the Order of Final Approval.

Class Counsel shall be responsible for mailing and publication of the specified notices to Class Members, including all expenses in connection therewith.

6. OPT-OUT PROVISIONS. Class Members shall be entitled to Opt-Out of the Class by filing within the time and as directed by the Court in the Notice of Pendency of Class Action, a written, legible and signed document clearly indicating an intent to be excluded from the Class as further provided below:

a. The Opt-Out must set forth the Class Member's full name, present address and telephone number, along with the specific address of the Class Home with respect to which the Class Member seeks exclusion from the Settlement, and the approximate dates the Class Member was owner of record of such Class Home, the Class Member's Social Security and Tax ID number if available, and must be signed by such Class Member and any co-owner of the Class Home.

b. The Opt-Out must be filed with the Court and received or postmarked no later than December 2, 1996, and a copy thereof must be mailed or delivered to the law offices of Class Counsel and counsel.

c. In the event that with respect to any specific Class Home, all Class Members (owners and former owners) effectively Opt-Out, that Class Home shall not be a Participating Class Home, and such Class Members shall not participate in or be bound by the Settlement of the Class Action.

d. In the event that with respect to any specific Class Home, one or more, but not all Class Member(s) (owners and/or former owners) effectively Opt-Out, that Class Home shall be deemed not to be a Participating Class Home and no Class Members shall participate in or be bound by the Settlement of the Class Action; provided, however, that in the event that prior to the occurrence of the Effective Settlement Date the Class Member(s) who did not Opt-Out with respect to such Class Home demonstrate to the satisfaction of Class Counsel and counsel

SD\1019338-1

-12-

that the Class Member(s) who filed Opt-Outs would not be entitled to recovery under the Settlement, and subject to Court approval, such Class Home shall be deemed a Participating Class Home, and such Class Member(s) shall participate in and be bound by the Settlement as Participating Class Member(s).

7. RELEASES. Upon occurrence of the Effective Settlement Date, all Participating Class Members and their successors in interest shall conclusively be deemed to have given full general releases of any and all Released Claims against in favor of suppliers and subcontractors, and all insurance carriers, successors, and all related entities and individuals, and to have waived the provisions of the Civil Code section 1542 which provides as follows:

> "A general release does not extend to claims which the creditor does not know or suspect to exist in his favor at the time of executing the release, which if known by him must have materially affected his settlement with the debtor."

Furthermore, upon occurrence of the Effective Settlement Date, each and every Participating Class Member and all successors in interest shall be permanently enjoined and forever barred from prosecuting any and all Released Claims against any person or entity.

Promptly following the occurrence of the Effective Settlement Date and as a condition precedent to release of any amounts to any Participating Class Member, Class Counsel shall obtain from each Participating Class Member who is to receive any recovery pursuant to this Settlement, an Agreement and Release in the form attached as an exhibit as to the Notice of Final Approval (Exhibit 2), to be promptly recorded by Class Counsel, who shall also promptly provide conformed copies thereof to counsel.

8. PAYMENT OF CLASS COUNSEL FEES AND EXPENSES. Payment of Class Counsel Fees and Expenses is subject to all the terms and conditions of this Stipulation re Settlement and Court approval, is included within the approximately

SD\1019338-1

-13-

($ .00) Settlement Amount specified in Paragraph 4.a, and shall be paid as set forth below.

a. Class Counsel Fees and Expenses. The amount to be paid by or on behalf of as Class Counsel Fees will be the amount approved and ordered by the Court after consideration and hearing on Class Counsel's application for attorney fees; provided, however, that such Class Counsel Fees and Expenses shall in no event exceed ($).

b. Class Counsel Expenses. Class counsel expenses referred to in paragraph 8a. above shall be paid by or on behalf of to Class Counsel as reimbursement of the agreed upon Class Counsel litigation expenses, subject to Court approval.

9. TOTAL FINANCIAL OBLIGATIONS OF ____________ The total and maximum financial obligation of under this Settlement shall consist of the amounts as set forth in paragraph 4 of this Stipulation re Settlement.

10. CONTINUING JURISDICTION OF THE COURT. The parties agree that upon the occurrence of the Settlement Date, this Settlement shall be enforceable by the Court pursuant to Code of Civil Procedure section 664.6 and the Court shall retain exclusive and continuing equity jurisdiction of this action over all parties and Class Members to interpret and enforce the terms, conditions and obligations of the Settlement.

IT IS SO STIPULATED.

DATED:____________________

____

DATED:____________________

____

SD\1019338-1

-14-

DATED: 10.14.96

Approved:

COHELAN & KHOURY

By: ______________________
TIMOTHY D. COHELAN
Attorneys for Plaintiffs

DATED: ______________

A California General Partnership

By: ______________________

DATED: ______________

A California Corporation

By: ______________________

DATED: 10/14/96

GRAY CARY WARE & FREIDENRICH
A Professional Corporation

By: ______________________
MERRILL F. STORMS
Attorneys for Defendants

SD\1019338-1

-15-

§ 9.12 Memorandum of Points and Authorities in Support of Final Approval of Partial Settlement of Class Action; Award of Attorney's Fees and Costs (*Marquart* case)

Timothy D. Cohelan, Esq. (CA State Bar #60827)
Isam C. Khoury, Esq. (CA State Bar #58759)
Margaret L. Coates, Esq. (CA State Bar #126683)
J. Mark McNeill, Esq. (CA State Bar #153531)
COHELAN & KHOURY
701 "C" Street
San Diego, California 92101-5307
Telephone: (619) 595-3001

Attorneys for Plaintiffs

SUPERIOR COURT OF CALIFORNIA

COUNTY OF ORANGE

WESLEY MARQUART; on behalf of themselves and all others similarly situated, Plaintiffs, v. XYZ CORPORATION, a California corporation; ABC CORPORATION, a Delaware corporation, et al. Defendants.	**Case No. 000000** **Assigned For All Purposes To: Judge Tully H. Seymour Department 30** **MEMORANDUM OF POINTS AND AUTHORITIES IN SUPPORT OF FINAL APPROVAL OF PARTIAL SETTLEMENT OF CLASS ACTION; AWARD OF ATTORNEYS' FEES AND COSTS, AND ENHANCEMENT FOR CLASS REPRESENTATIVES** **Date:** **Time:** **Dept: 30**

The law firm of Cohelan & Khoury, on behalf of the Plaintiff Class of investors in the above-captioned class action, move for entry of an order approving the partial settlement of this action, as embodied in the Stipulation of Settlement dated August 27, 1996 and the Exhibits thereto (the "Stipulation") and for an award of attorneys' fees and reimbursement of costs and expenses incurred to date. (See Exhibit A.) As of the date this document is filed there have been no objections to the settlement by Class Members. Given the constraints

settled\final.pas

surrounding this case the partial settlement is fair, reasonable and adequate and in the best interests of the Class.

I.

INTRODUCTION

This case arises out of the financial collapse of a group of related trusts and business entities organized, assembled and financed through a California corporation -- XYZ Corporation ("XYZ"). Beginning in 1989, a variety of trusts and other securities offerings (sometimes hereinafter referred to as the "trusts") were organized and sold by XYZ and its predecessors. These securities were purportedly exempt from federal and state securities laws.

The XYZ securities were marketed through a web of NASD-registered broker/dealers, or "participating dealers." The Plaintiff Class and the Settling Defendants, ABC Corporation and its registered representatives ("ABC"), who sold the majority of the notes, have reached an agreement and have executed a Stipulation of Settlement which provides for ABC to contribute $_____________ to the XYZ Settlement Account in return for a full and complete release of all claims made against it and its registered representatives arising out of the sale of specific XYZ investments, i.e. the TR3 Trust, TR4 Trust, MFTI, MFTII, XYZ VII Short Term Trust and XYZ VIII.[1]

The case has progressed successfully through demurrers and motions to strike. At the time the settlement was reached there were calendared the Plaintiffs' motion to certify the Class and the Defendants' two motions for summary adjudication. The Court, at the August 27, 1996 hearing regarding preliminary approval of this settlement, conditionally certified the Class for settlement purposes only, approved the Notice to the Class and the Proof of Claim forms and awarded Class Counsel interim attorney fees and expenses.

Preliminary approval of the settlement, the proposed Notice and the Proof of Claim

---

[1] XYZ VIII was not originally included in the Complaint. However, the settling parties have stipulated to Plaintiffs filing an Amendment to the Complaint adding Chartwell VIII for purpose of this settlement only. Plaintiffs will request permission to file the Amendment at the Final Fairness Hearing.

settled\final.pas

2

was given by the Court on August 27, 1996. Notice has been sent out to the Class Members and at the time of the filing of this document no Class Members have objected to the settlement nor have any excluded themselves from the Class. Prior to the Final Fairness Hearing Plaintiffs will submit a declaration regarding the final count of opting out Class members, if any. The Settlement Administrator has received and deposited the sum of $________________ into the XYZ Settlement Account.

This settlement is the product of several mediation sessions and concerted negotiations between and among counsel for the parties who concentrated on adopting and enhancing a settlement agreement for the optimal benefit of the Class. One of the complicating and compelling factors driving this settlement was the fact that there were limited funds available to satisfy Plaintiffs' claims. The settlement that has been reached is only a partial settlement of the action. Plaintiffs have been unable to engage either or in a settlement. As such, this action will continue as against those defendants. The settlement that has been reached is believed to be a fair, reasonable and adequate resolution of the Class claims given the above referenced constraints and the Plaintiffs respectfully request the Court enter an Order to that effect.

Class Counsel seek a final award of attorneys' fees and reimbursement of costs and expenses incurred. On August 27, 1996 the Court granted an interim award of attorneys' fees of $______________ and interim costs of $_______________. These amounts represented one-third of the total amounts to be requested for Class Counsel in this case. Plaintiffs are now requesting the Court award Class Counsel the remaining two-thirds attorneys' fees, i.e. $_______________ and the remaining two-thirds reimbursement for costs and expenses in the amount of $_________________.

II.

CLASS ACTION SETTLEMENT PROCEDURE

"To prevent fraud, collusion or unfairness to the class, the settlement or dismissal of a class action requires court approval." (*Malibu Outrigger Bd. of Governors v. Superior Court* (1980) 103 Cal.App.3d 573, 578-579.) The Court must determine that the settlement

settled\final.pas

3

is fair, adequate, and reasonable. (See *Officers for Justice v. Civil Service Com.* (9th Cir. 1982) 688 F.2d 615, 625; Fed. Rule Civ. Proc., rule 23(e).)[2] The purpose of the requirement is "the protection of those class members, including the named plaintiffs, whose rights may not have been given due regard by the negotiating parties." (*Officers for Justice v. Civil Service Com., supra,* 688 F.2d at p. 624.)

The trial court has broad powers to determine whether a proposed settlement in a class action is fair. (*Mallick* v. *Superior Court* (1979) 89 Cal.App.3d 434.) The prevailing procedure and criteria for use in class action settlements is embodied in the *Manual for Complex Litigation, 2d,* (1985), at §30.44. The Manual's settlement approval procedure is comprised of three distinct steps:

1. Preliminary approval of the proposed settlement at an informal hearing;
2. Dissemination of notice of the settlement to all affected class members; and
3. A "Formal Fairness Hearing" or final settlement approval hearing at which class members may be heard regarding the settlement and at which evidence and argument concerning the fairness, adequacy and reasonableness of the settlement is presented.

This procedure, which is commonly utilized by both federal and state courts, assures class members of the protection of procedural due process safeguards, and enables the Court to fulfill its role as the guardian of class interests. (L.A. County Superior Court Rules §15.41 et seq.)

The Court has already given preliminary approval of the settlement and notice has been sent to all Class Members. At the Final Fairness Hearing the Court should consider the relevant factors, such as the strength of the Plaintiffs' case, the risk, expenses, complexity and likely duration of further litigation, the risk of maintaining class action status through trial, the amount offered in settlement, the extent of discovery completed and the stage of the proceedings, the experience and views of counsel, the presence of a governmental participant

[2] In the absence of California law on the subject, California courts look to federal authority. (*Vasquez v. Superior Court* (1971) 4 Cal.3d 800, 821.)

settled\final.pas

4

and the reaction of the Class Members to the proposed settlement. (*Officers for Justice v. Civil Service Com., supra,* 688 F.2d at p. 624.) "This list is not exhaustive and should be tailored to each case. Due regard should be given to what is otherwise a private consensual agreement between the parties." (*Dunk v. Ford Motor Company* (4th Dist. Ct. Appeal 1996) 96 Daily Journal D.A.R. 10799, 10800.)

A presumption of fairness exists where: (1) the settlement is reached through arm's length bargaining; (2) investigation and discovery are sufficient to allow counsel and the court to act intelligently; (3) counsel is experienced in similar litigation; and (4) the percentage of objectors is small. (*Dunk v. Ford Motor Company, supra,* 96 Daily Journal D.A.R. 10799 at p. 10800, citing Newberg & Conte, *Newberg on Class Actions* (3d ed. 1992) §11.41, pp. 11-91.)

Also, in California, the plaintiff may settle with one of several joint tortfeasors or co-obligors on a contract without releasing the others. Provided it is in good faith, the settlement also discharges the settlor from liability to the other defendants for equitable contribution or comparative indemnity pursuant to *Code of Civil Procedure* § 877(a)(b). Hence a settling defendant is protected from future claims of class members and co-defendant cross-complaints other than those based upon written express indemnity agreements.

There should be a rough approximation of the Settling Defendants' total responsibility to the total they are paying in settlement with a discount for the fact that it is a settlement with an allocation amongst the various Plaintiffs and, of course, there should be an absence of collusion, fraud or tortious conduct. (*Tech-Bilt, Inc.* v. *Woodward, Clyde & Associates* (1977) 38 Cal.3d 488, 499.)

A. The Settlement Is The Product Of Arm's Length Bargaining.

The parties have engaged in many hours of mediation sessions in front of three different retired Judges; District Court Judge J. Lawrence Irving; and Superior Court Judges Kevin Midlam and Daniel J. Weinstein. At all times, the parties have conducted their negotiations at an arms-length distance and, despite a mutual desire to resolve the case, in an adversarial manner. The Settling Parties have been able to hammer out a settlement that,

settled\final.pas

5

given the constraints and realities of the case, is fair, reasonable, adequate and in the best interest of the Class.

Arriving at a settlement that was acceptable to the Settling Parties was no small achievement. ABC and its representatives felt strongly about their ability to prevail on the merits, yet found themselves with a limited amount of insurance coverage to satisfy the claims of the Plaintiff Class. One of the most compelling factors behind reaching this particular partial settlement at this time was the position taken by ABC that it had but one insurance policy covering itself and all of its representatives and that policy had limits of $____________ with a $____________ aggregate. Furthermore, it was a burning limits policy which had already been whittled down to approximately $____________ and was being reduced daily as defense costs were incurred.

Therefore, Plaintiffs were put in the position of negotiating a settlement at this time or risk obtaining a favorable judgment down the road for which there was no insurance coverage. Since that might have meant a smaller or possibly no recovery to the Class, Class Counsel determined that the best interests of the Class were served by entering into this settlement at this time.

B. Sufficient Investigation and Discovery Has Taken Place To Warrant A Settlement At This Time.

The Settling Parties have been worthy adversaries throughout this litigation. Depositions of the named Plaintiffs have been taken and discovery tendered by both sides. Dispositive motions have been filed and mountains of documents produced into the document repository. Plaintiffs had filed a motion for class certification and were prepared to advance the lawsuit within that context. Countless hours have been spent by all parties in sifting through the evidence in order to ascertain the viability of their respective positions. Accordingly, all of the Settling Parties were sufficiently informed of the nature of their claims and the viability of the defenses to be in a good position to evaluate the proposed settlement for its fairness, adequacy and reasonableness. All discovery was stayed during the pendency of the settlement negotiations in order to minimize defense costs during that period

settled\final.pas

6

which would only serve to reduce the availability of funds with which the action could be settled.

C. Class Counsel Is Experienced.

Cohelan & Khoury practices exclusively class action litigation. Timothy Cohelan has taken ten class action cases through certification, either full or conditional, and has been lead or co-counsel in twelve class action cases within the last 5 years. (See Declaration of Timothy Cohelan filed concurrently herewith.) Mr. Cohelan is qualified to evaluate the potential viability of the class claims and the viability of the defenses tendered. As such, he was well qualified to participate in and negotiate a settlement with the Settling Defendants. It has been his experience that a recovery of 10% to 20% in a securities case is a very favorable recovery. Furthermore, the constraints involving the lack of funds to satisfy any judgment the Plaintiffs might obtain compelled reaching this settlement at this time. (See Declaration of Timothy Cohelan.) The settlement is a fair, adequate and reasonable settlement and in the best interests of the Class.

D. The Degree Of Opposition Within The Class.

The Class Members received the Notice of the pending settlement and Proof of Claim forms shortly after October 17th. To date, no Class Members have objected to the settlement and none have chosen to exclude themselves, i.e., opt out although Class Counsel have been informed that at least three Class Members do plan to opt out of the settlement by the October 25th deadline. (See Declaration of Timothy Cohelan filed concurrently herewith.)

E. ABC's Contribution Is Proportionate To Its Responsibility.

There were just under $__________ dollars worth of XYZ investments sold in California. Of those sales, ABC and its registered representatives sold $__________ worth. As such, the Settling Defendants represent over 75% of the total sales of the notes. None of the other Defendants are contributing to the settlement at this time and the action will continue as against them.

settled\final.pas

7

Plaintiffs recommend approval of this partial settlement on the grounds that it is eminently fair, reasonable, and adequate given the nature of the claims against the defendants, the viability of the defenses raised against those claims and the lack of resources to satisfy Plaintiffs' claims. While not making the Plaintiffs whole, the settlement is well within the accepted range of recoveries for securities litigation.

III.

THE FORMAL FAIRNESS HEARING

The last step in the settlement approval process is the "Formal Fairness Hearing" at which the Court may obtain all information relevant to its settlement evaluation, and at which proponents of the settlement explain and describe its terms and conditions, offer argument and evidence in support of settlement approval, and at which the Class Members themselves, or their counsel, may be heard regarding the final approval or disapproval of the Settlement Agreement by the Court.

> The court will employ that procedure which it deems necessary to ascertain the fairness, reasonableness, and adequacy of the proposed settlement, this procedure will involve a taking of evidence by declaration, and points and authorities in support of the proposed settlement. It will also involve the opportunity for members of the class to be heard in objection to the proposed settlement, if they have satisfied prerequisites therefor set out in the notice to the class of the proposed settlement.

L.A. County Superior Court Rules §15.45.

> After the settlement hearing, the court will make and enter judgment or final order. Where the judge requires future acts to be performed by the parties, beyond payment of money by defendants, the judgment will provide for the court's retention of jurisdiction while satisfaction of the judgment is being effectuated. All proposed judgments which are submitted to the court with settlement agreement should include a provision for retention of jurisdiction if said retention is appropriate, and should provide in detail for the terms of said retained jurisdiction.

L.A. County Superior Court Rules §15.46.

Plaintiffs seek the Court's retention of jurisdiction in this matter since this is only a partial settlement. The action will continue as against Defendants ---

settled\final.pes

8

. In addition, Plaintiffs anticipate the Settlement Administrator, in the performance of his duties regarding the disbursement of funds to the Class, will incur expenses for which he will seek the approval of the Court for reimbursement.

If final approval is granted, the settlement becomes binding on all Plaintiff Class Members, except those who timely elected to opt out and properly gave notice thereof, and the claims of the participating Class Members against the Defendants will be released via the entry of a Final Order and Dismissal. The Court will retain continuing jurisdiction over the implementation, enforcement, and construction of the Settlement Agreement, and the administration, allocation, and distribution of the Settlement Fund.

IV.

PLAINTIFFS SEEK A FINAL AWARD OF ATTORNEYS' FEES

Plaintiffs also respectfully request the Court make a final award of attorneys' fees to Class Counsel. California class action compensation is governed by a mixture of the application of federal class action case law and equitable principles incorporated into California cases. The equitable principles behind the common fund can be traced to *Central Railroad and Banking of Georgia* v. *Petus* (1885) 113 U.S. 116 [28 L.Ed. 915, 5 S.Ct. 387], where the U.S. Supreme Court stated: "The lawyer who creates a common fund is allowed an extra reward, beyond that which he has arranged with his client, so that he might share the wealth of those upon whom he has conferred a benefit." In *Quinn* v. *State of California* (1975) 15 Cal.3d 162, the California Supreme Court stated, in pertinent part, ". . . The exception to this rule [the American Rule regarding attorneys' fees] has become as well established as the rule itself: That one who expends attorneys' fees in winning a suit which creates a fund from which others derive benefits may require those passive beneficiaries to bear a fair share of the litigation costs." (*Quinn, supra,* 15 Cal.3d at page 167.) The California cases establish that when two or more parties are entitled to a common fund, the courts can use their equitable powers to apportion costs and attorneys' fees. (*Samura* v. *Kaiser Foundation Health Plan, Inc.* (1993) 17 Cal.App.4th 1284.)

The federal common fund rule "rests upon the perception that persons who obtain the

settled\final.pas

9

benefit of a lawsuit without contributing to its costs are unjustly enriched at the successful litigant's expense." (*Boeing* v. *Van Gemert* (1980) 444 U.S. 472, 478.) The federal common fund doctrine is to be applied only if: "(1) The class of beneficiaries is sufficiently identified; (2) the benefits can be accurately traced; and (3) the fee can be shifted with some exactitude to those benefitting." (*In Re: Hill* (9th Cir. 1985) 775 F.2d 1037.) Courts in the Ninth Circuit now routinely sanction this approach.

In the instant case it is clear that the Class has been sufficiently identified and that the Class will benefit from the settlement. Furthermore, the attorneys' fees that are being requested are to be awarded from the gross Settlement Fund and are therefore being paid out of the fund that has been created for the benefit of the Class. As noted in the Declaration of Timothy Cohelan filed concurrently herewith, Class Counsel is very experienced in handling class action litigation and has devoted over 1700 hours in prosecuting this case on behalf of the Plaintiff Class. Furthermore, utilizing the lodestar method of determining attorneys' fees would result in an even higher amount being awarded, thus yielding a smaller recovery to the Class. Accordingly, an award of 25% is eminently reasonable and fair. The Court has already made an interim award of $______________, (1/3 of the total request). Plaintiffs request the Court approve a final award of the remaining $______________________, (2/3 of the total fee request).

V.

PLAINTIFFS SEEK REIMBURSEMENT FOR COSTS INCURRED TO DATE

The Stipulation of Settlement provides for the reimbursement to Class Counsel of expenses and costs incurred in the prosecution of this action. The Court has made an interim award of costs of $______________ (1/3 of the total request) based on the total of incurred costs and expenses of $______________. (See Declaration of Timothy Cohelan.) Plaintiffs request the Court make an award of the remaining costs of $______________ (2/3 of the total request).

In addition, for those named Plaintiffs who brought the case to Class Counsel and served the Class by participating in depositions, engaging in discovery and maintaining

settled\final.pas

10

contact with counsel throughout this litigation, Plaintiffs request the Court grant a small enhancement equal to 10% of their respective recoveries in this lawsuit. This enhancement would apply solely to Plaintiffs Wesley Marquart,

.[3]

The Settlement Administrator has already incurred expenses for the printing and mailing of the Notice and Proof of Claim forms to the Class and for the compilation and verification of those claim forms already returned. It is anticipated that Class Counsel will have an interim billing available for the Court's approval on November 5, 1996.

CONCLUSION

On the basis of the foregoing, and because the Settlement Agreement is highly beneficial to the Class Members and will efficiently, economically and favorably resolve what would otherwise be protracted and expensive litigation, the Plaintiffs respectfully urge the Court make a finding to that effect and enter an Order approving the settlement. The Plaintiffs further request the Court grant Class Counsel an award of attorneys' fees in the amount of $________________ (representing the remaining two-thirds of the total proposed fees) and approve the reimbursement of costs and expenses in the amount of $____________ (representing the remaining two-thirds of the total requested costs and expenses); an enhancement equal to

10% of their recovery for the four named Plaintiffs who fully participated in the lawsuit; to retain jurisdiction in this matter; and cause to be entered an Order thereon.

Dated: October 17, 1996

COHELAN & KHOURY
Attorneys for Plaintiffs

By:____________________
Timothy Cohelan

[3] The remaining named Plaintiffs are not included in this request since they withdrew themselves from that role during their depositions.

settled\final.pas

11

§ 9.13 Order of (1) Preliminary Approval of Settlement, and (2) Approval of Notice of Pendency of Class Action, Preliminary Approval of Settlement and Setting Fairness Hearing

SUPERIOR COURT OF THE STATE OF CALIFORNIA

FOR THE COUNTY OF

on behalf of themselves and all others similarly situated, Plaintiffs, vs. a California general partnership; a California Corporation; and DOES 1-100, inclusive, Defendants.	CASE NO. ORDER OF (1) PRELIMINARY APPROVAL OF SETTLEMENT, AND (2) APPROVAL OF NOTICE OF PENDENCY OF CLASS ACTION, PRELIMINARY APPROVAL OF SETTLEMENT AND SETTING FAIRNESS HEARING

The Court, having fully reviewed the parties' Joint Motion for (1) Temporary and Conditional Certification of Class Action for Settlement Purposes Only, (2) Preliminary Approval of Proposed Settlement, (3) Approval of Notice of Pendency of Class Action, Preliminary Approval of Settlement, and Setting Fairness Hearing, and the supporting Points and Authorities, stipulations, notices and declarations, and having carefully analyzed the Stipulation re Settlement and the proposed Notice of Pendency of Class Action, and in recognition of the Court's duty to make a preliminary determination as to the reasonableness of any proposed Class

-1-

Action settlement, and if preliminarily determined to be reasonable, to provide notice to Class Members in accordance with due process requirements, and to conduct a formal Fairness and Good Faith Determination Hearing as to the good faith, fairness, adequacy and reasonableness of any proposed settlement;

THE COURT HEREBY MAKES THE FOLLOWING DETERMINATIONS AND ORDERS:

1. The Court finds on a preliminary basis that the Stipulation re Settlement attached as Exhibit 1 and incorporated herein by this reference and made a part of this Order of Preliminary Approval, appears to be within the range of reasonableness of a settlement which could ultimately be given final approval by this Court; the Court notes that to date has voluntarily paid in excess of ($) in inspecting, improving and repairing homes constructed in the Valley in an effort to address homeowner complaints and concerns relating to expansive soils and related problems; the Court further notes that counsel representing individual plaintiffs in other pending construction defect litigation against in County have no objection to such settlement; it further appears to the Court on a preliminary basis that the settlement amount is fair and reasonable to Class Members when balanced against the probable outcome of further litigation relating to class certification, liability and damages issues; it further appears that significant investigation and research has been conducted such that counsel for the parties at this time are able to reasonably evaluate their respective positions; it further appears that settlement at this time will avoid substantial costs, delay and risks that would be presented by the further prosecution of the litigation; it further appears that the proposed Settlement has been reached as the result of intensive, serious and noncollusive negotiations including extensive mediation proceedings before two nationally recognized mediators of complex, construction and class action disputes;

/////

-2-

ACCORDINGLY, GOOD CAUSE APPEARING, THE JOINT MOTION FOR ORDER OF PRELIMINARY APPROVAL OF CLASS SETTLEMENT IS HEREBY GRANTED; AND AS A PART OF SAID PRELIMINARY APPROVAL THE COURT HEREBY ACCEPTS AND INCORPORATES THE PARTIES' STIPULATION REGARDING TEMPORARY AND CONDITIONAL CERTIFICATION OF CLASS FOR SETTLEMENT PURPOSES ONLY;

2. The Court finds that the proposed Notice of Pendency of Class Action, which advises of the pendency of the Class Action and temporary conditional certification of the Class for settlement purposes only, and of preliminary Court approval of the proposed Settlement, opt-out timing and procedures and of the Fairness and Good Faith Determination Hearing, in the long form attached hereto as Exhibit 1 and short form attached hereto as Exhibit 2 and incorporated herein by this reference and made a part of this Order of Preliminary Approval, fairly and adequately advises Class Members of the terms of the proposed Settlement and the benefits available to Class Members thereunder, as well as their right to "opt-out" and procedures for doing so, and of the formal Fairness and Good Faith Determination Hearing to be conducted on December 9, 1996, and the right of Class Members to file documentation in support or in opposition and to appear in connection with said hearing; the Court further finds that said Notice clearly comports with all constitutional requirements including those of due process;

ACCORDINGLY, GOOD CAUSE APPEARING, THE COURT HEREBY APPROVES THE PROPOSED NOTICE OF PENDENCY OF CLASS ACTION;

3. The Court finds that the Class Members who are most likely to be entitled to the benefits of the proposed Settlement are the current owners of record on October 15, 1996 of the Class Homes as defined in the Stipulation re Settlement; ACCORDINGLY, IT IS HEREBY ORDERED that on or before October 21, 1996 Class Counsel shall mail first class, postage pre-paid, the Notice of Pendency of Class Action (long form) to all persons who are shown in the records of the County

-3-

Recorder for the County of   to be owners of record of Class Homes on October 15, 1996; and Class Counsel shall file a list of such names and addresses with the Court as soon as practicable and no later than October 28, 1996. The Court further finds that prior owners of record of Class Homes since April 1, 1994, who are not current owners of record of Class Homes, are unlikely to be entitled to any benefits of the proposed Settlement; provided however, in certain exceptional circumstances, such a person could conceivably be entitled to some benefit under the proposed Settlement; ACCORDINGLY IT IS HEREBY FURTHER ORDERED, that to the extent that the present addresses of such persons are available by reference to records of the County Recorder for the County of   , on or before October 21, 1996 Class Counsel shall also mail first class, postage pre-paid, the Notice of Pendency of Class Action (long form) to those persons; and Class Counsel shall file a list of such names and current addresses with the Court as soon as practicable and no later than October 28, 1996; ADDITIONALLY, IT IS HEREBY ORDERED that the Notice of Pendency of Class Action (short form) shall be published in the   *Press* newspaper, a newspaper of general circulation in the   , once each week for three consecutive weeks between October 22, 1996 and November 19, 1996. IT IS FURTHER ORDERED that said Notice shall be mailed and published as indicated in this paragraph in both the English and Spanish languages. The Court finds that the mailing and publication of notice as set forth in this paragraph is the best means practicable by which to reach Class Members and is reasonable and adequate pursuant to all constitutional and statutory requirements including all due process requirements. The Court further determines that it would be most appropriate for Class Counsel Cohelan & Khoury to mail and publish the Notice as set forth herein, ACCORDINGLY, IT IS SO ORDERED; AND IT IS FURTHER ORDERED that upon doing so that Class Counsel file and serve a declaration so indicating no later than November 26, 1996.

/////

-4-

4. IT IS FURTHER ORDERED that the Fairness and Good Faith Determination Hearing shall be held before the undersigned at 10:00 a.m. on December 9, 1996, at the County Superior Court, located at California , to consider the good faith, fairness, adequacy and reasonableness of the proposed Settlement preliminary approved by this Order of Preliminary Approval, and to consider the application of Class Counsel Cohelan & Khoury for an award of attorneys' fees and reimbursement of reasonable litigation expenses incurred.

5. IT IS FURTHER ORDERED that pending final determination of whether this proposed Settlement should be granted final approval, no Class Member, either directly or representively, or in any other capacity, shall commence or prosecute any action or proceeding asserting any of the Released Claims, as defined in the Stipulation re Settlement, against defendants herein in any court or tribunal, with the exception of individual lawsuits already filed on behalf of individually named plaintiffs in the Superior Court for the County prior to the date of this Order;

6. IT IS FURTHER ORDERED that any party to this case, including Class Members, may appear at the Fairness and Good Faith Determination Hearing in person or by counsel, and may be heard to the extent allowed by the Court, in support of or in opposition to, the Court's determination of the good faith, fairness, reasonableness and adequacy of the proposed Settlement, the requested attorneys' fees and reimbursement of litigation expenses, and any Order of Final Approval and Judgment regarding such Settlement, fees and expenses; provided, however, that no person, except Class Counsel and counsel for defendants, shall be heard in opposition to such matters unless such person has complied with the conditions set forth in the Notice of Pendency of Class Action which conditions are incorporated herein;

7. IT IS FURTHER ORDERED that in the event of the occurrence of the Effective Settlement Date, as defined in the Stipulation re Settlement, Participating Class Members and their successors shall conclusively be deemed to have given full

-5-

general releases of any and all Released Claims against defendants, their suppliers and subcontractors, insurance carriers, successors, and all related entities and individuals, and to have waived the provisions of Civil Code section 1542, and all such Participating Class Members and their successors shall be permanently enjoined and forever barred from asserting any Released Claims against any person or entity, and a document entitled "Agreement & Release Affecting Real Property & Covenant Running with the Land" in the form attached to the Stipulation re Settlement reflecting such releases in recordable form shall be executed by all Participating Class Members who are to receive any recovery under this Settlement, and duly notarized, and shall promptly be recorded by Class Counsel with the County Recorder for the County of   in the chain of title of all Participating Class Homes and a conformed copy thereof shall be furnished by Class Counsel to counsel for defendants;

8. IT IS FURTHER ORDERED that if for any reason the Court does not execute and file an Order of Final Approval or Order Determining Good Faith of the Settlement, or if the Effective Settlement Date, as defined in the Stipulation re Settlement, does not occur for any reason whatsoever, the proposed Stipulation re Settlement and the proposed Settlement subject of this Order and all evidence and proceedings had in connection therewith shall be without prejudice to the *status quo ante* rights of the parties to the litigation as more specifically set forth in the Stipulation re Settlement and Stipulation Regarding Temporary and Conditional Certification of Class for Settlement Purposes Only;

9. The Court expressly reserves the right to adjourn or continue the Fairness and Good Faith Determination Hearing from time to time without further notice to Class Members.

DATED: __________

____
JUDGE OF THE SUPERIOR COURT

-6-

§ 9.14 Judgment on Order of Final Approval of Settlement

SUPERIOR COURT OF THE STATE OF CALIFORNIA

FOR THE COUNTY OF

on) behalf of themselves and all others similarly situated, Plaintiffs, vs. a California general partnership; a California Corporation; and DOES 1-100, inclusive, Defendants.	CASE NO. **JUDGMENT ON ORDER OF FINAL APPROVAL OF SETTLEMENT**

Proceedings regarding the proposed Settlement and Settlement of the referenced Class Action have been regularly conducted before this Court, the Honorable Judge presiding; plaintiffs and , individually and as representatives of others similarly situated, were represented by Timothy D. Cohelan and Isam C. Khoury of Cohelan & Khoury, and defendants were represented by Merrill F. Storms and Terry D. Ross of Gray Cary Ware & Freidenrich;

The Court *inter alia* conducted a hearing on October 15, 1996 on the parties' joint motion for (1) Temporary and Conditional Certification of Class Action

SDR2\709538-1

-1-

for Settlement Purposes Only, (2) Preliminary Approval of Proposed Settlement, (3) Approval of Notice of Pendency of Class Action, Preliminary Approval of Settlement and Hearing, and (4) Setting Hearing for Final Approval, and after fully considering all supporting papers, evidence and arguments, granted preliminary approval of the Settlement, and further, after determining that the proposed Notice of Pendency of Class Action met all constitutional and statutory requirements, including due process, the Court ordered said notice to be mailed and published in a manner likewise in accordance with all constitutional and statutory requirements, including due process; subsequently, and in accordance with the Court's Order and the Notice of Pendency of Class Action, the Court conducted a further hearing on December 9, 1996 at 10:00 a.m. for the purpose of considering the properly noticed motions for orders of Final Approval and Good Faith Determination of the Settlement, and considering the application of Class Counsel for attorneys' fees and expenses; and the Court after fully considering all supporting papers, evidence and arguments, and having reviewed Class Counsel's declaration concerning the giving of the Notice of Pendency of Class Action to Class Members in accordance with the Court's order, and having fully and carefully considered said matters, good cause appearing, the Court issued its Order of Final Approval of Settlement, finding said Settlement to be fair, reasonable and adequate, and in the form attached hereto as Exhibit 1;

THEREFORE, THE COURT HEREBY ADJUDGES AND DECREES THAT JUDGMENT PURSUANT TO THE ORDER OF FINAL APPROVAL OF SETTLEMENT OF CLASS ACTION ATTACHED AND INCORPORATED HEREIN AS EXHIBIT 1 IS HEREBY MADE AND SHALL BE ENTERED BY THE CLERK PURSUANT TO THE TERMS AND CONDITIONS SET FORTH THEREIN.

DATED: ____________________ ________________________________

JUDGE OF THE SUPERIOR COURT

SDR2\709538-1

-2-

SUPERIOR COURT OF THE STATE OF CALIFORNIA

FOR THE COUNTY OF

on) behalf of themselves and all others similarly situated, Plaintiffs, vs. a California general partnership; a California Corporation; and DOES 1-100, inclusive, Defendants.	CASE NO. NOTICE OF FINAL APPROVAL OF SETTLEMENT

THIS LEGAL NOTICE AFFECTS YOUR RIGHTS: PLEASE READ IT CAREFULLY.

TO ALL OWNERS OF RECORD AT ANY TIME SINCE APRIL 1, 1994 (CURRENT OR FORMER) OF CERTAIN COUNTY HOMES CONSTRUCTED BY WITH RESPECT TO WHICH THE NOTICE OF COMPLETION WAS RECORDED ON OR AFTER JANUARY 1, 1983 AND BEFORE APRIL 1, 1994, IN THE FOLLOWING CITIES AND SUBDIVISIONS:

/////

SDR2\709563-1

-1-

City of ______
City of
City of ______

City of ______

1. PURPOSE OF THIS NOTICE. This notice is being mailed to Class Members and published pursuant to Court Order in order to notify Class Members of the following: (1) the Court's Order of Final Approval of the Settlement of said certified Class Action, (2) the Court's award of Class Counsel's fees and costs, and (3) the process for Participating Class Members to submit claims for recovery under the Settlement.

2. PERSONS COVERED BY THIS SETTLEMENT. This Settlement covers all persons who are shown in the records of the County Recorder of the County of to have owned a home at any time between April 1, 1994 and October 15, 1996, located in the County of and specifically in the cities and subdivisions set forth above, constructed by ( ) with respect to which the Notice of Completion was recorded on or after January 1, 1983 and before April 1, 1994, except (a) such persons who have previously reached settlements, released or dismissed claims against (b) named plaintiffs in lawsuits pending in County against for construction defects and specifically in County Superior Court Case Nos.

(c) any owners, officers or directors of and (d) persons who effectively Opted-Out of the Class Action in accordance with the Notice of Pendency of Class Action.

3. RELIEF AVAILABLE UNDER THE SETTLEMENT. Participating Class Members will be entitled to receive the amount as to their Participating Class Home, shown on the attached Exhibit A, which sets forth such amount by Participating Class Home address for each of the respective subdivisions covered by

SDR2\709563-1

-2-

the Settlement; provided that all Participating Class Members as to each Participating Class Home shall complete and sign the Class Action Settlement Claim form attached hereto as Exhibit B and execute before a notary public the Agreement and Release form attached hereto as Exhibit C, and submit said forms to Class Counsel as provided below, subject to verification by Class Counsel and the Court.

4. HOW TO MAKE A CLAIM. The Court has concluded that the Participating Class Members who are most likely to be entitled to recovery under the Settlement are the owners of record of Participating Class Homes on October 15, 1996, the date the Court gave preliminary approval to the Settlement. Accordingly, the amount set forth as to each Participating Class Home in your subdivision on Exhibit 1 shall be paid to Participating Class Members who were owners of record of Participating Class Homes on October 15, 1996, unless, with respect to any specific Participating Class Home, application as set forth below is made by one or more Participating Class Members who were owners of record on or after April 1, 1994 but who were not owners of record on October 15, 1996, setting forth the reasons such person(s) are entitled to recovery under the Settlement, which application will be considered by Class Counsel and ultimately decided by the Court. Accordingly, in order to obtain recovery under the Settlement:

a. If you are an Participating Class Member who was an owner of record of a Participating Class Home on October 15, 1996, you *must* complete Part 1 of the attached one-page Claim Form and submit it to Class Counsel as soon as possible, but in no event later than February 10, 1997. In order for your claim to be considered, you *must provide all information* requested in Part 1 of the form *and* the form *must be signed by all owners of record* on October 15, 1996. If there are no other Participating Class Members making claim for recovery under the Settlement as to your Participating Class Home, you may expect your claim to be processed without delay.

/////

SDR2\709563-1

-3-

b. If you are a Participating Class Member who was not an owner of record of a Participating Class Home on October 15, 1996, and you believe you are entitled to any portion of the Settlement Amount, you *must* complete *both* Part 1 and Part 2 of attached one-page Claim Form and submit it to Class Counsel as soon as possible, but in no event later than February 10, 1997. In order for your claim to be considered, you *must provide all information* requested on the form *and* the form *must be signed by all co-owners of record at the time you were an owner of the Participating Class Home.* Recovery for Participating Class Homes as to which claims for recovery are made by both Participating Class Members who were owners of record on October 15, 1996 and Participating Class Members who were not owners on said date will be determined by the Court or by such person as the Court may designate, after recommendations from Class Counsel and a hearing with respect to which all Participating Class Members will be provided notice and opportunity to be heard.

5. DEADLINES FOR MAKING A CLAIM. In order for your claim to be considered, it *must be received by Class Counsel and postmarked no later than February 10, 1997.* Any claims received or postmarked later than February 10, 1997 will be untimely and invalid and will not be considered.

6. ADDITIONAL INFORMATION. If you feel you need further information, you may inquire of Class Counsel in writing or by phone as follows:

Timothy D. Cohelan
Isam Khoury
COHELAN & KHOURY
701 "C" Street
San Diego, CA 92101-5307
(619) 239-8148

THE COURT HEREBY APPROVES THIS NOTICE.

DATED: ____________________ ________________________________

JUDGE OF THE SUPERIOR COURT

SDR2\709563-1

-4-

10 ATTORNEY'S FEES

A. TEXT

Sec.

10.01 Fundamental Principles

10.02 Qualifications of Class Counsel

10.03 Commercial Reality in Compensation

10.04 Common Fund Compensation

[A] Exception to Rule that Party Pay Own Attorney's Fees

[B] Extra Shares and Benchmarks

[C] Enhancing Common Fund Fees with the Private Attorney General Statute

[D] Reasonableness Requirement

10.05 References

B. FORMS

10.10 Retainer Agreement and Duties of Class Representative (*Marquart* case)

10.11 Plaintiffs' Memorandum of Points and Authorities in Support of Motion for Order (1) Awarding Attorney's Fees, (2) Allowing Reimbursement of Costs and Expenses, (3) Appointing Settlement Administrator, and (4) Allowing Enhancements for Representatives (Real Property Class)

A. TEXT

§ 10.01 Fundamental Principles

While some states have express statutes governing the award of attorney's fees in class actions, California lacks such authority. Compensation in California class actions is governed by a mixture of federal case law and equitable principles incorporated into state cases. According to Code of Civil Procedure section 1021, when no statute provides for attorney's fees and mode of payment, these matters are left to express or implied agreement by the parties, with counsel entitled at a minimum to costs.

In a California class action where the members of the class have an undisputed, mathematically ascertainable, and clearly traceable claim to a lump sum settlement or common fund recovery, each absent class member should share in the burden of the contingent fee arrangement. In cases where the exact value of the benefit to each absent class member cannot be determined until claims are presented, the fee should be based on the entire judgment fund, thereby shifting the costs of litigation to each absentee in the exact proportion of his potential claim to the total recovery.

California authorizes attorney's fees only by statute or private agreement, with three well-established exceptions: the common fund, the substantial benefit (i.e., a noncash benefit conferred upon a group of absent persons), and the private attorney general theories concerning Code of Civil Procedure section 1021.5. All are discussed in *Jacobson* v. *Simmons Real Estate* (1994) 23 Cal.App.4th 1285 [28 Cal.Rptr.2d 699]. In recent years, entitlement to attorney's fees has become clearer, with the prospect that the economic aspects of a prefiling decision to accept or reject the case can be brought into clearer focus.

§ 10.02 Qualifications of Class Counsel

Plaintiff's counsel's compensation for representation of a California class action is wholly contingent on achieving benefit for the class. Compensation is payable only after the court approves the attorneys or law firms serving as class counsel at the class certification or settlement hearing. Approval hinges on both the qualifications of counsel and the absence of conflict of interest between plaintiff and class. (*McGhee* v. *Bank of America* (1976) 60 Cal.App.3d 442–443, 450 [131 Cal.Rptr. 482].) As always, class counsel and representative are bound to protect the interests of the class vigorously. (*Simons* v. *Horowitz* (1984) 151 Cal.App.3d 834, 846 [199 Cal.Rptr. 134].)

The terms of fee representation with the class representative should be stated in writing. A typical retainer agreement, such as the illustrative form in Chapter 13, discusses the methodology of compensation with or without court approval of class certification. This agreement falls under Business and Professions Code section 6147, except that it specifically allows class counsel to represent other parties in the class.

Like representation generally, conflicts of interest among differently situated class members affect the retainer agreement. In certain circumstances conflicts among the interests of class members can undermine adequacy of representation. The results may range from substitution of the class member or disqualification of class counsel to, in extreme circumstances, judicial sanctions. Differences of interest between the representative party and the class members or between the class and subclasses offer the greatest potential for disqualification, and they can even lead to judicial sanctions. In class actions as in individual litigation, prior representation of the defendants or concurrent representation of the same parties or issues in similar litigation in another forum can also result in disqualification.

Representing a class of absent persons requires that class counsel possess the appropriate experience and training. Few California cases discuss the specific qualifications of class counsel, but federal cases do provide guidance. Many attorneys mistakenly assume that they must have extensive experience in class actions. This is not the case. The court looks more for evidence of sufficient skill, experience in the kind of case at bar, and a demonstration of diligence in working for the class. Attorneys seeking court approval of their appointment as class counsel should submit a declaration outlining their professional experience and background and providing a basic road map of the strategy they propose. Such a declaration tells the court enough of where the lawyers have been and where they are heading in the case to permit approval of their appointment.

§ 10.03 Commercial Reality in Compensation

Because it will directly affect his or her compensation, plaintiff's counsel must assess both the likelihood and the size of a class recovery. Because contingent representation involves comparing the risk of loss (and nonpayment) to the probability of reward, one must have a sense of these commercial realities. For instance, if you are attempting to create a common fund, the size of the fund depends upon the number of class members multiplied by their individual damages over the years plus, if appropriate, any trebling or interest due.

Clearly the amount and likelihood of compensation depend in part on whether a practitioner expects to petition for a fixed benchmark percentage of the settlement or award. Generally, compensation by a defined or fixed percentage of the tangible benefit to the class stands a better chance of approval by the court. As a result, most class action practitioners consider the question of whether or not to undertake a class action by identifying as closely as possibly the size of the common fund and figuring their likely percentage of it.

§ 10.04 Common Fund Compensation

[A] Exception to Rule that Party Pay Own Attorney's Fees

Common fund compensation is an exception to the general American rule that each party pays his or her own attorney's fees. The practitioner who has succeeded in establishing a common fund recovery for a prospective class through settlement or trial may petition the court for compensation from the fund, thereby spreading the fee beyond the representative to be shared by the class.

[B] Extra Shares and Benchmarks

The equitable principles behind compensation from the common fund reach back to *Central Railroad and Banking of Georgia* v. *Petus* (1885) 113 U.S. 116 [28 L.Ed. 915, 5 S.Ct. 387]. The U.S. Supreme Court stated that the lawyer who creates a common fund is allowed an extra share beyond what was arranged with the client. In *Quinn* v. *State of California*, the California Supreme Court carried this point further to say that the common fund exception to the usual American rule of clients paying their own attorney's fees is as well established as the rule itself. When a winning or settling plaintiff bears the cost of attorney's fees in creating a fund that benefits others, it is only fair that plaintiff require the passive beneficiaries to bear a fair share of litigation expense. (*Quinn* v. *State of California* (1975) 15 Cal.3d 167 [124 Cal.Rptr. 1, 539 P.2d 761].) California case law typically holds that courts can use their equitable powers to apportion costs and attorneys' fees when two or more parties are entitled to a common fund. (*Samura* v. *Kaiser Foundation Health Plan, Inc.* (1993) 17 Cal.App.4th 1284 [22 Cal.Rptr.2d 20].)

Only in recent years, however, have these equitable principles have been used to set attorney's fees in California class actions. (*Beasley* v. *Wells Fargo Bank* (1991) 235 Cal.App.3d 1383 [1 Cal.Rptr.2d 446].) Although a lawyer may be entitled to the extra reward granted in *Central Railroad and Banking Co. of Georgia* v. *Petus*, the specific amount is unclear without reference to federal rules. *(Central Railroad and Banking Co. of Georgia* v. *Petus* (1885) 113 U.S. 116 [28 L.Ed. 915, 5 S.Ct. 387].) To date, the California cases on common funds have not expressly sanctioned a specific percentage of the common fund, nor have they set up direct benchmarks, such as percentages or other objective criteria. (See, e.g., *Dunk* v. *Ford Motor Company* (1996) 48 Cal.App.4th 1794 [56 Cal.Rptr.2d 483].) In fact, one court stated the award of attorney's fees based upon a percentage of a 'common fund' is of questionable validity in California. (*Dunk* v. *Ford Motor Company* (1996) 48 Cal.App.4th 1794, 1808 [56 Cal.Rptr.2d 483].) However, that court's analysis turned on the inability to calculate the fund's actual (cash) value. The settlement provided for coupons to the settlement class which had a one-year expiration period. Also, because the record was devoid of any evidence concerning the actual value, it became problematic. In such cases, counsel additionally are cautioned to keep summaries or some evidence of hours expended or "even an approximation" of the hours expended to allow the court to make a full conclusion as to the reasonableness of attorney's fees. (*Dunk* v. *Ford Motor Company* (1996) 48 Cal.App.4th 1794, 1808 [56 Cal.Rptr.2d 483].)

The federal courts, by contrast, have established a clear line of precedent for a fixed percentage. The federal common fund rule rests upon the perception that it is only fair for all class members to bear the cost of litigation. Otherwise, those who contribute nothing to an action's costs benefit disproportionately from the successful litigant's expense. (*Boeing* v. *Van Gemert* (1980) 444 U.S. 472, 478 [62 L.Ed. 676, 100 S.Ct. 745].) After years of wrestling with complicated fee applications of "mind-numbing complexity" using the lodestar method (time spent multiplied by counsel's hourly rate), many federal courts have determined that a fixed percentage serves the interests of both early settlement and judicial economy. A percentage award also contributes to judicial economy by offering a larger carrot. (*Mashburn* v. *National Healthcare Inc.* (1988) 684 F.Supp. 679.) The *Mashburn* litigation reached settlement within less than a year, yet the court awarded a percentage fee anyway, noting that the financial incentive to do a good job in a short period of time supports prompt resolution of class claims. The court stated that, like the surgeon who removes an appendix in a speedy few minutes and charges the same fee as the medical plodder who takes an hour, counsel who achieves a successful result quickly is as entitled to compensation as a practitioner who draws the proceeding out yet achieves only the same result. (*Mashburn* v. *National Healthcare Inc.* (1988) 684 F.Supp. 660.)

The federal common fund doctrine applies only if the class of beneficiaries is sufficiently identified, the benefits can be accurately traced, and the fee can be shifted with some exactness to those who benefit. (*In re Hill* (9th Cir. 1985) 775 F.2d 1037.) Settled federal authority fixes compensation at a 25 percent "benchmark" of the common fund, which may be adjusted up or down if circumstances warrant. Circumstances can include complexity of the matter, reputation and experience of counsel, amount of recovery, likelihood of success, and the stage of the proceedings at which compensation is requested. The Ninth Circuit Court of Appeals, which, of course, includes California, routinely sanctions the 25 percent benchmark as an alternative to the lodestar method. (*Paul, Johnson, Alston & Hunt* v. *Graulty* (9th Cir. 1989) 886 F.2d 268.)

Two recent California district court opinions similarly support a percentage fee benchmark. *In re Activision Securities Litigation* cited the 25 percent figure as a proper benchmark. In arriving at its opinion, the court described the reasoning in *Lindy Bros.* v. *American Radiator & Standard Sanitary Co.* as complicated, cumbersome, and often surrealistic. The *Lindy* method entails preparing and evaluating fee petitions, a widely accepted procedure the court criticized as a plague upon the bench and bar. The Uniform Law Commissioner's version of the Model Class Action Act, for example, stipulates that attorney's fees for the prevailing class depend on a long list of factors, including time and effort, benefits to the class, the size and complexity of the litigation, the original likelihood of success, and the state code of professional responsibility (Model Class Action Act). Applying such standards or using the lodestar or multiple-factor approach is extraordinarily difficult, causing voluminous discovery, long motion practice, and the expenditure of even more time by attorneys and court. Yet, despite this prodigious effort, nearly all common fund awards fall into the neighborhood of 30 percent. (*In re Activision Securities Litigation* (ND Cal. 1989) 723 F.Supp. 1373, 1377; see *Lindy Bros.* v. *American Radiator & Standard Sanitary Co.* (3d Cir. 1973) 487 F.2d 161.) Why go to such trouble when the outcome is known and can be arrived at much more easily and efficiently?

Most federal circuit courts accept the reasoning that a percentage fee is the best practice in common fund class action cases. Absent extraordinary circumstances that suggest lowering or increasing the percentage, the rate should be 25 to 30 percent.

A practitioner in a California common fund class action should submit a fee application to the court that includes citations to the recent federal Ninth Circuit and California district court common fund cases discussed above. The practitioner will help his or her own cause by guiding the reviewing court through the relevant cases and showing the clear rationale behind a fixed-percentage approach.

[C] Enhancing Common Fund Fees with the Private Attorney General Statute

Code of Civil Procedure section 1021.5, the private attorney general statute, allows fees to be awarded when an important right or significant benefit has been conferred on absent persons. The statute provides that, upon motion, the court may award attorney's fees to a successful party against one or more opposing parties in an action enforcing an important right affecting the public interest. Three conditions need apply. First, a significant pecuniary or nonpecuniary benefit must be conferred on the general public or a large class of persons. Second, the financial burden of privately enforcing this public right and the necessity of the action make the award appropriate. Third, in the interests of justice, the fees should not be paid out of any recovery.

This statute's relationship to common fund awards appears in an important case of "first impression." (*Beasley* v. *Wells Fargo Bank* (1991) 235 Cal.App.3d 1383 [1 Cal.Rptr. 446].) The *Beasley* court held that a California court can award a private attorney general or public interest fee under Code of Civil Procedure section 1021.5 even if a common fund exists. In awarding almost $2 million in attorney's fees, costs, and expenses above and beyond a percentage of the $5.2 million common fund, the *Beasley* court identified and analyzed the financial burden of the litigation, the interests of justice, and the public's interest in the consumer benefits protected by the action. The court applied a lodestar multiplier of 1.5 to counsel's hourly rate in calculating fees, taking into consideration the contingency risk factor in the litigation. Expert witness expenses and other nonrecoverable costs were added pursuant to the private attorney general statute.

If counsel can make an appropriate showing, compensation may include both common fund and private attorney general sources. To the extent that trial courts use the 25 to 30 percent common fund benchmark, *Beasley* appears to place plaintiff's counsel in appropriate cases in a position to seek attorney's fees in addition to a common fund percentage as total compensation.

[D] Reasonableness Requirement

The reasonableness of any claimed fee must be demonstrated. The court will look to the surrounding circumstances, the timing and setting of the fee application after settlement negotiations or trial, and the best interests of absent class members. Local rules further provide that, no matter what the parties have agreed, the court reviewing settlement may disapprove counsel's compensation or conduct its own de novo review. (See, e.g., Super. Ct. L.A. County Rules, rule 18.45.) The court will award only the fees it determines to be reasonable, which may mean lowering the compensation the parties have agreed to. (Super. Ct. San Mateo County Rules, rule 7.9, Settlement of Class Claims.) Superior Court of San Francisco County Rules, rule 463 further provides that if the parties cannot agree on fees, the court will award what it considers reasonable. Local rules typically require "evidence" to support the fee request, including the amount of the recovery, the probability of success when representation was undertaken, the number of hours the attorney spent on the matter, his or her professional standing, his or her hourly and daily rates for office work and court appearances, and the attorney's agreement with the class representative about fees. (Super. Ct. S.F. County Rules, rule 363; Super. Ct. L.A. County Rules, rule 15.45(b).)

Even in a common fund case, the prudent applicant for attorney's fees should submit as much information as possible on time and costs to ensure that the court can determine the fee's reasonableness. The typical practice is to prepare a statement summarizing hours expended and multiplying the time by an hourly rate based on years of experience. Usually counsel should make a time log available for in-camera review to back up the request. The statement should also specifically list costs advanced in the interests of the class. The lodestar computation of hours times the reasonable rate is boosted by a multiplier to determine the hour-based fees portion of the overall award. This detailed statement gives class members information they need to judge the prudence of the fee. After notice to the class, the court provides objection opportunities to class members before ruling on reasonableness.

In a footnote in *Dunk* v. *Ford Motor Company*, previously mentioned, the court offered a "moral from this case" to keep some approximation of hours expended in the event the court uses a lodestar analysis for attorney's fees. (*Dunk* v. *Ford Motor Company* (1996) 48 Cal.App.4th 1794 [56 Cal.Rptr.2d 483].)

There are a number of other practical things that can be done to expedite the payment of compensation to plaintiffs' counsel in a settlement. A "fast pay" provision can allow for some percentage of the costs or fee to be paid upon preliminary approval of a settlement. The danger, of course, is that if the settlement ultimately is not approved after notice to the class, there would be a need to refund all funds paid. Therefore, the risk is entirely on plaintiff's counsel, and it depends on a realistic assessment of the likelihood of approval. It is not recommended, however, in multiparty settlements where the settlements face continued opposition unless it is pure cost reimbursement and the cost reimbursement is calculated to assist in the ongoing ability to represent a class, such as expenses for notice or other objective expenses. Also, note that in California the common fund rules will require a very objective analysis of the cash available to the class to support the common fund approach to attorney's fees.

§ 10.05 References

NEWBERG For additional discussion of attorney's fees in class actions, see 3 Newberg on Class Actions (3d ed. 1992), Chapter 14.

TRG **THE RUTTER GROUP** See the following sections in California Practice Guide: Civil Procedure Before Trial (CPBT) regarding attorney's fees:

- Award of attorney's fees (CPBT, §§ 14:140–14:146).

See also the following sections in California Practice Guide: Federal Civil Procedure Before Trial (FCBPT) regarding attorney's fees in federal class actions:

- Fee award to plaintiff's attorney (FCPBT, §§ 10:600–10:617.3).

WESTLAW® See the WESTLAW Electronic Research Guide at the beginning of this volume.

B. FORMS

§ 10.10 Retainer Agreement and Duties of Class Representative (*Marquart* case)

PRIVILEGED AND CONFIDENTIAL
ATTORNEY-CLIENT COMMUNICATION

January, 1997

Re: Jones v. XYZ Corporation, et al.
San Diego Superior Court Case No. 00000000

Dear ______________:

The purpose of this letter is to memorialize our engagement to represent you as a class representative in the above-entitled action against XYZ Corporation and others. You have advised us that since ______________, 1996, you purchased ______________ from these companies for your own use and believe that you were overcharged as a result.

You have advised us that your only relationship to any of the Defendants is as a purchaser of ______________. We have advised you that based upon our experience in prosecuting class actions under the federal and state antitrust laws and our preliminary investigation into the facts and circumstances of this case it is our opinion that a lawsuit is meritorious. We will continue with our investigation. Enclosed is a copy of the complaint for your review. Assuming that we amend the complaint and name you as a class representative, you will have certain duties and responsibilities to the class. Certain of these duties are explained in greater detail in this letter and the attachment.

You have agreed to cooperate with the attorneys in this case and to comply with all reasonable requests for information. You also agree to provide us with copies of all relevant records and invoices and to participate in discovery in this action as necessary, by, among other things, answering interrogatories, producing documents to the Defendants and giving deposition and trial testimony if requested. You understand that you may be required to testify at trial in San Diego. We will make every effort to comply with your scheduling requirements. We will also advance the travel costs on behalf of the class.

We will advance all costs and expenses of the litigation and you will not be responsible for these moneys regardless of the outcome of this case.[1] At the conclusion of the case, the attorneys for Plaintiffs will apply to the Court for an award of fees and the reimbursement of expenses based upon, among other things, the time expended, the difficulty of the litigation and, of course, the results achieved. You understand that such an award of attorneys' fees may be as much as 33 1/3% of any settlement fund or judgment, although the amount actually awarded is within the sole discretion of the Court. (Our office as a practical matter rarely seeks more than 25% of any common fund created for the benefit of a class.)

---

[1] Rules of Professional Conduct of the State Bar of California, Rule 4-210(3).

1

Although you will not be responsible for our legal fees, costs and expenses as part of your fiduciary obligations, you should be aware of our billing practices. We will maintain records of our time and expenses that may be submitted to the Court in support of our application for attorneys' fees and reimbursement of expenses. We will bill the case at our prevailing hourly rates for attorneys, paralegals, law clerks, legal interns and other support staff. These rates are periodically adjusted; hourly charges are in minimum units of one-quarter hour. Costs and expenses include professional fees and costs charged by investigators, experts, consultants and others and expenses including copying, process servers, on-line research, travel, messengers, telephone, postage, facsimiles and other usual and customary expenses at our usual and customary charges for such items. Charges for meals and related items associated with meetings among attorneys may also be included in expenses.

We may apply to the Court for a special award to compensate the class representative(s) for their contribution to the action. You understand, however, that unless such an award is approved by the Court you will only be entitled to your pro rata share of funds available for distribution to all class members.

Obviously, as with any type of litigation, we are unable to guarantee any particular result or outcome. It is very important that you maintain the confidentiality of this retainer agreement and all communications with our law firm.

Please return a signed copy of this agreement to us as soon as possible. Thank you for your trust and confidence. We look forward to working with you.

Very truly yours,

COHELAN & KHOURY

Timothy Cohelan

Agreed:

Date:____________________ ________________________
Client Signature

2

DUTIES OF A CLASS REPRESENTATIVE

1. A **class representative** represents the interests of all members of his or her class in litigation to recover money damages or obtain injunctive relief for the class.

2. The **class** usually consists of all persons who are **similarly situated** with respect to a common course of conduct or practice. In other words, all those persons who are effected by the challenged behavior.

3. A class representative has claims that are **typical** of those of the class, and thus involve **common issues of law or fact**. For example, as a class representative, your claims against the defendants are typical of the class claims against them, simply because you paid artificially high prices for gasoline.

4. A class representative always considers the interests of the class just as he or she would consider his or her own interests and in some cases must put the interests of the class before their own interests. This means that you are a **champion of the class** or **fiduciary litigant**.

5. A class representative always **actively participates** in the lawsuit, as necessary, by, among other things, answering interrogatories, producing documents to the defendants and giving deposition and trial testimony if requested. **You may be required to travel to give such testimony**.

6. A class representative recognizes and accepts that any resolution of the lawsuit, by **dismissal or settlement**, is subject to **court approval**, and must be designed in the best interest of the class as a whole.

7. A class representative is not required to be particularly sophisticated or knowledgeable about the subject of the lawsuit. However, a class representative should follow the progress of the lawsuit and should provide all relevant facts to the lawyers for the class.

8. A class representative volunteers to represent or **champion** many other people with similar claims and injuries because of the importance of the case and that necessity that all class members benefit from the lawsuit equally; the savings of time, money and effort should benefit all parties and the court. Class actions are an important tool to assure compliance with the law even where an individual's losses may be relatively small.

I have reviewed and acknowledge my duties as a class representative.

Date:______________________ __________________________________

Signature

§ 10.11 Plaintiffs' Memorandum of Points and Authorities in Support of Motion for Order (1) Awarding Attorney's Fees, (2) Allowing Reimbursement of Costs and Expenses, (3) Appointing Settlement Administrator, and (4) Allowing Enhancements for Representatives (Real Property Class)

Timothy D. Cohelan, Esq. (CA State Bar #60827)
Isam C. Khoury, Esq. (CA State Bar #58759)
J. Mark McNeill, Esq. (CA State Bar #153531)
COHELAN & KHOURY
701 "C" Street
San Diego, California 92101-5307
Telephone: (619) 595-3001

Attorneys for Plaintiffs

SUPERIOR COURT OF CALIFORNIA

COUNTY OF

on behalf of themselves and all others similarly situated, Plaintiffs, v. XYZ CORPORATION, et al. Defendants.	**Case No. 00000** **PLAINTIFFS' MEMORANDUM OF POINTS & AUTHORITIES IN SUPPORT OF MOTION FOR ORDER:** **1) AWARDING ATTORNEYS' FEES;** **2) ALLOWING REIMBURSEMENT OF COSTS AND EXPENSES;** **3) APPOINTING SETTLEMENT ADMINISTRATOR; AND,** **4) ALLOWING ENHANCEMENTS FOR REPRESENTATIVES** **DATE:** **TIME:** **DEPT: 3** **Hon. James H. Harmon**

The law firm of Cohelan & Khoury, on behalf of the Plaintiff Class of homeowners in the above-captioned (conditional) class action, move for entry of an order (1) awarding attorneys' fees; 2) allowing reimbursement of costs and expenses; 3) appointing David R. Hickey, CPA, as settlement administrator; and, 4) allowing a modest enhancement to certain homeowners who were heretofore proposed class representatives for their substantial assistance to the case.

I.

INTRODUCTION

This Class Action was brought by and prosecuted on behalf of persons and entities who are or were owners of approximately 1,391 Class Homes, (XYZ homes located in Valley and better defined in the Stipulation Re Settlement), (either as original purchasers or as subsequent purchasers) since April 1, 1994. The allegations on behalf of Class Members are that the Class Homes have various types of construction defects which have caused or may cause damage to Class Homes or to Class Members. Defendants XYZ Corporation denied and continues to deny the allegations of the Complaint and additionally assert certain affirmative defenses.

Plaintiffs' counsel has made a thorough investigation into the facts and applicable law concerning the claims and defenses in this Class Action and based thereon has concluded that the proposed Settlement, which was vigorously negotiated and mediated, is fair, reasonable and adequate and is in the best interests of Class Members, taking into account all relevant factors, including the time and expense of further prosecution of the lawsuit, the difficulties and delay inherent in this type of complex litigation, the substantial benefit to Class Members without additional costs, uncertainty or delay, and the range of likely recovery by Class Members if the case is litigated further. (See, Declaration of Timothy D. Cohelan [hereinafter "Cohelan Decl."], submitted herewith). The proposed settlement provides cash benefits in a higher amount or percentage than occurs in many construction defect cases.

The case has progressed successfully through adversarial litigation, including various motions and ex parte applications. Mountains of documents were produced and countless hours have been spent by all parties in sifting through the evidence in order to ascertain the viability of their respective positions. At the time the settlement was reached there was calendared the Plaintiffs' motion to certify the Class. Sufficient investigation, discovery, and litigation has taken place to warrant an award of the requested fees and costs.

The Court, at the October 17, 1996 hearing regarding preliminary approval of this settlement, conditionally certified the Class for settlement purposes only, gave preliminary

2

approval of the settlement and approved the Notice (regarding preliminary approval) for mailing to the Class.

Notice has been sent out to the Class Members, owners of approximately 1,391 homes, and at the time of the filing of this document no Class Members had objected to the settlement and only six (6) had excluded themselves from the Class. Prior to the Final Fairness Hearing, Plaintiffs will submit a declaration regarding the exact final count of opting out Class members.

This global Settlement is the product of over two years' worth of vigorous opposition by defendants and other interested parties and extensive negotiations and mediations involving representatives of these competing interests, including insurance carriers. These mediation sessions and concerted negotiations between and among counsel for the parties concentrated on adopting and enhancing a settlement agreement for the optimal benefit of the Class. The settlement that has been reached is believed to be a fair, reasonable and adequate resolution of the Class claims. Class Counsel is of the opinion that, given the facts and the problems associated with proving liability at trial, coupled with the "better than average" result achieved for the Class, the requests for attorneys' fees and costs, and for certain enhancements and for the appointment of an administrator are warranted and equitable. (See, Cohelan Decl.).

Class Counsel seek an award of attorneys' fees and reimbursement of costs and expenses incurred in the total amount of $__________, i.e. $__________ for attorneys' fees and $______________ for reimbursement of costs and expenses. Class Counsel also request appointment of Mr. David R. Hickey, CPA, as Settlement Administrator, and further seek permission to give well-earned modest enhancements to certain representative plaintiffs, the owners of nine Class Homes.

II.

PLAINTIFFS' COUNSEL SEEKS AN AWARD OF ATTORNEYS' FEES

The last step in the settlement approval process at the "Formal Fairness Hearing" is the Court's decision regarding Class Counsel's fees and costs. Plaintiffs' Counsel herein respectfully request the Court make an award of attorneys' fees to Class Counsel.

California class action compensation is governed by a mixture of the application of

3

federal class action case law and equitable principles incorporated into California cases. The equitable principles behind the common fund can be traced to *Central Railroad and Banking of Georgia* v. *Petus* (1885) 113 U.S. 116 [28 L.Ed. 915, 5 S.Ct. 387], where the U.S. Supreme Court stated: "The lawyer who creates a common fund is allowed an extra reward, beyond that which he has arranged with his client, so that he might share the wealth of those upon whom he has conferred a benefit." In *Quinn* v. *State of California* (1975) 15 Cal.3d 162, the California Supreme Court stated, in pertinent part, ". . . The exception to this rule [the American Rule regarding attorneys' fees] has become as well established as the rule itself: That one who expends attorneys' fees in winning a suit which creates a fund from which others derive benefits may require those passive beneficiaries to bear a fair share of the litigation costs." (*Quinn, supra,* 15 Cal.3d at page 167.) The California cases establish that when two or more parties are entitled to a common fund, the courts can use their equitable powers to apportion costs and attorneys' fees. (*Samura* v. *Kaiser Foundation Health Plan, Inc.* (1993) 17 Cal.App.4th 1284.)

The federal common fund rule "rests upon the perception that persons who obtain the benefit of a lawsuit without contributing to its costs are unjustly enriched at the successful litigant's expense." (*Boeing* v. *Van Gemert* (1980) 444 U.S. 472, 478.) The federal common fund doctrine is to be applied only if: "(1) The class of beneficiaries is sufficiently identified; (2) the benefits can be accurately traced; and (3) the fee can be shifted with some exactitude to those benefitting." (*In Re: Hill* (9th Cir. 1985) 775 F.2d 1037.) Courts in the Ninth Circuit now routinely sanction this approach.

In the instant case it is clear that the Class has been sufficiently identified (owners of record of 1,391 homes) and that the Class will benefit from the settlement. Furthermore, the attorneys' fees that are being requested are to be awarded from the gross Settlement Fund and are therefore being paid out of the fund that has been created for the benefit of the Class. As noted in the Declaration of Timothy Cohelan filed concurrently herewith, Class Counsel is very experienced in handling class action litigation and has devoted over 4000 hours in prosecuting this case on behalf of the Plaintiff Class. (See, Cohelan Decl. at paras. 6 & 12, and "Exhibit

4

A" [Time Summary], attached thereto). An award of 25%, modest in most contingency cases, would yield a resulting fee much higher than what is herein requested, i.e., only 7.6%. (See, Cohelan Decl. at para. 12 and Ex. A.). Therefore this request is eminently reasonable and fair. Plaintiffs request the Court approve an award of attorneys' fees in the amount of $________ ($__________ minus costs of $____________).

III.

PLAINTIFFS SEEK REIMBURSEMENT FOR COSTS AND EXPENSES INCURRED TO DATE

In this case, the Stipulation of Settlement provides for the reimbursement to Class Counsel of expenses and costs incurred in the prosecution of this action. Plaintiffs request the Court order the reimbursement of costs and expenses in the amount of $____________. (See, Costs Summary, attached as "Exhibit B" to Cohelan Decl.).

Cases of this nature are very expensive to finance. For over two years, Plaintiffs' Counsel incurred the full risks and costs associated with the successful and complex prosecution of this case. Nothing was guaranteed, of course, but finally a good result was achieved. Plaintiffs' Counsel received no payment towards these costs during the pendency of the case, from class members or from any other source. (See, Cohelan Decl. at para. 8). As such, the request for costs is fair and Plaintiffs respectfully seek an order from the Court for reimbursement.

IV.

PLAINTIFFS REQUEST THE APPOINTMENT OF A SETTLEMENT ADMINISTRATOR

Plaintiffs also request the appointment of Mr. David R. Hickey, CPA, a named partner in the accounting firm of Coradino, Hickey & Hanson, as Settlement Administrator in this case. Mr. Hickey is well-respected in his field and very experienced in the tasks surrounding settlement fund distributions. (See, Mr. Hickey's curriculum vitae, attached to Cohelan Decl. as "Exhibit C"). Mr. Hickey will be vested with the general responsibilities and authority regarding the administration and distribution of the settlement funds within the terms of the terms of the Stipulation Re Settlement.

5

Mr. Hickey's duties will include the following: obtain tax identification numbers and establish bank accounts into which the gross settlement funds will be deposited and from which class members will be compensated; generally monitor and supervise the entire claims process, including the coordination with local bank personnel, involvement in determining the validity of claims, and the distribution of settlement funds to class members and fees and costs to class counsel; generally accounting for these funds and the distribution thereof, including preparing a report for the Court; filing required state and federal income tax returns for the funds; and applying to the Court for any additional fees and costs regarding administration of the settlement funds.

As Settlement Administrator, he shall have the authority to withdraw from the settlement fund accounts a maximum of $____________ monthly to cover costs of administration. Any additional administration costs will require application to and approval of this Court. The Settlement Administrator shall periodically provide the Court with an accounting of the distribution of all settlement funds.

Of course, and pursuant to the terms of the Stipulation Re Settlement, the Court will retain continuing jurisdiction over the implementation, enforcement, and construction of the Settlement Agreement, and the administration, allocation, and distribution of the Settlement Fund.

V.

ENHANCEMENTS FOR CERTAIN REPRESENTATIVE PLAINTIFFS ARE WARRANTED IN THIS CASE

In addition, for those Plaintiffs who initiated the case with Class Counsel (the s) and/or served the Class by participating in depositions, engaging in discovery and maintaining contact with counsel throughout this litigation, Plaintiffs request the Court grant a small enhancement of their respective recoveries in this lawsuit. This enhancement would apply solely to Plaintiffs

(See, Cohelan Decl. at para. 17.). These enhancements total

6

$______________ and will likely be covered by interest earned on the settlement funds deposited into the class action settlement account(s).

VI.

CONCLUSION

On the basis of the foregoing, the Plaintiffs respectfully request that this Court 1) grant Class Counsel an award of attorneys' fees in the amount of $______________; 2) allow the reimbursement of costs and expenses in the amount of $______________; 3) permit enhancements totalling $______________ to the owners of certain class homes who fully participated in the lawsuit; 4) appoint David R. Hickey, CPA, as settlement administrator; and, 5) retain jurisdiction in this matter; and cause to be entered an Order thereon.

Dated: November 27, 1996

COHELAN & KHOURY
Attorneys for Plaintiffs

By: ________________________
J. Mark McNeill

7

11 TRIAL STRATEGIES

Sec.

11.01 Venue and Court for Trial

11.02 Making the Trial Manageable

- [A] In General
- [B] Bifurcation
- [C] Severance
- [D] Pretrial Master or Reference Reports
- [E] Arbitration of Certain Issues
- [F] Contribution Bar Orders
- [G] Statements of Contested and Uncontested Issues
- [H] Summaries of Voluminous Documents for Exchange with Opposing Parties
- [I] Pretrial Discussion and Disposition of Disruptive Evidentiary Issues

11.03 Additional Considerations

- [A] In General
- [B] Determining Trial Issues Before Certification
- [C] Trial of Remaining Action
- [D] Appropriate Inferences and Presumptions

11.04 References

§ 11.01 Venue and Court for Trial

Much like the federal Multidistrict Litigation Panel, the California Judicial Council may transfer like cases to one court in the interests of judicial economy (28 U.S.C., § 1407 *et seq.*). California has adopted comprehensive rules to manage complex litigation in general, not just class actions, when matters with a common question of law or fact are pending in different courts (Code Civ. Proc., §§ 404–404.8; Cal. Rules of Court, rule 1501). These procedures should be employed in cases where major events of widespread import precipitate litigation in several California venues. When the same facts spawn both state and federal litigation, counsel can attempt to stay federal proceedings and pursue the state action.

§ 11.02 Making the Trial Manageable

[A] In General

California courts can benefit substantially from using the *Manual for Complex Litigation, Third* as a model for trial management on such issues as partial pretrial class settlements, bifurcation, expediting, and evidence summaries. Any or all of the following tools should be considered in the effort to make the matter easier to manage.

[B] Bifurcation

Since a class action trial likely involves complex or extensive evidentiary proof, it is appropriate to divide the trial into preliminary questions, such as those involving liability under Code of Civil Procedure section 598. At the pretrial conference or some other convenient date, the court should entertain the logical order of resolution for trial issues, deferring damage questions for separate analysis. Additionally, the trial of special defenses under Code of Civil Procedure section 597 should precede other issues, particularly if an evidentiary record is to be made.

[C] Severance

In a multiparty action, the court needs to review closely the appropriateness of a joint hearing or trial of issues through consolidation under Code of Civil Procedure section 1048. Individual counsel for defendants may seek to avoid prejudice and have a separate trial of issues relating to the liability of their clients pursuant to Code of Civil Procedure section 1048, subdivision (b).

[D] Pretrial Master or Reference Reports

Under the authority of California Code of Civil Procedure sections 638 and 639, the court, either after agreement of the parties or on its own motion, can order a reference or master for such issues as taking a long account or an extensive and detailed evidentiary record. After hearing appropriate objections, the court can also adopt the contents of the master's or reference's report and, in most cases, substantially expedite the trial of the matter. Parties to the action need to recognize the joint advantages of stipulating to reference. The court also needs to be aware of this important tool to accelerate factual resolution of complicated claims.

[E] Arbitration of Certain Issues

Some collateral issues in a larger controversy are subject to arbitration. The court should recognize the arbitration clauses in many commercial transactions not as an impediment to judicial resolution of claims, but as a potential complement to the larger questions in some cases. The court needs to be advised of such clauses early in the process so that the outcome of pending arbitrations can be confirmed at the trial of the matter.

[F] Contribution Bar Orders

As discussed in Chapter 9, the court needs to address nonsettling party issues concerning apportionment of liability. The trier of fact will be asked to assign proportional liability to all parties in some fashion. The apportionment process can be an important part of damage allocation at the actual trial.

[G] Statements of Contested and Uncontested Issues

Federal courts can use statements of contested and uncontested issues thirty days before pretrial conference to focus and narrow issues, a highly productive capability. California's equivalent would be contention interrogatories combined with discreet and focused requests for admissions and authentication of documents.

[H] Summaries of Voluminous Documents for Exchange with Opposing Parties

The *Manual for Complex Litigation* suggests summaries of complex documentation for presentation at trial. California, through local rules, will usually require as much agreement as possible between counsel to isolate evidentiary issues before the trial. There is simply no excuse for counsel presenting the court with an evidentiary controversy that could have been readily resolved through the "meet and confer" process. In any event, the court can isolate certain evidentiary issues well before the trial.

[I] Pretrial Discussion and Disposition of Disruptive Evidentiary Issues

Most superior courts have adopted the equivalent of an advanced trial review process that forces counsel to focus on the details of evidentiary issues likely to be presented at the trial. Expanded use of this process substantially expedites trial and minimizes inconvenience to juries.

§ 11.03 Additional Considerations

[A] In General

Early shaping of classwide issues substantially influences the trial. Counsel should make every effort to incorporate simplified elements of proof, presumptions, or inferences whenever possible. Again, the *Manual for Complex Litigation, Third* is an important tool for making class action trials simpler and more manageable.

[B] Determining Trial Issues Before Certification

The court can rule on injunctive relief pursuant to Code of Civil Procedure section 527 before the class is certified, possibly simplifying the certification phase. Absent a stipulation between the parties, however, other merits issues cannot be tried until the court has resolved the issues relating to class certification. (*Home Sav. & Loan Ass'n* v. *Superior Court Los Angeles County* (1974) 42 Cal.App.3d 1006 [117 Cal.Rptr. 485]. See Chapter 6 for a discussion of the *Home Savings* rule.)

[C] Trial of Remaining Action

In trying a class action, the practitioner needs to consider a variety of issues on how to proceed. This list covers the principal questions counsel should answer.

- How many class members will be testifying for the absent class members, and on what issues?

- How many class members must appear at the trial to prove the case? Can a sampling of class members be used?
- If more than one attorney is representing the class, which one will be lead counsel?
- Can certain issues in the case be bifurcated or severed, such as liability and damages?
- Would the case benefit from a pilot or test case prove-up?
- Are there simplified elements of proof or causation, reliance, impact, aggregate damages, or others?

Damage issues should be reviewed and discussed. Damages may be proved and assessed in the aggregate by statistical or sampling methods, pro rata allocation of illegal overcharges or excess profits, or other reasonable systems that the court in its discretion may permit. (Bus. & Prof. Code, § 16760, subd. (d).) *Rosack* v. *Volvo of America Corporation* laid out the practical methods for calculating individual damages expeditiously, including bifurcation and subclasses. In some cases, the court has certified the class for purposes of liability only, reserving the right to reassess possible subclasses for that purpose later. *(Rosack* v. *Volvo of America Corporation* (1982) 131 Cal.App.3d 741 [182 Cal.Rptr. 800] cert. denied 460 U.S. 1012 (1983).)

Code of Civil Procedure section 384 governs class action damage calculations at trial. This section provides that, prior to entry of judgment in a class action under Code of Civil Procedure section 382, the court shall determine the total amount payable to all class members and then make an award accordingly.

Damage distribution can present special problems in consumer class actions. Fluid recovery may be useful in meeting the objectives of action. Pursuant to the equitable doctrine of cy pres, the court can exercise certain discretion over the proceeds of a recovery.

The principal methods of determining damages include a rollback of the defendant's prices escheat to a government body for either specified or general purposes or the establishment of a consumer trust fund or claimant fund sharing. (*State* v. *Levi Strauss & Co.* (1986) 41 Cal.3d 460 [224 Cal.Rptr. 605].)

[D] Appropriate Inferences and Presumptions

California case law supports inferences and presumptions. *La Sala* v. *American Savings & Loan Ass'n* allowed representative proof as an inference that class members in an adhesion contracts case were similarly situated in bargaining power. (*La Sala* v. *American Savings & Loan Ass'n* (1971) 5 Cal.3d 864 [97 Cal.Rptr. 849, 489 P.2d 1113].) *Vasquez* v. *Superior Court* permitted inferences with respect to reliance in a fraud case. (*Vasquez* v. *Superior Court* (1971) 4 Cal.3d 800 [94 Cal.Rptr. 796, 484 P.2d 964].) *B.W.I. Custom Kitchen* v. *Owens-Illinois, Inc.* provided that injury may be proved on a classwide basis in an antitrust action. (*B.W.I. Custom Kitchen* v. *Owens-Illinois, Inc.* (1987) 191 Cal.App.3d 1341 [235 Cal.Rptr. 228].) Finally, *Rosack* v. *Volvo of America Corporation*, another antitrust case, held that inferences of impact damages and market complexity were appropriate. (*Rosack* v. *Volvo of America Corporation* (1982) 131 Cal.App.3d 741 [182 Cal.Rptr. 800]; cert. denied 460 U.S. 1012 (1983).)

The *Manual for Complex Litigation, THIRD* provides additional practical ways of expediting proof at trial and achieving ultimate resolution more quickly. These methods include expert summaries, summaries of voluminous testimony, and sampling to provide for proof of classwide issues.

§ 11.04 References

NEWBERG For additional discussion of trial considerations, see 2 Newberg on Class Actions (3d ed. 1992), Chapter 9. For discussion of proof and aggregate class damages, see 2 Newberg on Class Actions (3d ed. 1992), Chapter 10.

WESTLAW® See the WESTLAW Electronic Research Guide at the beginning of this volume.

12 CLASS ACTIONS GROUPED BY SUBSTANTIVE LAW

Sec.

12.01 Overview

12.02 Antitrust

12.03 Discrimination

12.04 Securities

12.05 Bank and Credit Card Overcharges

12.06 Product Liability

12.07 Partnerships and Investment Schemes

12.08 Brokerage Agreement Charges

12.09 Real-Property–Related Class Actions

- [A] Deeds of Trust
- [B] Nuisance and Trespass
- [C] Construction Defect
- [D] Landlord-Tenant
- [E] Mobile Home Rents
- [F] Unlawful Detainers
- [G] Subdivision Land Sales
- [H] Condominiums
- [I] Escrow Practices
- [J] Title Insurance Practices

12.10 Government Benefits and Taxes

12.11 Medical Treatment

12.12 Ticketholders

12.13 Employee-Employer

12.14 Rental Cars

12.15 References

§ 12.01 Overview

California's substantive law makes the state an attractive venue for certain types of class actions and a less favorable one for others. In a number of legal areas, California law treats plaintiffs more advantageously than federal law. In other areas, however, class action treatment in California is unlikely to succeed.

§ 12.02 Antitrust

A state antitrust case alleging restraint of trade offers an enormous procedural advantage over federal litigation because of California's express tolerance of class actions. California statutory law provides that any person injured in business or property by anything forbidden or declared unlawful by the Cartwright Act—the state equivalent of the Clayton Act—may bring a treble-damage action, regardless of whether the injured person dealt with the defendant directly or indirectly. (See Bus. & Prof. Code, § 16750.) Making it procedurally easy for indirect purchasers to prosecute antitrust suits serves California's public policy interests. (*Union Carbide Corp.* v. *Superior Court* (1984) 36 Cal.3d 15 [201 Cal.Rptr. 580, 679 P.2d 14].) By contrast, federal antitrust principles deny the class action device to indirect purchasers damaged by manufacturer's overcharges. (*Illinois Brick Co.* v. *Illinois* (1977) 431 U.S. 720 [52 L.Ed.2d 707, 97 S.Ct. 2061].)

A number of interesting class actions involving antitrust causes of action are worth examining. The first is *Rosack* v. *Volvo of America Corporation*, which alleged a vertical retail price management scheme violating the Cartwright Act. After a procedural history that included removal and remanding to superior court by the United States Supreme Court, the court of appeal found predominant questions of fact and law based upon the substantive issues of California antitrust law. Price fixing was determined to have been a per se violation and a complaint alleging a conspiracy and its existence predominated. Proof of violation and injury to the plaintiffs was enough. (*Rosack* v. *Volvo of America Corporation* (1982) 131 Cal.App.3d 741, 749 [182 Cal.Rptr. 800] cert denied 460 U.S. 1012 (1983).)

In *B.W.I. Custom Kitchen* v. *Owens-Illinois, Inc.*, the court of appeal reasserted the right of indirect purchasers to bring a state action even though federal antitrust law disallowed such litigation. (*B.W.I. Custom Kitchen* v. *Owens-Illinois, Inc.* (1987) 191 Cal.App.3d 1341 [235 Cal.Rptr. 228]; see *Illinois Brick Co.* v. *Illinois* (1977) 431 U.S. 720 [52 L.Ed.2d 707, 97 S.Ct. 2061].) The court permitted indirect purchasers of glass containers to maintain a class action that alleged a horizontal price-fixing conspiracy by numerous defendants to set noncompetitive prices in violation of the Cartwright Act. The ability to bring a California class action on behalf of indirect consumers has prompted antitrust practitioners to take a hard look at the state as a forum for such actions. As in *Rosack*, the existence of a conspiracy was sufficient to establish the predominant questions of both fact and law. (*B.W.I. Custom Kitchen* v. *Owens-Illinois, Inc.* (1987) 191 Cal.App.3d 1341 [235 Cal.Rptr. 228].)

California cases have dealt with other types of antitrust activity prohibited by the Cartwright Act besides price fixing. *Classen* v. *Weller* involved an unlawful tie-in between lot purchases and a real estate broker. The class included buyers who purchased subdivision lots and were forced to use the services of a specific real estate broker at a full 6 percent listing commission as a condition of the purchase. The builder selling the lots and requiring the unlawful tie-in received an adverse summary judgment under a cross-complaint alleging damages under the Cartwright and Sherman acts. Tying arrangements of the type alleged in the case are prohibited by the Cartwright Act and also sections 16726 and 16727 of the Business and Professions Code. The court cited *People* v. *National Ass'n of Realtors* (1981) 120 Cal.App.3d 459 [174 Cal.Rptr. 728] and *Suburban Mobile Homes, Inc.* v. *Amfac Communities, Inc.* (1980) 101 Cal.App.3d 532 [161 Cal.Rptr. 811] in support of the unlawfulness of tie-ins in other settings. (*Classen* v. *Weller* (1983) 145 Cal.App.3d 27 [192 Cal.Rptr. 914].) For a substantive discussion of the differences between certain types of antitrust activities in the state courts, see *The California State Courts and Consumer Class Actions for Antitrust Violations* (1982) 33 Hastings Law Journal 689.

State v. *Levi Strauss & Co.* discusses damages in a consumer price-fixing antitrust action. A Federal Trade Commission complaint had charged the defendant company with pressuring retailers to maintain high prices in violation of federal antitrust law. The State of California filed suit in superior court both as a class action and on behalf of itself and similarly situated consumers, using Code of Civil Procedure section 382 and in parens patriae on behalf of its residents. (Bus. & Prof. Code, § 16760.) Although the issue in the suit concerned a proposed settlement residue and not a trial, the case discusses the propriety of fluid recovery for achieving the public policy goals of a consumer class action. The case cites price rollbacks escheat to a government body, a consumer trust fund, or a claimant fund sharing as possible methods. (*State* v. *Levi Strauss & Co.* (1986) 41 Cal.3d 460 [224 Cal.Rptr. 605].)

Another advantage to antitrust class actions in California allows plaintiffs to have their cake and eat it too. Business and Professions Code section 16760, subdivision (d), allows damages in the aggregate to be proved by statistical or sampling methods with a pro rata allocation of overcharges. This evidentiary advantage, combined with indirect purchaser actions and such additional remedies as price rollbacks and consumer trust funds, make California a very attractive venue for antitrust class actions.

§ 12.03 Discrimination

Although the plaintiff was found to be an inadequate class representative, *Stephens* v. *Montgomery Ward & Company* contains important language with broad implications for plaintiffs asserting employment discrimination in a California class action. The court held that employment discrimination by its very nature is often class discrimination and therefore well-suited for class certification. Significantly, the court also allowed statistical analysis of the discrimination, which consisted of failure to promote women to managerial jobs in specific retail departments. California's laws, therefore, can facilitate a discrimination claim because they favor class action and allow statistical proof. (*Stephens* v. *Montgomery Ward & Company* (1987) 193 Cal.App.3d 411 [238 Cal.Rptr. 602].)

§ 12.04 Securities

There is reason to believe that the California superior court system will see an ever-increasing number of California state securities class actions. U.S. Supreme Court decisions have shortened the federal statute of limitations for securities claims and made state venues more attractive. Additionally, the U.S. Supreme Court seemingly sanctioned full faith and credit for state securities settlements even though they extinguish claims that would otherwise have been brought in federal court. (*Matsushita Electric Industrial Co., Ltd.* v. *Epstein* (1996) __U.S.__ [134 L.Ed. 2d 6, 116 S. Ct. 873].) This is the case even if those other claims must have been brought in the federal court system—with exclusive federal court jurisdiction. (*Lampf, Pleva, Lipkind, Prupis & Pedigrew* v. *Gilbertson* (1991) 501 U.S. 350 [115 L.Ed.2d 321, 111 S. Ct. 2773].)

California's securities laws work to plaintiff's advantage. Corporations Code section 25503 provides for absolute liability for sales without a permit. Civil fraud statutes allow for a rescission or damages for misrepresentation, offer seemingly lower threshold scienter requirements, and provide for "strict liability" in a civil sense (Corp. Code, §§ 25401, 25501). California also has uniquely beneficial statutes, such as Corporations Code section 15701, which allows for class action in limited partnerships.

In *Schneider* v. *Vennard* , a superior court refused to certify a state court class action because there were pending federal actions alleging violations of section 10(b) (15 U.S.C., § 78j(b)) and section 20(a) (15 U.S.C., § 78t(a)) of the Securities Exchange Act of 1934 as well as Securities and Exchange Commission rule 10b-5 (17 C.F.R., § 240.10b-5). *(Schneider* v. *Vennard* (1986) 183 Cal.App.3d 1340 [228 Cal.Rptr. 800].)

A well-known California case has, however, rendered the "fraud on the marketplace" method of recovery a defrocked class theory of recovery in California. (*Mirkin* v. *Wasserman* (1991) 5 Cal.4th 1082 [282 Cal.Rptr. 101, 858 P.2d 568].)

As this book goes to press, there are significant efforts to clarify the rules with regard to California securities laws. Several cases working their way through the California appellate system may have an impact on whether discovery is stayed in California state court in light of certain federal reforms or whether California security laws can cover the claims of out-of- state investors.

§ 12.05 Bank and Credit Card Overcharges

California has a well-developed body of class action law relating to credit card overcharges, mortgage prepayment penalties, unauthorized late charges, and other types of damages. *Beasley* v. *Wells Fargo Bank* rendered a substantial verdict under the theory that the charge for late payment of credit card bills constitutes a penalty or liquidated damages for breach of the credit card agreement and bears no relation to actual damages. The court held that fees amounting to liquidated damages are invalid under Civil Code section 1671, subdivision (d). (*Beasley* v. *Wells Fargo Bank* (1991) 235 Cal.App.3d 1383, 1398, 1441 [1 Cal.Rptr.2d 446].) In a similar case, *Hitz* v. *Interstate Bank*, credit card customers brought a class action challenging the bank's assessment of fees on customers who made late payments or exceeded their credit limits. A judgment of almost $14 million was rendered. The court of appeal reduced it to $9 million, which represented the amount the trial court had found to be the net revenue First Interstate enjoyed from delinquent and overdue balances above and beyond actual damages. *(Hitz* v. *Interstate Bank* (1995) 38 Cal.App.4th 274 [44 Cal.Rptr.2d 869].)

Much of this litigation has surrounded the efforts of defendant lenders to wrap themselves in federal preemption. In *Smalley* v. *Citibank*, the Supreme Court also supported preemption arguments wherein interest was construed to include late fees. *(Smalley* v. *Citibank* (1995) 11 Cal.4th 138 [44 Cal.Rptr.2d 441].)

§ 12.06 Product Liability

Recent California precedent makes a product liability class action under an implied warranty theory difficult, if not impossible.

American Suzuki Motor Corp. v. *Superior Court* overruled an experienced Los Angeles trial court judge and vacated a previous order certifying a products liability class action. The court held that because the class action plaintiffs failed to allege any personal injury or consequential property damage from the vehicle they claimed was designed defectively, they conceded by implication that the vehicle had been fit for its ordinary purpose since the date of purchase. Measuring damages by the cost of repairing the safety defect was not enough. (*American Suzuki Motor Corp.* v. *Superior Court* (1995) 37 Cal.App.4th 1291 [44 Cal.Rptr.2d 526].)

In *General Motors Corp.* v. *Superior Court*, a product liability action alleging defective and unsafe engines, the plaintiffs sought certification of a national class comprising all purchasers of the vehicles in question. The court certified a statewide California class of original purchasers of a 1981 Cadillac V8-6-4 automobile, a group of approximately 21,000 entities. *(General Motors Corp.* v. *Superior Court* (1988) 199 Cal.App.3d 247 [244 Cal.Rptr. 776].)

Osborne v. *Subaru of America, Inc.* proposed a nationwide class of owners of Subaru automobiles plagued by various engine breakdowns. Plaintiffs attributed the malfunctions to a defect in the design of the head gasket and valve systems. Certification was denied because a nationwide class would require adjudication of issues under numerous different rules of law from various states. *(Osborne* v. *Subaru of America, Inc.* (1988) 198 Cal.App.3d 646 [243 Cal.Rptr. 815].)

§ 12.07 Partnerships and Investment Schemes

Daniels v. *Centennial Group, Inc.* involved the merger of six limited partnerships into a single corporate entity, with three former limited partners as class representatives suing on behalf of approximately 28,000 owners of interests in the six partnerships. The court allowed the case to proceed and deemed the plaintiffs adequate representatives even though they did not hold shares in each of the six limited partnerships. The merger of the six into one entity proved a sufficient joining to allow the class action. (*Daniels* v. *Centennial Group, Inc.* (1993) 16 Cal.App.4th 467 [21 Cal.Rptr.2d 1].)

National Solar Equipment Owners' Ass'n, Inc. v. *Grumman Corp.* involved an investment scheme to purchase solar equipment. The case simplified the finding relative to the uniformity of misrepresentations and further defined the appropriate standards for class certification. (*National Solar Equipment Owners' Ass'n, Inc.* v. *Grumman Corp.* (1991) 235 Cal.App.3d 1273 [1 Cal.Rptr.2d 325].)

Danzig v. *Jack Grynberg & Associates* involved plaintiffs induced to subscribe in limited partnerships in oil and gas drilling partnerships. (*Danzig* v. *Jack Grynberg & Associates* (1984) 161 Cal.App.3d 1128 [208 Cal.Rptr. 336].)

§ 12.08 Brokerage Agreement Charges

McConnell v. *Merrill Lynch, Pierce, Fenner & Smith, Inc.* was a broker challenge to the monthly compounding of interest by a securities broker on a customer's debit balance accounts in contravention of section 2 of the usury law. (*McConnell* v. *Merrill Lynch, Pierce, Fenner & Smith, Inc.* (1983) 33 Cal.3d 816 [191 Cal.Rptr. 458, 662 P.2d 916].)

Dean Witter Reynolds, Inc. v. *Superior Court of Alameda County* posed a challenge to the assessment of fees in connection with a self-directed individual retirement account (IRA). The defendant asserted that a class action was unnecessary since the remedies for unfair competition were sufficiently remedial and lay within the reach of an individual. The court agreed. (*Dean Witter Reynolds, Inc.* v. *Superior Court of Alameda County* (1989) 211 Cal.App.3d 758 [259 Cal.Rptr. 789].)

§ 12.09 Real-Property–Related Class Actions

[A] Deeds of Trust

McGhee v. *Bank of America* ruled that preprinted contracts and deeds of trust with impound account provisions were contracts of adhesion allowing certification of the class. (*McGhee* v. *Bank of America* (1976) 60 Cal.App.3d 442 [131 Cal.Rptr. 482].)

[B] Nuisance and Trespass

City of San Jose v. *Superior Court of Santa Clara County* found that matters alleging trespass and nuisance are unsuitable as class actions. (*City of San Jose* v. *Superior Court of Santa Clara County* (1974) 12 Cal.3d 447 [115 Cal.Rptr. 797, 525 P.2d 701].)

[C] Construction Defect

Becker v. *McMillan Construction Co.* failed to achieve class certification because of the multiplicity of individual issues. However, denial of class certification for lack of common questions did not prevent the tolling of the statute of limitations for individual claims. (*Becker* v. *McMillan Construction Co.* (1991) 226 Cal.App.3d 1493 [277 Cal.Rptr. 491].)

[D] Landlord-Tenant

Hamwi v. *Citinational-Buckeye Investment Co.* concerned leases with rent escalation clauses negotiated over a number of time periods for tenants in twenty buildings. The court held there was no class because a community of interest was lacking. (*Hamwi* v. *Citinational-Buckeye Investment Co.* (1977) 72 Cal.App.3d 462 [140 Cal.Rptr. 215].)

In *Granberry* v. *Islay Investments*, the defendant entity, which owned and operated 1,200 to 1,500 residential rental units in the Santa Barbara area, made a general practice of charging an increase in rent in the first thirty-one days of tenancy without treating the charge as a security deposit. The trial court held the increase was indeed a security deposit and ordered restitution. The Supreme Court decided the measure of damages. (*Granberry* v. *Islay Investments* (1995) 9 Cal.4th 738 [38 Cal.Rptr.2d 650, 889 P.2d 970].)

[E] Mobile Home Rents

Rich v. *Schwab* mounted a classwide challenge of a rent increase for mobile home owners who alleged the increase was improper and retaliatory. The court of appeal reversed an adverse trial court judgment and directed certification of the class because the sixty-day notice required for the rental increase was imperfect. (*Rich* v. *Schwab* (1984) 162 Cal.App.3d 739 [209 Cal.Rptr. 417].)

In *Pinnacle Holdings, Inc.* v. *Simon*, a mobile home park owner attempted to have the mobile home owners bound as a defendant class in a mandamus action. When Pinnacle, the park's owner, requested a rent increase, four tenants protested. Following an adverse city determination of the amount of rental increase permissible under city ordinance, Pinnacle petitioned for administrative mandate and filed the class action in order to bind the defendant class under the pending administrative mandamus. The court sustained demurrers against the class on the basis of the factual pattern. Among other points, the court stated there was no sufficient allegation of class interest. (*Pinnacle Holdings, Inc.* v. *Simon* (1995) 31 Cal.App.4th 1430 [37 Cal.Rptr.2d 778].)

Tenants Association of Park Santa Anita v. *Southers* was filed against park owners and managers for alleged misconduct. The unincorporated association was allowed to file suit on behalf of its members and had appropriate standing. The finding was that necessity, convenience, and justice allowed use of the class action device. (*Tenants Association of Park Santa Anita* v. *Southers* (1990) 222 Cal.App.3d 1293 [272 Cal.Rptr. 361].)

[F] Unlawful Detainers

Even though unlawful detainers are limited to municipal court, standard practice warrants class certification. The court found that nothing in Code of Civil Procedure section 382 suggests it is inapplicable to municipal courts. (*Little* v. *Sanchez* (1985) 166 Cal.App.3d 501 [213 Cal.Rptr. 297].)

[G] Subdivision Land Sales

Richmond v. *Dart Industries, Inc.*, a bellwether California class action case, challenged subdivision land sales and alleged misrepresentations in subdivision documents. The Supreme Court sanctioned the matter as a class action and dealt with a variety of important class action concepts. A case already cited as an example of tie-ins unlawful under the Cartwright Act, *Classen* v. *Weller* (1983) 145 Cal.App.3d 27 [192 Cal.Rptr. 914], concerned a real estate development. (*Richmond* v. *Dart Industries, Inc.* (1981) 29 Cal.3d 462 [174 Cal.Rptr. 515, 629 P.2d 23].)

[H] Condominiums

Izzi v. *Mesquite Country Club* resulted in classwide arbitration. The class of condominium purchasers complained that the sellers failed to disclose that the condominiums would be subject to assessments for curbs, gutters, sewers, and flood control structures. The court held that the arbitration clause in the sales contract for the condominiums did apply, but that classwide arbitration could be sought. (*Izzi* v. *Mesquite Country Club* (1986) 186 Cal.App.3d 1309 [231 Cal.Rptr. 315].)

The defendant class in *Kaye* v. *Mount La Jolla Homeowners Ass'n*, which comprised the members of a condominium homeowners' association, failed certification. The court held the class certification to be superfluous because the homeowners' association already had adequate insurance to cover the compensatory damages the plaintiff claimed. (*Kaye* v. *Mount La Jolla Homeowners Ass'n* (1988) 204 Cal.App.3d 1476 [252 Cal.Rptr. 67].)

[I] Escrow Practices

Macmanus v. *A.E. Realty Partners* was a Cartwright Act antitrust matter alleging an unlawful tying of escrow services to real estate sales. (*Macmanus* v. *A.E. Realty Partners* (1987) 195 Cal.App.3d 1106 [241 Cal.Rptr. 315].)

[J] Title Insurance Practices

In *Bell* v. *American Title Ins. Co.* (1991) 226 Cal.App.3d 1589 [277 Cal.Rptr. 583], the class comprised California property owners who defaulted on property-secured loans. When class members reinstated or redeemed their loans, they were required to buy a title insurance policy called a trustee's sale guarantee aimed at preventing nonjudicial foreclosure. The plaintiffs alleged this practice was a conspiracy violative of the Cartwright Act and Business and Professions Code section 17200. The settlement involved a price discount and other benefits for the class, and it serves as a rare example of a non–opt-out class settlement. (*Bell* v. *American Title Ins. Co.* (1991) 226 Cal.App.3d 1589 [277 Cal.Rptr. 583].)

§ 12.10 Government Benefits and Taxes

Green v. *Obledo* involved a class of recipients of Aid to Families with Dependent Children challenging the Department of Benefit Payments for its limitation on expenses attributable to earnings. (*Green* v. *Obledo* (1981) 29 Cal.3d 126 [172 Cal.Rptr. 206, 624 P.2d 256].)

Rose v. *City of Hayward* successfully challenged on a class basis the computation of retirement benefits, including certain fringe benefits and a salary base. (*Rose* v. *City of Hayward* (1981) 126 Cal.App.3d 926 [179 Cal.Rptr. 287].)

Bingham v. *Obledo* challenged participation in a California program as a required qualification for federal Medicaid eligibility because the program failed to provide necessary transportation for recipients. (*Bingham* v. *Obledo* (1983) 147 Cal.App.3d 401 [195 Cal.Rptr. 142].)

Reyes v. *Board of Supervisors* challenged the county's practice of depriving general relief recipients of benefits if they did not comply with work project rules. The plaintiffs prevailed because the county failed to distinguish between willful and nonwillful violators. (*Reyes* v. *Board of Supervisors* (1987) 196 Cal.App.3d 1263 [242 Cal.Rptr. 339].)

Gardner v. *County of Los Angeles* was brought by county residents to enjoin the county from subtracting general assistance cash grants from the amounts the county spends on indigent health care. (*Gardner* v. *County of Los Angeles* (1995) 34 Cal.App.4th 200 [40 Cal.Rptr.2d 271].)

Keith G. v. *Bilbray* concerned a class of juveniles held in pretrial detention at county juvenile hall. Plaintiffs asserted violations of their due process rights relating to crowding, staffing, mental health care, and postdisposition treatment. (*Keith G.* v. *Bilbray* (1995) 36 Cal.App.4th 1587 [43 Cal.Rptr.2d 277].)

Farrar v. *Franchise Tax Bd* was governed by recently enacted changes to the Franchise Tax Code requiring opt-in in tax refund cases. The court found a distinction between the normal class action remedies and their equitable provisions, and it deferred to the express statutes governing refunds in tax cases. Specifically, the terms of Revenue and Taxation Code section 19055 provide that where an administrative claim for refund of income taxes is made on behalf of a class of taxpayers, it must be accompanied by a written authorization signed by each taxpayer stating the specific grounds on which the claim is founded. The court found that this "specific legislative displacement" authorized the handling of a tax-refund class action in a way contrary to normal class action practice, which includes the "opt out" mechanism. (*Farrar* v. *Franchise Tax Bd.* (1993) 15 Cal.App.4th 10 [18 Cal.Rptr.2d 611].)

Miller v. *Woods* involved a class of beneficiaries receiving disability benefits. This case overruled a denial of class certification based upon the trial court's "hope and expectation" that the defendants would remedy their conduct. Accordingly, such grounds are inappropriate for denying class certification. (*Miller* v. *Woods* (1983) 148 Cal.App.3d 862 [196 Cal.Rptr. 69].)

§ 12.11 Medical Treatment

Brown v. *Regents of the University of California* alleged malpractice action in the level of coronary care afforded patients. Certification was denied because individual issues relating to reliance, informed consent, causation, and damages predominated over common questions. (*Brown* v. *Regents of the University of California* (1984) 151 Cal.App.3d 982 [198 Cal.Rptr. 916].)

Rose v. *Medtronics, Inc.* mounted a personal injury action on behalf of an alleged class of 4,000 individuals whose pacemakers had been replaced. The defendant was the manufacturer of the defective devices. The court found the action singularly ill-suited for class action because the factual questions and legal issues were preponderantly diverse rather than common. (*Rose* v. *Medtronics, Inc.* (1980) 107 Cal.App.3d 150 [166 Cal.Rptr. 16].)

Jolly v. *Eli Lilly & Co* was a pharmaceutical defect product liability matter filed as a class action. It did not toll the statute because the defendant received no notice. (*Jolly* v. *Eli Lilly & Co.* (1988) 44 Cal.3d 1103 [245 Cal.Rptr. 658, 751 P.2d 923].)

§ 12.12 Ticketholders

Weaver v. *Pasadena Tournament of Roses* held that ticketholders' individual issues arising from the marketing of Rose Bowl tickets were too diverse for the factual nexus class action requires. (*Weaver* v. *Pasadena Tournament of Roses* (1948) 32 Cal.2d 833 [198 P.2d 514].)

Baltimore Football Club, Inc. v. *Superior Court*, a ticketholder action involving class members in a number of states, failed certification because varying state law precluded group analysis. (*Baltimore Football Club, Inc.* v. *Superior Court* (1985) 171 Cal.App.3d 352 [215 Cal.Rptr. 323].)

§ 12.13 Employee-Employer

Atari, Inc. v. *Superior Court* involved a class action in which the employee class members alleged that they were assured there would be no mass layoffs. *Atari* also helped define precertification standards by authorizing court-approved precertification notices. (*Atari, Inc.* v. *Superior Court* (1985) 166 Cal.App.3d 867 [212 Cal.Rptr. 773].)

Frazier v. *City of Richmond* involved a class action on behalf of all current and retired police officers and firefighters for the City of Richmond. The class alleged entitlement to pension benefits and an error in the calculation of retirement benefits. Though the class had not received notice, a prior action on similar grounds precluded much of the relief sought. (*Frazier* v. *City of Richmond* (1986) 184 Cal.App.3d 1491 [228 Cal.Rptr. 376].)

§ 12.14 Rental Cars

Lazar v. *Hertz Corporation* involved a customer who challenged the rental car company's policy of charging for gasoline when the car was returned with less than a full tank. The court of appeal overruled the denial of class certification. (*Lazar* v. *Hertz Corporation* (1983) 143 Cal.App.3d 128 [191 Cal.Rptr. 849].)

Stephen v. *Enterprise Rent-A-Car* centered on plaintiff's attack of the collision damage waiver (CDW) in rental contracts. The plaintiff alleged the rates charged for this risk allocation option were unconscionably high. In a series of preliminary pretrial class certification hearings in which the parties offered and objected to evidence, the court of appeal subsequently ruled that the "death knell doctrine" barred the plaintiff's ability to appeal. (*Stephen* v. *Enterprise Rent-A-Car* (1991) 235 Cal.App.3d 806 [1 Cal.Rptr.2d 130].)

§ 12.15 References

TRG **THE RUTTER GROUP** See the following sections in California Practice Guide: Civil Procedure Before Trial (CPBT) regarding different types of class actions:

- Individual issues affecting each class member (CPBT, §§ 14:28–14:39.10).

WEST'S KEY NUMBER SYSTEM See the following Key Numbers in West's California Digest 2d, Federal Civil Procedure (Topic 170A):

- Particular classes represented (Federal Civil Procedure ⚷ 181–189).

See also Parties (Topic 287):

- Particular classes represented (Parties ⚷ 35.61–35.89).

WESTLAW® See the WESTLAW Electronic Research Guide at the beginning of this volume.

APPENDIX

Relevant Federal and State Statutes and Rules

Contents

Federal Rules of Civil Procedure, rule 23 . . . . APP-2

California Civil Code section 1781 . . . . APP-4

California Code of Civil Procedure section 382 . . . . APP-4

Los Angeles County Superior Court Rules, Chapter 15, Class Actions APP-5

San Diego County Superior Court Rules, Class Action Rules APP-18

San Francisco County Superior Court Rules, Class Actions Manual APP-20

San Mateo County Superior Court Rules, Pretrial Proceedings in Class Action . APP-39

Federal Rules of Civil Procedure

RULE 23. CLASS ACTIONS

(a) Prerequisites to a Class Action. One or more members of a class may sue or be sued as representative parties on behalf of all only if (1) the class is so numerous that joinder of all members is impracticable, (2) there are questions of law or fact common to the class, (3) the claims or defenses of the representative parties are typical of the claims or defenses of the class, and (4) the representative parties will fairly and adequately protect the interests of the class.

(b) Class Actions Maintainable. An action may be maintained as a class action if the prerequisites of subdivision (a) are satisfied, and in addition:

(1) the prosecution of separate actions by or against individual members of the class would create a risk of (A) inconsistent or varying adjudications with respect to individual members of the class which would establish incompatible standards of conduct for the party opposing the class, or (B) adjudications with respect to individual members of the class which would as a practical matter be dispositive of the interests of the other members not parties to the adjudications or substantially impair or impede their ability to protect their interests; or

(2) the party opposing the class has acted or refused to act on grounds generally applicable to the class, thereby making appropriate final injunctive relief or corresponding declaratory relief with respect to the class as a whole; or

(3)the court finds that the questions of law or fact common to the members of the class predominate over any questions affecting only individual members, and that a class action is superior to other available methods for the fair and efficient adjudication of the controversy. The matters pertinent to the findings include: (A) the interest of members of the class in individually controlling the prosecution or defense of separate actions; (B) the extent and nature of any litigation concerning the controversy already commenced by or against members of the class; (C) the desirability or undesirability of concentrating the litigation of the claims in the particular forum; (D) the difficulties likely to be encountered in the management of a class action.

(c) Determination by Order Whether Class Action to be Maintained; Notice; Judgment; Actions Conducted Partially as Class Actions.

(1) As soon as practicable after the commencement of an action brought as a class action, the court shall determine by order whether it is to be so maintained. An order under this subdivision may be conditional, and may be altered or amended before the decision on the merits.

(2) In any class action maintained under subdivision (b)(3), the court shall direct to the members of the class the best notice practicable under the circumstances, including individual notice to all members who can be identified through reasonable effort. The notice shall advise each member that (A) the court will exclude the member from the class if the member so requests by a specified date; (B) the judgment, whether favorable or not, will include all members who do not request exclusion; and (C) any member who does not request exclusion may, if the member desires, enter an appearance through counsel.

(3) The judgment in an action maintained as a class action under subdivision (b)(1) or (b)(2), whether or not favorable to the class, shall include and describe those whom the court finds to be members of the class. The judgment in an action maintained as a class action under subdivision (b)(3), whether or not favorable to the class, shall include and specify or describe those to whom the notice provided in subdivision (c)(2) was directed, and who have not requested exclusion, and whom the court finds to be members of the class.

(4) When appropriate (A) an action may be brought or maintained as a class action with respect to particular issues, or (B) a class may be divided into subclasses and each subclass treated as a class, and the provisions of this

rule shall then be construed and applied accordingly.

(d) Orders in Conduct of Actions. In the conduct of actions to which this rule applies, the court may make appropriate orders: (1) determining the course of proceedings or prescribing measures to prevent undue repetition or complication in the presentation of evidence or argument; (2) requiring, for the protection of the members of the class or otherwise for the fair conduct of the action, that notice be given in such manner as the court may direct to some or all of the members of any step in the action, or of the proposed extent of the judgment, or of the opportunity of members to signify whether they consider the representation fair and adequate, to intervene and present claims or defenses, or otherwise to come into the action; (3) imposing conditions on the representative parties or on intervenors; (4) requiring that the pleadings be amended to eliminate therefrom allegations as to representation of absent persons, and that the action proceed accordingly; (5) dealing with similar procedural matters. The orders may be combined with an order under Rule 16, and may be altered or amended as may be desirable from time to time.

(e) Dismissal or Compromise. A class action shall not be dismissed or compromised without the approval of the court, and notice of the proposed dismissal or compromise shall be given to all members of the class in such manner as the court directs.

California Civil Code

§ 1781. Consumer's Class Action; Conditions; Notices; Judgment

(a) Any consumer entitled to bring an action under Section 1780 may, if the unlawful method, act, or practice has caused damage to other consumers similarly situated, bring an action on behalf of himself and such other consumers to recover damages or obtain other relief as provided for in Section 1780.

(b) The court shall permit the suit to be maintained on behalf of all members of the represented class if all of the following conditions exist: (1) It is impracticable to bring all members of the class before the court. (2) The questions of law or fact common to the class are substantially similar and predominate over the questions affecting the individual members. (3) The claims or defenses of the representative plaintiffs are typical of the claims or defenses of the class. (4) The representative plaintiffs will fairly and adequately protect the interests of the class.

(c) If notice of the time and place of the hearing is served upon the other parties at least 10 days prior thereto, the court shall hold a hearing, upon motion of any party to the action which is supported by affidavit of any person or persons having knowledge of the facts, to determine if any of the following apply to the action:

(1) A class action pursuant to subdivision (b) is proper.

(2) Published notice pursuant to subdivision (d) is necessary to adjudicate the claims of the class.

(3) The action is without merit or there is no defense to the action. A motion based upon Section 437c of the Code of Civil Procedure shall not be granted in any action commenced as a class action pursuant to subdivision (a).

(d) If the action is permitted as a class action, the court may direct either party to notify each member of the class of the action. The party required to serve notice may, with the consent of the court, if personal notification is unreasonably expensive or it appears that all members of the class cannot be notified personally, give notice as prescribed herein by publication in accordance with Section 6064 of the Government Code in a newspaper of general circulation in the county in which the transaction occurred.

(e) The notice required by subdivision (d) shall include the following:

(1) The court will exclude the member notified from the class if he so requests by a specified date.

(2) The judgment, whether favorable or not, will include all members who do not request exclusion.

(3) Any member who does not request exclusion, may, if he desires, enter an appearance through counsel.

(f) A class action shall not be dismissed, settled, or compromised without the approval of the court, and notice of the proposed dismissal, settlement, or compromise shall be given in such manner as the court directs to each member who was given notice pursuant to subdivision (d) and did not request exclusion.

(g) The judgment in a class action shall describe those to whom the notice was directed and who have not requested exclusion and those the court finds to be members of the class. The best possible notice of the judgment shall be given in such manner as the court directs to each member who was personally served with notice pursuant to subdivision (d) and did not request exclusion.

California Code of Civil Procedure

§ 382. Nonconsent to Joinder as Plaintiff; Representative Actions

If the consent of any one who should have been joined as plaintiff cannot be obtained, he may be made a defendant, the reason thereof being stated in the complaint; and when the question is one of a common or general interest, of many persons, or when the parties are numerous, and it is impracticable to bring them all before the court, one or more may sue or defend for the benefit of all.

LOS ANGELES COUNTY SUPERIOR COURT RULES

Effective January 1, 1994
Including Amendments Effective
January 1, 1997

Chapter Fifteen. Class Actions

15.0 Purpose of Rules.
15.1 Class Actions in the Central District Only.
15.2 Class Action Designation on Complaint.
15.3 Relief From Compliance With Class Action Rules.

INFORMAL CONFERENCE ON CLASS ISSUES

15.4 Nature of Conference.
15.5 Time and Place of Conference; Notice Thereof.
15.6 Conference on Motion of Named Party; Form Thereof.
15.7 Conference on Order of the Court.
15.8 Conference Order.

PRETRIAL MOTIONS FOR CLASS CERTIFICATION

15.9 Nature of Hearing.
15.10 Scheduling Hearing.
15.11 Submission of Memoranda of Points and Authorities.
15.12 Form of Documents.
15.13 Notice to Public Entity, Official, Employee Class Member.
15.14 Notice to Attorney General.
15.15 Continuance of Hearing.
15.16 Change in Time to Submit Documents.
15.17 Conduct of Hearing.
- (a) Use of Declarations.
- (b) Judicially Noticed Matters.
- (c) Discovered Evidence.
- (d) Discovery After Notice of Hearing.
- (e) Oral Testimony.
- (f) Burden of Proof in the Hearing.
- (g) Irrelevant and Unnoticed Issues.

15.18 Issues; Documents for Presentation.
- (a) Constitution of the Class.
- (b) Common, Similar and Unique Questions of Law and Fact.
- (c) Superiority of the Class Action to Other Available Methods for the Fair and Efficient Adjudication of the Controversy.
- (d) Membership of the Class Representative in the Class.
- (e) Ability of the Class Representative to Protect Fairly and Adequately the Interests of the Class.
- (f) Necessity for and Content of Notice of Class Certification.
- (g) Order Dispensing With Notice of Class Certification.

ADDITIONAL ISSUES

15.19 Consolidation, Severance, Abatement or Coordination.
15.20 Bifurcation.
15.21 Abuse of Class Action.
15.22 Intervention.
15.23 Joinder of a Class Member.
15.24 Precedence of Discovery.
15.25 Summary Judgment.

ORDERS

15.26 Order Determining Class Issues.
15.27 Order Requiring Additional Hearing.
15.28 Order Upon Stipulation.
15.29 Order Concerning Nature of Recovery.
15.30 Order Upon Other Class Matters.
15.31 Order Upon Nonappearance.
15.32 Order Superseding Pleadings.
15.33 Relationship of the Interlocutory (Pretrial) Order to Trial of the Class Issues.
15.34 Notice of Order.
15.35 Stipulations for an Order.

EARLY TRIAL OF BIFURCATED ISSUES

15.36 Motion for Early Trial of a Bifurcated Issue.
15.37 Procedure for Notice and Presentation of Motion.
15.38 Time for Trial.
15.39 Order After Early Trial.
15.40 Pretrial Proceedings in Class Actions.

SETTLEMENT HEARINGS AND JUDGMENTS

15.41 Nature of Class Action Settlement Hearings.

15.42 Motion for Settlement Hearing.
15.43 Place and Time of Hearing the Motion.
15.44 Order for Settlement Hearing.
15.45 Conduct of Settlement Hearings.
(a) Procedure.
(b) Attorney's Fees.
15.46 Judgment.

DISMISSALS

15.47 Court Approval.
15.48 Dismissal Procedure.
15.49 Court Approval or Disapproval.

Chapter Fifteen. Class Actions

RULE 15.0 PURPOSE OF RULES

These rules set out the scheduling and conduct of pretrial proceedings which will be held in every class action pending in Los Angeles Superior Court.

Adopted, eff. Jan. 1, 1995. As amended, eff. March 1, 1996.

RULE 15.1 CLASS ACTIONS IN THE CENTRAL DISTRICT ONLY

All class actions shall be filed in the Central District (see LASCR, rules 2.0(b) and 2.5(j)). Pretrial proceedings in class actions are assigned to Department 59, in the Central District. Hearings may be noticed for Department 59 only after the date and time of hearing have been cleared by the clerk of said department.

Adopted, eff. Jan. 1, 1995.

RULE 15.2 CLASS ACTION DESIGNATION ON COMPLAINT

All complaints for or against a class party will include in the caption the designation CLASS ACTION. This designation will appear, typewritten in capital letters on a line having no other words, on the first page of the complaint immediately below that space reserved for the County Clerk's file number stamp but above the title or description of the nature of the complaint (e.g., Complaint for Damages for Breach of Contract, etc.).

If the answer or a cross-complaint is the first pleading to allege a class, the rules set out herein shall apply as if said pleading were the complaint and the pleader were the plaintiff.

Adopted, eff. Jan. 1, 1995.

RULE 15.3 RELIEF FROM COMPLIANCE WITH CLASS ACTION RULES

Any named party may make a motion to have all parties relieved from compliance with the class action rules on the ground that the pending case does not involve a class action of the nature contemplated by Code of Civil Procedure § 382, Civil Code §§ 1750 et seq., or Federal Rules of Civil Procedure § 23(b)(3). Actions brought by a taxpayer under Code of Civil Procedure section 526(a) or by an association as the representative of its members will be excused from compliance with these class action rules.

The notice of hearing shall be filed with the clerk in Department 59 (Class Action Department) and should notice the hearing for a date and time previously obtained from the clerk of said department.

If a motion for relief from compliance with class action rules is granted, all pretrial proceedings and trial shall thereafter be heard in the trial department to which the case would otherwise have been assigned pursuant to the Los Angeles Superior Court local rules.

Adopted, eff. Jan. 1, 1995.

INFORMAL CONFERENCE ON CLASS ISSUES

RULE 15.4 NATURE OF CONFERENCE

One or more informal conferences may be held in chambers or open court between the court and counsel for every party to the action. At said conference, the parties will discuss class issues, establishment of precedence of discovery, the scheduling of hearings, or any other matters concerning pretrial determination of class issues. No evidence will be presented at the informal conference, but all parties in attendance shall have sufficient knowledge of class issues to discuss proposed stipulations for resolution thereof.

Adopted, eff. Jan. 1, 1995.

RULE 15.5 TIME AND PLACE OF CONFERENCE; NOTICE THEREOF

The notice of the conference shall be filed with the clerk in Department 59 (Class Action Department) and should notice the conference for a date and time previously obtained from the clerk of said department.

Notice of the conference may be given, notwithstanding the fact that notice of motion for class certification has already been given. If said notice is given by plaintiff, it must be served on all named defendants in the action. If notice is given by a defendant or the court, it will be served on only the parties who have appeared; however, within ten (10) days after receipt of said notice, plaintiff will serve a copy thereof on each named defendant who has not appeared in the action and will submit a declaration of said service. In the event that plaintiff is unable to effect service upon any defendant, as aforesaid, plaintiff will submit a declaration stating the reasons for failing to serve said defendant.

Adopted, eff. Jan. 1, 1995.

RULE 15.6 CONFERENCE ON MOTION OF NAMED PARTY; FORM THEREOF

The conference may be scheduled through notice given by plaintiff or any named party who has submitted an answer in the action. A conference may not be noticed by a class member who was not specifically named as a party.

The notice must be in writing and must designate those topics which counsel expects to discuss at the conference (e.g., order of discovery, stipulation concerning certain issues, etc.). The notice may but need not be supported by documents. The notice will be served and filed at least twenty (20) days before the scheduled time of the conference.

Adopted, eff. Jan. 1, 1995.

RULE 15.7 CONFERENCE ON ORDER OF THE COURT

The court may schedule a conference, notice of which will be served on all parties who have appeared. Said notice must be in writing and must designate those topics which the court expects counsel to discuss at the conference. The notice will be served and filed at least twenty (20) days before the scheduled time of the conference.

Adopted, eff. Jan. 1, 1995.

RULE 15.8 CONFERENCE ORDER

At the conclusion of the conference, the court shall make an order to embrace the stipulations, if any, of the parties. Until modified or terminated by the court, the conference order will be binding upon all parties to the action. The court may order the conduct of an additional conference upon all or certain of the class issues. The conference order will not be used to resolve any class issues in dispute.

Adopted, eff. Jan. 1, 1995.

PRETRIAL MOTIONS FOR CLASS CERTIFICATION

RULE 15.9 NATURE OF HEARING

In each class action brought under Code of Civil Procedure section 382 or Civil Code section 1750 et seq., in which either the plaintiff or the defendant is a class, a motion for class certification may be submitted within 60 days after a defendant has filed an answer; said defendant then may submit a motion relating to class certification. If said motion is made by plaintiff, it must be served on all named parties in the action. If said motion is made by a defendant, it must be served on only those parties who have appeared; however, within ten days after receipt of notice of said motion, plaintiff must serve a copy thereof on each named defendant who has not appeared in the action, and shall submit a declaration of said service. In the event that plaintiff is unable to effect service of any defendant, as aforesaid, plaintiff will submit a declaration stating the reasons for failing to serve said defendant.

Adopted, eff. Jan. 1, 1995.

RULE 15.10 SCHEDULING HEARING

The hearing will be noticed not less than 60 days or more than 75 days after the serving of notice of motion for class certification. Each responding party may submit documents on or within 45 days after service upon said party of the notice of hearing. The moving party may submit rebuttal documents on or before five days after service upon said party of the responding documents. These rebuttal documents will present no new evidentiary facts.

The notice of hearing shall be filed with the clerk in Department 59 (Class Action Department) and should notice the hearing for a date and time previously obtained from the clerk of said department.

The moving party will submit with the notice of hearing, documents supporting moving party's position on each issue to be presented in said hearing. All facts other than purely rebuttal matters upon which the moving party will rely in the hearing must be set out in declarations submitted with the notice of motion for class certification.

All documents filed by either party after the notice of hearing has been submitted will be filed directly with the clerk in the department for which the hearing has been noticed. It is the responsibility of each counsel to ascertain that all documents filed by said counsel have reached Department 59 prior to the hearing.

Adopted, eff. Jan. 1, 1995.

RULE 15.11 SUBMISSION OF MEMORANDA OF POINTS AND AUTHORITIES

In all hearings, all parties will submit, in addition to those documents specifically described elsewhere in these rules, memoranda of points and authorities citing and discussing relevant authority upon each issue presented in each hearing. Decisional authority under Code of Civil Procedure section 382, Civil Code sections 1750 et seq., and Federal Rules of Civil Procedure section 23 should be cited by counsel. Counsel are invited to cite and argue additional relevant authorities. Citation of California cases must be by reference to the Official Reports and should indicate volume number, the first page of the case and the specific page or pages on which the pertinent matter appears in the Official Reports, and the year of decision. If a party cites a case from another jurisdiction, said party shall attach to the memorandum a photocopy of said case. The memorandum should not merely cite an authority, but shall explain its relevance to the point for which it is cited. Citation of these rules shall include the paragraph number. Memoranda of points and authorities shall be preceded by an index setting out each case, statute, and treatise cited, keyed to the page on which such citation[s] may be located. Multiple documents submitted under one blue-back cover shall be tabbed for easy reference.

Adopted, eff. Jan. 1, 1995.

RULE 15.12 FORM OF DOCUMENTS

All documents submitted in hearings must conform with California Rules of Court and Rule 9.2 et seq., of Los Angeles County Superior Court Local Rules.

Adopted, eff. Jan. 1, 1995.

RULE 15.13 NOTICE TO PUBLIC ENTITY, OFFICIAL, EMPLOYEE CLASS MEMBER

When a public entity or a public official or public employee in his official capacity is an unnamed member of the plaintiff or defendant class, notice of the pendency of said class action shall be given to said public entity or public official or public employee. Said notice shall be served in the same manner as a civil summons is served.

Adopted, eff. Jan. 1, 1995.

RULE 15.14 NOTICE TO ATTORNEY GENERAL

If the action seeks relief of any nature, other than solely for money damages, for alleged pollution or adverse environmental effects which could affect the public generally, the notice of motion re class certification and a copy of all documents relating thereto, submitted by any party, shall be served on the Attorney General of the State of California irrespective of whether the Attorney General is a named party (Code Civ. Proc., § 389.6). The court may direct that notice be given to the Attorney General in other actions.

Adopted, eff. Jan. 1, 1995.

RULE 15.15 CONTINUANCE OF HEARING

Continuance of a hearing may not be made unilaterally except upon motion noticed and granted. However, a continuance to a date certain, or removal of the hearing from calendar, may be made by stipulation with the approval of the court. The date to which the hearing may be continued by stipulation must be approved by the court, through advice by the clerk of available dates.

Adopted, eff. Jan. 1, 1995.

RULE 15.16 CHANGE IN TIME TO SUBMIT DOCUMENTS

On motion by a party noticed for hearing before that party's time to submit documents expires, the court may order the documents to be submitted at a time different from that set out herein. Said motion for change in the time scheduled for submission of documents must be supported by a declaration setting out evidentiary facts showing good cause for the change.

Adopted, eff. Jan. 1, 1995.

RULE 15.17 CONDUCT OF HEARING

(a) Use of Declarations. Presentation of evidence in the hearing will be through declarations submitted and previously discovered evidence. Counsel shall attempt to resolve by stipulation, before hearing, as many class issues as possible.

(b) Judicially Noticed Matters. Either party in its moving or responding documents may request that the court take judicial notice of certain matters pursuant to Evidence Code §§ 451 et seq. It is the responsibility of the party who makes the request concerning those items described in Evidence Code § 452 to furnish the court with legible copies of the matters referred to therein.

(c) Discovered Evidence. Either party in its moving or responding documents may request that the court consider particular discovered evidence in the case file (depositions, answers to interrogatories, admissions, etc.). All references to discovered evidence will be to line and page thereof. It is the duty of the party who refers to matters in a deposition to lodge the deposition in court before the hearing. Opposing counsel in responding documents may raise objections, based upon the rules governing admissibility of evidence, to consideration by the court of said evidence. Before considering said requested discovered evidence, the court will rule on each objection thereto.

(d) Discovery After Notice of Hearing. The party who notices a hearing for class certification must complete all discovery upon which it intends to rely prior to the submission of the notice of hearing. Said moving party will not be entitled to conduct discovery during the period between the notice of hearing and the hearing, except upon leave of court.

(e) Oral Testimony. Oral testimony will not be received in the hearing except upon leave of the court after counsel has made an adequate evidentiary showing of his inability to present evidence through declaration, or earlier use of discovery procedure, and has presented good cause for consideration by the court of such oral testimony.

(f) Burden of Proof in the Hearing. The burden of proof on all class issues is on the party alleging the existence of a class. All issues of fact will be proved by a preponderance of the evidence presented in the hearing.

(g) Irrelevant and Unnoticed Issues. The court will not hear evidence or argument on any matter irrelevant to the class action issues or on any issue which is not included in the notice of motion. *Counsel shall not argue orally or in writing the merits of the lawsuit at a hearing of a motion for class certification.*

Adopted, eff. Jan. 1, 1995.

RULE 15.18 ISSUES; DOCUMENTS FOR PRESENTATION

(a) Constitution of the Class. The party alleging existence of a class shall submit one or more declarations which present facts describing in detail the composition of the class. The facts submitted in such a declaration must be legally admissible evidence. Such declaration[s] shall contain the following facts:

(1) The approximate number of persons in the class. If there are subclasses, the declaration shall also describe each and set out the approximate number of persons in each subclass;

(2) The general geographic location[s] of the class members. If the class is not confined to the state of California, the description shall include those locations outside California where class members are located;

(3) A description of the status of the class members where relevant to the action;

(4) A description of the members of each subclass between whom issues of law or fact must be litigated;

(5) A description of those class members, including an estimate of their number, whose claims must be approved or evidence presented only as to each individual member;

(6) The manner in which and the time when the individual class members will be identified if such identification is contemplated;

(7) Other relevant matters: If the declarations demonstrate that the class is interstate, the party maintaining the action will submit a memorandum on the subject of whether the Superior Court of Los Angeles County has jurisdiction to render a binding judgment in favor of, or against, nonresident, unserved class members.

(b) Common, Similar and Unique Questions of Law and Fact. Each party will submit a statement discussing each of the following:

(1) Those issues of law which are common to all class members;

(2) Those issues of law which are similar to all class members and, with respect to each such issue, a detailed statement concerning how said issues may be determined on other than an individual basis;

(3) Those issues of law which are unique to one or more class members, but which must be presented in the trial. In the description of these unique issues of law, the segments of the class to which they are applicable will be described with a statement of the number within the class to whom each unique issue applies;

(4) The issues of law which must be litigated between class members;

(5) Those issues of fact which are common to all class members;

(6) Those issues of fact which are similar to all class members, with a detailed statement concerning how each such issue can be determined other than on an individual basis;

(7) Those issues of fact which are unique to one or more class members but which must be presented in the trial. In the description of these unique issues of fact, the segments of the class to which they are applicable will be described with a statement of the number within the class to whom each unique issue applies;

(8) The issues of fact which must be litigated between class members.

Each party will also submit a memorandum discussing whether issues of law and fact which are common to all members of the class, or, if not common, are similar and susceptible to proof by evidence applicable to all members of the class, predominate over issues which must be tried on an individual basis. These memoranda will set out an estimate of the number of witnesses and the time for their testimony upon issues which exist only as to individual class members, or subclasses, including issues which must be litigated between class members.

(c) Superiority of the Class Action to Other Available Methods for the Fair and Efficient Adjudication of the Controversy. Each party will submit statements concerning:

(1) Procedures alternative to a class action which might be utilized to adjudicate the issues involved in the action. Such a statement will include an estimate of the time of trial of each alternative procedure;

(2) The effectiveness of the remedies available under the alternatives described compared to those available under the class action modality;

(3) The ability of the court to manage the alternative proceedings in relation to its ability to manage the conduct of the class action;

(4) The benefit to the public from each alternative proceeding;

(5)The propriety of relief other than money damages;

(6) A description of other actions purporting to be brought on behalf of the same class, raising the same or similar issues, and a statement of the reasons the instant action should be allowed to proceed parallel to the others, or be abated or dismissed;

(7) If the action purports to be brought on behalf of a class which includes residents of states other than the State of California, a statement as to whether, aside from jurisdictional limitations, the court should limit the class to residents of the State of California for reasons of public policy and manageability.

(d) Membership of the Class Representative in the Class. The class representative will submit one or more declarations, containing legally admissible evidence, with respect to the following matters:

(1) If membership in the class is dependent upon having participated in a transaction or series thereof, a description of each particular transaction which evidences when and in what manner the representative became a member of the class;

(2) If membership in the class is dependent upon ownership of property, membership in an organization or other status at the time of filing of the action, a description of each fact by which the representative acquired said status which made him or her a member of the class. The class representative will also set out facts evidencing continuation of the status of a class member;

(3) Factual differences, if any, in the representative's status as a class member and those of any other persons within the class. If there are subclasses, a factual statement of the subclass of which the representative is a member;

(4) Legal differences, if any, in the representative's status as a class member and those of any other persons within the class;

(5) Unique legal and/or factual issues, if any, pertaining to the representative which must be litigated.

(e) Ability of the Class Representative to Protect Fairly and Adequately the Interests of the Class. As a fiduciary of the class members (*LaSala v. American Savings and Loan Assn.* (1971) 5 Cal.3d 864, 97 Cal.Rptr. 849, 489 P.2d 1113), the class representative shall, at all times during the pendency of the litigation, make known to the court his or her relationship to the class members, including those conflicts with, or differences in, their positions. The class representative shall submit one or more declarations describing, in detail, the following:

(1) The amount of damages which the representative estimates will be awarded to the class and his or her share thereof, or, if the class is a defendant class, the total damages which may be suffered by the class and the representative's share thereof;

(2) Other class actions to which the representative or his or her spouse has been, or now is, a named party. The description of these include case name, court designation and number, the nature of the controversy, its outcome, and the representative's (or spouse's) status therein as a class representative or as a named party. If there remains an unsatisfied judgment or court costs from prior litigation, the representative should set out the amounts thereof and the reason for failure to have paid them.

(f) Necessity for and Content of Notice of Class Certification. If the court rules favorably on the motion for class certification, a status conference shall be set at which the court may review the proposed notice to class members. Counsel for the parties shall meet and confer with respect to the content of the proposed notice to members of the class prior to the hearing of said status conference.

At the status conference, the moving party shall submit the following:

(1) Original and copy of proposed order approving notice to the class;

(2) Original and copy of proposed notice to the class of pendency of class action;

(3) A statement on each of the following:

(a) Time when notice should be given;

(b) The manner in which notice will be given. This will include a discussion concerning whether said notice should be published, mailed, or otherwise brought to the attention of class members. If recommended to be published, it will include the recommended publication media, including an estimate of the cost thereof. If recommended to be mailed, it will include a statement of the manner in which addresses of the class members will be obtained and an estimate of the cost of preparation of the notice and of said mailing. If notice is to be given through other means, a description of said other means will be set out in detail, including an estimate of the cost. Each estimate of costs will contain a statement of the factual basis thereof. Such statement also will include an estimate, with the factual basis therefor, of the percentage of the class members which the party believes will receive knowledge of the pending action through use of each notice modality;

(c) The party who should bear the cost of giving the notice or the manner in which the cost thereof should be divided between the parties.

(4) Each proposed notice will include, at least, a representation concerning each of the following matters:

(a) A brief explanation of the case, including basic contentions or denials of the parties;

(b) A statement that any member of the class who so requests by a specified date, may exclude himself or herself from the class and the action by giving notice thereof ("opting out");

(c) Information concerning how class members who desire to be excluded from the class ("opt out") may give notice thereof;

(d) A statement that the claim of a member who does not request to be excluded from the class will be terminated by the judgment in the action under the rule of res judicata;

(e) A statement that any member who does not request exclusion may move the court for permission to appear as a named class co-representative;

(f) The estimated total amount of the recovery, the anticipated fee which will be sought by counsel for the class, the anticipated other expenses and costs to the class which will be paid from the funds recovered before distribution of the net proceeds to class members, and the net amount to be recovered by each member if the action is successful (a formula statement will be satisfactory).

(g) Order Dispensing With Notice of Class Certification. Although, as a general rule, notice to the class of the pendency of the action shall be ordered, notice to the class is not necessary in all actions, e.g., an action seeking injunctive relief, without a claim for damages. An order may be made, on motion of a party, supported by declaration and points and authorities, dispensing with the requirement that the class be notified of the action. When a public entity or a public officer or public employee in his official capacity is an unnamed member of the plaintiff or defendant class, notice of the motion to dispense with the requirement that the class be notified of the action must be served on said public entity, public officer, or employee in the same manner as a civil summons is served.

Adopted, eff. Jan. 1, 1995.

ADDITIONAL ISSUES

RULE 15.19 CONSOLIDATION, SEVERANCE, ABATEMENT OR COORDINATION

A motion to consolidate with, or sever from, one or more other pending actions, to abate the instant action until certain other pending actions have proceeded to judgment, and similar motions based on the similarity of issues with those in other pending actions, may be made. Motions to coordinate with other pending actions pursuant to Code of Civil Procedure section 404 et seq. are not made in Department 59, but are made as provided in said sections.

Adopted, eff. Jan. 1, 1995.

RULE 15.20 BIFURCATION

A motion to bifurcate trial of the issue of liability of the defendant from trial on class issues may be made.

Adopted, eff. Jan. 1, 1995.

RULE 15.21 ABUSE OF CLASS ACTION

Motions to restrict or regulate contact of named parties or counsel with the class, shall be set in the class action department.

Adopted, eff. Jan. 1, 1995.

RULE 15.22 INTERVENTION

A motion to intervene pursuant to Code of Civil Procedure section 387 by a person who has earlier excluded himself or herself from the class ("opted out") shall be heard in the class action department.

Adopted, eff. Jan. 1, 1995.

RULE 15.23 JOINDER OF A CLASS MEMBER

A class member may move that he or she be made a co-representative, and that, as such, be allowed to associate additional counsel to represent the class.

Adopted, eff. Jan. 1, 1995.

RULE 15.24 PRECEDENCE OF DISCOVERY

A motion to establish a precedence among issues in discovery, including a motion limiting discovery to class issues until an interlocutory order is made concerning such issues, shall be heard in the class action department.

Adopted, eff. Jan. 1, 1995.

RULE 15.25 SUMMARY JUDGMENT

All motions for total or partial summary judgment or adjudication of issues under Code of Civil Procedure section 437c, with respect to class actions, shall be heard by the class action department.

Adopted, eff. Jan. 1, 1995.

ORDERS

RULE 15.26 ORDER DETERMINING CLASS ISSUES

At the conclusion of each hearing, the court will make an order upon the issues presented to it in said hearing. The order will be final if it dismisses the maintenance of the action as a class action. If the order grants the motion for class certification, it will be interlocutory in nature and may be rescinded or modified as the changed circumstances of the class, its representative, or the particular action otherwise require.

Adopted, eff. Jan. 1, 1995.

RULE 15.27 ORDER REQUIRING ADDITIONAL HEARING

At the conclusion of a hearing, the court may make an order expressly deferring determination of the issues presented to it in said hearing and may order an additional hearing. The order may direct the nature of the evidence to be presented therein and otherwise direct the nature and extent of the presentation in said subsequent hearing.

The court may order that additional discovery be made before said subsequent hearing and that the evidence discovered be presented in said subsequent hearing.

Adopted, eff. Jan. 1, 1995.

RULE 15.28 ORDER UPON STIPULATION

The court generally will approve stipulations resolving the class issues and make its order thereon. This approval and order thereon will make unnecessary a hearing on said issues.

Adopted, eff. Jan. 1, 1995.

RULE 15.29 ORDER CONCERNING NATURE OF RECOVERY

The court may order that recovery, if eventually obtained, will be of a nature other than that sought in the complaint.

Adopted, eff. Jan. 1, 1995.

RULE 15.30 ORDER UPON OTHER CLASS MATTERS

The court may grant orders on class issues of a nature not provided for in these rules, if equitable considerations make the granting of such orders beneficial to the determination of class issues.

Adopted, eff. Jan. 1, 1995.

RULE 15.31 ORDER UPON NONAPPEARANCE

When one or more of the parties do not appear at a regularly noticed hearing, the court, in its discretion, may nevertheless make an order on the issues presented, or may continue the hearing until a later date set by the court, or may place the matter off calendar.

Adopted, eff. Jan. 1, 1995.

RULE 15.32 ORDER SUPERSEDING PLEADINGS

An interlocutory order which is inconsistent with a pleading will supersede said pleading, and in trial, the evidence will be directed to proof of the issue as determined by the order, rather than the pleading.

Adopted, eff. Jan. 1, 1995.

RULE 15.33 RELATIONSHIP OF THE INTERLOCUTORY (PRETRIAL)ORDER TO TRIAL OF THE CLASS ISSUES

The existence of an interlocutory (pretrial) order does not relieve the party who has alleged the existence of a class from the burden of proving at trial the matters hereinabove set out in rule 15.18. However, if the interlocutory order (pretrial) has excluded a portion of the alleged class, by defining the class to be less extensive than alleged by the party seeking class determination, evidence will not be admitted at trial concerning that portion of the alleged class which has previously been excluded by the interlocutory order.

Adopted, eff. Jan. 1, 1995.

RULE 15.34 NOTICE OF ORDER

Although the court may direct the clerk to forward by mail to counsel copies of the order when made, counsel who is directed by the court to give notice of the ruling shall do so, notwithstanding the clerk's notice.

Adopted, eff. Jan. 1, 1995.

RULE 15.35 STIPULATIONS FOR AN ORDER

As hereinabove indicated in rule 15.28, uncontroverted class issues shall be resolved by written stipulation executed by counsel and filed in court. Stipulations upon all class issues before hearing make the hearing unnecessary. Counsel shall attempt to stipulate to those class issues which are made the subject of an interlocutory order and remain to be tried.

Stipulations may be presented at any time to the clerk of Department 59 for approval by the judge sitting in said department. Said approval constitutes the order resolving the issues.

Adopted, eff. Jan. 1, 1995.

EARLY TRIAL OF BIFURCATED ISSUES

RULE 15.36 MOTION FOR EARLY TRIAL OF A BIFURCATED ISSUE

Any named party may move, pursuant to Code of Civil Procedure section 597, that the court order an early trial of class issues which have not been earlier resolved by order or stipulation.

Any named party may move, pursuant to Code of Civil Procedure section 598, that the court order an early trial of the issue of defendant's liability or may move for a separate trial of any cause or causes of action or separate issue, pursuant to Code of Civil Procedure section 1048(b).

The court may, on its own motion, order an early trial on class issues, liability, or any other cause of action or issue.

Any bifurcated trial shall take place pursuant to agreement between the I/C judge and the judge assigned to the Class Action Department. (Ref. LASCR, rules 2.5(j), 7.2(b).)

Adopted, eff. Jan. 1, 1995.

RULE 15.37 PROCEDURE FOR NOTICE AND PRESENTATION OF MOTION

Those rules ordinarily applicable when making a motion under Code of Civil Procedure sections 597 and 598 shall apply concerning the time and manner of noticing and making a motion for early trial of a bifurcated issue, except that all motions therefor will be noticed for Department 59. The party making said motion shall first contact the clerk in Department 59 to ascertain the availability of a particular date before giving notice of hearing on the motion.

Adopted, eff. Jan. 1, 1995.

RULE 15.38 TIME FOR TRIAL

Except for good cause, the court will not set the early trial of class issues for any date preceding the making of an interlocutory order on said issues, after the conduct of one or more hearings in connection therewith.

Adopted, eff. Jan. 1, 1995.

RULE 15.39 ORDER AFTER EARLY TRIAL

At the conclusion of a trial on bifurcated issues, the court will make its order establishing the proof, or failure thereof, upon the issues presented therein, which order will constitute a final determination of said issues for all trial purposes.

Adopted, eff. Jan. 1, 1995.

RULE 15.40 PRETRIAL PROCEEDINGS IN CLASS ACTIONS

All law and discovery and writs and receivers matters in a class action, shall be noticed and heard in the class action department (Department 59) unless: (1) A motion for relief from compliance with these rules has been granted; or (2) The class allegations have been stricken and the unnamed class members dismissed; or (3) The class is decertified.

If any of such events has occurred, law and discovery matters shall thereafter be noticed and heard in the appropriate I/C department and writs and receivers matters shall thereafter be noticed and heard in the Writs and Receivers Department.

Adopted, eff. Jan. 1, 1995.

SETTLEMENT HEARINGS AND JUDGMENTS

RULE 15.41 NATURE OF CLASS ACTION SETTLEMENT HEARINGS

All agreements between the parties which settle the claims of the class and terminate the action must be approved by the court after hearing (herein "settlement hearing"), which approval will be reflected by a judgment or final order. The court's approval is one based upon its acceptance of the fairness of the proposed settlement to the class for which the court will conduct an independent inquiry. The court, after said hearing, may refuse to approve the settlement if the court determines that it is not fair, reasonable, and adequate. The court may modify the terms thereof to achieve such fairness, reasonableness, and adequacy, and, if the parties agree to be bound by said modification, the court may approve said settlement.

A settlement will not ordinarily be approved if, as a result thereof, the class representative will receive a benefit not made available to the other members of the class.

Adopted, eff. Jan. 1, 1995.

RULE 15.42 MOTION FOR SETTLEMENT HEARING

Any party to a settlement agreement may submit a written notice of motion for approval of the agreement by the court. The notice of motion must be accompanied by all documents upon which the party will rely in the hearing on the motion, including, but not limited to, the following:

—Original and copy of executed settlement agreement;

—Original and copy of proposed order granting settlement hearing;

—Original and copy of proposed notice to the class of the pendency of the class action and notice of hearing on proposed settlement.

Adopted, eff. Jan. 1, 1995.

RULE 15.43 PLACE AND TIME OF HEARING THE MOTION

Notice of motion for a settlement hearing should be noticed for Department 59, with the period of notice as set out in Code of Civil Procedure section 1005. The party making said motion should ascertain from the clerk in Department 59 the availability of a particular date before giving notice of hearing on the motion.

Adopted, eff. Jan. 1, 1995.

RULE 15.44 ORDER FOR SETTLEMENT HEARING

After hearing the motion, the court will make its order granting or denying a settlement hearing. If it grants a settlement hearing, its order will include the time and place of said settlement hearing, the notice thereof to be given to the class members, and other matters which it deems necessary to the proper conduct of a settlement hearing.

Adopted, eff. Jan. 1, 1995.

RULE 15.45 CONDUCT OF SETTLEMENT HEARINGS

(a) Procedure. The court will employ that procedure which it deems necessary to ascertain the fairness, reasonableness, and adequacy of the proposed settlement. This procedure will involve a taking of evidence by declaration, and points and authorities in support of the proposed settlement. It will also involve the opportunity for members of the class to be heard in objection to the proposed settlement, if they have satisfied prerequisites therefor set out in the notice to the class of the proposed settlement.

(b) Attorney's Fees. Irrespective of whether the parties to the proposed settlement have agreed as to the amount of fees for representation of the class, the court will award only that amount which it determines to be reasonable, which amount may be less than that to which the parties agree. In every settlement hearing in which the representative seeks the award of fees to his or her attorney, said representative must present evidence to support his or her request. Said evidence will include, but is not limited to, the amount of the recovery, the contingent nature thereof (probability of success when the representation was undertaken), the number of hours which the attorney has devoted to the matter, his or her professional standing, his or her hourly rate for office work and court appearances, his or her daily rate for office work and court appearances, if said daily rate differs from mere accumulation of hours, and said attorney's agreement with the class representative concerning fees. Initial presentation of such evidence will be through a declaration.

Adopted, eff. Jan. 1, 1995.

RULE 15.46 JUDGMENT

After the settlement hearing, the court will make and enter judgment or final order. Where the judgment of the court requires future acts to be performed by the parties, beyond payment of money by defendant, the judgment will provide for the court's retention of jurisdiction while satisfaction of the judgment is being effectuated. All proposed judgments which are submitted to the court with the settlement agreement should include a provision for retention of jurisdiction if said retention is appropriate, and should provide in detail for the terms of said retained jurisdiction.

Adopted, eff. Jan. 1, 1995.

DISMISSALS

RULE 15.47 COURT APPROVAL

Dismissals in class actions are subject to prior court approval, including not only dismissals of entire suits, but also dismissal of certain causes of action or of certain parties. Dismissals requests are processed by Department 59 (Class Action Department).

The Clerk of the Superior Court may not process requests for dismissal of any type in class actions, without prior court approval.

Adopted, eff. Jan. 1, 1995.

RULE 15.48 DISMISSAL PROCEDURE

Counsel seeking dismissal, total or partial, with respect to a class action, shall file the following documents directly with the clerk in Department 59 (Class Action Department):

—Request for Dismissal in the usual form;

—The request must be accompanied by at least one declaration setting forth the facts upon which the party relies in seeking the dismissal.

The declaration must clearly set forth whether or not any consideration of any kind, direct or indirect, has been given or will be given to any named party or his or her attorney in respect of the action or the dismissal thereof. If so, the details of such consideration must be set forth.

Adopted, eff. Jan. 1, 1995.

RULE 15.49 COURT APPROVAL OR DISAPPROVAL

If the requested dismissal is approved, the court will sign an Order of Dismissal which will then be entered by the Clerk of the Superior Court. Notice of the signing of the order will be sent to the attorneys of record by the clerk in Department 59.

If the requested dismissal is tentatively disapproved, notice thereof will be sent to the attorneys of record with a request that they set the matter for hearing in Department 59 on a date acceptable to the court's calendar.

Adopted, eff. Jan. 1, 1995.

SAN DIEGO COUNTY SUPERIOR COURT RULES

DIVISION II. GENERAL CIVIL LITIGATION
SECTION THREE. CLASS ACTION RULES

RULE 3.1 FILING OF CLASS ACTIONS

Every complaint filed pursuant to Code of Civil Procedure § 382 or Civil Code § 1751, et seq., other than those involving primarily construction defect claims, shall include on the front page a designation as a "Class Action." All San Diego Superior Court local rules shall apply to such cases unless expressly contravened by the provisions of this section, or waived by the judge to whom the case is assigned. These include, but are not limited to all Division II—General Civil Litigation Rules. (Cross reference: Rule 1.20 Construction Defect Cases.)

Adopted, eff. July 1, 1996.

RULE 3.2 MOTIONS FOR CLASS CERTIFICATION

(a) Time for Motion.*

In order for the class to be certified, a motion must be made by the party desiring class action status. Said motion should normally be filed within sixty (60) days of the filing of the certificate of service, and in every case must be heard within one hundred twenty (120) days of the filing of the certificate of service unless upon a showing of good cause the court extends the time. The motion and any opposition shall conform with the local rules, including but not limited to 4.1, 4.2 and 4.4. The party making the motion has the burden of establishing the requisites for maintenance of a class action.

(b) Discovery After Notice of Hearing. The party who notices a hearing for class certification must complete all discovery upon which it intends to rely prior to the submission of the notice of hearing. Said moving party will not be entitled to conduct such discovery during the period between the filing of the notice of hearing and the hearing, except that upon a showing of good cause the court may continue the hearing on the motion of the moving party to permit such discovery to be completed.

(c) Content of Motion Documents. The motion documents must contain a detailed description of the nature and size of the proposed class, a description of its members and its geographical location, along with a statement of reasons and sufficient evidence to justify the Court in making the findings required by Civil Code § 1781(c) and any other applicable statutory and case law.

(d) Opposition to Motion. Any opposition to the motion for class certification must contain a statement supported by sufficient evidence and setting forth reasons why the Court should not make any or all of the required findings.

(e) Order. The Court will make an order upon the issues presented to it by the motion for class certification.

Adopted, eff. July 1, 1996.

RULE 3.3 STATUS CONFERENCE RE: NOTICE OF CLASS CERTIFICATION

(a) If the Court grants the motion for class certification, the Court will schedule a status conference for the purpose of reviewing the proposed notice to class members within 30 days and so notify the other appearing parties.

(b) Three (3) court days prior to the status conference, the prevailing party shall file with the court and serve personally or by FAX on the other appearing parties a proposed notice to the class of the pendency of a class action, along with a statement containing the following information:

(1) The time when notice should be given;

(2) The manner in which notice should be given;

* Suggested title added by Publisher.

(3) If the prevailing party does not feel that it should bear the entire cost of notice, the reasons why other parties should bear a portion of the cost; and

(4) In the event that (3) above is invoked, an estimate as to the amount of the cost involved in giving notice.

(c) The proposed notice shall also contain:

(1) A brief explanation of the case, including basic contentions or denials of the parties;

(2) A statement that any member of the class who so requests by a specified date may "opt out" [be excluded from the class] of the action by giving notice thereof;

(3) Information concerning how a class member who desires to opt out may give notice thereof;

(4) A statement that the claim of a member who does not opt out will be terminated by the judgment in the action under the rule of res judicata; and (5) A statement that any member who does not opt out may move the Court upon good cause shown for permission to appear as a named class co-representative.

(d) The Court may, in its discretion, dispense with requirement of notice, upon a proper showing, in an appropriate case such as one where only injunctive relief is being sought.

(e) The Court shall determine the best practical method of notice and date.

Adopted, eff. July 1, 1996.

RULE 3.4 PROGRESS CONFERENCES

(a) Within ninety (90) days after the status conference, the Court will schedule a progress conference in lieu of the case management conference scheduled in civil cases generally. Notice of the conference will be served by the Court, or a party designated by the Court, on all parties who have appeared at least twenty (20) days before the scheduled time of the conference.

(b) The conference will be held for the purpose of discussing class issues, establishing precedence of discovery, the scheduling of hearings, the status of settlement discussions, or any other matters concerning pretrial determination of class issues, as well as issues traditionally addressed at case management conferences generally.

(c) Counsel completely familiar with the case and possessing authority to enter into stipulations shall be present and shall be fully prepared to discuss the issues outlined above. If counsel is not fully prepared, the court may continue the hearing and impose sanctions against the offending party. If the hearing proceeds as scheduled, the orders made will not be subject to reconsideration due to counsel's unfamiliarity with the case at the time of the hearing.

(d) At the conclusion of the conference, the Court shall make an order to embrace the stipulations, if any, of the parties.

(e) Additional conferences will be scheduled in the discretion of the Court.

Adopted, eff. July 1, 1996.

SAN FRANCISCO COUNTY SUPERIOR COURT

MANUAL FOR THE CONDUCT OF PRE-TRIAL PROCEEDINGS IN CLASS ACTIONS

July 1982

Table of Sections

INTRODUCTION

Sec.
401. Purpose of this Manual.
402. "Class Action" Designation on Complaint.
403. Relief from Compliance with this Manual.
404. Certain Designations.

INFORMAL CONFERENCE ON CLASS ISSUES

411. Nature of Conference.
412. Conference on Motion of Named Party.
413. Conference on Order of the Court.
414. Time for Conference.
415. Filing Notice of Conference: Place and Time.
416. Conference Order.

PRE-TRIAL HEARINGS ON CLASS ISSUES

421. Nature of Hearings.
    1. Content of Hearings.
    2. Policy Underlying Scheduling and Conduct of Hearings.
422. Initial Hearing.
    1. Nature of Hearing.
    2. Hearing on Motion of a Named Party.
    3. Hearing on Order of Court.
    4. Time for Hearing.
423. Subsequent Hearing.
    1. Nature of Hearing.
    2. Hearing on Motion of a Named Party.
    3. Hearing on Order of Court.
    4. No Hearing After Dismissal.
    5. Re-examination of Issues Earlier Determined.
    6. Time for Hearing.
    7. Judge Presiding at Hearing.
424. Scheduling Hearing.
    1. Notice of Hearing by a Named Party.
    2. Notice of Hearing by the Court.
    3. Period of Notice of Hearing.
    4. Filing Notice of Hearing: Place and Time.
    5. Submission of Supporting Documents.
    6. Filing of Responsive and Rebuttal Documents.
    7. Submission of Memoranda of Points and Authorities.
    8. Notice Without Supporting Documents.
    9. Form of Documents.
    10. Notice to Public Entity, Official, Employee Class Member.
    11. Notice to Attorney General.
425. Continuance of Hearing and Submission.
    1. Change in Hearing Date.
    2. Change in Time to Submit Documents.
426. Conduct of Hearing.
    1. Use of Declaration.
    2. Judicially Noticed Matters.
    3. Discovered Evidence.
    4. Discovery After Notice of Hearing.
    5. Oral Testimony.
    6. Burden of Proof in the Hearing.
    7. Nature of Evidence.
    8. Issues Not Noticed Will Not Be Heard.
427. Issues: Documents for Presentation.
    1. Issue: Constitution of the Class.
    2. Issue: Common, Similar and Unique Questions of Law and Fact.
    3. Issue: Superiority of the Class Action to Other Available Methods for the Fair and Efficient Adjudication of the Controversy.
    4. Issue: Membership of the Class Representative in the Class.
    5. Issue: Ability of the Class Representative to Fairly and Adequately Protect the Interests of the Class.
    6. Issue: Necessity for and Content of Notice.
    7. Additional Issues.
428. Orders.
    1. Order Determining Issues.
    2. Order Requiring Additional Hearing.
    3. Order Upon Stipulation.
    4. Order Concerning Nature of Recovery.

5. Order Upon Other Class Matters.
6. Order Upon Non-appearance.
7. Order Superseding Pleadings.
8. Relationship of the Interlocutory (Pretrial) Order to Trial of the Class Issues.
9. Notice of Order.

429. Stipulations for an Order.

FILING CERTIFICATE OF READINESS

431. Filing Certificate of Readiness.

EARLY TRIAL OF BIFURCATED ISSUE

441. Scheduling Early Trial.
1. Motion for Early Trial of Bifurcated Issue.
2. Procedure for Notice and Presentation of Motion.
3. Place and Hour of Hearing.
4. Time for Trial.

442. Order After Early Trial.

SURVIVAL OF EXISTING PROCEDURES

451. Survival of Existing Procedures.

SETTLEMENT HEARINGS AND JUDGMENTS

461. Nature of Class Action Settlement Hearings.

462. Scheduling Settlement Hearing.
1. Motion for Hearing.
2. Notice of Motion.
3. Order for Settlement Hearing.

463. Conduct of Settlement Hearings.
1. Procedure.
2. Attorney's Fees.

464. Judgment.

470. All Dismissals Subject to Court Approval.
1. Documents to Be Filed.*
2. Court Approval or Disapproval.

*Suggested title added by publisher.

INTRODUCTION

SECTION 401. PURPOSE OF THIS MANUAL

This manual sets out the policy of the San Francisco Superior Court for the scheduling and conduct of pre-trial proceedings which will be held in every class action to determine class issues.[1]

This manual defines and catalogs those issues (herein designated "issues") which are unique to class actions, which are present in each said action, and which are subject to pre-trial determination.

These issues are:

1. Constitution of the class.

2. Common, similar and unique questions of law and fact.

3. Superiority of the class action to other available methods for the fair and efficient adjudication of the controversy.

4. Membership of the class representative in the class.

5. Ability of the class representative to fairly and adequately protect the interest of the class.

6. Necessity for and content of notice.

Certain issues, although not unique to class actions, are present in many of them. These are cataloged as

7. Additional issues.

(These issues, which herein sometimes are referred to simply by the above numerical designation and the content of documents which will be submitted concerning each, are discussed in section 427.)

This manual describes two types of pre-trial proceedings concerning class actions: first, an informal conference (herein designated "conference") at which the class issues are discussed (sections 411–416), and second, pre-trial hearings on class issues (sections 421–429). One or more of said hearings must be conducted in every action brought under Code of Civil Procedure section 382 or Civil Code section 1750 et seq. (Consumers' Legal Remedies Act), in which either the plaintiff or defendant is a "class."[2] Each said hearing will result in an order, generally pendente lite in nature, concerning class issues.

This manual also sets out the procedure for the making of motions to bifurcate the class issues from those of liability and early trial of one or more of said bifurcated issues (sections 441–442).

This manual also sets out the procedure for the making of motions to schedule the hearing to consider the fairness of the settlement agreement entered into by the parties for the termination of a pending class action. The manual further describes the policy of the court in connection with the conduct of said hearings, including the award of fees to the attorney for the class representative (sections 461–464).

The manual also sets out the procedure for the filing of requests for dismissal of a party or cause of action (section 470).

As in all statements of policy, the procedural policies set out herein may be modified if the court in a particular case deems said modification in the best interests of the parties or the court. However, in the absence of an order modifying

---

1 In *Vasquez* v. *Superior Court* (1971) 4 Cal.3d 800, 94 Cal.Rptr. 796, 484 P.2d 964, the court, at p. 820, 809, 977, said, "... plaintiffs must ... demonstrate the questions which they will be required to litigate separately are not numerous or substantial and that the action meets the other requirements for a class action set forth in detail above ..." and that it is appropriate to hold a pre-trial hearing to make such determination. See also *LaSala* v. *American Savings and Loan Ass'n.* (1971) 5 Cal.3d 864, 876, 97 Cal.Rptr. 849, 856, 489, P.2d 1113, 1120; *Bauman* v. *Islay Investments* (1975) 45 Cal.App.3d 797, 119 Cal.Rptr. 681.

2 The Consumers' Legal Remedies Act requires that the representative of the plaintiff class give notification and make certain demands as a prerequisite to the maintenance of a class action for damages under said act. The rules set out in this Manual do not deal with the notification and demands required by Civil Code sections 1780 and 1782.

these procedures or adopting others, the rules set out herein will apply to all class actions.

July 1982.

SECTION 402. "CLASS ACTION" DESIGNATION ON COMPLAINT

All complaints for or against a class party will include in the caption the designation "CLASS ACTION." This designation will appear, typewritten in capital letters on a line having no other words, on the first page of the complaint immediately below that space reserved for the County Clerk's file number stamp but above that general description of the nature of the complaint (e.g., "Complaint for Damages for Breach of Contract," etc.) sometimes used by counsel. It is essential to the prompt processing of class action pre-trial proceedings that this "CLASS ACTION" designation appear.

July 1982.

SECTION 403. RELIEF FROM COMPLIANCE WITH THIS MANUAL

Any named party may make a motion to have all parties relieved from compliance with the policy set out in sections 411–416 and 421–429 of this manual on the ground that the pending case does not involve a class action of the nature contemplated by Code of Civil Procedure section 382 or Civil Code sec. 1750 et seq. or Federal Rules of Civil Procedure section 23(b)(3). As a general rule, actions brought by a taxpayer under Code of Civil Procedure section 526(a) or by an association as the representative of its members will be excused from compliance with the policy set out herein. (E.g., many actions brought by labor organizations as the representatives of their members would be exempt from the rules set out in this manual. See *Professional Fire Fighters v. City of Los Angeles* (1963) 60 Cal.2d 276, 32 Cal.Rptr. 830, 384 P.2d 158.) Certain mandamus actions also may be excused. (See *Diaz v. Quitoriano* (1969) 268 Cal.App.2d 807, 74 Cal.Rptr. 358.) Notice of such a motion should be given in accordance with Code of Civil Procedure section 1005.

July 1982.

SECTION 404. CERTAIN DESIGNATIONS

The following designations are used in this manual:

1. "Declaration" is an affidavit (or declaration pursuant to Code Civ.Proc., sec. 2015.5) which relates to facts.
2. "Documents" is the collective description of declarations, memoranda and statements, or any combination of them.
3. "Manual" is this statement of the policy of the Court concerning pre-trial and settlement proceedings in class actions.
4. "Memorandum" is the memorandum of points and authorities.
5. "Plaintiff," "defendant," "complaint," etc.: if the answer or a cross-complaint is the first pleading to allege a class, the rules set out herein will apply as if said pleading were the complaint and that pleader were the plaintiff.
6. "Statement" is a written discussion or argument by counsel which is not under oath or penalty of perjury. The memorandum and statement may be combined in one document.
7. "Submit" (e.g., "to submit documents") is to both serve and file said documents with proof of service affixed to the filed documents.

July 1982.

INFORMAL CONFERENCE ON CLASS ISSUES

SECTION 411. NATURE OF CONFERENCE

One or more conferences, informal in nature, may be held in chambers between the court and counsel for every party to the action. At said conference the parties will discuss the class issues involved, establishment of precedence of discovery, scheduling of hearings and other matters concerning the class issues. No evidence will be presented at the conference, but the court will expect all attorneys in attendance to have sufficient knowledge of the class issues to discuss proposed stipulations resolving the class issues.

July 1982.

SECTION 412. CONFERENCE ON MOTION OF NAMED PARTY

The conference may be scheduled through notice given by the plaintiff or any named party who has submitted an answer in the action. The notice must be in writing and must designate those topics which counsel expects to discuss at the conference (e.g., order of discovery, stipulation concerning certain issues, etc.). The notice may, but need not, be supported by documents. The notice will be submitted at least twenty (20) days before the scheduled time of the conference. A conference may not be noticed by a class member who is not specifically named as a party unless said member earlier has received permission from the court to appear individually or to become a co-representative (section 427.7(e) and (f)).

July 1982.

SECTION 413. CONFERENCE ON ORDER OF THE COURT

The court may schedule a conference, notice of which will be served on all parties who have appeared. Said notice must be in writing and must designate those topics which the court expects counsel to discuss at the conference. The notice will be submitted at least twenty (20) days before the scheduled time of the conference.

July 1982.

SECTION 414. TIME FOR CONFERENCE

The conference may be held at any time after the at-issue memorandum has been filed. Notice of the conference may be given, although notice of the initial hearing already has been given. If the at-issue memorandum has not been filed within sixty (60) days after a defendant has answered, the said defendant then may submit a notice for conference, and said conference will be held at the time noticed, even though the at-issue memorandum has not been filed. If said notice is given by the plaintiff, it must be served on all named defendants in the action. If notice is given by a defendant or the court, it will be served on only the parties who have appeared; however, within ten (10) days after receipt of said notice plaintiff will serve a copy thereof on each named defendant who has not appeared in the action and will submit a declaration of said service. In the event that plaintiff is unable to effect service on any defendant as aforesaid, plaintiff will submit a declaration stating the reasons for failing to serve the said defendant.

July 1982.

SECTION 415. FILING NOTICE OF CONFERENCE: PLACE AND TIME

The notice of the conference shall be filed with the County Clerk and shall notice the conference only for a date and time previously obtained from the clerk of the Law and Motion department or such other department designated by the Presiding Judge to hear class action pre-trial motions.

July 1982.

SECTION 416. CONFERENCE ORDER

At the conclusion of the conference, the court shall make an order to embrace the stipulations, if any, of the parties (herein designated "conference order"). Until modified or terminated by the court, the conference order will be binding on all parties to the action. The court may order an additional conference upon all or certain of the class issues. The conference order will not be used to resolve any class issues in dispute.

July 1982.

PRE–TRIAL HEARINGS ON CLASS ISSUES

SECTION 421. NATURE OF HEARINGS

1. Content of Hearings. In each class action brought under Code of Civil Procedure section 382 or Civil Code section 1750 et seq. in which either the plaintiff or the defendant is a "class," one or more pre-trial hearings (herein designated collectively "hearing") on the class issues (defined in Sections 401 and 427) must be held. These hearings are:

(a) *Initial Hearing.* The first pre-trial hearing to resolve class issues is herein designated "initial hearing." The time for said hearing, issues to be presented and resolved therein and other matters concerning said hearing are discussed in sections 422, 424–429.

(b)*Subsequent Hearing.* At any time or times after the initial hearing an additional hearing may be held, which hearing is therein designated "subsequent hearing." The criteria for scheduling a subsequent hearing, the time for said hearing, the issues to be presented and resolved therein and other matters concerning said hearing are discussed in sections 423–429.

2. Policy Underlying Scheduling and Conduct of Hearings. The unique and salutary nature of the class action for adjudication of claims which otherwise would be impracticable for judicial consideration is recognized in California. (See [*Vasquez v. Superior Court* (1971) 4 Cal.3d 800, 807–808, 94 Cal. Rptr. 796, 800, 484 P.2d 964, 968]). Therefore, the scheduling of hearings and the precedence of determination of issues may be varied by the court, in its discretion, in order that the parties will have a reasonable opportunity to present fully all relevant evidence and argument on each class issue. Without a prior order to the contrary, however, that schedule set out herein for the conduct of the hearings and determination of issues will apply to all class actions.

July 1982.

SECTION 422. INITIAL HEARING

1. Nature of Hearing. An initial hearing will be held to make a determination of at least issues 1 through 5 (Section 427). In said hearing, additional issues, if included in the notice of hearing, may be determined.

2. Hearing on Motion of a Named Party. Plaintiff or any named defendant who has answered may submit notice of an initial hearing. If the party who has alleged the existence of a class is the party who notices the hearing, his notice must be accompanied by declarations of issues 1, 4 and 5 in addition to documents on all issues to be presented. If the party controverting the class allegations is the party who notices the hearing, his motion must be accompanied by documents on all issues presented, except said party need not submit declarations on issues 1, 4 and 5. All facts other than purely rebuttal matter upon which the moving party will rely at the hearing must be set out in declarations which accompany the notice of the hearing.

3. Hearing on Order of Court. The court may schedule an initial hearing, notice of which will be served on all parties. Said notice must direct that the class party submit documents upon at least issues 1 through 5 on or before a specified date. Responding and rebuttal documents then will be submitted without further order on or before those times set out in Section 424.3, unless the court orders otherwise. The court is not bound by the seventy five (75) day maximum time set out in Section 424.3.

4. Time for Hearing. Notice of the initial hearing may be submitted any time after the at-issue memorandum has been filed except that if an at-issue memorandum has not been filed within sixty (60) days after a defendant has filed his answer, said defendant then may submit a notice of an initial hearing. If said notice is given by the plaintiff, it must be served on all named parties in the action. If said notice is given by a defendant or the court, it must be served on only those parties who have appeared; however, within ten (10) days after receipt of said notice, plaintiff must serve a copy thereof on each named defendant who has not appeared in the action and will submit a declaration of said service. In the event that plaintiff is unable to effect service of any defendant as aforesaid, plaintiff will submit a declaration stating the reasons for failing to serve the said defendant.

The period of notice of hearing is set out in Section 424.3.

July 1982.

SECTION 423. SUBSEQUENT HEARING

1. Nature of Hearing. A subsequent hearing will be held to resolve class issues not earlier resolved. It also may be held upon a sufficient showing of changed factual circumstances having occurred or new evidence having been discovered after the earlier hearing. See Section 423.5, for the manner and time of presenting the facts concerning said changed circumstances or new evidence.[1]

2. Hearing on Motion of a Named Party. A subsequent hearing noticed by either party must request a determination of issue 6 if this issue was not earlier determined, or may request a redetermination of any issue earlier presented, subject to satisfying the requirement set out in Section 423.5. The notice of hearing must be accompanied by all the documents supporting the party's position on each issue. All facts other than purely rebuttal matter on which the moving party will rely at the hearing must be set out in the documents which accompany the notice of the hearing.

3. Hearing on Order of Court. The court may schedule a subsequent hearing, notice of which will be served on all parties. Said notice will direct that one of the parties submit moving documents on issues as directed by the court (even though said issues were resolved in earlier hearing) on or before a specified date. Responding and rebuttal documents then will be submitted without further order or before those dates set out in Section 424.3. The court is not bound by the seventy five (75) day maximum time set out in Section 424.3.

4. No Hearing After Dismissal. No subsequent hearing will be noticed or held to examine or reexamine class action issues after an order has been made dismissing the action as one maintainable by, or against, a class.

5. Re-examination of Issues Earlier Determined. A subsequent hearing will be conducted on issues determined in earlier hearings only upon a sufficient showing by the moving party that changed factual circumstances or new evidence make necessary modification of the earlier order. The changed circumstances or new evidence must not have been known or reasonably ascertainable at the time or the earlier hearing. The facts constituting the changed circumstances or newly discovered evidence must be set out in a declaration accompanying the moving party's notice of hearing.

The court on its own motion or upon the motion of the responding party may strike the notice of said subsequent hearing if the declaration in support thereof does not make a sufficient showing of changed factual circumstances or new evidence.

6. Time for Hearing. A subsequent hearing may be held at any time prior to the filing of the Certificate of Readiness, or may be held after the filing of a Certificate of Readiness upon a factual showing of changed circumstances or the discovery of new evidence which was not known or could not have been reasonably ascertained in time to notice a hearing to be held before the Certificate of Readiness was filed. If said notice is given by the plaintiff, it must be served on all named parties in the action. If said notice is given by a defendant or the court, it must be served on only those parties who have appeared; however, within ten (10) days after receipt of said notice, the plaintiff must serve a copy thereof on each named defendant who has not appeared in the action and will submit a declaration of said service. In the event that plaintiff is unable to effect service on any defendant as aforesaid, plaintiff will submit a declaration stating the reasons for failing to serve the said defendant.

The period of the hearing is set out in Section 424.3.

7. Judge Presiding at Hearing. The judge assigned to the hearing need not be the same judge who presided in an earlier hearing, even though the subsequent hearing may be for the purpose of modifying or rescinding an order earlier made.

July 1982.

SECTION 424. SCHEDULING HEARING

1. Notice of Hearing by a Named Party. Any named plaintiff or defendant who has submitted an answer may notice a hearing. The

1 See *Occidental Land, Inc.* v. *Superior Court* (1976) 18 Cal.3d 355, 134 Cal.Rptr. 388, 556, P.2d 750.

notice must be in writing, must designate those issues which will be the subject of the hearing and describe the documents supporting said motion. Issues which must be noticed are set out in sections 422.2 and 423.6. A hearing may not be noticed by a class member who is not specifically named as a party unless said member earlier has received permission from the court to appear individually or to become a co-representative. (See section 427.7(e) and (f).)

2. Notice of Hearing by the Court. The court may notice a hearing by order served on plaintiff and all defendants who have answered. The order must designate the issues which will be the subject of the hearing. (For issues which must be, and may be, noticed see Sections 422.3 and 423.3.)

3. Period of Notice of Hearing. The hearing will be noticed for not less than sixty (60) days or more than seventy five (75) days after the serving of notice thereof. Each responding party may submit documents on or within forty five (45) days after service upon said party of the notice of hearing. The moving party may submit rebuttal documents on or before five days after service upon him of the responding documents. These rebuttal documents will present no new evidentiary facts.

4. Filing Notice of Hearing; Place and Time. The notice of the hearing shall be filed with the county clerk and shall notice the hearing only for a date and time previously obtained from the clerk of the Law and Motion Department or such other department designated by the presiding judge to hear class action pre-trial motions.

5. Submission of Supporting Documents. If the moving party is the class representative, he will submit with the notice of hearing documents on all issues to be presented in said hearing. All facts other than purely rebuttal matters, upon which the moving party will rely in the hearing, must be set out in declarations submitted with the notice of the hearing.

If the moving party is the non-class party, he will submit with the notice of hearing documents on all issues to be heard except that he need not submit declarations on issues 1, 4 or 5; however, if the non-class moving party has facts on these issues which he wishes to present, he must present them with his moving papers and not reserve them for inclusion with his rebuttal documents.

6. Filing of Responsive and Rebuttal Documents. All documents filed by either party after the notice of hearing has been submitted will be filed with the county clerk. It is the responsibility of each counsel to ascertain that all documents filed by him have reached the proper department prior to the hearing.

When the date of hearing and department are known, it is helpful to the court to have that information set out on the front page of the documents just below the name of the document.

Example:

DEFENDANT'S RESPONSE TO
DOCUMENTS FILED FOR
INITIAL HEARING

Hearing Date: _______

Department: ___________

7. Submission of Memoranda of Points and Authorities. In all hearings, all parties will submit, in addition to those documents described elsewhere in this Manual, memoranda of points and authorities citing and discussing relevant authority upon each issue presented in each hearing. Decisional authority under Code of Civil Procedure section 382, Civil Code section 1750 et seq. and Federal Rules of Civil Procedure 23 should be cited by counsel. Counsel are invited to cite and argue additional relevant authorities. Citation of California cases must be by reference to the Official Reports and should indicate the volume number, the first page of the case and the specific page or pages on which the pertinent matters appear in the Official Reports, and the year of such decision. If a party cites a case from another jurisdiction, it is helpful to attach to the memorandum a photocopy of said case. The memorandum should not merely cite an authority without explaining its relevance to the point for which it is cited. It is not necessary to provide a plethora of citations when a single relevant authority states the law on the subject (unless, e.g., counsel makes citations in support of his argument that the weight of authority supports his position or that it is the state of the law in many jurisdictions, etc.). Citation of this Manual should include the paragraph number.

8. Notice Without Supporting Documents. A notice of hearing unaccompanied by each of the documents required by these rules will be deemed to have been untimely made and the hearing may be placed off calendar on the court's motion or that of the responding party.

9. Form of Documents. All documents submitted in hearings must conform with California Rules of Court, Rule 201. Documents submitted simultaneously by a party may be bound under one cover sheet with an appropriate table of contents or index to aid the court in locating each document.

10. Notice to Public Entity, Official, Employee Class Member. When a public entity or a public official or public employee in his official capacity is an unnamed member of the plaintiff or defendant class, notice of the pendency of said class action will be given to said public entity, public official or public employee before the at-issue memorandum is filed. Said notice will be served in the same manner as a civil summons is served.

11. Notice to Attorney General. If the action seeks relief of any nature, other than solely for money damages, for alleged pollution or adverse environmental effects which could affect the public generally, the notice of motion of the hearing and a copy of all documents relative thereto submitted by any party shall be served on the Attorney General of the State of California regardless of whether the Attorney General is named party. (Code of Civil Procedure Section 389.6.) The court may direct that notice be given to the Attorney General in other types of actions.

July 1982.

SECTION 425. CONTINUANCE OF HEARING AND SUBMISSION

1. Change in Hearing Date. Continuance of a hearing may not be made unilaterally except upon motion noticed and granted. However, a continuance to a date certain, or removal of the hearing from calendar, may be made by stipulation. The date to which the hearing may be continued by stipulation must be approved by the court (through advice by the clerk of available dates) in order to be effective. The parties cannot avoid the necessity of completing all hearings before filing the Certificate of Readiness through stipulating to a hearing date later than said filing. However, for good cause the court may order the hearing continued to a time subsequent to the filing of the Certificate of Readiness.

2. Change in Time to Submit Documents. On motion by a party noticed for hearing before that party's time to submit documents expires, the court may order the documents to be submitted at a time different from that set out herein. Said motion for change in the time scheduled for submission of documents will be supported by a declaration setting out evidentiary facts showing good cause for the change.

July 1982.

SECTION 426. CONDUCT OF HEARING

1. Use of Declaration. Presentation of evidence in the hearing generally will be through declarations submitted and previously discovered evidence. Inasmuch as all counsel generally will be apprised of all evidence several days before the hearing, counsel should attempt to resolve by stipulation before hearing as many class issues as possible. (See section 429.)

2. Judicially Noticed Matters. Either party in its moving or responding documents may request that the court take judicial notice of certain matters pursuant to California Evidence Code section 451 et seq. It will be the responsibility of the party who makes the request concerning those items described in California Evidence Code section 452 to furnish the court with adequate copies of the matters referred to therein. The court will not undertake to gather said matters.

3. Discovered Evidence. Either party in its moving or responding documents may request that the court consider particular discovered evidence in the case file (depositions, answers to interrogatories, admissions, etc.). All references to discovered evidence will be to line and page thereof. It is the duty of the party who refers to matters in a deposition to lodge the deposition in court before the hearing. Opposing counsel in responding documents may raise objections, based upon the rules governing admissibility of evidence, to consideration by the court of said evidence. The court will rule on each objection before considering said requested discovered evidence.

4. Discovery After Notice of Hearing. The party who notices a hearing must complete all discovery upon which it intends to rely prior to the submission of the notice of hearing. Said moving party will not be entitled to conduct discovery during the period between the notice of hearing and the hearing, except upon leave of court.

5. Oral Testimony. Oral testimony will not be received in the hearing except upon leave of the court after counsel has made an adequate evidentiary showing of his inability to present evidence through declaration or earlier use of discovery procedure and has presented good cause for consideration by the court of such oral testimony.

6. Burden of Proof in the Hearing. The burden of proof on all class issues is on the party alleging the existence of a class, whether the party making said allegations is the moving or responding party in the hearing. All issues of fact will be proved by a preponderance of the evidence presented in the hearing.

7. Nature of Evidence. The court in its discretion at any time prior to or during the hearing may order that the evidence to be presented by the parties will be of a character different from that provided in Sections 426.1 and 426.5 and other relevant sections of the Manual. (E.g., the court may order cross-examination upon the evidence in the declarations, production of original documents, oral testimony of certain persons, etc., or a combination of any of them.) Such order will provide a reasonable time for preparation of such evidence, including a continuance of the hearing if necessary.

8. Issues Not Noticed Will Not Be Heard. The court will not hear evidence or argument on any issue which was not included in the notice of motion for hearing.

July 1982.

SECTION 427. ISSUES: DOCUMENTS FOR PRESENTATION

Set out in Section 427.1–7 are the issues which must be resolved by order after one or more hearings. Also set out with each issue are subjects which should be included in the documents submitted in support of each party's position on said issue. These subjects are not exclusive but do represent the minimum information which the court deems necessary for presentation by the parties on each issue.[1]

1. Issue: Constitution of the Class. The party alleging existence of a class will submit one or more declarations which present facts describing in detail the composition of the class, including the following: (The facts submitted in a declaration must stand the test to which oral testimony would be subjected in the trial of an action. The declaration should contain enough competent evidence to convince the trier of fact. Averments which are satisfactory in pleadings are not competent evidence. The declaration should show the source of the declarant's information, that is, the declaration should contain a proper foundation.)

(a) The approximate number of persons in the class. If there are subclasses, the declaration also should describe each and set out the approximate number of persons in each subclass.

(b) The general geographical location (or locations) of the class members. If the class is not confined to California, the description will include those locations outside California where the class members are located.

1 See *Cooper* v. *American Savings and Loan* (1976) 55 Cal.App.3d 274, 127 Cal.Rptr. 579.

(c) A description of the status of the class members where relevant to the action (e.g., minors, particular ethnic, occupational, economic, professional or other group).

(d) A description of the members of each subclass between whom issues of law or fact must be litigated.

(e) A description of those class members, including an estimate of their number, whose claims must be approved or evidence presented only as to each individual member.

(f) Other facts which describe the class. These other facts should describe the class with sufficient thoroughness that it therefore can be accurately and particularly described.

Further, the class representative will submit a statement presenting his position concerning:

(g) The manner in which and the time when the individual class members will be identified. If individual identification is not contemplated, the reasons therefor (e.g., reliance on fluid class recovery or non-monetary relief. See *Blue Chip Stamps v. Superior Court* (1976) 18 Cal.3d 381, 134 Cal.Rptr. 393, 556 P.2d 755.)

(h) Other matters relevant to this issue: If the declarations demonstrate that the class is interstate, the party maintaining the action will submit, in addition to other memoranda, a memorandum on the subject of whether this court has jurisdiction to render a binding judgment in favor of, or against, nonresident, unserved class members.

2. Issue: Common, Similar and Unique Questions of Law and Fact. Each party will submit a statement discussing each of the following:

(a) Those issues of law which are common to all class members.[2]

(b) Those issues of law which are similar to all class members and, with respect to each such issue, a detailed statement concerning how said issues may be determined on other than an individual basis.

(c) Those issues of law which are unique to one or more class members, but which must be presented in the trial. In the description of

---

2 In the context of these paragraphs an issue is "common to all members of the class" when the determination of that issue with respect to the representative's own claim will determine, without more, that issue with respect to the claims of all other class members.

Issues that must be determined separately with respect to each member of the class are not "common," although they may be "similar" in the sense that they exist with respect to each member's claim. The distinction between "common" and "similar" is illustrated by [*Vasquez* v. *Superior Court* (1971) 4 Cal.3d 800, 94 Cal.Rptr. 796, 484 P.2d 964]. One of the issues was whether the defendant had made certain representations to each member of the class. Proof that the representations had been made to one person would not establish that they had been made to others. Therefore, this issue was not common to all members of the class; for plaintiffs to prevail, the court would have had to find that defendant had made separately the representations to each class member. These were similar issues, not a comon issue.

Another question in the case was whether the representations, if made, were false. That turned on the question of whether the type of food freezer sold by defendant had the characteristics represented. This was a common issue to all members of the class, the court stating, at page 812 [94 Cal.Rptr. 803, 484 P.2d 971]:

"The falsity of these representations could be shown on a common basis, since proof of the allegations regarding the quality and price of the freezers purchased by the named plaintiffs would not provide proof as to all."

The presence of "similar" but non common issues in a case does not mean that it cannot be tried as a class action. In *Vasquez*, the complaint alleged that each salesman employed by defendant memorized a standard sales spiel which he recited to every member of the class, and plaintiff argued that this would enable him to prove that the representations were made to each class member without the necessity of individual testimony by each plaintiff. At page 812, [94 Cal.Rptr. 803, 484 P.2d 971], the court stated: "If plaintiffs can prove their allegations at the trial, an inference that the representations were made to each class member would arise, in which case it would be unnecessary to elicit the testimony of each plaintiff as to whether representations were in fact made to him."

An issue is "unique" when it applies only to one or more but less than all members of the class.

these unique issues of law, the segments of the class to which they are applicable will be described with a statement of the number within the class to whom each unique issue applies.

(d) The issues of law which must be litigated between class members.

(e) Those issues of fact which are common to all class members.

(f) Those issues of fact which are similar to all class members, with a detailed statement concerning how each such issue can be determined other than on an individual basis.

(g) Those issues of fact which are unique to one or more class members but which must be presented in the trial. In the description of these unique issues of fact, the segments of the class to which they are applicable will be described with a statement of the number within the class to whom each unique issue applies.

(h) The issues of fact which must be litigated between class members.

Each party also will discuss whether the issues of law and fact which are either common to all members of the class or, if not common, are similar and susceptible to proof by evidence applicable to all members of the class, predominate over issues which must be tried on an individual basis. These statements will set out an estimate of the number of witnesses and the time for their testimony upon issues which exist only as to individual or subclasses (including issues which must be litigated between class members).

3. Issue: Superiority of the Class Action to Other Available Methods for the Fair and Efficient Adjudication of the Controversy. Each party will submit statements concerning:

(a) Procedures alternative to a class action which might adjudicate the issues involved in the action. These will include an estimate of the time of trial of each alternative proceeding.

(b) The effectiveness of the remedies available under the alternatives described compared to those available under the class action. This could include a discussion of the number of persons who may receive compensation after each alternative proceeding (whether directly or indirectly by virtue of the judgment) and the difference, if any, in the amount thereof.

(c) The ability of the court to manage the alternative proceedings in relation to its ability to manage the conduct of the class action.

(d) The benefit to the public from each alternative proceeding. (e.g., if the action challenges the constitutionality of a statute, is a class action therefor of any greater benefit to the public than one on behalf of named plaintiffs only?)

(e) The propriety of relief other than money damages. This should include a discussion of the alternatives of fluid recovery, injunctive relief without any type of money damages (except attorney's fees and costs), or a combination of several types of relief.

(f) A description of other actions purporting to be brought on behalf of the same class, raising the same or similar issues, and a statement of the reasons the instant action should be allowed to proceed parallel to the others or should be abated or dismissed. (See section 427.7(a) for motions to coordinate cases pursuant to Code Civil Procedure, sec. 404 et seq.)

(g) If the action purports to be brought on behalf of a class which includes residents of states other than California, a statement as to whether (aside from jurisdictional limitations) the court should limit the class to California residents for reasons of public policy and manageability.

4. Issue: Membership of the Class Representative in the Class. The class representative will submit one or more declarations which present facts describing in detail: The facts submitted in a declaration must stand the test to which oral testimony would be subjected in the trial of an action. The declaration should contain enough competent evidence to convince the trier of fact. Averments which are satisfactory in pleadings are not competent evidence. The declaration should show the source of the declarant's information, that is, the declaration should contain a proper foundation.

(a) If membership in the class is dependent upon having participated in a transaction or series thereof, a description of each particular transaction which evidences when and in what manner the representative became a member of the class.

(b) If membership in the class is dependent upon ownership of property, membership in an organization or other status at the time of filing of the action, a description of each fact by which the representative acquired said status which made him a member of the class. He also will set out facts evidencing that he continues to have the status of a class member.

(c) Factual differences, if any, in the representative's status as a class member and those of any other persons within the class. If there are subclasses, a factual statement of the subclass of which the representative is a member.

He also will submit a statement describing in detail:

(d) Unique factual issues, if any, pertaining to the representative which must be litigated.

(e) Legal differences, if any, in the representative's status as a class member and those of any other persons within the class.

(f) Unique legal issues, if any, pertaining to the representative which must be litigated.

(g) Any defense of fact or law which may be asserted against the representative individually.

5. Issue: Ability of the Class Representative to Fairly and Adequately Protect the Interests of the Class.[3]

The class representative is a fiduciary of the class members (*LaSala v. American Savings and Loan Assn.* (1971) 5 Cal.3d 864, 97 Cal.Rptr. 849, 489 P.2d 1113) and has a duty at all times during the pendency of the litigation to make known to the court his relationship to the class members including those conflicts with, or differences in, their positions. The class representative will submit one or more declarations which present facts describing in detail:

(a) The amount of damages which the representative estimates will be awarded to the class and his share thereof or, if the class is the defendant, the total damages which may be suffered by the class and the representative's share thereof.

(b) Other class actions to which the representative or his spouse has been or now is a named party. The description of these should include case name, court designation and number, the nature of the controversy, its outcome, and the representative's (or spouse's) status there as a class representative or merely as a named party. If there remains an unsatisfied judgment or court order against him or his spouse from earlier litigation, the representative should set out the amounts thereof and the reason for failure to have paid them.

6. Issue: Necessity for and Content of Notice. It is recommended that this issue not be dealt with until the party advocating the existence of the class has received a favorable ruling from the court on the first five issues. At the time of the court's favorable ruling on the first five issues, the court will generally shorten the time for notice on this sixth issue.

When the moving party submits a motion concerning this issue, such motion must include:

(a) Original and copy of proposed order approving notice to the class;

(b) Original and copy of proposed notice to the class of pendency of class action.

Although as a general rule notice to the class of the pendency of the action shall be ordered, notice to the class is not necessary in all actions, and an order may be made, on motion of a party, dispensing with the requirement that the class be notified of the action. When a public entity or a public officer or public employee in his official capacity is an unnamed member of the plaintiff

3 See *McGhee v. Bank of America* (1976) 60 Cal.App.3d 442, 131 Cal.Rptr. 482.

or defendant class, notice of the motion to dispense with the requirement that the class be notified of the action must be served on said public entity, public office or employee in the same manner as a civil summons is served.

When the moving party submits a motion for an order concerning the giving of or dispensing with notice, such party will submit a statement on each of the following (e.g., said party will submit the proposed orders set forth above, even though he seeks an order dispensing with notice):

(a) A document discussing whether notice should be given at all.[4]

(b) A statement which assumes that notice will be given and discusses:

(i) The time when notice should be given.

(ii) The manner in which notice will be given. This will include a discussion concerning whether said notice should be published, mailed or otherwise brought to the attention of class members. If recommended to be published, it will include the recommended publication media, including an estimate of the cost thereof. If recommended to be mailed, it will include a statement of the manner in which addresses of the class members will be obtained and an estimate of the cost of preparation of the notice and of said mailing. If notice is to be given through other means, a description of said other means will be set out in detail, including an estimate of the cost. Each estimate of costs will contain a statement of the factual basis thereof. Each statement also will include an estimate, with the factual basis therefor, of the percentage of the class members which the party believes will receive knowledge of the pending action through use of each notice media.

(iii) The party who should bear the cost of giving the notice or manner in which the cost thereof should be divided between the parties.

(c) Each proposed notice will include, at least, a representation concerning each of the following:

(i) Brief explanation of the case, including basic contentions or denials of the parties.

(ii) Any member who so requests by a specified date may exclude himself from the class and the action by giving notice thereof ("opting out").

(iii) Information concerning how class members who desire to be excluded from the class ("opt out") may give notice thereof.

(iv) The claim of a member who does not request to be excluded from the class will be terminated by the judgment in the action under the rule of res judicata.

(v) Any member who does not request exclusion may move the court for permission to appear as a named class co-representative.

(vi) The estimated total amount for the recovery, the anticipated fee which will be sought by counsel for the class, the anticipated other expenses and costs to the class which will be paid from the funds recovered before distribution of the net proceeds to class members, and the net amount to be recovered by each member if the action is successful (a formula statement will be satisfactory).

7. Additional Issues. Certain issues, although not always unique to class actions, frequently arise in them and are appropriate for a pre-trial order after hearing, upon notice as provided in section 451. Among these issues are:

(a) *Consolidation, Severance, Abatement or Coordination.* A motion to consolidate with, or sever from, one or more other pending actions, to abate the instant action until certain other pending actions have proceeded to

4 See *Cartt* v. *Superior Court* (1976) 50 Cal.App.3d 960, 124 Cal.Rptr. 376; Cal.Civ.Code, sec. 1781(c)(3); *Anthony* v. *General Motors Corp.* (1973) 33 Cal.App.3d 699, 109 Cal.Rptr. 254.

judgment and similar motions based on the similarity of issues with those in other pending actions may be made to Code of Civil Procedure section 404 et seq.

(b) *Bifurcation.* A motion to bifurcate trial of the issue of liability of the defendant from trial on the class issues may be made (section 441).

(c) *Bonds.* Government Code section 947 and other sections provide that when a public entity is a defendant, a bond may be demanded by said defendant. A motion to excuse or fix the amount of the bond may be made.

(d) *Abuse of Class Action.* A motion to restrict or regulate contact of the named parties or counsel with the class may be made. The form of order generally approved by the court is that found in section 1.41 of the Appendix of Materials in the Federal Manual for Complex Litigation (excluding the last two paragraphs).

(e) *Intervention.* A motion to intervene pursuant to Code of Civil Procedure section 387 by one who earlier has excluded himself from the class ("opted out") may be made.

(f) *Joinder of a Class Member.* A motion by any class member that he be made a co-representative may be made; he also may move that as co-representative he be allowed to associate additional counsel to represent the class.

(g) *Precedence of Discovery.* A motion to establish a precedence among issues in discovery may be made. (e.g., where discovery on the issue of liability may be expensive and time consuming, a motion may be made limiting discovery to only class issues until an interlocutory order is made concerning those issues.)

(h) *All Motions for Summary Judgment* (total or partial) under Code of Civil Procedure section 437c in class actions. (*Home Savings and Loan Ass'n v. Superior Court* (1976) 54 Cal.App.3d 208, 126 Cal.Rptr. 511.)

(i) *Others.* The above are but a few of the additional issues which may be present in a class action and which properly may be the subject of a motion in a class hearing.

July 1982.

SECTION 428. ORDERS

1. Order Determining Issues. At the conclusion of each hearing, the court will make an order upon the issues presented to it in said hearing. The order will be final if it dismisses the maintainability of the action as a class action. Upon request of counsel, the court will make findings of fact and conclusions of law in support of its order dismissing the class. If the order does not dismiss the maintainability of the action as a class action, it will be interlocutory in nature and may be rescinded or modified as the changed circumstances of the class, its representative or the particular action otherwise require.

2. Order Requiring Additional Hearing. Notwithstanding section 428.1, at the conclusion of a hearing the court may make an order expressly deferring determination of the issues presented therein (e.g., that the evidence consist of oral testimony and particular exhibits) and otherwise direct the character of the presentation in said later hearing.

The court may order that additional discovery be made before said later hearing and, notwithstanding section 426.4, that it be presented in said later hearing.

The court may also order that said later hearing be a trial on a bifurcated issue pursuant to section 441.

3. Order Upon Stipulation. The court generally will approve stipulations resolving the class issues and make its order thereon (section 429). This approval and order thereon will make unnecessary a hearing on said issues.

4. Order Concerning Nature of Recovery. The court may order that recovery, if eventually obtained, will be of a nature other than that sought in the complaint. Thus, even though the complaint may seek only money damages, the court may order that the recovery be of the fluid recovery nature, for injunctive relief only, or a combination of types of relief.

5. Order Upon Other Class Matters. The court may grant orders on class issues of a nature not contemplated in this manual if equitable considerations make the granting of said orders beneficial to the determination of class issues.

6. Order Upon Non-appearance. When one or more of the parties do not appear at a regularly noticed hearing, the court in its discretion nevertheless may make an order on the issues presented or may place the matter off calendar.

7. Order Superseding Pleadings. An interlocutory order which is inconsistent with a pleading will supersede said pleading, and in trial the evidence will be directed to proof of the issue as determined by the order rather than the pleading. (e.g., if the complaint alleges that a class is composed of certain persons but the order after hearing defines the class to be smaller than that set out in the complaint, the definition in the order will supersede the description in the complaint and proof in the trial will be concerning the existence of the class as defined in said order.)

8. Relationship of the Interlocutory (Pre-trial) Order to Trial of the Class Issues. The existence of an interlocutory (pre-trial) order (section 428.1) does not relieve the party who has alleged the existence of a class from the burden of proving at trial the matters included within class issues 1 to 5, inclusive.

However, if the interlocutory order has excluded a portion of the alleged class (by defining the class to be less extensive than alleged), evidence will not be admitted at trial concerning that portion of the alleged class which earlier had been excluded by the interlocutory order.

9. Notice of Order. Although the court may direct the clerk to forward by mail to counsel copies of the order when made, it will be the responsibility of that counsel, who is directed by the court to give notice of the ruling, to give said notice.

July 1982.

SECTION 429. STIPULATIONS FOR AN ORDER

In many actions, one or more class issues are uncontroverted. (E.g., in many class actions constitution of the class may be clear, thus resolving issue 1.) The uncontroverted issues should be resolved by written stipulation executed by counsel and filed in court. Stipulations upon all class issues before hearing make the hearing unnecessary. Also, counsel are urged to attempt to stipulate to those class issues which are made the subject of an interlocutory order and remain to be tried. (In most instances, substantially all relevant evidence on the issue probably will have been revealed in the declarations submitted for the hearing.)

All stipulations should recite not only the matters included therein but should make reference to the issues as catalogued in this manual.

Stipulations may be presented at any time to the clerk of the Law and Motion Department or to the clerk of such other department that the presiding judge shall designate to hear pre-trial class action motions for approval by the judge presiding in said department. Said approval constitutes the order resolving the issues.

July 1982.

FILING CERTIFICATE OF READINESS

SECTION 431. FILING CERTIFICATE OF READINESS

A Certificate of Readiness will not be filed by any party until the court has made an order determining each class issue (section 428.1). The Certificate of Readiness when filed will include the statement (typed after paragraph 8 of the certificate) "8.1. All class issues have been determined by order of the court."

Notwithstanding the above, in those cases where the court orders bifurcation of issues and the early trial of the issue of liability (section 441), the Certificate of Readiness may be filed before the court has made an order determining each class issue, and the Certificate of Readiness need not contain that statement concerning determination of class issues set out above. In this instance, the Certificate of Readiness when filed will include the statement (typed after paragraph 8 of the certificate) "8.1 Trial on the issue of liability only pursuant to order of (insert date)."

July 1982.

EARLY TRIAL OF BIFURCATED ISSUE

SECTION 441. SCHEDULING EARLY TRIAL

1. Motion for Early Trial of Bifurcated Issue. Any named party may move, pursuant to Code of Civil Procedure section 597, that the court order an early trial of the class issues which have not been earlier resolved by order or stipulation.[1]

Any named party may move, pursuant to Code of Civil Procedure section 598, that the court order an early trial of the issue of the defendant's liability or may move for a separate trial of any cause or causes of action or separate issue, pursuant to Code of Civil Procedure section 1048(b).[2]

The court on its own motion may order an early trial on the class issues, liability or any cause of action or issue.

2. Procedure for Notice and Presentation of Motion. Those rules ordinarily followed when making a motion under Code of Civil Procedure sections 597 and 598 apply concerning the time and manner of noticing and making a motion for early trial of a bifurcated issue, except that all motions therefore will be noticed for the Law and Motion Department or such department as shall be designated by the presiding judge to hear pre-trial class action motion (see section 441.3), even though the motion is not to be made in conjunction with a hearing on class issues.

3. Place and Hour of Hearing. All motions for early trial of bifurcated issues will be noticed for hearing in the Law and Motion Department or such other department as shall be designated by the presiding judge to hear pre-trial class action motions. The party making said motion should first contact the clerk in the Law and Motion Department or such other department designated by the presiding judge to hear class action motions to ascertain the availability of a particular date before giving notice of hearing on the motion.

4. Time for Trial. Except for good cause, the court will not set the early trial of class issues for any date preceding the making of an interlocutory order on said issues after the conduct of one or more hearings thereon.

July 1982.

SECTION 442. ORDER AFTER EARLY TRIAL

At the conclusion of a trial on bifurcated issues, the court will make its order establishing the proof (or failure thereof) upon the issues presented therein, which order will constitute a final determination of said issues for all trial purposes.

July 1982.

SURVIVAL OF EXISTING PROCEDURES

SECTION 451. SURVIVAL OF EXISTING PROCEDURES

Although resolution of issues 1–6 may be made only through a class hearing noticed in the manner and for the department described herein (section 424), existing procedures for determination of other issues, even though the litigation involves a class, will be noticed in the manner and for the department generally applicable for the resolution of said issues.[3] Thus, issues concerning the sufficiency of pleadings and motions concerning discovery matter will be heard in the Law and Motion Department.

Motions upon matters within issue 7 (whether or not specifically described therein) will be noticed for the Law and Motion Department or such department that shall be designated by the presiding judge to hear pre-trial class action motions and will be subject to that time for notice

1 An answer controverting the existence or constituency of the class ". . . sets up (a) defense not involving the merits of the plaintiff's cause of action but constituting a bar or ground of abatement to the prosecution thereof . . ." as defined in Code of Civil Procedure section 597.

2 See *Colwell Co. v. Superior Court* (1975) 50 Cal.App.3d 32, 123 Cal.Rptr. 228.

3 See *Kass v. Young* (1977) 67 Cal.App.3d 100, 136 Cal.Rptr. 469. A default judgment cannot be obtained before determination of class issues.

set out in section 424.3 if said motion is to be heard in conjunction with the pre-trial hearing on one or more of the issues 1–6. However, if such motions are made at any other time, the following notice periods shall be applicable:

(a) Twenty (20) days: consolidation, severance or abatement, bifurcation and summary judgment.

(b) Ten (10) days: all others.

Response to the twenty (20) day motions shall be filed with the county clerk no later than 4:30 p.m. of the fifth court day preceding the scheduled hearing. Response to ten (10) day motions shall be filed with the county clerk no later than 4:30 p.m. of the second court day preceding the scheduled hearing.

July 1982.

SETTLEMENT HEARINGS AND JUDGMENTS

SECTION 461. NATURE OF CLASS ACTION SETTLEMENT HEARINGS

All agreements between the parties which settle the claims of the class and terminate the action must be approved by the court after hearing (herein "settlement hearing"), which approval will be reflected by a judgment. The court's approval is one based upon its acceptance of the fairness of the proposed settlement to the class for which the court will conduct an independent inquiry. The court after said hearing may refuse to approve the settlement if the court determines that it is not fair. The court may modify the terms thereof to achieve fairness, and if the parties agree to be bound by said modification, the court may approve said settlement.

July 1982.

SECTION 462. SCHEDULING SETTLEMENT HEARING

1. Motion for Hearing. Any party to a settlement agreement may submit a written notice of motion for approval of the agreement by the court. The notice of motion must be accompanied by all documents upon which the party will rely in the hearing on the motion, including, but not limited to, the following:

(a) Original and copy of settlement agreement

(b) Original and copy of proposed order granting settlement hearing

(c) Original and copy of proposed notice to the class of the pendency of the class action and notice of hearing on proposed settlement.

2. Notice of Motion.* Notice of motion for a settlement hearing should be noticed for the Law and Motion Department or such department that shall be designated by the presiding judge to hear pre-trial class action motions with the period of notice as set out in the Code of Civil Procedure section 1005. The party making said motion must ascertain from the clerk of said department the availability of a particular date before giving notice of hearing on the motion.

3. Order for Settlement Hearing. After hearing the motion, the court will make its order granting or denying a settlement hearing. If it grants a settlement hearing, its order will include the time and place of said settlement hearing, the notice thereof to be given to the class members, and other matters which it deems necessary to the proper conduct of a settlement hearing.

July 1982.

SECTION 463. CONDUCT OF SETTLEMENT HEARINGS

1. Procedure. The court will employ that procedure which it deems necessary to ascertain the fairness of the proposed settlement. This procedure may involve only a conference in chambers, may involve both a conference and the examination of documents, or may involve the taking of testimonial and other evidence.

2. Attorney's Fees. All agreements for the payment of fees to the attorney for the class representative should be included in the settlement. If the parties to said agreement are unable to agree to the amount of a fee, the court will

* Suggested title added by Publisher.

award only that amount which it determines to be reasonable, which amount may be less than that to which the parties agree. In every settlement hearing in which the representative seeks the award of fees to his attorney, said representative must present evidence to support his request. Said evidence will include, but is not limited to, the amount of the recovery, the contingent nature thereof (probability of success when the representation was undertaken), the number of hours which the attorney has devoted to the matter, his professional standing, his hourly rate for his office work and court appearances, his daily rate for office work and court appearances if said daily rate differs from mere accumulation of hours, and said attorney's agreement with the class representative concerning his fees. (See 1 Witkin, California Procedure, 2nd ed., 101 et seq., for a list of some of the relevant considerations.) Initial presentation of this evidence will be through a declaration.

July 1982.

SECTION 464. JUDGMENT

After the settlement hearing, the court will make and enter judgment pursuant to Code of Civil Procedure section 632 and other relevant sections. Where the judgment of the court requires future acts to be performed by the parties beyond mere payment of a money judgment by defendant, the judgment will provide for the court's retention of jurisdiction while satisfaction of the judgment is being effected. All proposed judgments which are submitted to the court with the settlement agreement should include a provision for retention of jurisdiction if said retention is appropriate and should provide in detail for the terms of said retained jurisdiction.

July 1982.

SECTION 470. ALL DISMISSALS SUBJECT TO COURT APPROVAL

Dismissals in class actions are also subject to prior court approval.[1] This includes not only dismissals of entire suits but also includes anything less than total dismissals, e.g. dismissal of certain causes of actions or of certain parties. All dismissal requests are handled by the Law and Motion Department or such department as shall be designated by the presiding judge to hear pre-trial class action motions.

The County Clerk is not authorized to process requests for dismissal of any type in class actions without prior court approval.

1. Documents to Be Filed.* Counsel shall file the following documents with the county clerk and deliver endorsed filed copies of the documents to the clerk of the Law and Motion Department or such department as shall be designated by the presiding judge to hear pre-trial class action motions:

(a) Request for Dismissal in the usual form

(b) The request must be accompanied by at least one declaration setting forth the facts upon which the party relies in seeking the dismissal. The declaration must clearly set forth whether or not consideration of any kind, direct or indirect, is being given for the dismissal. The details of any consideration must be set forth.

2. Court Approval or Disapproval. If the requested dismissal is approved, the court will sign an Order of Dismissal which will then be entered by the County Clerk. Notice of the signing of the order will be sent to the attorneys of record by the clerk in the Department approving the dismissal.

If the requested dismissal is not being approved, notice of such tentative disapproval will be sent to the attorneys of record with a request that they set the matter for hearing in the department on a date acceptable to the court's calendar.

July 1982.

---

1 See *LaScala* v. *American Savings & Loan Assn.* 5 Cal.3d 864, 97 Cal.Rptr. 849, 489, P.2d 1113; *Marcarelli* v. *Cabell* (1976) 58 Cal.App.3d 51, 129 Cal.Rptr. 509; *Anthony* v. *Superior Court* (1976) 59 Cal.App.3d 760, 130 Cal.Rptr. 758.

* Suggested title added by Publisher.

SAN MATEO COUNTY SUPERIOR COURT RULES

DIVISION VII. PRETRIAL PROCEEDINGS IN CLASS ACTIONS

RULE 7.1 INTRODUCTION

This division sets out the pretrial procedures to be used by this court in class action suits brought under Code of Civil Procedure Section 382 or Civil Code Sections 1750, et seq., to determine class issues and for terminating class suits prior to trial. The RULE sets forth general procedures and does not purport to codify the law governing class actions. It is the intent of this court that this RULE be applied flexibly and in light of the particular circumstances of a given case. In appropriate cases,[1] any named party may move for relief from compliance with this RULE on the ground that the pending case does not involve a class action of the nature contemplated by this RULE.

Eff. July 1, 1996.

RULE 7.2 ISSUES SUBJECT TO PRETRIAL DETERMINATION

(a) Class Issues. To the extent required by applicable law, the court shall consider the following class issues to determine whether a class action properly exists:

(1) Constitution of the class (composition, number, location, description, possible subclasses, etc. of the class).

(2) Whether common issues of law or fact predominate over individual issues.

(3) Superiority of the class action to other available methods for the fair and efficient adjudication of the controversy.

(4) Membership of the class representative in the class.

(5) Ability of class representative to fairly and adequately protect the interests of the class.

(6) Necessity for and contents of notice.

(b) Additional Issues. When appropriate, the court may also consider additional pertinent issues, including consolidation, severance, coordination, bifurcation, communication with the class, intervention, joinder, and precedence of discovery.

Eff. July 1, 1996.

RULE 7.3 CAPTION OF PLEADINGS

All complaints for or against a class party shall include in the caption the designation "CLASS ACTION". This designation shall be typewritten in capital letters on the first page of the complaint immediately below the Clerk of the Court's file number but above the general description of the nature of the complaint.

Eff. July 1, 1996.

RULE 7.4 PRETRIAL PROCEEDINGS

Two types of pretrial proceedings may be scheduled to resolve issues involved in class actions.

(a) Informal Conferences. One or more conferences, informal in nature, may, in the discretion of the court, be held upon written notice of any named party or the court. The conferences will be held in chambers to discuss class issues involved, establishment of precedence of discovery, scheduling of hearings and other matters. At these conferences no evidence may be presented, but the court will expect all attorneys to have sufficient knowledge of the class issues to discuss proposed stipulations resolving any class issues.

(1) *Timing.* The conference may be held any time after all the defendants have made an appearance in the case, following written notice

1 For example, a taxpayer action under C.C.P. Section 526(a) or an action by an association as the representative of its members (see, e.g., Professional Fire Fighters v. City of Los Angeles, 60 Cal.2d 276, 32 Cal.Rptr. 830 (1963)); a mandamus action to compel performance of a public duty (see, e.g., Diaz v. Quitoriano, 268 Cal.App.2d 807, 74 Cal.Rptr. 358 (1969)); actions analogous to those defined by RULE 23(b)(1) and (b)(2) of the Federal RULES of Civil Procedure.

at least fifteen days before the date of the conference.

(2) *Order.* At the conclusion of the conference, the court shall make an order embracing any stipulations of the parties and establishing a schedule for discovery, the date for subsequent informal conferences, if any, and the initial pretrial hearing on class issues. The order will be binding on all parties until modified or terminated. Nothing contained herein shall preclude a party from stating on the record any objection to the court's conference order.

(b) Pretrial Hearings on Class Issues. One or more pretrial hearings will be held to resolve class issues. Presentation of evidence at the hearing will be through declarations submitted and previously discovered evidence. Oral testimony will not be permitted except on leave of court. The burden of proof on all class issues is on the party alleging the existence of the class, and all class issues must be proved by a preponderance of the evidence.

(1) *Initial Hearings.* An initial pretrial hearing will be held to resolve, at least, class issues (1)-(5) listed in Rule 7.2(a) (and, if appropriate, also issue 6). All motions must be accompanied by documents on all issues to be presented to the court. The party who has alleged the existence of the class must submit declarations on issues 1, 4 and 5.

(2) *Subsequent Hearings.* A subsequent hearing may be held to resolve class issues not earlier resolved or, upon a sufficient showing of changed factual circumstances having occurred or new evidence having been discovered after the earlier hearing, to reconsider class issues. If issue was not determined earlier, that issue must be determined at the subsequent hearing.

(3) *Filing of Documents.* All notices of motion for pretrial proceedings to resolve class issues must be filed and served at least thirty days before the date of the hearing. All response documents must be filed at least fifteen days before the date of the hearing. All documents in reply to the response must be filed at least five days before the date of the hearing.

(4) *Contents of Documents.* Every notice of motion for pretrial proceedings to resolve class issues must be accompanied by appropriate declarations and by a memorandum of points and authorities, including a statement separately discussing each class issue to be resolved in terms of the pleadings, the evidence before the court, and such other matters as are appropriate to set forth that party's position on each issue.

Eff. July 1, 1996.

RULE 7.5 NOTICE TO PUBLIC ENTITY OR OFFICIAL

When a public entity, or a public official or public employee in his or her official capacity is an unnamed member of the class, notice of the pendency of the class action shall be given to that entity, official, or employee, if known. If the action seeks relief, other than money damages, for adverse environmental effects which affect the public generally, notice shall be served on the State Attorney General.

Eff. July 1, 1996.

RULE 7.6 CLASS ACTION ORDER

At the conclusion of each hearing, the court will make an order upon the issues presented to it. The order will be final if it dismisses the maintainability of the action as a class action; if the order does not dismiss the action as a class action it will be interlocutory in nature and may be rescinded or modified as the changed circumstances of the action require. An order certifying a class supersedes the pleadings but does not relieve the party from the burden of proving at trial the matters included within class issues (1) through (5) of Rule 7.2(A).

Eff. July 1, 1996.

RULE 7.7 EARLY OR SEPARATE TRIAL

Any named party may move for, or the court on its own motion may order, an early trial of appropriate issues under Code of Civil Procedure Section 597 or Section 598, or a separate trial of any cause of action or issue under Code of Civil Procedure Section 1048(b). At the conclusion of the trial on bifurcated issues, the court will make its order establishing the proof (or failure therefor) upon the issues presented. The order will constitute a final determination of said issues for all trial purposes.

Eff. July 1, 1996.

RULE 7.8 CERTIFICATE OF READINESS

No certificate of readiness may be filed until all class issues have been resolved and appropriate orders made.

Eff. July 1, 1996.

RULE 7.9 SETTLEMENT OF CLASS CLAIMS

All agreements between the parties which settle the claims of the class and terminate the action must be approved by the court after a settlement hearing. The notice of any motion for approval of the agreement must be accompanied by a copy of the proposed notice to the class on the proposed settlement and by the proposed method of giving notice, which shall be the same as that previously used in the case, unless otherwise determined by the court. All agreements on fees to be paid to attorneys for the class as part of the settlement should be included in the settlement. Regardless of the sum agreed upon by the parties, the court will award only that amount of fees which it determines to be reasonable.

Eff. July 1, 1996.

RULE 7.10 RETENTION OF JURISDICTION

Where the judgment of the court requires the parties to perform future acts beyond mere payment of a money judgment, the judgment shall provide for the court's retention of jurisdiction while satisfaction of the judgment is being effected.

Eff. July 1, 1996.

RULE 7.11 DISMISSALS

Dismissals or partial dismissals in class actions are subject to prior court approval. Any request for dismissal must be accompanied by at least one declaration setting forth the facts upon which the party relies in seeking the dismissal, as well as the full terms of any settlement between the named parties. Notice to the class may be required before the dismissal is approved.

Eff. July 1, 1996.

TABLE OF STATUTES AND RULES

UNITED STATES CODE

Tit.:Sec.	This Work Sec.
15:78j(b)	12.04
15:78t(a)	12.04
28:1407	1.04
	11.01
28:1738	9.04

FEDERAL RULES OF CIVIL PROCEDURE

Rule	This Work Sec.
23	1.01
	1.03
	1.04
	1.05
	1.06
	2.07
	2.08
	3.11
	4.03
	4.04
	5.02
	7.01
	7.02
	7.04
	9.04

CAL. CONSTITUTION

Art.	This Work Sec.
VI, § 10	1.01

CAL. BUSINESS AND PROFESSIONS CODE

Sec.	This Work Sec.
6147	10.02
16760	5.03
	11.03
	11.02
17082	3.03

CAL. BUSINESS AND PROFESSIONS CODE

Sec.	This Work Sec.
17200	3.03
17204	3.03

CAL. CIVIL CODE

Sec.	This Work Sec.
1750 et seq.	1.01
	1.03
	1.05
	2.05
	3.12
	7.02
1752	3.12
1770	3.12
1781	1.03
	1.05
	3.12
	7.01
	7.03
1782	3.12
1784	3.12

CAL. CODE OF CIVIL PROCEDURE

Sec.	This Work Sec.
170.1	6.02
170.6	6.02
369.5	3.05
378	6.02
379	6.02
382	1.01
	1.03
	1.05
	1.07
	2.01
	2.06
	4.02
	5.02
	5.03
	7.01

CAL. CODE OF CIVIL PROCEDURE

Sec.	This Work Sec.
383	3.06
384	4.02
387	4.04
	6.02
404	1.04
	6.02
404–404.8	11.01
410.30	5.02
474	5.03
526a	3.04
527	3.02
	11.03
564	3.08
581	9.03
583	6.01
597	8.03
	11.02
598	8.03
	11.02
638	8.03
	11.02
639	8.03
	11.02
877	9.04
877.6	1.01
	9.04
1021	10.01
1021.5	10.01
	10.04
1048	11.02
1085	3.09

CAL. CORPORATIONS CODE

Sec.	This Work Sec.
17501	5.02

CAL. REVENUE AND TAX CODE

Sec.	This Work Sec.
19055	3.04

CAL. RULES OF COURT

Rule	This Work Sec.
365	6.01
	9.03
1501	11.01

CAL. STANDARDS OF JUDICIAL ADMINISTRATION

Sec.	This Work Sec.
19	6.02

LOS ANGELES COUNTY SUPERIOR COURT RULES

Rule	This Work Sec.
15.4	6.01
	8.02
15.6	8.02
15.10	7.02
15.18	4.02
	4.03
	5.03
	7.02
	7.03
	9.04
15.36	8.03
15.41	4.02
15.45	9.04
18.45	10.04

SAN FRANCISCO COUNTY SUPERIOR COURT RULES

Rule	Sec.
363	10.04
427	7.03
441	8.03
461	9.04

SAN MATEO COUNTY SUPERIOR COURT RULES

Rule	This Work Sec.
7.2	7.02

7.4 . . . . 6.01
7.7 . . . . 8.03
7.9 . . . . 9.04
. . . . 10.4

TABLE OF CASES

Abella v. Riverside Unified Sch. Dist. (1976) 65 Cal.App.3d 153 [135 Cal.Rptr. 177]—§ 7.02[F]

Altman v. Manhattan Savings Bank (1978) 83 Cal.App.3d 761 [148 Cal.Rptr. 100]—§ 4.03[H]

American Pipe & Construction Co. v. Utah (1974) 414 U.S. 538 [38 L.Ed.2d 713, 94 S.Ct. 756]—§ 5.03[F]

American Suzuki Motor Corp. v. Superior Court (1995) 37 Cal.App.4th 1291 [44 Cal.Rptr.2d 526]—§§ 4.02[F], 12.06

Anthony v. Superior Court of Los Angeles County (1976) 59 Cal.App.3d 760 [130 Cal.Rptr. 758]—§§ 4.03[G], 5.02[C], 9.03[C]

Armstrong v. Board of School Directors (7th Cir. 1980) 616 F.2d 305—§ 9.04[C]

Atari, Inc. v. Superior Court (1985) 166 Cal.App.3d 867 [212 Cal.Rptr. 773]—§§ . 6.01[H], 12.13

B.W.I. Custom Kitchen v. Owens-Illinois, Inc. (1987) 191 Cal.App.3d 1341 [235 Cal.Rptr. 228]—§§ 2.04, 4.02[C], 5.03[D], [E], 11.03[D], 12.02

Balon v. Drost (1993) 20 Cal.App.4th 483 [25 Cal.Rptr.2d 12]—§ 5.03[H]

Baltimore Football Club, Inc. v. Superior Court (1985) 171 Cal.App.3d 352 [215 Cal.Rptr. 323]—§§ 4.03[G], [I], 12.12

Bangert v. Narmco Materials Inc. (1984) 163 Cal.App.3d 207 [209 Cal.Rptr. 438]—§ 5.03[F]

Bartlett v. Hawaiian Village, Inc. (1978) 87 Cal.App.3d 435 [151 Cal.Rptr. 392]—§ 4.03[I]

Beasley v. Wells Fargo Bank (1991) 235 Cal.App.3d 1383 [1 Cal.Rptr.2d 459]—§§ 10.04[B], [C], 12.05

Becker v. McMillin Construction Co. (1991) 226 Cal.App.3d 1493 [277 Cal.Rptr. 491]—§§ 5.03[F], 7.02[E], 12.09

Bell v. American Title Ins. Co. (1991) 226 Cal.App.3d 1589 [277 Cal.Rptr. 583]—§§ 1.01[C], 3.11, 4.04[D], 6.01[G], 7.02[E], 9.04[H], 12.09[J]

Bingham v. Obledo (1983) 147 Cal.App.3d 401 [195 Cal.Rptr. 142]—§§ 2.07, 3.11, 7.04[E], 9.03[B]

Blue Chip Stamps v. Superior Court (1976) 18 Cal.3d 381 [134 Cal.Rptr. 393]—§§ 2.06, 4.03[B]

Boeing v. Van Gemert (1980) 444 U.S. 472 [62 L.Ed.2d 676, 100 S.Ct. 745]—§ 10.04[B]

Bronco Wine Co. v. Frank A. Logoluso Farms (1989) 214 Cal.App.3d 699 [214 Cal.Rptr. 899]—§§ 1.02, 3.03

Brown v. Regents of the University of California (1984) 151 Cal.App.3d 982 [198 Cal.Rptr. 916]—§§ 4.03[H], 5.03[E], 6.01[B], 12.11

Budget Finance Plan v. Superior Court In and For Santa Cruz County (1973) 34 Cal.App.3d 794 [110 Cal.Rptr. 302]—§ 6.03[H]

Carabini v. Superior Court (1994) 26 Cal.App.4th 239 [31 Cal.Rptr.2d 520]—§§ 1.01[C], 7.02[B]

Carlson v. Superior Court for Los Angeles County (1973) 33 Cal.App.3d 640 [109 Cal.Rptr. 240]—§ 6.03[C]
Caro v. Procter & Gamble Co. (1993) 18 Cal.App.4th 644 [22 Cal.Rptr.2d 419]—§§ 4.03[F], 7.02[E], [G]
Carson v. American Brands, Inc. (1981) 450 U.S. 79 [67 L.Ed.2d 59, 101 S.Ct. 993]—§ 9.04[C]
Cartt v. Superior Court of Los Angeles County (1975) 50 Cal.App.3d 960 [124 Cal.Rptr. 376]—§§ 1.01[C], 1.04[B], 2.07, 4.02[A], 7.03[A]
Central Railroad and Banking of Georgia v. Petus (1885) 113 U.S. 116 [28 L.Ed. 915, 5 S.Ct. 387]—§ 10.04[B]
Central Valley Chap. 7th Step Foundation v. Younger (1979) 95 Cal.App.3d 212 [157 Cal.Rptr. 117]—§ 5.03[B]
Citizens Against Forced Annexation v. County of Santa Clara (1984) 153 Cal.App.3d 89 [200 Cal.Rptr. 166]—§ 3.05
City of San Jose v. Superior Court of Santa Clara County (1974) 12 Cal.3d 447 [115 Cal.Rptr. 797, 525 P.2d 701]—§§ 1.03, 2.04, 4.03[C], 5.03[E], 6.01[A], 7.02[B], 9.03[B], 12.09
Civil Service Emp. Ins. Co. v. Superior Court of City and County of San Francisco (1978) 22 Cal.3d 362 [149 Cal.Rptr. 360, 584 P.2d 497]—§§ 2.05, 6.01[I], 7.03[C]
Classen v. Weller (1983) 145 Cal.App.3d 27 [192 Cal.Rptr. 914]—§§ 2.04, 5.02[D], 5.03[D], 12.02, 12.09[G]
Clemons v. Western Photo Camera Hut (1981) 117 Cal.App.3d 392 [172 Cal.Rptr. 782]—§ 1.01[C]
Clothesrigger, Inc. v. GTE Corporation (1987) 191 Cal.App.3d 605 [236 Cal.Rptr. 605]—§ 7.02[I]
Collins v. Safeway Stores, Inc. (1986) 187 Cal.App.3d 62 [231 Cal.Rptr. 638]—§§ 6.01[C], 7.02[E]
Collins v. Rocha (1972) 7 Cal.3d 232 [102 Cal.Rptr. 1, 497 P.2d 225]—§ 4.02[A], [E]
Colonial Life & Acc. Ins. Co. v. Superior Court of Los Angeles County (1982) 31 Cal.3d 785 [183 Cal.Rptr. 810, 647 P.2d 86]—§ 6.03[H]
Colwell Co. v. Superior Court of County of Los Angeles (1975) 50 Cal.App.3d 32 [123 Cal.Rptr. 228]—§§ 6.01[I], 8.02[B]
Coopers & Lybrand v. Livesay (1978) 473 U.S. 463 [57 L.Ed.2d 351, 98 S.Ct. 2454]—§ 7.04[A]
D'Amico v. Sitmar Cruises, Inc. (1980) 109 Cal.App.3d 323 [167 Cal.Rptr. 254]—§ 4.03[I]
Daar v. Yellow Cab Co. (1967) 67 Cal.2d 695 [63 Cal.Rptr. 724, 433 P.2d 732]—§§ 1.01[B], 4.03[H], 5.03[B], [D], [E], 7.04[A]
Daniels v. Sanitarium Ass'n, Inc. (1963) 59 Cal.2d 602 [30 Cal.Rptr. 828]—§ 3.05
Daniels v. Centennial Group, Inc. (1993) 16 Cal.App.4th 467 [21 Cal.Rptr.2d 1]—§§ 1.01[C], 5.03[G], 7.02[F], 12.07
Danzig v. Superior Court for Alameda County (1978) 87 Cal.App.3d 604 [151 Cal.Rptr. 185]—§ 6.03[F]

Danzig v. Jack Grynberg & Associates (1984) 161 Cal.App.3d 1128 [208 Cal.Rptr. 336]—§§ 7.02[C], 12.07
Dean Witter Reynolds, Inc. v. Superior Court of Alameda County (1989) 211 Cal.App.3d 758 [259 Cal.Rptr. 789]—§§ 4.03[F], 5.03[D], 12.07
Del Mar Beach Club Owners Ass'n. v. Imperial Contracting Co. (1981) 123 Cal.App.3d 898 [176 Cal.Rptr. 886]—§ 3.07
Devidian v. Automotive Service Dealers Ass'n. (1973) 35 Cal.App.3d 978 [111 Cal.Rptr. 228]—§§ 4.03[D], 5.03[G]
Diamond v. General Motors Corp. (1971) 20 Cal.App.3d 374 [97 Cal.Rptr. 639]—§§ 4.03[D], 5.03[G]
Dunk v. Ford Motor Company (1996) 48 Cal.App.4th 1794 [56 Cal.Rptr,2d 483]—§ 9.04[C], [J], 10.04[B], [D]
Eisen v. Carlisle and Jacquelin (1974) 417 U.S. 156 [40 L.Ed.2d 732, 94 S.Ct. 2140]—§ 1.04[B]
Environmental Coalition of Orange County Inc. v. Local Agency Formation Com. (1980) 110 Cal.App.3d 164 [167 Cal.Rptr. 735]—§ 1.02
Espinoza v. Machonga (1992) 9 Cal.App.4th 268 [11 Cal.Rptr.2d 498]—§ 9.04[J]
Estate of Davis (1990) 219 Cal.App.3d 663 [268 Cal.Rptr. 384]—§ 4.04[F]
Fanucchi v. Coberly-West Co. (1957) 151 Cal.App.2d 72 [311 P.2d 33]—§§ 4.03[J], 5.03[C]
Farrar v. Franchise Tax Bd. (1993) 15 Cal.App.4th 10 [18 Cal.Rptr.2d 611]—§§ 3.04, 12.10
Fenning v. Glenfed Inc. (1995) 40 Cal.App.4th 1285 [47 Cal.Rptr.2d 715]—§ 5.02[B]
Frazier v. City of Richmond (1986) 184 Cal.App.3d 1491 [228 Cal.Rptr. 376]—§§ 4.04[B], 9.04[H], 12.13
Fuhrman v. California Satellite Systems (1986) 179 Cal.App.3d 408 [231 Cal.Rptr. 113]—§§ 4.03[H], 6.01[C]
Gainey v. Occidental Land Research (1986) 186 Cal.App.3d 105 [231 Cal.Rptr. 249]—§ 7.03[B]
Gardner v. County of Los Angeles (1995) 34 Cal.App.4th 200 [40 Cal.Rptr.2d 271]—§§ 3.02, 12.10
General Motors Corp. v. Superior Court of Alameda County (1983) 141 Cal.App.3d 966 [190 Cal.Rptr. 742]—§ 5.02[C]
General Motors Corp. v. Superior Court (1988) 199 Cal.App.3d 247 [244 Cal.Rptr. 776]—§§ 4.03[G], 7.04[B], 12.06
Granberry v. Islay Investments (1995) 9 Cal.4th 738 [38 Cal.Rptr.2d 650, 889 P.2d 970]—§§ 4.02[E], 12.09
Green v. Obledo (1981) 29 Cal.3d 126 [172 Cal.Rptr. 206, 624 P.2d 256]—§§ 6.01[I], 7.01, 12.10
Grogan-Beall v. Ferdinand Roten Galleries, Inc. (1982) 133 Cal.App.3d 969 [184 Cal.Rptr. 411]—§ 7.04[C]
Hamwi v. Citinational-Buckeye Investment Co. (1977) 72 Cal.App.3d 462 [140 Cal.Rptr. 215]—§§ 1.01[C], 7.02[D], [F], 12.09
Hansberry v. Lee (1941) 311 U.S. 32 [85 L.Ed. 22, 61 S.Ct. 115]—§ 1.02
Hebbard v. Colgrove (1972) 28 Cal.App.3d 1017 [105 Cal.Rptr. 172]—§ 4.02[A]

Hitz v. Interstate Bank (1995) 38 Cal.App.4th 274 [44 Cal.Rptr.2d 869]—§ 12.05
Hogya v. Superior Court, County of San Diego (National Meat Packers, Inc., Real Party In Interest) (1977) 75 Cal.App.3d 122 [142 Cal.Rptr. 325]—§§ 1.01[C], 3.12, 7.02[F]
Home Sav. and Loan Ass'n v. Superior Court (1974) 42 Cal.App.3d 1006 [117 Cal.Rptr. 485]—§§ 1.01[C], 6.01[I], 7.03[A], 8.02[B], 11.03[B]
Home Sav. and Loan Ass'n v. Superior Court (1976) 54 Cal.App.3d 208 [126 Cal.Rptr. 511]—§§ 1.01[C], 6.01[I]
Hypolite v. Carleson (1975) 52 Cal.App.3d 566 [125 Cal.Rptr. 221]—§§ 1.01[D], 5.03[B], 7.04[E]
Illinois Brick Co. v. Illinois (1977) 431 U.S. 720 [52 L.Ed.2d 707, 97 S.Ct. 2061]—§ 12.02
In re Hill (9th Cir. 1985) 775 F.2d 1037—§ 10.04[B]
In re Activision Securities Litigation (ND Cal. 1989) 723 F.Supp. 1373—§ 10.04[B]
In re "Agent Orange" Products Liability Litigation (2d Cir. 1987) 818 F.2d 11—§ 9.04[A]
Izzi v. Mesquite Country Club (1986) 186 Cal.App.3d 1309 [231 Cal.Rptr. 315]—§§ 3.10, 12.09[H]
Jacobson v. Simmons Real Estate (1994) 23 Cal.App.4th 1285 [28 Cal.Rptr.2d 699]—§ 10.01
Johnson v. American Airlines, Inc. (1984) 157 Cal.App.3d 427 [203 Cal.Rptr. 638]—§§ 1.03, 4.03[I]
Jolly v. Eli Lilly & Co. (1988) 44 Cal.3d 1103 [245 Cal.Rptr. 658, 751 P.2d 923]—§§ 5.03[F], 12.11
Kass v. Young (1977) 67 Cal.App.3d 100 [136 Cal.Rptr. 469]—§ 6.01[D]
Kaye v. Mt. La Jolla Homeowners Ass'n (1988) 204 Cal.App.3d 1476 [252 Cal.Rptr. 67]—§§ 1.02, 2.06, 4.03[B], 4.03[E]. 6.01[F], 8.01, 12.09[H]
Keating v. Superior Court of Alameda County (1982) 31 Cal.3d 584 [183 Cal.Rptr. 360]—§ 3.10
Keith G. v. Bilbray (1995) 36 Cal.App.4th 1587 [43 Cal.Rptr.2d 277]—§ 12.10
La Sala v. American Sav. & Loan Ass'n (1971) 5 Cal.3d 864 [97 Cal.Rptr. 849, 489 P.2d 1113]—§§ 1.03, 4.02[F], 5.03[D], [E], 6.01[E], 9.03[B], 11.03[D]
Lambert v. California (1957) 355 U.S. 225 [2 L.Ed.2d 228, 78 S.Ct. 240]—§ 1.02
Lampf, Pleva, Lipkind, Prupis & Pedigrew v. Gilbertson (1991) 501 U.S. 350 [115 L.Ed.2d 321, 111 S.Ct. 2773]—§ 12.04
Lazar v. Hertz Corporation (1983) 143 Cal.App.3d 128 [191 Cal.Rptr. 849]—§ 12.14
Lewis v. Prudential-Bache Securities (1986) 179 Cal.App.3d 935 [225 Cal.Rptr. 69]—§ 3.10
Lindy Bros. v. American Radiator & Standard Sanitary Co. (3d Cir. 1973) 487 F.2d 161—§ 10.04[B]
Little v. Sanchez (1985) 166 Cal.App.3d 501 [213 Cal.Rptr. 297]—§ 12.09[F]
Los Angeles County Democratic Central Committee v. County of Los Angeles (1976) 61 Cal.App.3d 335 [132 Cal.Rptr. 43]—§ 7.02[C]
Macmanus v. A.E. Realty Partners (1987) 195 Cal.App.3d 1106 [241 Cal.Rptr. 315]—§ 12.09[I]
Mallick v. Superior Court In and For San Mateo County (1979) 89 Cal.App.3d 434 [152 Cal.Rptr. 503]—§ 9.04[C]
Marcarelli v. Cabell (1976) 58 Cal.App.3d 51 [129 Cal.Rptr. 509]—§ 9.03[B]

Mashburn v. National Healthcare Inc. (1988) 684 F.Supp. 660—§ 10.04[B]
Massey v. Bank of America Nat. Trust and Sav. Ass'n (1976) 56 Cal.App.3d 29 [128 Cal.Rptr. 144]—§§ 6.01[F], 7.02[C]
Matsushita Electric Industrial Co., Ltd. v. Epstein (1996) __U.S.__ [134 L.Ed.2d 6, 116 S.Ct. 873]—§§ 1.04[C], 4.04[C], 9.04[K], 12.04
McConnell v. Merrill Lynch, Pierce, Fenner & Smith, Inc. (1983) 33 Cal.3d 816 [191 Cal.Rptr. 458, 662 P.2d 916]—§ 12.08
McGhee v. Bank of America (1976) 60 Cal.App.3d 442 [131 Cal.Rptr. 482]—§§ 1.03, 6.03[H], 10.02, 12.09
Miller v. Woods (1983) 148 Cal.App.3d 862 [196 Cal.Rptr. 69]—§§ 4.02[E], 12.10
Mirkin v. Wasserman (1993) 5 Cal.4th 1082 [282 Cal.Rptr. 101]—§ 12.04
National Solar Equipment Owners' Ass'n, Inc. v. Grumman Corporation (1991) 235 Cal.App.3d 1273 [1 Cal.Rptr.2d 325]—§§ 1.01[C], 3.05, 6.03[C], [F], 12.07
Neecke v. City of Mill Valley (1995) 39 Cal.App.4th 946 [46 Cal.Rptr.2d 266]—§ 3.04
Osborne v. Subaru of America, Inc. (1988) 198 Cal.App.3d 646 [243 Cal.Rptr. 815]—§§ 4.03[G], 12.06
Paul, Johnson, Alston & Hunt v. Graulty (9th Cir. 1989) 886 F.2d 268—§ 10.04[B]
People v. Pacific Land Research Co. (1977) 20 Cal.3d 10 [141 Cal.Rptr. 20]—§ 7.03[C]
People v. National Ass'n of Realtors (1981) 120 Cal.App.3d 459 [174 Cal.Rptr. 728]—§ 12.02
Petherbridge v. Altadena Federal Sav. and Loan Ass'n (1974) 37 Cal.App.3d 193 [112 Cal.Rptr. 144]—§ 5.03[G]
Piambino v. Bailey (5th Cir. 1980) 610 F.2d 1306 cert. denied, 449 U.S. 1011—§ 9.04[C]
Pinnacle Holdings, Inc. v. Simon (1995) 31 Cal.App.4th 1430 [37 Cal.Rptr.2d 778]—§§ 4.03[E], 12.09
Quinn v. State of California (1975) 15 Cal.3d 162 [124 Cal.Rptr. 1, 539 P.2d 761]—§ 10.04[B]
Reich v. Club Universe (1981) 125 Cal.App.3d 965 [178 Cal.Rptr. 473]—§§ 4.02[F], 4.04[D], 5.03[D]
Renken v. Compton City School District (1962) 207 Cal.App.2d 106 [24 Cal.Rptr. 347]—§ 4.02[A]
Residents of Beverly Glen, Inc. v. City of Los Angeles (1973) 34 Cal.App.3d 117 [109 Cal.Rptr. 724]—§ 3.05
Reyes v. Board of Supervisors (1987) 196 Cal.App.3d 1263 [242 Cal.Rptr. 339]—§§ 2.02, 2.03, 2.07, 3.11, 4.02[A], 4.02[E], 12.10
Rich v. Schwab (1984) 162 Cal.App.3d 739 [209 Cal.Rptr. 417]—§ 12.09
Richmond v. Dart Industries, Inc. (1981) 29 Cal.3d 462 [174 Cal.Rptr. 515, 629 P.2d 23]—§§ 1.01[B], 1.02, 2.01, 4.03[J], 5.03[C], 6.01[G], 12.09[G]
Rosack v. Volvo of America Corporation (1982) 131 Cal.App.3d 741 [182 Cal.Rptr. 800]—§§ 1.01[C], 7.04[B], 11.03[C], [D], 12.02
Rose v. Medtronics, Inc. (1980) 107 Cal.App.3d 150 [166 Cal.Rptr. 16]—§§ 4.02[A], 4.03[H], 12.11
Rose v. City of Hayward (1981) 126 Cal.App.3d 926 [179 Cal.Rptr. 287]—§§ 5.03[C], 12.10

Salton City, etc., Owners Ass'n v. Penn Philips Co. (1977) 75 Cal.App.3d 184 [141 Cal.Rptr. 895]—§ 3.07

Samura v. Kaiser Foundation Health Plan, Inc. (1993) 17 Cal.App.4th 1284 [22 Cal.Rptr.2d 20]—§ 10.04[B]

San Francisco Unified School Dist. v. W.R.Grace & Company-Connecticut (1995) 37 Cal.App.4th 1318 [44 Cal.Rptr.2d 305]—§ 5.03[F]

Saunders v. Superior Court (California Reporting Alliance) (1994) 27 Cal.App.4th 832 [33 Cal.Rptr.2d 438]—§ 3.03

Schneider v. Vennard (1986) 183 Cal.App.3d 1340 [228 Cal.Rptr. 800]—§§ 4.04[D], 12.04

Seely v. White Motor Co. (1965) 63 Cal.2d 9 [45 Cal.Rptr. 17]—§ 5.03[F]

Simons v. Horowitz (1984) 151 Cal.App.3d 834 [199 Cal.Rptr. 134]—§§ 4.03[E], 5.03[H], 10.02

Slakey Brothers Sacramento, Inc. v. Parker (1968) 265 Cal.App.2d 204 [71 Cal.Rptr. 269]—§ 4.02[A]

Smalley v. Citibank (1995) 11 Cal.4th 138 [44 Cal.Rptr.2d 441]—§ 12.05

Southern California Edison Co. v. Superior Court of Los Angeles County (1972) 7 Cal.3d 832 [103 Cal.Rptr. 709, 500 P.2d 621]—§ 6.03[C]

Southland Corp. v. Keating (1984) 465 U.S. 1 [79 L.Ed.2d 1, 104 S.Ct. 852]—§ 3.10

State v. Levi Strauss & Co. (1986) 41 Cal.3d 460, 472 [224 Cal.Rptr. 605]—§§ 4.02[E], 5.03[C], 11.03[C], 12.02

Stephen v. Enterprise Rent-A-Car (1991) 235 Cal.App.3d 806 [1 Cal.Rptr.2d 130]—§§ 1.01[C], 6.03[A], 7.02[C], 7.04[A], 12.14

Stephens v. Montgomery Ward & Company (1987) 193 Cal.App.3d 411 [238 Cal.Rptr. 602]—§§ 4.02[C], 7.02[H], 12.03

Stilson v. Reader's Digest Ass'n, Inc. (1972) 28 Cal.App.3d 270 [104 Cal.Rptr 581]—§§ 4.02[E], 4.03[B]

Suburban Mobile Homes, Inc. v. Amfac Communities, Inc. (1980) 101 Cal.App.3d 532 [161 Cal.Rptr. 811]—§ 12.02

Tech-Bilt, Inc. v. Woodward-Clyde & Associates (1985) 38 Cal.3d 488 [213 Cal.Rptr. 256]—§ 9.04[C]

Tenants Association of Park Santa Anita v. Southers (1990) 222 Cal.App.3d 1293 [272 Cal.Rptr. 361]—§§ 3.07, 12.09

Title U.S.A. Ins. Corp. v. Armato, Gaims, Weil, West, and Epstein (1995) 36 Cal.App.4th 363 [42 Cal.Rptr.2d 498]—§ 3.08

Trotsky v. Los Angeles Fed. Sav. & Loan Ass'n (1975) 48 Cal.App.3d 134 [121 Cal.Rptr. 637]—§§ 4.04[D], 9.04[B]

Union Mut. Life Ins. Co. v. Superior Court (Bobby Ray Scott, Real Party in Interest) (1978) 80 Cal.App.3d 1 [145 Cal.Rptr. 316]—§§ 1.01[D], 4.03[G], 6.03[A], 6.03[H], 7.02[C]

Union Carbide Corp. v. Superior Court (1984) 36 Cal.3d 15 [201 Cal.Rptr. 580]—§ 12.02

Vasquez v. Superior Court (1971) 4 Cal.3d 800 [94 Cal.Rptr. 796, 484 P.2d 964]—§§ 1.01[B], 2.02, 5.03[C], [D], 7.03[C], 11.03[D]

Weaver v. Pasadena Tournament of Roses (1948) 32 Cal.2d 833 [198 P.2d 514]—§§ 2.02, 4.03[I], 5.03[B], 12.12

Woosley v. State of California (1992) 3 Cal.4th 758 [13 Cal.Rptr.2d 30]—§ 3.04
Zahn v. International Paper (1973) 414 U.S. 291 [38 L.Ed.2d 511, 94 S.Ct. 505]—§ 1.04[B]

INDEX

References are to Sections

ADVANTAGES OF CLASS ACTIONS, § 1.04

ADEQUACY OF REPRESENTATION, §§ 2.04, 4.02[F]

ADVERSE CALIFORNIA CASE LAW, § 4.03

AGGREGATE CLASS DAMAGES, § 5.03[C]

ALLEGATIONS, CLASS, § 5.02[E]

ALTERNATIVES TO CLASS ACTIONS
- Association as representative party, § 3.07
- Associations managing common-interest developments, § 3.06
- Association status, suits based on, § 3.05
- Class arbitration, § 3.10
- Class treatment without notice, § 3.11
- Consumer Legal Remedies Act, § 3.12
- Court-appointed receiver, § 3.08
- Injunctive relief, § 3.02
- Mandamus against government, § 3.09
- Mass torts consolidation test cases, § 3.13
- Taxpayer lawsuits, § 3.04
- Unfair competition injunctions, § 3.03

AMENDMENT TO COMPLAINT
- Presently unknown defendants, § 5.03[H]

ANTAGONISTIC CLASS MEMBERS, § 4.03[J]

ANTITRUST CASES, § 12.02

APPLICABLE LAW AND RULES, § 1.01[B]

APPROVAL PROCEDURE (SETTLEMENT), § 9.04

ARBITRATION, §§ 3.10, 11.02[E]

ASCERTAINABLE CLASS, § 2.02

ASSOCIATIONS
- As plaintiffs in general, §§ 3.06, 3.07
- Common interest developments as representative party, § 3.06
- Suits based on association status, § 3.05

ATTORNEY'S FEES
- Commercial realty in compensation, § 10.03
- Common fund compensation, § 10.04
- Form of retainer agreement, § 10.10
- Form of memorandum of points and authorities in support of motion for order awarding attorney's fees and costs, appointing settlement administrator, and allowing enhancements for representatives, § 10.11
- Fundamental principles, § 10.01
- Qualifications of class counsel, § 10.02
- Settlement paying class attorney's fees only, § 9.03[C]

BANK AND CREDIT CARD OVERCHARGE CASES, § 12.05

BAR ORDERS, §§ 9.04[J],[K], 11.02[F]

BENEFIT,
- Substantial benefit as a prerequisite, § 7.02[G]

BIFURCATION, § 11.02[B]

BROKERAGE AGREEMENT CASES, § 12.08

BURDEN
- Class certification burden on plaintiff, § 7.02[F]

CASE MANAGEMENT
- See Precertification Case Management

CASE LAW
- Effect of adverse, § 4.03

CAUSES OF ACTION, §§ 5.02[F], 6.03[G]

CERTIFICATION
- Form of declaration in support of plaintiffs' motion for class certification, § 7.12
- Form of declaration regarding time, manner, and estimated cost of notice, § 7.10
- Form of memorandum of points and authorities in opposition to plaintiffs' motion for order determining class issues, § 7.13
- Form of memorandum of points and authorities in support of plaintiffs' motion for class certification, § 7.11
- Form of order certifying class, § 7.16
- Form of order determining class issues (first hearing), § 7.14
- Form of order determining class issues (second hearing), § 7.15
- Procedure generally, §§ 7.02, 7.03, 7.04

CERTIFICATION HEARINGS
- Burden on plaintiff, § 7.02[F]
- Findings of fact, § 7.02[H]
- Nature, § 7.02[D]
- Notice, § 7.02[B]
- Scope of inquiry, § 7.02[E]
- Standard of review on appeal, § 7.02[I]
- Superior benefit, § 7.02[G]
- Timing, § 7.02[C]

CHALLENGES, PEREMPTORY, § 6.02[F]

CHALLENGES FOR CAUSE, § 6.02[G]

CLASS ACTION AUTHORITY, § 1.05

CLASS
- Allegations, § 5.02[E]
- Ascertainable, focusing and defining key issues in class complaints, § 5.03[A]
- Certification hearing, § 7.02
- Defendant class, § 5.03[H]
- Definition, § 4.02[A]
- Discovery, § 6.03
- Notice, § 2.07
- Settlement Procedure, § 9.04

CLASS COMPOSITION, DISCOVERY OF, § 6.03[G]

CLASS DISCOVERY, § 6.03[B]

COMMERCIAL REALITY AS COMPENSATION, § 10.03

COMMON FUND COMPENSATION, § 10.04

COMMON QUESTIONS OF LAW AND FACT, § 4.02[C]

COMMUNICATIONS WITH PROPOSED CLASS MEMBERS, § 6.01[G]

COMMUNITY OF INTEREST, § 2.03

COMPLAINTS
- Ascertainable class, defining, § 5.03[B]
- Backbone of case, § 5.03[E]
- Caption, § 5.02[A]
- Causes of action, § 5.02[F]
- Certification issues, § 5.03[A]
- Class allegations, § 5.02[E]
- Class representative issues, § 5.03[D]
- Damages, § 5.03[C]
- Form of complaint, §§ 5.10, 5.11
- Form of notice of motion on special demurrers, § 5.12
- Generally, §§ 5.02, 5.03
- Jurisdiction, § 5.02[B]
- Multiple defendants, § 5.03[G]
- Parties, § 5.02[D]
- Statute of limitations, § 5.03[F]
- Unknown defendants, § 5.03[H]
- Venue and forum, § 5.02[C]

COMPLEX DESIGNATION,
- Designation of case as, § 6.02[E]
- Form of declaration of attorney in support of order consolidating demurrer hearings, designating case as complex, and setting pretrial conference, § 8.12

CONCURRENT CLASS ACTIONS, § 4.04[D]

CONDITIONAL CLASSWIDE AND PRECERTIFICATION (settlement), § 9.04[E]

CONDOMINIUM CASES, § 12.09[H]

CONSOLIDATION, § 6.02[C]

CONSUMER LEGAL REMEDIES ACT, §§ 2.05, 3.12

CONSTRUCTION DEFECT CASES, § 12.09[C]
COORDINATION, § 6.02[B]
COURT-APPOINTED RECEIVERS, § 3.08
CREDIT OVERCHARGE CASES, § 12.05
DAMAGES, UNIQUE ISSUES, § 4.03[H]
DEATH KNELL DOCTRINE, § 7.04[A]
DECIDING WHETHER TO FILE A CLASS ACTION, § 4.01
DEEDS OF TRUST, § 12.09[A]
DEFENDANTS
  Defendant class, § 5.02[H]
  Multiple, accused of wrongdoing, §§ 4.03[D]; 5.03[F]
  Settlement consideration, § 9.02[E]
DEFENDANT'S CONDUCT, DISCOVERY OF, § 6.03[G]
DISCOVERY FROM PLAINTIFFS TO DEFENDANTS, § 6.03[D]
DOCUMENT DEPOSITORIES, DISCOVERY OF, § 6.03[E]
DELAY IN PROSECUTION, DISMISSAL FOR, § 6.01[F]
DEMURRERS TO CLASS ALLEGATIONS, § 6.01[C]
DIFFERENCES BETWEEN CALIFORNIA AND FEDERAL CLASS ACTION LAW, §§ 1.01[C], 1.07
DISCOVERY
  See precertification discovery
DISCRIMINATION, § 12.03
DISMISSAL
  Mandatory requirement of court approval for, § 6.01[F]
  Requirement of court approval on settlement, § 9.03
DRAFTING, CALIFORNIA CLASS ACTION COMPLAINT, § 5.02
DUE PROCESS REQUIREMENTS, § 1.02
EMOTIONAL DISTRESS CLAIMS, § 4.03[C]
EMPLOYMENT DISCRIMINATION CASES, § 12.03
ESCROW PRACTICE CASES, § 12.09[I]
EVIDENTIARY ISSUES, PRETRIAL DISPOSITION OF, § 11.02[I]
EX PARTE
  Application for court approval of preliminary terms of settlement and notice, § 9.04[A]
  Declaration of attorney in support of ex parte application approving precertification notice, § 6.11
  Memorandum in support of ex parte application for order approving precertification notice, § 6.10
  Notice of ex parte application for order consolidating demurrer hearings, designating case as complex, and setting pretrial conference, § 8.10
EXTENSIVE GROUP LITIGATION, § 4.04[E]
FAIRNESS, REASONABLENESS AND ADEQUACY, § 9.04[C]
FEDERAL AUTHORITY, § 1.06
FEDERAL AND STATE PREREQUISITES, § 1.07
FEE CONTRACTS, § 10.10
FIDUCIARY DUTY, § 6.01[A]
FORMS, ILLUSTRATIVE
  Complaint, §§ 5.10, 5.11
  Declaration in support of ex parte application approving precertification notice, § 6.11
  Declaration in support of order consolidating demurrer hearings, designating case as complex, and setting pretrial conference, § 8.12
  Declaration in support of plaintiffs' motion for class certification, § 7.12
  Declaration regarding time, manner, and estimated cost of notice, § 7.10
  Judgment on order of final approval of settlement, § 9.14
  Memorandum of points and authorities in opposition to plaintiffs' motion for order determining class issues, § 7.13

Memorandum in support of ex parte application for order approving precertification notice, § 6.10
Memorandum of points and authorities in support of final approval of partial settlement of class action; award of attorney's fees and costs, § 9.12
Memorandum of points and authorities in support of order consolidating demurrer hearings, designating case as complex, and setting pretrial conference, § 8.11
Memorandum of points and authorities in support of motion for order awarding attorney's fees and costs, appointing settlement administrator, and allowing enhancements for representatives, § 10.11
Memorandum of points and authorities in support of plaintiffs' motion for class certification, § 7.11
Notice of ex parte application for order consolidating demurrer hearings, designating case as complex, and setting pretrial conference, § 8.10
Notice of motion on special demurrers, § 5.12
Order certifying class, § 7.16
Order determining class issues (first hearing), § 7.14
Order determining class issues (second hearing), § 7.15
Order for case management, § 8.13
Order of preliminary approval of settlement, and approval of notice of pendency of class action, preliminary approval of settlement and setting fairness hearing, § 9.13
Retainer agreement, § 10.10
Stipulation regarding temporary and conditional certification of class for settlement purposes only and order, § 9.10
Stipulation re settlement, § 9.11

GOOD FAITH
Settlement, determination of, § 9.04

GOVERNMENT BENEFITS AND TAXES CASES, § 12.10

HEARING
Class certification, nature of, § 7.02
Class notice, § 7.03[B]

HISTORY/DEVELOPMENT OF CALIFORNIA CLASS ACTIONS
See Foreword

INJUNCTIONS
As alternative to class action, § 3.02
Unfair competition, § 3.03

INTERMEDIATE CLASS RULING, § 7.04[B]

INTERROGATORIES, § 6.03[F]

INTERROGATORIES, DISCOVERY OF, § 6.03[F]

INTERVENTION, §§ 4.04[F], 6.02[D]

INTRODUCTION, CALIFORNIA CLASS ACTIONS, § 1.01

INVESTMENT SCHEME CASES, § 12.07

JURISDICTION,
Due process, § 1.02
National class, California court requirements, § 4.03[G]

LANDLORD-TENANT CASES, § 12.09[D]

LIMITATION ON PRE-CERTIFICATION MERITS RULINGS, § 6.01[I]

LIMITATIONS
Tolling the statute of, § 5.03[E]

LITIGATION
Related, the effect of, § 4.04

LOCAL RULES, IMPORTANCE OF, § 1.01[D]

MANAGEABLE TRIAL
Proposing, § 8.01

MANDAMUS AGAINST GOVERNMENT, § 3.09

MANDATORY CLASS CERTIFICATION, § 7.04[D]

MANDATORY DISMISSAL, § 6.01[F]

MASS TORTS/CONSOLIDATION/TEST CASES, § 3.13

MEMBERS

Class antagonistic to class action, § 4.03[J]

MERITS
Postmerits rulings, notice, § 7.04[E]

MOBILE HOME RENT CASES, § 12.09[E]

MOTIONS
See Precertification Motions

MULTIPLE DEFENDANTS ACCUSED OF WRONGDOING, § 4.03[D]

NATIONAL IMPORTANCE OF CALIFORNIA CLASS ACTIONS, § 1.01[A]

NATURE OF THE HEARING,
Class certification procedure, § 7.02[D]

NOTICE
Class, § 7.03
Hearing on, § 7.03[B]
When required and what it must say, § 7.03[A]

NOTICE IN OPT-OUT CASES, § 9.04 [I]

NOTICE TO CLASS/CLASS SETTLEMENT PROCEDURE, § 9.04[B]

NUISANCE AND TRESPASS CASES, § 12.09[B]

OUTLINING THE CASE
Benefits to litigants and court, § 4.02[G]
Class definition, § 4.02[A]
Class period, § 4.02[B]
Class representation, § 4.02[F]
Common questions of law and fact, § 4.02[C]
Residual questions, § 4.02[D]
Relief sought, § 4.02[E]

PARTNERSHIP AND INVESTMENT SCHEMES, § 12.07

PEREMPTORY CHALLENGES TO TRIAL JUDGE, § 6.02[F]

"PITFALL" CASES, § 4.03

POST CERTIFICATION SETTLEMENT, § 9.04[F]

PRECERTIFICATION
Communications with proposed class members, § 6.01[G]
Conduct, § 6.01
Conferences, § 6.01[B]
Default, § 6.01[D]
Discovery, § 6.03
Dismissal, § 6.01[E], [F]
Demurrers, § 6.01[C]
Fiduciary responsibility, § 6.01[A]
Form of memorandum in support of ex parte application for order approving precertification notice, § 6.10
Form of declaration of atotrney in support of ex parte application approving precertification notice, § 6.11
Merits rulings, § 6.01[I]
Motions, § 6.02
Notices, § 6.01[H]
Stage, § 6.01

PRECERTIFICATION CASE MANAGEMENT
Appointing a discovery master, § 8.02[C]
Informal conferences, § 8.02[A]
Form of case management order, § 8.13
Form of declaration of attorney in support of order consolidating demurrer hearings, designating case as complex, and setting pretrial conference, § 8.12
Form of memorandum of points and authorities in support of order consolidating demurrer hearings, designating case as complex, and setting pretrial conference, § 8.11
Form of plaintiffs' notice of ex parte application for order consolidating demurrer hearings, designating case as complex, and setting pretrial conference, § 8.10
Precertification determinations, § 8.02[B]

PRECERTIFICATION DISCOVERY
Causes of action, § 6.03[G]
Class discovery, § 6.03[B]
Defendant's conduct, § 6.03[G]
Defendant to plaintiff class, § 6.03[C]
Determining class composition, § 6.03[G]

Discovery from plaintiffs to defendants, § 6.03[D]
Document depositories, § 6.03[E]
Interrogatories, § 6.03[F]

PRECERTIFICATION MOTIONS
Challenges for cause, § 6.02[G]
Challenges, peremptory, § 6.02[F]
Complex designation, § 6.02[E]
Consolidation, § 6.02[C]
Coordination, § 6.02[B]
Intervention, § 6.02[D]

PREDOMINANCE OF COMMON QUESTIONS
Building the backbone of your case, § 5.03[A]

PREREQUISITES TO FILING AN ACTION
Adequacy of representation, § 2.04
Ascertainable class, § 2.02
Class notice, § 2.07
Community of interest, § 2.03
Comparison of federal and state prerequisites, § 2.08
Consumer Legal Remedies Act, § 2.05
Substantial benefit, § 2.06

PRESUMPTION
Inferences building the back bone of the case, § 5.03[E][3]

PRETRIAL DISPOSITION OF EVIDENCE ISSUES, § 11.02[I]

PRETRIAL MASTER OR REFERENCE REPORTS, § 11.02[D]

PROCEDURE
California, §§ 1.03, 7.01 et seq.

PRODUCTS LIABILITY CASES, § 12.06

PROPERTY-RELATED CASES
Deeds of trust, § 12.09[A]
Nuisance and trespass, § 12.09[B]
Construction defect, § 12.09[C]
Landlord-tenant, § 12.09[D]
Mobile home rents, § 12.09[E]
Unlawful detainers, § 12.09[F]
Subdivision land sales, § 12.09[G]
Condominiums, § 12.09[H]
Escrow practices, § 12.09[I]
Title Insurance practices, § 12.09[J]

PROPOSING MANAGEABLE TRIAL, § 8.01

QUALIFICATIONS OF CLASS COUNSEL, § 10.02

REASONABLENESS REQUIREMENT, § 10.04[D]

RECOVERY
Plaintiffs' unique facts regarding, § 4.03[C]
Realistic evaluation of recovery sources, § 9.02

REFERENCE REPORTS
Pre-trial master, § 11.02[D]

RELATED LITIGATION
Concurrent class actions, § 4.04[D]
Effect of, § 4.04
Extensive group litigation, § 4.04[E]
Importance of early analysis, § 4.04[A]
Intervention, § 4.04[F]
Successive class actions or federal class actions precluding state class treatment, § 4.04[B]
Successive class actions or state class actions precluding federal class treatment, § 4.04[C]

REMEDIAL STATUTES
Superiority to class treatment, § 4.03[F]

REPRESENTATIVE
Class/adequacy of, § 4.02[F][1]

SECURITIES CASES, § 12.04

SETTLEMENT ISSUES AND PROCEDURE
Attorney's fees conflicts, § 9.03[G]
Conditional classwide and precertification settlement, § 9.03[E]
Defendant considerations, § 9.02[E]
Discovery of insurance information, § 9.02[B]
Dismissal, § 9.03
Effective date of settlement, § 9.03[L]
Ex parte or noticed court approval of preliminary terms, § 9.03[A]
Form of judgment on order of final approval of settlement, § 9.14

COHELAN ON CALIFORNIA CLASS ACTIONS

2000 UPDATE PAMPHLET

Timothy D. Cohelan
Cohelan & Khoury
San Diego, California

THE EXPERT SERIES

WEST GROUP

San Francisco, California
2000
ISBN 0-314-22196-4

WEST GROUP
610 Opperman Drive
P.O. Box 64526
St. Paul, MN 55164-0526
1-800-328-9352

ISBN 0-314-22196-4

Library of Congress Catalog Card No. 97-060489

PREFACE

Since last year's 1999 supplement to *California Class Actions*, decisions by the Ninth Circuit and the California Supreme Court, and changes to California state practice and procedure require discussion.

The Ninth Circuit Court of Appeals vacated an earlier decision and now affirms state court settlements compromising federal claims. (*Epstein v. MCA, Inc.* (9th Cir. 1999) 179 F.3d 641.) The California Supreme Court continued its expansive interpretation of California's unfair competition statute (Bus. & Prof. Code, § 17200), an alternative to class action treatment, and reiterated its view of the Unfair Competition Act in *Cel-Tech Communications, Inc.* v. *Los Angeles Cellular Telephone Company* (1999) 20 Cal.4th 163 [83 Cal.Rptr.2d 548, 973 P.2d 527], as a law with cumulative remedies not necessarily dependent on companion causes of action.

At the trial court level, presiding judges now are encouraged to assign class cases to interested, experienced, and willing judges. California practitioners, after January 1, 2000, will need to complete a Civil Cover Sheet identifying class action cases as "provisionally" complex under rule 1800 of the California Rules of Court. The California Standards for Judicial Administration recommended by the Judicial Council now specifically encourage presiding judges to select judges for complex litigation assignments after consideration of the judge's ability, interests, training, experience (including experience with complex civil cases), and willingness to participate in educational programs related to the management of complex civil cases. (Cal. Rules of Court, Appendix, Div. I, § 19, subd. (c).) Additionally, this section discourages the use of commissioners "in any phase of complex litigation" unless necessary to assist in the management of the case. (*Id.*) This potentially impacts certain pretrial practices in certain superior court jurisdictions, such as those of Los Angeles County.

In addition, according to these new rules, judges assigned to handle complex cases should be given assistance where possible, including research attorneys and administrative staff. (Cal. Rules of Court, Appendix, Div. I, § 19, subd. (j).)

This new coverage is merged in this pamphlet with the 1999 updates, which include interpretations of the Unfair Competition Act in *Stop Youth Addiction Inc. v. Lucky Stores, Inc.* (1998) 17 Cal.4th 553 [71 Cal.Rptr.2d 731]; increase in favor for national classes in California courts as seen in *Diamond Multimedia Systems, Inc. v. Superior Court of Santa Clara County* (1999) 19 Cal.4th 1036 [80 Cal.Rptr.2d 828]; and the use of classwide arbitration as discussed in *Blue Cross of California v. Superior Court of Los Angeles County* (1998) 67 Cal.App.4th 42 [78 Cal.Rptr.2d 779].

Timothy D. Cohelan
San Diego

COORDINATED RESEARCH IN CALIFORNIA FROM WEST GROUP

WITKIN TREATISES

Summary of California Law, 9th
California Procedure, 4th
California Evidence, 3rd
California Criminal Law, 2d (with Norman Epstein)
[*Also available on CD-ROM*]

CALIFORNIA JURISPRUDENCE (3D)

[*Also available on CD-ROM*]

JURY INSTRUCTIONS

California Jury Instructions—Civil (BAJI), 8th
California Jury Instructions—Criminal (CALJIC), 6th
[*Also available in computer disk and looseleaf formats*]

CALIFORNIA CIVIL PRACTICE

Business Litigation
Civil Rights Litigation
Employment Litigation
Environmental Litigation
Family Law Litigation
Probate and Trust Proceedings
Procedure
Real Property Litigation
Torts
Workers' Compensation
[*Also available on CD-ROM*]

CALIFORNIA LITIGATION AND TRANSACTIONS FORMS

California Transactions Forms: Business Entities
California Transactions Forms: Business Transactions
California Transactions Forms: Estate Planning
California Transactions Forms: Family Law
[*Also available on CD-ROM*]

CALIFORNIA PRACTICE GUIDES AND HANDBOOKS

California Affirmative Defenses 2d
Ann Taylor Schwing

California Community Property Law 3d
William W. Bassett

California Insurance Law 4th Desk Reference
Bruce Cornblum

California Insurance Law Handbook
John K. DiMugno and Paul E. B. Glad

California Insurance Law Reporter

California Legal Filing Directory
Patricia A. Britton

California Medical Malpractice
George McDonald

California Prejudgment Money Remedies
Justice John Zebrowski, Barry Adler, and Paul S. Malingagio

California Premises Liability Law and Practice
Michael Thomas, Mark Kelegian, and Paul Gutierrez

California Subpoena Handbook
John M. Sink

California Tort Reporter

Taxing California Property
Kenneth A. Ehrman and Sean Flavin

California Family Law Practice Library on CD-ROM

California Personal Injury Practice Library on CD-ROM

THE EXPERT SERIES

Cohelan on California Class Actions
Timothy D. Cohelan

Dunne on Depositions in California
Kevin J. Dunne

Overly on Electronic Evidence in California
Michael R. Overly

Simons on California Evidence
Judge Mark B. Simons

Younger on California Motions
Judge Eric E. Younger (ret.)

REAL ESTATE PRACTICE

California Real Estate 2d
Harry Miller and Marvin Starr

California Real Estate Forms
Alexander Hamilton

California Real Property Digest

Real Estate NewsAlert
[*Also available on CD-ROM*]

California Construction Law Manual 5th
James Acret

California Construction Law Reporter

California Foreclosure
Margaret Sheneman

California Real Estate Practice Library on CD-ROM

CRIMINAL PRACTICE

West's California Criminal Law
Douglas Dalton

West's California Criminal Procedure
Laurie L. Levenson

California Criminal Trialbook
Harry M. Caldwell, Sue Steding and Gary Nichols

California Criminal Forms and Instructions 2d
Edward A. Rucker and Mark E. Overland

California Drunk Driving Defense 2d
Lawrence Taylor

California Criminal Practice Library on CD-ROM

JURY SELECTION PRACTICE BOOKS

Bennett's Guide to Jury Selection and Trial Dynamics: California Criminal Litigation

Bennett's Guide to Jury Selection and Trial Dynamics: California Civil Litigation
Cathy E. Bennett, Robert B. Hirschhorn and Dr. Jo-Ellan Dimitrius

---

WEST'S CALIFORNIA CODE FORMS

Business and Professions
Joel S. Primes

Civil
Jeanne P. Robinson

Civil Procedure
Gregory L. Ogden and Daryl Fisher-Ogden

Commercial
Stephen N. Hollman and Ray D. Henson

Corporations
Janet E. Kerr

Education
Jay E. Grenig

Elections, Fish & Game, Food & Agricultural, Insurance
Susan J. Orton

Family
Margaret McAllister

Government
Jay E. Grenig

Probate
Ann E. Stodden and Timothy A. Whitehouse

Public Utilities
Boris H. Lakusta

Revenue and Taxation
Anthony X. McDermott

RUTTER PRACTICE GUIDES

Alternative Dispute Resolution
Civil Appeals and Writs
Civil Procedure Before Trial
Civil Trials and Evidence
Corporations
Enforcing Judgments and Debts
Family Law
Federal Civil Procedure Before Trial
Federal Civil Trials and Evidence
Federal Ninth Circuit Civil Appellate Practice
Insurance Litigation
Landlord-Tenant

Law Practice Management
Personal Injury
Probate
Professional Responsibility
Real Property Transactions
[*Also available on CD-ROM*]

WEST'S ANNOTATED CALIFORNIA CODES

[*Also available on CD-ROM*]

BARCLAY'S OFFICIAL CALIFORNIA CODE OF REGULATIONS

[*Also available on CD-ROM*]

CALIFORNIA OFFICIAL REPORTS

[*Also available on CD-ROM*]

CALIFORNIA DIGEST OF OFFICIAL REPORTS 3D

[*Also available on CD-ROM*]

WEST'S CALIFORNIA REPORTER

[*Also available on CD-ROM*]

WEST'S CALIFORNIA DIGEST 2D

[*Also available on CD-ROM*]

WEST GROUP'S CALIFORNIA DESKTOP CODES

Unannotated Desktop Codes
California Civil Code
California Code of Civil Procedure
California Corporations Code
California Education Code
California Evidence Code
California Insurance Code
California Penal Code
California Probate Code
California Revenue and Taxation Code
California Vehicle Code
California Water Code
California Business Statutes
California Employment Laws

California Environmental Laws
California Family Laws and Rules
California Juvenile Laws and Rules

Annotated Desktop Codes

California Civil Practice Statutes and Rules
Blumberg California Family Code Annotated
California Commercial Code Annotated
DiMugno & Glad California Insurance Laws Annotated
Dwyer & Bergsund California Environmental Laws Annotated
Imwinkelreid & Hallahan California Evidence Code Annotated
McGovern California Probate Code Annotated
Miller and Starr Real Estate Laws Annotated

Court Rules

California Rules of Court—State and Federal
Northern California Local Court Rules—Superior Court
Bay Area Local Court Rules—Superior Court
Central California Local Court Rules—Superior Court
Southern California Local Court Rules—Superior Court
Los Angeles County Court Rules—Superior Court

JUDICIAL COUNCIL FORMS

California Judicial Council Forms (Official Publisher)
Legal Solutions Judicial Council and local forms disk products (DOS and Windows)
See the Judicial Council Forms provided by West Group on the Internet at www.courtinfo.ca.gov/forms.

INTERNET

Visit West Group's online store on the World Wide Web at http://www.westgroup.com.

For more information about West Group's California practice tools, please call your West Group Representative or West Group Customer Service at 1-800-328-4880. You may also fax inquiries to 1-800-340-9378 (WEST). If you have research questions concerning WESTLAW® or West Group Publications, please call the West Reference Attorneys at 1-800-733-2889.

CHAPTER 2

PREREQUISITES TO FILING A CALIFORNIA CLASS ACTION

PAGE 2-4

§ 2.04 Adequacy of Representation

[Insert after last sentence of § 2.04:]

Class settlements have triggered United States Supreme Court review of the role settlement may play in determining the propriety of class certification. These decisions often hinge on questions that at their heart deal with adequacy of representation.

"The adequacy inquiry under rule 23(a)(4) serves to uncover conflicts of interest between named parties and the class they seek to represent . . . [citations omitted]. . . . 'The class representative must be a part of the class and "possess the same interest and suffer the same injury" as the class members.'" In *Amchem Products, Inc. v. George Windsor* (1997) 521 U.S. 591 [117 S.Ct. 2231, 138 L.Ed.2d 689], the court found that the named parties with diverse medical conditions were inadequate to represent a single, giant class rather than discrete subclasses. The interests of those within the single class were not aligned. In that case the most salient difference was that the currently injured were primarily motivated by generous, immediate payments with exposure only or later injured plaintiffs being allowed separate rights in an "inflation protected fund for the future." (*Amchem Products, Inc. v. George Windsor* (1997) 521 U.S. 591 [117 S.Ct. 2231, 138 L.Ed.2d 689].)

In *Amchem* "the settling parties achieved a global compromise with no structural assurance of fair and adequate representation for the diverse groups and individuals affected." The objectors in *Amchem* further maintained class counsel and the class representatives had disqualifying conflicts of interest in that the claimants whose injuries had become manifest and claimants without manifest injuries should not have common counsel and should not be aggregated in a single class. The settlement was negotiated by class counsel representing those immediately injured.

A 1990 California case had reached the same conclusion. *Rebney v. Wells Fargo* (1990) 220 Cal.App.3d 1117 [269 Cal.Rptr. 844] found a lack of standing to argue a class settlement expansion for failure to suffer the same injury as class members, i.e., not paying the same fees or having the same market rate account as class members and therefore with atypical claims. The difference between the

recent *Amchem* case and *Rebney* is that in *Amchem* the objections were advanced in the settlement by aggrieved parties.

The Ninth Circuit Court of Appeals in *Epstein v. MCA, Inc.* (9th Cir. 1997) 126 F.3d 1235, after remand of *Matsushita Electric Industrial Co. v. Epstein* (1996) 516 U.S. 367 [116 S.Ct. 873, 134 L.Ed.2d 6], stated, "binding absentees to any part of a class action judgment is an act of judicial power. . .. [citations omitted] and that power can only be exercised over absentees when their interests have, in fact, been adequately represented by parties lawfully authorized to represent them . . .." (*Epstein v. MCA, Inc.* (9th Cir. 1997) 126 F.3d 1235, 1241.)

The Ninth Circuit determined that it could withhold full faith and credit from a Delaware judgment because it was entered into in a settlement which violated the due process right of the absent class members to adequate representation at all times.

In *Epstein*, the plaintiffs were allowed to challenge adequacy of representation even though they failed to intervene at the fairness hearing in the underlying state matter.

The Ninth Circuit found that the underlying judgment issued after the settlement in the Delaware court was approved did not result in issue preclusion and was subject to a collateral attack because the issue of adequacy of representation was "never actually litigated in the chancery court." (*Epstein v. MCA, Inc.* (9th Cir. 1997) 126 F.3d 1235.)

Note, however, that in 1999, the 1997 decision in *Epstein* v. *MCA, Inc.* (9th Cir. 1997) 126 F.3d 1235 was vacated and a substituted opinion affirming the binding nature of the state court settlements is now at *Epstein* v. *MCA, Inc.* (9th Cir. 1999) 179 F.3d 641, cert. den. Nov. 15, 1999, No. 99-417, ____ U.S. ____ [120 S.Ct. 497, 145 L.Ed.2d 384].

This reversal of the prior holding resulted from the reexamination led by Justice O'Scannlain, a previous dissenter, now joined by Justice Wiggins, both affirming the binding effect of the state court settlement. Justice Wiggins, who changed his vote, was satisfied that "adequacy of representation," previously discussed in the earlier opinion, was "litigated." Comments by objectors at a settlement hearing in the state court proceedings were, in his view, sufficient on that point and thereby barred subsequent review. (*Epstein* v. *MCA, Inc.* (9th Cir. 1999) 179 F.3d 641, 650.)

See Chapter 9 in the main text for discussion of settlement issues and procedure.

CHAPTER 3

ALTERNATIVES TO CLASS ACTIONS

PAGE 3-4

§ 3.03 Unfair Competition Injunctions

[Insert after last sentence of § 3.03:]

In *Stop Youth Addiction, Inc. v. Lucky Stores, Inc.* (1998) 17 Cal.4th 553 [71 Cal.Rptr.2d 731], California Supreme Court affirmed the broad, private standing provisions of section 17204 of the California Business and Professions Code. The plaintiff, Stop Youth Addiction, a private, for-profit corporation, brought a series of actions under the Unfair Competition Law against the defendant for cigarette sales to minors in violation of the California Penal Code. The court cited plain language and legislative history of 17204 permitting a "private plaintiff who has himself suffered no injury at all may sue to obtain relief for others."

The court stated, "the question presented is whether a private for profit corporation may maintain on behalf of the general public an unfair competition action against a retailer who, in violation of the Penal Code, sells cigarettes to minors. We conclude such an action is authorized under California Business and Professions Code sections 17200 through 17209."

The superior court had originally sustained the defendant's general demurrer without leave to amend, stating that Penal Code section 308, which prohibits the knowing sale of cigarettes to minors, "preempts" all private enforcement of section 308. The court of appeal reversed and the California Supreme Court affirmed the reversal. The case has significant implications for violations of the law that nonetheless give a plaintiff no private right of action.

The court outlined case law interpreting the Unfair Competition Law (UCL) including its former existence as California Civil Code section 3369. 1977 and 1992 amendments to now California Business and Professions Code section 17200 were also discussed, including the 1992 amendment that expanded the definition of unfair competition to include "any unfair, unlawful or fraudulent business act or practice ..." with amendments to expand section 17203 incorporating the scope of injunctive relief to encompass past activity and out-of-state activity. (*Stop Youth Addiction Inc. v. Lucky Stores, Inc.* (1998) 17 Cal.4th 553 [71 Cal.Rptr.2d 731].)

"Neither from our discussion nor the authorities we cited . . . does it follow that a private plaintiff lacks UCL standing whenever the conduct alleged to constitute unfair competition violates a statute for the direct enforcement of which there is no private cause of action." (*Stop Youth Addiction, Inc. v. Lucky Stores, Inc.* (1998) 17 Cal.4th 553 [71 Cal.Rptr.2d 731].)

Cortez v. Purolator Air Filtration Products Co. (1998) 64 Cal.App.4th 882 [75 Cal.Rptr.2d 551] (review granted Aug. 19, 1998) is presently under review by the California Supreme Court and has implications for the use of the restitution mechanism. The trial court had awarded the plaintiff substantial "attorney's fees," but denied her request for restitution under the Unfair Business Practices Act claim. An appeal followed from that ruling. The court reversed the denial of restitution. The issue before the Supreme Court will be whether a private party may obtain an award of restitution for nonparties under the Unfair Business Practices Act if the absence of class certification and an issue concerning whether an action for disgorgement of unpaid wages constitutes a claim for damages that may not be recovered under the Act or a claim for restitution that may be covered under California Business and Professions Code section 17200.

In *People v. Duz-Mor Diagnostic Laboratory, Inc.* (1998) 68 Cal.App.4th 654 [80 Cal.Rptr.2d 419], the court found that the payment of commissions to a marketing contractor by a licensed, clinical laboratory who performed services for Medi-Cal beneficiaries was a violation of the unfair competition provisions of California Business and Professions Code section 17200 inasmuch as the court found that payment of commissions to a marketing director also violated California Welfare and Institutions Code section 14107.2. The court concluded that the statutory violation was also a violation of the unfair competition statute. California Welfare and Institutions Code section 14107.2 is a criminal law that prohibits the offering of discounts to physicians' private pay patients. Section 14102.2 provided criminal penalties for "any person who offers or pays any remuneration including, but not restricted to, any kickback, bribe, or rebate, directly or indirectly, overtly or covertly in cash or in valuable consideration of any kind ... to refer any individual to a person for the furnishing or arranging for furnishing of any service or merchandise for which payment may be made in whole or in part by Medi-Cal."

Duz-Mor's payment of a sales commission to an independent contractor for his marketing services violated this section. Since the court determined it was "unlawful," they did not need to determine its unfairness.

In *Day v. AT&T Corp.* (1998) 63 Cal.App.4th 325 [74 Cal.Rptr.2d 55], the court determined that an action that seeks only to enjoin misleading or deceptive practices in the advertising of phone card rates and seeks no monetary

recovery does not implicate the federal filed rate doctrine and can proceed under sections 17200 and 17500. (*Day v. AT&T Corp.* (1998) 63 Cal.App.4th 325 [74 Cal.Rptr.2d 55].)

In *Cel-Tech Communications, Inc.* v. *Los Angeles Cellular Telephone Company* (1999) 20 Cal.4th 163 [83 Cal.Rptr.2d 548, 973 P.2d 527], the Supreme Court and other California courts continue to interpret expansively the scope of California's unfair competition statute, Business and Professions Code section 17200. In *Cel-Tech*, a majority found that even if a party's actions lacked the necessary purposes to violate the Unfair Practices Act (Bus. & Prof. Code, §§ 17043 and 17044 [dealing with below cost sales and loss leaders]) that nonetheless they may be deemed unfair under the Unfair Competition Law.

Likewise, the Supreme Court, in *Quelimane Co.* v. *Stewart Title Guaranty Co.* (1998) 19 Cal.4th 26 [77 Cal.Rptr.2d 709, 960 P.2d 513], reconfirmed that plaintiffs may prosecute a UCL action on behalf of the general public without need to have suffered personal damages. *Quelimane* reconfirmed the application of the unfair competition laws to insurance practices in spite of the provisions of the Unfair Insurance Practices Act (UIPA) (Ins. Code, § 790.03).

Finally, *Schnall* v. *The Hertz Corp.* (2000) __ Cal.App.3d __ [93 Cal.Rptr.2d 439], upheld the application of the Unfair Competition Law to allegations that a car rental company concealed exorbitant fuel rates charged to customers. Schnall had filed a class action seeking damages and injunctive relief against The Hertz Corporation with his chief allegation being that Hertz's fuel service charge was "excessive and punitive" and that the rental agreement was unlawful, unfair, and fraudulent within the meaning of the Unfair Competition Law. The First Appellate District of the California Court of Appeal upheld the plaintiff's ability to state a cause of action under the Unfair Competition Law. It acknowledged *Cel-Tech Communications, Inc.* v. *Los Angeles Cellular Telephone Company* (1999) 20 Cal.4th 163 [83 Cal.Rptr.2d 548, 973 P.2d 527], noting the law refers to any unlawful, unfair, or fraudulent practice and makes clear a practice may be deemed unfair even if not specifically proscribed by some other law.

PAGE 3-4

§ 3.04 Taxpayer Lawsuits

[Insert after the last sentence of § 3.04:]

In *State of California v. Superior Court of Los Angeles (Patrick Woosley, Real Party In Interest)* (1998) 66 Cal.App.4th 421 [78 Cal.Rptr.2d 88], the court found that to conform to the earlier decision in *Woolsey v. State of California* (1992) 3 Cal.4th 758 [13 Cal.Rptr.2d 30], the class of persons entitled to a DMV refund must be limited to persons who filed timely claims within the

three years preceding the filing of each of the three individual cases that had been consolidated.

The Department of Motor Vehicles (DMV) sought a writ of mandate directing the trial court to vacate the order certifying a class of persons entitled to refund of vehicle license fees on motor vehicles originally sold outside of California that were higher than the fees charged for similar vehicles first sold within the state. DMV contended the class certified by the trial court did not conform with the instructions issued by the California Supreme Court in *Woolsey v. State of California* (1992) 3 Cal.4th 758 [13 Cal.Rptr.2d 30].

The court found that although there was no requirement that each claimant consent to representation by Woolsey prior to class certification, once the class was properly defined and notified, the persons who filed timely claims within the three years preceding the filing of each of the three individual cases were class members.

In *Jordan* v. *Department of Motor Vehicles* (1999) 75 Cal.App.4th 449 [89 Cal.Rptr.2d 333], a refund was sought of Department of Motor Vehicles and Board of Equalization tax payments for smog impact fee of $300.00 even though cars passed the California state smog test. The court held that the fee was unconstitutional but the trial court exceeded its jurisdiction in ordering "a class claim for refunds, one option as to taxpayers who previously paid the fee requires the express consent of each class member." (Citing *Woosley* v. *State of California* (1992) 3 Cal.4th 758 [13 Cal.Rptr.2d 30, 838 P.2d 758] [the court doesn't have unfettered discretion to order refunds].)

PAGE 3-6

§ 3.08 Court-Appointed Receivers

[Insert ", other than in a limited civil case" at end of first sentence to reflect 1998 legislation]

PAGE 3-8

§ 3.10 Class Arbitration

[Insert after last sentence of § 3.10:]

A California court can, as authorized by state law, order a classwide arbitration in a case that falls under the Federal Arbitration Act (9 U.S.C.A.). In *Blue Cross of California v. Superior Court of Los Angeles County (Farquhar, Real Party In Interest)* (1998) 67 Cal.App.4th 42 [78 Cal.Rptr.2d 779], plaintiffs argued that arbitrating claims stemming from mandatory clauses as class actions is more economical than taking on individual claims such as routine healthcare matters. The court concluded that Congress's purpose in enacting the Act was

to abolish the archaic law under which the courts refuse to enforce arbitration agreements and make voluntary agreements specifically enforceable. The court noted California case law authorizes classwide arbitration in appropriate cases, and that such language does not conflict with the Act.

Ramirez v. *Circuit City Stores* (1999) 76 Cal.App.4th 1229 [90 Cal.Rptr.2d 916], rev. granted March 15, 2000, S085000, found an arbitration agreement that incorporated a clause that removed the ability to sue the employer, or file a class action lawsuit against the employer, was unconscionable. The California Supreme Court granted review on March 15, 2000. However, further action is deferred pending consideration and disposition of a related issue in *Armendariz* v. *Foundation Health Psychcare*, S075942.

CHAPTER 4
PRELIMINARY CASE ANALYSIS

PAGE 4-8

§ 4.02 Outline the Case

[F] Class Representation

[1] The Class Representative

[Replace last sentence of third paragraph under heading to following:]

Similar local rules require the class representative, as a fiduciary of the class members, to inform the court of conflicts with the class's position.

PAGE 4-9

§ 4.03 Adverse California Case Law

[B] Is the Cause Unsympathetic, or Is the Class Deprived of Little?

[Insert after last sentence of subsection [B]:]

In *Reese* v. *Wal-Mart Stores, Inc.* (1999) 73 Cal.App.4th 1225 [87 Cal.Rptr.2d 346], a ladies' day discount promotion of defendants' automobile lubrication was styled as sex and gender discrimination. The court of appeal upheld the trial court's denial of class certification, which focused on an analysis of the different benefits to the court of certification. Since the California Supreme Court held in *Koire* v. *Metro Car Wash* (1985) 40 Cal.3d 24 [219 Cal.Rptr. 133, 707 P.2d 195], that a ladies' day discount violated the Unruh Civil Rights Act and that the violations potentially carried a $1,000 minimum fine and an attorney's fee clause, there was a sufficient incentive for anyone truly aggrieved to file such a claim. A restitution remedy, found in Business and Professions Code section 17200, provides additional injunctive relief beneficial to the class without certification. The representative male plaintiff paid $18.79 for auto lubrication that contrasted with a $15.00 charge to female customers partaking of the promotion.

PAGE 4-11

[G] Is the Case a National Class in a California Court?

[Insert after last sentence of subsection [G]:]

Diamond Multimedia Systems, Inc. v. Superior Court of Santa Clara County (Joanne Pass, Real Party In Interest) (1999) 19 Cal.4th 1036 [80 Cal.Rptr.2d 828]

specifically held that a civil remedy is available to out-of-state purchasers who bought or sold the stock whose price was affected by market manipulation, even though the purchaser sales took place outside of California. The defendant was a California-venued business, and this widely observed ruling allowed the class of purchasers to pursue their claims under California Corporations Code section 25400, a part in the corporate securities law of 1968 (Corp. Code, § 25000 et seq.) to pursue their claims in a California court. Although mooted by recent changes in federal law (Private Securities Litigation Reform Act of 1995 (15 U.S.C.A. §§ 77z-1, 77z-2, 78j-1, 78u-4, 78u-5)), the case and the accompanying language nonetheless appears, as a matter of policy, to encourage the extension of California jurisdiction.

Clothesrigger, Inc. v. GTE Corp. (1987) 191 Cal.App.3d 605 [236 Cal.Rptr. 605] was cited with favor by the court and appears to be one of the more expansive discussions by the California Supreme Court of the question of venuing national classes in California courts.

Additionally related to the pendency of national classes is *Canon U.S.A, Inc. v. Superior Court of Los Angeles County (Rhulen Company, Inc., Real Party In Interest)* (1998) 68 Cal.App.4th 1 [79 Cal.Rptr.2d 897], which compels trial courts to deal with national class issues at the pleading stage. (See § 5.02 in the main text.)

PAGE 4-12

[H] Does the Class Have Common Law Negligence Claims or Unique Damage Issues?

[Insert after last sentence of subsection [H]:]

In *Block v. Major League Baseball* (1998) 65 Cal.App.4th 538 [76 Cal.Rptr.2d 567], the court found no community of interest and determined common questions of law and fact did not predominate in a case in which the class was proposed of 800 former baseball players and involved the use of their "names, voices, signatures, photographs and/or likenesses, on products such as books, films, trading cards, collector merchandise, memorabilia and apparel" that had occurred in California since 1992. The court indicated the task of evaluating those claims would have been "daunting at best." "The trial court stated each use of a class member's name, voice, signature, photograph or likeness for each product ... will have to be examined for each class member to determine whether the use violates either his statutory right of publicity or his common law right of publicity." Further, the ability to award damages was complicated by a number of other factors including the "value of each player's right of publicity," the "level of his celebrity." The court noted "Hall of Fame players such as Stan Musial, Ted Williams and Joe DiMaggio might be entitled to one level of compensation; journeymen players who had a lengthy (albeit unspectacular) career a different

level; while relatively unknown players such as appellant Block, who had the proverbial 'cup of coffee' in the major leagues, might be entitled to yet another level of compensation." The plaintiffs were criticized for failing to provide a method of accounting for the variation when awarding damages. (*Block v. Major League Baseball* (1998) 65 Cal.App.4th 538, 544 [76 Cal.Rptr.2d 567].)

PAGE 4-14

§ 4.04 The Effect of Related Litigation

[B] Successive Class Actions or Federal Class Actions Precluding State Class Treatment

[Insert after second to last paragraph in subsection [B]:]

In *Hanlon v. Chrysler Corp.* (9th Cir. 1998) 150 F.3d 1011, the Ninth Circuit Court of Appeal confirmed a nationwide class action settlement that precluded and effectively extinguished an attempted "opt out" class action filed by Plaintiff Robert Kempton, a Georgia resident who purported to represent all Georgia residents and entities in a class action filed during the pendency of the federal class action. Kempton's stated desire was to either "opt out" all Georgia residents from the *Hanlon* action or object on their behalf. In affirming the court's approval of the settlement, the court found the underlying facts concerning the class of minivan owners was distinguishable from the *Amchem* asbestos class action. In its approval the court found, "reasonably inconsequential differences in state law remedies" and a "sufficiently cohesive" class to "survive rule 23(b)(3) scrutiny." (*Hanlon v. Chrysler Corp.* (9th Cir. 1998) 150 F.3d 1011.)

The court found that Kempton had effectively excluded himself from the nationwide class, but "his opt out had no effect on the remaining Georgia class members." (*Hanlon v. Chrysler Corp.* (9th Cir. 1998) 150 F.3d 1011.)

"There is no class action rule, statute, or case that allows a putative class plaintiff or counsel to exercise class rights *en masse*, either by making a classwide objection or by attempting to effect a groupwide exclusion from an existing class. . .." (*Hanlon v. Chrysler Corp.* (9th Cir. 1998) 150 F.3d 1011.)

Brinton v. *Bankers Pension Services, Inc.* (1999) 76 Cal.App.4th 550 [90 Cal.Rptr.2d 469], involved claims in a prior class action that barred subsequent recovery. The plaintiff participated in a prior class action. The prior settlement of the uncertified class action included extensive and broad settlement language. Thon and Titan were defendants in the *Tauf, et al. v. Hill Williams Development Corp.*, an uncertified class action (Orange County Superior Court No. 7051766) which was settled in May of 1996. This broad interpretation of the class settlement, although the specific defendant was unmentioned, was found to preclude the subsequent case, as was the plaintiffs' participation in prior arbitrations in

other claims. Using third party beneficiary and primary right theories, the defendants were liable to a class of persons. The settlement did not identify him by name; however, defendant showed he was of a class of persons barred by the settlement language.

PAGE 4-15

[D] Extensive "Group" Litigation

[Replace subsection letter "[D]" with "[E]."]

PAGE 4-16

[Insert after last sentence of subsection [E]:]

In *Citizens for Open Access to Sand and Tide, Inc. v. Seadrift Ass'n* (1998) 60 Cal.App.4th 1053 [71 Cal.Rptr.2d 77], the court held that a prior action brought by the Attorney General of California and a subsequent settlement agreement reduced to a judgment barred a later lawsuit by an association claiming to represent the public interest and seeking to establish a public recreation easement over coastal land. The *Citizens* court found that the application of res judicata applied because the issue in both actions was the same because it dealt with the recreational use of the area, which was common to all members who asserted no other issue of law and claimed no other individual property interests.

CHAPTER 5

DRAFTING A CALIFORNIA CLASS ACTION COMPLAINT

PAGE 5-3

§ 5.02 Structuring the Complaint

[A] The Caption

[Add after 1st paragraph:]

Effective January 1, 2000, the Judicial Council of California form 982.2(b)(1), a Civil Case Cover Sheet, must be filed with the complaint and be checked to indicate its complex case designation. The definition of "complex" set forth in rule 1800 of the California Rules of Court includes a class action. Other criteria on the civil cover sheet include the following: large number of separately represented parties; extensive motion practice raising difficult or novel issues that will be time consuming to resolve; substantial amount of documentary evidence; a large number of witnesses; coordination in related actions pending in one or more courts in other counties, states, or countries, or in a federal court; and substantial post-disposition judicial disposition.This mandatory form now requires that a copy of the cover sheet be served on all parties to the action or proceeding. See also discussion in Chapter 8, Case Management: Controlling the Issues.

For the Judicial Council form, see West's California Judicial Council Forms, vol. 1, Civil Case Cover Sheet, 982.2(b)(1). See also the Judicial Council website at <http://www.courtinfo.ca.gov/forms.>

[B] Jurisdiction

[Insert after last sentence of subsection [B]:]

In *Canon U.S.A, Inc. v. Superior Court of Los Angeles County (Rhulen Company, Inc., Real Party In Interest)* (1998) 68 Cal.App.4th 1 [79 Cal.Rptr.2d 897], the court held that the trial should consider whether to accept a nationwide class in a defective product suit at the pleading stage. At the pleading stage a court is permitted to strike nationwide class references based upon *Osborne v. Subaru of America, Inc.* (1988) 198 Cal.App.3d 646 [243 Cal.Rptr. 815] factors. *Osborne* held that California courts should not, absent a "special obligation" to do so, undertake the "massive burden" of adjudicating nationwide class action lawsuits when to do so would require the trial court to adjudicate issues by application of numerous different rules of law from the varying states.

In the *Osborne* case, the decision not to certify the class was made following an evidentiary hearing during which the plaintiffs were given an opportunity to present evidence garnered through discovery. At issue was the application of "the variations of applicable law among the various states which could result in an unmanageable class." The *Osborne* court discussed the "special obligation" to undertake the burden of a nationwide class. The *Canon* decision, however, seems to force this analysis to the pleading stage.

These courts encourage an analysis as to whether a nationwide class would promote "judicial economy in California courts and whether California claimants would be aided in their recovery by class litigation and further the extent of the connection the parties may have with California." (*Osborne v. Subaru of America, Inc.* (1988) 198 Cal.App.3d 646 [243 Cal.Rptr. 815]; *Canon U.S.A, Inc. v. Superior Court of Los Angeles County (Rhulen Company, Inc., Real Party In Interest)* (1998) 68 Cal.App.4th 1 [79 Cal.Rptr.2d 897].)

The California Supreme Court's decision in *Diamond Multimedia Systems, Inc. v. Superior Court of Santa Clara County (Joanne Pass, Real Party In Interest)* (1999) 19 Cal.4th 1036 [80 Cal.Rptr.2d 828], concluded that California has a "legitimate and compelling interest in preserving a business climate free of fraud and deceptive practices" in supporting the ability of out-of-state purchasers and sellers of securities whose price was affected by unlawful market manipulation may avail themselves of the California Corporations Code in a way that is not limited to transactions made in California. The Supreme Court cited with approval the decision in *Clothesrigger, Inc. v. GTE Corp.* (1987) 191 Cal.App.3d 605 [236 Cal.Rptr. 605], wherein the importance of extending state created remedies to out-of-state parties harmed by wrongful conduct occurring in California was underscored.

Combining these cases suggests to the practitioner that the appropriate pleading should underscore the "legitimate and compelling interest" of allowing non-California class members to assert claims utilizing California's law where necessary.

To the extent the laws of other jurisdictions are involved, however, the "special obligation" analysis of *Osborne* seems to still be warranted.

For discussion of nationwide class actions, see § 4.03[G] in the main text.

CHAPTER 6

THE PRECERTIFICATION STAGE

PAGE 6-4

§ 6.01 General Rules for Precertification Activity and Conduct

[C] Demurrers to Class Allegations: The Reasonable-Possibility Standard

[Add after continuing paragraph at top of page:]

In *Wilner* v. *Sunset Life Insurance Co.* (March 29, 2000) __ Cal.App.4th __ [93 Cal.Rptr.2d 413], the complaint alleged a common course of conduct of the insurance company adequately alleged the existence of an ascertainable class and demonstrated potential ability to prove a community of interest. The prior complaint erroneously sustained without leave to amend class allegations. Note: The allegations of the complaint also adequately alleged a claim under Business and Professions Code section 17200 for unfair business practices. (See Chapter 3.)

CHAPTER 7

CALIFORNIA CLASS ACTION PROCEDURE

PAGE 7-8

§ 7.03 Class Notice

[A] When Notice Is Required and What It Must Say

[Replace "Super. Ct. L.A. County Rules, rule 15.18(4)(f)" at end of last paragraph with "Super. Ct. L.A. County Rules, rule 15.18(f)(4)":]

PAGE 7-10

§ 7.04 Successive Certification Motions

[A] Difference Between Federal and State Rules

[Insert after last full paragraph on page:]

Federal Rules of Civil Procedure, rule 23, was amended in 1998 to include a provision dealing with appeals. It provides that, "[a] court of appeals may in its discretion permit an appeal from an order of a district court granting or denying class action certification under this rule. . . ." This hybrid procedure allows a direct appeal, even though it is an interim ruling under federal procedure. The appeal, however, does not stay the proceedings in the appellate district court unless the district court or court of appeals requests it. (See Federal Rules of Civil Procedure, rule 23(f), Appeals.)

CHAPTER 8

CASE MANAGEMENT: CONTROLLING THE ISSUES

PAGE 8-2

§ 8.01 Proposing a Manageable Trial

[Add after second paragraph:]

The California Rules of Court have been modified in several critical aspects that should enhance the possibility for early control and management of class action cases.

Rule 1800 of the California Rules of Court provides by definition that class actions are "complex" cases. Rule 1800 states:

Rule 1800. Definition

> (a) [Definition] A "complex case" is an action that requires exceptional judicial management to avoid placing unnecessary burdens on the court or the litigants and to expedite the case, keep costs reasonable, and promote effective decision making by the court, the parties, and counsel.
>
> . . .
>
> (c) ([Provisional designation] Except as provided in subdivision (d), an action is provisionally a complex case if it involves one or more of the following types of claims:
>
> . . .
>
> (6) Claims involving class actions . . . .

(Cal. Rules of Court, rule 1800, adopted effective January 1, 2000.)

Pursuant to rule 1810 of the California Rules of Court, "complex case designation," "[a] plaintiff may designate an action a complex case by filing with the initial complaint the *Civil Case Cover Sheet* (Form 982.2(b)(1)) required by rule 982.2 that is marked to indicate the action is a complex case." (Cal. Rules of Court, rule 1810, adopted effective January 1, 2000.)

Likewise, section 19 of Appendix, Division I, of the California Rules of Court has also been amended to ensure assignment to appropriate and interested judicial officers. As amended, it states:

> (c) [Selection of judges for complex litigation assignments] In selecting judges for complex litigation assignments, the presiding judge should consider the needs of the court and the

> judge's ability, interest, training, experience (including experience with complex civil cases), and willingness to participate in educational programs related to the management of complex cases. Commissioners should not be employed in any phase of complex litigation, except under the judge's direct supervision to assist in the management of the case.

(Cal. Rules of Court, Appendix, Div. I, § 19, subd. (c).) This important modification also provides that, "[j]udges assigned to handle complex cases should be given research attorney and administrative staff assistance where possible." (Cal. Rules of Court, Appendix, Div. I, § 19, subd. (j).)

PAGE 8-3

§ 8.02 Precertification Case Management

[C] Appointing a Discovery Master

[Insert after last paragraph of subsection:]

Trial courts handling complex cases within the meaning of section 19 of the Standards of Judicial Administration have "broad discretion" in managing these cases. *Lu v. Superior Court* (1997) 55 Cal.App.4th 1264 [64 Cal.Rptr.2d 561] authorized the appointment of a discovery referee in the absence of a pending discovery dispute. The court concluded that the general authority under California Code of Civil Procedure section 187 is granted to exercise their discretion. The *Lu* court stated (*Lu v. Superior Court* (1997) 55 Cal.App.4th 1264, 1269 [64 Cal.Rptr.2d 561]):

> Complex cases invariably involve complex discovery disputes and, unless managed, a case with many separately represented parties has the potential for burdensome and duplicative discovery—it is therefore appropriate for a case management order to provide for the appointment of a discovery referee.

CHAPTER 9

SETTLEMENT ISSUES AND PROCEDURE

PAGE 9-5

§ 9.02 Tactical Considerations

[C] Early Appointment of Settlement Master

[Insert after last paragraph of subsection [C]:]

Lu v. Superior Court (1997) 55 Cal.App.4th 1264 [64 Cal.Rptr.2d 561] held that "a trial court has authority to appoint a discovery referee even in the absence of a current discovery dispute." In *Lu*, a case management order in a complex case appointed a discovery referee who was also designated a "mediator." His duties in the latter capacity were to "attempt to assist the parties in resolving it." Thus, this case extends the trial court's authority under the California Standards of Judicial Administration section 19 to make these appointments as a part of the normal case management process.

PAGE 9-10

§ 9.04 Class Settlement Procedure

[C] Settlement Hearing

[Insert after last paragraph of subsection [C]:]

The United States Supreme Court in *Amchem Products, Inc. v. George Windsor* (June 25, 1997) 521 U.S. 591 [117 S.Ct. 2231, 138 L.Ed.2d 689], discussed the bounds of settlement class certification in a matter that responded to the "asbestos-litigation crisis." The Supreme Court stated, "[w]e granted review to decide the role settlement may play, under existing rule 23, in determining the propriety of class certification." (*Amchem Products, Inc. v. George Windsor* (1997) 521 U.S. 591 [117 S.Ct. 2231, 138 L.Ed.2d 689].)

The Court stated that settlement only class certifications by district courts didn't need to involve normal trial management issues, however, absent class members needed to be protected and required "undiluted, even heightened, attention in the settlement context." After a detailed review of the requirements of rule 23, the Supreme Court concluded that "the settling parties, in sum, achieved a global compromise with no structural assurance of fair and adequate representation for the diverse groups and individuals affected . . .." (*Amchem Products, Inc. v. George Windsor* (1997) 521 U.S. 591 [117 S.Ct. 2231, 138 L.Ed.2d 689].)

The fundamental problem was the interests of presently injured asbestos claimants being in a different position than those who may have future claims. The class representative must be a part of the class and possess the same interest and suffer the same injury as the class members. (*Amchem Products, Inc. v. George Windsor* (1997) 521 U.S. 591 [117 S.Ct. 2231, 138 L.Ed.2d 689].)

This class action settlement was "not intended to be litigated." No additional counsel were appointed to represent subclasses who could have responded to the problem of future claimants as opposed to those who presently manifested injuries.

The specific adequacy of representation issues advanced by the objectors to the *Amchem* settlement were that the class counsel and class representatives had disqualifying conflicts of interest. The claimants whose injuries had become manifest and claimants without manifest injuries should not have had common counsel and should not have been aggregated into a single class. (*Amchem Products, Inc. v. George Windsor* (1997) 521 U.S. 591 [117 S.Ct. 2231, 138 L.Ed.2d 689].)

These same objections were rejected by the district court, but disabling according to the Supreme Court review. The certification was subsequently vacated by the Third Circuit Court of Appeals and review was then granted by the Supreme Court.

The United States Supreme Court is expected to decide *Ortiz v. Fibreboard Corp.* (5th Cir. 1998) 134 F.3d 668 (U.S. S.Ct. cert. granted June 22, 1998), in the near future. The *Ortiz* case has been called the second global asbestos settlement and is known as *Ahearn* after a member of the plaintiff class. The Supreme Court will deal with the extent and limits of settlement classes beyond the issues raised in *Amchem. Amchem* was consummated as a rule 23(b)(3) opt out class, while the issues in *Ortiz* are expected to deal with the settlement structure as a rule 23(b)(1)(B) mandatory class.

Future claims were negotiated separately after pending claims were negotiated in this insurance/defendant structured global resolution. The trust fund for future asbestos claimants was established and backed by an agreement by the defendant and two of its insurance carriers. The Fifth Circuit Court of Appeal had affirmed the court's approval of the mandatory class and rejected a due process challenge by objectors. Commentators have suggested that this case has great significance for the resolution of mass tort litigation.

PAGE 9-11

[D] Standing to Object

[Insert after last paragraph of subsection [D]:]

Appellants must be aggrieved parties (Code Civ. Proc., § 902) and parties of record, and their rights or interests must be injuriously affected by the judgment. (*Rebney v. Wells Fargo* (1990) 220 Cal.App.3d 1117, 1128 [269 Cal.Rptr. 844].) Since the appellants were not situated so as to have suffered the type of injury of the expanded class, they could not object. (*Rebney v. Wells Fargo* (1990) 220 Cal.App.3d 1117, 1129 [269 Cal.Rptr. 844].)

Note that Ralph Abascal was named plaintiff and objector arguing his own inadequacy, yet contemporaneously arguing on behalf of different parties on appeal. The court asked, "how can he have it both ways?"

The appellants were not aggrieved by the errors they asserted with regard to the expansion of class certification and the fairness of the settlement and thus they lacked standing to assert those errors as a basis for reversal. (*Rebney v. Wells Fargo* (1990) 220 Cal.App.3d 1117, 1132 [269 Cal.Rptr. 844].)

CHAPTER 10

ATTORNEY'S FEES

PAGE 10-7

§ 10.04 Common Fund Compensation

[B] Extra Shares and Benchmarks

[Insert after last paragraph of subsection [B]:]

In *Williams v. MGM Pathe Communications Co.* (9th Cir. 1997) 129 F.3d 1026, the Ninth Circuit Court of Appeal recently held that the calculation of the contingent fee should have been one-third of the entire $4.5 million settlement for a fee of $1.5 million, rather than calculating it as one-third of the class members' claims against the fund for a fee of only $3,300. The Ninth Circuit characterized the district court's action as an abuse of discretion by basing the fee on the class members' claims against the fund rather than on a percentage of the entire fund or on the lodestar and, accordingly, reversed and remanded. The court held, "[i]n *Boeing Co. v. Van Gemert* (1980) 444 U.S. 472, 480-81, the Court concluded that the attorneys for a successful class may recover a fee based on the entire common fund created for the class, even if some class members make no claims against the fund so that money remains in it that otherwise would be returned to the defendants." (*Williams v. MGM Pathe Communications Co.* (9th Cir. 1997) 129 F.3d 1026, citing *Boeing Co. v. Van Gemert* (1980) 444 U.S. 472, 480-481 [100 S.Ct. 745, 62 L.Ed.2d 676].)

PAGE 10-8

[D] Reasonableness Requirement

[Replace "Super. Ct. S.F. County Rules, rule 363" at end of first paragraph with "Super. Ct. S.F. County Rules, rule 463":]

PAGE 10-9

[Add the following new subsection after subsection [D]:]

[E] Agreements Between Class Counsel

The propriety of a written agreement between class counsel that divides lump sum attorney's fees on a percentage basis was attacked on appeal as unfair due to the "tremendous incentive" for class counsel with few hours to settle earlier than trial. (*Rebney v. Wells Fargo* (1990) 220 Cal.App.3d 1117 [269 Cal.Rptr. 844].)

The court conceded that an award of attorney's fees in class action litigation is "tied to the substantial efforts to benefit the class" but no prejudice was shown.

COMMENT

Increasingly, complicated questions of compensation of plaintiffs' counsel are being referred to either sitting or retired judges. A common tactic in complicated settlements involving numerous plaintiffs' law firms is to agree to a reference to a master with an agreement not to appeal his or her findings. This mechanism has evolved in recognition of the fact that the trial court has little power to allocate fees, only to approve or disapprove compensation.

CHAPTER 12

CLASS ACTIONS GROUPED BY SUBSTANTIVE LAW

PAGE 12-5

§ 12.04 Securities

[Insert the following before first paragraph of § 12.04:]

Congress substantially limited the ability of investors to pursue claims in California state courts when securities traded nationally are at issue. On October 13, 1998, Congress passed the Securities Litigation Uniform Standards Act of 1998 (15 U.S.C.A. § 78a) dealing with securities class actions involving nationally traded securities based upon false or misleading statements. These must now be brought exclusively in federal court under federal law. President Clinton signed the bill into law on November 3, 1998. There is no longer a reason to believe that the California superior court system will see an ever-increasing number of California state securities class actions. The 1998 legislation was designed to prevent class actions being filed around the protections afforded insurers of securities under the Private Securities Litigation Reform Act of 1995 (15 U.S.C.A. §§ 77z-1, 77z-2, 78j-1, 78u-4, 78u-5) by filing securities class actions in a state court under state laws. 15 U.S.C.A. § 78a states, "[T]he Private Securities Litigation Reform Act of 1995 sought to prevent abuses in private securities fraud lawsuits; . . . since enactment of that legislation, considerable evidence has been presented to Congress that a number of securities class action lawsuits have shifted from Federal to State courts; . . . this shift has prevented that Act from fully achieving its objectives . . .."

Section 16(c) of the Securities Act of 1993 (15 U.S.C.A. § 77p) is amended to read as follows: ". . . Any covered class action brought in any State court involving a covered security . . . shall be removable to the Federal district court for the district in which the action is pending . . .."

The California Supreme Court's decision in *Diamond Multimedia Systems, Inc. v. Superior Court of Santa Clara County (Joanne Pass, Real Party In Interest)* (1999) 19 Cal.4th 1036 [80 Cal.Rptr.2d 828], has allowed a class of California residents and others throughout the United States to pursue civil remedies supported by California securities laws. (See discussion in the main text at § 4.03[G] and § 5.02[B].)

The California Supreme Court sanctioned the court of appeal decision in *Clothesrigger, Inc. v. GTE Corp.* (1987) 191 Cal.App.3d 605 [236 Cal.Rptr. 605] when it rejected a claim similar to *Diamond Multimedia* and recognized the

importance of extending state-created remedies to out-of-state parties harmed by wrongful conduct occurring in California. (*Diamond Multimedia Systems, Inc. v. Superior Court of Santa Clara County (Joanne Pass, Real Party In Interest)* (1999) 19 Cal.4th 1036 [80 Cal.Rptr.2d 828].)

PAGE 12-7

§ 12.06 Product Liability

[Insert after last paragraph of § 12.06:]

In *Canon U.S.A, Inc. v. Superior Court of Los Angeles County (Rhulen Company, Inc., Real Party In Interest)* (1998) 68 Cal.App.4th 1 [79 Cal.Rptr.2d 897], motions to strike national class pleadings were granted with the court sanctioning the *Osborne* "special obligation" factors to be determined at the pleading stage.

PAGE 12-14

§ 12.13 Employee-Employer

[Insert after last paragraph of section:]

Recently, wage and hour claims alleging failure to pay overtime have been venued increasingly in California courts and have received class certification. California state law in class action procedure can be applied to these claims, which pursuant to the Fair Labor Standards Act require "opt in," often times substantially inhibiting participation. In 1998, the author secured class certification on such a claim against a California employer.

Cortez v. Purolator Air Filtration Products Co. (1998) 64 Cal.App.4th 882 [75 Cal.Rptr.2d 551], currently under review by the California Supreme Court, will either confirm or deny the ability of California's Unfair Competition Law (Bus. & Prof. Code, § 17200 et seq.) to provide restitution of illegally withheld overtime wages. "Cortez alleged that overtime pay had been improperly withheld from approximately 175 Purolator employees during the time relevant under the statute of limitations. The second cause of action stated Cortez's individual claim for failure to pay overtime wages pursuant to Labor Code section 1198. Cortez sought restitution of the overtime wages, civil penalties and attorneys' fees in connection with this claim." (*Cortez v. Purolator Air Filtration Products Co.* (1998) 64 Cal.App.4th 882 [75 Cal.Rptr.2d 551].)

As the California employer, Purolator and its predecessors were subject to the California Industrial Welfare Commission Wage Orders, which required overtime pay if certain conditions were met.

The *Cortez* court found that the claim was for restitution and not damages. The plaintiff sought to have the difference between the overtime wages allowed and the standard wages paid provided by way of restitution. The plaintiff claimed that the defendant profited from breaking the law and the profit was wrongfully obtained and needed to be disgorged. The court of appeal cited this principle with favor and stated, "Plaintiff's unpaid wages therefore are simply one method by which to measure the disgorgement of wrongful profit. Because the unpaid wages would restore plaintiff to the position where she would have been if not for Purolator's illegal conduct, this remedy is equitable in nature and therefore appropriately recoverable under [Bus. & Prof. Code] section 17203." (*Cortez v. Purolator Air Filtration Products Co.* (1998) 64 Cal.App.4th 882 [75 Cal.Rptr.2d 551].) This ruling conflicted with two prior courts of appeal cases that had characterized unpaid wages as damages and not recoverable under section 17200.

PAGE 12-14

[Add new section after § 12.14:]

§ 12.15 Right of Publicity

In *Block v. Major League Baseball* (1998) 65 Cal.App.4th 538 [76 Cal.Rptr.2d 567], the plaintiff had played major league baseball for the Chicago Cubs between 1942 and 1946. The plaintiff and other major league players who played prior to 1947 filed a class action alleging that major league baseball violated their statutory and common law right of publicity by using "their names, voices, signatures, photographs and/or likenesses in a variety of ways." The court failed to find a community of interest and found that common questions of law or fact did not predominate given the substantial differences in the "level" of "celebrity." (*Block v. Major League Baseball* (1998) 65 Cal.App.4th 538 [76 Cal.Rptr.2d 567].)

[Change "§ 12.15 References" to "§ 12.16 References."]

APPENDIX

Relevant Federal and State Statutes and Rules

APP-18

SAN DIEGO COUNTY SUPERIOR COURT RULES

San Diego County revised their trial court rules. Class action rules now appear in the Coordinated Rules of San Diego County, rule 10.9. Rule 10.9 generally covers the same topics as former rules 3.1–3.4, but there are some differences. For example, the former status conference is now called the class certification conference, and the progress conference is scheduled within 90 days after the initial case management conference.

APP-20

SAN FRANCISCO COUNTY SUPERIOR COURT RULES

The San Francisco Class Actions Manual continues to be published by the court to provide counsel with such guidance as it may contain. It is expected, however, that revisions to the manual will be published for comment later in 2000.

TABLE OF STATUTES AND RULES

UNITED STATES CODE

U.S.C.

Tit.:Sec.	This Work Sec.
29:204	12.13

U.S.C.A.

Tit.:Sec.	This Work Sec.
9	3.10
15:77z-1, 77z-2, 78j-1, 78u-4, 78u-5	4.03[G], 12.04
15:78a	12.04

FEDERAL RULES OF CIVIL PROCEDURE

Rule	This Work Sec.
23	7.04[A], 9.04[C]
23(a)(4)	2.04
23(b)(1)(B)	9.04[C]
23(b)(3)	4.04[B], 9.04[C]
23(f)	7.04[A]

SEC RULES

Rule	This Work Sec.
14-B	2.04

CAL. BUSINESS AND PROFESSIONS CODE

Sec.	This Work Sec.
17043	3.03
17044	3.03
17200	3.03, 4.03, 6.01, 12.13
17200-17209	3.03
17200 et seq.	3.03, 12.13
17203	3.03, 12.13
17204	3.03
17500	3.03

CAL. CIVIL CODE

Sec.	This Work Sec.
3369	3.03

CAL. CODE OF CIVIL PROCEDURE

Sec.	This Work Sec.
187	8.02[C]
639	8.03
902	9.04[D]

CAL. CORPORATIONS CODE

Sec.	This Work Sec.
25000 et seq.	4.03[G]
25400	4.03[G]

CAL. INSURANCE CODE

Sec.	This Work Sec.
790.03	3.03

CAL. LABOR CODE

Sec.	This Work Sec.
1198	12.13

CAL. PENAL CODE

Sec.	This Work Sec.
308	3.03

CAL. WELFARE AND INSTITUTIONS CODE

Sec.	This Work Sec.
14102.2	3.03
14107.2	3.03

CALIFORNIA RULES OF COURT

Rule	This Work Sec.
982.2(b)(1)	5.02
1800	8.01
1801	8.01

CAL. STANDARDS OF JUDICIAL ADMINISTRATION

Sec.	This Work Sec.
19	8.01, 8.02[C], 9.02[C]

TABLE OF CASES

Amchem Products, Inc. v. George Windsor (June 25, 1997) 521 U.S. 591, 117 S.Ct. 2231, 138 L.Ed.2d 689—§§ 2.04, 4.04[B], 9.04[C]

Block v. Major League Baseball (1998) 65 Cal.App.4th 538 [76 Cal.Rptr.2d 567]—§§ 4.03[H], 12.15

Blue Cross of California v. Superior Court of Los Angeles County (Farquhar, Real Party In Interest) (1998) 67 Cal.App.4th 42 [78 Cal.Rptr.2d 779]—§ 3.10

Boeing Co. v. Van Gemert (1980) 444 U.S. 472—§ 10.01[B]

Brinton v. Bankers Pension Services, Inc. (1999) 76 Cal.App.4th 550 [90 Cal.Rptr.2d 469]—§ 4.04

Canon U.S.A, Inc. v. Superior Court of Los Angeles County (Rhulen Company, Inc., Real Party In Interest) (1998) 68 Cal.App.4th 1 [79 Cal.Rptr.2d 897]—§§ 4.03[G], 5.02[B], 12.06

Cel-Tech Communications, Inc. v. Los Angeles Cellular Telephone Company (1999) 20 Cal.4th 163 [83 Cal.Rptr.2d 548, 973 P.2d 527]—§ 3.03

Citizens for Open Access to Sand and Tide, Inc. v. Seadrift Ass'n (1998) 60 Cal.App.4th 1053 [71 Cal.Rptr.2d 77]—§ 4.04[D]

Clothesrigger, Inc. v. GTE Corp. (1987) 191 Cal.App.3d 605 [236 Cal.Rptr. 605]—§§ 4.03[G], 5.02[B], 12.04

Cortez v. Purolator Air Filtration Products Co. (1998) 64 Cal.App.4th 882 [75 Cal. Rptr.2d 551] (S.Ct. review granted 1998)—§§ 3.03, 12.13

Day v. AT&T Corp. (1998) 63 Cal.App.4th 325 [74 Cal. Rptr.2d 55]—§ 3.03

Diamond Multimedia Systems, Inc. v. Superior Court of Santa Clara County (Joanne Pass, Real Party In Interest) (1999) 19 Cal.4th 1036 [80 Cal.Rptr.2d 828]—§§ 4.03[G], 5.02[B], 12.04

Epstein v. MCA, Inc. (9th Cir. 1999) 179 F.3d 641—§ 2.04

Epstein v. MCA, Inc. (9th Cir. 1997) 126 F.3d 1235—§ 2.04

Hanlon v. Chrysler Corp. (9th Cir. 1998) 150 F.3d 1011—§ 4.04[B]

Jordan v. Department of Motor Vehicles (1999) 75 Cal.App.4th 449 [89 Cal.Rptr.2d 333]—§ 3.04

Koire v. Metro Car Wash (1985) 40 Cal.3d 24 [219 Cal.Rptr. 133, 707 P.2d 195]—§ 4.03

Lu v. Superior Court (1997) 55 Cal.App.4th 1264 [64 Cal.Rptr.2d 561]—§§ 8.02[C], 9.02[C]

Matsushita Electric Industrial Co. v. Eptstein (1996) 516 U.S. 367, 116 S.Ct. 873, 134 L.Ed.2d 6—§ 2.04

Ortiz v. Fibreboard Corp. (5th Cir. 1998) 134 F.3d 668 (U.S. S.Ct. cert. granted June 22, 1998)—§ 9.04[C]

Osborne v. Subaru of America, Inc. (1988) 198 Cal.App.3d 646 [243 Cal.Rptr. 815]—§ 5.02[B]

People v. Duz-Mor Diagnostic Laboratory, Inc. (1998) 68 Cal.App.4th 654 [80 Cal.Rptr.2d 419]—§ 3.03

Quelimane Co. v. Stewart Title Guaranty Co. (1998) 19 Cal.4th 26 [77 Cal.Rptr.2d 709, 960 P.2d 513]—§ 3.03

Ramirez v. Circuit City Stores (1999) 76 Cal.App.4th 1229 [90 Cal.Rptr.2d 916]—§ 3.10

Rebney v. Wells Fargo (1990) 220 Cal.App.3d 1117 [269 Cal.Rptr. 844]—§§ 2.04, 9.04[D], 10.04[E]

Reese v. Wal-Mart Stores, Inc. (1999) 73 Cal.App.4th 1225 [87 Cal.Rptr.2d 346]—§ 4.03

Schnall v. The Hertz Corp. (2000) __ Cal.App.__ [93 Cal.Rptr.2d 439]—§ 3.03

State of California v. Superior Court of Los Angeles (Patrick Woosley, Real Party In Interest) (1998) 66 Cal.App.4th 421 [78 Cal.Rptr.2d 88]—§ 3.03

Stop Youth Addiction Inc. v. Lucky Stores, Inc. (1998) 17 Cal.4th 553 [71 Cal.Rptr.2d 731]—§3.03

Williams v. MGM Pathe Communications Co. (9th Cir. 1997) 129 F.3d 10263—§ 10.04[B]

Wilner v. Sunset Life Insurance Co. (2000) __ Cal.App.4th __ [93 Cal.Rptr.2d 413]—§ 6.01

Woolsey v. State of California (1992) 3 Cal.4th 758 [13 Cal.Rptr.2d 30]—§§ 3.03, 3.04

Form of memorandum of points and authorities in support of final approval of partial settlement of class action; award of attorney's fees and costs, § 9.12
Form of order of preliminary approval of settlement, and approval of notice of pendency of class action, preliminary approval of settlement and setting fairness hearing, § 9.13
Form of stipulation regarding temporary and conditional certification of class for settlement purposes only and order, § 9.10
Form of stipulation re settlement, § 9.11
Hearing, § 9.03[C]
Notice in declaratory/injunctive relief cases, § 9.03[H]
Notice in opt-out cases, § 9.03[I]
Notice to class, § 9.03[B]
Postcertification settlement, § 9.03[F]
Realistic evaluation of recovery sources, § 9.02[A]
Scope of bar order-federal class settlements, § 9.03[K]
Scope of bar order-state class settlements, § 9.03[J]
Serial settlements, § 9.02[D]
Settlement master, appointment of, § 9.02[C]
Standing to object, § 9.03[D]
Tactical considerations, § 9.02

SETTLEMENT MASTER
Early appointment of, § 9.02[C]

SEVERANCE, § 11.02[C]

SIMPLIFYING ISSUES
Following certification, § 8.03

STATE VERSUS FEDERAL LAW, §§ 1.01[C], 1.07

STATUTE OF LIMITATIONS
Tolling of *American Pipe & Construction Co.* v. *Utah*, § 5.03[F]

SUBDIVISION LAND SALES CASES, § 12.09[G]

SUBSTANTIAL BENEFIT PREREQUISITE, § 2.06

SUCCESSIVE CLASS ACTIONS
Federal class actions precluding state class treatment, § 4.04[B]
State class actions precluding federal class treatment, § 4.04[C]

SUMMARIES OF VOLUMINOUS DOCUMENTS, 11.02[H]

TAXPAYER LAWSUITS, § 3.04

TIMING
Class certification hearing, § 7.02[B]

TITLE INSURANCE CASES, § 12.09[J]

TORTS, MASS TORT-CONSOLIDATION CASES, § 3.13

TREATMENT
Class without notice, § 3.11

TRIAL MANAGEMENT
Appropriate inferences and presumptions, § 11.02[D]
Arbitration, § 11.02[E]
Bar orders, § 11.02[F]
Bifurcation, § 11.02[B]
Determining trial issues before certification, § 11.03[B]
Pretrial discussion and disposition of evidence issues, § 11.02[I]
Pretrial master or reference reports, § 11.02[D]
Severance, § 11.02[C]
Statements of contested and uncontested issues, § 11.02[G]
Summaries of voluminous documents, § 11.02[H]
Trial of remaining issues, § 11.02[C]

TRIAL STRATEGY, §§ 11.01, 11.02, 11.03

UNFAIR COMPETITION INJUNCTIONS, § 3.02

UNIQUE DAMAGE ISSUES, § 4.03[H]

UNLAWFUL DETAINER CASES, § 12.09[F]

VENUE, §§ 5.02[C], 11.01

WITHOUT NOTICE
Class treatment, § 3.11